Writer's Northwest Handbook

4th Edition

4th Edition

Writer's Northwest Handbook

Media Weavers
Blue Heron Publishing, Inc.
Hillsboro, Oregon

Writer's Northwest Handbook
4th Edition

Published by
Media Weavers
Blue Heron Publishing, Inc.
Route 3 Box 376
Hillsboro, OR 97124
503/621-3911

Editors:
Dennis Stovall & Linny Stovall

Editorial Assistants:
Linda O'Brien
Bill Woodall

Advertising Sales:
Darlene Fesler
Dennis Stovall

Cover Art:
Larry Milam

ISBN 0-936085-08-8
ISSN 0896-7946
LCC Number 91-70156

Table of Contents

TEACHERS/YOUNG WRITERS

PUBLISHING TIPS

ORGANIZATIONS

INDEX TO MARKET LISTINGS

MARKET LISTINGS

ADVERTISEMENTS

Acknowledgement

Support for the 4th edition of *Writer's Northwest Handbook* came from all sectors of the literary community — writers, book artists, editors, arts and library organizations, and advertisers such as printers, bookstores, typesetters, colleges, researchers, publishers, literary agents, and publicists.

We are grateful for three grants provided by the Idaho Commission on the Arts, the Oregon Arts Commission, and the Oregon Center for the Book in the Oregon State Library.

Without the tremendous support from Northwest writers, we would not have the fine essay section of the book. We thank all of you for contributing to the discussion of important literary issues and for your expertise in subjects ranging from book design to facing TV interviewers.

This edition had the expert help of two assistant editors, Linda O'Brien and Bill Woodall. They helped develop the concept of the essay section, contacted writers and assisted from the first to final proofing. They, along with Terri Lee Grell, editor of *Lynx*, also did research and interview articles. The book might have taken years instead of months without them.

For the cover art, we thank Larry Milam who has consistently graced the pages of our newspaper, *Writer's NW*, with book-related art.

And last, we thank all of you who use *Writer's Northwest Handbook* for providing feedback, suggestions, and corrections that enable us to keep coming back with the most useful and updated material.

Introduction

Welcome to the 4th edition of *Writer's Northwest Handbook*. This is the one resource for everyone hooked on the printed word, from the hobbyist to the professional. Whether you are a writer or a publisher. A publicist or a researcher. Teacher or librarian. If what you're looking for is a resource or a market in the Northwest — Alaska, British Columbia, Idaho, Montana, Oregon, or Washington — you'll undoubtedly find it here.

The book is divided into four sections: 1. articles, 2. market listings, preceded by index, 3. resources, and 4. advertisements.

The article section is all new and features 50 writers — Northwest favorites as well as new voices. The essays and interviews that grace these pages speak to important concerns — from debunking the old mythology of the west to protecting copyright.

The nearly 2800 publisher listings are newly updated. The resource section lists more than 500 of the region's conferences, classes, organizations, distributors, and events. And the advertising section offers services and products such as printing, typesetting, publicists, literary agents, and conferences.

IF YOU ARE A:	YOU WILL FIND:
WRITER	2800 market listings, some paying and some not; tips on writing mysteries and westerns, finding an agent or an editor, dealing with censorship and copyright, staying alive, and how to stay clear of sexist language.
PUBLISHER	3300 addresses, including the region's newspapers, from which to develop a market list; essays on book design and copy editors, successful promotion, necessary registrations, funding, and how others do it.
RESEARCHER	A comprehensive guide to the culture, politics, economic life, trends, and personalities of an entire region of the continent via their publications. This is why we attempt to be inclusive whether or not a publisher is a paying market.
LIBRARIAN	Subject areas for which presses and periodicals are producing books and periodicals; essays on copyright and small presses, plus the ideas and dreams of some of the continent's leading authors.
TEACHER STUDENT PARENT	Listings of periodicals that accept submissions from students; a special essay section with testimonials from published student writers as well as how to use regional books in the classroom, or publish a book in kindergarten.
BUSINESS	The trade periodicals or community newspapers that you need to target a marketing campaign; for instance, all the sports-related magazines or agricultural trade journals.

No matter who you or what you do, when you open *Writer's Northwest Handbook* you are accessing the best regional directory of the community of the printed word. We are committed to improving *WNH* with each biennial edition. Your suggestions make that easier, and are always welcome.

—The Editors

Sorry, We Don't Take Westerns

by Mary Clearman Blew

In 1972 I sent one of my first short stories to a prestigious national magazine and got it back almost by return mail. Written across the printed rejection form was this note: *Sorry, we don't take Westerns.*

The title of that story was "I beat the Midget," and a part of it had been born during the summer I was seventeen and my father had decided I should break a Shetland stallion to ride. For me the experience had been equal parts humiliation — my feet dragged the ground when I rode the Midget, what if somebody from school *saw* me? — and fear; the Midget might be pint-sized, but he was cold-mouthed and powerful, and when he bowed his neck and stampeded, I couldn't stop him. Out of those wild sidehill rides on the Midget, as he crashed through timber, thornbrush, and windfall with the bit in his teeth, with blue sky revolving and pine stubs breaking over my head, came the feelings I drew upon years later to tell the story of a boy's anger at his father, his frustration with an animal that could return none of his feelings, and his recognition of his own capacity to inflict pain.

I don't think that kind of rejection note would be written today. In the space of twenty years, our idea of the West, and of writing about the West, has changed radically. It is not just that gunslingers have gone out of style or that we have become too cynical to believe in the clear-cut virtues of *High Noon.* Nor — contrary to the outraged letters that pepper the journals of Western history — are the new writers of the West necessarily its destroyers. The growing awareness among historians and writers that the story of the West is not told in epic alone, nor in one voice, nor contained in any mythos, has exploded the old formulae and cleared space for the stories the men and women who lived through the process called "the frontier" knew all along.

It has been pointed out many times before now that one of the most profound developments in recent Western literature has been the emergence of talented Native American writers who have taught us to listen to a story that runs counter to the old myth of frontier settlement. But a remarkable achievement of contemporary novelists like James Welch and Louise Erdrich is their reinvention of a fictional past in which the voices of an older generation of writers — D'arcy McNickle, for example, or Mourning Dove — have a context. And in this context, a wealth of Indian oral literature emerges as the heritage of the many and varied people who hadn't been sitting around yawning while they waited for Lewis and Clark to show up and assign them a part in the Westward Movement.

Telling a story is a way we have of giving shape to ourselves out of chaos. The story-teller selects, discards, arranges, and rearranges the myriad details that clamor for telling. A new arrangement, a new story, another version of the way things are. Contemporary writers of fiction owe a lot to the oral historians and social historians who helped retrieve the memories and the written records of ordinary men and women and locate them in a past that seems incomparably richer and more diverse than it did twenty years ago. The voices of women in particular now resound far beyond the old stereotypes, generating a wide range of novels, stories, and memoirs dealing with women's experience in the West; a few of my recent personal favorites include Shannon Applegate (*Skookum*), Molly Gloss (*The Jump-Off Creek*), Pauline Mortensen (*Back Before the World Turned Nasty*).

Writers in the West are reconsidering the old assumptions about property and stewardship, individualism and self-reliance. Our contemporary stories are about families and cultural inheritance during a hundred hard years of farming and ranching, or about disconnections and disturbing visions in the urban West, or about the diminishing natural world and our place in it. These stories are remarkable not because they are new, but because there are so many of them and because they can be told simultaneously. Contemporary fiction about the West is complex, diverse, rich, and various in ways that barely seemed possible twenty years ago.

Nothing in the way we live now is as simple as it once seemed. But as our context expands, so does our sense of ourselves. If we are to have a future, that future may depend on our understanding of past and place. For me, the recent wealth of books written about the place where I live is a source of hope for a future. ∎

Contemporary writers of fiction owe a lot to the oral historians...who helped retrieve the memories and the written records of ordinary men and women....

Mary Clearman Blew, *born in Lewistown, Montana, teachers creative writing at Lewis-Clark State College in Lewiston, Idaho. Her books include* Lambing Out and Other Stories, Runaway, *and a series of essays, tentatively entitled* All But the Waltz *(to be published later in 1991).*

Interview with Katherine Dunn: Stephen King, Cornflakes Boxes, & "Real Writers"

by Susan Stanley

Katherine Dunn — tall, graceful, goldenhaired, wise-faced — rolls herself a cigarette and gazes fondly at author Stephen King's books on a shelf opposite her easy chair. A phone rings in another part of the cavernous Northwest Portland house shared with two friends and her son Eli. But Dunn will not be distracted from the subject at hand: namely, literary snobbery over what constitutes "real writing."

As author of *Geek Love*, the shocking, heartwarming — and National Book Award-nominated — tale of the Binewskis, a carnival family breeding their own freak show, Dunn has earned her right to talk about what makes good writing good writing.

"The Geek," as she casually refers to her weird brain-child, was preceded by two earlier novels. (*Truck* and *Attic*, published when she was in her 20's, convinced Dunn that she should take a break to learn the novelwriting craft.) Writing *Geek Love* over a seven-year period, she kept hearth and home intact by painting houses, tending bar, slinging hash, cranking out a column called "The Slice" for *Willamette Week*, and — yes! — writing about the sport of boxing.

And yes, she is a slobbering fan of the writings of the horrific Stephen King.

"They're thoroughly smeared with peanut butter and jelly," she says of her King collection. "And sprinkled with tobacco leaves. And give every evidence of being mauled by everybody in the family.

"I think Stephen King is an excellent storyteller, and a marvelous craftsman who is read because he really touches people. There's this Olympian notion that anybody who is voluntarily read by millions of people, and who has the poor taste to make a lot of money at writing, has to be trash!"

It's not a new notion, she admits. Nor does it spring from a purity of spirit.

"Primarily we find that it is writers who are not making so much money, and who do not have as large an audience, who say these things," says Dunn. "One hates to say that it might be a green-eyed monster showing its head, but.… "

It all comes down, she says, to a hierarchical system of snobberies formally defining literature — "lit-ur-uh-chur…there's an umlaut in there!" Somewhere out there,

mostly self-appointed critics grumpily decree what does and doesn't make "qual lit."

"And the 'qual lit' writers, of course, look down upon anybody who happens to write in a different genre."

Good writing is good writing, period, according to Katherine Dunn.

"There is no reason why there cannot be excellent writing, and deeply-moving works, in any genre of fiction." There's no stopping her now.

"And I will go further and say there are probably marvelous romance writers. There are certainly terrific mystery writers. There are magnificent science fiction writers. There are *astounding, profound, and culturally-elevating* S&M slasher writers!"

> *He meant him and Norman Mailer and — on a good day, and if they're feeling particularly open-minded — maybe Tom Wolfe.*

Topic? Form? Genre? All irrelevant, according to Dunn:

"It has simply to do with the quality of the writing. And good writing is good writing — no matter where it appears. If it appears on the back of a Kellogg's Cornflakes box, it is still good writing."

The novelist ticks off her own faves, non-qual lit-wise.

There was Elmer Keith, the late and "astounding" handgun columnist in *Guns and Ammo* Magazine.

"I'm terrified of guns, but I occasionally read that magazine because I have to research something," she explains. But Keith's writing pulled her in, despite herself.

"The man was an astounding writer, and he brought great beauty and simplicity and integrity of emotion to his writings about any kind of handgun, any topic that he broached."

Then there was Don Holm, longtime *Oregonian* outdoors writer, whose descriptions of salmon swimming upstream to spawn, for example, "would literally bring tears to my eyes."

Nobody seems to mention that journalism is actually *writing*, Dunn points out, "and yet 99 percent of everything that we read, once we graduate from high school, is going to be journalism.

"They didn't build cathedrals out of bricks or stones, they built them out of gossamer webs spun from the ears of gods or something! This stuff is rock and brick, and whatever you

Continued on pg. 14

If Poets Were Made

by Lowell Jaeger

I graduated from the Iowa Writers' Workshop, though just barely. The faculty refused to sign my thesis. I was angry with the workshop because I wasn't producing much or growing as a writer. I didn't strain a muscle to help myself either, because my failure was tolerable so long as I could blame my teachers, the university, or the "literary establishment," rather than pointing the finger where it belonged. Back then I was full of all the standard paranoia toward workshops that one still hears on the pages of this or that journal over and over again. Chicken Little sounds the alarm; workshops are cloning McPoets and McPoems, and like a final curtain falling on the literature of Western Civilization, the sky is dropping down, down, down.

Cock-a-doodle-do. I'd enlisted in the Iowa Writers' Workshop to be made into a writer, and because I wasn't performing like I'd hoped, I strutted around the classroom making noise, pecking at my teachers for not doing their jobs. Jack Legget, the workshop director back then, wisely counseled me not to make a lifelong practice of such cocky nonsense, then he overrode the faculty's censure, winked, shook my drumstick, and sent me out into the world where he knew I was doomed to someday contend with students just like myself. "If the fool persists in his folly, he shall become wise." Thus spake William Blake.

Ironically, a reviewer for *American Book Review* panned my first book, *War On War*, for the "glib vacuity" and "sanitized execution" one would expect of a writer who had been groomed by the Iowa Workshop: "A reasonable subtitle for the collection might be 'The Iowa Writers' Workshop Meets Vietnam,'" said the review; "Jaeger is a former student of this outfit, and his teachers, *the usual suspects*, wax predictably effusive about the prize-hopeful importance of the book." (The italics are mine.) Marvin Bell had written a cover blurb, but he was on leave or teaching in Hawaii for the entire span of my enrollment at Iowa. Denise Levertov penned a strong endorsement also; I'd never spoken to her in my life. Nor had I ever been a student of William Stafford's, and he also wrote a few kind words about the book. In his self-righteous struggle against glib vacuity, the Chicken Little who wrote this review was both glib and vacuous. I'd bet this man worries about being pursued by the "poetry mafia," an old label thrown at successful writers by unhappy wanna-be's.

And Jack Legget was right: I've been teaching now for ten years; every quarter one student or another of mine mirrors for me my behavior at Iowa. I get blamed if my students fail ("But I did it just like *you* said I should!"), and if

my students succeed, then I'm blamed for having engineered their careers. One of my students published poems in a magazine that's been rejecting me for years. I overheard a classmate's jealous analysis: "He only got published because

> *At fourteen, I was so strung-out on new hormones I spent most of the year exiled into whatever corner the teachers shoved my desk and thereby drew a DMZ between me and the rest of civilization.*

he sucks up to Jaeger, and Jaeger's got pull." Strange I can be seen as so powerful when most days I worry that if my salary were determined by how much my students gain from me, then I shouldn't be paid at all.

All this racket in the barnyard begins with the sophomoric notion that a writer can be made — can be guaranteed success — if only he or she enrolls in a prestigious school and makes solid contacts with influential bigshots. "I can get you a gonnection," offers Myer Wolfsheim, and Nick must be comforted to know that Gatsby's not a self-made man. That's how I felt at Iowa; I was convinced that all my classmates who were writing well, placing poems, and winning awards — those guys were all sucking up to the faculty and making "gonnections." So, too, the reviewer mentioned above is comforted to assume I'm a mafioso.

If they're secure enough, some writers share names of editors, prospective markets, etc. Maybe one student in a thousand is recommended by a big-name teacher to an agency. But I know of no writer ever who edged his or her way into the spotlight without having some pretty damn good work to show. Hemingway said the one tool every writer needs is a built-in shockproof crap detector. The notion that workshops can destroy genuine talent, or that workshops can mold the mediocre into literary marketability is crap. A writer weak enough to be broken by a workshop will likely be broken elsewhere anyway. Writers who think they are spending tuition dollars on instant literary success are fated to meet with some painful surprises. And critics who think workshops both ruin writers and then propel them into fame…well, they're just plain naive.

On the other hand, if I've been made at all, I must credit my eighth-grade English teacher, Bernadine Tomasik. At fourteen, I was so strung-out on new hormones I spent most of the year exiled into whatever corner the teachers shoved my desk and thereby drew a DMZ between me and the rest of civilization. (Once the vice-principal jerked me from class and dragged me down the hallway with my head in a hammer

Continued on pg. 15

The Journey to Now: Influences on the Life and Work of William Stafford

An Interview by David Hedges

HEDGES: What were some of your early influences?

STAFFORD: I suppose, in relation to writing, one of the big influences was that my parents were both readers — eager, voracious, famished readers. We'd go to the library every week and get a stack of books, bring them home, and read them. And so we kids — there were three, I had a brother and a sister — we'd get our books, they'd get their books, and we'd come home and read.

HEDGES: Do you recall any of those books?

STAFFORD: Well, the first thing I remember my father forcing on me was H.G. Wells' *Outline of History*, a multi-volume thing. I suppose I was in the second or third grade. It had little pictures of flint arrowheads, and they really got me excited.

HEDGES: Where were you living at that time?

STAFFORD: This was in Kansas, in little towns — Hutchinson, Liberal, Garden City, El Dorado, Lawrence.

HEDGES: How did Kansas influence you?

STAFFORD: Kansas was not overcrowded — when I was there, at least. And we relied on ourselves for sociability. All kinds of ice cream socials. The church was usually the center of social life in those little towns, and I don't mean the formal Sunday services. We'd go to whatever church had the most sociability.

HEDGES: Did religion play a role in your life?

STAFFORD: Neither of my parents was orthodoxly religious, but they had decided social views. We were integrated in Kansas, for one thing, and they always had a special interest in it. It was a lot more than formal tolerance. It was an active interest in other races and other countries. And they would read me little poems about life in other parts of the world.

HEDGES: Is there a teacher who stands out?

STAFFORD: There were several, even back in grade school. I can remember the one who read *The Highwayman* to us. She was so overcome she couldn't finish it. It was just too much for her. And this touched me.

HEDGES: What writers influence you?

STAFFORD: Prose writers are the main influence on me, not poets. I think the more interesting writers are writing prose today. Maybe back in Virgil's time, that wasn't true.

…If you go back and re-read Milton, or someone like that, there's a lot of confidence. It's not ironic, it's not funny, it's straight into the heart of things. And the poets now are often witty, and intelligent, but they don't usually feel the tide of life.

HEDGES: You've talked about your Native American heritage. Was that an influence?

STAFFORD: Well, the Native Americans were an influence. I don't know if Dorothy's listening — she always gets tickled if I claim to be Native American — but my father said, "Remember, Bill, we're part Indian." And in these little towns, we could always jump off the edge of town and be in the country. We'd go out hiking, kicking around, building tepees, digging caves, things like that. Being self-sufficient in the wilderness always appealed to me — surviving.

HEDGES: You were a conscientious objector during World War Two. Was your decision a curve in the road, or a major fork?

STAFFORD: It felt as if I were just keeping on doing what I had been doing. It seemed to me *other* people were taking the fork. In the thirties, there was a very strong peace movement in colleges, so most people were peace lovers. Then the war came, and people took the fork in the road, and I just kept on going straight. You know, that's happening all over again, in our time. For some reason, people get that quirky feeling when a war comes. They change. There is another aspect to that, though. It was a fork in the road in the sense that I suddenly found myself a part of a society that had departed from me. And that veering off on the part of

---

…my parents were both readers — eager, voracious, famished readers.

---

society left me feeling different. The country had been taken away from me — you know, the ordinary assumptions about people around you. And they all, even the people close to me in my home town, turned into foreigners.

HEDGES: Did your C.O. experiences have an influence on you?

STAFFORD: Terrific influence, I realize now. At the time, you're sort of tunnel visioned. But I've looked back and realized that it was four years of living among foreigners. I mean, there were government supervisors, and they were foreign, definitely. And there were military men. And there were the church people, who were foreign to me when I started but I was domesticated to them at the end. And all these people that were just shoveled into the camps from all kinds of places....So what we had in common was that we wouldn't go to war. Otherwise, we had tremendous arguments for four years on all other topics.

HEDGES: Do you feel you took any wrong turns? Were there any dead ends that caused you to back up and reassess?

STAFFORD: There were a lot of dead ends that really were dead ends, but I didn't realize they were at the time. I mean, I should have reassessed often. When I was growing up, I don't think I was nearly as experimental as I should have been about big things — my choice of a vocation — I mean, to make money. These were Depression days, so

You could be a farmer, you could be a writer.

I'm justifying myself now. If there was a job, you took it. You didn't say, "No, this isn't my career." You said, "Oh, a job!" I delivered papers. I dug ditches, literally. I was in construction work…worked for an oil refinery…thinned sugar beets out in the fields. Whatever there was to do, I did. As a consequence, I was never alert to the longer term implications of whatever job I got. I'd just keep on with that job until it was shot out from under me, or I had to move, or was drafted. So, I went through life never changing my job of my own volition, but always being pushed like a billiard ball, by circumstances. And somehow, I got in that channel of being a teacher. By the time I sort of waked up, I knew how to teach. I didn't know anything else.

HEDGES: Was teaching a spur or a hindrance to your creativity?

STAFFORD: (reflects) I guess even the fact that I hesitated means that I'm not with a lot of writers who automatically say teaching enough English will turn you into a writer. It seemed to me better than digging ditches, or thinning sugar beets. I thought it was a pretty good job. I taught high school, by the way, first, and that was hard, but college was always easy.

HEDGES: Were you ever reluctant to call yourself a writer?

STAFFORD: No, I just thought that was one of the things you could do. You could be a farmer, you could be a writer. And I still feel that way.

HEDGES: Do you consider yourself part of a movement, or a school?

STAFFORD: When I'm writing, it's a whole new adventure each time. It's like plunging into the ocean each time…like, "The language is out there. Get into it See what happens." It seems experimental all over again, each time, each day I write. It doesn't seem like supporting a movement, or finding a trend that I want to join, or anything like that.

…If you go into writing in order to write something good, to be a great writer, or to prevail in a certain market, you're not doing it, it's not art. What you've tied yourself to is mechanical activity in which you measure some goal, and carpenter your way toward it.

…I think art is the kind of activity in which the primary goal doesn't have to do with anything outside itself.…Art comes about through exercising an appetite for an activity. If you hold yourself to a regimen of training, you're not downhill skiing. You're not doing the thing that will enable you, after you've been involved in it long enough, to be a natural.

HEDGES: You're riding the chair lift up, and riding it back down.

STAFFORD: (laughs) Something like that. And writing, heart writing, creative writing, is more like downhill skiing on a slope you don't know. You've got to improvise. All sorts of things happen. And if you know what you're going to do before you start, it's because somebody's already been there.

…What I like about writing poetry is that each time, I feel I've almost got it. It's almost there. I'm tantalized by that feeling. And maybe I *have* got it. I don't know. I just write again tomorrow, 'cause what I wrote today really moved me, really shook me up.

HEDGES: Would you go back and change anything?

STAFFORD: It feels as if…(laughs) writing something all over again. I wouldn't have started where I started, I wouldn't have gone where I went. It's the hindsight advantage we have.

HEDGES: I was thinking of the last lines from *Any Journey*: "The road straightens behind you. / It is now. It has all come true."

STAFFORD: It straightens behind you in the sense that it's a story, and it's coherent. But you could have chosen another road. In fact, one of my poems, *Ask Me*, sort of has that in it: "Some time when the river is ice ask me / mistakes I have made. Ask me whether / what I have done is my life." ∎

I was thinking about someone like Wordsworth. You know, people can say, "Too romantic, shallow psychology," and so on. But he had a lot of fervency about what he thought he was doing.

David Hedges is a West Linn (OR) writer whose poems, short stories, essays and articles have appeared in The Christian Science Monitor, Northwest Magazine, *and numerous literary periodicals.*

Science Fiction and Fantasy

by Greg Bear

Speaking to a good friend recently, I came to a sudden realization that the war had been won. Science fiction and fantasy have permeated the world consciousness; past discriminations against the literature we love have fled. What few backwaters of literary bigotry remain are rather like those Eastern European and Asian countries still wrapped in the shroud of Stalin and Mao — poor, depressed, deeply in trouble.

Our conversation went like this: he read me the lyrics of a song for a Broadway musical for which he's writing the book, a musical rife with science fiction elements and brisk references to science fiction lore; we talked about a review of one of my books in *People* magazine; we discussed science fiction and fantasy's regular appearance in the Book-of-the-Month Club; Poland and the Soviet Union are now paying cash U.S. dollars for American science fiction; and so on.

The war's over. It's time to get on with the peace. And the peace means writing with every tool at our disposal, writing as passionately as we can, to reach that large and eclectic audience of readers who, whether they know it or not, are ripe for the very best science fiction and fantasy.

> *They [sf and fantasy] require not just a keen eye and a sharp prose style, but a wild imagination and education in areas as diverse as science and technology, history, comparative religions, linguistics, musicology...*

There's one catch. More bad science fiction and fantasy are being written now than ever before. The popularity of these genres — if indeed they are genres, having few if any limitations of style and form — has attracted thousands of beginners with no previous experience, or hacks with no passion or love.

Publishers, fighting for lucrative rack space, have published thousands of terrible books. The amount of bad or mediocre science fiction and fantasy published now is astonishing, more than ever before. Some of it makes best-seller lists; some of it even wins prestigious awards. Most of it doesn't begin to approach the top of the form.

Science fiction and fantasy are the hardest kinds of literature to write well. They require not just a keen eye and a sharp prose style, but a wild imagination and education in areas as diverse as science and technology, history, comparative religions, linguistics, musicology...an apprenticeship in either field could take ten or fifteen years, just to achieve minimal competence, let alone excellence.

Let's start at the beginning: what is science fiction? The name is established, unavoidable, and not completely misleading. It is fiction that uses science's ideal world-view of selfless objectivity to tell timeless stories dealing with the deep nature of existence, consciousness, organization, humanity, life. Science fiction is not limited by what the writer has personally experienced, though that will inevitably shape the writer's fictions. It is not limited by religion, culture, or even by the present laws of science. Its only limitation — more a liberation, actually — is its demand that the writer, and the reader, step outside of their selves and see through other eyes, in other spaces, places, and times. It demands extraordinary empathy for otherness, not just Milton's sympathy for Satan, but an awareness of the character and importance of all beings human and otherwise, real and potential. Prejudice should be its antithesis; discovery its only fixed law.

Good science fiction is not just good literature; it's exercise for the marathon future.

Fantasy is more inner-directed, past-oriented. Fantasy explores the subconscious in more traditional modes. Religion, history, and language heavily color fantasy; science is less important, though not negligible. Fantasy has its own kind of freedom. Both modes are rich and important. And good fantasy is no easier to write than good science fiction, though with our present state of education, it may be more accessible to more writers and readers than science fiction.

Why do I concentrate on science fiction? The strictures of the sf fugue appeal to me. The discipline expands my art. I do not start with the strictures: my mind runs free, examining a wide range of dreamlike possibilities. I then ask myself, how can the scientific world-view allow these things to *be*? And I find in them the problems and emotions that most intrigue and puzzle me. I work using both subject and story structure to get beneath the reader's skin, to grab the reader's heart and mind simultaneously.

Science fiction has a reputation for cold rationality, but that's a misconception. At the heart of science fiction, as well as science, is the mystic urge for transcendence, for growth and survival, love and appreciation.

Personal example: my most recently published novel, *Queen of Angels*, is set some sixty years from today, in Los Angeles and Haiti. Its subject is sanity and self-awareness, both personal and cultural, explored through the plot elements of mass murder, political turmoil, and psychological therapy. Its infrastructure includes nanotechnology — the as

Continued on pg. 15

John Haines: Alaskan Voice of Reason

Interview by Linda O'Brien and Linny Stovall

A poet, an essayist and a homesteader in the Alaskan wilderness, John Haines' words paint moving and exacting pictures. He has kept a vigil on the northern frontier, and his writing emerges from the knowledge that we must learn to draw on resources deeper than the human experience. His work resonates with images from nature that tell us much about ourselves and belie an intimacy with the natural world that very few modern writers have achieved.

Haines is the author of six major collections of poetry, and two collections of reviews, essays, and a memoir, The Stars, The Snow, The Fire. *He was a featured speaker at Bumbershoot 1990 in Seattle where WNH caught up with him.*

WNH: What was your goal in placing yourself outside the cultural mainstream, so far removed from the intellectual and academic community most writers gel in?

HAINES: My twenty-plus years homesteading in Alaska was important to me in the sense of getting back to something basic in the place itself. It was a big adventure. It was hard work and it was fun. Mostly, it was very demanding and I learned a lot about myself. I also learned a lot about this pristine country in a way that you cannot by going out on a weekend. The idea is to immerse oneself in the place.

WNH: While homesteading, what influenced your thinking?

HAINES: I had a lot of reflective time. I was married, but I had a good amount of correspondence with other writers. My conversation was primarily with books. There are certain works that influenced me that had no relation to Alaska as such. They had everything to do with the encounter of the European with North America all the way back to Daniel Boone. I did a fair amount of reading on Native American backgrounds. My task was to try to clarify all that and define it for myself and see where I fit in.

This is the last stage of a certain western course of empire. It's interesting and dispiriting to see the things happening there. Some days you think we haven't learned anything in 200 years. Some people have. I place some confidence in that. It's no longer permissible to set fire to a forest in order to get dry wood, for example. But the early people up there did that just as a matter of course. They just cut everything, you see. And you can't do that now. But we still have the same people who want to drill the last puddle of oil. They haven't learned anything. They're unfortunately the ones running the affairs.

WNH: Although you moved to Alaska in the late 1940s, you didn't write about your experiences there until 1966. At what point did you define your writing focus?

HAINES: I began as a poet my first winter up there. That was 1947-1948. I stayed long enough to do all the preliminaries on the homestead, and started writing that winter. Then I left and went back east to school. I kept writing while I was studying art. Gradually I became more and more of a writer and less of an artist. When I began writing again in the late '50s I graduated to writing pretty much full time, and to teaching literature.

WNH: Do you think of yourself as a Northwest writer?

HAINES: I think of myself as an American writer, an essayist, and I happen to like the Northwest over the east. But I don't have to be in the Northwest to write. I wrote very well in England. I was sufficiently distant from everything and had things in perspective better.

WNH: How have you as a poet stayed alive and what do you recommend to new writers?

HAINES: Fundamentally that's what every writer has to find out. My way of going about it was extreme, and I would say, limited. I wouldn't encourage anybody to go out and try what I did. On the other hand, someone might do it and discover something.

I've had some difficult times, during periods when I wasn't teaching. But I've been lucky in getting grants at times when I really needed them. Ohio University rescued me two years ago when I was thinking about selling my car to get by. And I may end up teaching at Ohio University, if I don't find something else. As I get older, I like less and less the necessity of constantly having to move from place to place in order to work.

WNH: What changes would you like to see come about within this profession?

HAINES: This is the only country I know of in the Western world where so many poets and writers teach. It seems to me a self-imposed barrier, and I would like to see us stop limiting ourselves. I'd like to see writers teach

---

Haines' writing is clear testament to his commitment to participating in life, and to his keen knack for observation. He urges us to: "Stand still where you are — at the end of pavement, in a sunbreak of the forest, on the open, cloud-peopled terrace of the plains. Look deeply into the wind-furrows of the grass, into the leaf-stilled water of pools. Think back through the silence, of the life that was and is not here now, of the strong pastness of things — shadows of the end and beginning."

Continued on pg. 16

The Montana Canon and Its Discontents

by Rick Newby

Almost precisely two years ago, in the autumn of 1988, two superb anthologies — *Montana Spaces* (Nick Lyons Books in collaboration with the Montana Land Reliance) and *The Last Best Place* (Montana Historical Society Press) — were published in celebration of the Montana statehood centennial, documenting a rich and diverse Montana literary tradition. The two anthologies — both regional bestsellers and, for the most part, critically acclaimed — set a standard, announced to Montanans and to the world, "This is the canon of Montana writing;" as the editors of *The Last Best Place* noted, theirs was not the first (or last) anthology of Montana writing, but "if we have done our work well, it will be definitive for awhile."

Luckily for the health of literature under the Big Sky, progress in literary history is, as Viktor Shklovsky said, "a succession of canonizations and displacements," the canon being shaped, not only by considerations of form and of quality, but by the rise of new schools, new visions, new and contrary voices. And over the past two years, those Montana writers and constituencies even partially excluded from the newly constructed canon — women, avant gardists, Native Americans, and residents of the state's eastern counties — have refused to be silenced, making their voices heard, sometimes politely, sometimes crudely, and often with great

> *...the Montana "surrealists," a band of Missoula-based avant gardists, mostly male, who eschewed the usual subjects of Montana poems — landscape, weather, and natural objects — in favor of inner, psychic landscapes...*

vehemence, wit, and anger. The displacements have already begun; what was definitive two years ago seems less than inclusive today.

In an early review of *Montana Spaces*, T.J. Gilles, staff writer for the *Great Falls Tribune*, complained that the book's contributors (including such luminaries as Tom McGuane, David Quammen, Gretel Ehrlich, Tim Cahill, William Hjortsberg, and Annick Smith) were, for the most part, relative newcomers to Montana, and, worse, from his east-of-the-Continental-Divide perspective, they mostly spoke from western Montana and the "confines of narrow river values with good fly fishing."

Where, he asked, were the Native American writers like Bill Yellow Robe and James Welch, the writers from the eastern two-thirds of the state, cowboy poets like Wally

McRae and rancher-fictioneers like John Moore? (Welch and McRae do appear in *The Last Best Place*.

Mary Clearman Blew, a member of the editorial board of *The Last Best Place* and a contributor to *Montana Spaces*, had her own sharp questions when she presented her paper, "There Ain't No Such Thing as a Woman in Montana," to

> *There is such a thing as a women who writes fiction in Montana. She is largely invisible.*

the state historical society's annual conference in late 1988. Blew had just finished reading, in *Montana Spaces*, novelist Ralph Beer's essay, "In Spite of Distance: The New Literature of Montana," and she'd been startled to discover that Beer had not mentioned, among the new Montana writers he cited, one woman. Reading more closely, Blew found — applying, tongue somewhat in cheek, the techniques of feminist hermeneutics — "traces of the excluded other," three brief references in which women or girls were either rescued or kidnapped, "acted upon and passed around like token[s] in a game, but essentially unretained." It seems odd, she said, "speaking of outsiders and insiders," to be the only native Montanan on the panel that day when "I don't even exist."

Blew concluded her remarks with the assertion, "There is such a thing as a women who writes fiction in Montana. She is largely invisible. She's Pat Henley, Lynda Sexson, Linda Peavey, Ruth McLaughlin. She's enrolled in a fiction writing class somewhere, and she's probably keeping quiet."

Astonishingly, *The Last Best Place* — which purports to be definitive and does in fact present remarkable diversity in its 1162 pages — falls short in its representation of women writers. Where, indeed, were the women writing fiction today, those who have published novels and collections of stories, the Lynda Sexsons (*Margaret of the Imperfections*, winner of a Pacific Northwest Booksellers Award), the Sara Vogans (*In Shelley's Leg*), the Melissa Kwasnys (*Modern Daughters and the Outlaw West*)?

The Last Best Place excluded another group of Montana writers, the Montana "surrealists," a band of Missoula-based avant gardists, mostly male, who eschewed the usual subjects of Montana poems — landscape, weather, and natural objects — in favor of "inner, psychic landscapes not grounded in the real, but in what Andre Breton called the 'marvelous.'" These poets found much energy in an outlaw Montana tradition that included anarchists and folk artists, copper kings

Continued on pg. 14

Ivan Doig: Researching the Past

by Linda O'Brien

Ivan Doig brings our past to life, populating a realistic West with characters who struggle through their day to day existence by balancing passions, dreams, and responsibilities. Doig's books are tightly-plotted testaments to his belief that in order to write about a region, "you have to learn its skin and language and soul."

All of which translates into planning and hard work. "I tend to think of situations and chronologies early," Doig says. "In the current book, *Ride With Me Mariah Montana*, it was the situation of putting three people of a couple generations in a motorhome and turning them loose in Montana during the Centennial year. *Dancing At The Rascal Fair* is putting people aboard a ship in Scotland and sending them to Montana. Alongside of this, is thinking about chronology, which is often an outline for me. *English Creek* takes place within one summer in Montana. *Winter Brothers* is one winter on the coast. *Dancing at The Rascal Fair* deliberately expanded to cover thirty years. So situation and chronology are early considerations, and on the planks of that stage come the characters."

"If I had one thing to change about my freelance period, it would be to be tied less to trying to get published and make money out of it, and to work more on manuscripts and the craft of writing."

Doig's affinity for the land and its language, and his commitment to historical accuracy are the cornerstones of his work. As he puts it, "To me, getting the details right puts an intrinsic rightness to the book. The notion that care in small things translates to care in greater things is one of the benefits of research."

Doig believes research is not an isolated part of the writing process. "It's akin to an actor's performance. Is the time spent memorizing not part of the performance? No, I think it is. And a writer's research is maybe akin to that—to an actor learning his part.

"You have to cast a broad research net and find details. A lot of archival research goes into my books. I try to be as imaginative as possible about where to look. There's a brief mention early in *English Creek* of auction sales of the property and equipment of farmers and ranchers who had gone bankrupt. I wondered, what would those have been like? I talked to a historian friend who said to look at the records of the Montana agency that took over when all the banks failed in the 1930s. Those state guys had to go out and inventory the properties the banks held. There were listings of what kind of harness, what kind of plow, what kind of kitchen equipment those ranches possessed, so there's an exact picture of what was on a ranch in the mid 1930s.

"A lot of my research is done by going out and listening to the people of the area I'm writing about. For characters,

I've often gone back into historic photo files and collected faces. In *English Creek* there's a kid named Ray Heaney who's described as looking more like his face had been carved out of a pumpkin than born. That kid is from a Dorothea Lange photo from the depression years. A kid from somewhere out in Oregon, with an absolutely winning face, a cowlick and great incised dimples. I've never seen that kid but he existed for me in that photo."

During the past ten years Doig has immersed himself in writing about a century of western existence. When asked at what expense, he says, "One of a writer's decisions has to be what he can take on. What his time and energy will allow. One of the things I've had to do as a supposedly successful novelist is turn my back on journalism. Sometimes that's frustrating, because I can't clone myself to do some of the topical writing I'd like to do. I wrote a couple of hundred magazine pieces during the ten or so years I was a full-time magazine freelance writer, and probably 40 or 50 of those were ecological pieces. That was my inning to speak to the ecological issues of this area. My greater effect, these days, seems to be in the longer, slower process of writing books."

Reminiscing about the role of regional markets in his career, Doig says, "The markets that were available to me through the late '60s and '70s were a place to flex writing muscle and try some things out. Economically the markets were pretty dismal, and that's one reason I turned to books.

"Regional publishing has something to offer, but I'm not sure it always offers it quickly and amply enough. I was a writer out here for twelve years before *This House Of Sky* was accepted by an editor in New York, and my memory is that only one regional publisher ever came around and asked me 'Hey, are you thinking about doing any kind of book, ever?' And that was after the manuscript had already begun making the rounds nationally."

With the success his career has seen, it's hard to imagine Ivan Doig with regrets. But there's always hindsight. "If I had one thing to change about my freelance period, it would be to be tied less to trying to get published and make money out of it, and to work more on manuscripts and the craft of writing. I wish to God I had worked on a novel at that point. I wish I'd done more poetry than I did.

"Given what I tend to see as the severe economics of regional freelancing, I think I would urge people to say, 'This isn't going to pay me anything anyhow, why don't I write

Continued on pg. 15

Writing Here in God's Country

by John Rember

My discussion of Northwest writing begins ten thousand miles away. During the last year I was sent to the tropics by a travel magazine to report on an up-and-coming beach resort. I had a great time, but the article I produced ultimately was killed by the magazine's senior editor because it was downbeat. I made the mistake of explaining the life cycle of a tropical beach.

This cycle takes land of astonishing beauty and shows it as the real estate that supports a strange architectural succession. Bungalows turn into small hotels, small hotels turn into large ones, and large ones turn into clusters of great concrete high-rises with attendant red-light districts, jet-ski marinas, faked-goods shops, tours to places that were once in movies, beggar-infested currency exchange booths, and sewage-marked tidelines.

My travel article had become an environmental piece, and like most environmental pieces, it did not contain a lot of good news. One of the clear conclusions that could be drawn from it was that the tourist industry is anything but non-polluting. People who advertise in travel magazines do not welcome conclusions of this sort. People who edit travel magazines don't either.

I tell this anecdote not because of its implications for travel writers or for tropical excursions, but because it contains a transformation that Northwest writers — and writers anywhere else, for that matter — are going to have to face. All writing has become environmental writing. What we might call the Gaia Issues — the concerns of the living Earth — have become the backdrop against which we view the meaning of short stories, novels, and even simple descriptions of days at the beach.

If such a statement seems too strong, consider the first question I ask the students in my writing classes: How do you make meaning in a world without an ozone layer? Or the second: How do you keep an eloquent and individual voice in a world where the population will double to 10 billion in forty-five years? Or the third: How do you set a novel or essay or short story in a world whose climate is radically changing, without the setting becoming the plot?

These are alien, twisted, crazy-making questions. But they stem from the world we live in and the world which engenders our experience — and therefore our writing. If we do not answer them we will become writers who are silly and irrelevant, or worse yet, escapist, or worst of all, mute.

The above material suggests several points that I think

are important to writers who share the Northwestern environment. We need to have, and I think can have, a shared vision, a vision that will allow us to speak in a common language, and use it to answer questions we all face. Literary history is full of examples of people who sparked each other to brilliance, who saw in each other that quality that I would characterize as *having something to say*. And having seen that in others, they began to see it in themselves.

In the Northwest, we have a multitude of good writers, but we do not have, I suspect, the benefit of a shared vision. We tend to see each other as economic and cultural rivals rather than as allies, and we tend to take refuge from the terribly complicated questions we face by indulging in a mythology that isn't even our own.

In the interests of escape, we have forgotten who we are and where we live. We yearn, instead, to be part of an American culture that does not cherish the Northwest for its inherent qualities but instead uses it as a backdrop for a strange succession of images whose ultimate function is to degrade. We cannot define a common vision or even our common selves — we cannot even name the things we love — without coming into conflict with that encircling culture.

You get an idea of how mutagenic and unhealthy that culture can be when you find, in the fields and mountains of Idaho, that most urban of creatures, the Marlboro Man. Madison Avenue images have defined both the wild West and the wild Westerner. When we buy these images or the products they sell, when we dress up in funny hats and pointy-toed boots and five-pound belt buckles, we stop seeing the real fields and real mountains and real trails and real trees and the real people that exist here. They become overlaid with what are often commercial images, which are — in not the nicest sense of the word — fictions.

It is a pervasive phenomenon, seen perhaps most clearly in our treatment of land heretofore free of commercial exploitation. The Northwest wild lands have come to be defined — and confined — by the lawyers who wrote the Wilderness Bill. The wilderness experience, whether it be called to mind by empty beach or primitive mountain lake, has come to be defined by the people who create 4-wheel drive ads, or who write the terrifyingly urban REI catalog. Wilderness has become stage setting, and is used to market products or to make soul deadening jobs bearable for fifty weeks a year or to bear the grisly projections of people who

> *The wilderness experience…has come to be defined by the people who create 4-wheel drive ads, or who write the terrifyingly urban REI catalog.*

Continued on pg. 16

James Welch: Writing the Native American Experience

Interview by Ed Edmo

The autumn sun shinning through the window brought a cheeriness into the ticky-tacky hotel room in downtown Portland. In town touring with his new book, Indian Lawyer, *James Welch discussed his career and Indian writing. His other books include* Riding the Earthboy 40 *(poetry),* Winter in the Blood, The Death of Jim Loney, *and* Fools Crow.

On publishing: "One of the problems I have is that not many Indian people are writing novels…so, in some ways, I think it's up to Indian people to write in that genre which big publishing houses would accept. For instance, they are very reluctant to accept poetry from anybody, because they have to make money. So I think if more Indian people got involved in writing novels and collections of stories, more Indian people would be published."

On non-Indians writing about Indians: "That's been a problem for a long time. I was on a panel with Leslie Silko 15 years ago and our response was that a person has to have knowledge of the Indian situation, not only traditional but contemporary, centered within themselves to write about the Indian experience…and a lot of people don't have that. So, when Kinsella writes these books, I know it creates a real problem. A lot of people feel that those books deal with stereotypical situations or they focus on the kind of ridiculous nature of some of Indian experience."

"Kinsella wrote *Moccasin Telegraph*, a collection of short stories based out of Canada. He was at a conference and four people from the audience got mad at him. He certainly has a right to write about it — Indian experience — but it is too bad that he becomes a spokesperson for Indian people. And for a lot of people, he's the only person they got their knowledge of Indian people from and that's a bad situation."

On publishing opportunities for Native writers: "I think publishers are becoming more open. I think all of the publishing houses that I'm familiar with wouldn't reject material because it was written by an Indian. Of course, they're in a business and they have to pay attention to a lot of other elements. Number one, is this piece going to be good enough. Number two, is it going to be of interest to other people. I really honestly think that they're looking for Indian material. Now, I think this started back in the days of *The American Review*. The editors were really looking for not only Indian material, but Western material, material written out here in this part of the country. And they did, they published a lot of it in that magazine.

Harper & Row did have that series, the Native American series, which was really a good-hearted influence. They took on books…including my book of poems and several other books of poems that weren't going to make them any money, and…half of the proceeds or whatever, went to a worthy cause. So it was a good, beneficial program all the way around. I think they got a certain amount of publicity out of it, a certain amount of respect as a good will company, and a lot of Indian writers got to be published through that.

Right now I can't see any pipeline for Indian people to publish through. I think they just have to take their chances along with other writers and if they present the Indian experience well and interestingly, I can't see a publisher rejecting it because it is about Indians. So, I think they have a good chance, and I wish there was more encouragement. "

On beginning writing: "In high school I used to write poems, not very good poems, mushy poems. Then I got to college, took creative writing and found out that I liked it! It wasn't until I was actually taking courses from Richard Hugo in 1966 that I realized ordinary people could write poems. So I wrote poems. Dick became my mentor, we became really good friends."

"Then I started a novel because I wanted a larger canvas, so to speak. I wanted to deal with characters and put them through various situations. I was writing about everything but the reservation, everything but Indians, because I didn't think that would be interesting to anybody. And finally Hugo said, 'Well, geez, you ought to write about these experiences, this is what you really know.' That just changed everything. It really opened everything up to me, and from then on I knew I had my material, that I'd probably be writing about that pretty much for the rest of my life."

On writing a novel: "First I think about the new novel, say for a year. I just try to work out in my mind who the characters are going to be, what kind of situation I want to put them through. Then I'll make some notes. In fact, I'll make a lot of notes, fill up a notebook with details, ideas for scenes, how the characters are going to interact with each other. Only then when I know what the beginning will be, know the end and know four or five points along the way, I feel comfortable enough to start.

I know some writers would write pages just clarifying the character in their own mind. I don't do that, but I do know

Continued on pg. 13

Wilderness Sends Wide Rainbows Upward Out of Stone:
A Dialogue on Myth at Wallowa Lake With a Muledeer

by George Venn

(Note to readers: many of the ideas summarized here were expressed in a poetry reading on July 14, 1990, at the Fishtrap Gathering, Wallowa Lake. While several dialogues did occur after that reading, my Questioner here is a composite from many such conversations. As we talk, muledeer wander around us on ground that was first owned by an Ice Age glacier, then by creek water and granite boulders, then by the Nez Perce, then by an Oregon State Game Refuge, and then by the Methodist Church and then by —)

Questioner: I don't understand what are you really saying in these poems.

GV: I said Northwest writers are attempting to create a mythology of enduring habitation in a society that has always dreamed its believers will escape into space — the next paradise.

Questioner: Why should that be necessary? I mean, mythology isn't true, is it?

GV: Myth embodies the authentic values of a people. In particular, myths discriminate between acts that preserve and perpetuate life and acts that degrade and destroy life. All serious writing continues this mythological process.

Questioner: So what does this have to do with the Northwest?

GV: Writers here inherited a mythology of subjugation which once made "settlement" heroic, but that mythology is destroying us.

Questioner: But there must be some goodness in our traditions. Look at us. We're the most powerful nation on earth. I just can't reject everything I believe.

GV: I'm not asking you to reject what you believe. Just recognize its accompanying myths.

Questioner: I don't know what you mean.

GV: Western literature best portrays the assumptions of subjugation myth. Let me list a few: (1) violence against anyone or anything who opposes advancing civilization is acceptable; (2) escape from the restraints of civilization is possible, desirable; (3) natural resources are unlimited, free, and exploitable by any agricultural or industrial means; (4) only male heroic emotions are approved: stoicism, simplicity, naivete, power; (5) anxiety over and fear of females is constant; (6) plundering a community —human or ecological — is acceptable. Sound familiar? Most of them are derived from the *enslavement analogy*, the *dictatorship analogy*, the *Roman army mentality*.

Questioner: Like a John Wayne western. Sounds dangerous.

GV: But they didn't always sound that way. Civilization has used such assumptions to justify expansion for centuries.

Questioner: But violence is happening all over now. Pollution, endangered species, toxic waste, soil erosion, battered women, abandoned children, drugs, gang violence, racism, energy shortages — you name it.

GV: Does that sound like a world without end, a world of continuous habitation?

Questioner: Not really. Maybe the end of the world is coming — like Revelation says. (A muledeer doe approaches.)

GV: I'd say that subjugation mythology is destroying living communities everywhere. The present generation of Northwest writers has witnessed this undeniable destruction.

Questioner: That sounds too easy, too black and white for me. Besides, there are lots of good Christian people.

GV: Can you deny that Christendom devours more natural resources than any civilization in history? Can you deny that Christendom has the most violent attitude toward nature of any religion?

Questioner: Maybe this is changing. The Pope named St. Francis the patron saint of the environment this year. Is that part of this new mythology of habitation — as you call it? (The deer stands still. Her deep shining eyes stare at the Questioner — as though in a trance.)

GV: Token symbolism is better than nothing?

Questioner: Well, how *is* this mythology of habitation formed?

GV: Let me list a set of assumptions which seem to be shaping habitation mythology: (1) the native and indigenous — in all their forms — must be defended from degradation and violence; (2) the human must be restrained, must relearn cultivation, must practice cyclic processes that do not degrade ecosystems; (3) limited natural resources can only be used if that use preserves the long-term (200 year) integrity, stability, and diversity of ecosystems; (4) full emotional range of awareness is necessary — the childlike, the feminine, the masculine, the plant, the animal, the river, the rock, the sky, the star — and complete emotional expression is essential — the tragic, the comic, the satiric, the farcical; (5) the female

> *Writers here inherited a mythology of subjugation....*

sense of home, compassion, cultivation, and nurture must be understood, taught, and practiced; (6) community integrity and individual genius must be asserted in all microcosms in order to generate continuing wisdom and art. Most of the new assumptions are based on the *marriage analogy*, the *regenerative dance of opposites analogy*, the *imagery of wholistic and organic interdependence*.

Questioner: But I just heard two women historians say, "No more mythology. Let's just have the facts." (The doe takes a step toward the Questioner, who seems to recoil from her approach.)

GV: It's too late. The transition from subjugation myth to habitation myth is already happening in the Northwest.

Questioner: This deer is looking at me. How do you know?

GV: The primary habitation myth figure, the archetypal wise old woman in her many masks, is already demanding *cleanup, restoration, repair, rehabilitation, justice, respect for children, plants, animals*. She becomes a corrective to the excesses of subjugation myth. In a younger version, she becomes the outraged Antigone determined to see justice done.

Questioner: Is the subjugation myth changing? Look at this thing. (The Questioner points to the staring doe. Her great, soft, silken-purse ears slowly and continuously listen on all sides.)

GV: I think so. The penitent, self-pitying male, guilty of all the extremes of subjugation myth, has become both a predictable literary pose and a fictional character. While film westerns and their silent strong stereotypes lose their audience, real cowboys have suddenly become poetic and loquacious. Writers of all ethnic backgrounds are now taking indigenous and prehistoric life seriously. Writers and poets everywhere are practicing the disciplined spiritual observation it takes to become intimate with a place.

Questioner: So you think there's hope for us?

GV: Writers have always asked the same question: what generates and perpetuates abundance, and what degrades and destroys it? To make and keep a habitable world, everything is subjected to that test. Elsewhere, writers have been making that imaginative test for centuries, and Northwest writers will have to make that test here now. Wallowa County was the last county "settled" in the lower 48 states, so this is the last place where subjugation myth worked its destruction. Isn't it fitting that we talk here now about this new mythology? Salmon, forests, rivers, owls, soil, children, women, men, air, grass — everything is saying we have to invent a new story for our lives or we will perish. What we do to the cosmos, what we do to others, we do to ourselves.

Questioner: (The doe comes closer to the Questioner and shining black nose sniffs the air around the conversation.) What is this deer doing to me? (The Questioner moves away from the doe.) What does she want?

GV: Wilderness sends wide rainbows upward out of stones. ■

George Venn is the author of two books of poems: Sunday Afternoon: Grande Ronde *and* Off The Main Road, *and a collection of poetry, fiction, and essays,* Marking The Magic Circle. *He has been a member of the English faculty at Eastern Oregon State College for 17 years.*

> ***Everything is saying we have to invent a new story for our lives or we will perish.***

James Welch *Cont. from pg. 11*

physically what type of person it will be, in terms of economics, where that person fits into the scale, and is that person sensitive or is that person psychologically okay or messed up in a certain area, which is of course the most important thing, because it's that person's psychological makeup that you'll be working with during the course of the novel."

On writing the Native American experience: "It's certainly filled with too much conflict on a human scale, but on a say, literature scale, or writer scale, I think it's just that kind of conflict that a writer would like to explore. For instance, in my first two novels, what I wanted to do was create characters that if a tourist passed through Harlow, Montana, say, and saw this 33 year-old Indian man kind of leaning up against the wall, looking like a derelict, and that would be the image of that man — what I wanted to do is get inside of that person and show what made him this way and what's important to him. Does he have any kind of personal life? Does he have any connection with his traditions, and so on. So it's those conflicts in the human being and the kind of outward image that one sees and the inward reality of that person, I think, creates the conflict with a lot of Indian characters." ■

Ed Edmo, poet, playwright, storyteller, is Shoshonne Bannock and lives in Portland. "After Celilo" will appear in Paper Medicine, *a collection of contemporary Native American short fiction out in 1991.*

Katherine Dunn *Cont. from pg. 2*

use it for is whatever you use it for. But it's all the same stuff....

"And it is ludicrous to set up these pompous, pretentious hierarchies to make ourselves feel a little bit better because, 'Well, they may make more money, but we are the *real* writers!'"

The constant drone, the mutter of complaint, emanates from writers not making much money. And from those frolicking in the groves of academe, to hear Dunn tell it.

"And I think that one of the reasons that it's a perpetuated form in academia, and this is my personal opinion as a nonacademic, is that people who teach are those who apparently can't make a living writing. I mean, we've all done it from time to time — or many of us have — and I'm not saying it's a bad thing to do, although I do have my questions. Nonetheless...."

Which leads her to poetry, defined as "a beige book that nobody in particular wants to read."

But she thinks that if you take a close listen to what's transpiring in America today, you'll discover poetry's vibrant new form.

Namely, in the music.

"It is in the lyrics of rock songs, and it is in the lyrics of rap songs. Rap is the truest form of poetry that has existed in a very long time," she says. And it is a continuation of the centuries-long oral tradition.

..."Homer was doing rap. That's exactly what he was doing," she suggests. "Silly little plink-a-plink baseline in the back, and the whole thing is content and lyric...*boom-boom-boom.*"

The handy dismissal of rap lyric-writing or outdoors reporting or boxing essays as not "real writing" is part of a web Dunn calls the "delicate hypocracies of humankind."

Take the time celebrated author Kurt Vonnegut hit town a year or two ago.

"There we were in this packed hall at the Masonic Temple, and he stood up in front of 1,500 or 2,000 people — many of them ardent young people who were admirers of his work. And, knowing Portland, probably everybody in the room was probably at least an aspiring writer," she recalls.

"He told that crowd that there were only 400 writers in America making a living off their work.... What a crock of horseshit! There were probably 400 people in that *room* making a living...."

"Ah, but he meant 'real writers'! He meant him and Norman Mailer and — on a good day, and if they're feeling particularly openminded — maybe Tom Wolfe."

The next time this happens, Dunn swears, all hell is going to break loose.

"I am going to commit a violent act upon the person. And before they carry me away, I will point out to the children that there are thousands of us in this state. Thousands

Montana Canon *Cont. from pg. 8*

and turn-of-the-century Butte writer Mary MacLane, highwaymen and Jim Welch's high-line mythos. Centered around Missoulian Peter Koch, who published many of their works in his journal, *Montana Gothic*, and in fine letterpress editions from his Black Stone Press during the mid-1970s, the surrealists included Michael Poage (*Born* and *Wings of Hair*), Craig Czury (*Janus Peeking*, winner of the Montana Arts Council's First Book Award in 1980), and Lee Bassett (whose many books include *Gaugin and Food*, *Hatsutaiken*, and *The Mapmaker's Lost Daughter* and who had little connection with the clique around Koch). Not a single work by these accomplished poets appears in *The Last Best Place*. Nor do poems by other Montana avant gardists, like Bill Borneman and Paul Piper, whose ties to the controversial Language Poets no doubt made them suspect to the anthology's editors.

William Kittredge — the driving editorial force behind both *Montana Spaces* and, with Annick Smith and a distinguished editorial board, *The Last Best Place* — once wrote, "The art of a region begins to come mature when it is no longer what we think it should be." And Montana novelist Tom McGuane has said, "The best literature is alarming to the complaisant and annoying to all boosters." Perhaps the next Montana literary anthology — the next definer of the canon — will contradict our expectations more radically than these two have, more clearly reflect the voices of Native Americans, women, eastern Montanans, and the always embattled Montana avant garde, and do its best to alarm and annoy. There is no doubt it will serve to outrage other constituencies who find themselves excluded. If we are lucky, they, too, will speak out, lending their energies, their passion, to a Montana literary tradition that has already begun to come mature. ∎

Rick Newby is director of Sky House Publishers, an imprint of Falcon Press Publishing Co., Inc. of Helena, Montana. Newby recently completed Sobering Moments in Montana History: Actual Events, Genuine Characters, *a collaboration of twelve texts and twelve etchings with printmaker Doug Turman.*

---

of us. And that there are never enough good writers." ∎

Susan Stanley is a writer for regional and national publications and teaches writing. Her book Maternity Ward *will be published in January 1992.*

Science Fiction *Cont. from pg. 6*

yet theoretical technology of very small organic machines — and a new kind of psychological investigation into the Country of the Mind. It is uncompromising in its language, suggesting the patois and syntax of 2047-48. Its literary structure is a series of handball reverberations that build to solutions as the book progresses, through at least three levels of metaphor. Four very different main characters let us see the world through their eyes; the central character, black poet Emanuel Goldsmith, appears only briefly in person, but his spirit — and his madness — haunts the book and gives it its shape.

I leave it to readers to decide whether the book succeeds; what I mean to suggest is that science fiction writers, to reach the top of the form, should command an array of techniques and information that would dazzle past masters in and out of science fiction.

At the same time, for me, story is supreme; story-telling is the spine of my work. I hope, through science fiction and fantasy, to quietly steal into the reader's house and rearrange the furniture, maybe even redecorate; occasionally, demolish and rebuild.

If that's a manifesto, so be it.

It's also a challenge. There's more *excellent* science fiction and fantasy being written now than every before, and the best is truly astonishing. Many of the world's finest writers make science fiction their home. We stand on the shoulders of giants, competing with extremely talented friends, and our audience is the best and the brightest.

That defines a renaissance. ∎

Greg Bear, author of science fiction and fantasy, is married to Astrid Anderson Bear and is the father of two, Erik and Alexandra. He has published sixteen books and been awarded a Nebula, a Hugo, and the Prix Apollo.

Ivan Doig *Cont. from pg. 9*

for the love of it? Why don't I take a short story course? Why don't I write some poetry?'

"Behind all this is the assumption that people are going to be working seriously and professionally." With a Ph.D. in History, a journalistic background, more than twenty years experience in "this ink-stained craft," plus six critically successful books to his credit, it's obvious this is the standard Doig sets for himself. And one he lives up to, admirably. ∎

Linda O'Brien freelances advertising copy and business communications from a quiet spot in Maple Valley, Washington.

Poets Were Made *Cont. from pg. 3*

lock.) I have no idea what the hell Miss Tomasik was trying to teach me. I had Beatle-mania on the brain; I was scribbling goofy parodies of "I Want to Hold Your Hand" and "Twist and Shout" until Miss Tomasik ventured into my corner and was suddenly looming over my desk, reading my pen scratches. I expected the worst. At that moment she could have wounded me almost as much as I deserved. "Well," she said, "a budding poet. These aren't bad." Somewhere she fanned in me the ember that would someday light my life.

Or my senior year, 1969 — the height of the Vietnam "conflict," — I was scared, depressed, and soon to be of draft-age. I remember sitting in calculus class sunk into such a funk

> ### Somewhere she fanned in me the ember that would someday light my life.

I couldn't lift my pencil or focus on the test at hand. I hadn't been listening all term; body counts on the network news each night were all the numbers I could handle. Mr. Komro confiscated my test sheet, and I heard him wad it and pitch it in the waste basket near his desk in the back of the room. Soon he was headed my way again. I half expected he was going to hit me, but I can't explain why. I hardly knew the man though I'd seen him daily for the past three school years, and I assumed he neither knew anything about me nor cared to know more. He laid a copy of *Harper's* in front of me. "Read this," he said, putting his hand on my shoulder. "I can't understand it, but maybe you can." In front of me were poems and letters of e.e. cummings. I'd never seen a copy of *Harper's* before in my life; I barely knew the name e.e. cummings; it was the first time I'd ever read "I Sing of Olaf…." All that weird typography seemed at a glance like formulas in our text, but by God I understood them. Even though I hadn't done my homework.

Miss Tomasik and Mr. Komro lifted me up when they could easily have crushed me, and in that sense they were two of the most valuable connections I've ever made. Shortly after *War On War* hit the bookstores, I found a letter in my box from Bernadine Tomasik. She'd read my work, and she said simply, "I'm proud of you." I hadn't heard from her for better than twenty years. Some will call it corny, but that letter meant more to me — went a lot further toward "making" this poet — than any workshop, cover blurb, or review. ∎

Lowell Jaeger lives in Bigfork, Montana. He has two collections of poems in print: War on War (1988) and Hope Against Hope (1990), both from Utah State University Press.

God's Country *Cont. from pg. 10*

must ignore the subsurface violence of urban life. When we accept these images, we forget what is really out there, and we forget the questions that what is out there asks us.

Those questions, as I have indicated, are terrifying and weird. Out there are cities built under volcanoes. Out there the ground shakes. Out there are winters that have people hunkered down in mountain cabins, praying for the Greenhouse Effect. Out there are distances resistant to jet travel,

Out there is empty, wild, windy, whirling space, some of it psychic.

loneliness resistant to a crowded world. Out there is empty, wild, windy, whirling space, some of it psychic.

And we Northwesterners, writers or not, are also strange and full of contradictions. One of our major industries, tourism, depends on the deliberate synthesis of experience for a multitude of lemming-like people, each of whom is looking for the non-synthetic real thing. Another, real estate development, depends on us selling our ancestral lands. Two others, logging and mining, depend on the infinitely projected extraction of finite resources. And in the face of it all, we try to literalize a dream of an Edenic existence, calling the place where we live God's country, yearning and sometimes mortgaging our lives for plots of land bordering National Forest, where we can pretend to look out on a world untouched by human concept.

These words, these questions, these contradictions, these weirdnesses and wildernesses, these are the stuff of writing. In the Northwest, we writers have only to look around to have something to say. Saying it, we can spark each other, if not to brilliance, then at least to the courage to name the things we love, and to face the questions they ask us. ∎

John Rember, a fourth-generation Idahoan, teaches at the College of Idaho in Caldwell. He is a columnist for the Idaho Mountain Express, *freelances for magazines, and has a collection of stories published,* Coyote in the Mountains.

John Haines *Cont. from pg. 7*

something besides creative writing. Why not get a degree in political science? Or history? And teach it? I think writing would benefit.

Up until the last three or four decades, most writers were intellectually independent. A few were in universities but the majority were not. They used to support themselves by being journalists or critics. But now we're almost entirely university dependent.

If you look almost anywhere else — for instance, the foremost poet in Estonia is a linguist and also an anthropologist. In Iceland many writers might be librarians or teach something like music, or are journalists. The same is true in Sweden.

The specialization is a constant danger, and for so many writers to get cozy in the university is not very good for the craft. And practically everybody today wants to do exactly that. I have students who want to stay in the same community. That's very nice, but in the meantime they haven't gone out and done anything. They've been in college and workshops all their life. Writing benefits from a certain amount of participation in ordinary life. ∎

The aha! that sets us all upon the path; our rusty capacity to create language out of silence....
— Terri Lee Grell

The story-teller selects, discards, arranges, and rearranges the myriad details that clamor for telling. —Mary Clearman Blew

The Life of a Freelancer

by Anne Garber

This article was first published in Wordworks, *the newsletter of the Federation of B.C. Writers.*

The freelancer's world is very dog-eat-dog, or as Woody Allen's character in *Crimes & Misdemeanors* says: "Dog doesn't return other dog's phone calls." What this really means is that your personal freelance environment is virtually one of your own creation. It's your reputation that's on the line every time you submit a query, make a phone contact, or offer up an article. And it's a very tough, competitive market out there. No one hands you work on a silver platter, so there are a few things you need to know (and do) to make your creative environment work for you.

British Columbia has a reputation outside of the province which is highly adjustable, according to the context from which it is viewed. For example, in Toronto, everyone west of the Rockies is "a little flaky" (they're jealous, naturally); in California, where the naive perception is that we're fostering 'runaway production,' BCers are considered creative, competitive, and friendly, albeit a trifle homespun. In New York, the prevailing notion is that we're great comedy writers (don't ask me why, since most of the formerly-Canadian comedy producers in NYC actually hail from Toronto). Wherever these perceptions come from, the central fact is: *You are what people THINK you are.* As a freelancer, it is your job to make sure you capitalize on those perceptions, erroneous though they might be.

The next important task of the freelancer is to know the market. You may be a brain surgeon, but if you try to write a golf feature — wait a minute — I take that back. If you're a brilliant brain surgeon, you probably know scads about golf. But you know what I mean: stick first to what you know best. Succeed there and many doors otherwise bolted shut will be open to you. It's also important to understand the publications you approach. Read back issues. Know who the readers they are courting might be. Match your fresh ideas to some editorial context — and be certain they haven't recently run a feature on the same topic, or you'll reveal you haven't done your homework.

When it comes to remuneration, many normally-assertive creative people simply seize up. The common, unspoken axiom is that we might be contaminated by contact with filthy lucre. Or perhaps we'll be shunned by the muse for accepting compensation for work which surely must be divinely inspired? Do you believe this? This is an important matter, since many of us unknowingly sabotage our best efforts (missed deadlines, off-topic, too terse, too wordy, redundant) because we find it 'unseemly' to be burdened with sacks of gold. So, please think carefully about this area. Don't undervalue your work.

Going rates run anywhere from 25 cents to a dollar per (finished) word, and many publications take into account the amount of legwork and research involved in even a very short piece. If you don't get a formal letter of assignment from an editor (and few offer them), it's wise to send a written confirmation to the person who gave you the assignment, outlining your understanding of the task and the money you expect to be paid for doing it. Work in when you understand that fee will be due (generally upon publication). Keep a copy and at least you'll be able to produce it if there's a misunderstanding. Many freelancers find these letters of confirmation a clarifying exercise anyway. And the editor has a chance to get back to you if you've misread his or her instructions — AND, if the work is submitted as requested, the editor can't change the parameters mid-project and say, "No, I didn't want that, I want this."

The last word of advice I'll offer is about meeting deadlines. Nothing is worse for your reputation than having one editor say to another, "I like Bob Smith's work, but he's a little unreliable." "I know what you mean," says the other guy, and Mr. Smith is passed over for someone, possibly even less skilled, but certain to make the assignment deadline. Enough said, I'm sure.

Yes, it's a tough life for freelancers in our region, but here's a cliche worth noting: "The harder you work, the luckier you get." ∎

The freelancer's world is very dog-eat-dog, or as Woody Allen's character in Crimes & Misdemeanors *says: "Dog doesn't return other dog's phone calls."*

Anne Garber is a radio journalist and featured columnist for the Vancouver Province *newspaper. She has written four regional guide books which include* Vancouver Super Shopper *&* Shopping the World.

Your Grandmother Might Have Been Mayor or Why Write?

by Kathleen Alcalá

When I was first asked to write this article, I declined, citing lack of time and the fact that there are "few Hispanic writers in the Northwest." As soon as I said that, I knew it wasn't true. There are few Hispanic/Latino writers being *published* in the Northwest, but I know that people are at home writing.

So I will address this article to you, the writers of color who don't send out their work. Why write? Why submit your work for publication given all the odds against getting published?

First of all, people need to hear your voice. They may not like your voice, or even your grammar, but you are part of the cultural crazy quilt, too. Many editors say they receive few submissions from writers of color, and when they do, they are not of good quality. The editors who really want to publish your work will give thoughtful critiques and ask you to try again. These critiques might make you mad, so go ahead and throw that manuscript in a drawer and stomp around. When you've cooled off, look at the critique and see if there might be something useful in it. Rewrite the piece

---

> *You probably went through school being told that your ancestors were ignorant slave or migrant labor.*

---

and send it out again. It takes time to get published, but eventually the right piece will find the right editor.

Practice, practice, practice. The more you write, the easier it gets. Write letters to the editor: It's an easy way to get published, and if you like seeing your work in print, a good incentive. Write to your relatives, even if they owe you money (or you them). Keep a journal, at least when you travel or have the opportunity to speak with elders. This leads to the next reason to write: history is usually written by the conquerors.

You probably went through school being told that your ancestors were ignorant slave or migrant labor that came to this country at the bidding of rich, white industrialists. They never tell you what happened before that. Don't take other people's word for things. Do your own research. You might find that your great-grandfather was a respected healer, that your grandmother was mayor of the town where she grew up, and held off the Federalistas single-handedly with a shotgun and a broom. Not only do these stories need to be told, they are a wonderful addition to the culture of any

country. This heritage is yours to discover and share. By becoming a writer, you can *rewrite history*.

Finally, support other writers of color. Buy their books, take classes from them, seek them out to wish them well and ask for words of encouragement. The Northwest is blessed with some of the best writers in the country, such as Charles Johnson, Colleen McElroy and (insert your name here). The more people of color are writing, the more editors and publishers have to take us seriously. Go to your local bookstore and ask for these books, even if you know the owner doesn't carry them. The next day, put on your sunglasses and ask again. Bookstore owners need to make money, and if they perceive a demand, they will carry books by minority writers.

Finally, if you are in a position to do so, encourage others to write, and share the work of writers you like. Volunteer to go into classrooms — these are your future readers; read on the radio services for the blind — they need to hear your accent and the type of literature that interests you. Read to the shut-ins and elderly, and they may share their stories with you.

Writing by people of color, no matter what your subject, is a political act — an important contribution to your community. So don't let people trivialize the time that you spend writing. Treat it as a devotion, as a religious act if need be. If it's just one half hour a day, it might be enough time to polish that story or finish that poem. And send out those manuscripts! Editors are standing by.... ∎

Kathleen Alcalá edited the Spring 90 International Issue of The Seattle Review *and will have her first collection of short stories,* Mrs. Vargas and the Dead Naturalist, *published by Calyx Books in 1992.*

> *Writing by people of color, no matter what your subject, is a political act.*

How to Do a Who Done It
An Interview With M.K. Wren

by Monica Mersinger

M.K. Wren lives on the Oregon Coast and has published a detective series featuring bookseller/detective Conan Flagg. Her most recent book is not a mystery, but a post-apocalypse novel, A Gift Upon the Shore.

A mystery is a dramatic morality play. It allows the reader to be involved with the worst possible crime, yet be assured that good will triumph over bad, justice will be done, and order will conquer chaos. It confirms that life has a purpose and the loss of life is always for a reason. It is a tradition, a genre, with its own set of rules.

"There's a contract between a mystery reader and its writer. The reader promises not to look at the end of the book to find out who done it. The writer promises believable settings and characters and a good plot. Without these three factors, the mystery will fail," explains M.K. Wren.

Wren (Martha Kay Renfroe when not using her pen name) explains these rules in a thoughtful manner. "When I began to write I didn't think a woman could get a mystery published, so I chose the pen name of M.K. Wren."

So far, she has published six mysteries set in Northwest locations and featuring her detective protagonist, Conan Joseph Flagg. Her stories are sold in six foreign countries.

"Believable characters are one of the three basic elements to any good fiction," says Wren. "The protagonist is very important. This character has to become a real person to the reader." She explains that the writer should make many decisions about this character before beginning. Decide how the protagonist will look, walk, talk, deal with the bad guys, and interact with the other characters. Determine also the protagonist's car, work site, and home.

"Remember to have small flaws in the characters you create, especially the protagonist. It makes the characters more human and therefore, more believable," advises Wren. She maintains that it is always better to show than tell the reader. Instead of advising the reader the hero is brave, have the hero perform a brave act. Include only those characters which contribute to the advancement of the story, and the more verbiage the writer includes about a character, the more importance the reader will give that character.

Wren suggests that characters are introduced into a mystery in the same way we get to know another person, through the outward characteristics such as gender, race, age, class and physical appearance. Then, there are those inward characteristics which take a while for us to learn about one another. These elements make up the personality of a character such as motivation, personal historical, moral, and ethical philosophy.

Wren discusses Conan Joseph Flagg. "He's a combination of much of my past mystery reading. I took the name Conan out of respect for Sir Arthur Conan Doyle's stories of Sherlock Holmes. I didn't know about *Conan the Barbarian* when I chose the name, nor did I know about *Mash's* Colonel Flagg character when I chose his last name. Joseph just seemed to rhyme nicely with Conan. It was from his middle name that I chose his Nez Perce Indian ancestry and determined his appearance."

> *"Remember to have small flaws in the characters you create, especially the protagonist."*

What's the most challenging part to writing a mystery? Wren believes it is the setting. The setting is where the story takes place and where most amateur mystery writers fail. The setting could be as small as a drawing room or as large as Europe. However, the details must be sufficient to place readers at the scene with the kind of understanding the writer wants them to have. "The reader can't see anything. The only information a reader has to operate from is the writer's words," she says. Another rule: nothing happens in limbo. Events occur at specific times and places. In any mystery, the setting descriptions hold vital information for the reader.

"When I wrote *Seasons of Death*, the story took place in Silver City, Idaho. I really researched it. I must have taken 35 photographs of that town. Then before I ever began writing, I organized the information in a working notebook. It included diagrams of the buildings, the types of flora and fauna, the weather, short character descriptions, and the time sequences for the murder. The notebook also included the clues which pointed to each suspect and the killer with an explanation of why each suspect other than the killer couldn't have done it."

Then there is the plot. This is how the story will advance. Mystery drama is the building of tension and the assurance that the murderer will be revealed and punished in some manner. As in any story, there are three parts to the plot: the orientation, the development and the climax/resolution.

A good orientation makes the writer gets the reader curious to read more. Since murder is central to any mystery

Continued on pg. 35

15 Library Research Tips for Writers

Thanks to King County librarians Karen Hardiman, Lora Bennett, Norma Arnold, and Mary Campbell for compiling the information on this page.

Public libraries are a vital link between people and the information they need. Libraries purchase, collect, and organize sources of information and entertainment in a variety of formats. You can access these sources by using indexes, catalogs, and assistance from librarians. Specific titles may vary from library to library, but most public libraries have:

Encyclopedias: Use encyclopedias for a general overview of your subject. Write down key subject words as you read, and then look for them in the encyclopedia index volume to find other articles about your subject. Note the "see also" references at the end of the articles.

Reference Books: The *Encyclopedia of Science and Technology*, *World Almanac*, and *Current Biography* are examples of specialized reference books useful for many levels of research.

Books: Check the library's subject catalog and especially note "see also" references for related materials.

Magazine Index/Reader's Guide: These are indexes to periodical articles, arranged by subject and author. Magazines are available in hard copy or on microfilm. Individual articles can be requested, and often faxed, from one library to another.

Electronic Indexes: InfoTrac is a CD-Rom index to periodicals. DIALOG is an electronic index to 350 databases on such subjects as agriculture, business, science and technology, and the humanities. MEDLINE indexes medical and health-related journal articles. Consult the librarian for as-sistance with these and other electronic indexes.

Magazines: Browse through current issues for topic ideas and trends.

Newspaper Indexes: Local and national events can be tracked using print, CD-ROM and/or electronic indexes. DataTimes is an on-line index with full text articles from major national newspapers and wire services.

Newspapers: Most libraries subscribe to a variety of newspapers and keep back issues in hard copy and on micro-film.

Pamphlet File: Pamphlets and brochures are arranged by subject and are useful as current, updated sources.

Atlases: In addition to maps showing political boundaries, atlases often contain graphic information about agriculture, energy, the environment, oceans, travel routes, history, and more.

CD's/Records/Audio & Video Cassettes: Include formats other than print when looking for materials or background for a presentation.

Telephone Books: Check here for public agencies, organizations, businesses, and hotlines.

Embassies/Tourist Offices/Chambers of Commerce: Especially valuable for national and international economic, geographical, and cultural information.

Community Resources: Look for museums, bookstores, galleries, restaurants, historical societies. These provide a unique perspective to the subject.

Interviews/Oral Histories: Interview someone connected to the subject by background, knowledge, experience, or concern ■

Writing Without Bias

Books

Dealing With Censorship. James E. Davis, Ed.

Disability Resources for Media. (Employment Security Dept., KG-11, Olympia, WA 98504.)

Guidelines for Creating Positive Sexual and Racial Images in Educational Materials. Nancy Roberts.

The Handbook of Nonsexist Writing. Casey Miller.

"Sheit": A No-nonsense Guidebook to Writing and Using Nonsexist Language. Val Dumond.

Watch Your Language!: 1001 Ways Not to Write or Speak. Thomas Starr Terrill.

Without Bias: A Guidebook for Nondiscriminatory Communication. International Association of Business Communicators.

Magazine Articles

"Bible Critics Give Nonsexist New Testament Thumbs up." *National Catholic Reporter*, April 17, 1987.

"Rebels With a Cause." *Boston Magazine*, June, 1987. (High school students attempting to change sexist language in Massachusetts constitution.)

"The Well-Heeled Drug Runner." *U.S. News & World Report*, April 30, 1990. (Poor Black youth are targeted in athletic-shoe advertising.)

"Yellow-Peril Journalism: Is Latent Racism Coloring Business Coverage of Japan?" *Time*, Nov. 27, 1989. ■

To Develop a Niche, Get Out of Its Way

by Terri Lee Grell

Learn the rules, then forget 'em.
Matsuo Basho (1644-94)

I think Basho knew there'd be days like this. Days when Poetry Workshop Etiquette would be just as critical to getting published as writing a poem. Days when the Big Name Poetry Society (underwritten by the Big Name Editor/Publisher Society) would define (and police) the parameters of the torrential Mainstream. Days when fledgling poets would grow weary of initiation rites and become editors; and Big Name poets would grow weary of each other and ask, "Where did all the poetry readers go?"

In some ways, the "poetry mainstream" in Basho's world (17th century Japan) was like this. I think Basho sent a message to us, through the ages, because he knew something about how poetry discovers and re-discovers itself, and how necessary this is, and how poets sometime get in the way of this happening. Basho developed a niche for a poetry called "renga" by nurturing its self-discovery, and by reminding his students to get out of its way.

Up to that point, renga (linked verses composed by a group of people working together) was looked upon as merely a game. Some renga were merely plays on words: satirical, erotic, doggerel. Basho saw the potential for renga to transcend these first impulses, and at the same time, retain that quality of "discovery" heralded by this emerging form. Later, after renga had been elevated to a "true artform" and had become the rave in Japan, a fledgling poet may have approached Basho and asked, "How do I become a renga master?" History tells us that Basho once said, "Learn the rules, then forget 'em." I think he meant that once you learn the rules, don't let them get in the way of discovering your niche.

The future is *now*, and the competition among fledgling poets to set sail on the Mainstream has led to a revival of renga and other old/new poetry forms in the West. Diverse poetry forms are widening the mainstream under the herald of "New Formalism." Ha! The only striking formality among these niche-makers is a stubborn fascination for adventure: the aha! that sets us all upon the path; our rusty capacity to create language out of silence, regardless of all the noisy poetry around us. These old/new forms are also bringing fresh voices out of the Big Name Poets Society; and as in the case of renga, the drift towards collaborative (less lonely) poetry forms is bypassing initiation rites in order to bring Poets face to face with poets.

This, in essence and in process, is the development of a niche. Niche-makers "learn the rules" of the past because, without 'em, we're only making noise. Niche-makers also

"forget the rules" when a poem wants to go its own direction, transforming itself into another life-form. To the free-verse poet, New Formalism may look like a "new life-form," but that's only because we've forgotten the rules that evolved free verse as a niche long ago. The niche develops into a mainstream. And the cycle repeats itself indefinitely.

Developing a niche means recognizing that poetry can't sit still. Now and then you must let go of the reins and see where the poem ends up. That means accepting a certain amount of failure, a certain amount of rejection because the poem has no genre, no sponsor, no "workshop." But if the poem is true, no matter how it evolved or how fiercely it insists on navigating against the flow, trust it. Put it out there. Research the alternative press and see if the poem has kin. Write a letter to the poet who seems to have made the same "discovery" that you made. Develop a round-robin. Start a fanzine! Soon you will see that a niche-maker is simply a poet who gets out of the way and lets the niche develop itself. The fun part is that you have front row seats in the roller-coaster.

> *Developing a niche means recognizing that poetry can't sit still.*

Twenty years ago there were very few renga writers in the world. A handful of curious poets in the West who had each "discovered" renga in old an new works, began to link verses with each other. They formed a fanzine (*APA Renga*), and then a quarterly magazine (*Lynx*). Though they were aware of Basho's "rules" of renga, they focused instead on Basho's method of discovering — by listening to renga's first impulses and developing them into "rules" that guide a contemporary evolution. And so an old form evolved a new body (albeit a very young body, still learning to walk) and renga writers created a network that, at last count, reaches out to hundreds of poets worldwide. There is a "calling" now for renga. There are renga workshops. Everything old is new again.

Recently, I presented a series of renga workshops and I can see that certain consistencies in poets' approach to the form represent "new rules." They're not the same rules that evolved renga in 17th century Japan, but they're kin. I can see that the niche will develop into a mainstream of sorts, probably along with a bunch of other "niches" that will, somewhere downstream, blend together and call itself something.

Then I'll probably sit down and write a new poem, let go of the reins, and get out of the way. ∎

Terri Lee Grell lives in Toutle, Washington and is the editor and publisher of Lynx, *a quarterly journal of renga. Her work has been published in* Mirrors, Exquisite Corpse, Next Exit, *and* Lost and Found Times.

Spider Robinson Talks Science Fiction

by Marjorie Rommel

Master punster, jazz and dance aficionado Spider Robinson (B.D. Wyatt), winner of the Hugo and Nebula, lives in Vancouver, B.C., with his wife, Jeanne, a dancer and writer, and their daughter, Terri, 16.

He is author of, among others, Callahan's Secret, Callahan's Lady, Mindkiller, *and* Stardance *(with Jeanne Robinson).*

WNH: Why did you choose science fiction as your genre?

SPIDER: In school, I bombed out of science courses left and right. All the science I know, I got from sf. My mom taught me to read at age four, in a particularly diabolical way. She'd read till the Lone Ranger was hanging by his fingertips, then she'd have to go do the dishes. When I was 5, she took me to the library, told me to go ask the nice lady to give me a book.

The nice lady — I don't know what her name is, or I'd have sent her a case of Scotch — gave me *Rocket Ship Galileo*

> ### *Defining what is more than human is the most fun you can have out of bed.*

---

by Heinlein. I was in heaven. Then I discovered all the books in that section had rocket ships on their spines. This was back in the early '50s and if a sf book got in hardback, it had to be very, very good. If it got into the libraries, it was superb. The science fiction section had the highest quality to crap ratio in the building. I was about ten before I read anything else.

WNH: According to Ben Bova's forward to *Callahan's Crosstime Saloon*, you were guarding a Long Island sewer while you wrote your first published story, "The Guy With the Eyes." You wrote for a Long Island newspaper for a while, too, I believe.

SPIDER: I got the newspaper job on the strength of having sold the sf story, my one and only sale, "The Guy With the Eyes," to Ben Bova at *Analog*. [The newspaper] advertised for a research assistant, which meant run the realty section. Before that, yes, I guarded a hole in the ground, to make sure nobody stole it. I kept myself busy writing.

WNH: It's often said that you are the heir of sf greats Ted Sturgeon and Robert Heinlein. Who else do you count among your literary antecedents?

SPIDER: Robert Heinlein was a true renaissance man. He was famous for his generosity. I hope someday to be worthy of carrying his pencil case. Theodore Sturgeon was another man I admire immensely. He taught me how to hug and a lot about how to write. I also, quite early on, read and

admired the work of Poule Anderson and Cyril Kornbluth, a brilliant short story writer. Those were my gods until I got old enough to discover Edgar Pangborn. He's as good as Mark Twain, wrote a post-holocaust novel called *Davy*. Those characters still wake me up at 2 a.m. He makes you howl, makes you sing and dance.

Frederick Pohl was always a favorite, and he's the only one still alive and working, he and Poule Anderson and Fritz Leiber. Shortly after that, I discovered Alfie Bester. His theory of art was to grab you by the lapels on page one, start punching you in the face, and keep it up till the last page. He gave me the titles for all three Callahan books in about five minutes the night I met him.

WNH: Your characters carry a message of rigorous personal honesty and openness essential to the further development of the human soul. How do they relate to your own philosophy?

SPIDER: If you combine people, you combine strengths. I picked that up from Sturgeon. We're all locked in solitary confinement in these bone boxes. If we could get shut of that — I'm tired of hearing about the death of morality, the death of God, that there is no meaning in life. Get people together, and they'll solve any problem. The most puzzling thing is, you share pain, there's less of it. You share joy, there's more of it.

WNH: Your work presents the unusual view (at least in sf) that the human race given a little serious effort might save itself in the end. Do you believe this?

SPIDER: John Gardner later repudiated as youthful work his book, *On Moral Fiction*, but I think it was a case of diplomacy. He was right the first time. If there's no morality in the future, I ain't going. We're supposed to be making road maps to countries that don't exist. If those places have no center, no morality, then phooey. I don't want to live there. I want to show people futures they want to live in.

Science fiction always has talked about making things better: If only…Nanotechnology, the science of the future, really intrigues me. Eric Drexler, the creator of nanotechnology, says in 30 to 50 years everybody on the planet should have the approximate net worth of the gross national product of the U.S., and be immortal.

What do you do with that much freedom, that much power? Keith Henson wants to tour the galaxy before the whole thing melts down, meet a group of friends at the far edge for a memory merge, then hunt down the last proton in the universe and watch it decay. To find out more, read Ed Regis' *Great Mambo Chicken and the Transhuman Condition*. It's subtitled "Science slightly over the edge."

Continued on pg. 35

Fragments From the Sacred Text: The Writer's Life as a Subject

by Sharon Doubiago

What would happen if one woman spoke the truth? The world would break open.
—Muriel Rukeyser

I have a filmmaker friend who says in a hundred years we'll go to the library to check out films on real people. Fiction, make-believe, what we know of now as the movies, will seem primitive and silly.

I am five, spinning cartwheels under the Los Angeles sky, to the rhythm of the mantra I've learned from Socrates: Know Thyself!

In the last thing I wrote before I took my vow not to be a poet, a vow I understood then most consciously as having to do with the lying words that created the Vietnam War, I uncovered a repressed story from my childhood so devastating I believed it could kill certain persons. I kept the vow for only six years, 1968 to 1974, but it's taken twenty-two years to get back to the open, vulnerable place of the secret, and the realization that I quit writing to protect not just those persons, but also, to protect the self they had created in me. I quit writing poetry so as not to know myself.

During the time of this vow I had a great and beautiful correspondence. Ramona and I exchanged thirty-plus page letters two and three times a week. I began to know a part of myself that can be known only in language. Equally important — in the task of becoming a writer, that is, knowing the reader — I came to know language in her. The word for this alchemy of equal exchange is *Love*.

On November 22, 1975, Ramona's brother killed himself. She asked me to write a poem about it, a request I couldn't refuse. It became my first *real*, completed poem, a first public writing in which I allowed my terrorized unknown self to emerge, and submerge, as deeply into the language as the subject, the occasion, required.

Soon afterwards *My Brother Took His Life November 11, He Tied a Plastic Bag Over His Head* was published in a local paper. The following week a local man killed himself by tying a plastic bag over his head.

I'm standing in the front room of my cabin reading the news story of this man. I see his body, my poem lying beside him. My ears are beginning their old unbearable ringing, my heart to pound, and my sight is going — my Self diminishing within the body, growing smaller and smaller in the deadliest of prisons, the lie pressed upon me since infancy, IT'S YOUR FAULT.

My greatest fear as a writer, that my words will kill if I tell the truth, seemed to come true with my first important publication. But then something happened. A crack began in the fictional world. I didn't faint. I didn't renew my vow. I went to my desk, and in great trepidation and loathing, wrote it out.

Four months later my husband of nine years left me and my children because I had become a poet. His parting words were, "If you write about me, I will come back and kill you."

I knew great compassion for his position and denied, except in the nightmares, my fear and the injustice. I called it the Missing Poem and wrote around the actual story. Years later, on the eve of the publication of my first book, I realized I had weakened my art for his unworthy sake; he still dominated and controlled me. In the most fragile of epiphanies, I finally realized *it's my story, too.*

More recently I had another love who treated me badly. He said this was because I was failing his great love of me. I kept trying. The harder I tried the worse things got — though in a profound way the more I knew love of him.

My greatest fear as a writer, that my words will kill if I tell the truth.

One summer day his second great love appeared in the garden. I was delighted to meet Beatrice, the beautiful woman in his personal mythology whose power was so great she'd led him from his first wife and infant son. I've always loved my sisters, a fact my men have never believed, or, maybe, trusted.

I am leading her into my studio. Behind me she is saying, I'VE TAKEN A VOW THAT IF I EVER ENCOUNTER ANOTHER WOMAN LIVING WITH ——— I WILL TELL HER OF THE SISTER SUPPORT GROUP IN HIS NAME.

"Sit down," she said then, gently, indicating my typewriter. "I'm going to dictate the Sisters' message to you.

"First, this is who you are: a powerful, independent, creative, erotic, woman, who loves men, who still believes in love. This, you must know, is a description of all the sisters, the two dozen I've been meeting with for years. He doesn't know this about himself, it is not that he is malefic, but a

Continued on pg. 36

Writing About Work

by K.B. Emmott

"The consumer world we inhabit would like to pretend work doesn't exist, that we spend all our time purchasing commodities and imagining lifestyles."

Shop Talk, an anthology of work poetry by the Vancouver Industrial Writers' Union, goes on to say:

"These poems oppose this view. They place work — the activity at which we spend the bulk of our waking lives — at the forefront of concern and of the imagination."

Editor Zoe Landale points out that VIWU members are not among the college professors who regularly publish 90 percent of the poetry in this country. We work, inside and outside the home, in blue-collar and white-collar jobs, in the city and on the farm. While we do not write exclusively about our work, it is a central experience in our lives.

Zoe acknowledges the debt of the new work writing movement to Tom Wayman, who founded VIWU in 1979 along with Mark Warrior and Al Grierson. Tom Wayman's three anthologies of work poetry, "have formalized a genre from what had previously been an isolated process by individual writers. Completely unlike the sentimental, moralistic dogma written about 'the workers' in the twenties, the poems Tom collected were written from knowledgeable inside perspective of a particular job." Teachers, housewives, doctors, mothers, police officers have something to say about their lives.

In Wayman's collection of essays, *Inside Job*, he points out that literary academics are hostile to work writing because of an alienated perception that equates the obscure in art with quality. Yet here we are, writing modern poetry that is freely understandable and accessible — just like the everyday conversations we have with the people we know.

Life on the job can be tough, Wayman notes:

"We are not automatons, however, The present schemes for organizing production are human constructs, and we as human beings can improve or discard them. As we examine what happens at the jobs, we can see how to change work for the better. And literature and criticism could be of assistance in this. One of the slogans of the 1968 Paris May was '*vivre sans temps mort*' — life without dead time. The challenge that this ideal proposes is to collectively bring as much human thought and experience together as we can, in order to take back these hours that we work for others, to make them or their equivalents economically, physically, mentally our own."

Writing has been liberating for me as a doctor. Audiences seem surprised, somehow, to hear about the sheer joy I get from delivering babies — a frequent topic. Then there's the hard part — the brutality of the training, the overwork, the need to hide one's feelings, the constant sense from the un-informed that work that pays well can't possibly have a down side. What a relief to tell it like it is!

"Danger — Women at Work" says the sign in the delivery room: *A Labour of Love* is the title of an anthology on pregnancy and birth. This is labour as labour — women's work. This, too, is our lives.

VIWU was formed for mutual support and to share one another's writing, both prose and poetry. A shifting mem-

---

Writing has been liberating for me as a doctor. Audiences seem surprised, somehow, to hear about the sheer joy I get from delivering babies.

---

bership of about a dozen people has formed and kept strong links over the years as various people moved to other parts of the country. We have a regular reading series each year, we have taken part in many literary events and labour arts festivals, and we have formed a fruitful relationship with the folksinging group, Fraser Union, with whom we perform often under the name "Split Shift" — the name of our first cassette tape. As of this writing, our next gig is to be New Year's Eve at Vancouver's First Night Festival — a chance to remind a thousand or so of our fellow citizens that what we do all day is a very important part of who we are. ∎

Kirsten Emmott, *secretary-treasurer of VIWU, began writing work-related poetry in 1973. She worked as a newspaper reporter for the* Vancouver Sun, *attained her M.D. degree in 1973, and is now in general practice in Vancouver, B.C.*

The Western: Still Fertile Territory

by Richard Wheeler

In spite of thousands of novels, hundreds of films, and dozens of TV series, the western field is wide open. To be sure, some themes have been done to exhaustion, but fascinating things are happening in the field and there is now more interest in western history than ever before.

But the people who read frontier history and biography rarely buy popular western fiction. The main reason is that traditional western novels are not really about the frontier West, even though the frontier serves as backdrop. They are pastel versions of the historic West, which was wilder, more colorful and vivid, more bizarre, and more astonishing than anything the western novelist could ever invent.

The western novel has been around for almost a century. Most literary scholars date it back to Owen Wister's great 1902 novel, *The Virginian*, which had all the elements of the modern western story. Others date the category's origins even earlier, to the dime novels of Ned Buntline, whose florid stories were contemporaneous with the actual frontier. In any case, the western has been around almost as long as the mystery, and is considered this country's only original contribution to literature.

From the beginning, America loved its frontier heritage, its cowboys and Indians, buffalo and longhorns. Westerns quickly became a national pastime. Americans devoured frontier stories in pulp magazines, novels and films. Western novels made Zane Gray, Frederick Faust, Ernest Haycox, William McLeod Raine, Will Henry, and Jack Schaefer household names. By the 1950s, westerns accounted for a large percentage of the income of mass market paperback publishers.

Most of the early western stories were mythical. They weren't anchored in a geographical West. Neither did they have much to do with history. Their theme was the struggle of the male pecking order, set against a background of wilderness; private warfare out beyond the rim of civilization and its moral and legal restraints. The western setting was largely backdrop. Cowboys, longhorns, wild Indians, buffalo, ranches, gold mines, and gaudy saloons were there only to supply color and were not really intrinsic to the story.

As is true of all mythic literature, these stories affirmed a body of belief about virtue, and courage, and bravery. They affirmed the nature of American manhood, valuing strength, loyalty, and integrity. The mythic western created a seductive and magical image of freedom: a man on a horse making his way through trouble, to triumph at the end. They dealt with legends, explaining ourselves and what we are, justifying our history. They were lessons that helped shape the American character. And whatever their failings, these mythic westerns were often great stories. But they didn't deal with the real west, the practical west. Nor did they deal with the morally ambiguous conquest of Indian and Hispanic lands by white Europeans.

Twenty-five or thirty years ago, those writing in the field became aware that the traditional story was scarcely fair to other people, especially the Indians whose homelands had been invaded by the onslaught of white civilization. The stories in which good whites overwhelmed bad Indians glossed over the realities. Many of those "bad" Indians were men of great virtue, courage, and vision. Tribes had been treated badly, and there was the matter of justice; of things owed and still owing to these people. This awareness precipitated a shift in western storytelling. There had always been a strain of sympathy for the Indians, but it was present only in a minority of stories. By the 1960s that strain became dominant, while stories that lauded white imperialism virtually disappeared.

The next wave of westerns usually portrayed Indians and Hispanics as virtuous victims who were unjustly persecuted and harried by designing and evil white men. This trend resulted in a reversal of the old roles. In many modern novels the Indians, along with their wisdom and religion, are revered, while whites appear devoid of spiritual values and are the true savages. Mythic-Indian novels are as mendacious as the mythic-white variety.

A number of western authors have sought a more balanced sort of story. Among them is John Byrne Cooke, whose novel *The Snowblind Moon* takes place on the eve of the Custer Battle. It is notable for its realistic treatment of both Cheyenne and white characters, who are portrayed as complex, diverse mortals, with all the virtues and vices, strengths and weaknesses that one finds in real life. The other novelist of note who sought balance is Larry McMurtry. In *Lonesome Dove*, his Comanche, Blue Duck, is so evil even his own people dislike him.

Cooke and McMurtry were the pioneers. Now there is a trend toward a balanced portrayal of all types of people in the western story, and perhaps for the first time, one can find westerns in which no racial group is portrayed in mythic

> *The mythic western created a seductive and magical image of freedom: a man on a horse making his way through trouble, to triumph at the end.*

Continued on pg. 35

Writing for Newspapers: A Great Start for Many Writers

by John Wolcott

Probably more professional writers have started their careers by writing for newspapers than for any other medium. Yet it is a training and proving ground overlooked by so many beginning writers, as well as by some more advanced journalists.

Your local newspaper could be one of the best places to find those first writing opportunities you've been searching for, a convenient market close to home. Unfortunately, it's human nature to want to see your writing in a well-known magazine with a national readership. Smaller, local markets are easily ignored.

Learning to write clearly is only one advantage of becoming a good newspaper journalist. Writing for newspapers will also teach you how to do thorough interviewing, how to meet deadlines, how to write tightly and how to sense what makes a story worth writing — and what doesn't. Those are invaluable skills that will serve you well in whatever writing path you pursue later.

The advantages of writing for newspapers are enticing in many other ways, too.

Their editors usually respond much faster to queries than magazine editors are able to do. Normally, in fact, newspaper editors accept stories rather than inquiries, not having the staff to carry on correspondence with freelancers. Although it may seem like a disadvantage to put effort into writing an article "on spec," your acceptance letter from the editor is often a check rather than approval to proceed with the story.

Editors continually stuff many pages of each day's paper with out-of-the-area stories that they would gladly trade for a well written local story about some local person, event, or trend. Most newspapers, after all, want to provide as much local news as possible, supplemented by the AP and UPI wire services and syndicated news features from the *New York Times, Washington Post* and other sources — not the other way around.

Another advantage is that once your sales prove your work is meeting the paper's professional standards, you can boost your income by maintaining regular contact with your editor. Many story assignments are generated by staying in touch with editors and helping them fill their pages with good material.

There are advantages to newspaper writing for the more experienced writer, too. The vast number of newspaper markets in the country provides opportunities for multiple submissions because the majority of the papers have no overlapping, competing circulations. Newspaper editors are always looking for stories that can tell their readers how some other community solves a common problem, such as: What is your new fire protection dispatching system? How do you involve citizens in park renovations or the preservation of historical residential or commercial districts?

Writing for a local newspaper also opens opportunities to become a "stringer." Editors continually need part-time writers to cover town council and school board meetings or sports events that are too numerous to be handled by the paper's limited staff. It will be to your advantage to write about a familiar environment and interview people you know.

How can you evaluate a newspaper as a potential market? Basically, by reading it, which is the advice freelancers are always given. What's important, though, is not just reading a paper, but knowing how to interpret what you see.

For instance, if there are by-lined articles from "Special Correspondents," that usually means the paper uses stringers. "Special to the Daily Universe" probably means the paper buys freelance stories.

Look at the kind of stories they buy and what sections they're in. That'll give you a clue to where the paper's freelance funds are kept. Some papers hire freelancers for travel or business section stories. Others hire "church page" writers for stories on current religious topics. Still others use stringers for covering meetings and sports, with different editors and different budgets fueling the writer's paychecks.

> *It will be to your advantage to write about a familiar environment and interview people you know.*

Ideas can be easy to generate. Many of them, in fact, are in the same newspaper you're targeting. You might notice, for instance, a three-inch story among the stock market quotes about a local pea processing plant announcing an expansion. An inquiry at the plant may provide you with enough additional information to convince the paper's business editor that the story needs a feature treatment.

Through research, interviews, and perhaps a tour of the plant, you'll gain insight into the significance of the plant's expansion, the company's rate of growth over the past decade, new markets it's been developing, or new employment planned as a result of the expansion. That information could well become a half- or full-page feature in the local paper's business section.

Continued on pg. 35

Photo Release

PHOTO RELEASE

For value received I grant permission to ....,
its successors, licensees and assigns, to publish and copyright for all purposes,
my name, pictures, and information concerning myself and my property photographed at
....
on the ....day(s) of .... 19...........

Signature *(or name if subject is a minor)*..
Parent *(if subject is a minor)*...
Date .... Editor/Dept. ....
Photographer ....

Tax Tips

Writing is a business if you intend to earn money by it. That means the tax folks will expect proof of both earnings and expenses. When expenses exceed earnings, additional proof of the seriousness of your intent is required. Because tax laws are different in Canada and the United States of America, it's important you ask either an accountant or the revenuers for the latest requirements.

Basically, you'll be in fine shape if you simply keep complete, accurate records — including check stubs or photocopies of checks received in payment, receipts for all business related expenses (best kept by project).

Acceptable expenses include (so long as used exclusively in the business):

- Cost of purchase, rental, or lease of equipment such as cameras, enlargers, typewriters, tape recorders, computers, software, printers, modems, FAX machines, telephones, answering machines, postal scales, pencil sharpeners, coffee-makers, and staplers.
- Costs of purchase, etc., for office furniture such as chairs, tables, rugs, wall art, desks, shelves, file cabinets, waste baskets, and lamps.
- Cost of necessary supplies such as paper, printer ribbons, diskettes, labels, postage, tape, envelopes, pens, pencils, light bulbs, batteries, audio tapes, staples, paper clips, film, and coffee.
- Amounts paid for repairs, insurance, service contracts, software updates, photo developing, typing and transcription services, etc.

- If you have an office outside your home, you may deduct all related expenses. For an office in your rented home, deduct a percentage of your rent equivalent to the percentage of the total space you use for the office. If you work in the home you own, consult an acountant or the IRS.
- The price of admission to events you must attend to do research, the cost of classes necessary to your professional development, the dues you pay to professional organizations, the price of subscriptions to publications (like *Writer's NW*) you need for either researching markets or keeping abreast of your profession, the cost of books you need (like *Writer's Northwest Handbook*), etc.

Naturally, if you're reimbursed for project related expenses, you cannot deduct them unless you account for the reimbursement as income.

In the income category, keep equally careful track of who paid you when and how much for what.

Maintaining a daily journal of activities makes all of this easier, as does creating a file folder for each month into which you put relevant receipts, vouchers, and notes.

If you're writing is computerized, it's easy to automate your business recordkeeping, but you'll still need to save all hard copy documentation. And be sure to back up you files frequently, keeping an archival set of disks at another location for security. ■

Sample Query Letter

Date

Editor's name
Editor's address

Dear (editor's name):

The lead of your query may be the actual lead that you will use in your article. It must attract the editor's attention and draw interest to your topic and approach. Write the query just as you would write a letter to a friend, but keep it short and to the point.

Use the second paragraph to detail your subject and make the point of the article. Your writing style should continue to be as it would in the article. Mention statistics, quotes, or important facts that reflect your preliminary research. Without giving away the entire story, write enough here to entice the reader — an editor — into wanting more. If you have done your job properly, the editor will ask you to send the complete manuscript.

Include a paragraph discussing how you will present the story, naming individuals to be interviewed or resources to be used. Explain why this article will interest the publication's readers. Tell the editor how long the article will be and whether photos or art work are available. Also, say when the piece could be completed.

Finally, state your qualifications for writing this article. Mention your recent publishing credits or, if none exist, why you are in the best position to write this piece. Include clips of articles similar to that which is being proposed in this query. Follow the instructions in the publication's writer's guidelines or those listed in a market directory such as *Writer's Northwest Handbook*.

How to Work With Editors

by Cecelia Hagen, *Northwest Review*

To work well with an editor, just use a little common sense: be prompt and courteous, take good advice when it's offered, and hold fast to your gut-level feelings when that's what you have to do. Those are the basics; read on for the finer points.

Because the *Northwest Review* requires written consent from the author before making any changes to a story, and because, like most writers, we operate on a strict budget, communication about revisions and rewrites is most often done through letters. Sometimes, however, deadlines are close enough to make phone calls a necessity, or our editorial suggestions need the back-and-forth clarification of conversations. I try to use letters whenever possible for another obvious reason as well: Imagine you're at home one afternoon, eating peanuts and reading the newspaper. The phone rings. It's an editor from some magazine you sent a story to a few months back, and she wants to publish it. She's talking rewrites, she's getting specific and detailed, and you're still trying to get the last peanut off your molars while stretching the phone cord over to your filing cabinet to hunt down what you hope will be the same version of the story she seems to know inside out while you, embarrassingly enough, aren't sure whether you finally titled it "Mimosa Memories" or "The School Bus I Hated to Wait For."

While I have enough mischief in me to think that surprising people can be fun, experience has taught me that most writers express their surprise over the phone in the form of a guarded numbness. I'm hoping for enthusiasm and gratitude, and I get mostly a kind of disgruntled quiet. So I try to keep the contact in the written form as much as possible.

Not counting blank rejection slips or those with a brief "Thanks but no thanks" scrawled on them, I send three kinds of letters to authors: unconditional acceptances, conditional acceptances, and letters of encouragement. *Unconditional* means we will publish the story whether or not you agree to making any of our suggestions (if we have any). Authors are usually grateful for the suggestions and for the careful reading their work has been given. Although I don't agree with one author's comment in a recent letter that "caring about commas in the 1990s requires an act of moral courage," it does seem true that you'll never get a closer examination of your work. I usually send a copy of the story back to you: it makes my comments easier for both of us to recognize. Also, you can simply initial the changes you agree with, and write comments about the others in the margin or in your letter back to me.

A *conditional* acceptance hinges on your ability to make revisions which we feel successfully elevate the work's impact on the reader. Occasionally rewrites to a story only

succeed in making it even less of what we were looking for, and most authors accept this fate graciously enough. Some opt not to even attempt a rewrite, but continue to submit stories because of the serious interest we have expressed in their work.

Often our suggestions strike a nerve: we've focussed on a part of the story you know is weak, and our thoughts have brought you some new inspiration. This kind of working re-

---

We are, after all, working toward a mutual goal: getting the best stories into print.

---

lationship makes everyone feel good. We are, after all, working toward a mutual goal: getting the best stories into print. One common step in the process of achieving that goal is giving you the benefit of our ideas on how to make the story stronger.

While I like to think that our editorial process works to eliminate the weak spots and leave the quirks in, the division between the two is often hazy. If you receive a *conditional* acceptance letter, don't feel you have to roll over and acquiesce to things you don't agree with. If we suggest a change you don't want to make, you're free to suggest an alternative or ask if we can live with it as it is. We respect as many requests to leave the story alone as we possibly can. What's annoying is an author who responds to virtually all of our suggestions with one kind of excuse or another, from "I feel this phrase is necessary to the rhythm" to "It really did happen that way." If you aren't inclined to at least give serious consideration to our editorial suggestions, then you shouldn't have sent your work to us in the first place. If you admire the magazine, you're admiring the work of its authors *and* its editors, because stories are seldom published exactly "as is."

I should point out here that the editorial "we" is not an arch grammatical term at the *Northwest Review*. The fiction staff consists of a handful of committed and intelligent volunteers, and stories that manage to reach our "Special" box are read by all of us and discussed in detail at our meetings. Suggestions to writers are based on the consensus of this core of thoughtful, well-read individuals. Advice of this caliber is not to be taken lightly, and the biggest "name" authors are the most gracious about our editing.

Letters of encouragement are less exciting and, wouldn't you know it, more common than acceptances. A smart writer will realize that if an editor takes time to try and delineate

Continued on pg. 34

Making Ends Meet

by Charles Potts

The primary challenge for a creative writer at the initial stages of a career is to find enough time to create and still make ends meet. I've been asked to tell you how I got by in the belief that some of my experience could prove useful to you. I decided early to eschew a career in academe for a life on the street. I wound up in business, not my original intention, but it pays the bills, provides subject matter, and stimulates my competitive imagination.

I grew up on a ranch, joined the social security system in 1954 at age eleven, and worked my way through college at Idaho State University on farms and ranches. I worked in warehouses, bookstores, print shops, computer centers; sold real estate for commission and wrote appraisals; taught at Western Washington Community College and the Washington State Maximum Security Prison, on the way to getting my act together.

Not having a profession, twelve years ago I began buying residential rental dwellings and fixing them up. I'm a real estate broker who manages his own investments. Real estate is exceptionally complicated and produces in depth transactions with a wide variety of people from bankers to welfare recipients and everybody on the food pyramid in between, enabling me to learn the life of my community.

I am also a certified practitioner of Neuro Linguistic Programming and frequently conduct seminars called "Seize the Day," for ambitious people who need to find more time lying around the house. There is one over-arching principle of time control: always work on the most important thing you can. After establishing rapport and warming people up with humor, I ask participants to make a list of all the goals they want to accomplish and sort that list by things they want to finish within a week, a month, six months, a year, five years, and before they die. No point to organize your time (life) until you know what you want to do with it.

I further ask them to prioritize their list, as well as to identify whether the activity or goal is primarily visual, auditory, or kinesthetic (having to do with feelings and emotions). After discussion, I ask people to re-prioritize their list as if they'd just been told for certain that they only had six months to live.

Nothing separates the trivial from the significant as quickly as a death sentence. Use this process to put that great novel or collection of poems on your front burner. We all know we're going to die, we just don't know when. You can use that lyrical uncertainty (*duende*) to sing or otherwise distinguish yourself from the rest of the biomass.

Once you are fixated on a goal, imagine it and write down your imaginings in complete sensory detail, how it looks and will look, how it feels, what it sounds like, etc. I spend at least as long planning a book this way as I do writing it. It is relatively easy to get inspired briefly for a lyric poem. The trick for longer works is to keep your inspiration at the flash point when you're creating and be able to turn it off for rest and back on again when you want to. If you put it in your unconscious mind via the sensory planning process, it can be there when you need it. I call it want power. I use this process for practically everything I do. One of my personal

---

Realize that only 15 minutes a day adds up to almost 12 eight hour days in a year.

---

challenges was learning to love sitting at my computer four to six hours a day.

We learn what we do. Find a job where you can care about what you're learning. Find the time to begin in whatever time you presently have. Realize that only 15 minutes a day adds up to almost 12 eight hour days in a year. Could you get a book written in 12 days? Organize, as Joe Hill once admonished us.

I use a lovely story in "Seize the Day" from John Muir's autobiography of his boyhood, too long to retell in its entirety here. Suffice it to say that he was browbeaten by his father when he wanted to read Shakespeare and the Bible. His father said, get up as early in the morning as you want to and read before you do your chores. The next day John was up at 1:00 AM, and found four hours a day for the rest of his life. I imagine writers who plan to help save the planet could find as much time for it as the master. ∎

Charles Potts hails from Walla Walla, WA where he was one of the organizers of the Walla Walla Poetry Party in the fall of 1990. His most recent book of poems is A Rite to the Body.

Freelance Rate Chart

The following rates are based on information obtained from writers-for-hire and communications consulting firms located in the Northwest. These fees should only be used as guides for setting your own rates, based on your experience and location, the nature of individual projects, and what you believe the market will bear.

Advertising copywriting	$15-$50/hour
Annual reports	$20-$45/hour
Articles (ghosted)	$10-$35/hour
Articles (with writer's byline)	$10-$25/hour, % of fee paid, or combination
Book (ghosted)	$15-$35/hour or flat fee
Book (with credit)	$10-$30/hour, % royalty, or combination
Brochures	$15-$45/hour or flat fee
Business letters	$15-$35/hour or flat fee of $10-$50/letter
Company newsletters	$30-$100/page or $15-$30/hour
Corporate history	$500 & up flat fee or contract wage of $10/hour
Editing (copy)	$7-$20/hour
Editing (substantial)	$15-$30/hour
Family history	$12/hour & up
News releases	$20-$40/page
Promotional or public relations	$15/hour & up (expenses extra)
Readings of poetry or nonfiction	$20/hour & up
Research for writing projects	$10/hour & up
Resume writing	$30/each and up
Scriptwriting	$15/hour & up or by negotiated rate
Speeches	$20-$80/hour
Technical writing	$15-$60/hour
Typing (nontechnical)	$1-$2.50/page
Typing (technical by transcription)	$1.50-$5/page
Writing/publishing consulting	$30-$75/hour

Writer's Book Marketing Checklist

Sample resources and the checklist that follow will help you find and approach the appropriate publisher or agent.

Resources

Books in Print
Books Out of Print
Bookstores give you an idea of who publishes what
International Directory of Little Magazines/Small Presses
Literary Agents of North America
Literary Marketplace
Publishers Weekly
Subject Guide to Books in Print
Writers' Markets
Writer's Northwest Handbook (and other regional guides)

Marketing Checklist

Research the market
Make list of likely publishers or agents
Get latest catalogs and submission guidelines
Personalize and polish cover letter
Revise synopsis until it's perfect
Polish first 50 to 75 pages of manuscript
Be sure submission conforms to publishers guidelines
Send it off and continue working on something else
Be patient

The Future of Copyright

by Dennis Hyatt

The Copyright Act of 1909 aged gracefully. But age it did, and eventually the statute became so unsuited for its primary mission that it had to be replaced. The same fate awaits its replacement, the Copyright Act of 1976. With history as a guide, predicting the future of copyright law is easy.

On one side of the legislative equation is the necessity of protecting the property rights of authors and publishers. On the other side is the desirability of promoting the greatest possible use and dissemination of artistic works. "Creative work is to be encouraged and rewarded, but private motivation must ultimately serve the cause of promoting the broad public availability of literature, music, and the other arts." (From Twentieth Century Music Corp. v. Aiken, 422 U.S. 151, 1975, at 156)

The 1976 Act reset the statutory balance in light of the tremendous progress in the arts and technology over the 80 years since the 1909 Act. But the new Act will also become outmoded. The newest forms of literary expression, a new array of authors' rights, and new information dissemination technologies already foreshadow the long-range problems of the current copyright law.

When is a Book not a Book?

The 1976 Copyright Act specifies seven categories of subject matter that can be copyrighted: literary works, musical works, dramatic works, pantomimes, and choreography, graphic and sculptural works, audiovisual works, and sound recordings. Into which category a particular work falls is important because the statute specifically attaches different rights to different categories.

At first blush the categories seem fairly distinct. But problems arise when a new form of expression fits into overlapping categories, none of which will are entirely adequate to the task. Already the Federal District Court of Texas has held that an animated stuffed bear which is activated by insertion of a tape in a cassette player is an audiovisual work.

New concepts of the book also offer fresh modes of artistic expression that defy easy categorization. For example, consider artist's books, which attempt to connect the craft of publishing with artists interested in books and with writers interested in art. The literary part of an artist's book may be significant, minimal, or non-existent. Often the texture, shape, and materials of the book become its content, and the physical piece may be more a work of sculpture than anything else, more appropriate for a museum than for a library.

Pamela Petro says in *Books as Works of Art*, "These feats of craftsmanship and perception tend to treat text, illustration, and binding in ways that are outside conventional expectations and are intended to shake the 'reader' into new channels of communication."

New Rights for American Artists

Copyright law in the United States assiduously protects the economic interests of authors. However, for the most part American law rejects the so-called "moral rights" of artists, rights long recognized and protected in the civil law countries of continental Europe.

Moral rights include a right to prevent distortion, mutilation or destruction of works (integrity); a right of attribution and against misattribution (paternity); and a right of control over the time and circumstances of initial dissemination (disclosure). These rights arise not because artists need economic protection as incentive for their labor, but because they deserve protection as a right inherent to the act of creation.

Certainly one impetus for adopting moral rights in the United States will come from the outrageous behavior of owners of works who insist on altering the originals to "improve" them. Recent examples include painting sculptural pieces, colorization of black-and-white films, and changing the substantive content of writings by authors who have produced works-for-hire without changing attribution of authorship.

Another impetus for adopting moral rights is the increasing pressure for world-wide harmonization of copyright laws through international agreement. In 1989 the United States became a signatory to the Berne Convention but sidestepped the recognition of moral rights of paternity and integrity found in Article 6 of the treaty by expressly stating that the Convention's provisions have no force in United States law apart from the rights of artists that already existed at the time of signing.

Avoiding the recognition of moral rights can only be temporary, and the next century will see the development of moral rights in the United States.

Dissemination Technologies

The classic infringement of copyright — copying — undercuts the potential sales market and royalties to authors, and the 1976 Act attempts to balance interests by setting limits on permissible photocopying by libraries. However, other library system services still have the potential for dramatically reducing sales. Thus, several countries have adopted public lending right legislation that aims to compensate authors based on the number of times their works are borrowed from libraries, or on the number of

Continued on pg. 36

Literary Agents

by Carolan Gladden

From the moment you admit the desire to be published, you begin to hear variations on the theme, "You must find an agent." Many times this is good advice and the correct action is to embark on a search. But just as often, because of a lack of ready information, beginning writers miss some important steps between writing and achieving publication. A short primer on the four-step process may be helpful.

First: Determine just where what you've written fits in the marketplace and find out the specific requirements for such a project. For instance, what is the proper length and format for its intended category? This may require research at your local library and bookstore.

Second step: Rewrite and polish every page to the very best of your ability. Be sure to eliminate typos and misspellings. And study similar published/produced projects. Ask yourself seriously whether your subject and quality of writing compare favorably.

Step three: It's important to understand what an agent does and whether, when, and how an agent can help you. For instance, few agents handle short pieces — fiction or non — from a new writer. If magazines or newspapers are your target, you should plan to do your own marketing. Poetry is a specialty of a few agencies, ignored by many others. And for movie or television scripts, you need a Writer's Guild of American signatory.

Many successful New York-based agencies represent only previously published/produced writers. But this unfortunate situation has given rise to a new level that appears to be materializing within the industry, agents based away from New York who may also fill the important role of manuscript evaluator and/or "first editor," the person who first reads and critiques your manuscript.

In days gone by the first editor and the editor in the publishing house were often one and the same. Caring people like Max Perkins at Scribners for many years read partial manuscripts and wrote long letters to Hemingway, Fitzgerald, and others, encouraging them and offering advice on projects in the works. In fact, in the past many potentially profitable authors were groomed by the industry, brought up to speed, their rough edges smoothed by long-term interaction with compatible editors. No longer does anybody have this sort of luxury. Today's authors can't get away with handwriting scrawled on yellow pads, nor with presenting a whiff of talent buried in a mass of poor syntax

and bad spelling. Today, your manuscript has to stand on its own from the moment it hits the door of a publishing house or a producer's office.

In addition to turning out an impeccable manuscript, you can lessen the odds against you by learning as much as you can about the market and the marketing process. In short, act as if you're a professional and you may very well be accepted as one. And now's the time to find the right agent for you!

Step four: Literary agency listings can be accessed easily at your library in reference books including the annual *Writer's Market* by Writer's Digest Books and *Literary Market Place* by R.R. Bowker Co. More difficult is deciding which to contact. Ask another writer? Somebody close to home? New in the business? Low priced? With encouraging words? Interested and experienced in projects like yours?

It's okay to ask about areas of expertise, specialties, published/produced projects, speed of decision, fees.

Often it boils down to simply following a hunch. But whatever your decision, for your first contact with an agent, don't telephone! It's much more effective to send a dynamic one-page query letter about the project. Your goal is to be invited to send your manuscript, proposal, or treatment. Ideally your query will exhibit your writing talent, passion for the project, and knowledge of method and form.

It's all right to send queries to several agents. And it's okay to ask about areas of expertise, specialties, published/produced projects, speed of decision, fees. But never, ever send the manuscript, proposal, or treatment to more than one agent at a time! Always include a self-addressed stamped envelope (SASE) with your query and give the agent a reasonable time — say a month — to respond.

If the answer turns out to be "No," give serious consideration to any reasons offered. Some agents may give good guidance if you're open to it. However, agents are only human. If one turns you down, believe in your project and move on to another.

While it is generally true that most publishable/producible material will sooner or later find its place in print/film, an agent who believes in your project is invaluable in preventing the random submissions process. Your relationship with your agent will be an ongoing one, as he or she advises and assists on the marketing package for your project, represents it to appropriate publishers or producers, negotiates for the best terms, markets some of the subsidiary rights, receives funds and distributes your share to you. Therefore, finding

Continued on pg. 34

Succeeding on TV in an Author Interview

by Lisa Uhlmann

Great news! Your publicist has managed to book you for a TV interview. The potential to sell hundreds, even thousands of books is dazzling. But wait — there are important things that need to be done before, during, and after those TV lights go on.

First, write down ten of the best questions you think you might be asked. Then practice answering those questions with your publicist or a friend who will be brutally honest with criticism about your responses. Keep your answers short and to the point.

Second, set up one or even several bookstore autographing sessions for the same day or a few days after your TV appearance, to get more mileage out of the free advertising for your book.

Remember to take extra copies of your book to the interview, and to make sure one is correctly placed on the television studio set during your on-air time. Also, take along a VHS cassette to get a free dub of the interview when it's being aired. Most TV stations will record your tape as a matter of courtesy if you bring it with you.

Always wear flattering colors and try to avoid chroma-key (bright) blue and bland white as well as distracting geometric patterns.

Both women and men should wear makeup. Ask for assistance at the studio as soon as you arrive for interview. There's nothing worse than appearing washed out or too shiny during your moment of glory.

Consider the interview an easy, fun way to gain media experience, sell books, and reach potential fans. Even the most experienced author can get nervous when appearing under the hot lights, so try to treat the audience as a group of your friends. Relax as much as possible and enjoy the experience.

Show emotion and compassion and be lively — not too technical. Use as many personal stories as you can about yourself and/or others when discussing the topic or the mood of your book. Always describe your work, characters or topic in human terms.

Never say "in my book" 33 times. That's the Number One complaint of TV hosts and producers, and a definite way to make sure you will never be invited back.

Thank your interviewers and the producer regardless of your feelings about the final outcome. Send a thank you note. You never know when you will want to be invited back to talk about your next book. ∎

Lisa Uhlmann has been a TV producer for over 12 year in Chicago, Seattle, and Portland. She worked on "Northwest Afternoon" and "Town Hall" and won three Iris awards.

Agents *Cont. from pg. 33*

an agent in whom you have both personal and fiscal confidence is imperative.

Three-quarters of all manuscripts are sold through agents these days, with varying business arrangements. Some agencies make an up-front charge to new writers for reading and/or evaluating their manuscripts. Often this charge is refunded upon sale of the project. But agents generally don't do editing or rewriting, give major manuscript advice, or produce marketing packages without compensation.

Agency fees range between ten and fifteen percent for placement of a book with a publisher and ten percent for film or TV (WGA rate). Some agencies charge for such items as copying, mailing, and telephone. But, remember, you're entitled to verify all policies when you agree to representation, and your agency contract should also stipulate your rights to terminate the agreement. ∎

Carolyn Gladden owns Gladden Unlimited, a one-stop firm offering literary agency and authors' services on book and film projects. The firm is also publisher of The Writer's Simple, Straightforward, Common Sense Rules of Marketability.

Work with Editors *Cont. from pg. 29*

where the story falters, it's because the story has promise. Receiving a note that says "I enjoyed the voice of this story but felt the ending was a disappointment" is not a bad thing; it's an affirmation that you're doing something right. Encouragement isn't an invitation to rewrite, but it is a sign that you would do well to send another story to that magazine in the near future. As odd as it might sound, coming from someone whose life is dogged by a stack of manila envelopes, a good story really does make my mouth water, and I look at every submission with the expectation that it will be the magic one I hope to find. ∎

Cecelia Hagen is a poet and short story writer who also works as the fiction editor of the Northwest Review.

Newspapers *Cont. from pg. 26*

Once you land an assignment, however, don't miss your deadline! Meeting deadlines is one of the most difficult challenges of writing, and not meeting them is one of the fastest ways to shorten your writing career.

When you're doing well locally and want to begin branching out, spend a few hours studying the out-of-town papers most libraries keep on file. Study them the way you scrutinized your local paper. See what sections might be likely to use freelance stories, what types of stories are being run, and which editors are in charge of those sections.

Write to the editors about the stories you've already had published and enclose photocopies of your clippings. Suggest how one or more of the stories might be of interest to people in their community. If all of this sounds tedious or uninspiring or simply like too much hard work, then you've learned something important about yourself, your interests, and your priorities.

If it's sparked your enthusiasm, generated ideas for new stories, or inspired you to call your local editor, then you're on your way. ∎

John Wolcott and his wife, Roberta, who own Features Northwest in Marysville, Washington, provide freelance articles and photos to periodicals. This article is based on his book, Writing For Newspapers.

Western *Cont. from pg. 25*

terms, and all characters are realistic mortals. This movement toward historical accuracy is a mark of the deepening maturity of the western novel and bodes well for the future.

The real West is virtually untouched territory. The most colorful decades in the history of the American frontier were the 1840s and 1850s, the period of expansion. These were the years of the Oregon and Mormon migrations, the California gold rush, the annexation of Oregon and Texas, the Mexican war, the Santa Fe trade, and the first great wars with the plains tribes. This was the period of mustangs and countless buffalo. The time when John Fremont explored an unknown continent. The time of initial mining ventures, the robe trade, and the period when the plains tribes were at their zenith.

The West of this period is the finest trove of material available to a novelist. It will form the foundations for a type of western hitherto unknown, in which pale mythologies are stripped away and bright realities are shaped into great stories. The future of the western novel could not be more promising. ∎

Richard Wheeler won the Spur Award for best western novel in 1989 for Fool's Coach. The Final Tally *and* The Rocky Mountain Company *are new titles in 1991.*

Spider Robinson *Cont. from pg. 22*

Think of it — we have two million years as human apes with killer instincts. Sf writers say, "we (humans) can fix that." But it took us two million years to establish an intercom, and what do we use it for? Bad news. The idea used to be to lie to the younger generation, keep them innocent (about how bad things are) as long as possible. Our generation said cut the crap, tell us the truth. Somewhere in the middle, there is the joy of life. Between naive and jaded.

What are the best parts of humans? When we can change *any* of those parts at will, what do we want to preserve? Defining what is more than human is the most fun you can have out of bed.

Somewhere along the line, we got too sophisticated, we aged too quickly. *In Time Enough for Love,* Heinlein says, "it's amazing how much mature wisdom resembles being too tired." The only cure for that is telling funny stories. Tall Tale Night at Callahan's. I see myself, as a writer, in an airplane, engines failing, smoke pouring out of the engines. I run ahead and entertain everyone with bad jokes long enough for the pilot to regain control. ∎

Marjorie Rommel, who teaches at Highline College in Washington, is a journalist and short story writer.

Who Done It *Cont. from pg. 19*

plot, Wren's advice is that the deed should be done within the first three chapters. It should include who the victim is, the discovery of the crime, the apparent circumstances of the death, and the introduction of central characters of the story, including the detective.

Development is the heart of the mystery and the body of the book. It is the investigation part of a book in which the detective is searching for the truth: the real time, place, and cause of death, and, of course, who done it! Suspects are developed in depth. Development should build the tension and drama until its climax/resolution.

The climax/resolution is what any good mystery worth its salt is all about. Primary questions posed through the orientation are answered, releasing the tension caused by the drama. The answer to a mystery is always the same. The killer is identified and brought to some kind of justice, which the good guy causes to happen. When the reader completes the mystery, there should be no unanswered questions; all should have been revealed.

Martha Kay Renfroe (alias M.K. Wren) is now working on her seventh Conan Joseph Flagg murder mystery, where *all* will be revealed — once again. ∎

Monica Mersinger is a Salem, Oregon resident and freelance writer whose articles have appeared in Oregon Coast, Oregon Business, *and* Travelin' Magazine.

Life as Subject *Cont. from pg. 23*

malefic force is in him in regards to women. He is attracted to the most powerful women so he can destroy them. In this destruction he finds what he thinks is his manhood.

"Second, this is what is going to happen to you."

I typed it out, the Sisters' itinerary for me. A year and a half later, through the worst betrayal yet — partly because I was convinced I had learned the lesson — I went searching for this writing. When I found it, I held in my hands the exact story I had just lived, right down to the very sentence with which he had kicked me out. *"You're no longer erotic to me."*

The immorality of exposing a loved one, one with whom one has had the sacred experience of *knowing*, is perhaps my largest understanding. I've always called this Love, and quoted Rilke: *"The role of the lover is to protect the privacy of the loved one."* My journey has been to see that this cosmic law has not been reciprocated for me, that my soul has not been protected by the ones who vowed to do this. Now I come back to my childhood secret, but my love is not less. Now I search for the true balance, my betrayals and theirs, of unconditional love. Now I know it is the Goddess holding the Scales of Love who is blindfolded, not either of the lovers.

"What about your private life?" a guy asked me tonight at The Mark Antony. "I admit I've been fascinated by you, I've watched you a lot. But you won't like what I see." He told me anyway. "You have about fifteen veils." His hand indicated them before his face.

"Veils are okay," I responded. "You can take off veils. They're soft, erotic. The Goddess wears veils."

Before the conversation took this hostile turn, he'd told me of his nascent efforts to be a poet and asked me about when I accepted the calling, if it was hard. Now this question fell together with the one of my private life.

"It was the hardest thing I've ever done. I accepted my calling at the precise moment I understood that as a private person I would always be betrayed by the man I love. I accepted it when I understood that my unconditional love was tipping the Scales. I accepted it rather than give up my faith that there are men capable of love, that there is a man I can love who can love me. I went public with my soul, my most private self, as a way of making the world make me accountable for something I am not strong enough to do alone. I went public as part of the Sister Support Group — we, the Great Ones, who, despite everything, still believe there are Great Men."

I wasn't wrong in 1968 about Vietnam. War begins in the Lover's bed, in the House where Father is King. I just didn't know myself. ■

Sharon Doubiago's latest book is Psyche Drives the Coast, Poems 1975-1987, *from Empty Bowl.*

Copyright *Cont. from pg. 32*

copies of their works that are purchased by libraries. Public lending right legislation may yet come to the United States.

New dissemination technologies are already creating additional opportunities for libraries to deliver copyrighted works directly to users without copying. Inexpensive home computers provide telephone access to library networks where information and literary works are stored in full-text electronic format, such as compact disk. By dialing into such networks, the borrower will eventually read a "book" which exists as an artifact only as an electronic signal. As the price of hardware and software decrease, these dissemination technologies are becoming ubiquitous, and within only a few years all forms of literary expression will probably require licensing fees, as well as royalties, to protect the economic interests of authors and publishers.

Conclusion

Copyright law in the 21st Century will replay the themes of the 20th Century. Creativity will again outstrip the capacity of copyright statutes to keep a fine balance of competing public interest, especially for new forms of artistic expression. The bundle of rights called copyright law will expand in the United States to encompass international community concerns for the moral rights of artists. New technologies for dissemination of literary works will require licensing fee arrangements, as well as royalties, for authors and publishers. ■

Dennis Hyatt is a Law Librarian at the University of Oregon.

Learning the Landscape: Regional Literature in Classrooms

by Ruth Vinz

The Bridger Range of southwestern Montana, the flatland sagebrush and mudflats near Malheur Lake, the personified inlet the Kwakiutl people called "Hollow of the Northwest Wind," and the coastal rainforests of Washington: such a collection of landscapes weaves more than a handful of stories. Stories of people who were corrupted by gold, of ranchers and nesters warring the land into a topography of battlefields, of hunger, dreams, and elk hunts, of shallow and not so shallow graves.

Through the stories, we can define ourselves and the country we live in. "Remember your stories," Kim Stafford said to a group of students in Wallowa County. "They can save your life a little at a time."

As a critical preamble to emphasizing the importance of bringing regional literature into the classroom, I would like to stress that schools, suffering myopia, have never gained sight of the richness, of the small, near sacred geography hidden away from textbooks and curriculum guides. Dizzied by images of national literature, immutable truths, and worship of the canon, most schools, like cockleburrs, cling to tradition. Yet, to pay heed to the literature of the physical and spiritual landscape of a region is to turn up a reward: a fragment intricately carved into the shape of metaphors that define and redefine who we are and how we live.

Such literature offers a record of the ways in which people connect to a place and make it home, rooted in lives and rhythms of the land that we, also, feel under our feet and hear pounding in our hearts and imaginations. As Ivan Doig carries us "far back among the high spilling slopes of the Bridger Range..." and through a lifetime of ranch, blizzard and into sun "so hot above the plain that sweat cooked from you...," we recognize the awe of seeing into ourselves through what is vaguely familiar there.

To preserve the wonder and lengthen the memory is the province of the classroom teacher. To help students through the self-defining process, the teacher can invite them to hear stories of their Northwest land and the people who shape it, and to experience the act of telling for themselves the stories that shape their identities. The students are the active voices, in transition, creating a present and a future that contains shadows of the past. If we avoid binding down the voices and the words of the land into dissected bits held under the knife of literary criticism, we highlight this sense of place.

My grandfather would cage fish for spawning. He'd take a hen fish and knead her belly until the eggs would spill forth like jelly into the bucket he'd carried there. Kneading again and again, he'd bring forth eggs until he'd let her go, back into the water. Then he'd uncage the male. He knew just the right movements to release a trickle. A thousand eggs were fertilized, sent back into the waters where the river doesn't roar. He had two purposes in the last of his life: to fish and to keep the river populated. In a way it's like a hand from God, something natural and unnatural at the same time.— Sarah, age 14

Early this morning I watched the calves herded into the range corral for branding. The irons were heated by a sagebrush bonfire to a red hot glow. Inside a smaller pen, Byron threw each calf to the ground, looping a rope around its back feet that was tied to a post. Once the front legs were tied, the calf was stretched out, much like a torture rack of the Middle Ages. Each calf would bawl pitifully, struggle to get up as the branding iron pressed into its hide. The stench rose and a breeze blew it my way.

These calves represent our shelter, our bread and our home. The branding makes them legally ours. The brand defends our property much like a good fence does. Yet, brands, like words, are only the symbol of an idea.
—Eric, age 14

My job as teacher is to let the literature loose into the classroom. I select two or three authors who deal with locale sensitively to get us started. *The International Directory of Little Magazines & Small Presses* and *Writer's Northwest Handbook* help

Continued on pg. 45

Part of what you're doing as a writer is to make that silent language of mountains and trees and water part of your language. It's speaking all the time, and I hear it speaking.
—Tess Gallagher

Through My Eyes: Publishing in Kindergarten

by Michelle O'Brien-Palmer

Our literary adventure began with an assignment from my son's pre-school teacher. Nicholas was asked to bring his favorite poem to class. Being non-conformists, we decided to write a poem together instead. His idea was to write about all of the different shapes he saw in the clouds. I recorded his words for him and amazingly, the words fell easily into rhythm and rhyme. Nick enjoyed rhyming words and this type of poetry seemed very natural to him. I typed up the poem as he illustrated a construction paper border. He was so proud of our poem that he memorized it and presented it to his pre-school class himself.

We continued to write poetry together for fun. It was a wonderful opportunity for me to hear and record how Nicholas perceived his world. He especially enjoyed the fact that what he said was important enough to be written down. He had my undivided attention and interest! We worked together to pull poems out of his words. There were poems about his adventures at the zoo, getting sand up his nose at the beach, and movie seats that folded his legs into his face. We wrote about getting bumped by grownups, washing peas down with milk, and touching the sky from atop his daddy's shoulders. Perhaps the most moving poem was the one written as an expression of Nick's grief at the loss of his Great Grandpa Henry.

When Nicholas started kindergarten he shared our poems with his new classmates. Shortly thereafter, his teacher called me in to observe what she termed, "the children's animated response" to our poetry. Upon doing so, I realized that our poems struck a chord of common experience in these children. I was overwhelmed at how moved they were by the poetry. The children's enthusiasm was irresistible. We decided to turn our poetry into a book with these ardent supporters as the illustrators.

Each child in the kindergarten class created one illustration for the book. Our book was entitled *Through My Eyes* because it was written and illustrated from a child's perspective. *Through My Eyes* was self-published in early June 1990. Initially, our book was selling in four bookstores in the Seattle area. The children were ecstatic when we planned a field trip to the local bookstore. The looks on the children's faces when they saw "their book" on the store bookshelves was something I'll treasure forever.

Now that their book is available in fifty bookstores throughout four states, the children understand through firsthand experience that you can take an idea and create a tangible product. They feel that something they contributed to is valued by our society. This is interpreted as, "I am valuable."

The children now consider themselves "published illustrators."

The children now consider themselves "published illustrators." As such, they have autographed books, appeared on television, radio, and in the newspaper. Brianne, the cover illustrator, had an author visit her new school recently. When the author started talking about his illustrations, Brianne raised her hand and said with confidence, "I know how to illustrate, I illustrated the cover and one poem of a book last year." Evan notes that he "illustrated the Getting Bumped poem and really likes poems now." Nicholas also had an author come to visit his school. His reaction was, "Mom, I am an author and an illustrator at six years old. My teacher said, 'that's pretty neat,' and I think so too." When we discussed writing recently, Nick said, "Someday soon I won't need you to help me write my books anymore, I'll write them all by myself." ∎

Michelle O'Brien-Palmer has plans for future books and runs a consulting business.

Whenever I think of designing a book, I always keep in mind the story Maurice Sendak shared about his "getting acquainted ritual" with his first book. He tried to bite into Mark Twains's **The Prince and the Pauper.**— *Elsi Vassdal Ellis*

I Completed My First Novel at Age 10

by Jennifer DiMarco

I was born to be a writer. Both my parents and my maternal grandfather gave me the genes. Those chromosomes became a gift that developed into finely honed skills which continue to grow and develop. But I never really gave writing a second thought until I was ten years old.

Back in 1983 there was a teacher named Carol Pearl. She had the arduous task of teaching a certain shy little girl Language Arts. This proved to be almost impossible as the youngster would barely talk, let alone try to master grammar and spelling. Finally, having exhausted all other approaches, a bewildered and exasperated Ms. Pearl asked the child to write a short story that told something about who the little girl was.

Little Jenni's first attempt at creative writing turned into a 265-page science fiction novel that went on to win a top twenty placement in a national writing contest for thirteen to eighteen year olds! One novel quickly turned into five

All along the way I have been blessed with supportive teachers and a nurturing environment.

novels, four screenplays, a collection of poems that won the 1990 Bumbershoot Arts Competition, and a short story that won First Place, Nonfiction Category in the 1990 Pacific Northwest Writers' Conference.

All along the way I have been blessed with supportive teachers and a nurturing environment. I am fortunate to attend Seattle Alternative School Summit K-12, where creativity is the norm. In my junior high years at Summit, Sandra Whaley proved to be a friend and confidant, as well as an inspiring Creative Writing teacher. Now, during my high school tenure, Eleanor Weston helps guide my craft and challenge my imagination.

My parents and immediate family have always blanketed me in encouragement and praise. I cannot stress enough how much a positive, nurturing atmosphere can make anything possible in a young writer's life.

After being interviewed in our community newspaper, people stopped me with the same hail: "Aren't you THE WRITER?" Still somewhat shy, I would nod politely and give a blushing grin. I had arrived! But more important, these friendly strangers would go on to explain how reading the article about my writing had inspired them. Many had been fired with a new passion to rekindle an old love. I was

Continued on pg. 44

On Becoming a Published Author

by Elizabeth Haidle

Ever since I can remember, I have been drawing and writing. All three of us kids had journals that we would write and draw in after going on vacations. Mom and Dad helped us jot down memories for which we drew pictures. On evenings, we would make up songs or stories and dictate as our parents wrote. Illustrating them was the most fun part.

In fourth and fifth grades, I had some wonderful teachers who encouraged doing extra-credit. My best friend and I turned out tons of projects like research collages from magazines, picture books of wild forest animals, or even funny plays involving a snobby fat lady and her clumsy maid that we put on for the class.

But in fifth grade, I first made up the characters that later became published! I still remember laying on the floor, drawing a world of city and country elves, subject to their king, queen, and princess baby. I made elaborate mushroom homes for them and insect pets.

In sixth grade, I felt unchallenged at school, so I home-schooled fourth quarter. Mom suggested I do a project to show teachers in case they wondered if I was really studying. I decided to make my own book about the elves I created. I spent hours researching mushrooms, flowers and insects.

Though my parents always knew it should be published, I thought the idea preposterous. At least until I was twenty or thirty it could only be a future goal. Sure, lots of authors told us kids to start printing now, but after all, they hadn't published until adult age. So I kept my book and seldom thought about redoing it for publication until, one day in eighth grade, Mom found an article about a girl who had her book published in a contest. The 1988 contest deadline was only a month away, so I launched into the rewriting and illustrating, working busily after school until the last hour possible. Thousands entered each year, so I figured I hadn't much of a chance. But I thought I could try it with other publishers if I didn't win. So, of course I was surprised to find out in the fall that I had won first place in my age group!

In November 1988, I flew with Mom on an expense-paid trip to the publishing company in Kansas City, Missouri. Editors helped me improve my elves and gave suggestions for rewriting. At home, the next three months involved editing my whole story four times. The next one and a half months I spent redoing my illustration sketches three times each and then finally watercoloring them. Then came the day in July that was well worth all my work. I received the first published copy of my book!

Lately, I have been talking at grade schools about how I got published and encouraging kids to write and illustrate. I

Continued on pg. 45

On Teaching Writing: Learning Lessons From Working Writers

by Tim Gillespie

For me, learning to write in elementary school meant mostly penmanship practice and occasional assignments in the vein of "Our Field Trip to the Bakery" or "My Favorite Pet." Spelling and neatness were what counted. In junior high, I hacked out reports on stipulated topics — amphibians or FDR or Costa Rica. In high school English, we diagrammed. Writings were sporadically required: "An essay on *Macbeth*, 500 words long, and don't forget to outline first." The papers were turned in; two weeks later we got them back, corrected in scarlet. "Creative Writing" was an elective.

Today, happily, things are different. Writing instruction has changed dramatically in American schools, a change partly attributable to the descriptions of professional writers about their working processes. Sometime in the last twenty years, those of us who teach writing in the schools realized that the writing instruction many students suffer has had little to do with the way real writers work.

A few years ago, I was interviewing students on their attitudes about the craft of writing. I asked some, "Do you think the way professional writers work differs from the way you do?"

"Yeah," responded one student with a grin. "They can get it right the *first* time!"

We all chuckled, but my experience tells me the truth is something almost exactly the opposite. If anything could be said to characterize most professional writers, it's an unwillingness to accept how it comes out the first time, a stubborn commitment to revision. Hemingway said he wrote the ending to *Farewell to Arms* 39 times, just "getting the words right."

So, we educators worried that our classroom methods were too far removed from the methods of working writers, and we began to pay attention to their lessons. As the journalist Donald Murray said in his book, *A Writer Teaches Writing*, students and teachers need to "teach themselves the lessons professional writers have taught themselves…and learn by experiencing the process of writing as practiced by the publishing writer."

This practitioners' viewpoint has influenced curriculum. For one thing, students write far more often these days than students did twenty years ago. Daily composition time is a commonplace in many schools today. Working writers taught us the necessity of daily discipline. As Somerset Maugham said, "Good writing is the application of the seat of the pants to the seat of the chair."

Another change is that not every topic is assigned by the teacher these days. Students are often given a chance to choose their own topics, partly because professional writers testify about the importance of following one's own interests and curiosity to those topics, unique and personal, that compel the words to pour forth. Also, outlining is less likely to be required in a modern writing class, partly because of writers' descriptions of the power of writing itself to help one discover the form or shape of a thought. C. Day Lewis said, "I do not sit down at my desk to put into verse something that is already clear in my mind. If it were clear in my mind, I would have no incentive or need to write about it. We do not write in order to be understood, we write in order to understand."

Teachers these days care as much as they ever did about the protocols of writing — proper spelling, grammar, and punctuation — but they are more likely than their predeces-

---

If anything could be said to characterize most professional writers, it's an unwillingness to accept how it comes out the first time, a stubborn commitment to revision.

---

sors to wait to worry about these matters. It is not unusual to see teachers talking with students about the content and form of a writing first, letting students draft and redraft before they edit for correctness. This accommodates the common writers' claim that a spilling of language must come first and that early drafts will thus necessarily be messy. As Katherine Paterson says, "A good (editor or teacher) reserves criticism for appropriate times. She knows that no one can work creatively and critically at the same moment. She never peers over your shoulder while you're on a first draft…. I have respect for her critical ability, but if I allow her to make remarks on my work while it is still tentative and fragile, she is likely to kill something before it has a chance to breathe properly." Thus you won't see many teachers correcting too early, and when they do proofread a student paper, it's for a purpose — publication.

This is the final lesson from real writers, this growing recognition of the importance of publishing to student writers. In traditional school instruction, the end result of a writing experience was a corrected paper and a grade. This made it seem that the purpose of writing in school was simply to be evaluated.

Continued on pg. 44

Classroom Publishing: Setting Up a Program

by Ruth Ann Carter

Teaching elementary students to write competently and creatively has always been a goal at Peter Boscow School. In each classroom and at each grade level, we have provided students with activities designed to teach not only the mechanics of writing, but also to spark our students' creativity. It is to this end that we applied for and were granted two School Improvement and Professional Development Grants. Following are some highlights of our activities.

By surveying our staff, we found that everyone felt quite confident in teaching the mechanics of writing. We made our goal the improvement of teacher's skills in the areas of teaching, evaluating, and publishing student writing.

Because of the grant, we were able to bring experts in the writing process to our school to help us design programs and materials for our students. Teachers worked with Dr. Beverly Chin of the University of Montana and Bev Merrill of Mesa, Arizona. It was a wonderful experience for the staff to work together on the writing process; it provided a much desired common ground in the understanding and application of the writing process in our school.

One of our most successful activities to get students to write has been and still is to expose them to good writing. Through the generosity of the P.T.A., we have been able to have at least one author visit per year. Our students have been inspired by Steven Kellogg, Syd Hoff, Johanna Hurwitz, Jasper Tompkins, and Ted and Gloria Rand. The grant enabled us to have Jack Prelutsky appear at our school in the afternoon and for the entire community in the evening. Our students still feel very close to these wonderful authors and illustrators. They feel comfortable sharing their original poetry with Jack Prelutsky and even jumping rope with Gloria Rand. Knowing that authors are people too helps students to know their work has value. After all, everyone engages in the same basic process from initial thought to published material.

Another of our goals, evaluating, was met through training in Trait Analysis. Initially, a group of teachers and parents were trained in Trait Analysis. That team was able to evaluate student writing samples, provide data for the grant, and to assist in training the other staff members.

Publishing student writing is probably the most fun of all! In our classrooms, we provide paper (both lined and construction), staples, tape, paper punch, yarn, and a variety of other writing and art supplies. This informal set-up is commonly referred to as the "underground press." Students can publish whenever they wish once their work is finished.

Each grade level is provided with a publishing kit. We use large plastic tool boxes and have equipped them with a heavy duty stapler, heavy duty paper punch, various cloth tapes, press-on letters, etc. Teachers can publish class books as well as individual books in a more formal manner by using the material in the kits.

We finally have a real publishing center. It is equipped with a roll laminator and laminating film, a comb binder with an assortment of sizes and colors of binders, and a Macintosh computer. We also have a computer lab supplied with multiple copies of the Children's Publishing Center software and other word processing programs. Through the grant, we trained teachers and parents to use the Children's Publishing Center software .Now teachers are training students to use the software themselves and to publish their own work.

Student books are bound and enjoyed by our students and their families in many ways. One of the nicest is when teachers use student writing as the read aloud literature for the day. Many times students choose their classmates' work for sustained silent reading. The library also circulates books written and published by students. Twelve of our students read their books at LitEruption, Portland's annual book and author festival. It was the first time students were on the same schedule as adult authors. They also read their books at a school assembly. Imagine reading your work to six hundred people! We are currently exploring other possibilities for getting our students' work out into the community.

A key component of the grant was the training we provided for our parents. We trained approximately fifty parents at two sessions — one in the fall and one in the spring. In addition to an overview of the writing process that enabled parents to help in the classroom, parents were trained in several different binding techniques and in laminating. Parents continue to help us publish children's books.

In planning and completing our grants, we also surveyed our students. In the spring of 1989, seventy-four percent of our students in grades three through six said creative writing was important even though fifty percent considered it hard. Seventy-nine percent enjoyed creative writing. When we resurveyed the students one year later, seventy-four percent said creative writing was important, only twenty-seven percent considered it hard, and eighty-eight percent enjoyed creative writing.

At Peter Boscow, we continue to teach students to write competently. We feel successful in sparking creativity and in providing a finished product of which children are proud. As Kimberly Franklin, age seven, stated: "When you start writing, you never want to stop." ∎

Ruth Ann Carter has been a school librarian for ten years and works with both teachers and librarians.

Resources for Young Writers

by Terri Lee Grell

So you're really enjoy writing and may be looking for more opportunities outside of the classroom. We offer you here a sampling of contests, conferences, places to get your writing published, and ideas for expanding your writing horizons.

• Your local newspaper is a good place to start getting your work published. Many daily and weekly newspaper editors are always on the look-out for students willing to write columns about school activities. Also, some newspapers sponsor writing contests for young writers and poets (like the *Longview Daily News* in Longview, WA) or run regular open columns for and by members of the community, young and old alike (i.e. *The Cowlitz County Advocate* weekly in Castle Rock, WA, publishes a weekly open column called "Community Ad-Libs.") Check with your local newspaper editor and ask what kind of material he or she is looking for.

• Young writers in all states can find out about annual programs, contests, and conferences sponsored by state affiliates of the National Council of Teachers of English by contacting NCTE, 1111 Kenyon Road, Urbana, IL 6801.

• "Breviloquence," 99 words or less, is an annual writing contest open to any student in the NW. It is sponsored by *Writer's NW*, a quarterly newspaper published by the people who put out this book. One division is for 3rd-8th grades, another for 9th-12th grades. The deadline is Feb. 1, and the winners (who receive prizes of books) are published in the spring issue. Contact: *Writer's NW*, Rt 3, Box 376, Hillsboro, OR 97124.

ALASKA

• *Writings from Alaska Schools* is an annual publication from the Alaska Council of Teachers of English. All Alaskan students are invited to submit samples, which are then judged and edited by ACTE. Contact Phyllis Rude, 2567 Arlington Drive, Anchorage, AK 99517.

• *The Alaska State Writing Consortium Newsletter*, Department of Education, PO Box F, Juneau, AK 99811. Contact Judith Entwine at 907-465-2841. The Consortium is the Alaskan version of the Writing Project in other states; the newsletter announces contests for young writers and lists student newsletters and magazines.

• *Poets of the Stars*, considered the oldest continually published poetry journal in Alaska for young writers, publishes work from elementary children of the Anchorage School District. For information on this and other resources in the Anchorage SD, contact Becky Sipe at 907-269-2242.

• Fine Arts Institute Camp is held the first two weeks in June at Mount Edgecumbe High School and includes creative writing workshops led by nationally-known authors. Contact the Camp at PO Box 2133, Sitka, AK 99835 or call Anne Morrison at 907-747-3372. A similar arts camp is held at the University of Alaska in Fairbanks each year. Contact Helen Barrett at 907-452-2000.

• Rainbow Factory: A Very Special Arts Festival each year for Alaskan people with disabilities includes workshops for young creative writers. Contact Sharon Abbott at Anchorage Museum 907-343-4326 or David Edlessen at 907-343-6185.

• *Musher Monthly* is a publication by and for children of Bethel, AK. Contact Mike Murray, PO Box 305, Bethel, AK 99559 or call 907-543-2845.

• Students on the Aleutian Islands have their writings published in an annual yearbook organized by the Aleutian School District. Contact Robert Much at 907-562-2924.

BRITISH COLUMBIA

• For information on programs for young writers, contact Linda Power, communications coordinator for the Assembly of B.C. Arts Councils at 604-738-0749. She is compiling a resource list and is eager to help young writers "find their way through the menagerie."

• The Association of B.C. Teachers of English has information about resources for students. Contact Judith Blakeston, ABCTE president, at Duncan School District, Vancouver Island, 604-746-4435.

• *Chalk Talk Magazine* is written by children for children. Submissions are welcome from children between the ages of 5 and 14. Contact the magazine at 1550 Mills Rd., RR 2, Sidney, B.C. V8L 3S1.

• The Association of B.C. Book Publishers can send students a booklet of resources and directory of members, which includes publishers of books by and for young writers. Contact Margaret Reynolds, executive director at 604-734-1611.

• Normal Art Society organizes a Small Press Festival each year which includes works by and for young writers. Contact Gordon Murray at 604-873-3129.

• Other suggestions for events and publications: Ministry of Education 604-356-2500; Canada Teachers Union 604-731-8121; Writers Union of Canada 604-874-1611; Cultural Services Branch, Canada Council 604-356-1724.

IDAHO

• Northwest Inland Writing Project publishes *Inland*, a newsletter that includes student writing. It is co-sponsored by NWIWP and Idaho Council of Teachers of English. Contact Driek Zirinsky, editor, at 208-343-2279.

• The most popular resource for young Idaho writers, according to Elinor Michel at the University of Idaho, is the Young Writers Conference at EWU in Cheney, WA (see listing under Washington).

• The Pilot Knobs Writers Group plans to have a mentorship program where young writers in junior and senior high school can work with writers by mail. Contact the group c/o Christina Adams, Rt 1 Box 591, Victor, ID 83455 or 208-354-8522.

• The Idaho State Department of Education sponsors a state-wide writing contest called WRITE ON! IDAHO. "Write about a person, place, or object in your area of Idaho that symbolizes or means Idaho to you." Winning entries in each district are displayed for two weeks in the capitol building and then made available for other publications. For example, the Idaho Theatre for Youth used student entries as the script for their touring production, "The I in Idaho." *The Idaho Statesman* also used entries for an article called "A Child's View."

MONTANA

• The Montana Division of the American Association of University Women sponsors an annual essay contest with prizes, open to all Montana students, grades 10-12. Contact Student Contest Coordinator, 20200 W. Dickerson #58, Bozeman, MT 59715.

• The Office of the Montana Superintendent of Public Instruction will send you a schedule of statewide programs and residencies for young writers. Contact Jan Cladouhous or June Atkins, Education Specialists, Montana OPI, Helena, MT 59620, or call 406-444-3664.

• The Montana Chapter of the National Council of Teachers of English sponsors a program that recognizes excellence in student literary magazines. Contact Linda Edwards, 301 8th Ave. S., Lewiston, MT 59457.

• Missoula Reading Council sponsors a statewide young authors conference for elementary through eighth grade. The conference includes workshops, speakers, and a display of books students have made. There are no qualifications or fees for the display, except that the student submit through a teacher.

• The Montana Writing Project works to inspire young writers and teachers of young writers. Different programs are set up annually, according to need and request. Contact Dr. Beverly Ann Chin, Director, MWP, Dept. of English, University of Montana, Missoula, MT 59812, or call her at 406-243-0211.

OREGON

• The Oregon Council of Teachers of English and Eastern Oregon State College sponsors an Oregon Student Magazine Contest. The contest is open to students and teachers publishing student writing in a magazine format where the entire project is by students and teachers. Awards

six prizes of $100 each. Contact David Axelrod, EOSC, English Department, La Grand, OR 97850.

• The Oregon Council of Teachers of English also sponsors an Oregon Writing Festival for young writers. The event is scheduled for May 4, 1991, to be held at Portland State University. Contact Dr. Ulrich Hardt, PSU, PO Box 751, Portland, OR 97207 for information and future dates. Includes speakers, workshops, and readings.

• Young writers may submit writings to *Oregon English Journal*, published twice a year. Deadlines for submissions are March 1 and September 1. All age groups are represented. Same address as listing above.

• Oregon Press Women sponsors a journalism contest for high school students. Categories for features, photography, news, editorials. Contest is judged by professional journalists. First place winners are entered into National Federation of Press Women Contest. Guidelines are sent to Oregon high schools. Contact Jann Mitchell at *The Oregonian*, 1320 SW Broadway, Portland, OR 97201, or call 503-221-8327.

• *The Asterick*, a newspaper for prize-winning high school journalists, is published by the Oregon Press Women, Inc. PO Box 2534, Portland, OR 97225-0354.

• A city-wide student newspaper, *Metropolitan News*, accepts work by student journalists. Contact Judd Randall at *The Oregonian*, 1320 SW Broadway, Portland, OR 97201.

• *Skipping Stones* seeks writing in every language, artwork, and photography from and for children. Contact the magazine c/o Aprovecho, 80574 Hazelton Rd., Cottage Grove, OR 97424, or call 503-942-9434.

• The Oregon Students Writing & Art Foundation has published two anthologies of student writing, and is accepting material until Sept. 1991 for a third. Contact Chris Weber, PO Box 2100, Portland, OR 97208, or call 503-232-7737.

• LitEruption, Oregon's largest book fair and literary festival held each March in Portland, includes a children's room with young writers as well as adult authors. Contact Northwest Writers Inc., PO Box 3437, Portland, OR 97208.

• Physicians for Social Responsibility sponsors an annual writing contest open to Oregon students grades 7-12. Prizes are awarded. For the theme and guidelines, contact PSR, 921 SW Morrison, Ste 500, Portland, OR 97205.

• *Young American*, America's Newsmagazine for Kids, accepts work from young writers. Contact them at PO Box 12409, Portland, OR 97212, 503-230-1895.

• Young Writers Competition is a writing workshop, a program of the Oregon Arts Commission, which takes various forms. Offered to middle schools in 1991, teams of students and teachers work together in a week-end residency. Contact OAC at 835 Summer St NE, Salem, OR 97301.

Continued on pg. 45

Campus Journal — A Showcase for Student Writing

by Scott Johnson

I have a great job. I publish a magazine for teens called *Campus Journal* — a publication I wish had been in existence when I was in school. *Campus Journal* is a full color magazine that showcases literary and visual art by junior high and senior high school students.

A typical issue includes color and black & white art, color and black & white photography, poetry, short fiction, and non-fiction covering topics from jobs to human interest to science to entertainment. We solicit submissions directly from students and through our network of education professionals. *Campus Journal* also has a student staff which helps edit, design, and produce the magazine.

Campus Journal encourages good writing on any subject, in almost any genre or style. We've published haiku poems about beautiful sunsets, limericks about exam anxiety, and free-form works about alcoholic parents; short fiction on a variety of topics; science fiction; and articles on sports, dating, entertainment, science, juvenile correction programs, and teen organizations.

This is a much broader range of artistic opportunities than a high school newspaper offers. There is little or no room for short fiction, poetry, or visual art in a school newspaper. That's why I love publishing the magazine. It provides teens with a healthy outlet for their literary (and visual) creativity, an outlet that's seen by over 150,000 of their peers.

Campus Journal provides teens with what I like to call the four Rs: recognition of their talent, reward for their efforts, respect for them as valuable members of society, responsibility for helping publish the magazine.

I believe in the four Rs. Too many of us complain about the quality of public education in America but don't do anything to make it better. I like to think that publishing this magazine makes a difference. We boost students' self esteem by printing their work. We also provide them with the first step in a career as a writer, editor, designer, artist, or salesperson.

If America wants the quality of public school graduates to improve, society must reward students for displaying their scholarly talents. Newspapers devote many pages to high school sports but almost nothing to scholarly accomplishments, especially in the literary and visual arts. We need to make the trophies for academic achievement bigger than those for athletic achievement. ■

Scott Johnson is president of Student Publishing Services Inc., a company devoted to publishing works written, edited, designed, and produced by teenagers.

First Novel *Cont. from pg. 39*

overjoyed. I had accomplished my most cherished goal. Not only had I shared a part of myself with others, I had imparted some of the love and inspiration I felt.

Of course, it has not always been easy. The hardships of being a writer, especially a young writer trying to break into the seemingly impenetrable writers' community, have been many. I've gotten my share of rejection slips and less than kind critiques. And you can just imagine the looks on people's faces when I tell them I completed my first novel at age 10! My work tends to be on the controversial side, but I fervently believe that all great writers take risks. If not for the never-ending support (both emotional and financial) of my loving friends, teachers, and family, I would not be where and who I am today. ■

Jennifer DiMarco, a 17 year-old old student who lives in Seattle, has written five books, including her self-published, Sarah's Dead.

Teaching Writing *Cont. from pg. 40*

But why not, we began to wonder, shoot for the same things that impel real writers to put pen to paper — the desire to communicate to a larger audience, to share your expression with others, to see your words in print? So, the idea of publishing kids' works, in the classroom or outside, is more than just another educational fad. It is an attempt to connect the work of students to the work of professional writers. It is a commitment to give students a glimpse of themselves as real writers, as young authors whose words might move a reader and change the world. ■

Tim Gillespie is the Language Arts Specialist at the Multnomah Education Service District, past president of the Oregon Council of Teachers of English, co-director of the Oregon Writing Project at Lewis & Clark College, and a freelance writer.

Regional Literature *Cont. from pg. 37*

me find out about current literary activity in the region. Also, *A Dictionary of American Poets and Writers*, which lists regional writers, can be useful. Alternative publishing thrives for good and necessary reasons. Here are some good starting works that helped my students, and me along with them, into this landscape of life and spirit: Kim R. Stafford, *Having Everything Right*; Nicholas O'Connell, *At The Field's End: Interviews With 20 Pacific Northwest Writers*; Hugh Nichols, *Passages West:* Nineteen Stories of Youth and Identity; Ivan Doig, *This House of Sky* and *Dancing at the Rascal Fair*; William Kittredge, *Owning It All* and *We Are Not in*

Yet, to pay heed to the literature of the physical and spiritual landscape of a region is to turn up a reward: a fragment intricately carved into the shape of metaphors that define and redefine who we are and how we live.

This Together; Norman Maclean, *A River Runs Through It*; Mary Blew, *Lambing Out and Other Stories* and *Runaway*; Dorothy M. Johnson, *The Hanging Tree*; David Long, *The Flood of '64*; and Wallace Stegner, *The Uneasy Chair.*

The list is fragmentary and idiosyncratic, as is the landscape itself. As I roam the qualities of earth and spirit in the literature of the Northwest, crossing its roads, rivers and inlets, its bumps, bends, and soaring heights, I become more convinced how important it is to share all this with the next generation and to invite them in. Invite them to share and shape in the collective consciousness that is the land and its spirit. ∎

Ruth Vinz says her interest in the geographic and spiritual landscapes is the result of growing up in Idaho ranch country where her family always had stories to tell. She recently published a chapbook of poems, Propositions.

Published Author *Cont. from pg. 39*

show them the writing process and a slide show, and end by brainstorming up a new character with the kids that they can write about. Though it's been tough missing out on school, it's worth the experience to see the kids get so inspired. ∎

Elizabeth Haidle, author and illustrator, is a 16 year old junior attending Hillsboro High School in Hillsboro, Oregon.

Resources for Young Writers *Cont. from pg. 43*

WASHINGTON

• In April, Eastern Washington University sponsors the annual Young Writers Conference, a three-state conference for eastern Washington, Oregon, and Idaho writers. One segment is for grades 4-6, another for grades 7-12. In addition, there are workshops for teachers, administrators, and parents. A public reception is held Friday night and features award-winning authors of children's' books. Registration forms are sent to each school. Contact Marianne Nelson, EWU, MS 25, Cheney, WA 99004 or call 509-359-6032.

• In the spring, Seattle Pacific University sponsors the annual Young Authors Conference for young writers grades 1-8 in western Washington and Oregon. The 1991 conference features these workshops: sharing and critique; transformation of your writing with the help of award-winning authors; writing exploration; and a storytelling workshop. Apply through school beginning in January. Contact Nancy Johnson, School of Education, SPU, Seattle, WA 98119.

• The Washington State Office of the Superintendent of Public Instruction will send you a statewide bulletin of conferences and programs available for young writers. Request bulletin from Fred Bannister, Supervisor of Reading/Language Arts, Washington OSPI, Old Capitol Bldg. FG-11, Olympia, WA 98504-3211.

• Washington Poets Association sponsors an annual poetry contest for young poets with prizes. Categories are for grades 6-9 and 9-12. Winners are invited to an awards luncheon and a student reading in Tumwater. Deadline: April 2, 1991. Contact Betty Fukuyama, 112 Regents Blvd. Apt 1, Tacoma, WA 98466.

• Centrum Foundation in Port Townsend sponsors annual writing workshops for high school students. Two separate week-long residencies are awarded to 40-60 students selected on the basis of manuscript submissions. Apply by December 1; workshops are held in March and April. Contact Barbara Sailors, Education Coordinator, Centrum, PO Box 1158, Port Townsend, WA 98368.

• Pacific Northwest Writers Conference sponsors annual writing contests as well as workshops for high school students. Contest deadline is in the winter and categories are poetry, short story, and non-fiction. Workshops are in the spring. Contact Carol McQuinn, PNWC, 17345 Sylvester Road SW, Seattle, WA 98166, or call 206-242-9757.

• The Puget Sound Writing Program for Young Writers schedules a week-long workshop annually for students entering grades 5-11. In 1991-92, the workshop will be July 15-26 at the University of Washington, Seattle. Deadline is in the spring. Contact Linda Clifton, co-director, PSWP, Dept. of English, GN-30, U. of W, Seattle, WA 98195, or call 206-543-0141. ∎

Terri Lee Grell lives in Toutle, Washington and is the editor and publisher of Lynx, *a quarterly journal of renga.*

Writing instruction has changed dramatically in American schools, a change partly attributable to the descriptions of professional writers about their working processes.
— Tim Gillespie

We need to make the trophies for academic achievement bigger than those for athletic achievement.
— Scott Johnson

Ten Things Every Book Should Have
(To Keep Librarians Happy)

by Jeanne Engerman

This list may seem completely obvious, but I can assure readers that every one of these items has been omitted from at least one book in my acquaintance.

1) Title. What is your book called, and do you use the same title consistently throughout the book?

Is the front cover information the same as on the title page?

2) Author. Who gets credit for this work? If it is the work of a large committee, is there an editor?

Cataloging librarians are funny about that — they like to be able to attribute a book to a source. And, they like it if you use the same form of the name throughout the book.

3) Date. In what year was the book published? A cataloger takes nothing for granted. Without a date in the book itself, it will be described as being written in "19??"

4) Publisher information. Publishers receive their payment through sales of the book after its production; printers are paid at the time they print the volumes. If you paid a printer to produce five hundred copies, you would be the publisher (perhaps using a business name chosen for the occasion.) "Kinko's Copy Center" is not the publisher.

5) City, state. Where was the book published? Generally this would be the home city and state of the publisher. A book printed in Japan for a publisher based in Portland does not show "Tokyo" for its place of publication.

6) Unique number. This might be an LC number (issued by the Library of Congress for books which LC catalogs) or an ISBN (International Standard Book Number) issued by publishers. It is useful in cataloging systems to have a unique number associated with your book.

7) Author biography. A brief biographical sketch accomplishes several things. First, it satisfies the reading public's curiosity. Second, it may help a cataloging librarian to decide who you are — or aren't. If your name is Petunia Periwinkle, there probably isn't much chance of mixing you up with anyone else. However, if your name is John Smith you are one of dozens of people with that name who have written books. If you can at least be distinguished in library catalogs by your year of birth as "John Smith, 1949- ", it will assist someone who is trying to find your works amidst a sea of John Smiths. Middle names are most helpful.

8) Order information. Some authors are so modest, they can't imagine that anyone else is interested in their book. Then why did you print 1,000 copies? Do you have that many relatives? Let people know how they can get their very own copy. A discreet note on price and where to place an order is appropriate and appreciated.

9) Readable appearance. This point is very much a matter of personal preference, but I have yet to meet a reader who likes paragraphs that are three pages long and typefaces that require a magnifying glass to read. Take a step back from your book. Does it look appealing? Will it frighten away even your mother? Use some white space, or use a larger typeface even if it increases the book by a few pages.

10) Index. OK, I'm stretching things by putting this on a list designed for every book. However, it is so very important for non-fiction works that I want to emphasize it. You've spent a lot of time researching and writing your book; now spend a little time so other people can benefit from your efforts. Even a minimal list of personal and place names can be useful. Likewise, a bibliography of your sources and a table of contents are desirable features in non-fiction works. ∎

Jeanne Engerman is co-director of the State Library's Washington/Northwest Room, home of the Washington Author collection. A native of Wisconsin, Jeanne has lived in Washington since 1975 and still hasn't adjusted to the rain.

Take a step back from your book. Does it look appealing? Will it frighten away even your mother? Use some white space, or use a larger typeface even if it increases the book by a few pages.

Desktop Publishing Technology

by Kathleen Dickensen

Recently I was asked to speak to a writer's group about self-publishing in general, and electronic (desktop) publishing in particular. When the invitation was extended, the program chairperson regretfully informed me I could not become a member of their association because I was a "self-publisher."

The program chairperson introduced me that night via a story: "When I was a child my mother made all my clothes. Things she made were never quite right and they always looked homemade. I've held the same attitude about self-published books until *Accessible Art, A Layman's Look at Seattle's Public Art.*"

I approached the podium hoping that no loose thread was hanging and agreed that the issue, as it should be with

---

The stigma associated with self-publishing is that the manuscript must have been roundly rejected by a mainstream publisher.

---

any work, is quality. The stigma associated with self-publishing is that the manuscript must have been roundly rejected by a mainstream publisher. In the case of *Accessible Art*, I never approached an outside publisher as I wanted complete control of the content and look. And if my effort was well received by the public, I wanted to realize the monetary rewards.

Assuming you have a well-written manuscript, I believe the publisher and/or the technology is irrelevant. A few years ago I would have had reservations recommending desktop publishing for professional-quality documents. The technology has evolved and the gap between traditional methodology and electronic publishing bridged. (Assuming a trained operator is at the keyboard.)

With that disclaimer, let's discuss how electronic technology can aid the writer and publisher.

Simply stated, desktop publishing is a tool which combines text and graphics, via microcomputer, to produce publishable pages. The advantages are control, speed, and decreased vendor services such as type, half-tones, photostats and color separations. Decreased outside services equal decreased costs.

The following is an overview of the publishing process. First there is the manuscript, let's say in typewritten format. Assuming there are no editorial changes, the text is given to a graphic designer who specs the type for the typesetter. The typesetter gives galleys back to the designer or production artist for design approval, the galleys also go to the editorial

staff for proofing. If there are errors, corrections are made by the typesetter; the text goes back and forth until editorial and graphic errors are adjusted.

Simultaneously, the design staff is working on the book cover and graphic elements to be included in the book. Graphic elements can include photographs, illustrations, existing line art or clip art — in other words, anything that is not text.

Final art has been approved and final galleys are received from the typesetter. Then, a production artist combines the text and the graphics in a manner acceptable for printing. This is called camera-ready art. Camera-ready black-and-white photographs are termed halftones. Line art is made into photostats. If there are color photographs or illustrations they must be separated (color separations.)

The printer receives the camera-ready art, usually provided on a paste-up board. Depending on the printer and the job specifications, the paper page is shot and film is produced. The pages are assembled, metal plates are burned and the job is run.

Viola´, you have your book!

The same events occur when using desktop publishing technology. The advantage is that most of the described processes can be done on the computer by a skilled and knowledgeable operator. Electronic publishers now have the option of printing their files or documents to typeset-quality paper or film at a cost of about one to sixteen dollars a page depending on quantity, resolution, and color requirements. If output to film, that is one less step the printer takes and the savings passed on.

For writers who only want to write, don't invest in expensive computer equipment. With the dramatic price decreases of the Apple Macintosh line, price is no longer a major factor in the buying decision. Prior to the price wars, I would have recommended an IBM-compatible computer and a popular word processing software package such as Microsoft Word™ or WordPerfect™ for the writer wanting to enter the electronic age. Now, find out how many markets/publishers accept electronic submissions and in what form. Then make your decision accordingly.

Looking to do more of the graphic design and layout as well? My choice is an Apple Macintosh product. Go into a design firm and the only IBM-compatibles you might find will be in the accounting department. The reason, relative ease of use and the availability of high-end graphic software packages.

Owning a computer system, understanding printing, and having in-depth experience working with graphic designers

Continued on pg. 61

Copy Editors to the Rescue

by Jim Estes

There's an anecdote I use to show why publishers need copy editors:

Once I picked up a book by a reputable national publisher, which promised to tell me all I needed to know about personal computers.

The author misspelled the name of Knight-Ridder, one of the nation's major newspaper chains, several times; misspelled the name of Charles Babbage, the patron saint of computer designers; and located Silicon Valley in a former citrus grove.

And that was all in the first chapter.

I concluded that if the author was so ignorant or careless of his facts, I didn't think I could trust him to tell me anything.

I used the anecdote to lead an article I wrote for a self-publishers' publication in the Bay Area — and got a note from the proofreader for the publication informing me that she'd removed the reference to citrus groves (to groves entirely, in fact) because she'd heard that there used to be orchards there.

True, I responded to her; but they were apricots and nuts, not citrus, which was my point: Oranges, lemons and grapefruit don't flourish in the Bay Area's climate.

That proofreader unknowingly proved my point: Any good copy editor would have checked to be sure what was grown in what is now Silicon Valley.

On another occasion, a self-published book came in for review at the newspaper where I was a copy editor. The author claimed to have been a top executive at Saks Fifth Avenue in California for most of his adult life.

He spelled it "Sak's" throughout.

He also misspelled some of California's more notable names, such as Spreckels.

We didn't review his book.

Need another example? A glossy, good-looking restaurant guide came in — with a "Forward" on a prominent right-hand page.

Well, you get the idea. The writers all had good ideas, but couldn't communicate them effectively.

The purpose of a book is to communicate. Anything that gets between the writer and the reader — bad grammar, bad spelling, sloppy punctuation, bad word choice, ambiguity — is a barrier to that communication. Having put out good money for your book, the reader probably is in a show-me frame of mind anyway; don't put barriers between you.

The copy editor's function is to help an author realize as well as possible the intention behind every book: to communicate to the public something the writer thinks the public should know.

Detailed revision and rewriting are usually not in the copy editor's job description. What is included is sharpening the focus by tightening sentence structure, correcting spelling and punctuation, replacing the almost-right word with the just-right word, cleaning up grammar and syntax — all without damaging the writer's style. And, of course, correcting errors of fact.

The copy editor also supplies an ingredient every author needs: a reader who isn't familiar with the text and the subject matter. The writer, being close to the material, not only is likely to miss typographical and other minor errors, but probably thinks every sentence is clear; a detached reader often finds ambiguity and a need for clarification.

The good copy editor, if he/she doesn't know something, knows where and how to look it up. If the editor's shelves of reference works aren't enough, there's always the public library.

All these resources help; but the best resources are an inquiring, suspicious mind and an obsession for getting it right. ■

Jim Estes is retired from more than 35 years of newspaper work, mostly on copy desks. He lives at Alpha Farm, an intentional community in the Coast Range of Oregon, and claims to be working harder there than he ever did on a full-time job.

Do It With Style!

The contents of your book and the audience for whom it is intended are both important factors in determining the style guide you will use.

The Associated Press Stylebook and Libel Manual. Christopher W. French, Ed.
Bias-Free Publishing. McGraw-Hill.
The Chicago Manual of Style. University of Chicago Press.
Copyediting: A Practical Guide. Karen Judd.
Harbrace College Handbook. John C. Hodges, et. al.
The MLA Style Manual. Walter S. Achtert and Joseph Gibaldi.
Modern American Usage. Wilson Follett.
Style: Toward Clarity and Grace. Joseph M. Williams.
Technical Writing for Business and Industry. Pamela S. Beason and Patricia A. Williams.
Writing in Style at the Federal Reserve. Board of Governors of the Fed. Reserve System.

An Introduction to the Designing of Books

by Elsi Vassdal Ellis

The responsibility of the book designer is to develop a visual form which not only presents the textual (and pictorial) information in a manner that is suitable for the identified audience, but also keeps the audience interested. Because the book as a medium incorporates many decision-making and production phases as well as the coordination of a variety of talents, designing a book appears to be an intimidating process. The best advice is to keep in mind the production capabilities available within the budget and to never lose sight of the needs of the reader.

Some of the key aspects of book design are as follows:

From Manuscript to Visual-textual Form

Although books take a variety of forms today, from trade editions to limited editions, one-of-a-kind artists' books to xerographic books, most of us think of the traditional, textually-based book. Translating a book from its original manuscript to the book format may seem a fairly straight forward process. It is not, however, a process resolved in a vacuum. Decisions must be made about page size in relation to manuscript length, style and size of typefaces, and the break up of matter into chapters and/or subheads. If illustrative material is needed, the nature of the illustrations must be determined. There are also many small factors to consider, such as running heads, page numbers and their placement, and the front matter and back matter to be included. All these factors create the visual flavor of a book.

Alice in Wonderland may have asked what good was a book without illustrations, but the decision to illustrate a book should be based upon the wishes of the author, the appropriateness of illustrations as a textual accompaniment, and the budget. Tolkein never intended his books to be illustrated because he felt that it was important for the reader to form his or her own mental image of his imaginary land. In this way the reader is active — not passive.

Yet other authors, as well as book designers and illustrators, place a great deal of emphasis on the integration of image and text. Barry Moser, a very talented engraver, incorporates a variety of techniques in the integration of text and illustrations. In *Frankenstein*, the illustrations have the same height and width as the textblocks. There are no paragraph indents in the text. They are replaced by a dingbat (an ornamental character), resulting in textblocks that are the same shape on every page. In *Alice in Wonderland* the text flows around the illustration. The type and the illustrations

relate to each other in style and manipulation such that they become one entity rather than two separate elements.

In terms of budget, the reproduction costs of illustrations can vary from inexpensive black-and-white line art to the more expensive halftones of continuous tone art. Color reproduction requirements add significantly to production costs and should not be considered lightly. Ultimately, however, the decision to include illustrations or not to include illustrations should be based upon the intended audience and the appropriateness of illustrations for the text.

Typography

Type has two responsibilities in a book. The primary purpose is the denotative function. Type provides a cultural and learned format for the presentation of ideas.

The typeface selected must first be legible and readable. Every letter in the alphabet must be recognizable and the style selected must "encourage" the reader to read, regardless of the reading level and speed of the reader. Some factors to consider include the age of the reader in relation to the point size of the type, the x-height of the lower case letters, the weight of the type, its inclination (roman vs. italic), stroke weight, stroke contrasts, and whether to use a serif design or a sans serif design. The length of the lines and the line spacing are also important.

> *Never think of a style of type independent of its audience and reproduction requirements.*

There are some standard values to consider when designing a book. Text sizes for adults are normally 10 to 12 point type. Type faces for children are larger in size; the point size varies with the age of the reader. Line lengths in picas should be double the point size for optimum readability. Lines of text that are too long often cause the reader to reread lines over and over because the eyes find it difficult to come back to the appropriate place on the left hand margin. In most cases, line spacing or leading should be two points more than the size of type. Remember, these rules are only guidelines.

There are several thousand typefaces available for use on the printed page. Not all are suitable for books. Never think of a style of type independent of its audience and reproduction requirements. With the advent of desktop publishing and the use of 300 dpi laser printers, there are typefaces which have been designed to look "good" as text. Palatino and Times Roman are good default faces for text. Avant Garde is not! Traditionally, serif faces have been used for text, but there are some beautiful sans-serif faces worthy of textual use.

Typefaces also serve a connotative function. They not only provide the author's ideas with a tangible form, but the typeface can also suggest an attitude, an atmosphere. Typefaces may be described as traditional or elegant. Some faces are quirky. Others suggest a particular historical period. Many faces were designed to be used only for display or titles.

All book design begins with binding!

Some faces by their very physical nature suggest to the designer their appropriateness for a particular reproduction process, paper surface, ink color, length of text.

Paper Pros and Cons

The paper surface, color, and printing quality are quite important factors to consider when designing a book. If a book is only text, there is a wider range of options for the printing surface. Some typefaces have been designed to print on soft, absorbent papers (Oldstyle faces such as Jenson or Garamond). Others require papers that have smooth or calendered surfaces (Walbaum, New Caledonia, Bodoni). When a book is primarily text, select a paper that has low reflective qualities. The paper should not be bright white nor should it be a coated, glossy paper. Too much reflection off a page can fatigue the reader.

When reproducing black and white and color illustrations, the more detail in the image, the smoother or harder the paper surface. Line art can be successfully reproduced on soft surfaces if there is no fine detail. A harder and/or smoother surface might be more appropriate to hold the detail for a black-and-white wood engraving. The reproduction of continuous tone art as single color or four color halftones will require a paper that will not allow the halftone dots to spread or "gain." If dot gain occurs during printing, the overall contrast and tonal reproduction quality will suffer, and the resulting colors will not match the original art.

Binding

Of all the people in the printing industry, binders are probably the most vociferous when it comes to books. All book design begins with binding! That is the gospel according to the finishers and it's true.

Binding is the structural feature that makes the traditional concept of a book a book! Bindings can take many forms. Books can be soft or hard cover. They can be sewn or glued or mechanically bound. They can be very experimental or they can be quite traditional. How the reader will use the book, how it will open, is always a consideration. Mechanical bindings such as GBC or Wire-O are great for books up that open flat. They don't have the same finished look as a case bound hard back book, however.

The binding is the primary determiner of margin sizes, particularly the inside margin of a book. The eventual thickness of the book will help narrow the options for binding as well. Remember that binding represents a sizable portion in any budget.

Designing a book is a complex process, as these brief sketches show. Maurice Sendak felt that a book must smell good, taste good, feel good, and look good. The successful book design will provide a fulfilling, sensual, and intellectual experience of the designer *and* the reader. ∎

Elsi Vassdal Ellis teaches typography, design, and offset printing at Western Washington University. At her EVE Press studio, she creates books in many forms, from offset to one-of-a-kind to letterpress, all hand bound.

Production Resources

The Art of Desktop Publishing. Tony Bove.
Book Design & Production for the Small Publisher. Malcolm E. Barker.
The Designer's Guide to Text Type. Jean Callan.
Designing with Type. James Craig.
Desktop Publishing by Design. Ronnie Shushan, Don Wright.
Directory of Book, Catalog, and Magazine Printers. John Kremer.
Editing by Design. Jan V. White.
Getting It Printed. Mark Beach, Steve Shepro, Ken Russon
How to Understand and Use Design and Layout. Alan Swann.
Literary Marketplace. R.R. Bowker Co. (Suppliers & Manufacturers).
Looking Good in Print. Roger C. Parker.
The Print Production Handbook. David Bann.
Publication Design. Allen Hurlburt.
Tips on Type. Bill Gray.
Using Type Right. Philip Brady.

Where to Get Your Book Reviewed

Acquiring reviews and other "free media" requires some planning and organization well in advance of the publication of your book. Get the current review submission criteria from everyone you intend to address.

Some reviewers — *Publishers Weekly, Library Journal, School Library Journal, Booklist,* & *Kirkus* — will want galleys three to four months before publication. The galleys don't have to be the final ones with which you'll go to press; they should be roughly formatted to the final page size, include all front and back matter, and be bound in some manner.

When your new book comes out there are many possible places to send a copy. Along with the book, send a cover letter, review sheets, and a book photograph 4 x 6 or larger. Send one copy unless otherwise noted.

Publishers Weekly, Attn: Weekly Record, 249 W. 17th St., New York, NY 10011.

Library Journal, Attn: Book Reviews, 249 W. 17th St., New York, NY 10011.

School Library Journal, Attn: Book Reviews, 249 W. 17th St., New York, NY 10011.

H.W. Wilson Co., Attn: Cumulative Book Index, 950 Unversity Ave., Bronx, NY 10452.

The New York Times, Attn: Sunday Book Review Section, 229 W. 43rd St., New York, NY 10036.

Small Press Magazine, Meckler Corp., 11 Ferry Ln. W., Westport, CT 06880-5808.

Choice, Attn: Book Reviews, 100 Riverview Ctr., Middletown, CT 06457.

Two Copies to American Library Association, Attn: ALA Booklist, 50 E. Huron St., Chicago, IL 60611.

Kirkus Reviews, 200 Park Ave. S., New York, NY 10003.

The Horn Book Magazine, Attn: Book Reviews, Park Square Bldg., 31 St. James Ave., Boston, MA 02116. (Books for children and young adults.)

Small Press Review, PO Box 100, Paradise, CA 95969.

Baker & Taylor Co., Academic Library Services Selection Dept., 6 Kirby Ave., Somerville, NJ 08876.

The New York Times Magazine, 229 West 43rd St., New York, NY 10036.

Gale Research Co., Attn: *Contemporary Authors*, The Book Tower, Detroit, MI 48226.

America Library Association, Attn: *Openers*, 50 East Huron St., Chicago, IL 60611.

Kliatt Young Adult Paperback Book Guide, 425 Watertown St., Newton, MA 02158.

Newspaper Enterprise Association, Amercian Library Association, 50 East Huron St., Chicago, IL 60611.

Small Press Book Review, P.O. Box 176, Southport, CT 06490.

Chicago Tribune Books, 435 North Michigan Ave., #400, Chicago, IL 66011.

Los Angeles Times Book Review, Times Mirror Square, Los Angeles, CA 90053.

Rave Reviews, 163 Joralemon St., Brooklyn Heights, NY 11201.

Voice Literary Supplement, 842 Broadway, New York, NY 10003.

The Washington Post, Book World, 1150 15th St. NW, Washington, DC 20071.

USA Today, Books for Review, P.O. Box 500, Washington, DC 20044.

West Coast Review of Books, 1501 North Hobart Blvd., Los Angeles, CA 90027.

New York Review of Books, 250 West 57th St., New York, NY 10107-0001.

Local and regional newspapers.

Publications of appropriate organizations or special interest.

You may want to send a copy to larger wholesalers — such as Baker & Taylor, Ingram, or Pacific Pipeline — and chain bookstore buyers. You'll find lists in *Literary Marketplace* (R.R. Bowker) and in the *Book Publishing Resource Guide* (Ad Lib Publications). ∎

5 Steps to a Successful Book Promotion

by Mary Ann Kohl

Bright Ring Publishing has found promotional success in its niche marketing of books for parents, teachers, and child care providers. I would like to share with you five steps to a successful book promotion, steps that have worked well for Bright Ring.

1. Know Your Market

Before any steps are taken, be sure you know who you will target in your promotion, who will buy your book, and who will be able to reach your market for you. For instance, Bright Ring focuses on parents of young children, teachers and daycare providers, and public libraries. We do not especially worry about bookstores, but good promotion alerts bookstores to ordering from us. Know your market, and direct your hardest hitting promotion to that market only.

2. Book Reviews

Good book reviews have been essential in unveiling and announcing the proud arrival of our books into the marketplace. We send out hundreds of review copies before publication and have been fortunate to receive outstanding reviews from the highly respected American Library Association's journal, Booklist (a starred review in this journal is a recommendation for library purchase), Kirkus Reviews, Puget Sound Council for the Review of Children's Media, various magazines such as Creative Kids and Early Education, numerous newspapers across the country, and important listings such as Books in Print and Forthcoming Books. Although many of these reviews come from "not so famous" sources, they are from sources that reach the parenting and education market specifically, and are therefore like gold.

3. Book Clubs

Book club sales are a form of advertising which costs nothing. Macmillan Book Clubs sent out their monthly offering (just after my book reviews), which included my book MUDWORKS as a main selection. They mail to 80,000 parents and educators. Whether those reached order from Macmillan or not, they have seen the announcement at no cost to me. Macmillan buys about 4000 books, which also reduces the cost of my print run, and pays printing cost plus about a dollar per book. They pay net 30 days.

4. Distribution

Following the reviews and book clubs, publication officially begins and all my distributors and wholesalers have already been alerted to the new book. They have been advised in advance for their catalogs and their sales reps so that they can also push the new title. I always pay for a photograph advertisement in all my distributor's catalogs. The pictorial association has been imperative in selling a new book. I am represented by many school supply catalogs which come out at all different times of the year, so it is important to let all these people know when a new book is coming so that they have proper information ready for their new catalogs and new book announcements. What better information to give them than a shining review from Booklist or Library Journal! These reviews carry incredible weight.

5. Awards

There are many organizations which sponsor awards for quality and excellence in publishing. I submitted MUDWORKS to as many as came my way, and to my surprise and delight, MUDWORKS won something in each one! These awards carry validation of excellence to librarians, new distributors, buyers of all kinds, and give an oomph to new reviews and news releases. For instance, MUDWORKS won Best Children's Book at the American Booksellers Association from the independent press group, PMA, which included a wonderful announcement in Pubisher's Weekly. (It was also chosen a finalist for Best Interior Design and Best Book Cover.) About Books chose MUDWORKS Best Self-Published Book of 1989, and from the Washington Press Association — second place, Children's Books. Each of these awards carried a news release or brought new distribution or sales.

6. Frosting on the Cake

One of my most successful promotions has been the exciting new experience of being a guest on a children's television show, targeted to very young children, where I demonstrate art ideas from my books (which are mentioned in each segment and shown as part of the credits each day). This show has also increased my speaking engagements, guest presentations at conferences and workshops, and consulting in the schools. All the personal one-on-one speaking sells books while allowing me to spread my message that creativity is important for children's learning.

MUDWORKS has sold well over 80,000 copies since publication a year ago in September, 1989. This rivals the success of major publishing houses with scores of titles. The success of MUDWORKS lies in the hard hitting promotional direction to my market, parenting and child care. Sales to libraries and bookstores have ridden on the demand created by parents and teachers. Know your market. Promote to that market. The result? Success! ∎

Mary Ann Kohl is the owner of Bright Ring Publishing.

Publishing Checklist

The following is a list of many important tasks for publishers. This is by no means comprehensive and should be supplemented by research into book publishing practices.

Book Concept
- Potential market has been checked
- Niche is identifiable among competing titles
- Read and learn about publishing and book promotion
- Determine if sufficient funds are available to produce and promote your book, based on projected costs

Writing Process
- Writing schedule has been developed
- Preliminary subject research
- Detailed research and interviews
- Book outline and chapter development
- First draft of manuscript
- Draft evaluation and fact check
- Revisions (as many as necessary to produce final draft)
- Production of art work

Preliminary Details
- Establish your publishing company
- Register for International Standard Book Number, Cataloging in Publication data, and Advance Book Information.
- Get at least four typesetting bids (also photo screens and PMTs)
- Get at least six printing bids (ink, paper, cover, and binding)

- Mail manuscripts to key contacts for cover reviews
- Consult with editor, graphic artist, book designer
- Establish price of book (review all costs, necessary profit margin, and what the market can bear)
- Find wholesalers and plan all sales methods to be used

While Book is Typeset and Printed (or sooner)
- Design pre-publishing or first sales brochure
- Obtain list of target book reviewers (send galleys if possible)
- Obtain endorsements, if appropriate
- Set up accounting system and business materials
- Determine advertising mediums and budget
- Obtain mailing lists for direct promotion (check into joint mailings with publishers of compatible books)
- Design media kits

When Books are Ready to Sell
- Register for copyright
- Mail review and promotional copies (also media kits)
- Begin advertising, mailings, and direct promotions
- Plan participation in book fairs and target events
- Supply wholesalers and sales outlets

Additional tips
- Check into local writers' and publishers' organizations
- Attend regional retail book shows
- Consult other self-publishers and experts for advice
- Arrange seminars and publicity tours

Remember to Register!

ISBN: Every book wants to have an International Standard Book Number (ISBN). Ask for information from ISBN U.S. Agency, R.R. Bowker Co., 245 West 17th St., New York, NY 10011. There is a fee.

CIP: The Cataloging in Publication (CIP) number and information describes your book so that librarians will know where to place it on their shelves. Some books are excluded, so write and ask for the CIP Publishers Manual first. Then send a galley to Library of Congress cataloging, CIP Office, Library of Congress, Washington, DC 20540.

LC: The Library of Congress (LC) number helps the Library of Congress keep track of your book. Request information from the address above.

Bar Code: The computer has made your publishing work easier; it's also made the inclusion of the "bar code" neces-

sary on the cover of your book if you intend to sell it in many bookstores, especially the chains. Bowker will send you a list of bar code manufacturers.

Copyright: Write to the Register of Copyrights, Library of Congress, Washington, DC 20559 and ask for the forms to copyright your book. Send two copies of the book and the completed forms, along with the $20 fee, back to the Copyright office.

Send one copy to the Library of Congress acquisition and processing. Include your discount schedule and brochure. Library of Congress, Attn: Acquisitions and Processing Division, Crystal Mall Annex, Washington, DC 20540.

Send another copy to the Library of Congress, Exchange and Gift Division, Gift Section, Washington, DC 20540. ■

News Release

Your Letterhead

News Release
Date

For Immediate Release
Contact: Your name
        Your phone number(s)

Strong lead sentences make news releases more effective. Let the first sentence position your book as a solution to a problem or as an answer to a need. The first paragraph should mention the name of your book, as well as your name.

A news release should answer the who, what, where, when, and why news questions. Who will be interested in this book and why? What is the book about? When was the book published? Why was this book written and published? The information must "sell" the editor on the importance and timeliness of your book. Your credentials, as the author, will also help to gain credibility and human interest.

Ideally, this release should only require one page. It should be typed, double spaced, and on your company letterhead. If practical, it may be personalized to the editor.

The final information should contain the price and availablility details. Be sure to include your company address, as well.

The book's title
Author's name
Size, cover style, and binding
ISBN number and Library of Congress Card Catalogue number
Publication date
Price

# # #
(signifies the end)

Publishing in British Columbia

by Colleen MacMillan

Publishing in British Columbia is just entering its third decade, a fact which reflects something of the history of publishing in Canada as a whole. For many years, the books that were marketed to Canadian readers were imported from the U.K. and the U.S. Then an era of political change arrived, and with it, the determination of a number of Canadians to earn a place for an indigenous product on the bookstore shelves. Three companies began this process: McClelland and Stewart (Toronto), Hurtig Publishers (Edmonton, Alberta), and J.J. Douglas (Vancouver, now known as Douglas and McIntryre). Before long small presses were springing up all over the country, and B.C. was no exception. To underscore the point, sales of books produced by British Columbian publishers totalled $338,000 CDN in 1971; in 1989, they reached $15,000,000 CDN.

One might ask what accounts for this apparent explosion in the publishing industry in a province of 3 million people. One can look at the kind of publishing that takes place in the province. The fifty members of the Association of Book Publishers of British Columbia and the growing number of members of the Small Press Action Network, as well as those who fall into the self-published category, all create a great deal of activity. It is difficult to think of a category of publishing that is not represented; children's literature and educational books are genres are the weakest genres.

One of the reasons why books published here have succeeded is obvious to even the casual observer. Deprived of material that reflected something about the region in which they lived, British Columbians responded enthusiastically to books that offered them information on provincial politics, history, natural history, west coast Indian art, guide books, and regional memoirs, as well as color scenic books.

In some respects, B.C. is to Toronto what the Pacific Northwest is to New York. There is a separate identity in a province that is blocked from the rest of the country by a barely passable mountain range, and which is so distinct in terms of its history and its ever-changing character. To use another geographic metaphor, B.C. is the California of Canada. The province constantly draws people from the harsh climate of the Prairies and the big city coldness of Toronto and Montreal. These newcomers represent an ever-expanding market for books, as they eagerly seek to become acquainted with their new surroundings. B.C. has another advantage: it is one of the most visited provinces in Canada. The publishing industry capitalizes on this transient population.

There is another reason why British Columbian publishers have drawn new breath from one high risk year to another. The strong core of independent booksellers has offered a base of support to the publishing community for the distribution of books to a home market. Even though two major chains are well represented in B.C., along with two department stores and one food chain with book departments, the independents have managed to hold their own.

It is also a fact that British Columbians revel in their own success. We celebrate our accomplishments annually, with the annual B.C. Book Prizes which are held in the spring of each year. The prizes recognize outstanding books by B.C. authors and publishers, and have succeeded in raising the profile of the industry as a whole. There is also the B.C. Bestseller list, a project initiated by the publishers' association but compiled by an independent firm. The bestseller list appears in newspapers and is distributed to bookstores on a weekly basis. Books published in B.C. generally appear in at least two of the top ten positions throughout the year, with representation increasing during the fall season.

A later addition to the book publishing scene was the arrival of B.C. Bookworld, a tabloid featuring B.C. books and authors that appears four times a year. The newspaper is distributed free to bookstores and through a mailing list, and has provided an enormous boost to the book industry in the province. The brainchild of Allan Twigg, the paper has expanded eastward in the form of Prairie Bookworld. The great thing about B.C. Bookworld is that it clearly established B.C. as a distinct and thriving book region, whereas we've traditionally fought the biases of eastern media who typically regard anything outside of Toronto as endearingly folksy, but not really serious.

The publishers' association has also been a highly significant factor in the viability of the industry. This active lobbying group recently recorded a major victory after years of effort when the government announced a program of assistance to publishers which will inject a much-needed shot of capital. While the program is not as generous as provincial programs in other parts of the country, it is a significant achievement for the publishing community.

In this part of the world, publishing reflects the interests and personalities of the individuals involved as much as it does anywhere else. B.C. is a mecca for writers from all parts of Canada, and no one is in a better position to capitalize on that bit of good fortune than the B.C. publishing and book selling community. Admittedly, not every writer who takes up provincial status decides to move to a B.C. publishing house, but there is a vibrancy and excitement about books and the role of books that keeps many a publisher incurably hopeful from one season to the next. ∎

Colleen MacMillan has been in publishing for 12 years. She holds the position of publisher at Whitecap Books Ltd. in Vancouver, B.C.

Who the Hell Do I Think I Am?
or, Some Things I've Learned While Running
The Redneck Review

by Penelope Reedy

There's no freedom of the press unless you own the press.
—A.J. Liebling

Keeping *The Redneck Review* afloat has been a major project of my life for the past 15 years, and each year of publication has presented a new set of challenges. For instances, the printing process itself hasn't remained the same two years in a row. Due to economic considerations, *Redneck* has been produced on everything from a hand cranked mimeograph machine to a used Multilith Offset press. Even though I now own and operate a Macintosh computer as well as the aforementioned Multilith press, I am still dependent upon a local print shop for laser copies and printing plates.

Local readers expressed puzzlement about who the characters were in works of fiction, they didn't remember "those people" ever having lived on the prairie.

These necessary adjustments in printing methods are one indication of how an editor/publisher must remain flexible, must change course, when she finds herself beating her head against a rock wall. For example, I originally thought that a magazine of contemporary Western literature would appeal to persons living out the tail end of the myth in the rural West: farmers, ranchers, cowboys, would-be mountain men — literate readers "just like me" who were living in relative isolation and using their mailboxes as "life-lines." After a couple of years of peculiar and inappropriate response to my project — in several instances local readers expressed puzzlement about who the characters were in works of fiction, they didn't remember "those people" ever having lived on the prairie — I concluded that this wasn't the case. The readers I was targeting were anything *but* interested in reading stories and poems which dug at that heart of daily contemporary Western life. They would rather read stories resurrecting the nostalgic past, the wild West myth, and romanticized versions of their own ancestry. I had to find new readers, as well as new writers, and I did.

I began listing *Redneck* in directories of literary or little magazines, and I also began writing letters to authors of books I admired, and to scholars whose articles interested me a great deal, all of whom were also writing about and participating in the contemporary literature of the American West. I sent out press releases to area publications describing the kind of literature I was looking for. I joined the Western Literature Association and began making friends with scholars and writers with similar burning interests in the literature of this region. I also began making direct contact with other publishers in the American West. As a result, the correspondence I maintain has become one of the most rewarding aspects of *Redneck*.

What has worked for *The Redneck Review*, then, has been a very personal approach to publishing. I enjoy writing letters to writers and subscribers, coming up with theme issues based on topics that evolve out of this correspondence, and learning about new writers and books via this intellectually alive network.

I've been criticized by some for being a "one-woman show," for not having a board of directors or an editorial board or other form of jury for the magazine. While I admit that such things might offer a measure of "external" credibility, they would hardly provide the intellectual safety net that many think. During this past year, I've visited with several editors working within "the system" who have expressed dismay at the shallowness of their administrations and who are frustrated with trying to make significant changes while fearing for their jobs.

Just how does a small "independent" publication with a limited audience survive financially, then? By their very nature, such small press publications appeal to a smaller, although very dedicated, crowd of readers. In the regular business world, quantity, or the number of subscribers, is what usually commands large sums of money from advertisers. Some magazines are able through the sheer will and salesmanship powers of a dedicated volunteer, or the publisher herself, to gain substantial ad support. Other small publications' editorial policies appeal to certain grant-making organizations. But these are exceptional cases. Some years I've faced the sort of financial difficulties that textbooks tell us are sure to make a publisher cry "uncle." Two years ago, due to a divorce, a move, and a lifestyle change that drained my financial resources, I found myself sitting on an issue that was printed, bound, and ready to go, but I had no money for postage. After much soul searching I asked for help, and to my surprise and satisfaction, my subscribers and writers came through with the amount needed to get *Redneck* on its feet again. These wonderful supportive people are listed as

Continued on pg. 61

Boise Magazine

Interview by Bill Woodall

Alan Minskoff is the editor of Boise Magazine. He was born in White Plains, New York and moved to Idaho in June of 1972. Shortly afterwards he helped start Idaho Heritage Magazine.

WNH: How did you get started in the magazine business?

ALAN MINSKOFF: I was involved with a group of people called "Friends of Old Buildings." This group begat *Idaho Heritage Magazine* in 1974. We decided to do a newsletter to get the word out that Boise had significant buildings that were worth saving. We asked two dozen people what they thought Boise should look like ten years from then. Nearly everyone responded, and we had too much stuff for a newsletter. So in 1975 we brought out our first issue. It was a magazine on the tail of a cause, not only old buildings but small towns and, in a smaller way, the environment.

WNH: You had a concern for the arts, too.

AM: That's right. We did an arts issue; we did a magazine on Native Americans; we went to twenty-four small towns over two years; we did a program on children with the governor. We did a lot of thematic stuff that had not been done in Idaho. After about the third year we decided that we wanted to make magazines a regular, profit-making venture.

WNH: What was your next magazine?

AM: We started *Northwest America* next, and put out one issue. It was a neat idea, but we didn't have the money. To do a regional magazine from Boise, Idaho, you have to fight a lot of built-in prejudice from the coast that everything good emanates inland from Seattle or Portland or San Francisco.

WNH: You followed that with *The New Boise Rag*?

AM: Right. That was maybe the most fun publication I've ever done. Gino Sky wrote for it; Peter Bowen wrote for it. Several people who wrote for *Idaho Heritage* wrote under pseudonyms; I wrote under a woman's name.

WNH: When did you come to *Boise Magazine*?

AM: In the mid '80s I went back to New York for a few years. Then I returned to Idaho and set up Idaho Annual, the company that now owns *Boise Magazine*. We started with a humanities project on the Bicentennial of the Constitution. Then we ran into the former publisher of *Boise Magazine*, who was interested in selling it. One thing led to another and before we knew it, in November of 1987, we put out our first issue.

WNH: Give us a sense of your vision of the magazine.

AM: We have several goals at *Boise Magazine*. Because I wrote poetry and was interested in serious writing, I wanted to bring in poets and fiction writers, people like John Rember, Andrea Scott, Peter Bowen, Bill Studebaker, Penny Reedy — all kinds of people.

We wanted to change the editorial environment, to make it a different kind of magazine. One that would have creative writing and serious nonfiction and some humor, to go along with a big editorial well. We'd have a serious piece in every issue about topics that really mattered to Idaho: Saylor Creek, the nuclear issue, the rivers, logging. We want to create an editorial environment that fostered real journalism.

Another of our missions is to make it a real product, something that will come out in a timely fashion. We're dedicated to coming out before the turn of the month every issue like all good magazines around the country.

WNH: You were coming out six times per year. That's changed, hasn't it?

AM: We produced seven issues in 1990. In 1991 we'll come out eight times. I think that's where we'll stay for awhile. That's a part of being professional, to get ourselves up to eight issues per year. We also wanted to get the magazine onto the newsstands, and we've done that. We're probably in nearly 150 places, including lots of funky places where you won't normally see magazines. It's an important part of promotion.

I also think it's important that we have advertisers, because that shows that the community accepts us even though we remain controversial. We want to make people think.

WNH: You're concerned about being professional.

AM: Yes. Professionalism is very important to us in every way. It's important that you pay writers; it's important that you pay artists; it's important that you pay photographers, even if you pay them all like we do, a minimal amount of money. It's important they know that their work has value.

WNH: Do you want submissions from outside of Idaho?

AM: I don't like things from people who are just passing through, although if a poet has an experience at Craters of the Moon or a strong emotional response to some incredible little town — we're open to that. We take poems or fiction from anywhere.

As far as the nonfiction goes, we still take stuff that comes in over the transom, but rarely. We're not an especially good market for beginning writers. But we do have "entry level" departments. Like the "Dispatches" we get from all over the

> *Magazines hold a mirror up to society or take the pulse of a community.*

Continued on pg. 61

Seal Press

by Barbara Wilson

Seal Press began in a somewhat desultory fashion in 1976 when Rachel da Silva and I hand printed a poetry chapbook, *Private Gallery* by Melinda Mueller. Like most small presses of the seventies, we had no budget and very little publishing expertise. We handset and printed our first books in editions of five hundred and sold them in ones and twos at readings and on consignment in Seattle bookstores.

Within two years, however, we had defined our focus as feminist and graduated to offset presses (though we still printed the books ourselves), a workable bookkeeping set-up, and a loose distribution system. In the late seventies, most women's books were distributed by Bookpeople in California, and by the short-lived business, Women in Distribution. There were a number of feminist bookstores in operation by then and a handful of other feminist presses, most notably, Persephone and Naiad.

By 1981, when Rachel and I attended the second Women in Print Conference in Washington D.C., we had our own small office and twelve or so titles in print. The next few years were to change our business decisively. We published a bestselling book on domestic violence, *Getting Free* by Ginny NiCarthy, and began to pay ourselves wages and to employ a bookkeeper and part-time office helper. By 1984, with the help of Faith Conlon, a full-time member of Seal, we were publishing eight titles a year, a mix of women's studies titles, fiction, and translations. Our books began to be reviewed in *Publishers Weekly* and the *New York Times* and could be found in bookstores all over the country.

1991 finds us publishing twelve titles a year, but in much greater print runs (an initial run of 10,000 is not unusual). Much of our backlist of over a hundred titles is still in print, and we have eight full and part-time workers. Although Rachel da Silva left Seal in 1985, Faith Conlon, Seal's co-publisher, has been there since 1982. We recently created Women in Translation, a nonprofit publishing house that shares office space with Seal and has taken over the costly but rewarding work of publishing translations.

Although our focus on women's issues has not changed through the years, we have been pleased to see that society has changed a great deal. There is nothing about the feminist press movement to explain or defend any longer; indeed, many independent houses find that women writers and feminist subjects are among their bestselling books. Seal has grown up with women's studies courses at universities and with the success of feminist and gay and lesbian bookstores and periodicals. The small press movement is something that has also come of age; our titles are no longer distinguishable by the amateurness of the book jackets, and many of us have sales representatives who have no trouble in marketing our books to the trade.

The Women in Print movement is not just about publishing books written by one-half the population. It's about women learning the business of publishing and making a success of it. It's a far-ranging and often exuberant social experiment in shifting the focus away from traditional male themes to a much broader spectrum of concerns. At Seal we have published challenging feminist mysteries, lyrical and offbeat novels and short stories, and nonfiction anthologies on women in the trades, black women's health, and dating violence against young women. We have published important literary translations by well-known foreign writers as well as international English fiction from New Zealand, Zimbabwe and Grenada. We have published bilingual Spanish editions of our self-help books as well as easy-to-read versions for women without strong language skills; we've even produced two audio tapes for women who don't read at all. Within our focus on women, we attempt to be as multicultural as we can; we find it stretches us, and our readers, to acknowledge just how diverse and contradictory and exciting and powerful we are.

Publishing Where I Work

I have published most of my books in this country with Seal Press (twice with other feminist presses). As a lesbian and as a feminist I have experienced a blessed lack of censorship, which has allowed me to explore topics I'm interested in, not just those that New York editors decide are currently fashionable. Most of my work has been in print for at least ten years, which has enabled me to continue to find and keep a readership. There have been some disadvantages, certainly, including an unkind review here and there from writers we've rejected. But the few disadvantages are outweighed by the pleasure of being part of a publishing company that promotes and supports its writers. I have had many other publishing experiences, including having a book with the Quality Paperback Book Club and being included in anthologies by St. Martin's, Dial and Faber and Faber. In England, I'm published by Virago, a women's house that is as large as Norton or Grove/Weidenfeld in the States; in Germany, by both small leftist presses and the huge mass market house, Fischer. I would not rule out going to a mainstream New York house in the future, but for the moment, Seal is where I feel best. ∎

Barbara Wilson is co-publisher of Seal Press and editorial director of Women in Translation, a new nonprofit publishing company. She is the author of numerous stories and novels, most recently Gaudi Afternoon.

Caxton, Publisher in Idaho for Nearly a Century

by Kathy Gaudry

In 1895, only five years after Idaho's statehood and twelve years after the founding of Caldwell, Albert E. Gipson established the *Gem State Rural*, a monthly fruit and farm publication. At the turn of the century, A.E. Gipson and printer Earle Norton combined talents and established a printing plant in Caldwell, Idaho, which operated under the name of Gem State Rural Publishing Company. Their assets included $118 in cash for operating expenses, a broken-down press, a sackful of worn type, and a wheezy gas engine.

In 1903, they sold *Gem State Rural* to a Spokane company, then changed the company name. The name, The Caxton Printers, Ltd., was chosen because of William Caxton, esteemed British printer and publisher. Almost ninety years after this simple beginning, the Caxton Printers, Ltd. employs 100 people in a multi-divisional plant that covers one complete city block. The business has operated continuously under the Gipson family management, now in its fifth generation.

Book publishing did not start at Caxton until the mid-1930s. J.H. Gipson, son of A.E. and father and grandfather of some of the current company officers, was instrumental in developing the Publishing Department of Caxton and guiding it through the very rough waters of the Depression and World War II. Under his leadership, book publishing prospered and attracted such writers as Vardis Fisher and Ayn Rand. Small presses went into a demise for many years for a variety of reasons, but Caxton continued on through this period and often published books, not because they would sell, but because they were good and needed publishing. The emphasis was on finding a quality manuscript — no matter what genre, no matter what market.

Today, under the leadership of Jim, Gordon, and Dave Gipson, the company is maintaining its position as a vigorous and valued press. Consistent with its history, Caxton has been searching out and publishing works important to Idaho and the Northwest region; these works win awards for content, design, and printing. Quality is stressed at every step in production, and the Publishing Department has the responsibility to maintain high standards through all phases. The Caxton philosophy has always been to publish well, and the Gipson family has narrowed the publishing emphasis to western topics to accomplish this goal. We do best with what we know well: the West.

Consistent with its history, Caxton has been searching out and publishing works important to Idaho and the Northwest region

The Caxton Printers, Ltd. is unique in America, for it is one of a handful of presses that do all tasks under one roof: editing, producing, printing, and binding are all completed in-house. As a result, quality control and personal attention are easy to give to each of the titles.

Good things don't happen easily and Caxton has had its share of trouble. A major fire burned the plant to the ground in 1937. All records were lost and each department, including Publishing, had to rebuild its files. Publishing is difficult at the best of times, but recently, for a period of about ten years, the Caxton publishing staff had devastating losses due to illness and death. The needs of the department are now being evaluated over a period of time, and problems are being corrected. New staff has been brought in and both old and new staff are coming up with some innovative solutions to typical publishing problems. Policy changes are occurring, but only when all concerned are convinced that the change will benefit Caxton, its writers, and its customers.

As with any successful company, Caxton has found a market niche: Western nonfiction. The company looks for manuscripts that have a broad and lasting public appeal. Submissions must be carefully researched and well-written, for literate and questioning readers. Caxton is proud to be Western and the books reflect that pride. ■

Kathy Gaudry has been freelance editing and writing for ten years in the New Orleans area, and recently became General Editor at The Caxton Printers, Ltd.

The early western stories were mythical....Their theme was the struggle of the male pecking order, set against a background of wilderness; private warfare out beyond the rim of civilization and its moral and legal restraints.
— Richard Wheeler

Desktop Publishing *Cont. from pg. 48*

and printers made the self-publishing choice a relatively easy one for me to make.

What It's Worth (based on Seattle-metropolitan area)

Computer training: $20/hr. and up
Design/production services from service bureau: $35-$45/hr.
Design:* starts at $35+/hr and up
Freelance computer production: starts at $25/hr+
Traditional typesetting: $50/hr (low)-$120/hr (high)
Service bureau output from disk: $1.00/pg-$16.00/pg.
Traditional production: $15/hr-$30/hr
Illustration (computer or traditional) is priced according to usage, rights sold, and the illustrator's reputation.

Word processing: $8/hr-$18/hr
(Color separations are available via the desktop and savings of $100-$300 per job over traditional methods is estimated. Because of the complexity and quality issues, it will be awhile before the cost advantages are realized.)

*Design is more than hand-to-paper time, and frequently designers will bid on a project rather than just bill for time spent. ∎

Kathleen Dickenson, *owner of At Your Fingertips, A Desktop Publishing Placement Service in Seattle, is also publisher of* Accessible Art, A Layman's Look at Seattle's Public Art.

Redneck Review *Cont. from pg. 57*

"Friends of *The Redneck Review*" on the title page along with others who have been generous cash contributors.

All I've asked over the years is that *Redneck* pay for itself (which means it continues to interest my readers and writers) and continue to interest me. I've also found that the more involved I am in the hands-on production of the magazine, the more money I am able to save. My present subscription list and paid advertising could in no way begin to cover full shop prices for typesetting, printing and binding. But for the minute cost of ink and a little elbow grease to clean the press, I can run a two-color cover for considerably less than the cost of professional printing. Extra pages cost only the price of a few reams of paper and my time. I'm not an expert printer, but the job gets done. And in addition, there's a distinctly satisfying feeling in knowing that I can do the entire process myself, a kind of inner confidence that will continue to be valuable even if in the future I choose to hire a printer.

I enjoy doing *Redneck* on my own, having lived with it as a fascinated companion through its slow but steady development. I enjoy the personal contact and rapport I've developed among writers, readers, and other publishers. And yes, I do look at the magazine as a creative extension of myself. I publish what interests me and what I feel will interest my readers. For the last 15 years, *The Redneck Review* has been both my university and my counselor. When I decide to give it up, or when I die, I hope it will survive in the minds of regional writers as an interesting phenomenon that oozed out of the rural American West. It's been fun, guys. ∎

Penelope Reedy, *a 4th generation Northwesterner, has had her poetry, fiction, and essays appear in* Western American Literature, American Literary Review, *and* Sun Valley Magazine, *among others.*

Boise Magazine *Cont. from pg. 58*

world that generally have some kind of local or regional hook. Book reviews are another entry level venue. So are the "Short Takes" and the "Idaho Traveler."

WNH: Do you prefer queries?

AM: Yes. We'll respond right away to a well-written query. I'm always looking for new writers and the unique perspective. I'm more interested in the rodeo cowboy making the phone call home than seeing him on the bull.

WNH: Is getting people to think part of your mission?

AM: Absolutely. If you call yourself *Boise Magazine*, you'd be hypocritical if you didn't say that this is an extraordinary time in the life of Boise, Idaho. Yet you can't just do a fluff magazine about how great things are, because everything's not great here. Growth, for instance, is a complicated issue. When you build in the foothills, that's an environment that is fragile. If you don't grow, you'll die. But it has to be managed and planned. We have to look toward the future.

Magazine editors by definition have to have a little of the futurist in them, because you're always guessing about what will be an important story six to eight months ahead.

WNH: How would you summarize the mission of *Boise Magazine?*

AM: For me, magazines hold a mirror up to society or take the pulse of a community. That's what we try to do in every issue. We're Boise's magazine. ∎

Bill Woodall has an MA in English. He's a freelance writer, editor, and carpenter who lives, works, and plays Scrabble all over the Northwest.

ARTICLES

62

"B. C." Could Stand for "Book Country"

An overview of support programs in Canada reveals that there are two types. The first, cultural support, is intended to compensate for deficits in the publication of culturally valuable books such as literary works and books that address issues of concern to Canadians. The second, industrial support, is intended to assist book publishers to establish themselves as stable and effective businesses and the industry as profitable so that they may increase their effectiveness in marketing culturally valuable titles and diminish their need for public subsidy.

— From the Executive Summary of Book Publishing in British Columbia 1989, issued by the Canadian Centre for Studies in Publishing.

Speculation naturally arises as a result of the changes in technology. Often excited by the latest development in computer hardware or software, technocrats and techno-worshippers have predicted the imminent death of the book as a medium of expression since the 1960s. These predictions of demise are usually offered with the somber tone of regret or with the smug voice of victory. Forget it. The bound book is healthy, and it will persist as the preferred form of literary expression far into the future.

— Dennis Hyatt, Law Librarian, U of O

A Letter From the Front: the Censorship Battle

by Laura Kalpakian

What's at stake here is not simply what I, as an author, may write, but what you may read, or buy, or sell as a book, a tape, a record, or CD.

For twenty-five years the National Endowment for the Arts has funded, celebrated, and expressed the affirmation of American art. It should be celebrating its Silver Jubilee with one of those PBS gala fêtes. Instead, it is fighting for its very life. For all our cultural lives. Not simply those of us who write, but those who read. Not simply musicians, but those who love music. Not simply painters, but those with the gift of sight and means of expression. The struggle to save the NEA is not a question of allocation of resources — who is to be trusted with federal money — but a question of choice and freedom of expression. It is not the first such battle. It will not be the last. But it is the one history has given us in 1990.

In 1989, a shrill, well-organized minority chorus launched an assault against the Mapplethorpe exhibit in the name of obscenity, or rather, anti-obscenity. From that particular exhibit, the attack extended to tarnish and defile the NEA as a whole. In this country, questions of obscenity are correctly attended by considerations of censorship and the abridgement of constitutionally guaranteed rights. So, in 1990, the opposition chorus has modified their language to mollify their critics. They imply that the NEA is only in need of an expert interior decorator, that what they mean to do is "restructure" and "re-allocate resources." These phrases have the ring of sweet reason and not at all the flavor of smash, bash, trash, thrash and slash. In fact, they mean to do their redecorating with a wrecking ball.

This redecoration would allot the largest share of NEA funds to states and large institutions; it would curtail sharply, or cut altogether, grants to *individual* artists. The thinking here depicts artists as naughty children (at best, nasty subversives at worst) who cannot be trusted with public funds, who might use our (that is, the taxpayers') money to scrawl graffiti on bathroom walls. I resent this: as a taxpayer, an adult head of household, a hard working writer, and as a recipient of a 1990 NEA individual grant.

The work I submitted to the NEA was one of five winners flagged by the literature program and pulled (in November 1989) before the National Council on the Arts on the grounds of possible obscenity. The Council upheld the NEA's right to grant those individual awards in each of the five cases. (Given the climate of opinion a scant six months later, one wonders what the verdict might have been today.) That five should have been pulled and passed before the Council was unprecedented. Equally unprecedented: this year all NEA winners who have accepted money were required to sign an oath swearing that any works they should produce with this money will not be obscene, which is then defined as "*including but not limited to*" a catalogue of sexual activities which, taken literally, would eviscerate the Old Testament. Psalms and Proverbs alone might remain intact. Of course, the Old Testament was not written by members of the American Family Association who doubtlessly would have done it all differently.

I do not wish to alarm the American Family Association, Senator Jesse Helms and their troops and allies into angina attacks, but artists also have families. As a writer, the attack on the NEA appalls me, but as a mother I am truly horrified by a climate of opinion which not only encourages galloping intolerance, but prescribes it. Mandates conformity of thought. Tarnishes opposition with epithets like porno, pervert and obscene. Controversy and art are not new to 1990. Indissolutely linked, controversy and art are part of the process we historically label culture. A hundred years ago, the French Impressionists created public furor with their works. Early in this century, outrage greeted the music of Ravel and Debussy. Have the troops assaulting the NEA only just discovered what we have known all along: that art is crucial to the spiritual and cultural life of any people? Dialogue, discussion, creation, controversy will — and always have — nourished and resulted from

Continued on pg. 70

"Get Organized!" Say the Arts Commissions

by Bill Woodall

WNH surveyed the Arts Commissions of Oregon, Washington, Montana, Idaho, Alaska, and British Columbia to ascertain the health and the direction of their Literary Arts programs. In the roundtable interview that ensued we heard positive assessments about the "burgeoning" arts scenes around the region, depressing reports on the level of funding for the literary arts — except for a wonderful exception in British Columbia, and a nearly universal plea for literary artists to organize and become more active advocates for their own cause.

These people provided information for their commissions:
British Columbia Ministry of Culture — Dawn Wallace
Idaho Commission on the Arts — Margot Knight
Montana Arts Council — Bill Pratt
Oregon Arts Commission — Peter Sears
Washington State Arts Commission — Karen Gose

Tell us about current or proposed projects.

WA: In 1990 we're working with the Northwest Film and Video Center in Portland to make a Bill Moyers-style "Power of the Word" video on the "Across the River" program. [See box.]

MT: We're trying to get local arts agencies established in the state. We're also trying to establish a computer network for the arts, a bulletin-board system.

We also have a program that we're funding for arts coverage by low-power television, public television, in local communities that are unserved by public television.

ID: We've just added Worksite Grants as a funding category. Individuals can apply for money to attend workshops and in-residence programs.

OR: In 1989 we published *Oregon Small Presses & Publications*. This will help small presses in Oregon with their distribution. We're in the third phase of "Across the River" and I'm excited about the film/video component. "What the River Says," a documentary on poet William Stafford, began from a Fellowship award from the Oregon Arts Commission.

BC: In 1990 we announced two new funding programs of over half a million dollars. There's a Block Funding Program for B.C. Book Publishers ($450,000) and Project Assistance for Creative Writers ($100,000).

Give us an example of a local arts agency or a project in your state especially involved with the literary arts.

WA: We have some very active local arts groups, like the Bainbridge Island Arts Council. They publish a magazine called *Exhibition* and the *Northwest Poets & Artists Calendar*.

MT: Hellgate Writers has an office, a conference, and

tours writers around the state. The Yellowstone Regional Writers Project places select titles in point of purchase displays at art centers and museums. [Both are described in separate articles.]

ID: The Teton Valley Arts and Humanities Council received a reading series grant. The people in the Pilot Knob Writer's Group there have really started talking to one another; they're doing a lot for producing and sharing literature.

OR: The Oregon Coast Council of the Arts just sponsored the writing workshop for Young Writers. For this program, Congressperson Les AuCoin has raised $5,000 in each of the last three years. The Oregon Council of Teachers of English has already raised $200,000 towards the Oregon Literature Series.

BC: The Kootenai School of Writing in Vancouver has a strong poetry program. We also have a Festival of Writer's Arts in Sechbelt in August and an International Writer's Festival in October.

Describe the goals of your organization for the new decade. What problems or opportunities do you foresee?

MT: We have started a number of arts and cultural endowments that allow us to leverage individual dollars that may not have been available otherwise. Survival is a big issue right now, because of the NEA funding controversy. We have more and more organizations with good ideas and the money has leveled off. The changing funding structure, attitudes, and demographics will affect how arts organizations respond in the future since the NEA controversy is just the tip of the iceberg.

ID: We're in the middle of developing a five-year-plan, from 1993-98. We're looking to strengthen the local arts councils so that they become more of a resource for the artists within their communities as well as becoming almost an extension service for us to help people know what's available at the state and federal levels. We'll do this basically by helping them get paid staff. Only nine of the forty-one local councils now have paid staff. We've asked the legislature for money to provide salary and office support systems grants for local arts councils.

What about quality and quantity of applications?

WA: I look forward to seeing more applications from small presses and literary arts organizations. In a given year we'll have only five. When we've had good applications we've funded them, such as the Copper Canyon Press Reprint Series. The more applications we receive, the more we can fund. I'd like to see more presses apply for non-profit status.

ID: We have the most problems with applications when the person or organization doesn't call us to talk about the applications. If they would read the application and call us, and even send in a preliminary application, we're happy to critique it. It's our job to bring the strongest possible applications into the commission.

OR: *In the long run* (his emphasis) an increase in the number of and the quality of grants may result in more funding for the literary arts in Oregon.

Do you have any comments on the NEA funding controversy in 1990?

WA: There have been things that the artistic community could have gotten excited about years ago, but it chose not to be active until this NEA issue. It should continue to be as active and as galvanized as this issue has made them.

MT: We look very carefully at controversial grants. We want to know what we're getting into. In our enabling legislation protecting artistic freedom is a responsibility of the council. We obviously support the NEA. But we're not looking at them through rose-colored classes. Their addressing of the rural arts has been minuscule at best. We don't discount the radical right.

ID: Writers need to talk to other writers and get them working and realizing that community has as much to lose as any of the visual artists do if there's any kind of content restriction.

If a statewide writer's group did come along that was really meeting the needs of the constituents, I'd like to see the Arts Commission support them for a time while they established their own bureaucracy to get the work out.

Vigilance is important because this issue censorship is *never going away* (MK's emphasis). The people who benefit from NEA funding have to say, "I want my tax dollars going for this kind of activity." We're such a tiny part of the federal budget that we could be traded off in a heartbeat if we don't make our presence, and the value of that presence, known all the time.

Would you like to speak to any other major issues?

MT: I think the big issue that we have to address is statewide cultural planning. Individual artists are often isolated, which makes [organizing] difficult. How do we deal with the burgeoning arts scene? How can we sit down and, with the resources that are available, agree to agree, to come up with some strategies for increasing the pie. Obviously that's tied in with arts' advocacy. We hire a lobbyist, but we really don't have a year-round advocacy program, which is critical, in my estimation.

ID: I always want artist excellence to be the primary reason for funding by this agency. Freedom of artistic expression is something that we're committed to; that's a part of our enabling legislation. ∎

Bill Woodall has an MA in English. He's a freelance writer, editor, and carpenter who lives, works, and plays Scrabble all over the Northwest.

> *We're such a tiny part of the federal budget that we could be traded off in a heartbeat if we don't make our presence, and the value of that presence, known all the time.*
> *— Margot Knight*

Across the River

Across the River is the one program we have that specifically geared to the literary arts. It's a joint venture with the Oregon Arts Commission, with additional support from the NEA. We jury writers into a reading series, taking one from each state for each reading and pay their fees to go and read at a site, generally a rural site, in one of the states. We've been able to develop some audiences for fine poetry and prose. It's a good, one-time exposure for the writers, and the communities learn something about how to put on a literary reading, since the local arts or reading organization must apply for the program. The Commission provides guidance and support for the promotion of the writers and the event. We do have a competition for writers who want to appear in the series. — Karen Gose

Government Arts Funding

Every state and province that responded said they had programs for both organizations and individual artists. In both cases, the literary arts requests compete with all other arts and come out near the bottom of the pile for a variety of reasons. Call or write for specific information, including amounts, application requirements, filing deadlines, and other help.

Alaska State Council on the Arts
619 Warehouse Ave., Ste 220
Anchorage, AK 99501
907-279-1558
contact: Chris D'Arcy

Ministry of Culture
Cultural Services Branch
Parliament Buildings
Victoria, British Columbia
V8V 1X4 Canada
604-356-1727
contact: Dawn Wallace

Idaho Commission on the Arts
304 W. State St.
Boise, ID 83720
208-334-2119
contact: Cort Conley

Montana Arts Council
35 S. Last Chance Gulch
Helena, MT 59620
406-444-6430
contact: Bill Pratt

Oregon Arts Commission
835 Summer St. NE
Salem, OR 97301
503-378-3625
contact: Peter Sears

Washington State Arts Commission
110-9th&Columbia
Mail Stop GH-11
Olympia, WA 98504-4111
206-753-3860
contact: Mary Frye

Yellowstone Art Center's Regional Writers Project

by Adrea Sukin and Pat Palagi, Coordinators

In the fall of 1984, the Yellowstone Art Center inaugurated the Regional Writers Project, a retail outlet and mail order catalog promoting quality regional books. The books juried into the Project are either authored, published, or set in Montana, Idaho, Wyoming, Washington, Oregon, or the Dakotas. The Project has expanded its retail outlet into six affiliate museums including: in Montana, the Hockaday Center for the Arts, Kalispell; the Holter Museum of Art, Helena; the Lewistown Art Center, Lewistown; Paris Gibson Square, Center for Contemporary Arts, Great Falls; the Western Heritage Center, Billings; and in Wyoming, the Ucross Foundation, Ucross.

The Regional Writers Project promotes fine regional literature, supports small presses, and develops a national and regional audience for quality, regional, contemporary western writing with some historic and literary classics also included. The Regional Writers Project is further enhanced by sponsoring a lecture series featuring authors and small press publishers. Profits from book sales and grant monies help fund the speakers series and the mail order catalog.

A panel of jurors nominates books to be included in the Project. The final selection also includes the Montana Art Council's First Book Award winners and recipients of the Western States Arts Federation Book Awards, given biennially to outstanding books published by small presses in the western states. A committed group of scholars, readers, writers, publishers, library professionals, and arts administrators have been involved in the Project as advisors and jurors.

In 1989-90, the updated annual mail order catalogs were distributed nationally. Speakers invited to lecture at the Regional Writers Project museums were Charles Levendosky, Wyoming Poet Laureate; Tom Trusky, editor of Ahsahta Press; Karen Swenson, New York poet; and Debra Earling, Paul Zarzyski and Greg Keeler, Montana authors sponsored by the Hellgate Writers. Moving forward into 1990-91, featured speakers will be Mary Clearman Blew, author; and Linny and Dennis Stovall, editors of Media Weavers.

The National Endowment for the Arts gives considerable funding to the Regional Writers Project. The Montana Arts Council and the Montana Committee for the Humanities have also supported the Project.

The Regional Writers Project Staff is available to respond to questions or comments and will send the catalog upon request. Direct any correspondence to:

Regional Writers Project
Adrea Sukin and Pat Palagi
401 North 27th Street
Billings, Montana 59101 ∎

Redefining the Mainstream: The Before Columbus Foundation

by Shawn Wong

With the threat of numerous celebrations dedicated to the 500th anniversary of the "discovery of America" by Columbus, there may never be a more appropriate moment in American literary history for the Before Columbus Foundation to restate its mission. The Before Columbus Foundation was founded in 1976 by a group of writers, editors, and small press publishers with the goal of promoting and disseminating contemporary American multicultural literature through its American Book Awards, literary panel discussions and seminars, and the quarterly *Before Columbus Review*, America's only multicultural book review. With these programs the Before Columbus Foundation has provided recognition and a wider audience for the wealth of cultural and ethnic diversity that constitutes American writing. As director Gundars Strads notes, "The Before Columbus Foundation believes that the ingredients of America's 'melting pot' are not only distinct, but integral to the unique constitution of American culture — the whole comprises the parts."

At a recent literary panel co-sponsored by the Before Columbus Foundation, "Redefining the Mainstream" of American literature was the task for panelists Jessica Hagedorn, Jayne Cortez, J.J. Phillips, Oscar Hijuelos, N. Scott Momaday, John Barth, and Charles Johnson.

Jayne Cortez was the first to note that the only "mainstream" she recognized was the Mississippi River, because it is in the middle of the country and has a Native American name. She also noted that the American publishing establishment publishes what she considers "minority literature" and what remains unpublished is really, in fact, the "main-

> *N. Scott Momaday observed that American literature begins for him a thousand years ago and that somewhere in the more recent years of this enormous and rich history the "puritan invasion" of America took place.*

stream." N. Scott Momaday observed that American literature begins for him a thousand years ago and that somewhere in the more recent years of this enormous and rich history the "puritan invasion" of America took place.

Today, with the ethnic identity of America rapidly changing and pushing toward the disappearance of a white majority, some organizations and individuals have coined the phrase and started the movement of "the majorification of America's minorities." The process and the phrase is hidden behind a plea for public schools to return to "basic skills" education. "Basic skills" in this case is not only the three R's, but also a monocultural standard. America's minorities, soon to be the majority, must be "majorified."

Co-founder Ishmael Reed said in a speech given in Seattle last year, "Our vision of the future has room for the Asian, the African, as well as the Western (European). We don't see these as dangerous times, as do the paranoid monoculturalists. We see these as times fraught with hope and change. As we approach the end of the century, we have an opportunity to create a better world than the one envisioned by those who lived to see the close of the nineteenth century. But if we want to see that kind of world come about, we have to work for it. Before Columbus has done some of the ground breaking, but other institutions have to begin to lay the stones. We must go even farther — beyond Columbus." ■

Shawn Wong is president of the Before Columbus Foundation and is a professor of American Ethnic Studies at the University of Washington in Seattle.

Hellgate Writers, Inc.
One Organization's Beginnings

by Lee Evans

I would venture to say that there are more writers per capita in Missoula, Montana than anywhere else in the country. If you feel that you want to challenge this contention, you may live in a community that is ripe for setting up a nonprofit literary organization. In doing so, you might help lend cohesion to a creative, but disorganized collection of people, thereby creating new opportunities and audiences for these writers.

Named for the wind-swept canyon outside of Missoula, Hellgate Writers was conceived during a funding crisis at the University of Montana in December, 1986. The University was suffering from its usual financial problems, and the NEA had just turned down a grant to the English Department for a series of writers' residencies, giving priority instead to community-based programs.

Although most of the people involved with Hellgate Writers at this point were part of the University community, we had a definite commitment to being more than just a front for the University. We wanted to involve the community at large and decided to hold our first event, The Montana Writers Festival, featuring a weekend of readings with some of Montana's most prestigious authors, in downtown Missoula. Through a major volunteer effort, we were able to raise several thousand dollars worth of advertising. We attracted over 400 town folks to hear A.B. Guthrie and James Welch read, which we took as a sure sign that Hellgate Writers was something our community wanted to support.

We found a sympathetic lawyer to help us draw up articles of incorporation, which outlined the structure of the organization and board of directors. William Kittredge, who sat down at his computer shortly after the first meeting and generated a twenty-page document outlining the need for Hellgate Writers, was unanimously elected president of the board. Other writers and business leaders were asked to join as well. With our articles of incorporation, we were able to apply for our tax-exempt 501-C3 status, the magic key to applying for grants and setting up a bank account.

Next, we brought in the experts. We met with the Director of Organizational Services for the Montana Arts Council Bill Pratt and secured a small grant to bring in Susan Broadhead, executive director of The Loft, the highly successful literary center in Minneapolis. Susan stressed the importance of recognizing our constituency and collecting membership dues. We gathered business and arts leaders in the community to meet with Susan, and held our first public meeting and benefit during her visit.

Our first major conference, "The Life of the Poet: Developing a Social Conscience," was a three-day event featuring Carolyn Forche, Etheridge Knight and C.K. Williams. It was co-sponsored with another local group, Poetry for People, a coalition of graduate students which was giving poetry workshops in community settings. We have worked

---

I would venture to say that there are more writers per capita in Missoula, Montana than anywhere else in the country.

---

with several local arts groups over the past few years and have always benefited from the experience.

Running an active literary center out of the living rooms of volunteer staff is not something that can go on forever. We spent many of our last drops of volunteer energy writing a grant to our state's Cultural and Aesthetic Trust, which we hoped would provide us with a part-time staff and funds to help support conferences, readings, festivals, workshops, and a newsletter on a regular basis. We received $13,700 from the trust, about one-third of what we asked for. This grant allowed us to continue the programs we had developed, as well as to start new ones, such as the writing workshops. We were also able to start paying a program director and a development director, whose first duty was to write a grant to US West for an office, a place Hellgate Writers now calls home. ■

Lee Evans writes poetry and is Program Director for Hellgate Writers. The staff also includes Annick Smith, Development Director, and several volunteers. Contact them at P.O. Box 7131, Missoula, MT 59807, (406) 543-6333.

Hemingway said the one tool every writer needs is a built-in shockproof crap detector.
— Lowell Jaeger

The Fishtrap Gathering

by Rich Wandschneider

The Fishtrap Gathering is an annual July convocation, a blend of readings and focused and informal discussions on the issues confronting writers in the West. Its home is Wallowa Lake, Oregon.

Bill Kittredge opened the 1990 event with tales from a western boyhood — turkey ranching, Christmases, and small town life on the high desert of eastern Oregon. Terry Tempest Williams read "The Clan of the One-breasted Women," the personal account of a Utah nuclear testing "downwinder." Then Ursula Le Guin read a poem from a Native American writer and a playful and humorous story of her own.

These were the openers at the third annual Fishtrap Gathering. The crowd of 150 plus writers, editors, publishers, librarians, teachers, and just plain readers cried, laughed, and waited for the opportunity to talk about it with each other and with the writers.

A series of workshops has grown up around the writers who come to read and participate in the weekend Gathering. Fishtrap workshops, unlike the Gather itself, deal with nuts and bolts issues such as : book proposals, the children's picture book, writing history, oral history, and scriptwriting. 1991 promises "the literature of angling" and other workshops which provide some income for Fishtrap.

Fishtrap has been successful because of the qualities of the place and the participants. Wallowa Lake is seven hours from Portland; it's the same or less from Missoula, Boise, Spokane, Pullman, and Lewiston, and not much further from Seattle, Salt Lake, Reno, or Calgary. The Wallowa Mountains and nearby Snake River Country offer vivid examples of the varied and beautiful landscapes that become character in much good Western writing.

In its first three years, Fishtrap operated under the auspices of the Eastern Oregon Regional Arts Council and the Wallowa Valley Arts Council. Separate incorporation is underway, with the volunteer committee that has put the event together serving as a founding board. Grants from the Oregon Arts Commission, the Oregon Committee for the Humanities, the Oregon Tourism division, the OCRI Foundation, the Collins Foundation, the Jackson Foundation, and the Rose E. Tucker Trust have provided the fuel for the event in its development.

The Gathering has consistently attracted quality and diversity: James Welch, Bill Stafford, George Venn, Molly Gloss, Elizabeth Woody, Kim Stafford, Sue Armitage, Ursula Hegi, Craig Lesley, Jonathan Nicholas, Charles

Deemer, and John Rember have all read. It has provided an opportunity for novelists, poets, historians, journalists, biographers, and playwrights to consider the work of their peers and contemporaries in related disciplines.

From the beginning, Fishtrap has avoided a star system. At this writers' gathering, eight or ten or twelve writers read and/or participate in panel discussions with each other and with editors and with editors and critics. One of the joys of Fishtrap has been the surprise voices: Woody, Hegi, and Rember were new writers for most attendees. Scholarship and Fellowship programs are being developed to defray costs and provide recognition for new writers, and to ensure a future of surprise voices. This past year the Idaho Arts Commission provided a small grant to this end.

Each year Northwest writers have been joined by Eastern critics, editors, and publishers. It was Fishtrap's good fortune to have Alvin Josephy, editor emeritus of *American Heritage* and author of *The Nez Perce Indians and the Opening of the Northwest*, be a part-time resident of nearby Joseph. Josephy had tried for years to get his own agent and other Eastern literary friends to see this part of the country and to meet its writers. Fishtrap provided the occasion, and Herb Mitgang of the *New York Times*, Naomi Bliven of the *New Yorker*, agents Mary Evans and Julian Bach, and editors and publishers from Houghton Mifflin, Little Brown, and Grove have all been to Wallowa Lake. Publishers and critics are traipsing cross country more regularly now than they did when Fishtrap sent out its first invitations in 1988.

Northwest writing is of increasing interest to a national audience. Northwest writers go to New York to accept awards and sign contracts, and to Alaska and Antarctica to do research, but their writing community is in the Northwest, and Fishtrap's primary goal is to be a place and time for that community, or significant parts of it at any rate, to get together to talk about the work. It is, as *Oregonian* columnist Jonathan Nicholas says, a kind of revival meeting. The believers and practitioners come together for a few days to celebrate Writing in the West, and then go off for another year to their own places to write it, teach it, and enjoy it. ∎

Rich Wandschneider is a prime organizer of Fishtrap. He also publishes books under the Pika Press imprint.

> **It is, as Oregonian columnist Jonathan Nicholas says, a kind of revival meeting.**

Logger & Cowboy Poetry Readings

by Terri Lee Grell

Logger poetry originated as a way for loggers to relieve boredom and tension in isolated logging camps of the Pacific Northwest. Old time loggers, whose school days were filled with recitation, would repeat the works of popular poets such as Robert Service and Robert Swanson. Before long they were writing and reciting their own material, based on their own experiences working in the woods.

Poetry was not only one of the few forms of entertainment in the camp, but also was one of the few forums for loggers to express themselves creatively. Poetry was composed to spur laughter over the tragedies that almost happened, to praise fellow workers, to memorialize victims of crippling and fatal accidents, to draw attention to working conditions and to seek answers to life's questions. Rarely was logger poetry about "raping the land" — more likely it reflected the logger's awe of the woods he worked in every day of his adult life.

Logger poetry is enjoying a revival in the Pacific Northwest through poets such as Lon Minkler, Otto Oja, Darcy Cunningham, and Woodrow Gifford (a recipient of the Washington State Governor's Ethnic Heritage Award). These and other logger poets make appearances throughout the year at events such as the Northwest Folklife Festival, the Logger Poetry Gathering at the Mason County Fairgrounds, and bluegrass music festivals and country fairs. Last year, a well-attended logger poetry reading was held in Silver Lake, Washington as part of a commemoration of the 10th anniversary of the Mount St. Helens eruption.

For more information about logger poetry events, contact the Washington State Folklife Council. The council also has a resource list of logger poets in the NW, and is quite active in promoting the form as a way to preserve an important part of our cultural history.

One cowboy poem says: "The sad truth of this matter/ May bring strong men to tears/There hasn't been a real cowboy born/In almost a hundred years."*

By no means, however, is cowboy poetry dead. The annual Cowboy Poetry Gathering in Elko, Nevada, draws more participants and spectators (in the thousands) than most readings by "popular" poets. Modern-day cowboys recite odes to the Women of the West, the Australian Outback, and the Cowboy's Place in Nature, among other standing categories for readings in Elko. Cowboy poets come from as far away as North Dakota, Montana, and Australia to recite the rhymes of a rugged life that has some kinship with the logger's world. Sponsored by the Western Folklife Council, the Elko gathering brings in poets of all kinds, who "do their homework" on how to recite to a *very* large audience.

Working cowboys and ranchers who are interested in being considered as featured poets for the Elko gathering (held in January/February) can contact Cowboy Poetry Gathering, PO Box 888, Elko, Nevada 98901.

Cowboy poetry is just beginning to penetrate the competitive poetry market in the Pacific Northwest, sometimes as an added attraction at logger poetry events in Washington and Oregon. Specifically, in Idaho, the Salmon Arts Council has in recent years sponsored an annual cowboy poetry event. Contact the Council at PO Box 2500, 200 Main Street, Salmon, ID 83467. And there is also the Montana Cowboy Poetry Gathering, the contact being Gwen Petersen at Box 1255, Big Timber, MT 59011. ∎

From "The Open Question," a cowboy poem by Vess Quinlan that appeared in the program for the 1990 Cowboy Poetry Gathering, Elko, Nevada.

Terri Lee Grell *lives in Toutle, Washington and is the editor and publisher of* Lynx, *a quarterly journal of renga.*

Censorship Battle *Cont. from pg. 63*

art, yea, even unto the days of the Old Testament.

The fight to save the NEA in 1990 is not a battle over a tiny segment of Americans who make their livings by writing or painting or music. We are at the front, but the battle moves on and over us. The true target of those who would strangle the NEA is not so much a question of money (an amount that would not float a single battleship), but a question of the choices available to all Americans. What's at stake here is not simply what I, as an author, may write, but what you may read, or buy, or sell as a book, a tape, a record, or CD. "Perhaps," you may say, "I am not a reader or a lover of

music or a patron of the arts." Look on your refrigerator door: if you see a child's painting — a circle sun, a flower in primary colors, a happy stick figure with outstretched arms — and if this picture was painted in the public schools and at taxpayers' expense, then the survival of the National Endowment of the Arts is your fight too.

Write your congresspeople and senators. Do not let us go gently into this dark night. Do not let us go at all. ∎

Laura Kalpakian *is a novelist and short story writer living in Washington state. Her most recent book,* Dark Continent and Other Stories *(Viking, 1989) will be a Penguin paperback in 1991. This article is taken from her acceptance speech for an award from the Pacific Northwest Booksellers Association.*

If you have not already read the general introduction at the beginning of the book, we suggest you do so before using this section, since it will help you understand the intent of the directory section.

Three sections follow: the *indexes*, including breakdowns by state, publishing category, and several important editorial interests; the *alphabetical publisher listings*; and the *resource listings*, divided by type.

Indexes

At the beginning of the index section is the Market Subject Key, a guide to the numbers used in the main index to indicate general areas of editorial interest. This guide is displayed in both alphabetical and numeric order. Use it to find subjects that interest you; then scan the book publisher or periodical publisher indexes for names with matching numbers. Your selections can be found alphabetically in the publisher listings.

For the sake of space, subsidiary indexes, states, and subject groups do not include the subject numbers. They are simple alpha listings by title. To see the associated number(s) or subject(s), refer to the main indexes or go directly to the listing.

Publisher & Resource Listings

In the publisher listings, the associated subject numbers have been translated into text and placed directly below each entry in slightly indented, capped text. This allows you to scan the listings for your subjects without reference to the indices or the subject key.

Conventions

Indexes and listings are alphabetical, with cardinal numbers preceding letters. When possible we've indexed abbreviations according to the whole words they represent, e.g, BC as British Columbia. If you cannot find a title one way, try the other. In the case of a title beginning with an article, the next word has been used for alphabetizing, except in the rare cases of names that require ordering by the article (The Dalles, OR, etc.). When more than one publication shares a name, scan them all — just to be sure. In cases of publishing companies going by the names of their publishers, the publisher's surname has been used for alphabetizing, i.e., "Mary Smith Publishing" is indexed as "Smith Publishing, Mary." Once again, check both ways before giving up.

Some abbreviations are commonly used in the listing text. Among them are *ASAP* (as soon as possible), *assn* and *assoc* (association), *Ave* (Avenue), *avg* (average), *b&w* (black and white photo), *Bldg* (Building), *Blvd* (Boulevard), *CDN* (Canadian), *col* (column), *Corp* and *Co* (Corporation), *ds* (double spaced), *Fl* (Floor), *IRC* (International Reply Coupon), *Ltd* (limited), *mbr* (member), *ms* and *mss* (manuscript(s)), *pg* (page), *Pl* (Place), *PO* (Post Office), *POB* (Post Office Box), *pp* (pages), *ppd* (postage paid), *Pt* (Point), *Rd* (Road), *Rm* (Room), *RR* (Rural Route), *Rt* (Route), *s&h* (shipping and handling), *SASE* (self-addressed stamped envelope), *St* (Street), Ste (Suite), *Stn* (Station), *sub* (subscription), *US* (United States), *wd(s)* (word(s)), *wk(s)* (week(s)), and *yr* (year).

Updates & Accuracy

We clean our mailing lists at least twice each year. We do so again when we mail the surveys for a new edition of this book. That means that all listed addresses were deliverable in the last three months before the book went to press. However, we cannot guarantee that there have been no changes since. Publishing is a volatile business, with presses coming and going — often quickly. Further, the editorial information provided by publishers may change with new editors or owners. It is also the case that some publishers/editors provide only the sketchiest information on their operations. But if they're out there, we list them — even if it's only an address. Writers seeking markets are advised to pursue publishers that indicate an interest in submissions. If some other publisher looks enticing, but little or no information is available, be sure to query (with SASE) before sending your manuscript.

We consider *Writer's Northwest Handbook* to be a community building tool. As such, it depends on the contributions and feedback of all who use it. We welcome your suggestions and criticisms. Tell us your ideas for improvements, new features, etc. And, please, take the time to inform us of changed or erroneous listings.

During the two years between editions of *WNH*, updates are published in *Writer's NW*, our quarterly tabloid, which is available by mail for $10 per year (US$).

Market Subject Key

Subject	Code	Subject	Code
ABSTRACTS/INDICES	001	HUMOR	068
ADVENTURE	002	IDAHO	069
AGRICULTURE/FARMING	003	INDUSTRY	070
ALASKA	004	LABOR/WORK	071
AMERICANA	005	LAND USE/PLANNING	072
ANIMALS	006	LANGUAGE(S)	073
ANTHROPOLOGY/ARCHÆOLOGY	007	LAW	074
ANTIQUES	008	LIBERAL ARTS	075
ARCHITECTURE	009	LITERARY	076
ARTS	010	LITERATURE	077
ASIA	011	LUMBER	078
ASIAN AMERICAN	012	MARITIME	079
ASTROLOGY/SPIRITUAL	013	MEDIA/COMMUNICATIONS	080
AVANT-GARDE/EXPERIMENTAL	014	MEDICAL	081
AVIATION	015	MEN	082
BICYCLING	016	MILITARY/VETS	083
BILINGUAL	017	MINORITIES/ETHNIC	084
BIOGRAPHY	018	MONTANA	085
BIOLOGY	019	MUSIC	086
BLACK	020	MYSTERY	133
BOATING	021	NATIVE AMERICAN	087
BOOK ARTS/BOOKS	022	NATURAL HISTORY	088
BRITISH COLUMBIA	023	NEW AGE	132
BUSINESS	024	NORTHWEST	089
CALENDAR/EVENTS	025	OLD WEST	090
CANADA	026	OREGON	091
CHICANO/CHICANA	027	OUTDOOR	092
CHILDREN (BY/ABOUT)	028	PEACE	093
CHILDREN/TEEN	029	PHILOSOPHY	094
COLLECTING	030	PHOTOGRAPHY	095
COLLEGE/UNIVERSITY	031	PICTURE	096
COMMERCE	032	POETRY	097
COMMUNITY	033	POLITICS	098
COMPUTERS	034	PRISON	099
CONSERVATION	035	PSYCHOLOGY	100
CONSUMER	036	PUBLIC AFFAIRS	101
COUNTER CULTURE	037	PUBLISHING/PRINTING	102
CRAFTS/HOBBIES	038	RECREATION	103
CULTURE	039	REFERENCE/LIBRARY	104
DANCE	040	RELIGION	105
DISABLED	126	RURAL	106
DRAMA	041	SATIRE	107
ECONOMICS	042	SCHOLARLY/ACADEMIC	108
EDUCATION	043	SCIENCE	109
ENGLISH	044	SENIOR CITIZENS	110
ENTERTAINMENT	045	SEX	111
ENVIRONMENT/RESOURCES	046	SOCIALIST/RADICAL	112
FAMILY	047	SOCIETY	113
FANTASY/SCI FI	048	SOCIOLOGY	114
FASHION	049	SPORTS	115
FEMINISM	050	STUDENT	116
FICTION	051	TECHNICAL	117
FILM/VIDEO	052	TEXTBOOKS	118
FISHING	053	TRADE/ASSOCIATIONS	119
FOOD/COOKING	054	TRAVEL	120
FORESTRY	055	URBAN	121
GARDENING	056	VISUAL ARTS	122
GAY/LESBIAN	057	WASHINGTON	123
GENEALOGY	058	WOMEN	124
GEOLOGY/GEOGRAPHY	059	WRITING	125
GOVERNMENT	060	OTHER/UNSPECIFIED	999
HEALTH	061		
HISTORY, AMERICAN	062		
HISTORY, CANADIAN	063		
HISTORY, GENERAL	064		
HISTORY, NW/REGIONAL	065		
HOME	066		
HOW-TO	067		

Code	Subject	Code	Subject
001	ABSTRACTS/INDICES	069	IDAHO
002	ADVENTURE	070	INDUSTRY
003	AGRICULTURE/FARMING	071	LABOR/WORK
004	ALASKA	072	LAND USE/PLANNING
005	AMERICANA	073	LANGUAGE(S)
006	ANIMALS	074	LAW
007	ANTHROPOLOGY/ARCHÆOLOGY	075	LIBERAL ARTS
008	ANTIQUES	076	LITERARY
009	ARCHITECTURE	077	LITERATURE
010	ARTS	078	LUMBER
011	ASIA	079	MARITIME
012	ASIAN AMERICAN	080	MEDIA/COMMUNICATIONS
013	ASTROLOGY/SPIRITUAL	081	MEDICAL
014	AVANT-GARDE/EXPERIMENTAL	082	MEN
015	AVIATION	083	MILITARY/VETS
016	BICYCLING	084	MINORITIES/ETHNIC
017	BILINGUAL	085	MONTANA
018	BIOGRAPHY	086	MUSIC
019	BIOLOGY	087	NATIVE AMERICAN
020	BLACK	088	NATURAL HISTORY
021	BOATING	089	NORTHWEST
022	BOOK ARTS/BOOKS	090	OLD WEST
023	BRITISH COLUMBIA	091	OREGON
024	BUSINESS	092	OUTDOOR
025	CALENDAR/EVENTS	093	PEACE
026	CANADA	094	PHILOSOPHY
027	CHICANO/CHICANA	095	PHOTOGRAPHY
028	CHILDREN (BY/ABOUT)	096	PICTURE
029	CHILDREN/TEEN	097	POETRY
030	COLLECTING	098	POLITICS
031	COLLEGE/UNIVERSITY	099	PRISON
032	COMMERCE	100	PSYCHOLOGY
033	COMMUNITY	101	PUBLIC AFFAIRS
034	COMPUTERS	102	PUBLISHING/PRINTING
035	CONSERVATION	103	RECREATION
036	CONSUMER	104	REFERENCE/LIBRARY
037	COUNTER CULTURE	105	RELIGION
038	CRAFTS/HOBBIES	106	RURAL
039	CULTURE	107	SATIRE
040	DANCE	108	SCHOLARLY/ACADEMIC
041	DRAMA	109	SCIENCE
042	ECONOMICS	110	SENIOR CITIZENS
043	EDUCATION	111	SEX
044	ENGLISH	112	SOCIALIST/RADICAL
045	ENTERTAINMENT	113	SOCIETY
046	ENVIRONMENT/RESOURCES	114	SOCIOLOGY
047	FAMILY	115	SPORTS
048	FANTASY/SCI FI	116	STUDENT
049	FASHION	117	TECHNICAL
050	FEMINISM	118	TEXTBOOKS
051	FICTION	119	TRADE/ASSOCIATIONS
052	FILM/VIDEO	120	TRAVEL
053	FISHING	121	URBAN
054	FOOD/COOKING	122	VISUAL ARTS
055	FORESTRY	123	WASHINGTON
056	GARDENING	124	WOMEN
057	GAY/LESBIAN	125	WRITING
058	GENEALOGY	126	DISABLED
059	GEOLOGY/GEOGRAPHY	132	NEW AGE
060	GOVERNMENT	133	MYSTERY
061	HEALTH	999	OTHER/UNSPECIFIED
062	HISTORY, AMERICAN		
063	HISTORY, CANADIAN		
064	HISTORY, GENERAL		
065	HISTORY, NW/REGIONAL		
066	HOME		
067	HOW-TO		
068	HUMOR		

Book Publishers

Periodical Publishers

Scripts

Alaska

Abbott Loop Christian Center
Adventures
Air Alaska
Aladdin Publishing
Alaska Angler Publications
Alaska Association of Small
  Presses
Alaska Business Monthly
Alaska Council of Teachers of
  English
Alaska Dept of Fish & Game
Alaska Dept of Labor, Research
  & Analysis
Alaska Geographic
Alaska Geological Society
Alaska Heritage Enterprises
Alaska History
Alaska Illustrated
Alaska Jrl of Commerce
Alaska Magazine
Alaska Medicine
Alaska Metaphysical Council
  Newsletter
ANC News
Alaska Native Language Center
Alaska Natural History
  Association
Alaska Nurse
Alaska Outdoors
Alaska Pacific University Press
Alaska Quarterly Review
Alaska Review of Soc & Econ
  Conditions
AK Sea Grant
Alaska State Writing
  Consortium Newsletter
Alaska Today
Alaska Trails
Alaska Viking Press
Alaska Women
Alaskan Bowhunter
Alaskan Byways
Alaskan Women
Aleutian Eagle
Anchor Publishing
Anchorage Daily News
The Anchorage Times
Arctic Environmental Info &
  Data Center
Ascii
Autodidactic Press
Balcom Books
Black Current Press
Camp Denali Publishing
Capital City Weekly
Cecom Publishing
Challenge Alaska
The Denali Press
Devil's Thumb Press
Envoy
Explorations
Fairbanks News-Miner
Fathom Publishing Company
Firsthand Press
From The Woodpile
The Frontiersman
O.W. Frost Publisher
Geophysical Institute
Great Northwest Pub. & DiSt
  Company
Growing Images
Heartland Magazine
Homer News
In Common
Intertext
Henry John & Company
Juneau Empire

Ketchikan News
Kodiak Mirror
Lazy Mountain Press
Mountain Meadow Press
Rie Munoz, Ltd
Musher Monthly
Mushing
New River Times
The Newspoke
Northwest Arctic NUNA
Nugget
Old Harbor Press
Out North Theatre Company
The Ovulation Method
  Newsletter
Paisley Publishing
Paws IV Publishing Co
The Pedersens
Permafrost
Perseverance Theatre
Pressing America
Rainforest Publishing
Review of Social & Economic
  Conditions
Salmonberry Publishing
  Company
Sea Grant Program
The Senior Voice
Sentinel
Solstice Press
The Sourdough
Southeastern Log
Spirit Mountain Press
SwanMark Books
This Is Alaska
Thumb Press
Tundra Drums
Tundra Times
U of A Institute of Marine
  Science
Elmer E Rasmuson Library
University of Alaska Museum
University of Alaska Press
User-Friendly Press
Vanessapress
We Alaskans
White Mammoth
Winterholm Press
Wizard Works
Wolfdog Publications

British Columbia

123 studio
ABZ Books
The Advocate
Aerie Publishing
Agent West Weekly
AKHT Publishing
Alberni District Historical
  Society
Amphora
Antonson Publishing Ltd
Apple Books
Arbutus Publications, Ltd
Arsenal, Pulp Press, Ltd
Art Gallery of Greater Victoria
Artdog Press
Artest Magazine
Artistamp News
Arts BC
Arts & Crafts News
Arts Victoria
Azure Press
Bachelore
Barbarian Press
Baum Publications

Bear Grass Press
Beautiful British Columbia
Ben-Simon Publications
Blackfish Books
The Boag Foundation Ltd
Boat World Magazine
Boating News
Bold Brass Studios &
  Publications
Bowen Island Historians
Braemar Books Ltd
Brighouse Press
Bright Books
British Columbia Agri Digest
BC BookWorld
BC Business Examiner
BC Business Magazine
BC Farmways
British Columbia Genealogical
  Society
BC Historical News Magazine
BC Hotelman
BCIT Link
British Columbia Library
  Association Newsletter
British Columbia Medical
  Journal
British Columbia Monthly
BC Outdoors
BC Professional Engineer
British Columbia Railway
  Historical Assn
British Columbia Report
  Weekly News Magazine
BC Sport Fishing Magazine
BC Studies
BC Teacher
BC Orchardist
Burnaby Historical Society
Butter-fat Magazine
Cacanadadada Press Ltd
The Caitlin Press
Callboard
Canada Poultryman
Canadian Aquaculture
  Magazine
The Canadian Biker
Canadian Human Rights
  Reporter Inc
Canadian Literature
The Canadian Press
Canadian West Magazine
The Canadian Writer's Journal
Canho Enterprises Publishing
Capilano Courier
The Capilano Review
Cappis Press Publishers
CGA Magazine
Chalk Talk
Chanticleer
Cherry Tree Press
Chinatown News Magazine
Chinese Edition Lifestyle
  Magazine
Cinnabar Press Ltd
Common Ground
Communication Magazine
Community Digest Magazine
The Computing Student
Construction Sightlines
Country Roads
Cove Press
Crompton Books
Crook Publishing
Democrat
Dewdney Publishing
Diver Magazine
Diversity: The Lesbian Rag
Douglas Geidt

Douglas & McIntyre Publishers
  d'Void
The Eclectic Muse
Ekstasis Editions
The Elder Statesman
Encyclopedia Bananica
English Literature Studies
  Monograph Series
Enterprise
Equinews
Esquimalt Lookout
Estrada Publications and
  Photography
Event
Event
Expanducators Publishing
(f.) Lip
Famous Faces Magazine
Financial Times of Canada Ltd
Flight Press
Flying-W Publishing Co
Footprint Publishing Company
Foundation House Publications
Fountain Books
The Fraser Institute
Friends of Wells Gray Park
  Society
Fur Bearers
Gallerie: Women's Art
The Georgia Straight
The Globe & Mail
Good Medicine Books
Grassroots Oracle
Hancock House Publishers Ltd
Haralson Enterprises
Harbour Publishing
Harbour & Shipping
Heritage House Publishing Co
The Heron Press
Herspectives
Hi Baller Forest Magazine
Horizons Sf
Horsdal & Schubart Publishers
  Ltd
Il Centro, Newletter of Italian
  Canadian Community
Independent Senior
Integrity Publications
Interior Voice
International Self-Counsel
  Press, Ltd
Island Books
The Island Grower RR4
Joint Development Trading
  Company Ltd
Journal of BC English
  Teachers' Association
Kabalarian Philosophy
Kamloops Museum & Archives
Key to Victoria
Kinesis
Klassen & Foster Publications
Lambrecht Publications
Lazara Press
Light-House Publications
Lightship Press Ltd
Lillooet Tribal Council Press
Line
Log House Publishing
  Company Ltd
Logging & Sawmill Journal
Logistics & Transportation
  Review
Lumby Historians
The Malahat Review
The Martlet
Milestone Publications
Mining Review
MIR Publication Society

Monday Magazine
Mosaic Enterprises, Ltd
Musings
Nanaimo Historical Society
National Radio Guide
Nechako Valley Historical
  Society
Nerve Press
New Star Books
Newport Bay Publishing Ltd
Nursery Trades BC
Oolichan Books
Open Road Publishers
ORC Enterprises Ltd
Orca Book Publishers
Other Press
Outlook
The Overseas Times
Pacific Affairs
Pacific Coast Centre of
  Sexology
Pacific Educational Press
Pacific Publishers
Pacific Yachting
Panda Press Publications
Panorama Publication Ltd
Parallel Publishers Ltd
The Peak
Pemberton Pioneer Women
Petarade Press
Philam Books, Inc
Photography at Open-Space
Pioneer News
Playboard Magazine
Plus (Vancouver, BC)
Polestar Press
Pope International Publications
Poptart
Potboiler Magazine
Powell River Heritage Research
  Assn
Press Gang Publishers
Press Porcepic Ltd
Preston & Betts
PRISM International
The Province
Provincial Archives of British
  Columbia
Ptarmigan Press
the raddle moon
Railway Milepost Books
Raincoast Books
Rand & Sarah Publishers Ltd
Raxas Books
The Reader
Red Cedar Press
Reference-West
Reflections Publishing
Repository Press
Resource Development
Rhino Press
Richmond Review
RNABC News
Rocking Chair Studio
Room of One's Own
Sandhill Publishing
Screef
Select Homes
Shires Books
The Silver Apple Branch
Ski Canada Magazine
Skookum Publications
Skyword
Slug Press
The Smallholder Publishing
  Collective
Socialist Party of Canada
Sono Nis Press

Gordon Soules Book Publishers
  Ltd
Special Interest Publications
Spokes
Step Magazine
sub-TERRAIN
The Sun - Editorial
Sunfire Publications Ltd
Swedish Press
Talonbooks
Tantalus Research
Technocracy Digest
Theytus Books
Tickled by Thunder
Trabarni Productions
Trail City Archives
Training Associates Ltd
Transport Electronic News
Travelling
Truck Logger
Truck World
Trucks' Almanac
Truth on Fire (Hallelujah)
Truth on Fire (Hallelujah)
  Publishing
TV Week
University of British Columbia
  Press
Update
Urban Design Centre Society
The Vancouver Child
The Vancouver Courier
Vancouver History
Vancouver Magazine
Vancouver Scene
Vancouver Symphony
VCC
Victoria House Publishing
Vitamin Supplement
Donald E Waite Photographer
  & Publisher Co
R J Watts & Associates
Wavefront
West Coast Review
West Magazine
Western Fisheries
Western Geographical Series
Western Living
Western Trucking
Westworld Magazine
Whistler Publishing
Whitecap Books
Woman To Woman Magazine
Women's Chronicle
Wood Lake Books, Inc
Word Works
Write-On Press
Writing Magazine
Wynkyn Press
Yellow Hat Press

Idaho Publishing

Ad Lib
The Adjusting Entry
Adopted Child
The Advocate
Ahsahta Press
Aldrich Entomology Club
  Newsletter
American Dry Pea & Lentil
  Assn Bulletin
Appaloosa Journal
Backeddy Books
Beyond Basals Inc
Blackfoot Morning News
Blue Scarab Press

Ag/Forestry/Gardening

Arts: Fine, Allied, & Applied

Business/ Labor

Children

Ethnic/ Minority

Fiction

History/ Biography

1000 Friends of Oregon Newsletter, 534 SW 3rd Ave, Ste 300, Portland, OR 97204. Quarterly newsletter. Byline given. Query w/SASE. Accepts news items, photos (color and B&W, $50–200), interviews, op/ed, articles. Topics: issues of Oregon land use, development and environment. Sample $1.50.
ENVIRONMENT/RESOURCES, LAND USE/PLANNING, URBAN

123 studio, 123 S Turner St, Victoria, BC V8V 2J9. Book publisher. Poetry.
POETRY

Abbott Loop Christian Center, 2626 Abbott Rd, Anchorage, AK 99507. Publisher of Christian books.
RELIGION

Aberdeen Daily World, PO Box 269, Aberdeen, WA 98520. 206-532-4000. Daily newspaper.
COMMUNITY

Abraxas Publishing, PO Box 1522, Bellevue, WA 98009-1522. Book publisher.
OTHER/UNSPECIFIED

ABZ Books, PO Box 1404, Vancouver, BC V6C 2P7. 604-263-0014. Contact: Jackson House. Publisher of hard- & softcover books. Topics: literature, reference, sports. No unsolicited submissions. Catalog available.
LITERATURE, REFERENCE/LIBRARY, SPORTS

Academic Enterprises, PO Box 666, Pullman, WA 99163-0666. 509-334-4826. Self-publisher of books on agriculture, biology, and biography. Not a freelance market.
AGRICULTURE/FARMING, BIOLOGY, TEXTBOOKS

ACAPella, PO Box 11, Days Creek, OR 97429. Editor: Eleanor Davis. 503-825-3647. Quarterly. Circ 300. Sub $10. "No one receives any remuneration for the publication in ACAPella of their original gospel music or poetry." Accepts nonfiction, poetry. "Purpose of our organization is to assist and encourage members in the writing of gospel music and poetry, and provide timely articles about the state of the art." Sample available $1.
MUSIC, POETRY, RELIGION

AcreAGE, PO Box 130, Ontario, OR 97914. 503-889-5387. Editor: Marie A Ruemenapp. Monthly tabloid "distributed free to rural residents of Oregon and Idaho and related agri-business firms of the region.... We're interested in anything agriculturally oriented that will help our readers farm or ranch better, or entertain them." Payment: Money on publication. Rights purchased: 1st. Query w/SASE. Phone query OK. Reports in 2 wks. Publishes in 1–2 mos. Nonfiction, photos. Photos: $7.50 for 1st and $5 for others; 35mm B&W with articles; occasionally buys cover photos (color slides). "We encourage you to send us your exposed B&W film, preferably Tri-X and we will develop it here. Negatives will be returned." Tips: "AcreAGE is a very localized magazine, and as such, rarely uses material that isn't about farmers and ranchers in eastern Oregon and southern Idaho.
AGRICULTURE/FARMING, BUSINESS, ENTERTAINMENT

ACRL Newsletter, Washington State University, Owen Science & Engineering Library, Pullman, WA, 99164-3200, Periodical for academic and research librarians.
REFERENCE/LIBRARY, SCHOLARLY/ACADEMIC, SCIENCE

The Active Pacifist, 454 Willamette, Eugene, OR, 97402. Editor: Gary Kutcher. Monthly periodical devoted to the struggle for peace through nonviolence.
PEACE

Ad Lib, University of Idaho Law Library, Moscow, ID, 83843. Editor: Trish Cervenka. Irregularly published law periodical.
LAW

Ad-Dee Publishers Inc, 2736 Lincoln St, Eugene, OR 97405. Book publisher.
OTHER/UNSPECIFIED

The Adjusting Entry, PO Box 2896, Boise, ID 83702. Editor: Joyce Kasper. 208-344-6261. Ads: same. Quarterly aimed at CPAs. Circ 1,500. Sub by membership. No pay. Byline given. Phone query, dot matrix, and photocopies OK. Reporting time varies. Technical information.
BUSINESS, ECONOMICS

Adopted Child, PO Box 9362, Moscow, ID 83843. 208-882-1181. Editor: Lois Melina. Monthly. Subs $20; circ 3,000. Freelance mss accepted. Pays: money, copies on publication. Rights purchased: All. Byline given. Query with clips, ms, SASE. Photocopies, computer disk OK. Accepts: nonfiction. The newsletter uses a journalistic style with the author interviewing appropriate news sources on all types of adoptions. Some topics covered: bonding & attachment, how to talk to children about adoption, parenting, issues faced by the adopted adolescent. Guidelines available, sample $1.75.
CHILDREN (BY/ABOUT), FAMILY, SOCIOLOGY

Adrienne Lee Press, PO Box 309, Monmouth, OR 97316. 503-838-6292. Editor: Thomas Ferté. Published books of poetry irregularly. Query with 5 samples plus SASE. Report within 4–6 wks; publishes in 1 yr. If it's not exceptional and different, forget it.
POETRY

Adventures in Hell, Ritz Publishing, 202 W Fifth Ave, Ritzville, WA 99169-1722. 509-659-4336. Publisher: Star Andersen. Contact: David Andersen. "Alternative" semiannual book/journal for Vietnam War literature. Seeking Vietnam War related material — poetry, fiction, or 1st person historical narratives. Length open. Reports in 1 mo; publishing time varies. Query W/SASE. No dot matrix. Typed ms, or laser (suitable for scanning). "I believe wholeheartedly that this writing helps in the healing process of a war wound of the nation, as well as helping new authors get established."
FICTION, AMERICAN HISTORY, MILITARY/VETS

Adventure Northwest, 2521 A Pacific Hwy E, Tacoma, WA 98424-1007. Editor: Kerry Ordway. 206-863-4373. Monthly on NW travel for "upper middle class" audience about 45 yrs old. Circ 75,000. Buys 75 mss/yr. Payment: Money on publication. Byline given. Rights purchased: 1st. Query with mss, SASE. Dot matrix OK. Simultaneous submissions OK to non-competing markets. Publishes submissions in 2–6 mos. Nonfiction: 800–1,000 wds, $25–100. Guidelines/sample available.
TRAVEL

Adventures, Sheldon Jackson College, 801 Lincoln, Sitka, AK, 99835.
COLLEGE/UNIVERSITY

Adventures In Subversion, PO Box 11492, Eugene, OR 97440. Contact: John Zerzan, Dan Todd. 503-344-3119/503-345-1147. Self-publisher of occasional flyers and papers which present a "critical contestation of contemporary capitalism and its spurious opposition." Not a freelance market.
LABOR/WORK, SATIRE, SOCIALIST/RADICAL

Advocate, Mt. Hood Community College, 26000 SE Stark, Gresham, OR 97030. 503-667-7253. Student newspaper.
COLLEGE/UNIVERSITY

Advocate, PO Box 327, Sprague, WA 99032. 509-257-2311. Weekly newspaper.
COMMUNITY

The Advocate, PO Box 895, Boise, ID 83701. 208-342-8958. Editor/Ads: Linda Watkins-Heywood. Monthly. Sub $28/yr; circ 3,000. Byline given. Submit query letter, outline, phone. Photocopies OK. Reports in 2 mos. Accepts: nonfiction, articles, reviews. Topics: law-related. Tips: max 6 pgs, typed, ds. Guidelines available; sample $2.75.
IDAHO, LAW

The Advocate, Vancouver Bar Association, 4765 Pilot House Rd, West Vancouver, BC V7W 1J2. 604-925-2122. Editor: D P Roberts, QC. Bimonthly journal of the bar association. Circ 7,800. Subs $15/yr (CDN).
LAW

Aerie Publishing, Deep Bay, Vancouver Island, RR 1, Bower, BC V0R 1G0. Contact: John C Whelan. Book publisher.
OTHER/UNSPECIFIED

Aero Sun-Times, 44 N Last Chance Gulch #9, Helena, MT, 59601. 406-443-7272. Editor: Wilbur Wood. Quarterly magazine. Sub $15/yr. Circ 1,000. Accepts nonfiction, poetry, photos, cartoons, interviews, news items, articles, reviews, other. Topics: renewable energy, sustainable agriculture, economic development. Reporting time varies. Sample $2.50.
AGRICULTURE/FARMING, ENVIRONMENT/RESOURCES, POETRY

African American Journal, 525 NE Killingsworth St, Portland, OR 97211. Editor: Linda Johnson. Weekly newspaper. Circ 8,000. Uses freelance material of interest to the Portland Black community. No submission info available; query w/SASE.
BLACK, COMMUNITY

Ag Marketer, PO Box 1467, Yakima, WA 98907. 509-248-2452. Monthly agricultural business magazine.
AGRICULTURE/FARMING, BUSINESS

Ag-Pilot International, 405 Main St, Mt Vernon, WA 98273. 206-336-2045. Contact: Tom Wood. Monthly magazine for crop dusters. Circ 8,500. Acquires all rights to nonfiction related to the industry and those engaged in it. Query w/ms. Uses color or B&W photos. Accepts poetry, short humor.
AVIATION, BUSINESS

Agarikon Press, PO Box 2233, Olympia, WA 98507. Book publisher.
OTHER/UNSPECIFIED

Agent West Weekly, 1425 W Pender St, Vancouver, BC V6E 2S3. Editor: Douglas W Keough. 604-688-0481. Periodical.
OTHER/UNSPECIFIED

Aglow Magazine, PO Box 1548, Lynnwood, WA 98046-1557. 206-775-7282. Editor: Gloria Chisholm. Bimonthly magazine for charismatic Christian women. Circ 36,000. Sub $10.97/yr. Uses freelance material. Pays money on acceptance, byline given, acquires 1st and reprint rights. Submit query w/SASE. Photocopies OK. Reports in 6 wks; publishes within 1 yr. Accepts nonfiction, interviews, articles. Guidelines/sample available for SASE.
RELIGION, WOMEN

Aglow Publications, PO Box 1548, Lynnwood, WA 98046-1557. 206-775-7282. Publisher of 12 softcover originals a yr. Print run: 10,000. Payment: Royalties. Rights purchased: 1st and reprint. Query with sample chapters, SASE. Photocopies OK. Reports in 6 wks. Publishes in 6–12 mos. Nonfiction. Look for "Christian solutions to problems faced by today's women. To 50,000 wds." Guidelines/catalog available.
RELIGION, WOMEN

Agri Equipment Today, PO Box 1467, Yakima, WA 98907. 509-248-2457. Monthly on farm implements.
AGRICULTURE/FARMING, BUSINESS

Agri-News, PO Box 30755, Billings, MT 59107-0755. 406-259-4589. Editor: Rebecca Tescher. Weekly agricultural tabloid interested in "cottage industry." Circ 18,000. Writers must have expertise in agriculture. Pays money. Query w/SASE. Phone query OK. Nonfiction: 750 wds for $20–35 on Montana & Wyoming ag-related stories/profiles. Fillers: 500–1,000 wds for $15–25 on "farm taxes, ag-related business, gardening, knitting & crafts." Photos: B&W, good quality, $5, as used. Tips: "Must be useful to Montana & Wyoming agrarians." Guidelines/sample available.
AGRICULTURE/FARMING, CRAFTS/HOBBIES, MONTANA

Agri-Times Northwest, Box 189, Pendleton, OR 97801. 503-276-7845. Editor: Virgil Rupp. Weekly newspaper, Eastern WA, OR, ID. Uses freelance material. Pays 75¢/col inch. Photos $5–10. Submit phone query. Responds in 1 wk; publishes in 1 mo. Topics: farmers and agribusiness, ag-related community fairs and festivals in eastern OR, WA, & ID. Tips: Newspaper style, max. 3 ds pages. Guidelines available, sample 50¢.
AGRICULTURE/FARMING

Ahsahta Press, Dept of English, Boise State University, 1910 University Dr, Boise, ID 83725. 208-385-1246. Contact: Tom Trusky. Publishes 3 softcover books a yr. Print run: 500. Pays copies for 1st & 2nd printing; 25% royalties commence with 3rd printing. Acquires 1st rights. Reads samplers only (15 poems) sent Jan–Mar w/SASE. Reports in 2 mos. Accepts: poetry of the American West only. Guidelines included in catalog. Sample: $6.45 ppd.
POETRY

Air Alaska, PO Box 99007, Anchorage, AK 99509. 907-272-7500. Contact: Gene Storm. Circ 10,000. Monthly tabloid on flying small aircraft in the North. Buys 1st and serial rights. Pays after publication. Reports in 1 mo. Simultaneous subs OK. Pays more for electronic subs. Buys nonfiction related

to subject — profiles, how-tos, product and technical pieces, travel, sports, photo features, fillers, news items. Acquires some related adventure fiction. Submit brief query/w SASE.
ALASKA, AVIATION, FICTION

AKHT Publishing, 2420 Parkview D, Kamloops, BC V2B 7J1. Book publisher.
OTHER/UNSPECIFIED

Aladdin Publishing, PO Box 364, Palmer, AK, 99645. 602-347-5115. Editor: Marilyn Carter. Self-publisher of books. Not a freelance market. Catalog available.
OTHER/UNSPECIFIED

Alaska Airlines Magazine, 2701 – 1st Ave #250, Seattle, WA 98121. 206-441-5871. Editor: Paul Temple. In-flight magazine for West Coast travelers.
ALASKA, ENTERTAINMENT, TRAVEL

Alaska Angler Publications, PO Box 8-3550, Fairbanks, AK 99708. 907-456-8212. Editor: Chris Batin. Book publisher and monthly newsletter. Subs. $49/yr. Uses freelance material. Byline given, pays money on acceptance, acquires all rights. Query w/SASE. Responds in 1 mo. Accepts nonfiction, news items, interviews, articles. Catalog available; sample $8.50.
ALASKA, FISHING, RECREATION

Alaska Association of Small Presses, PO Box 821, Cordova, AK 99574. Contact: Constance Taylor. Circ 200. Irregularly publishes items of interest to small press publishers and writers. Query w/SASE.
ALASKA, RECREATION, WRITING

Alaska Business Monthly, PO Box 2412886, Anchorage, AK, 99524-1288. Editor: Paul Laird. As the name says.
ALASKA, BUSINESS, COMMERCE

Alaska Construction and Oil, 3000 Northrup Way #200, Bellevue, WA 98004-1407. 206-285-2050. Monthly.
ALASKA, BUSINESS, ENVIRONMENT/RESOURCES

Alaska Council of Teachers of English, PO Box 3184, Kodiak, AK, 99615. Editor: Kate O'Dell. Book publisher.
CHILDREN (BY/ABOUT), EDUCATION, ENGLISH

Alaska Department of Fish & Game, PO Box 3-2000, Juneau, AK 99802-2000. 907-465-4112. Editor: Sheila Nickerson. Bimonthly magazine. Sub $12. Circ 10,000. Occasionally takes freelance material. Pays money/copies on publication; acquires 1st rights. Byline given. Submit ms, SASE, phone. Dot matrix, photocopies, simultaneous subs OK. Reports in 4–6 wks; publishes in 6 mos. Accepts nonfiction on Alaska-related outdoors only. Photos: B&W $10–25; color $15–35; cover $100, back $50. Guidelines available; sample $3.
ALASKA, FISHING, OUTDOOR

Alaska Department of Labor, Research & Analysis, PO Box 25501, Juneau, AK 99802-2000. 907-465-4500. Editor: J P Goforth. Publisher of monthly journal and softcover books. Query w/SASE. Responds in 4–6 wks; publishing time varies. Catalog, sample available.
ALASKA, ECONOMICS, LABOR/WORK

Alaska Fisherman's Journal/Ocean Leader, 1115 NW 46th St, Seattle, WA 98107. 206-789-6506. Monthly. No submission info
ALASKA, BUSINESS, FISHING

Alaska Geographic, Alaska Geographic Society, PO Box 93370, Anchorage, AK 99509. 907-258-2575. Editor: Penny Rennick. Quarterly. Circ 13,000. Sub $39 for membership in Alaska Geographic Society. Pays money (approx $100/printed page) on publication; byline given; acquires 1st rights. Query w/SASE. Photocopies and simultaneous submission OK. Reports in 1 month. Nonfiction, photos. "Each issue devoted to specific topic, thus written proposals suggesting a topic are best initial approach. Mss are lengthy with finished issues ranging from 100–300 pages. Geography/natural resources in the broadest sense. Photos: 35mm color, $200 cover, $100 full pg, $50 half pg; good captions with photos. Guidelines available and will answer letters promptly.
ALASKA, NATURAL HISTORY, TRAVEL

Alaska Geological Society, PO Box 101288, Anchorage, AK 99510. Book publisher.
GEOLOGY/GEOGRAPHY, SCIENCE

Alaska Heritage Enterprises, 945 W 12th Ave, Anchorage, AK 99501. Publisher of Alaskan history. Book publisher.
ALASKA, GENERAL HISTORY

Alaska History, Alaska Historical Society, PO Box 100299, Anchorage, AK 99510. 907-276-1596. Editor: James H Ducker. Subs $10/yr; circ 800. Publishes 2 softcover journals a yr. Uses 3 freelance mss per issue. Pays copies; acquires 1st rights. Byline given. Submit ms w/SASE. Dot matrix, photocopied subs OK. Reports in 3 mos; publishes in 8 mos. Accepts nonfiction. Tip: Photos and maps desired. Sample $5.
ALASKA, AMERICAN HISTORY

Alaska Illustrated, 4341 MacAlister Dr, Anchorage, AK 99515. 970-243-1286. Editor: Kevin Cassity. Publishes 1–3 softcover Alaska, travel books a yr. Accepts freelance submissions. Payment terms vary. Submit query w/ SASE. Dot matrix, photocopied, simultaneous OK. Reports in 4–6 wks. Publishing time varies. Accepts nonfiction and photos.
ALASKA, TRAVEL

Alaska Journal of Commerce, PO Box 99007, Anchorage, AK 99509-9007. 907-272-7500. Editor: S J Suddock. Ads: L Brown. Weekly business newspaper. Sub $49. Circ 5,000. Uses 1–3 freelance mss per issue. Payment on publication, rates vary. Acquires 1st rights. Byline given. Submit ms by assignment only; query w/SASE. Photocopied, computer disk w/hard copy OK. Reports in 2 wks. Publishing time varies. Accepts nonfiction, cartoons. Photos: B&W or color print. "Some travel features." Tips: press releases welcome. Samples available.
ALASKA, BUSINESS, ECONOMICS

Alaska Magazine, 808 E St, Ste 200, Anchorage, AK 99501. 907-272-6070. Editor: Grant Sims. Monthly on natural resources and non-urban life in Alaska/Western Canada. Circ 150,000 to college educated readers, 35 and older. Pays money on acceptance. Byline given. Buys 1st rights. Submit ms w/SASE. Dot matrix OK. Publishes submissions in 4–12 mos. Nonfiction: 2,000 wds for $50–400. Photos: 35mm color, $25–200 (cover). Sample $2.
ALASKA, RURAL

Alaska Medicine, 4107 Laurel St, Anchorage, AK 99504. Editor: William Bowers, MD. 907-562-2928. Periodical.
ALASKA, HEALTH, MEDICAL

Alaska Metaphysical Council Newsletter, PO Box 98006, Anchorage, AK 99509-3006. Monthly newsletter of metaphysical organizations, services, and calendar events. Sub $12/yr.
NEW AGE

ANC News, Alaska Native Coalition, c/o 310 K St, Ste 708, Anchorage, AK, 99501. Periodical.
NATIVE AMERICAN

Alaska Native Language Center, PO Box 900111, University of Alaska, Fairbanks, AK 99775-0120. 907-474-7874. Publishes softcover books. No unsolicited mss. Scholarly publishing in and about Alaska's Native languages. Reporting time and payment vary. Catalog available.
ALASKA, LANGUAGE(S), SCHOLARLY/ACADEMIC

Alaska Natural History Association, 605 W 4th Ave #120, Anchorage, AK 99501-2231. Book publisher.
ALASKA, NATURAL HISTORY

Alaska Northwest Publishing Company, 130 Second Ave S, Edmonds, WA 98020. 206-774-4111. Contact: Marlene Blessing. Print runs: 2,000–10,000. Publishes 12–20 hard- & softcover originals & reprints per yr. Accepts unsolicited mss. Query with clips/SASE. Accepts nonfiction. "From 50,000–100,000 wds informal prose re: history, geography, resources, people of Alaska, Canada, the Pacific Northwest states. Also 1st-person experience narratives, preferably upbeat and outdoor-oriented. Royalty: 10% of gross. No juveniles, poetry, fiction, politics, economics. Photos: B/W, color trans, B/W drawings. No sex, drugs, vulgarity, racism, psychological studies, ex-

plorations of physical or mental illness; no muckraking. Controversial material must explore all angles fairly." Guidelines/catalog available.
ADVENTURE, ALASKA, ANTHROPOLOGY/ARCHÆOLOGY

Alaska Nurse, Alaskan Nurses Assn, 237 E 3rd, Anchorage, AK 99501. Periodical.
ALASKA, HEALTH, MEDICAL

Alaska Outdoors, Box 120324, Anchorage, AK 99519-0324. 907-276-2672. Editor: Christopher M Batin. Periodical. Uses freelance material. Byline given, pays money on acceptance, acquires all rights. Query w/SASE. Responds in 1 mo. Accepts nonfiction, news items, interviews, articles. Query w/SASE.
ALASKA, OUTDOOR, RECREATION

Alaska Pacific University Press, 4101 University Dr, Anchorage, AK 99508. 907-564-8304. Editor/ads: Jan Ingram. Publisher of 1–2 hard- & soft books a yr. Accepts unsolicited submissions. Pays royalties on publication. Acquires all rights. Submit ms, SASE. Dot matrix, photocopies OK. Reports in 3 mos. Publishes in 1 yr. Accepts nonfiction, fiction, and poetry with Alaskan focus — its people, places, and history. Book length determined by topic and information presented.
ALASKA, AMERICAN HISTORY, NATIVE AMERICAN

Alaska Quarterly Review, Dept of English, University of Alaska, 3221 Providence Dr, Anchorage, AK 99508. 907-786-1731. Editors: Ronald Spatz/ James Liszka. Quarterly review of literature and philosophy. Circ 1,000. Acquires 1st rights. Pay varies on publication according to available funds. Seeks criticism, reviews, fiction, poetry, essays. Accepts unsolicited mss.
LITERARY, PHILOSOPHY, POETRY

Alaska Review of Social & Economic Conditions, University of Alaska, 707 A St, Anchorage, AK 99501. 907-278-4621. Editor: Ronald Crowe. Periodical.
ALASKA, ECONOMICS, SOCIOLOGY

AK Sea Grant, 138 Irving #11, Fairbanks, AK, 99775. Book publisher.
ALASKA, BIOLOGY, ENVIRONMENT/RESOURCES

Alaska State Writing Consortium Newsletter, c/o Alaska Dept of Education, PO Box F, Juneau, AK 99811. 907-564-2841. Editor: Annie Calkins. Bimonthly during August-May. Sub $51 out of state. Circ 1,100. Uses freelance material. Pays copies on publication. Byline given. Submit ms. Photocopied OK. Reports in 1–2 wks. Publishes in 1–2 mos. Accepts nonfiction, fiction, poetry, cartoons. Topics: "Writing across the curriculum, writers residencies with children and adolescents, computers and writing, ties between oral language and writing and reading."
EDUCATION, WRITING

Alaska Today, Dept of Journalism, University of Alaska, Fairbanks, AK 99701. Periodical.
ALASKA, COLLEGE/UNIVERSITY, PUBLIC AFFAIRS

Alaska Trails, 7624 Duben Ave, Anchorage, AK 99504. Book publisher.
ALASKA

Alaska Viking Press, PO Box 11-3231, Anchorage, AK 99511. 907-345-0451. Editor: Gunnar S Pedersen. Self-publisher of books on fishing. Does not accept unsolicited submissions.
FISHING

Alaska Women, HCR 64 Box 453, Seward, AK 99664. 907-288-3168. Editor: L B Leary. Quarterly journal. Subs $30/yr. Uses freelance material. Byline given. Submit ms, query letter, SASE. Responds in 2 wks; publishing time varies. Accepts nonfiction, photos. Topics: "this is a living history journal…featuring women throughout Alaska involved in a variety of endeavors." Guidelines, sample available.
ALASKA, WOMEN

Alaskan Bowhunter, PO Box 870, Kasilof, AK 99610. 907-262-9191. Editor: Dave Hopkins. Quarterly magazine. Subs $10/yr; circ 1,000. Uses freelance material. Byline given, no pay. Submit query, ms, SASE. Dot matrix, disk subs OK. Accepts nonfiction, op/ed, articles, prefers B&W photos. Topics: hunting, bowhunting, archery. Sample $1.50.
ALASKA, ANIMALS, SPORTS

Alaskan Byways, PO Box 211356, Anchorage, AK 99521. Editor: Lisa M Short. Periodical.
ALASKA, TRAVEL

Alaskan Women, HCR 64 Box 453, Seward, AK 99664. 907-288-3168. Contact: Lory B Leary. Quarterly magazine. Circ 50,000. Interested in freelance writing, photos, cartoons, poetry by Alaskan women. Pays byline, title page listing, and subscription. Submit query, mss, and SASE. Reports in 1 month.
ALASKA, POETRY, WOMEN

Albany Democratic-Herald, Box 130, Albany, OR 97321. 503-926-2211. Daily newspaper.
COMMUNITY

Alberni District Historical Society, PO Box 284, Port Alberni, BC V9Y 7M7. 604-723-3006. Publisher of occasional softcover books. Canadian history and biography. Not a freelance market.
BIOGRAPHY, CANADA, COMMUNITY

Alchemy, Portland Community College, 12000 SW 49th Ave, Portland, OR 97219. College literary magazine. Editor could change yearly. SASE for guidelines.
COLLEGE/UNIVERSITY, FICTION, LITERARY

Alcove Publishing Co, 6385 NE Barclay, West Linn, OR 97068. 503-655-5564. Editor: Bruce Taylor. Publisher of softcover, nonfiction books on English usage, writing, and editing. Accepts unsolicited freelance material. Pays royalties; acquires all rights. Submit query letter. Dot matrix, simultaneous subs OK. Responds in 2 wks; publishes in 6 mos. Catalog available.
COLLEGE/UNIVERSITY, ENGLISH, WRITING

Aldrich Entomology Club Newsletter, University of Idaho, Department of Entomology, Moscow, ID 83843. Irregular periodical devoted to insects.
BIOLOGY, COLLEGE/UNIVERSITY, SCIENCE

Aleutian Eagle, PO Box 406, Dutch Harbor, AK 99692. 907-562-4684. Weekly newspaper.
COMMUNITY

Alioth Press, PO Box 1554, Beaverton, OR, 97075. 503-644-0983. Editor: Mark Dominik. Publishes hardcover reprints. Does not accept unsolicited submissions.
OTHER/UNSPECIFIED

ALKI: The Washington Library Association Journal, The Library MS-84, Eastern Washington University, Cheney, WA 99004. 509-359-7893. Editor: V Louise Saylor. Quarterly journal. Sub $14. Circ 1,200. Uses freelance material. Pays copies on publication. Byline given. Submit query w/clips, ms, or phone. Dot matrix, photocopied, simultaneous, electronic/modem subs OK. Accepts nonfiction, photos, cartoons. Topics: libraries and all related issues for people concerned with libraries. Tips: 1,000–2,500 wds, depending on topic. Photos: B&W glossy w/captions. Guidelines & sample available.
BOOK ARTS/BOOKS, FORESTRY, LIBERAL ARTS

Allegro Publishing, 1075 NW Murray Rd, Ste 266, Portland, OR 97229-5501. 503-690-7726. Contact: Phillip Bride. Publisher of softcover books of fiction, nonfiction, poetry, and biography. Accepts unsolicited submissions. Gives byline. Pays on acceptance (50%) and publication (50%) with copies, advance, and royalties. Acquires 1st rights. Responds in 4 wks; publishes in 6 mos. Query with sample chapters or complete ms, or by phone. Photocopy or disk (IBM or MAC) submissions OK.
ARTS, BIOGRAPHY, MUSIC

Allied Arts Newsletter, PO Box 2584, Bellingham, WA 98227. 206-676-8548. Editor: Miriam Barnett. Circ 500+. Sub $15. Monthly newsletter. Accepts unsolicited, freelance mss. No pay. Phone query OK. Photocopy OK. Reports on 15th of the month. Accepts poetry, photos, cartoons. "Will print anything related to visual, performing, or literary arts."
ARTS, MUSIC, VISUAL ARTS

Allied Arts of Seattle, 107 S Main, Rm 201, Seattle, WA 98104. 206-624-0432. Publishes a newsletter 6 times a yr. "We are not publishers but we have published a few titles such as 'Art Deco', 'Impressions of Imagination: Terra Cotta Seattle', and 'Access to the Arts'."
ARTS

Aloha Breeze, PO Box 588, Hillsboro, OR 97123. Weekly newspaper.
COMMUNITY

Alternative Energy Resources Organization, 44 N Last Chance Gulch, Stes B & 9, Helena, MT 59601. Book publisher.
CONSERVATION, ENVIRONMENT/RESOURCES

Altitude Medical Publishing Company, 5624 Admiral Way, Seattle, WA 98116. Book publisher — health & medical subjects.
HEALTH, MEDICAL

Amadeus Press Inc, 9999 SW Wilshire, Portland, OR 97225. 503-292-0961. Editor: Richard Abel. Publishes 20 music-related hardcover books per yr. Accepts unsolicited submissions. Acquires all rights. Submit query w/clips. Dot matrix, photocopied OK. Reports in 3–4 wks.
MUSIC

Amateur Brewer Information, PO Box 546, Portland, OR 97207. 503-289-7596. Contact: Fred Eckhardt. Publisher of books on beermaking.
CRAFTS/HOBBIES, FOOD/COOKING

Frank Amato Publications, PO Box 02112, Portland, OR 97202. 503-653-8108. Publishes hard- & softcover originals, reprints; also 2 fishing magazines. Accepts unsolicited submissions. Query w/clips, ms, SASE. "Interested in nonfiction book proposals — most subjects." Catalog available.
FISHING

Amazing Heroes, Fantagraphics Books, 7563 Lake City Way, Seattle, WA 98115. 206-524-1967. Contact: Thomas Harrington. Monthly magazine of comic book fans. Circ 15,000. Acquires 1st and 2nd serial rights to nonfiction articles and criticism. Query w/clips & SASE.
CULTURE, LITERARY, WRITING

American Contractor, PO Box 3165, Portland, OR 97208-3165. 503-226-1331. Editor: Cardice Crossley. Ads: Bruce Broussard at 503-280-9000. Weekly trade publication. Subs. $100/yr; circ 20,000. Uses freelance material. Byline given; pays on acceptance. Submit clips, query by phone, assignment only. Computer disk subs OK. Guidelines, sample available.
BUSINESS, TRADE/ASSOCIATIONS

American Dry Pea & Lentil Association Bulletin, PO Box 8566, Moscow, ID 83843. Editor: Harold Blain. Trade monthly. Circ 350.
AGRICULTURE/FARMING, BUSINESS

American Geographic Publishing, PO Box 5630, Helena, MT 59604. 406-443-2842. Editor: Mark Thompson. Publishes regional photo books with text. Accepts unsolicited submissions. Pays royalties/advance. Submit query, sample chapters, SASE. Photocopy OK. Responds in 2 wks to queries, 4–6 wks to mss. Publishes in 9 mos.
GEOLOGY/GEOGRAPHY, OUTDOOR, PHOTOGRAPHY

American Indian Basketry Magazine, PO Box 66124, Portland, OR 97266. 503-233-8131. Editor: John M Gogol. Quarterly of photo-essays on Native American basketry and crafts. Interested in history, biography, artistic methods and materials used. Heavily dependent on quality photos. Tips: Thorough understanding of Native American arts and crafts is important.
CRAFTS/HOBBIES, GENERAL HISTORY, NATIVE AMERICAN

American Institute for Yemeni Studies, Portland State University, History Dept, PO Box 751, Portland, OR 97207. Book publisher.
COLLEGE/UNIVERSITY, MINORITIES/ETHNIC

American Rhododendron Society Journal, 201-A S State St, Bellingham, WA 98225. Editor: Sonja Nelson. Quarterly sent with membership in American Rhododendron Society. Subs $25/mbrship. Circ 6,000. Uses several freelance mss per issue. Byline given, no pay. Submit ms w/SASE. Phone query, dot matrix, photocopies, computer disk OK. Reports in 2–4 wks. Publishes usually within 1 yr. Topic: rhododendrons & azaleas. Guidelines available, sample $4.
GARDENING

American-Nepal Education Foundation, 2790 Cape Meares Loop, Tillamook, OR 97141. Contact: Hugh B Wood. Book publisher.
EDUCATION, MINORITIES/ETHNIC

Americas Focus, 2000 SW 5th Ave, Portland, OR, 97201. Editor: Donald Bassist. Periodical.
OTHER/UNSPECIFIED

Amity Publications, 78688 Sears Rd, Cottage Grove, OR 97424. Book publisher.
OTHER/UNSPECIFIED

Ampersand Publishing, PO Box 943, Mukilteo, WA 98275. Book publisher.
OTHER/UNSPECIFIED

Amphora, The Alcuin Society, PO Box 3216, Vancouver, BC V6B 3X8. 604-688-2341. Quarterly newsletter. Sub $35/yr (CDN). Circ 300+. Accepts freelance material. No pay. Acquires 1st rights. Byline given. Submit ms w/ SASE. Dot matrix, photocopied OK. Publishes 1st issue w/available space. Accepts nonfiction, photos. Topics: book arts, calligraphy, book collecting, book binding, etc. Sample $5(CDN).
BOOK ARTS/BOOKS, PUBLISHING/PRINTING

Anaconda Leader, 121 Main St, Anaconda, MT 59711. 406-563-5283. Bi-weekly newspaper.
COMMUNITY

Anacortes American, PO Box 39, Anacortes, WA 98221. 206-293-3122. Weekly newspaper.
COMMUNITY

Analysis and Outlook, PO Box 1167, Port Townsend, WA 98368. Editor: R W Bradford. Monthly.
OTHER/UNSPECIFIED

Ananse Press, PO Box 22565, Seattle, WA 98122. Book publisher.
OTHER/UNSPECIFIED

Anchor Publishing, PO Box 30, Homer, AK 99603. 907-235-6188. Contact: Ted Gerken. Self-publisher. Not a freelance market.
OTHER/UNSPECIFIED

Anchorage Daily News, 1001 Northway Dr, Anchorage, AK 99508. 907-786-4200. Contact: Features Editor. Daily newspaper.
COMMUNITY

The Anchorage Times, 1001 Northway Dr, Anchorage, AK 99508. 907-263-9000. Contact: Features Editor. Daily newspaper.
COMMUNITY

Angst World Library, 1160 Forest Creek Rd, Selma, OR 97535. Publisher of fiction. Book publisher.
AVANT-GARDE/EXPERIMENTAL, FICTION

Animal Aid, 408 SW 2nd, Rm 318, Portland, OR 97204. Periodical.
ANIMALS

Animator, Oregon Art Institute, Northwest Film & Video Center, 1219 SW Park Ave, Portland, OR 97205. Editor/Ads: Kathy Clark. 503-221-1156. Quarterly on film, video, public relations, media. Circ 2,000. Sub $6 individual, $10 institution. Payment: Copies on acceptance. Byline given. Submit ms w/SASE. Nonfiction, photos, cartoons. Sample available.
ARTS, FILM/VIDEO, VISUAL ARTS

Ansal Press, 8620 Olympic View Dr, Edmonds, WA 98020. 206-774-4645. Contact: Ann Saling. Book publisher.
OTHER/UNSPECIFIED

The Antique Doorknob Publishing Company, PO Box 2609, Woodinville, WA 98072-2609.
ANTIQUES, OTHER/UNSPECIFIED

Antonson Publishing Ltd, 1615 Venable St, Vancouver, BC V5L 2H1. Book publisher.
OTHER/UNSPECIFIED

Aozora Publishing, PO Box 95, Myrtle Point, OR 97458. Book publisher.
OTHER/UNSPECIFIED

APA-EROS, c/o Correspan, PO Box 759, Veneta, OR, 97487. Contact: Sylvia. Bimonthly periodical. Accepts freelance material. Submit query w/ clips, SASE. Accepts nonfiction, fiction, poetry, other. Sample $2.
CULTURE, ENTERTAINMENT, MEN

Aperture Northwest Inc, PO Box 24365, Seattle, WA 98124-0365. 206-381-9220. Contact: Gordon Todd. Monthly newspaper. Sub $20/yr. Circ 13,000. Accepts unsolicited submissions; uses 5 freelance mss per issue. Rates flexible; pays on publication. Acquires all rights. Byline given. By assignment only. Submit phone or letter query. Dot matrix, photocopies, and computer disk submissions OK. Reports in 30 days; publishes within 2 months. Accepts journalism. Topics: Pacific NW, advertising, marketing news, features, strong journalist-hard news style. B&W glossies preferred. Sample issues $2/copy.
BUSINESS, COMMERCE, NORTHWEST

Aphra Behn Press, 13625 SW 23rd, Beaverton, OR 97005. Contact: Suzanne Graham. 503-646-0471. Publisher of 1–2 nonfiction, softcover originals a yr. Press run: 500–5,000. Accepts freelance submissions. Payment: 8–12% royalties, on retail minimum price, with "average advance." Reports in 2 wks. Publishes in less than 1 yr. Query w/SASE. Dot matrix, photocopies and simultaneous submissions OK. Mss from 60,000–100,000 wds on "popular science — technology — prefer medical, biological, engineering, cosmological, philosophical." Tips: "Informative, with self-help orientation, socio-economic commentary or philosophy of science."
HEALTH, MEDICAL, SCIENCE

Apostolic Book Publishers, 9643 N Lombard, Portland, OR, 97203. Book publisher.
RELIGION

Appaloosa Journal, Appaloosa Horse Club Inc, PO Box 8403, Moscow, ID 83843. 208-882-5578. Editor: Betsy Lynch. Ads: Chris Olney. Sub $15. Circ 15,000. Monthly. Accepts unsolicited mss on spec. Uses 2 freelance mss per issue. Pay: Money, copies on publication. Byline given. Submit query w/clips & SASE. Dot matrix, photocopies OK. Reports in 6–8 wks. Accepts nonfiction, photos (5x7 or larger B/W glossies/color prints/color transparencies). Pays "$0–$300 depending on length, content, & presentation, illustrations & photos, and whether or not is audience-specific (relating to Appaloosa horses and their owner/trainers). Accepts training, breeding, health and management, human interest and personality profiles as they relate to the Appaloosa breed." Guidelines/sample: $2.50+$1 post.
ANIMALS, RECREATION

Apple Books, 1370 E Georgia, Vancouver, BC V5L 2A8. Book publisher.
OTHER/UNSPECIFIED

Apple Press, 5536 SE Harlow, Milwaukie, OR 97222. 503-659-2475. Editor: J Majors. Publishes health sugar-free cookbooks, and travel related softcover books. Does not accept unsolicited submissions. Submit query w/ SASE. Dot matrix, photocopied, simultaneous, electronic, computer disk OK. Reports in 4 wks; publishes within 1 yr.
FOOD/COOKING, HEALTH, TRAVEL

Applegate Computer Enterprises, 4039 Oakman St S, Salem, OR 97302. 503-846-6742. Self-publisher of 1 softcover book a yr on personal computers. Print run: 2,000. Not a freelance market. Catalog available.
COMPUTERS

Applied Therapeutic Inc, PO Box 5077, Vancouver, WA 98668-5077. 206-253-7123. Contact: Caren Haldeman. Books on medial subjects.
HEALTH, MEDICAL

Apropos Magazine, 339 Telegraph Rd, Bellingham, WA 98226. Monthly of health, beauty, fashions for women. Sub $5/yr.
CONSUMER, FASHION, WOMEN

Arabian Horse Country, 4346 SE Division, Portland, OR 97206. Monthly.
ANIMALS, CRAFTS/HOBBIES, RECREATION

Arbutus Publications Ltd, PO Box 35070, Stn E, Vancouver, BC V6M 4G1. Book publisher.
BIOLOGY, OTHER/UNSPECIFIED

The Archer, 2285 Rogers Lane NW, Salem, OR 97304. 503-363-0712. Editor: Winifred Layton. Quarterly. Sub $8. Circ 200. Uses 45 freelance mss per issue. Pays copies on publication. Byline given. Submit ms, SASE. Reports in 1 month. Publishes in 6–12 mos. Poetry, not over 30 lines. Tips: "Be sure name, address are on each page. Too many ignore this necessity!" Sample $2.
POETRY

Arches, Office of Public Relations, University of Puget Sound, Tacoma, WA 98416. Editor: Gregory W Brewis. Periodical.
COLLEGE/UNIVERSITY

Architectural Lighting, 859 Willamette St, PO Box 10460, Eugene, OR, 97440. 503-343-1200. Editor: Charles Linn. Ads: Robert Joudanin. Monthly Magazine. Sub $49. Circ 50,000. Uses freelance material. Pays copies, other. Acquires 1st rights. Byline given. Submit query w/clips, ms, phone. Dot matrix, electronic subs OK. Reports in 1–3 mos. Accepts nonfiction. Guidelines available. Sample $5.
ARCHITECTURE

The Archive Press, 2101 192nd Ave SE, Issaquah, WA 98027. Book publisher.
OTHER/UNSPECIFIED

Arctic, Environmental Info & Data Center, University of Alaska, 707 A St, Anchorage, AK 99501. Book publisher.
ALASKA, NATURAL HISTORY, SCIENCE

Areopagitica Press Inc, 9999 SW Wilshire, Portland, OR 97225. 503-292-0745. Editor: Richard Abel. Ads: Michael Fox. Publishes 8 hardcover history-related books a yr. Accepts unsolicited submissions. Acquires all rights. Submit query w/clips. Dot matrix, photocopied OK. Reports in 3–4 wks.
AMERICAN HISTORY, GENERAL HISTORY

Argus Magazine, 2312 Third Ave, Seattle, WA 98121. Editor: John S Murray. 206-682-1212. Periodical.
OTHER/UNSPECIFIED

Argus Observer, Box 130, Ontario, OR 97914. 503-889-5387. Daily newspaper.
COMMUNITY

Argus Weekend, 14900 Interurban Ave S, Ste 290, Seattle, WA 98168. Contact: Sherri L Handley. Newspaper.
COMMUNITY

Ariel Publications, 14417 SE 19th Place, Bellevue, WA 98007. Book publisher.
OTHER/UNSPECIFIED

Arlington Times, PO Box 67, Arlington, WA 98223. 206-435-5757. Editor: Audrey Black. Weekly newspaper. Subs. $26/yr; circ 3,000. Uses freelance material. Byline given, pays on publication. Query w/SASE. Responds in 4 wks; publishes in 6 wks. Accepts news items, interviews that specifically apply to the local area. Sample $1.50.
COMMUNITY

ARMA Newsletter, 777 Pearl St, Eugene, OR, 97401. 503-687-5047. Editor: Karen Goldman. Irregularly published.
OTHER/UNSPECIFIED

Arnazella's Reading List, 3000 Landerholm Circle SE, Bellevue Community College, Bellevue, WA 98007. Annual literary magazine. Circ 400. Submit query, ms, w/SASE. Up to 1 yr response time. Accepts fiction, nonfiction, poetry, cartoons, photos (8x10 B&W), plays, art—fixed charcoal, pen & ink, calligraphy, photography of sculpture and pottery. Limited to entries from Northwest states, HI, CA, and WY. Guidelines available, sample $5.
ARTS, COLLEGE/UNIVERSITY, LITERARY

Arrowood Press Inc, PO Box 2100, Corvallis, OR 97339. 503-753-9539. Editor: Lex Runciman. Publisher of 1–2 hard- & softcover books per year of general literary interest. Unspecified payment schedule. Query w/SASE before submitting. Accepts nonfiction, fiction, poetry, plays.
FICTION, LITERATURE, POETRY

Arsenal, Pulp Press Book Publishers Ltd, Box 3868 MPO, Vancouver, BC V6B 3Z3. 604-687-4233. Contact: Brian Lam. Book publisher. Pays royalties. Query w/SASE (Int'l reply coupon if from USA), outline, sample chapters. Dot matrix, photocopied subs OK. Reports in 2 mos; publishes in 1 yr. Accepts: nonfiction, fiction, biography, environment, humor, Native American, feminism. Tips: specialize in short runs for a small, literary-oriented audience. Catalog available w/SASE.
BRITISH COLUMBIA, ENVIRONMENT/RESOURCES, FICTION

Art Gallery of Greater Victoria, 1040 Moss St, Victoria, BC V8V 4P1. Book publisher. Nonfiction. Guidelines available.
ARTS

Art West Magazine, PO Box 310, Bozeman, MT 59771. Editor: Helori M Graff. 406-586-5411. Bimonthly of wildlife and Western & American realism, aimed at collectors. Interested in historical as well as contemporary pieces. Uses photo-essays and profiles of artists, galleries and museums. Nonfiction, photos. Query w/SASE. Guidelines/sample available.
ARTS, COLLECTING, AMERICAN HISTORY

Artdog Press, 252 Memorial Crescent, Victoria, BC V8S 3J2. Book publisher.
OTHER/UNSPECIFIED

Arterial Magazine, 1202 E Pike St #697, Seattle, WA 98112. 206-325-9557. Editor: Sheila Jolley. Ads: Ernest Marquez. Monthly magazine. Sub $10. Uses freelance material. Byline given. Pays money, copies on publication. Query by phone. Dot matrix, photocopied subs OK. Responds in 2 mos; publishes in 3–4 mos. Accepts fiction, poetry, cartoons, photos (B&W negs), interviews, articles, plays, reviews, B&W illustrations. Guidelines available.
ARTS, ENVIRONMENT/RESOURCES, LITERARY

Artest Magazine, 301 – 310 Water, Vancouver, BC V6B 1B6.
CULTURE

Artist Trust, 512 Jones Bldg, 1331 Third Ave, Seattle, WA, 98101. 206-467-8734. Director: David Mendoza. Editor: Loch Adamson. Not-for-profit foundation, quarterly journal of information by, for, and about individual artists in all media in Washington State. Subs $10/yr; circ 15,000. Uses freelance material. Byline given, pays money for solicited material. Submit ms, query, clips, SASE. Dot matrix OK. Responds in 2 wks; publishes in 1–2 mos. Accepts nonfiction, interviews, B&W prints. Sample available.
ARTS, CULTURE, VISUAL ARTS

Artistamp News, Banana Productions, PO Box 3655, Vancouver, BC V6B 3Y8. 604-876-6764. Editor: Anna Banana. Circ 30; subs $150. Semiannual album of art stamps. Assignment only, query by phone.
ARTS, COLLECTING, VISUAL ARTS

Artists Notes, Lane Regional Arts Council, 411 High St, Eugene, OR, 97401. 503-485-2278. Editors: K Wagner/D Beauchamp. Monthly periodical. Sub $20–29. Query w/SASE.
ARTS, LITERARY

ArtistSearch, Montana Arts Council, New York Block, 48 N Last Chance Gulch, Helena, MT 59620. 406-444-6430. Editor: Julie Smith. Monthly arts publication. Circ 2,000. "This is a newsletter that includes space for artists to communicate with other artists. Very little poetry, fiction or essay publication."
ARTS, MONTANA

Artoonist Monthly, 2325 NE 42nd Ave, Portland, OR 97213. Periodical. Articles, cartoons.
ARTS, HUMOR

Arts BC, Cultural Services Branch, Parliament Bldg, Victoria, BC V8V 1X4. Editor: Dawn Wallace. Quarterly periodical.
ARTS, CULTURE, LITERARY

Arts & Crafts News, Burnaby Arts Council, 6528 Deer Lake Ave, Burnaby, BC V3B 1E7. Editor: Margaret Franz. Quarterly newsletter. Circ 10,000. Uses freelance material. Byline given, no pay. Submit query letter. Responds in 2 mos; publishes in 6 mos. Dot matrix, simultaneous submissions OK. Accepts: nonfiction, fiction, poetry, cartoons, news, photos, interviews, reviews, memoirs. Topics: arts, craft making and marketing. Sample $2.50.
ARTS, CRAFTS/HOBBIES, CULTURE

Arts East, Eastern Oregon Regional Arts Council, EOSC: Loso 220,1410 L Ave, LaGrande, OR 97850-2899. 503-962-3624. Editor: Anne Bell. Uses

freelance material. No pay. Byline given. Submit query letter, SASE. Dot matrix, photocopy OK. Accepts fiction, poetry, photos, interviews. Topics: art-related events, programs and profiles in Eastern Oregon, SE Washington and West Idaho.
ARTS, COLLEGE/UNIVERSITY, LITERARY

The Arts, King County Arts Commission, 506 2nd Ave #1115, Seattle, WA 98104. Editor/Ads: Joan Mann. 206-344-7580. Monthly newsletter of the King County Arts Commission. "We welcome articles, photographs, drawings, but such material must be accompanied by a SASE."
ARTS, CULTURE, WASHINGTON

Arts Victoria, Bay Publishing, #202 – 1026 Johnson St, Victoria, BC V8V 3N7. 604-386-1433. Bimonthly magazine of architecture, design, photography, literature, and the visual and performing arts. Circ 16,000.
ARCHITECTURE, ARTS, CULTURE

ASA Publications, 7005 132nd Pl SE, Renton, WA 98056-9236. Book publisher.
OTHER/UNSPECIFIED

Ascii, PO Box 222, Eagle River, AK 99577. Book publisher.
OTHER/UNSPECIFIED

Asia Cable, 1248 SW Larch, Portland, OR 97034. Editor: John Vezmar. Periodical.
ASIA, BUSINESS

Asian Music Publications, School of Music, University of Washington, Seattle, WA 98105. Book publisher.
ASIA, COLLEGE/UNIVERSITY, MUSIC

AOI News Digest, Associated Oregon Industries, 1149 Court NE, Salem, OR 97301. 503-588-0050. Editor: Jack Zimmerman. Ads: Mediamerica, 503-223-0304. Bimonthly newsletter. Does not use freelance material.
BUSINESS, OREGON

Associated Press, 1320 SW Broadway, Portland, OR 97201. 503-228-2169. News bureau.
OTHER/UNSPECIFIED

The Asterisk, Oregon Press Women Inc, PO Box 25354, Portland, OR, 97225-0354. Editor: Jean C Connolly. Quarterly newspaper for prize-winning high school journalists & photographers. Sample $2.
CHILDREN (BY/ABOUT), CHILDREN/TEEN, STUDENT

Astrology Night, Oregon Astrological Association, PO Box 6771, Portland, OR 97228. Periodical.
ASTROLOGY/SPIRITUAL, BUSINESS

At Your Fingertips, 2226 Third Ave, Ste 100, Seattle, WA 98121. 206-443-3220. Contact: Kathleen Dickenson. Publisher of art books.
ARTS, VISUAL ARTS

Athena Press, 431 E Main, Box 597, Athena, OR 97813. 503-566-3452. Weekly newspaper.
COMMUNITY

Author's Choice Monthly, Box 1227, Eugene, OR 97440. 503-344-6742. Editor: Kristine Kathryn Rusch. Ads: Dean W Smith. Science fiction and fantasy monthly. Uses freelance material. Byline given. Pays money, advance, royalties. Acquires 1st or anthology rights. Submit query letter, complete ms. Simultaneous subs OK. Responds in 2 mos; publishes in 8 mos. Accepts fiction, cartoons, nonfiction, photos. Guidelines available.
FANTASY/SCI FI, FICTION, WRITING

Auto Glass Journal, PO Box 12099, Seattle, WA 98102-0099. 206-322-5120. Editor: Burton Winters. Monthly trade magazine for the auto glass replacement industry. Uses how-to articles, history, profiles, trends, news. Query w/SASE.
BUSINESS

Auto Trader, PO Box 23369, Tigard, OR, 97223. 503-244-2886. Weekly periodical. Does not use freelance material.
CONSUMER

Autodidactic Press, PO Box 872749, Wasilla, AK 99687. 907-376-2932. Editor: Charles Hayes. Self-publisher of books. Does not accept unsolicited submissions.
EDUCATION, HOW-TO, PSYCHOLOGY

Automotive News of the Pacific Northwest, 14789 SE 82 Dr, Clackamas, OR, 97015-9624. Editor: Bradley Boyer. Monthly periodical.
CONSUMER

Aviation News, Oregon Aeronautics Division, 3040 25th St SE, Salem, OR, 97310. 503-378-4880. Editor: Ed Schoaps. Quarterly newsletter. Limited use of freelance material. Byline given, no pay. Submit query, SASE, phone. Disk sub OK. Responds in 2 wks; publishing time varies. Accepts news items, interviews, articles related to Oregon pilots, aviation. Guidelines, sample available.
AVIATION, GOVERNMENT, OREGON

Axis, Western States Chiropractic College, 2900 NE 132nd, Portland, OR 97230. 503-256-3180. Newspaper.
HEALTH, MEDICAL

Azure Press, PO Box 2164, 2417 Beacon Ave #3, Sidney, BC V8L 3S6. Book publisher.
OTHER/UNSPECIFIED

Baby, Creative Services International, 601 Main St, Vancouver, WA 98660. Editor: Mike Weber. 206-696-1150. Periodical.
CHILDREN (BY/ABOUT), OTHER/UNSPECIFIED

Bachelore, 1825 W Broadway, Vancouver, BC V6J 1Y5. Contact: Scott Stewart, editor. Bimonthly. Solicits freelance submissions relevant to the singles life-style, ages 18–30. Topics: sports, love and romance, food, wine, recreation, humor, etc. Tips: 1,000–2,500 words. Pays 10¢/wd, but negotiable.
ENTERTAINMENT, RECREATION

Back Door Travel, 120 4th Ave N, Edmonds, WA 98020. Editor: Mike McGregor. 206-771-8303. Quarterly on budget travel, "helping people to travel as 'temporary locals'…interested in personal accounts about meeting people, traveling on a budget, discovering new places." Circ 6,000. Sub free. Uses 2–3 mss per issue. Payment: Copies. Byline given. Rights purchased: 1st, 2nd, 3rd. Query with ms, SASE. Dot matrix, photocopies, simultaneous submissions OK. Nonfiction, poetry, photos, cartoons. "Articles should be practical, how-to, destination-oriented travel pieces…Our readers range from just planning a first trip to just returning from the tenth trip. Information about alternate modes of travel (bicycle, trekking) are welcome." Sample Free.
TRAVEL

Backeddy Books, PO Box 301, Cambridge, ID 83610. Book publisher. Old west.
OLD WEST, OTHER/UNSPECIFIED

Bad Haircut, 3115 SW Roxbury St, Seattle, WA 98126. Editors: Kim & Ray Goforth. Irregular journal. Subs $14/4 issues; circ 1,000. Uses freelance material. Pays copies on publication; acquires 1st rights. Byline given. Submit ms/SASE, biographical cover letter. Reports in 1–2 mos; publishes in 2–8 mos. Accepts: fiction, nonfiction, poetry, news items, biography, interviews, photos, cartoons. Topics: politics, human rights and environmental issues. Tips: poems in batches of 5; prefers fiction of 2,000 words, 5,000 max. Guidelines available for SASE. Sample $4.
COUNTER CULTURE, PEACE, POLITICS

Bainbridge Review, PO Box 10817, Bainbridge Island, WA 98110. 206-842-6613. Weekly newspaper.
COMMUNITY

Baker Democrat-Herald, PO Box 807, Baker OR 97814. 503-523-3673. Editor: Dean Brickey. Ads: Lynette Perry. Daily newspaper. Circ 3,500. Uses freelance material. Byline given, pays money on publication. Submit query letter, SASE, phone. Responds in 2 wks; publishing time varies. Accepts: news items, interviews, articles, op/ed. Photos $5 ea. Sample 35¢.
COMMUNITY, NW/REGIONAL HISTORY, RECREATION

Balcom Books, 320 Bawden St #401, Ketchikan, AK 99901. Book publisher.
OTHER/UNSPECIFIED

Ballard News-Tribune, 2208 NW Market, Seattle, WA 98017. 206-783-1244. Weekly newspaper.
COMMUNITY

Bandon Historical Society, PO Box 737, Bandon, OR 97411. Historical publisher on Bandon, Oregon and environs.
NW/REGIONAL HISTORY

Bandon Western World, Box 248, Bandon, OR 97411. 503-347-2423. Weekly newspaper.
COMMUNITY

Barbarian Press, 12375 Ainsworth Rd, RR #5, Mission, BC V2V 5X4. 604-826-8089. Editors: Jan & Crispin Elsted. Publisher of limited edition books. Accepts unsolicited submissions. Pays in copies on publication. Submit query w/clips, ms, SASE. Dot matrix, photocopied OK. Reports in 6 wks; publishing time varies. Accepts nonfiction, poetry, translations. Topics: Block printing, especially wood engraving, emphasis is on quality of production & text. Photos — suitable graphic media for letterpress.
LITERATURE, POETRY, PUBLISHING/PRINTING

Barclay Press, 600 E 3rd S, Newberg, OR 97132. 503-538-7345. Book publisher. Submit query letter, outline, sample chapters, SASE. Photocopy OK. Responds in 1 mo. Topics: spiritual, compatible with the convictions of the Friends (Quaker) Church. Catalog available.
PEACE, RELIGION, SOCIETY

Bardavon Books, PO Box 1378, Ashland, OR, 97520. 503-773-7035. Contact: James L Rodgers. Book publisher. Assignment only, does not accept unsolicited mss. Query w/SASE. Topics: Elizabethan (primarily Shakespearean) literature.
DRAMA, LITERATURE

Barleycorn Books, 290 SW Tualatin Loop, West Linn, OR 97068. Book publisher.
OTHER/UNSPECIFIED

Barlow Press, PO Box 5403, Helena, MT 59604. 406-449-7310. Editor: Russell B Hill. Book publisher. Does not accept unsolicited mss. Pays by arrangement. Submit query w/SASE. Dot matrix, photocopies, simultaneous, computer disk OK. Reports in 2 mos. Publishes by arrangement. Accepts nonfiction, fiction, poetry. Topics: traditional fiction set in the modern or historic Northwest; also interested in nonfiction compilations of letters, diaries, clippings, journals, etc from the Northwest.
BOOK ARTS/BOOKS, FICTION, MONTANA

Barometer, Western Wood Products Association, 1500 Yeon Bldg, Portland, OR 97204. Weekly which publishes statistical reports. Not a freelance market.
ABSTRACTS/INDICES, BUSINESS

Basement Press, 215 Burlington, Billings, MT 59101. 406-256-3588. Contact: Dan Struckman. Semiannual magazine. Sub $10/4 issues. Circ 200. Freelance material accepted. Query with complete ms and SASE. Photocopies and dot matrix submissions OK. Responds in 30 days; publishes within 1 year. Buys 1st rights. Gives byline; pays in copies on publication. Uses fiction, poetry, cartoons, interviews, op/ed, articles, reviews, and memoirs. Back issues $5.
HUMOR, MONTANA, POETRY

Bassett & Brush, W 4108 Francis Ave, Spokane, WA 99205. Book publisher.
OTHER/UNSPECIFIED

Marlene Y Bastian, 668 McVey Ave #115, Lake Oswego, OR 97034. Self-publisher. Not a freelance market.
CONSUMER, HOW-TO

Maryanne Bauer Productions, PO Box 02467, Portland, OR 97202. Book publisher.
RECREATION

Baum Publications, 831 Helmcken, Vancouver, BC V6B 2E6. Book publisher.
OTHER/UNSPECIFIED

Bay Press, 115 W Denny Way, Seattle, WA 98119. 206-284-5913. Editor: Thatcher Bailey. Publishes 3–6 art and cultural criticism books per yr. Press run 5,000. Pays 5% cover/advance and payments twice yearly. Reports in 4

wks. Publishes within 1 yr. Submit query, SASE. Dot matrix, photocopied OK. Accepts nonfiction only. Catalog available.
CULTURE

Bayless Enterprises Inc, 501 SW 7th St, Renton, WA 98055-2918. Contact: George Bayless. 206-622-6395. Self-publisher of two softcover maritime books per yr. Print run 7,500. Not a freelance market.
NW/REGIONAL HISTORY, MARITIME, RECREATION

BCS Educational Aids Inc, PO Box 100, Bothell, WA 98206. Book publisher.
EDUCATION

Beacon, University of Portland, 5000 N Willamette Blvd, Portland, OR 97203. 503-283-7376. Student newspaper. No pay. Byline given. Opinion pieces for editorial page and articles on entertainment in the Portland area considered. Preference given to students and faculty. Query w/SASE.
COLLEGE/UNIVERSITY, EDUCATION, ENTERTAINMENT

Beacon, Southwest Oregon Community College, Coos Bay, OR 97420. 503-888-2525 ext 304. College literary magazine. Editor could change yearly. SASE for guidelines.
COLLEGE/UNIVERSITY, FICTION, OREGON

Beacon Hill News, 2720 S Hanford S, Seattle, WA 98144. 206-723-1300. Weekly newspaper.
COMMUNITY

Bear Creek Publications, 2507 Minor Ave E, Seattle, WA 98102. Editor: Kathy Shea. Publisher of 1–2 nonfiction, softcover originals per year for parents/expectant parents. Press run: 2,000. Accepts freelance material. Query with outline, sample chapters, SASE. Photocopies, simultaneous subs OK. Reports in 1 month. Publishes in 6 mos. Payment and rights negotiable.
FAMILY, HOW-TO

The Bear Facts, The Citizens' Utility Board of Oregon, 921 SW Morrison #550, Portland, OR 97205-2734. 503-227-1984. Consumer affairs periodical.
CONSUMER, OREGON

Bear Grass Press, Box 211, Robson, BC V0G 1X0. 604-365-6549. Contact: Kathy Armstrong. Publishes hard- & softcover, subsidy books. Accepts unsolicited submissions. Pays copies, royalties. Acquires 1st rights. Submit query letter, outline, sample chapters, SASE, phone. Dot matrix, photocopied, simultaneous, disk (Mac) subs OK. Responds in 2 mos; publishes in 12–18 mos. Accepts fiction, poetry, biography, nonfiction, memoirs. SASE for catalog.
BIOGRAPHY, FICTION, POETRY

Bear Tribe Publishing, PO Box 9176, Spokane, WA 99209. 509-326-6561. Contact: Matt Ryan. Publisher of books on environment, Native American philosophy. 3–6 titles per yr. Query w/SASE.
ENVIRONMENT/RESOURCES, NATIVE AMERICAN

The Bear Wallow Publishing Company, 57919 High Valley Rd, Union, OR 97883. 503-562-5687. Editor: Jerry Gildemeister. Self-publisher. Does not accept unsolicited submissions.
AMERICANA, AMERICAN HISTORY, OLD WEST

Beartooth Networks Inc, Box 1742, Billings, MT, 59103. Editor: Lee Lemke. Book publisher.
OTHER/UNSPECIFIED

Beautiful America Publishing Company, PO Box 646, Wilsonville, OR 97070. 503-682-0173. Editor: Beverly Paul. Ads: Bobbi Humphries. Publisher of 12 hard- & softcover books per yr. No unsolicited mss. Pays copies, royalties, advance on acceptance. Acquires 1st rights. Submit query letter, outline, SASE. Accepts nonfiction, children's, poetry, photos. Catalog available.
ARCHITECTURE, CHILDREN (BY/ABOUT), GARDENING

Beautiful British Columbia, 929 Ellery St, Victoria, BC V9A 7B4. Editor: Bryan McGill. 604-384-5456. Periodical.
BRITISH COLUMBIA

Beaver Briefs, Willamette Valley Genealogical Society, PO Box 2083, Salem, OR 97308. Quarterly.
GENEALOGY, OREGON

Beaver Publications, 15605 NW Cornell Rd, Beaverton, OR 97006. Book publisher.
OTHER/UNSPECIFIED

Beaverton Arts Commission Newsletter, PO Box 4755, Beaverton, OR 97075. 503-644-2191.
ARTS

Beaverton Business Advocate, Beaverton Area Chamber of Commerce, 4800 SW Griffith Dr #100, Beaverton, OR 97005. Editor: Jerri Doctor. 503-644-0123. Periodical.
BUSINESS

Beef Industry News, Oregon Cattlemens Association, 1000 NE Multnomah, Portland, OR 97232. 503-281-3811. Periodical.
AGRICULTURE/FARMING, BUSINESS, OREGON

Before Columbus Review, Before Columbus Foundation, American Ethnic Studies, GN-80, University of Washington, Seattle, WA 98195. 206-543-4264. Contact: Shawn Wong. Promotes the efforts of minority and multicultural writers and topics. Seeking book reviews, articles, and critical comments about multicultural literature. Query w/SASE.
LITERATURE, MINORITIES/ETHNIC, WRITING

Before the Sun, PO Box 14007, Salem, OR 97309. 503-399-5184. Periodical. Circ 400. Sub $2.95. Byline given. Rights purchased: 1st. Query w/ SASE. Dot matrix, photocopies OK. Nonfiction, fiction, poetry, plays, cartoons, other reproducible artwork. "Topics range anywhere from science fiction to political essays. Our main objective is to provide a variety of mss that could be read by anyone. Length not to exceed 3,000 wds with 1,500 the average." Photos: high contrast B&W. "We'd like to see BTS on a waiting room table. Stories should be short/clean." Sample: $2.95.
DRAMA, FICTION, POETRY

Beginning Press, 5418 S Brandon, Seattle, WA 98118. 206-723-6300. Publishes 3 softcover original books a yr. Press run: avg 6,000. Does not accept unsolicited submissions.
CONSUMER, HEALTH, RELIGION

Bellevue Art Museum, Bellevue Sq, 3rd Fl, 10310 NE 4th St, Bellevue, WA 98004. Book publisher.
ARTS, GENERAL HISTORY

Bellevue Journal-American, 4339 134th Place SE, Bellevue, WA, 98004. 206-641-4130. Editor: Joanne Kotker. Newspaper.
OTHER/UNSPECIFIED

Bellingham Herald, PO Box 1277, Bellingham, WA 98227. 206-676-2600. Daily newspaper.
COMMUNITY

The Bellingham Review, The Signpost Press, 1007 Queen St, Bellingham, WA 98226. 206-734-9781. Editor: Susan Hilton. Semiannual magazine of poetry, drama, art, fiction. Sub $5/yr; circ 600. Pays 1 copy + sub on publication. Byline given, acquires 1st rights. Submit complete ms, SASE. Photocopy, simultaneous submission OK. Reports in 1–2 mos; publishes in 3–12 mos. Accepts fiction, poetry, photos, plays. Guidelines available, sample $2.
DRAMA, FICTION, POETRY

Bellowing Ark, PO Box 45637, Seattle, WA 98145. 206-545-8302. Editor: Robert R Ward. Bimonthly journal. Sub $12/yr; circ 1,000. Uses about 30 mss per issue. Pays in copies, byline given acquires all rights. Submit ms, SASE. Responds in 2–6 wks; publishes in 1–3 mos. Accepts nonfiction, fiction poetry, photos (B&W), memoirs. Topics: "literary works in the American Romantic tradition, ie, think of Roethke, Whittier, Emerson, Lindsay. Mostly poetry, fiction and serializations...but other forms sometimes used (plays, essays). Some short autobiography used for "Literal Lives" section...we do not hesitate to publish newcomers if the work is right." Sample $2.85. "Do not send query letter. Do not request guidelines."
FICTION, POETRY

Bellowing Ark Press, PO Box 45637, Seattle, WA 98145. 206-545-8302. Editor: Robert R Ward. Publishes softcover original books. Not accepting unsolicited submissions at present. Pays royalties. Publishes fiction, poetry. Catalog available.
FICTION, POETRY

Ben-Simon Publications, PO Box 318, Brentwood Bay, BC, V0S 1A0. Publishes 1–2 hard- & softcover originals, reprints a yr. Press run: 1,000-3,000. Accepts unsolicited submissions. Submit query, sample chap; SASE. Dot matrix, photocopied OK. Reports ASAP. Accepts nonfiction. Catalog available.
OTHER/UNSPECIFIED

Bench Press, 3100 Evergreen Point Rd, Bellevue, WA 98004. Book publisher.
OTHER/UNSPECIFIED

Bend Bulletin, 1526 NW Hill St, Bend, OR 97701. 603-382-1811. Daily newspaper.
COMMUNITY, OTHER/UNSPECIFIED

Benton Bulletin, Box 351, Philomath, OR 97370. 503-929-3043. Weekly newspaper.
COMMUNITY

Berry Fine Publishing Company, 5963 Walina SE, Salem, OR 97301. Book publisher.
OTHER/UNSPECIFIED

Berry Patch Press, 3350 NW Luray Terrace, Portland, OR 97210. Book publisher.
OTHER/UNSPECIFIED

Beynch Press Publishing Co, 1928 SE Ladd Ave, Portland, OR 97214. Contact: Alyce Cornyn-Selby. Self-publisher, not a freelance market.
BUSINESS, HUMOR

Beyond Basals Inc, 586 University Dr, Pocatello, ID 83201. 208-233-9717. Editor: Gale Sherman. Self-publisher of educational material for teachers. Not a freelance market.
EDUCATION

Beyond Words Publishing Inc, Pumpkin Ridge Rd, Rt 3 Box 492B, Hillsboro, OR 97124. 503-647-0140. Editor: Cynthia Black. Publishes 5–10 hard- & softcover books a yr. Accepts unsolicited submissions. Payment negotiated, on publication. Acquires all rights. Submit query w/clips, SASE, phone. Mac computer disk OK. Reports in 3 mos. Publishes in 6 mos. Accepts nonfiction, fiction, photos, children's. Topics: self-help, New Age.
HEALTH, PHOTOGRAPHY

Bible Temple Publications, 7545 NE Glisan St, Portland, OR 97213. Book publisher.
RELIGION

Bicentennial Era Enterprises, PO Box 1148, Scappoose, OR 97056. 503-684-3937. Self-publisher of softcover books. Not a freelance market.
ECONOMICS, GOVERNMENT, POLITICS

The Bicycle Paper, 7901 - 168th Ave NE #103, Seattle, WA 98111. 206-882-0706. Editor: Dave Shaw. Ads: Paul Clark. Monthly tabloid. Sub $8/yr; circ 7,500. Uses freelance material. Byline given, pays money on publication, acquires 1st rights. Submit query letter, ms, SASE, phone. Photocopied sub OK. Responds in 1–4 wks; publishes in 1–3 mos. Accepts news, articles, interviews, photos (B&W, $15/photo printed). Topic: bicycling. Tips: "readership is sophisticated and knowledgeable about bicycling; articles must reflect same level of sophistication." Guidelines available.
BICYCLING, SPORTS

Big Rain, PO Box 11902, Eugene, OR 97440. 503-484-3954. Contact: Clint Frakes. Literary arts magazine. Accepts submissions (unpublished work) in poetry, prose, essay/manifesto and visual. $50 editor's award for most spirited piece. Query w/SASE.
FICTION, LITERARY, POETRY

Big Sky Business Journal, PO Box 3263, Billings, MT, 59103. Editor: Evelyn Pyburn. Newspaper.
BUSINESS

The Big Timber Pioneer, PO Box 190, Big Timber, MT, 59011. Editor: Becky Oberly. Newspaper.
COMMUNITY, OTHER/UNSPECIFIED

Bigfork Eagle, PO Box 406, Bigfork, MT, 59911. 406-837-5131. Newspaper.
COMMUNITY

Bigoni Books, 4121 NE Highland, Portland, OR 97211.
OTHER/UNSPECIFIED

BikeReport, PO Box 8308, Missoula, MT 59801. Editor: Daniel D'Ambrosio. 406-721-1776. Published 9 times a year for touring bicyclists. Circ 18,000. Sub $22. Uses 9 mss per issue. Pays money, copies on publication. Byline given. Acquires 1st rights. Query with ms, SASE. Dot matrix, photocopies OK. Nonfiction, fiction, cartoons. "We like imaginative pieces that use cycling as a starting point to investigate or reveal other topics." They could include anything relating to tours in the USA, foreign countries, or any essay with cycling as a theme. Guidelines available; sample/$1.
BICYCLING, FICTION, TRAVEL

The Billings Times, 2919 Montana Ave, Billings, MT, 59101. Newspaper.
COMMUNITY

Binford & Mort Publishing, Box 42368, Portland, OR 97242. Contact: Paula Gardenier. 503-221-0866. Publisher of 10–12 hard- & softcover books and reprints per year on themes of Western Americana, history, biography, travel, recreation and reference. Does some subsidy publishing. Payment: variable advance to established authors; 10% royalties. Query w/SASE. Dot matrix OK. Reports in 2–4 mos. Publishes in 1 yr. Nonfiction: on above themes, with emphasis on NW/Pacific Coast. Fiction: only if heavily historical.
BIOGRAPHY, NW/REGIONAL HISTORY, RECREATION

Bingo Today, Dart Publishing Inc, 7900 SE 28th St #200, Mercer Island, WA 98040. 206-232-6071. Editor: Rim Miksys. Semimonthly for bingo players/managers. Sub $9/6 mos; circ 20,000. Not a freelance market. Sample $1.
ENTERTAINMENT, RECREATION

Bioenergy Bulletin, Bonneville Power Administration, PO Box 3621, Portland, OR, 97208-3621. Editor: Tom White. Bimonthly periodical.
GOVERNMENT

Bippity-Boppity Books, 915 W 12th, Spokane, WA, 99204. Book publisher.
OTHER/UNSPECIFIED

Birds' Meadow Publishing Company Inc, 1150 N Olson Rd, Coupeville, WA 98239. Book publisher.
OTHER/UNSPECIFIED

Black Current Press, Gutenberg Dump, PO Box 1149, Haines, AK, 99827. Book Publisher, poetry.
POETRY

Black Heron Press, PO Box 95676, Seattle, WA 98145. 206-363-5210. Contact: Jerry Gold. Publisher of 2 hard- & softcover fiction books per yr. Press run 500–5,000. Accepts unsolicited mss. Pays royalties. Submit ms w/SASE. Dot matrix, photocopies, simultaneous OK. Reports in 2–4 mos. Publishes in 18 mos. Accepts nonfiction, fiction. Tips: emotionally moving without being sentimental or intellectually stimulating." Catalog with SASE.
FICTION, LITERATURE, MILITARY/VETS

Black Powder Times, PO Box 842, Mount Vernon, WA 98273. 206-336-2969. For black powder firearms enthusiasts.
CRAFTS/HOBBIES, RECREATION, SPORTS

Black Sheep Newsletter, Rt 1 Box 288, Scappoose, OR 97056. Editor: Peggy Lundquist. Quarterly newsletter, books. Circ 2500. Sub $10/yr US. Uses freelance material. Pays copies on publication. Acquires all rights. Byline given. Submit ms. Dot matrix, photocopies OK. Accepts nonfiction, photos (B/W & color). Topics: animal fiber raising and use of animal fibers. Sample $2.50.
ANIMALS, CRAFTS/HOBBIES

Blackfish Books, 1851 Moore Ave, Burnaby, BC.
OTHER/UNSPECIFIED

Blackfoot Morning News, 27 NW Main, Blackfoot, ID 83221. 208-529-4919. Newspaper.
COMMUNITY

John and Dottie Blake Assoc Inc, Box 785, White Salmon, WA 98672. 509-493-2820. Self-publisher only. Not a freelance market.
OTHER/UNSPECIFIED

Blatant Image: a Magazine of Feminist Photography, 2000 King Mountain Trail, Sunny Valley, OR, 97497-9799. Irregular periodical.
FEMINISM, PHOTOGRAPHY

BLM News, Oregon & Washington, Bureau of Land Management, PO Box 2965, Portland, OR, 97208. 503-280-7031. US Government agency periodical. Not a freelance market.
FORESTRY, GOVERNMENT, PUBLIC AFFAIRS

The Bloodletter, Friends of Mystery, PO Box 8251, Portland, OR 97207. Editor: Debbara Hendrix. Newsletter published 3–5 times a yr. Circ 500. Accepts unsolicited freelance material. Byline given. Photocopied OK. Accepts nonfiction, cartoons. Topics: any aspect of mystery. Sample available.
FICTION

Blue Begonia Press, 225 S 15th Ave, Yakima, WA 98902. 509-452-9748. Editor: Jim Bodeen. A fine hand letterpress publisher/printer of poetry originals. Press run: 250–300. Accepts poetry for two books per yr. "We don't encourage submissions. There's too much to do as it is. We're not interested in adding another book to a poet's resume…A manuscript needs to be important enough for one person working nights to want to do it by hand." Pays in copies on publication. Query w/SASE. Catalog and samples available.
POETRY

Blue Heron Press, PO Box 5182, Bellingham, WA 98227. 206-671-1155. Contact: Mitch Lesoing/Carol Anderson. Publisher of softcover books. No unsolicited mss. Query with clips, SASE. Reports in 6–8 wks. Publishes in 6–12 mos. Accepts nonfiction, fiction, photos. Topics: computer education materials, children's books, outdoor recreation (boating, hiking, fishing). Tips: stock photos & graphics sometimes purchased at std rates.
CHILDREN/TEEN, COMPUTERS, RECREATION

Blue Heron Publishing Inc, Rt 3 Box 376, Hillsboro, OR 97124. 503-621-3911. Contact: Dennis Stovall/Linny Stovall. Publishes 1–3 writing related books under Media Weavers imprint (Writer's Northwest Handbook and Writer's NW, a quarterly newspaper). Publishes 3–6 young adult novels, reprints and originals per year. Publishes the Walt Morey Adventure Library (reprints from the author of Gentle Ben). Interested in doing other reprints of classic young adult fiction, and entertaining queries w/SASE on multi-ethnic fiction for young readers, especially from NW authors. Will also consider queries with outlines, sample chapters, and SASE for books aimed at publishers, librarians, booksellers, writers, editors, and teachers of writing, English, and journalism.
CHILDREN/TEEN, FICTION, WRITING

Blue Mountain Eagle, 741 W Main St, Box 69, John Day, OR 97845. 503-575-0710. Weekly newspaper.
COMMUNITY

Blue Raven Publishing, PO Box 5641, Bellevue, WA 98006. 206-643-2203. Book publisher.
OTHER/UNSPECIFIED

Blue Scarab Press, 234 S 8th St, Pocatello, ID, 83201. Editor: Harald Wyndham. Publisher of poetry and fiction. Query w/SASE.
FICTION, LITERARY, POETRY

Blue Unicorn Press, PO Box 40300, Portland, OR 97240. 503-238-4766. Contact: Wanda Z Larson. Publisher of books of prose and poetry. Not accepting queries or submissions at this time. Catalog available w/SASE.
FICTION, POETRY

Blue Water Publishing, PO Box 230893, Tigard, OR 97224. 503-684-9749. Editor: Brian Crissey. Ads: Pam Meyer. Publishes original books. Accepts unsolicited submissions. Submit query letter, phone, outline, sample chapters or ms/SASE. Dot matrix, photocopies, simultaneous, electronic/modem,

computer disk OK. Reports in 4 wks; publishes in 1 yr. Accepts nonfiction, fiction, poetry. Topics: New Age and UFOs.
ASTROLOGY/SPIRITUAL, NATIVE AMERICAN, NEW AGE

Blues Notes, PO Box 8872, Portland, OR 97207. 503-285-3470. Editor: Ardis Hedrick. Ads: Dave Clingan. Monthly newspaper. Sub $12/yr. Circ 4,000. Uses 2–3 freelance mss per issue. Byline given. Submit ms. Dot matrix, photocopied OK. Reports in 2 wks. Publishes in 2–6 wks. Accepts nonfiction, photos. Topics: blues music, legends, performers, interviews, reviews. Sample $1.
CULTURE, ENTERTAINMENT, MUSIC

Bluespaper, 3438 SE Caruthers St, Portland, OR 97214. 503-231-5605. Editor: Mark Goldfarb. Quarterly. Sub free. Circ 10,000.
MUSIC, NORTHWEST

The Boag Foundation Ltd, 576 Keith Rd, West Vancouver, BC V7T 1L7. Publishes socialist books on social and historical topics. Query w/SASE.
GENERAL HISTORY, SOCIALIST/RADICAL, SOCIETY

Boat World, 205 – 1810 Alberni, Vancouver, BC V6G 1B3. Magazine. No submission into.
BOATING

Boating News, 26 Coal Harbour Wharf, 566 Cardero St, Vancouver, BC V6G 2W6. Periodical.
BOATING, OUTDOOR, RECREATION

Boating News, PO Box 61411, Vancouver, WA 98666. 503-286-6408. Contact: Kim Matthews, editor. Ads: Geoff Hetrick. Monthly newspaper. Sub $8/yr. Welcomes freelance material. Submit ms/SASE.
BOATING, OUTDOOR, RECREATION

Bob Book Publishers, 22910 Bland Circle, West Linn, OR, 97068. Editor: Bobby Lynn Maslen. Publisher of illustrated books for very young readers.
CHILDREN/TEEN

Boise Business Today, Boise Chamber of Commerce, PO Box 2368, Boise, ID 83701. Editor: Lee Campbell. Monthly devoted to issues of interest to the Boise area business community.
BUSINESS, IDAHO

Boise Cascade Quarterly, Boise Cascade Corporation, One Jefferson Square, Boise, ID 83728. Editor: Don Hicks. Corporate quarterly. Circ 100,000.
BUSINESS, FORESTRY

Boise Idaho Register, PO Box 2835, Boise, ID 83701. Newspaper.
COMMUNITY

Boise Magazine–Idaho Annual Inc, 211 W State St, Boise, ID 83702. 208-344-4642. Editor: Alan Minskoff. Ads: Cindy Mack. Magazine published 8 times a yr. Sub $15.95/yr; circ 4,700. Uses freelance material. Pays money on publication. Acquires 1st rights. Byline given. Submit query letter, SASE. Photocopied, dot matrix subs OK. Reports in 1–2 wks; publishes in 2 mos. Accepts nonfiction, fiction, poetry, news items, reviews, photos ($20 5x7). Topics: city/regional, not connected with any government. Guidelines available. Sample $3.
COMMUNITY, IDAHO

BSU Focus, Boise State University, 1910 University Dr, Boise, ID 83725. 208-385-1577. Editor: Larry Burke. Quarterly magazine. Circ 43,000. Accepts unsolicited/freelance mss. Pays money on publication. Rights purchased: 1st. Byline given. Query w/clips. Dot matrix, photocopy, simultaneous, etc OK. Reports in 1 wk. Publishes in 3–4 mos. Accepts nonfiction, many topics. Sample.
COLLEGE/UNIVERSITY

Boise State University Western Writers Series, Department of English, Boise State University, 1910 University Dr, Boise, ID 83725. 208-385-1246. Contact: James H Maguire. Publisher of books of "critical introductions to the lives and works of authors who have made a significant contribution to the literature of the American West." Print run: 1,000. "Those who write for us are usually members of the Western Literature Association or read the association's journal, Western American Literature." No pay. Rights pur-

chased: All. Query w/SASE. Photocopies OK. Reports in 1 month. Publishes in 5–10 yrs. Guidelines & catalog available.
BIOGRAPHY, COLLEGE/UNIVERSITY, LITERARY

BSU/Search, Boise State University, 1910 University Dr, Boise, ID 83725. Editor: Larry Burke. Semiannual. Circ 1,000.
COLLEGE/UNIVERSITY

Bold Brass Studios & Publications, PO Box 77101, Vancouver, BC V5R 5T4. Book publisher.
OTHER/UNSPECIFIED

Bonanza Publishing, 62560 Stenkamp Rd, Bend, OR, 97701. Editor: Rick Steber. Book publisher, hard- & softcover on the old west history. Press run: 5,000–10,000. Does not accept unsolicited submissions.
OLD WEST, AMERICAN HISTORY, NW/REGIONAL HISTORY

Bonnie Scherer Publications, 1021 Alderson Ave, Billings, MT 59102. 406-245-7289. Editor: Mary Roberts. Self-publisher only of books about children. Not a freelance market.
CHILDREN (BY/ABOUT)

Book Dealers World, North American Bookdealers Exchange, PO Box 606, Cottage Grove, OR 97424. 503-942-7455. Contact: Al Galasso. Quarterly magazine for mail order book promotion. Subs: $25US, $30CDN per year for nonmembers.
BOOK ARTS/BOOKS, PUBLISHING/PRINTING

The Book Shop/Children's Newsletter, The Book Shop, 908 Main St, Boise, ID 83702. Editor/Ads: Lori Benton. 208-342-2659. Biannual newsletter reviewing new children's titles, mostly read by parents, teachers, and librarians. Circ 250. Sub free. Uses 2 mss per issue. Byline given. Query with ms, SASE. Phone queries, photocopies OK. "We are interested in book reviews only. Copy should be limited to seven paragraphs." Guidelines and sample available.
CHILDREN/TEEN, LITERARY

Bookletter Newsletter, Bookloft, 107 E Main St, Enterprise, OR, 97828.
BOOK ARTS/BOOKS

Bookmark, Library, University of Idaho, Moscow, ID 83843. Editors: Richard Beck/Gail Eckwright. Semiannual periodical. Circ 1,000.
BOOK ARTS/BOOKS, LITERARY, LITERATURE

BookNotes, PO Box 3877, Eugene, OR 97403. 503-655-5010. Editor: Cliff Martin. Quarterly provides marketing help for small publishers, self-publishers. Not a freelance market. Sample $5.
BUSINESS, PUBLISHING/PRINTING, WRITING

Boredom Magazine, PO Box 85817, Seattle, WA, 98145. 206-525-7947. Editor: Patrick McCabe. Magazine of poetry, art, fiction, nonfiction, cartoons, criticism, reviews, novel excerpts, plays, news, etc. Uses photos. Pays in copies. Query w/SASE.
FICTION, LITERARY, POETRY

Botany Books, 1518 Hayward Ave, Bremerton, WA 98310. 206-377-6489. Self-publisher of softcover books, how-to and gardening. Accepts no mss.
GARDENING, HOW-TO

Bowen Island Historians, RR 1, Bowen Island, BC V0N 1G0. Book publisher.
CANADIAN HISTORY

Box Dog, PO Box 9609, Seattle, WA, 98109. Editor: Craig Joyce. Semiannual magazine. Subs. $5/yr; circ 500. Accepts unsolicited submissions. Byline given, pays copies. Submit query letter, outline, SASE. Responds in 1 mo; publishing time varies. Accepts fiction, poetry, interviews, articles, reviews, photos, cartoons. Catalog available, sample $2.
AVANT-GARDE/EXPERIMENTAL, FILM/VIDEO, LITERATURE

Box Dog Press, PO Box 9609, Seattle, WA, 98109. Editor: Craig Joyce. Publishes softcover books. Accepts unsolicited submissions. Byline given, pays copies. Submit query letter, outline, SASE. Responds in 1 mo; publishing time varies. Accepts fiction, poetry, photos, cartoons. Catalog available.
AVANT-GARDE/EXPERIMENTAL, FILM/VIDEO, LITERATURE

Box Dog Press, PO Box 9609, Seattle, WA, 98109. 206-454-4078. Publishes softcover books. Press run: 40–100. Accepts unsolicited submissions. Reports in 4 wks. Accepts fiction, poetry, photos, cartoons. Catalog available.
FICTION, HUMOR, POETRY

Bozeman Chronicle, 32 S Rouse, Bozeman, MT, 59715. 406-587-4491. Editor: Rob Dean. Daily newspaper.
COMMUNITY

Braemar Books Ltd, PO Box 4142, Stn A, Victoria, BC V8X 3X4. Book publisher.
OTHER/UNSPECIFIED

Braemar Books, PO Box 25296, Portland, OR 97225. 503-292-4226. Contact: Craig Patillo. Self-publisher of 1 softcover book per year for record collectors, music stores, radio stations. Print run: 500. Not a freelance market.
COLLECTING, LITERATURE, MUSIC

The Bread and Butter Chronicles, Seven Buffaloes Press, PO Box 249, Big Timber, MT 59011. Editor: Art Cuelho. Semiannual with essays and columns on contemporary American farmers and ranchers. Sub $2.50. Query w/SASE. Sample: $1 w/SASE.
AGRICULTURE/FARMING, MONTANA, NORTHWEST

Breitenbush Publications, PO Box 82157, Portland, OR 97282. 503-230-1900. Contact: Tom Booth. Publisher of 8–12 hard- & softcover originals and reprints per yr. Pays advance, royalties. Query with outline or synopsis, sample chapters, SASE. Photocopies OK. Reports in 8–10 wks; publishes in 12–16 mos. Accepts nonfiction: human interest, natural history, social commentary, memoirs — creative and literary; fiction: author must be represented in magazines, 250–300 page limit; poetry: very limited. Catalog available $1.
FICTION, LITERARY, POETRY

Bremerton Sun, PO Box 259, Bremerton, WA 98310. 206-377-3711. Daily newspaper.
COMMUNITY

Brewster Quad-City Herald, PO Box 37, Brewster, WA 98812. 509-689-2507. Weekly newspaper.
COMMUNITY

Brick Lung Press, PO Box 12268, Seattle, WA 98102. Chapbook publisher. Book publisher.
LITERARY

Bricolage, c/o Creative Writing Office, Department of English, GN-30, University of Washington, Seattle, WA 98195. Periodical.
COLLEGE/UNIVERSITY, LITERARY

Bridge Tender, 9070 SW Rambler Lane, Portland, OR 97223. Quarterly.
OTHER/UNSPECIFIED

The Bridge, Portland Community College, 12000 SW 49th, Portland, OR 97219. 504-244-6111. Ads: Chris Mootham. Newspaper published 32 times a yr. Uses freelance material. Pays 50¢/column inch on publication. Acquires 1st rights. Byline given. Query w/clips, SASE. Dot matrix OK. Accepts nonfiction, photos. Topics: consumerism, entertainment, computers. Photos: B&W only, $10 on publication. Sample for postage.
COLLEGE/UNIVERSITY, COMPUTERS, CONSUMER

The Bridge, Danish American Heritage Society, 29681 Dane Lane, Junction City, OR, 97448. Editor: Egan Bodtker. Semiannual periodical. Sub $15/yr. Uses freelance material. Byline given. Submit query letter, complete ms, SASE. Responds in 1 mo; publishes in 1 yr. Accepts biography, nonfiction, articles, reviews, memoirs.
AMERICAN HISTORY, CANADIAN HISTORY, MINORITIES/ETHNIC

Bridges: A Journal for Jewish Feminists and Our Friends, PO Box 18437, Seattle, WA 98118. 206-721-5008. Editor: Clare Kinberg. Semiannual journal. Subs $15/yr; circ 3,000. Uses freelance material. Byline given, pays copies. Submit ms/SASE. Photocopy OK. Responds in 3 mos; publishes in 6 mos. Accepts: fiction, poetry, cartoons, nonfiction, photos, interviews, biography, op/ed, reviews, memoirs. Topics: Jewish, feminism, politics. Guidelines, sample available.
RELIGION, WOMEN

Brighouse Press, Box 33798, Stn D, Vancouver, BC V6J 4L6. 604-731-9994. Contact: Terri Wershler or Elizabeth Wilson. Publisher of 5 softcover regional nonfiction originals per yr. Accepts unsolicited mss. Query w/clips, SASE. Pays royalties, advance on publication. Dot matrix, photocopied subs OK. Reports in 6 weeks.
NORTHWEST

Bright Books, 329 W Broadway, Vancouver, BC V5Y 1P8. Contact: Thomas Tomosy. Book publisher.
OTHER/UNSPECIFIED

Bright Ring Publishing, PO Box 5768-MW, Bellingham, WA 98227. 206-734-1601. Contact: Mary Ann Kohl. Publisher of 1 softcover children's book per yr. Pays royalties, copies. Query with letter, sample chapters, ms, SASE, phone. Dot matrix, photocopies, simultaneous submissions, electronic OK. Reports in 2–4 wks; publishes in 1 yr. Accepts nonfiction. Topics: creative activity ideas for children. Guidelines and catalog available.
CRAFTS/HOBBIES, EDUCATION, FAMILY

British Columbia Agri Digest, DoMac Publications Ltd, #810 – 207 W Hastings St, Vancouver, BC V6B 1J8. 604-684-8255. Editor: Edna Mackey. Ads: Lloyd Mackey. Glossy tabloid published 9 times a yr, with thematic issues for segments of BC's ag industry: dairy, growers, swine & poultry, farm business, and horse. Circ varies with theme. Does not use freelance material. Pays money.
AGRICULTURE/FARMING, BRITISH COLUMBIA, BUSINESS

BC Bookworld, 940 Stn St, Vancouver, BC V6A 2X4. 604-684-2470. Editor: Alan Twigg. Circ 40,000. Sub $2/issue. A quarterly tabloid newspaper, "with new stories about books and authors related to BC." Accepts unsolicited/freelance mss. Pays money on publication. Rights purchased: None. Byline given. Submit: ms w/SASE. Photocopy OK. Accepts nonfiction, photos (photos necessary). Hints: "Keep it educational & brief & true."
BOOK ARTS/BOOKS, BRITISH COLUMBIA, WRITING

BC Business Examiner, 203 – 1 Alexander, Vancouver, BC V6A 1B2. Business periodical.
ASIAN AMERICAN, BUSINESS

BC Business Magazine, 550 Burrard St, Vancouver, BC V6C 2J6. Editor: R A Murray. 604-669-1721.
BRITISH COLUMBIA, BUSINESS

BC Farmways, RR #1, Old Salmon Arm Rd, Enderby, BC V0E 1V0. Periodical.
AGRICULTURE/FARMING, BRITISH COLUMBIA

British Columbia Genealogical Society, PO Box 94371, Richmond, BC V6Y 2A8. Book publisher.
BRITISH COLUMBIA, GENEALOGY

BC Historical News Magazine, PO Box 105, Wasa, BC V0B 2K0. Quarterly. Submit ms w/SASE. Accepts nonfiction: articles of no more than 2,500 wds, accompanied by photos if available, substantiated with footnotes if possible. Quarterly deadlines are Feb 15, May 15, Aug 15, and Nov 15. Topics: any facet of BC history. See BC Historical Federation listing under Contests.
BRITISH COLUMBIA, CANADIAN HISTORY, NW/REGIONAL HISTORY

BC Hotelman, 124 W 8th St, North Vancouver, BC V7M 3H2. Editor: Vivian Rudd. 604-985-8711. Periodical.
BRITISH COLUMBIA, BUSINESS

BCIT Link, BC Institute of Technology, 3700 Willingdon Ave, Burnaby, BC V5G 3H2. 604-434-5734. Newspaper.
COLLEGE/UNIVERSITY

British Columbia Library Association Newsletter, 883 W 8th Ave, Vancouver, BC, V5Z 1E3.
REFERENCE/LIBRARY, TRADE/ASSOCIATIONS

The British Columbia Medical Journal, 115-1665 W Broadway, Vancouver, BC V6J 5A4. 604-736-5551. Editor: W Alan Dodd, MD. Ads: Doug Davison. Monthly professional journal. Sub $30. Circ 6,600. Freelance ms accepted. No pay. Byline given. Submit ms. Computer disk OK. Accepts

medical/medically-related/ scientific articles — 2,500 wds. Photos: 5x7 B&W glossy. Sample/ $4.
MEDICAL, TRADE/ASSOCIATIONS

British Columbia Monthly, PO Box 4884, Bentall Stn, Vancouver, BC V7X 1A8. Monthly literary publication.
AVANT-GARDE/EXPERIMENTAL, FICTION, LITERARY

BC Outdoors, 202 – 1132 Hamilton St, Vancouver, BC V6B 2S2. 604-687-1581. Editor: George Will. Magazine, 7X/yr. Subs $19.95/yr; circ 40,000. Uses freelance material. Byline given; pays money on publication; acquires 1st rights. Submit query letter. Responds in 2 wks; publishes in 3 mos. Accepts nonfiction, news items, cartoons, reviews photos (color slides, B&W glossy). Topics: Hunting, fishing, conservation and other outdoor recreation in British Columbia. Tip: read the mag before submitting material. Guidelines, sample available.
BRITISH COLUMBIA, FISHING, OUTDOOR

BC Professional Engineer, 2210 W 12th Ave, Vancouver, BC V6K 2N6. Editor: Mike Painter. Ads: Gilliam Cobban. 604-736-9808. Monthly periodical. Circ 13,000; subs C$25/yr.
BRITISH COLUMBIA, BUSINESS, TRADE/ASSOCIATIONS

British Columbia Railway Historical Assn, PO Box 114, Victoria, BC V8W 2M1. Publisher of softcover books on BC railway history. Print run: 3,000. Unspecified payment schedule. Rights purchased: All. Query with ms, SASE. Dot matrix, photocopies OK. Nonfiction, photos. Catalog available.
CRAFTS/HOBBIES, CANADIAN HISTORY, RECREATION

British Columbia Report Weekly News Magazine, 103 – 1161 Melville, Vancouver, BC V6E 2X7.
BRITISH COLUMBIA, OTHER/UNSPECIFIED

BC Sport Fishing Magazine, 1161 Melville, Vancouver, BC V6E 2X7. As the title suggests.
BRITISH COLUMBIA, FISHING, RECREATION

BC Studies, University of British Columbia, 2029 W Mall, Vancouver, BC V6T 1W5. 604-228-3727. Editor: Prof Allan Smith. Quarterly journal. Sub $20 indiv, $24 inst/yr; circ 900. Uses freelance material. No pay. Submit query w/clips. Dot matrix, photocopied OK. Reports in 1–3 mos. Publishes up to 1 yr. Accepts nonfiction: scholarly articles on any aspect of human history in BC. Catalog, sample available.
BRITISH COLUMBIA, SCHOLARLY/ACADEMIC, SOCIOLOGY

BC Teacher, 105 – 2235 Burrard St, Vancouver, BC V6J 3H9. Editor: Larry Kuehn. 604-731-8121. Periodical.
BRITISH COLUMBIA, EDUCATION

BC Orchardist, #3–1115 Gordon, Kelowna, BC V1Y 3E3. Editor: Ron Wade. 604-763-1544. Periodical.
AGRICULTURE/FARMING, BRITISH COLUMBIA, BUSINESS

Broadsheet Publications, 620 Arthur, McMinnville, OR 97128. Contact: Wilma Grand Chalmers. 503-472-5524. Self-publisher of 1 softcover book per year for adult music listeners. Not a freelance market.
ENTERTAINMENT, MUSIC

The Broadside, Central Oregon Community College, College Way, Bend, OR 97701. 503-382-2743. Editor: Todd Pittman. Ads: Paula Brown. Biweekly newspaper. Circ 2,000.
COLLEGE/UNIVERSITY

Broken Moon Press, PO Box 24585, Seattle, WA 98124-0585. 206-548-1340. Contact: John Ellison or Lesley Link. Publishes books. Accepts unsolicited submissions. Pays on publication. Submit query letter, sample chapters, ms, SASE. Photocopy OK. Responds in 9 mos; publishes in 1–2 yrs. Accepts: fiction, poetry, biography, memoirs. Catalog available.
BIOGRAPHY, FICTION, POETRY

Brooding Heron Press, Waldron Island, WA 98297. Contact: Samuel Green/ Sally Green. Literary publisher. Book publisher.
LITERARY

Brown Penny Press, 18130 Hwy 36, Blachly, OR 97412. Book publisher.
OTHER/UNSPECIFIED

Brown's Business Reporter, PO Box 1376, Eugene, OR 97440. 503-345-8665. Editor: Dennis Hunt. Weekly newsletter. Sub $45. Circ 1,300. Uses 0–1 freelance mss per issue. No pay. Byline given. Dot matrix, photocopied, simultaneous, electronic, computer disk OK. Publishes in 2–3 wks. Accepts business "briefs, " 150–300 wds. Sample, SASE.
ABSTRACTS/INDICES, BUSINESS

Brussels Sprout, Vandina Press, PO Box 1551, Mercer Island, WA 98040. 206-232-3239. Editor: Francine Porad. Haiku poetry journal 3 times/yr. Subs $14. Uses freelance material. Byline given, cash ($10) awards, acquires 1st rights. Submit ms w/SASE. Dot matrix, photocopy OK. Reports in 3–5 wks; publishes in 3–5 mos. Accepts haiku, senryu. Guidelines available. Sample: $6.50.
ARTS, POETRY

Buckman Voice, Buckman Community Association, 3534 SE Main, Portland, OR 97214. Periodical.
COMMUNITY

Bulletin, Genealogical Forum of Portland Inc, 1410 SW Morrison, Ste 812, Portland, OR, 97205. 503-227-2398. Editor: Ruth C Bishop. Ads: Wilfred Burrell. Quarterly periodical. Sub $15/mbr. Circ 900. Uses freelance material. Submit ms, SASE. Reports in 8 wks. Accepts nonfiction, poetry, other. Sample $1/SASE.
GENEALOGY

Bulletin of the King Co Medical Society, PO Box 10249, Bainbridge Island, WA 98110. 206-682-7813. Professional publication, 11 times per yr.
BUSINESS, HEALTH, MEDICAL

Burley South Idaho Press, 230 E Main, Burley, ID 83318. 208-678-2202. Newspaper.
COMMUNITY

Burnaby Historical Society, 6719 Fulton Ave, Burnaby, BC V5E 3G9. Contact: Una Carlson. Publisher of historical pieces on the Fraser River area. Not a freelance market.
BRITISH COLUMBIA, NW/REGIONAL HISTORY

Burns Times-Herald, PO Box 473, Burns, OR 97720. 503-573-2022. Weekly newspaper. Subs $15/yr; circ 3,400. Uses freelance material. Byline given, pays copies, acquires 1st rights. Submit query letter, ms, SASE, phone. Accepts: news items.
COMMUNITY

Business Journal, PO Box 14490, Portland, OR 97214. Editor: Steve Woodward. 503-233-0074. Weekly periodical covering business in the greater Portland area. Circ 10,500. Freelance market, buys 2–4 mss per issue. Payment: Money on publication. Query w/SASE. Phone query, dot matrix OK. Reports in 1–2 wks. Publishes in 2–6 wks. Nonfiction: 800–1,200 wds at $3 per published column inch on local business. Guidelines available w/SASE; sample: $1.
BUSINESS

Business Magazine, 601 Main St, Vancouver, WA 98660. Editor: Scott Frangos. 206-696-1150. Ads: Francis Fisher. Bimonthly periodical. Circ 3,500. Freelance market for photos only: need 4-color cover and feature photos. Rates negotiable.
BUSINESS, ECONOMICS, PHOTOGRAPHY

Business News, 220 Cottage NE, Salem, OR 97301. 503-581-1466. Editor: Jeff Marcoe. Biweekly periodical. Sub $6. Circ 1,350. Uses freelance material. Byline given. Submit by phone. Photocopied OK. Accepts nonfiction. Sample available.
BUSINESS, ECONOMICS, PUBLIC AFFAIRS

Butter-Fat, PO Box 9100, Vancouver, BC V6B 4G4. 604-420-6611. Editor: Grace Chadsey. Ads: Karen Redkwich. Quarterly magazine for dairy industry. Sub $8/yr. Circ 2,500. Accepts freelance material by assignment only. Byline given. Query by letter or phone. Accepts fiction, nonfiction. Guidelines available.
AGRICULTURE/FARMING, BUSINESS, TRADE/ASSOCIATIONS

Butterworth Legal Publications, 15014 NE 40th St, Ste 205, Redmond, WA 98052-5325. 206-881-3900. Editor: Ray Krontz. Publishes hard- & softcover,

looseleaf books. Accepts unsolicited submissions. Nonfiction: books and services for lawyers and others in the legal community, primarily treatises, practice manuals, and rule or statute compilations. Authors are compensated by means of negotiated royalties. Publishes state-specific titles for OR, WA, & AK. Proposals for national titles are passed on to Publishing Director in Massachusetts.
LAND USE/PLANNING, LAW

Byline, Rogue Community College, 3345 Redwoods Hwy, Grants Pass, OR 97526. 503-479-5541. College newspaper.
COLLEGE/UNIVERSITY

Caber Press, 1417 NW Everett, Portland, OR 97209. Book publisher. Self-help, motivational.
OTHER/UNSPECIFIED

Cacanadadada Press Ltd, 3350 W 21st Ave, Vancouver, BC V6S 1G7. Contact: J Michael Yates. 604-738-1195. Ads: Margaret Fridel. Publishes 8–10 softcover books per yr. Press run: 1,000. Accepts unsolicited submissions. Pays copies, royalties on publication. Submit ms. Dot matrix, computer disk subs OK. Reports in 4 mos. Publishes in 6 mos. Accepts nonfiction, fiction, poetry, plays. Topics: Literature, women. Catalog available.
FICTION, POETRY, WOMEN

Cacanadadada Review, PO Box 1283, Pt Angeles, WA 98362. Contact: Jack Estes. Twice yearly magazine. "We like unusual work, anything risk-taking, iconoclastic, satirical, parodic, challenging or irreverent." Accepts submissions w/SASE. Reports in 3–4 wks. Accepts short stories, poetry, essays, reviews, letters, artwork, cartoons. Pays copies. Sample issues available, $5.
FICTION, LITERARY, POETRY

Cain-Lockhart Press, 19510 SE 51st St, Issaquah, WA 98027. 206-392-0508. Self-publisher of two softcover books a year on Asian languages and travel. Not a freelance market.
ASIA, LANGUAGE(S), TRAVEL

The Caitlin Press, PO Box 35220 Stn E, Vancouver, BC V6N 3K4. 604-261-7066. Editor: Carolyn Zonailo. Publishes softcover books. Does not accept unsolicited submissions. Pays copies. Submit query letter, SASE. Responds in 6 wks; publishes in 1 yr. Accepts fiction, poetry, memoirs. Catalog available.
FICTION, LITERATURE, POETRY

Calapooia Publications, PO Box 160, Brownsville, OR 97327. 503-369-2439. Contact: Margaret Standish Carey, Patricia Hoy Hainline. Publishers of regional histories. Not presently accepting mss. Query w/SASE. Catalog available.
NW/REGIONAL HISTORY

Calapooya Collage, PO Box 309, Monmouth, OR 97316. 503-838-6292. Editor: Thomas Ferté. Annual literary journal produced and written by the staff and students, but including works and articles by noted professional writers and others. Circulated nationally. Published Aug 1. Deadline June 1. Accepts freelance material. Pays in copies. "All submissions must be typed ds, and accompanied by a SASE." Nonfiction, fiction: 1,700 wds. Poetry: any type, length. Sponsor of the annual $700 Carolyn Kizer Poetry Awards. Sample $4.
COLLEGE/UNIVERSITY, LITERARY, POETRY

Call - A.P.P.L.E., 290 SW 43rd, Renton, WA 98052. 206-251-5222. Editor: Kathryn Hallgrimson Suther. Ads: Dave Morton. Monthly computer-related magazine. Sub $21. Uses freelance material. Pays money on publication. Acquires 1st rights. Byline given. Electronic submissions OK. Accepts nonfiction, fiction, photos. Topics: GS hardware & programming; Apple II programming, tutorial, applications. Guidelines available. Sample $3.
COMPUTERS

Callboard, Box 114, Victoria, BC V8W 2M1. Annual. Accepts freelance material. Byline given. Rights purchased: All. Submit ms w/SASE. Dot matrix, photocopies OK. Nonfiction, photos w/article. Sample available.
NW/REGIONAL HISTORY

Calyx, A Journal of Art & Literature by Women, PO Box B, Corvallis, OR 97339. 503-753-9384. Editor/Ads: Margarita Donnelly. Semiannual maga-
zine. Sub $18/3 issues; circ 3,000. Most articles by freelance writers. Pays copies on publication, money when grants allow. Byline given. Submit ms w/SASE. Dot matrix, photocopies, simultaneous submissions OK. Reports in up to 6 mos; publishes in 6–9 mos. Accepts fiction, poetry, photos, art, book reviews, essays, interviews; work by women — fine literature and art. Guidelines available w/SASE. Sample $8.00 + $1.25 S&H.
FICTION, LITERATURE, WOMEN

Calyx Inc: Calyx Books, PO Box B, Corvallis, OR 97339. 503-753-9384. Editor/Ads: Margarita Donnelly. Publishes hard- & softcover original books by women. Accepts unsolicited submissions Jan 1st to March 15th each yr. Pays royalties. Dot matrix, photocopies, computer disk OK. Reports in 1 yr; publishes in 1–2 yrs. Accepts fiction, poetry, art. Topics: fine literature & art by women. Catalog available. SASE for book submission guidelines.
FICTION, LITERATURE, WOMEN

Camas-Washougal Post-Record, PO Box 1013, Camas, WA 98607. 206-834-2141. Weekly newspaper.
COMMUNITY

Camp Denali Publishing, PO Box 67, McKinley Park, AK 99755. Book publisher.
ALASKA, OUTDOOR

Campus Journal, Student Publishing Services Inc, PO Box 3177, Kirkland, WA 98083-3177. 206-889-9762. Editor: Scott Johnson. Ads: Chris NeVan. Quarterly magazine for junior and senior high school students in the West. Free to school dist; sub $19/indiv; circ 150,000. Uses freelance material from students only. Pays copies. Submit synopsis, complete ms. Dot matrix, photocopied OK. Accepts student fiction, nonfiction, poetry, biography, reviews, op/ed, artwork, photography (prints or negs, color slides preferred). Has a student staff working with the publisher. Guidelines available. Sample $2.
CHILDREN (BY/ABOUT), CHILDREN/TEEN, STUDENT

Campus Magazine, W 827 25th Ave, Spokane, WA, 99203. Free periodical.
COLLEGE/UNIVERSITY

Canada Poultryman, 605 Royal Ave, New Westminster, BC V3M 1J4. Editor: Anthony Greaves. 604-526-8525. Trade periodical.
AGRICULTURE/FARMING, ANIMALS, BUSINESS

Canadian Aquaculture Magazine, 4611 William Head Rd, Victoria, BC V8X 3W9. Editor: Peter Chettleburgh. 604-478-9209. Ads: Deirdre E Probyn. Bimonthly magazine. Circ 3,500. Uses 2–3 mss per issue. Payment: 10¢/wd on publication. Byline given. Acquires 1st rights. Query w/SASE. Phone query, dot matrix, photocopies, electronic OK. Nonfiction, photos, or drawings, Topics: "Readable profiles on fish farmers, processors and research facilities; technical, how-to articles; in-depth analysis of political and resource issues with a bearing on Canadian aquaculture industry." Guidelines available; sample/$3.50.
AGRICULTURE/FARMING, BUSINESS, CONSERVATION

Canadian Biker Magazine, PO Box 4122, Stn A, Victoria, BC V8X 3X4. 604-384-0333. Editor/Ads: W L Creed. Magazine, 8 issues/yr. Sub $19.95/12 issues. Circ 20,000. Query w/SASE. Guidelines available. Sample $3.00.
SPORTS

Canadian Human Rights Reporter Inc, 3683 W 4th, Vancouver, BC V6R 1P2. Periodical.
PUBLIC AFFAIRS, SOCIETY

Canadian Literature, U of British Columbia, 2029 W Mall, Rm 223, Vancouver, BC V6T 1W5. 604-228-2780. Editor: W H New. Ads: B Westbrook. Quarterly journal. Circ 2,250. Rarely accepts unsolicited submissions. Pays in money, copies on publication. Acquires 1st rights. Query w/clips, SASE. Reports in 1 wk. Publishes in up to 2 yrs. Accepts poetry, criticism. For Canadian writers and writing; average 10 printed pages. $5 per printed page, $5 poems. Sample cost varies.
COLLEGE/UNIVERSITY, LITERARY, POETRY

Canadian Press, 1445 W 43rd Ave, Vancouver, BC, V6H 1C2.
OTHER/UNSPECIFIED

Canadian West, PO Box 3399, Langley, BC V3A 4R7. 604–534-9378. Editor: Garnet Basque. Publisher of hard- & softcover books & quarterly magazine. Sub $13/yr. Circ 8,000. Use freelance material. Pays money on publication. Acquires 1st rights. Byline given. Submit query letter, outline, complete ms, SASE, phone. Dot matrix, photocopied subs OK. Accepts nonfiction, biography. Topics: pioneer history of BC, Alberta and the Yukon; historical-ghost towns, mining, lost treasure, Indians, shipwrecks, rocks, gems & bottles, robberies, battles, etc. Articles should be accompanied by suitable artwork/photos. Factual accuracy required. Guidelines available, sample $4.

BRITISH COLUMBIA, CANADIAN HISTORY, NW/REGIONAL HISTORY

The Canadian Writer's Journal, Box 6618 – Depot 1, Victoria, BC V8P 5N7. 604-477-8807. Editor/ads: Gordon M Smart. Quarterly magazine. Sub $15/yr; circ 250. Uses freelance material. Byline given, pays money/exchange on publication. Acquires 1st rights. Submit ms, SASE. Photocopy, dot matrix OK. Responds in 2–6 wks; publishes in 2–12 mos. Accepts occasional fiction and biography, poetry related to writing, articles, reviews. Topics: how-to for writers, but avoid overworked subjects such as overcoming writer's block and dealing with rejections. Guidelines available. Sample $4.

HOW-TO, LITERARY, WRITING

Canby Herald/North Willamette News, 241 N Grant St, PO Box 1108, Canby, OR 97013. 503-266-6831. Weekly newspaper.

COMMUNITY

Canho Enterprises, c/o PO Box 171, Okanagan-Mission, BC VOH ISO. 604-493-7964. Contact: A Davison. Publishes softcover, original, educational, historical dramas. Pays money, 25 copies. Acquires all rights. Query letter w/outline, sample chapter, SASE. Reports in 2 mos; publishes in 1–2 yrs. Accepts nonfiction TV-screenplays. Tips: based on true life, informative, illustrated; exceptional research, proofreading. Catalog available.

DRAMA, EDUCATION, NORTHWEST

Cannon Beach Gazette, 132 W Second, Box 888, Cannon Beach, OR 97110. 503-436-2812. Biweekly newspaper.

COMMUNITY

CANOE Magazine, 10526 NE 68th, Kirkland, WA, 98083. 206-827-6363. Editor: Les Johnson. Ads: Glen Bernard. Bimonthly. Sub $18/6 issues; circ 65,000. Uses freelance material. Byline given. Pays money on publication. Acquires all rights. Submit query, SASE. Reports in 6 wks; publishes in 1 mo. Accepts nonfiction, interviews, reviews, photos (slides). Guidelines available. Sample $3.

OUTDOOR, RECREATION

Capilano Courier, Capilano College, 2055 Purcell Way, North Vancouver, BC V7H 3H5. Contact: News Coordinator. 604-986-1911. Ads: Imtiaz Popat. 604-980-7367. Biweekly. Circ 2,000. Accepts freelance material. Byline given. No pay. Query w/SASE. Photocopies OK. Nonfiction, fiction, poetry, photos, cartoons. Topics: Education, student related issues. Guidelines/sample available.

COLLEGE/UNIVERSITY, EDUCATION, POETRY

The Capilano Review, 2055 Purcell Way, North Vancouver, BC V7J 3H5. Editor: Dorothy Jantzen. 604-986-1911. Quarterly literary and visual arts magazine, "publishing only what its editors consider to be the very best work being produced." Circ 1,000. Sub $12. Accepts freelance material. Payment: $40 maximum/$10 minimum and copies on publication. Byline given. Submit ms w/SASE. Photocopies, electronic OK. Reports in 6 mos. Fiction, poetry, photos, plays. "We are most interested in publishing artists whose work has not yet received the attention it deserves. We are not interested in imitative, derivative, or unfinished work. We have no format exclusions." Guidelines available; sample/$5.

AVANT-GARDE/EXPERIMENTAL, LITERARY, VISUAL ARTS

Capital City Weekly, PO Box 2010, Juneau, AK 99803. 907-789-4144. Weekly newspaper.

COMMUNITY

Capital Press, Box 2048, Salem, OR 97308. Editors: Donna Henderson, Mike Forrester. 503-364-4674. Weekly newspaper. Sub $25/yr; circ 32,500. Pays $1.25/inch on publication. Byline given, acquires all rights. Query by phone. Photocopy, disk/modem, fax subs OK. Reports in 1–2 wk; publishes in 1–2 mos. Accepts nonfiction: 10–20 column inches. Topics: agriculture,

livestock and small woodlands in Oregon, Washington, Idaho, western Montana, northern California. Photos: B&W glossies ($15) or color slides ($20).

AGRICULTURE/FARMING, FORESTRY

Capitol Hill Times, 2720 S Hanford, Seattle, WA 98144-6599. 206-461-1308. Weekly newspaper.

COMMUNITY

Cappis Press, Publishers, Box 35548, Stn E, Vancouver, BC V6M 4G4. 604-420-2580. Editor: Mary Hoel. Publishes 3 hard- & softcover originals, subsidy books a yr. Press run: 5,000–10,000. Accepts some unsolicited submissions. Pays royalties on publication. Acquires all rights. Query w/SASE. Photocopied, simultaneous OK. Reports in 3 wks. Accepts nonfiction. Catalog available.

CANADA, ENVIRONMENT/RESOURCES, HUMOR

Carnot Press, PO Box 1544, Lake Oswego, OR 97034. Book publisher.

OTHER/UNSPECIFIED

Caronn's Town & Country with The Crib Sheet, 14109 NE 76th St, Vancouver, WA 98662. Editor: Karen LaClergue. 206-892-3037. Monthly. Circ 200. Sub $10. Uses 15 mss per issue. Payment: Money and copies on publication. $5/500 wds and up; $2.50/below 500 wds. Photos & mss: $7.50. $2.50 inside cover. $5 cover photo. Byline given. Submit ms, SASE. Dot matrix, photocopies, simultaneous submissions, electronic OK. Reports in 5–6 wks. Nonfiction, fiction, poetry, photos, plays, cartoons. "For Town & Country portion: garden/plant tips & photos; decorating ideas & photos; remodeling ideas & photos. Crib Sheet portion: articles pertaining to childrearing. Also adult and juvenile fiction." Guidelines available; sample/$2.

FAMILY, FICTION, PHOTOGRAPHY

Cascade Automotive Resources, 125 SW Wright Court, Troutdale, OR, 97060. Book publisher.

OTHER/UNSPECIFIED

Cascade Farm Publishing Company, 21594 S Springwater Rd, Estacada, OR 97023. Book publisher.

AGRICULTURE/FARMING, GARDENING, OTHER/UNSPECIFIED

The Cascade Publishing Company, 3623 72nd Place SE, Mercer Island, WA 98040. Book publisher.

OTHER/UNSPECIFIED

Cascades East, PO Box 5784, Bend, OR 97708. 503-382-0127. Editors: Geoff Hill, Jan Siegrist. Ads: Geoff Hill. Quarterly magazine. Sub $12/yr; circ 10,000. Uses freelance material. Byline given. Pays 3¢–10¢ wd on publication. Acquires 1st rights. Submit ms, SASE. Photocopies OK. Reports in 6–8 wks; publishes in 6–12 mos. Accepts nonfiction (1,000–2,000 wds) photos (B&W glossy/color prints or transparencies, $8 to $50). Topics: recreation, general interest in Central Oregon. Guidelines available; sample $4.

COMMUNITY, NW/REGIONAL HISTORY, OUTDOOR

Cashmere Record, PO Box N, Cashmere, WA 98815. 509-782-3781. Weekly newspaper.

COMMUNITY

Castalia Publishing Company, PO Box 1587, Eugene, OR 97440. 503-343-4433. Contact: Scot Patterson. Publisher of 2–3 hard- & softcover books a year. Print run 2,000–5,000. No unsolicited mss. Pays royalties, advance. Rights purchased: All. Reports in 3 mos. Publishes in 1 yr. Psychology textbooks & books on childrearing issues for parents. Materials are research-based. Catalog available.

FAMILY, PSYCHOLOGY, SCHOLARLY/ACADEMIC

Castle Peak Editions, 1670 E 27th Ave, Eugene, OR 97403. Contact: Jim Hall at 503-342-2975 or Judith Shears at 503-846-6322. Publisher of books — poetry, fiction, and texts (grammar and lit anthologies). Accepts submissions of collections of poetry or short stories "of extraordinary quality." Query w/SASE. Reports in 1–2 mos; publication time varies.

FICTION, POETRY, TEXTBOOKS

Catalyst, PO Box 20518, Seattle, WA 98102. Editors: M & Kathleen Kettner. 206-523-4480. Literature magazine published 2–3 times a year; special issues of erotica. Subscription: $7 for 3 issues. 75% of each issue is freelance. Submit ms w/SASE. Buys one time rights. Byline given. Pays in copies.

Accepts fiction, poetry, photos, cartoons and B&W art. "Open to all types of material, lean toward modern/experimental. Translations welcome. No length limits on poetry. Prose up to 10,000 wds." Samples available: 2nd Erotica, $2, & Mary Jane, $3.
FICTION, POETRY, SEX

Catalytic Publications, 2711 E Beaver Lake Dr SE, Issaquah, WA 98027. 206-392-2723. Self-publisher of educational materials. Not a freelance market.
EDUCATION

Catchline, Ski Business News, Drawer 5007, Bend, OR 97708. Trade periodical.
BUSINESS, SPORTS

Catholic Sentinel, 5536 NE Hassalo, Portland, OR 97213. Newspaper.
RELIGION

The Caxton Printers Ltd, 312 Main St, Caldwell, ID 83605. 208-459-7421. Editor: Kathy Gaudry. Publishes nonfiction, hard- & softcover original books. Accepts unsolicited submissions. Pays advance, royalties. Submit query letter, outline, sample chapters, SASE. Photocopy OK. Responds in 1–3 mos; publishes in 8–12 mos. Accepts nonfiction, biography, memoirs, photos. Topics: History, travel biography, life-style, Western Americana. Guidelines and catalog available.
AMERICANA, NW/REGIONAL HISTORY, OLD WEST

CCLAM Chowder, Shoreline Community College Library, 16101 Greenwood Ave N, Seattle, WA, 98133. 206-546-4556. Contact: John Backes. Librarian newsletter.
COLLEGE/UNIVERSITY, REFERENCE/LIBRARY

CCW Publications, 3401 NE 11th St, Renton, WA 98056. 206-228-8707. Publisher of 2 softcover books a year. Print run: 2,000. Not a freelance market. Catalog available.
ASTROLOGY/SPIRITUAL, EDUCATION, PHILOSOPHY

Cecom Publishing, Box 3059, Homer, AK 99603. Publisher of books on health, allergies, environmental illness.
HEALTH

Cedar Island Press, PO Box 113, West Linn, OR 97068. 503-636-7914. Contact: Helen Garcia. Self-publisher of 1 softcover original per year on cooking. Not a freelance market.
FOOD/COOKING

Celestial Gems, 404 State St, Centralia, WA 98531. Contact: Gypsy Al Coolidge. Book publisher.
OTHER/UNSPECIFIED

Center for East Asian Studies, Western Washington University, Bellingham, WA 98225. 206-676-3041. Editor: Henry G Schwarz. Book publisher. Accepts unsolicited mss. Pays copies. Submit query letter, outline, sample chapters, complete ms, SASE. Photocopies, dot matrix subs OK. Responds in 2 wks; publishes in 1 yr. Accepts nonfiction, biography, monographs, memoirs. Guidelines, catalog available.
ASIA, COLLEGE/UNIVERSITY

Center for Pacific Northwest Studies, Western Washington University, Bellingham, WA 98225. 206-647-4776. Contact: Dr James W Scott. Publishes softcover original books. Does not accept freelance material. Topics: academic works on the Pacific NW, usually by resident faculty and graduate students. Catalog available.
BIOGRAPHY, AMERICAN HISTORY

Center for Urban Education, 2710 NE 14th, Portland, OR 97212. 503-249-2857. Contact: Karen Quitt or Rod Barrows. Publisher of Oregon Media Guide, media directory & educational materials for non-profit groups. Book publisher. Phone or query w/SASE.
EDUCATION, LITERATURE, MEDIA/COMMUNICATIONS

The Center Press, 14902 33rd Ave NW, Gig Harbor, WA 98335. 206-858-3064. Book publisher.
OTHER/UNSPECIFIED

Centerplace Publishing Co, PO Box 901, Lake Oswego, Or 97034. 503-636-8710 or 800-96-CHILD. Editor: Paul J Lyons. Publisher of softcover parenting related/children's books. Accepts unsolicited mss. Pays on publication. Acquires 1st rights. Query w/clips. Dot matrix, computer disk subs OK. Reports in 2 wks; publishes in 3 mos. Does all design/coordinate illustrations. "We focus on practical, how-to information for parents and children on self-improvement and improvement of relationships."
CHILDREN/TEEN, FAMILY, PSYCHOLOGY

Central America Update, PO Box 6443, Portland, OR 97228. Editor: Millie Thayer. 503-227-5102. Periodical of "analytical feature articles on movements for social change and USA policy in Central America and on issues facing the solidarity movement." Circ 1,500. Sub $5/year. Uses 1 ms per issue. Payment: Copies. Byline given. Phone query, dot matrix, photocopies OK. Nonfiction, photos (B&W of local Central America related events). Sample 25¢.
MINORITIES/ETHNIC, PEACE, POLITICS

Central County Press, 2817 Wheaton Way #104, Silverdale, WA 98383. 206-692-9042. Weekly newspaper.
COMMUNITY

Central Idaho Star News, PO Box 985, McCall, ID 83638. 208-634-2123. Contact: Tom Grote. Newspaper.
COMMUNITY

Central Oregonian, 558 N Main, Prineville, OR 97754. 503-447-6205. Semiweekly newspaper.
COMMUNITY

CGA Magazine, 1176 West Georgia, Ste 740, Vancouver, BC V6E 4A2. 604-669-3555. Editor: Lesley Wood. Ads: Bryan Cousineau. Sub $30/yr. CDN, $45 elsewhere; circ 40,000. Monthly for accountants. Uses some freelance material. Byline given, pays money on acceptance. Submit outline, query, SASE. Responds in 1 mo; publishes in 3–4 mos. Accepts nonfiction articles related to accounting. Guidelines available.
BUSINESS, TRADE/ASSOCIATIONS

Chain Saw Age/Power Equipment Trade, PO Box 13390, Portland, OR 97213. 503-287-6115. Dealer magazine for small engine outdoor power equipment. Editor: Ken Morrison. Ads: Allen Nelson. Sub $24/yr; circ 22,000. Uses freelance material. Pays money on acceptance, $5/photo, more for specialized, high-quality or color. Byline given. Submit ms w/SASE. Dot matrix, photocopied, simultaneous, computer disk subs OK. Reports in 1 month. Accepts nonfiction, photos (B/W glossy, 3x5 or larger). Tips: No consumer, user-oriented articles. Sample: $1.
BUSINESS, TECHNICAL

Chalet Publishing Co, 18186 S Chalet Dr, Oregon City, OR 97045. 503-631-3247. Contact: Doris Charriere. Book publisher.
OTHER/UNSPECIFIED

Chalk Talk, 1550 Mills Rd, RR 2, Sidney, BC, V8L 3S1. 604-656-1858. Editor: Virginia Lee. Monthly magazine. Circ 3,600; sub $10.95/yr. Pays copies; acquires 1st rights. Accepts (from children only): fiction, nonfiction, poetry, cartoons, news items, interviews, reviews. "Written by children for children 5–14 years." Guidelines available. Sample $1.50.
CHILDREN (BY/ABOUT), FICTION, POETRY

Challenge Alaska, 720 W 58th Ave, Unit J, Anchorage AK 99518. Newsletter for the disabled.
ALASKA, DISABLED

Changing Homes Magazine, 510 SW Third Ave, Portland, OR 97204. 503-283-6202. A quarterly targeted to people moving in Oregon and Washington. Two regional editions featuring articles on financing, taxes, moving tips, remodeling, home security.
BUSINESS, CONSUMER, NORTHWEST

Channel Town Press, PO Box 575, LaConner, WA 98257. 206-466-3315. Weekly newspaper.
COMMUNITY

Chanticleer, 11700 Palfrey Dr, Vernon, BC V1B 1A8. Contact: Michael Galloway/Francis Hill. Published 10 times a year. Circ 300. Sub $5. Accepts freelance material. Pays in copies. Submit ms, SASE. Dot matrix, photocopies, simultaneous submissions, electronic OK. Reports in 4 wks. Non-

fiction, fiction, poetry. Topics: "General, good taste, suitable for family reading. Contemporary as well as material of traditional nature. Max 2,000 wds." Sample available/SASE.
FAMILY, FICTION, POETRY

Chelan Valley Mirror, PO Box 249, Chelan, WA 98816. 509-682-2213. Weekly newspaper.
COMMUNITY

Cherry Tree Press, Box 5113, Stn B, Victoria, BC. V8R 6N3. Self-publisher of writers books.
BRITISH COLUMBIA, WRITING

Chess International, 2905–B 10th St, Everett, WA, 98201-1462. 206-355-1816. Editor: Robert A Karch. Chess correspondence directory; $15.
ENTERTAINMENT

The Chewalah Independent, PO Box 5, Chewalah, WA 99109. 509-935-8422. Weekly newspaper.
COMMUNITY

Childbirth Education Association, 14310 Greenwood Ave N, Seattle, WA 98133-6813. Book publisher.
CHILDREN/TEEN, EDUCATION, FAMILY

Chin Up Beacon, 9529 SE 32nd, Milwaukie, OR 97222. Monthly for the handicapped.
DISABLED

Chinatown News Magazine, 459 E Hastings, Vancouver, BC. Chinese community publication.
ASIA, COMMUNITY, MINORITIES/ETHNIC

Chinese Edition Lifestyle Magazine, 206-960 Richards, Vancouver, BC V6B 3C1. Magazine.
ASIA, COMMUNITY, MINORITIES/ETHNIC

Chinkapin Press Inc, PO Box 10565, Eugene, OR 97401. Book publisher.
OTHER/UNSPECIFIED

Chinook Observer, PO Box 427, Long Beach, WA 98631. 206-642-3131. Weekly newspaper.
COMMUNITY

The Christ Foundation, PO Box 10, Port Angeles, WA 98362. Self publisher. Not a freelance market. Query w/SASE.
NEW AGE

Christian Outlook, PO Box 1870, Hayden, ID 83835. 208-772-6184. Editor: Linda Hutton. Quarterly newsletter. Sub $5. Circ 300+. Uses 6–8 freelance mss per issue. Pays money, copies on acceptance. Acquires 1st rights. Byline given. Submit ms, SASE. Dot matrix, photocopied, simultaneous OK. Reports in 1 mo. Publishes in 6 mos. Accepts nonfiction, fiction, poetry. Tips: "Uplifting and spiritual material, but nothing preachy." Guidelines/sample SASE & 2 first class stamps.
FICTION, POETRY, RELIGION

Christian Parenting Today, PO Box 3850, Sisters, OR 97759-9981. 503-549-8269. Contact: Janett Alvarez. Circ 175,000. Bimonthly magazine of evangelical Christian parenting of children from birth through teen years. Accepts nonfiction, poetry, photos, fillers. Pay varies. Length varies. Pays acceptance for 1st or second serial rights. Sample available for 8x11 SASE ($1.45). Guidelines free.
CHILDREN/TEEN, FAMILY, RELIGION

Christian Zion Advocate, PO Box 971, Port Angeles, WA 98362. Book publisher.
RELIGION

Chronicle, 195 S 15th St, Box 1153, St Helens, OR 97051. 503-397-0116. Semiweekly newspaper.
COMMUNITY

The Chronicle, PO Box 88, Aberdeen, WA, 98520. Newspaper.
OTHER/UNSPECIFIED

The Chronicle, PO Box 1115, Port Angeles, WA 98362. Contact: Dell Price. Newspaper. Query w/SASE.
COMMUNITY

The Chronicle/The Guide, 244 W Oregon Ave, PO Box 428, Creswell, OR 97426. 503-895-2197. Editor/Ads: Gerri Hawkins. Sub $12; circ 3,400 combined. Weekly newspaper. Accepts freelance material relating to Creswell only. Byline given. Pays money, copies, on publication. Acquires 1st rights. Assignment only, phone. Dot matrix OK. Responds immediately, publishes in a few wks. Accepts nonfiction, photos (B&W). Sample $2.
COMMUNITY

Cinnabar Press Ltd, Box 392, Nanaimo, BC V9R 5L3. 604-754-9887. Book publisher.
OTHER/UNSPECIFIED

Circa Press, PO Box 482, Lake Oswego, OR 97034. 503-636-7241. Editor: Robert Brooks. Publishes hard- & softcover original nonfiction books. Accepts unsolicited submissions. Pays royalties. Acquires all rights. Submit query letter, SASE. Dot matrix, photocopies OK. Reports in 3–6 wks; publishes in 6–9 mos. Catalog available.
ECONOMICS, POLITICS, SCIENCE

Circinatum Press, Box 99309, Tacoma, WA 98499. Book publisher.
OTHER/UNSPECIFIED

Circle, Box 176, Portland, OR 97207. Periodical of poetry.
POETRY

CIRI-BETH Publishing Company, PO Box 1331, Tacoma, WA 98401-1331. Book publisher.
OTHER/UNSPECIFIED

Citizen Action, Oregon Public Employees Union, SEIU Local 503, 1127 25th St, Salem, OR 97301. Bimonthly union publication.
LABOR/WORK

CBA Bulletin, Citizen's Bar Association, PO Box 935, Medford, OR, 97501. 503-779-7709. Conservative tabloid on opposition to government oppression.
LAW, POLITICS

The City Collegian, Seattle Central Community College, 1718 Broadway Ave, Seattle, WA 98122. Student newspaper.
COLLEGE/UNIVERSITY

The City Open Press, Opus 2 Publications, 6332 SE Division St, Portland, OR 97206. Editor: T C Distel. 503-777-6121. Monthly tabloid for "Portland's progressive gay people." Tips: "We want to provide an outlet for the creative individuals among us. This includes poets, prose writers, artists, photographers. We are instituting a quarterly feature called 'Creatively Ours!' which will highlight the best of each item submitted to us." A prize will be offered.
GAY/LESBIAN PHOTOGRAPHY, POETRY

Civetta Press, PO Box 1043, Portland, OR 97207-1043. 503-228-6649. Editor: Thomas Bjorklund. Book publisher: crafts, how-to, writing. Accepts unsolicited submissions. Pays royalties. Submit query letter, SASE. Responds in 2 wks; publishes in 6 mos. Accepts nonfiction.
CRAFTS/HOBBIES, HOW-TO, WRITING

Clackamas County News, 224 SW Zobrist, Box 549, Estacada, OR 97023. 503-630-3241. Weekly newspaper.
COMMUNITY

Clark City Press, PO Box 1358, 109 West Callender, Livingston, MT 59047. 406-222-7412. Book publisher of poetry, essays, short story collections.
ARTS, FICTION, POETRY

Arthur H Clark Co, PO Box 14707, Spokane, WA 99214. 509-928-9540. Contact: Robert Clark. Publisher of hardcover, nonfiction originals on history and Americana. Query with synopsis/outline/SASE.
AMERICANA, AMERICAN HISTORY

Clatskanie Chief, 90 Artsteele St, Box 8, Clatskanie, OR 97016. 503-728-3350. Weekly newspaper.
COMMUNITY

Classical Association of the Pacific NW Bulletin, University of Idaho, Moscow, ID 83843. Editor: C A E Luschnig. Semiannual scholarly publication.
COLLEGE/UNIVERSITY, SCHOLARLY/ACADEMIC

Classics Unlimited Inc, 2121 Arlington Ave, Caldwell, ID 83605. Book publisher.
OTHER/UNSPECIFIED

The Clatsop Common Sense, Clatsop Community College, Astoria, OR 97103. 503-325-0910 x311. Quarterly newspaper.
COLLEGE/UNIVERSITY

Claustrophobia: Life-Expansion News, 1402 SW Upland Dr, Portland, OR, 97221-2649. 503-245-4763. Periodical.
HEALTH

Cleaning Business Magazine (formerly, Service Business), 1512 Western Ave, Seattle, WA 98101. 206-622-4241. Editors: Gerri LaMarche & Jim Saunders. Ads: Betty Saunders. Quarterly magazine; circ 5,000; sub $20/yr. Uses freelance 5–10 freelance mss per issue. Requires knowledge of the cleaning industry, or good research ability. Pays $10–90 for up to 2,500 wds on publication. Acquires 1st or all rights. Byline given. Submit query w/clips, ms w/SASE, or phone query. Good dot matrix, photocopied or computer disk OK. Accepts nonfiction, photos, cartoons. Topics: exposé, cleaning and maintenance for self-employed professionals in this field, interviews with successful cleaning business operators, business, fact-based management advice geared to on-site cleaning. Prefers solid technical articles, positive slant, helpful, friendly. Polished ms only. Photos B&W or color, not over 5x7; $5 per photo used. Guidelines for SASE. Sample $3.
BUSINESS, LABOR/WORK, TECHNICAL

Cleaning Center Books, 311 S 5th Ave, Pocatello, ID 83201. 208-232-6212.
OTHER/UNSPECIFIED

Cleaning Consultant Services Inc, 1512 Western Ave, Seattle, WA 98101. 206-682-9748. Contact: William R Griffin. Publisher of soft- & hardcover originals. Accepts unsolicited submissions. Pays money, royalties on publication. Acquires 1st/all rights. Complete ms, query w/SASE. Disk/modem sub OK. Responds in 1 mo; publishes in 6 mos. Accepts nonfiction: references, directories, how-to and textbooks on cleaning and maintenance, health and self-employment, and entrepreneurship. Catalog free.
BUSINESS, EDUCATION, SENIOR CITIZENS

Clearwater Tribune, PO Box 71, Orofino, ID 83544. 208-476-4571. Newspaper.
COMMUNITY

Clients Council News, PO Box 342, Eugene, OR 97440. 503-342-5167.
OTHER/UNSPECIFIED

Clinton St Quarterly, PO Box 3588, Portland, OR 97208. 503-222-6039. Editor: David Milholland. Ads: Rhonda Kennedy. Quarterly magazine, newspaper. Sub rate $8. Circ 2 editions/50,000. Accepts freelance ms. Pays money on publication. Byline given. Query w/clips, ms, SASE. Simultaneous submissions OK. Reports in 1 mo. or less. Accepts nonfiction, fiction, cartoons. "CSQ covers a broad beat including Western American culture and US/international affairs. Specific topics covered in depth have included nuclear culture, US in Central America, sex roles and sexual identity, Western environmental concerns and art in its many forms. We print original fiction and exciting first-person accounts. Payment rates depend on story." Guidelines available. Sample $2.50.
ENVIRONMENT/RESOURCES, FICTION, HUMOR

Cloudburst Press, imprint of Hartley & Marks.
HEALTH, HOW-TO, SENIOR CITIZENS

Cloudline, PO Box 462, Ketchum, ID 83340. Editor: Scott Preston. 208-788-3704. Biannual exploring "various themes relating to the conflict/impact of man's presence in the wilderness and natural environment." Circ 300. Sub $6. Rarely accepts freelance material, "but we are open." Payment: Copies on publication. Byline given. Rights purchased: First. Reports in 2-4 wks. Fiction, poetry, B&W graphics. Guidelines available w/SASE.
ENVIRONMENT/RESOURCES, OUTDOOR, POETRY

Coalition for Child Advocacy, PO Box 159, 314 E Holly St, Bellingham, WA, 98227. 206-734-5121. Contact: Editor.
CHILDREN/TEEN, FAMILY, HEALTH

Coast Publishing, PO box 3399, Coos Bay, OR 97420. 503-888-5370. Contact: W J Howard. Strictly self-publishing books on science and math simplified for the layman. Information available w/SASE.
SCIENCE

Coast Tidings, The News Guard, PO Box 848, Lincoln City, OR 97367. Editor: Duane C Honsowetz. 503-994-2178. Periodical.
COMMUNITY, RECREATION

Coast to Coast Books, 2934 NE 16th, Portland, OR 97212. Contact: Mark Beach & Kathleen Ryan. Self-publisher of books on printing/publishing.
BOOK ARTS/BOOKS, PUBLISHING/PRINTING

Coastal Press, 1205 NW 191, Richmond Beach, WA 98177. Book publisher.
OTHER/UNSPECIFIED

Coeur d'Alene Press, 2nd & Lakeside Ave, Coeur d'Alene, ID 83814. 208-664-8176. Newspaper.
COMMUNITY

Coeur d'Alene Homes Messenger, Coeur d'Alene Homes for the Aged, 704 W Walnut, Coeur d'Alene, ID 83814. Quarterly directed to residents of local homes for the aged and their families. Circ 4,000.
FAMILY, PSYCHOLOGY, SENIOR CITIZENS

Coffee Break, Box 248, Bandon, OR 97411. 503-347-2423. Newspaper.
OTHER/UNSPECIFIED

cold-drill Books, Department of English, Boise State University, Boise, ID 83725. 208-385-1999. Contact: Tom Trusky. Publisher of 1 softcover original book a yr. Print run: 500. No unsolicited mss. Publishes only authors whose work has appeared in cold-drill Magazine. Pays copies on publication. Acquires 1st rights. Assignment only. Dot matrix, photocopies, simultaneous submissions OK. Accepts: nonfiction, fiction, poetry, photos, plays, cartoons, other. Catalog available.
AVANT-GARDE/EXPERIMENTAL, COLLEGE/UNIVERSITY, LITERATURE

cold-drill Magazine, English Department, Boise State University, Boise, ID, 83725. 208-385-3862. Editor: Tom Trusky. Annual magazine. Sub $10/yr; circ 500. Uses 30 freelance mss per issue. Pays copies on publication. Byline given. Acquires 1st rights. Submit: ms, SASE. Dot matrix, photocopies, simultaneous submissions OK. Accepts nonfiction, fiction, poetry, photos, plays, cartoons, other. Tips: "Know the magazine; we're not your average literary magazine...Our format is boxed looseleaf, which means we do 3-D comics, scratch 'n sniff poems, accordion-fold extravaganzas — plus traditional literary publishing (poems, short stories, plays, etc)." Guidelines available. Sample $10.
AVANT-GARDE/EXPERIMENTAL, COLLEGE/UNIVERSITY, IDAHO

Colin's Magazine, Poets. Painters. Composers, 10254 35th Ave SW, Seattle, WA 98146. 206-937-8155. Editors: Carl Diltz, Joe Keppler. Quarterly magazine. Uses freelance material. Pays copies on publication. Acquires all rights. Submit query letter, complete ms, SASE. Responds immediately, publishes in 3 mos. Accepts poetry, photos, interviews, op/ed, articles, plays, reviews. Topics: computer technology and the literary arts; design; art publications; poetry. A review of contemporary culture & technology. (See Poets. Painters. Composers.) Sample $7.
COMPUTERS, LITERARY, MUSIC

Collegian, Willamette University, 900 State St, Salem, OR 97301. 503-370-6053. Periodical.
COLLEGE/UNIVERSITY

Collegiate, City University, 16661 Northrup Way, Bellevue, WA 98008. Periodical.
COLLEGE/UNIVERSITY

Colonygram, PO Box 15200, Portland, OR 97214. 503-771-0428. Bi-monthly newsletter of Oregon Writers Colony. Circ 1,000. Sub w/membership/$15. One or two short pieces per issue. Published by NW writers for NW writers. Payment: Copies on publication. Byline given. Submit ms w/SASE. Dot matrix, photocopies, simultaneous submissions, electronic OK. Nonfiction only, except December, special fiction issue. "Short pieces on marketing your writing: 250 wds, free copies on request. Book review on books about writing: 500 wds, $5. Strong interview with a published writer: 500–1,000 wds, query first, $10." Tip: "Read Colonygram first. Do you have something to contribute to other writers?" Sample/SASE.

BOOK ARTS/BOOKS, PUBLISHING/PRINTING, WRITING

Columbia Basin Herald, PO Box 910, Moses Lake, WA 98837. 509-765-4561. Daily newspaper. Query/SASE.

COMMUNITY

Columbia Communicator, 4628 SW 49th, Portland, OR, 97221. 503-236-7377. Editor: Donna Snyder. Monthly periodical.

OTHER/UNSPECIFIED

The Columbia Press, PO Box 130, Warrenton, OR 97146. 503-861-3331. Weekly community newspaper. Sub $21.50/yr; circ 1,450. Uses freelance material. Byline given. Pays money on publication, acquires 1st rights. Query w/SASE. Responds in 1 wk; publishing time varies. Accepts cartoons, news items, articles, photos (B&W).

COMMUNITY

COLUMBIA The Magazine of Northwest History, Washington State Historical Society, 315 N Stadium Way, Tacoma, WA 98403. 206-593-2830. Quarterly magazine. Editor: David L Nicandri. Sub $5/mbr; circ 2,600. Uses freelance material. Pays $25 & copies on publication. Acquires 1st rights. Byline given. Submit query w/clips, ms, SASE. Reports in 2–4 wks; publishes in 9 mos. Accepts nonfiction, biography, op/ed, articles, photos. Topics: NW history; preferred length 3,000 wds or less. Guidelines available. Sample available.

NW/REGIONAL HISTORY, LITERARY, WASHINGTON

The Columbian, 701 W Eighth St, PO Box 180, Vancouver, WA 98666. 206-694-3391. 503-224-0654. Daily newspaper.

COMMUNITY

Columbiana, Chesaw Rt Box 83F, Oroville, WA 98844. 509-485-3844. Editor: J Payton. Ads: R Gillespie. Quarterly bio-regional journal. Sub $7.50. Circ 4,000. Uses 10 freelance mss per issue. Pays money/copies on publication. Acquires 1st rights. Byline given. Query w/clips, SASE. Dot matrix, computer disk OK. Reports in 1 mo. Publishes in 1–6 mos. Accepts nonfiction, fiction, photos, cartoons. Topics: progressive, relevant to inland Northwest, Columbia River Drainage. Prefers features of 1,000 wds with accompanying illustrations. Pays 1¢/word plus 6 mos subscription. Photos: B&W prints only, $5+. Guidelines available. Sample $2.

ENVIRONMENT/RESOURCES, NORTHWEST, RECREATION

Columns Magazine, University of Washington Alumni Association, 1415 NE 45th, Seattle, WA 98105. 206-543-0540. Editor: Tom Griffin. Ads: Mike Nienaber, 206-455-9881. Quarterly magazine. Circ 165,000. Accepts freelance material. Pays money on publication. Byline given. Acquires 1st rights. Submit query, SASE. Reports in 1 mo; publishes in 3–6 mos. Accepts nonfiction, interviews. "No manuscripts, query only, must be related to UW."

COLLEGE/UNIVERSITY, WASHINGTON

The Comics Journal, Fantagraphics Books, 7563 Lake City Way, Seattle, WA 98115. 206-524-1967. Contact: Helena Harviliez. Monthly magazine on comic book industry. Acquires 1st rights to nonfiction articles, features, criticism, news, column pieces, etc. Uses photos (send w/ms). Query w/clips & SASE.

CULTURE, LITERARY

The Coming Revolution, Box A, Livingston, MT, 59047. 406-222-8300. Periodical.

OTHER/UNSPECIFIED

Commercial Review, 1725 NW 24th, Portland, OR 97210-2507. Weekly periodical on Portland business and commerce. Not a freelance market.

BUSINESS, COMMERCE

Common Ground, Box 34090, Stn D, Vancouver, BC V6J 4M1. Editor: Joseph Roberts. 604-733-2215. Ads: Phil Watson. Quarterly celebrating the art of living. Circ 52,000. Sub $10. Uses 6 mss per issue. Payment: $0–100, copies on publication. Byline given. Query w/ms, SASE. Nonfiction, fiction, photos, cartoons. Book reviews: 250–500 wds; interviews: 500–1,500 wds; topic article: 750–2,000 wds. Photos: B&W inside, $5–25; color cover only (usually from color transparency), $25–100. "Lots of highlights work best.

Lots of mid-tone and good contrast." Tips: "We touch on a lot of subjects and are always looking for good editorials." Guidelines/sample available.

ENTERTAINMENT, HUMOR, PHOTOGRAPHY

Communications Magazine, 1133 Melville St, 6th floor, Vancouver, BC V6J 2K1. 604-681-3264. Editor: Penelope Noble. Ads: Kirsty Gladwell. Monthly magazine for Institute of Chartered Accountants of British Columbia. Circ 6,500. Freelance material accepted. No pay. Byline given. Submit query by letter or phone. Reports in 1 wk, publishes in 2–3 mos. Accepts articles relating to accounting. Generally written by accountants. Situations in the US may be of interest. Guidelines, samples available.

BUSINESS, TRADE/ASSOCIATIONS, OTHER/UNSPECIFIED

Communicator, SFCC – MS 3050, W 3410 Ft George Wright Dr, Spokane, WA, 99204. 509-459-3602. Editor: Klaus Scherler. Biweekly periodical. Circ 3,000. Uses freelance material. Byline given. Accepts news items, interviews, articles, photos (B&W).

COLLEGE/UNIVERSITY

COMMUNICOM, 19300 NW Sauvie Island Rd, Portland, OR 97231. 503–621-3049. Publisher of softcover books for film/video/multi-image professionals. Not a freelance market. Catalog available.

BUSINESS, HOW-TO, MEDIA/COMMUNICATIONS

Community Digest Magazine, 216-1755 Robson St, Vancouver, BC V6G 3B7. 604-875-8313. Editor: S M Bowell. Ads: N Ebrahim. Weekly magazine. Sub $25/yr; circ 25,000. Uses freelance material. No pay. Submit query letter, complete ms, SASE, phone. Dot matrix, photocopies OK. Accepts nonfiction, news items, photos. Topics: for an ethnic audience, stress Indian (East), African, South Asian.

COMMUNITY, CULTURE, MINORITIES/ETHNIC

Commuter, Linn-Benton Community College, 6500 SW Pacific Blvd, Albany, OR 97321. 503-928-2361x13. Newspaper.

COLLEGE/UNIVERSITY

Comparative Literature, 223 Friendly Hall, University of Oregon, Eugene, OR 97403. Quarterly academic publication. Not a freelance market.

COLLEGE/UNIVERSITY, ENGLISH, LITERARY

The Compass, Concordia Lutheran College, 2811 NE Holman, Portland, OR 97211. 503-288-9371. Newspaper.

COLLEGE/UNIVERSITY

The Competitive Advantage, PO Box 10091, Portland, OR, 97210. 503-274-2953. Editor: Jim Moran. Monthly periodical. Sub $96. Circ 10,000. Uses 1–2 freelance mss per issue. No pay. Byline given. Submit ms, phone. Dot matrix, photocopied OK. Accepts nonfiction, cartoons.

OTHER/UNSPECIFIED

Comprehensive Health Education Foundation (CHEF), 22323 Pacific Hwy S, Seattle, WA 98198. 206-824-2907. Contact: Robynn Rockstad or Steven Goldenberg. Publisher of books, videos, and health education curricula used in schools. No unsolicited submissions. Catalog available.

EDUCATION, HEALTH

The Computing Student, Soft-Teach Publications, 5530 Ewart St, Burnaby, BC V5J 2W4. 604-433-7626. Contact: Betty Grace. Magazine published 8 times per year. Circ @ 50,000. Topics: introducing students to computer use — word processing, telecommunications, writing, etc. Wants short articles (max 500 wds). Pays byline initially. Query/SASE.

COMPUTERS, EDUCATION

The Computing Teacher, University of Oregon, 1787 Agate St, Eugene, OR 97403-1923. 503-686-4414. Editor: Anita Best. Ads: Sandi Lysne. Publishes 9 times a year. Circ 12,000. Sub $21.50. Uses 3–5 mss per issue. Writers must be well versed in computer education. "Submissions are reviewed anonymously by at least three qualified reviewers…TCT emphasizes teaching about computers, teaching using computer, teacher education, computer software programs and the general impact of computers in education today." Pays copies on publication. Query w/ms, SASE. Dot matrix, simultaneous submissions, electronic OK. Reports in 10 wks. Nonfiction, photos. Approx. 600–3,000 wds. Guidelines available. Sample $3.50.

COMPUTERS, EDUCATION

Concrete Herald, PO Box 407, Concrete, WA 98237. 206-853-8800. Weekly newspaper.
COMMUNITY

Confluence Press Inc, Lewis Clark State College, 8th Ave & 6th St, Lewiston, ID 83501. 208-799-2336. Contact: James R Hepworth. Publisher of 5 hard- & softcover original books a yr. Press run 5,000. Accepts unsolicited submissions. Pays royalties, advance, on publication. Rights acquired: All. Submit query w/clips, SASE. Photocopies OK. Reports in 6–8 wks; publishes in 12–18 mos. Accepts nonfiction, fiction, poetry. "We're looking for the best writing in the Northwest. We have excellent national distribution." Catalog available/SASE.
LITERATURE, NORTHWEST, POETRY

Conscience & Military Tax Campaign, 4534 1/2 University Way NE, #204, Seattle, WA, 98105. Editor: Katherine Bourdonnay. Quarterly periodical.
PEACE, PUBLIC AFFAIRS

Conscious Living Foundation, PO Box 9, Drain, OR, 97435. 503-836-2358. Editor: Dr Tim Lowenstein. Publishes 1–6 softcover books a yr. Accepts unsolicited submissions. Submit query w/clips. Dot matrix, photocopied, simultaneous, electronic subs OK. Reports in 3 wks. Publishes in 8 mos. Accepts nonfiction. Catalog available.
OTHER/UNSPECIFIED

Constant Society, 4244 University Way NE, PO Box 45513, Seattle, WA 98105. Book publisher.
OTHER/UNSPECIFIED

Construction Data & News, 925 NW 12th Ave, Portland, OR, 97209. Periodical.
BUSINESS, TRADE/ASSOCIATIONS

Construction Sightlines, 124 W 8th St, North Vancouver, BC V7M 3H2. 604-985-8711. Editor: Tom R Tevlin. Quarterly trade magazine. Uses freelance material. Byline given. Submit outline, SASE. Dot matrix sub OK. Accepts articles.
TRADE/ASSOCIATIONS

Consultant Services Northwest Inc, 839 NE 96th St, Seattle, WA, 98115. 206-524-1950. Editor: Charna Klein. Publishes 1 softcover book a yr. Does not accept unsolicited submissions.
ABSTRACTS/INDICES, BUSINESS COMPUTERS

Consumer Resource NW, 5215 W Clearwater #107–25B, Kennewick, WA 99336. 509-783-3337. Editor: Jo Hollier. Ads: Deb Layman. Monthly magazine. Circ 41,000. Uses 1–2 freelance mss per issue. Pays copies. Rights acquired: First. Byline given. Submit mss, SASE. Reports in 1 mo. Accepts nonfiction, poetry, photos. Topics: "Mature, retirement; 100–150 wds." PMT's on photos.
CONSUMER, PUBLIC AFFAIRS, SENIOR CITIZENS

Contacts Influential, 140 SW Arthur, 3rd Fl, Portland, OR 97201. 503-227-1900. Monthly newsletter. Sub $150. Circ 400. Not a freelance market.
BUSINESS

A Contemporary Theatre, 100 West Roy St, Seattle, WA 98119. Contact: Barry Pritchard. Buys full-length scripts for the stage.
DRAMA

Contemporary Issues Clearinghouse, 1410 S Second, Pocatello, ID 83221. Book publisher.
OTHER/UNSPECIFIED

Continuing Education Press, Portland State University, PO Box 1383, Portland, OR 97207. 503-725-4890. Contact: Tony Midson. Publishes hard- & softcover books for "individuals with a desire for self-improvement or development of professional skills." Pays royalties. Submit outline, sample chapters and synopsis. "We're looking for materials for educators, students or professionals, especially items with a continuing education function or for self-instruction and improvement. Should be appropriate for academic review before acceptance. Writers should be established authorities, or have special insight."
EDUCATION

Contractors Weekly, 1213 Valley, Seattle, WA 98109. 206-622-7053. Trade periodical.
BUSINESS, TRADE/ASSOCIATIONS

Controversy in Review, PO Box 11408, Portland, OR, 97211. 503-282-0381. Editor: Richard E Geis. Bimonthly periodical. Sub $9. Circ 1,000. Uses 1 freelance ms per issue. Pays copies on publication. Byline given. Submit ms, phone. Dot matrix, photocopied, simultaneous OK. Reports in 1–2 wks. Accepts nonfiction, cartoons.
LITERARY, POLITICS

Cooper Point Journal, Evergreen State College, Campus Activities Bldg, Rm 306A, Olympia, WA, 98505. Weekly newspaper.
COLLEGE/UNIVERSITY

Coos Bay World, 350 Commercial, Coos Bay, OR 97420. 503-269-1222. Editor: Charles Kocher. Daily newspaper. Circ 17,500. Uses freelance material. Byline given. Pays money on publication, acquires 1st rights. Query by phone, letter, complete ms w/SASE. Dot matrix, photocopied subs OK. Responds in 1 wk; publishing time varies. Accepts news items, poetry, interviews, photos (B&W negatives). Sample $1.
COMMUNITY

Copper Canyon Press, Box 271, Port Townsend, WA 98368. 206-385-4925. Editor: Mary Jane Knecht. Publishes hard- & softcover originals, reprints; poetry and poetry in translation. Accepts no unsolicited material. Query w/ SASE. Reports in 1 mo; publishes in 2 yrs. Acquires all rights. Catalog available.
POETRY

Copyhook, 4416 134th Pl SE, Bellevue, WA, 98006. Editor: Helen Szablya. Periodical.
TRADE/ASSOCIATIONS

Copyright Information Services, 440 Tucker Ave, PO Box 1460-A, Friday Harbor, WA 98250-1460. 206-378-5128. Contact: Jerome K Miller. Publisher of 5 hardcover original books a yr. about USA copyright law. Accepts unsolicited submissions. Pays 15% net royalties. Submit query w/clips, SASE. Dot matrix, computer disk OK. Reports in 6 wks. Publishes promptly. Accepts nonfiction. Catalog available.
LAW, WRITING

Coquille Valley Sentinel, Box 519, Coquille, OR 97423. 503-396-3191, 503-572-2717. Weekly newspaper.
COMMUNITY

Coriolis Publishing Company, 425 SE 3rd, Portland, OR 97214. Book publisher.
OTHER/UNSPECIFIED

Corvallis Gazette Times, 600 SW Jefferson Ave, Box 368, Corvallis, OR 97339. 503-753-2641. Daily newspaper.
COMMUNITY

Cottage Grove Sentinel, PO Box 31, Cottage Grove, OR 97424. 503-942-3325. Weekly newspaper.
COMMUNITY

The Council for Human Rights in Latin America Newsletter, PO Box 3239, Eugene, OR 97402.
MINORITIES/ETHNIC, POLITICS

Council for Indian Education, 517 Rimrock Rd, Billings, MT 59102. 406-252-7451. Editor: Hap Gilliland. Ads: Marilyn Degel. Publishes 6 softcover books a yr. Accepts unsolicited mss. Pays $.015/wd. on acceptance of short items, 10 percent of wholesale price royalty on books; copies. Acquires 1st rights. Submit ms, SASE. Dot matrix, photocopies, simultaneous submissions OK. Reports in 1–6 mos; publishes in 6 mos. Accepts nonfiction, fiction, poetry on Native American life and culture, past or present. Also how-to books on Indian crafts. Must be true to Indian culture and thought, appropriate for use in schools with Indian students. Also short books on teaching. Catalog available.
CHILDREN/TEEN, EDUCATION, NATIVE AMERICAN

Country Rds, DoMac Publications Ltd, #810 – 207 W Hastings St, Vancouver, BC V6B 1J8. 604-684-8255. Editor: Barb Schmidt. Ads: Fran Kay. Free distribution in Frazer Valley community newspapers. Circ 25,000. Bimonthly tabloid serving the Fraser Valley's independent and small scale farmers. News, features, and articles for and about people and events in rural BC. No submission into.

AGRICULTURE/FARMING, BRITISH COLUMBIA

Courier 4, Chemeketa Community College, PO Box 14007, Salem, OR 97309. 503-399-5134. Newspaper.

COLLEGE/UNIVERSITY

The Courier, 174 N 16th St, Box 268, Reedsport, OR 97467. 503-271-3633. Weekly newspaper.

COMMUNITY

Courier-Herald, PO Box 157, Enumclaw, WA 98022. 206-825-2555. Weekly newspaper.

COMMUNITY

Courier-Pioneer-Advertiser, PO Box 1091, Polson, MT, 59860. Newspaper.

OTHER/UNSPECIFIED

Courier-Times, PO Box 32, Sedro Woolley, WA 98284. 206-855-1641. Weekly newspaper.

COMMUNITY

The Court Scribe, 2201 Friendly St, Eugene, OR 97405. Book publisher.

OTHER/UNSPECIFIED

Cove Press, 2125 Seal Cove Circle, Prince Rupert, BC V8J 2G4. Book publisher.

OTHER/UNSPECIFIED

Cowles Publishing Company, 927 Riverside, Spokane, WA 99210. Book publisher.

OTHER/UNSPECIFIED

Cowlitz County Advocate, PO Box 368, Castle Rock, WA 98611. 206-274-6663. Weekly newspaper. Editor: Terri Lee Grell. Ads: Barbara Thompson. Sub $20. Circ 5,000. Uses freelance material. Byline given. Pays copies on publication. Acquires 1st rights. Submit: query w/clips, ms, SASE, phone. Dot matrix, photocopies, electronic, computer disk OK. Accepts nonfiction, photos, news, features, columns. A weekly column called 'Ad-libs' is written by anyone with a unique story to tell; topics preferably local area or Mt. St Helens, but all submissions considered. No more than 4 typed pgs. Sample $1.

CALENDAR/EVENTS, COMMUNITY, NW/REGIONAL HISTORY

Cowlitz-Wahkiakum Senior News, PO Box 2126, Longview, WA, 98632. Monthly periodical.

COMMUNITY, SENIOR CITIZENS

Crab Creek Review, 4462 Whitman Ave N, Seattle, WA 98103. 206-633-1090. Editor: Linda Clifton/Carol Orlock, fiction. Literary magazine of poetry/fiction published 3 times a yr. Sub rate $8. Circ 350–500. All articles freelance. Pays copies on publication. Rights purchased: First. Byline given. Submit ms, SASE. Dot matrix, photocopies OK. No simultaneous submissions. Reports in 6–8 wks. Publishes in 2–24 mos. Accepts fiction: up to 3,500 wds, strong voice, imagery; nonfiction: up to 3,500 wds; poetry: under 40 lines — ("free or formal, clear imagery, wit, voice that is interesting and energetic, accessible to the general reader rather than full of very private imagery and obscure literary allusion"); art: B&W, pen or brushwork. Tips: "Translations accepted — please accompany with copy of the work in the original language." Accepting work only by invitation until Sept. 1989. Guidelines available. Sample $3.

FICTION, PHOTOGRAPHY, POETRY

Crabtree Publishing, PO Box 3451, Federal Way, WA 98063. Contact: Catherine Crabtree. 206-927-3777. Publisher of 2 hard- & softcover originals a year on cooking, home design, health/fitness, entertainment/restaurant guides. Print run: 5,000. Accepts freelance material with permission. "Send request letter stating type of material." Include SASE. Rights purchased: All. Guidelines/catalog available.

ENTERTAINMENT, FOOD/COOKING, HEALTH

Craft Connection, PO Box 25124, Seattle, WA 98125. 206-367-7875. Editor: Cindy Salazar. Ads: Terrie Purkey. 206-746-6884. Sub $12/yr; circ 15,000. Uses freelance material. Byline given. No pay, acquires 1st rights. Photocopies, computer disk OK. Reports in 1 mo. Accepts nonfiction, photos (B&W), cartoons, graphics. Topics: craft how-to's; general interest business, how to start, wholesale, marketing; history or topical stories about handcrafts or local artist. Sample $2.

BUSINESS, CRAFTS/HOBBIES, HOW-TO

Crafts Advocate, 950 Fish Hatcher Rd, Grants Pass, OR, 97527. Sub $18/yr. Circ 500. Bimonthly periodical featuring listings of Oregon Crafts fairs and evaluations of them by readers. Not a freelance market. Back issues available only to subscribers.

BUSINESS, CRAFTS/HOBBIES, OREGON

Crafts Report, 87 Wall St, Seattle, WA 98121. 206-441-3102. Editor: Christine Yarrow. Ads: Sheila Haynes. Monthly tabloid. Sub $19.25/yr; circ 20,000. Uses freelance material. Business subjects for crafts professionals. Pays on publication. Byline given. Send photo with submission. Query w/ SASE. Guidelines available. Sample $2.50.

BUSINESS, CRAFTS/HOBBIES

Creative Children, c/o Keith McAlear, 811 15th Ave E, Polson, MT, 59860. Book publisher.

CHILDREN/TEEN

Creative News N' Views, Creative Employment for the Deaf Foundation Inc, PO Box 1001, Tualatin, OR 97062. 503-624-0131(v) 503-624-0351(TDD). Editor: Paula Reuter-Dymeck. Ads: Don Carbone. Monthly newsletter for membership.

LABOR/WORK, DISABLED

The Crescent, George Fox College, Box A, Newberg, OR 97132. 503-538-8383. Newspaper.

COLLEGE/UNIVERSITY

Crompton Books, 142A – W 15th St, North Vancouver, BC V7M 1R5. Contact: Dr John Matsen. Book publisher.

OTHER/UNSPECIFIED

Crook County Historical Society Newsletter, 246 N Main, Prineville, OR 97754. Irregular periodical.

NW/REGIONAL HISTORY

Crook Publishing, 1680 Cornell Ave, Coquitlam, BC V3J 3A1. Book publisher.

OTHER/UNSPECIFIED

Cross Cultural Press, 1166 S 42nd St, Springfield, OR. 503-746-7401. Editor: Ken Fenter. Publishes hard- & softcover original, subsidy books. No unsolicited mss. Query w/SASE. Dot matrix, photocopies, computer disk OK. Reports in 1–4 wks; publishes within 1 yr. Topics: Japanese-American experiences, Asian-American experiences.

ASIA, ASIAN AMERICAN, CULTURE

Crosswind, PO Box 10, Oak Harbor, WA 98277. 206-675-6611. Weekly newspaper.

COMMUNITY

Crow Publications Inc, PO Box 25749, Portland, OR, 97225. 503-646-8075. Book publisher.

130

Crowdancing Quarterly, 570 W 10th Ave, Eugene, OR, 97401. 503-485-3981. Editors: John Campbell & Holly V Pink. Periodical. Sub $7/$12. Circ 300. Uses 35+ freelance mss per issue. Pays copies. Byline given. Submit ms, SASE. Reports in 8–10 wks. Accepts fiction, poetry, other. Guidelines available. Sample $4.

FICTION, POETRY

Crusader, Northwest Nazarene College, Nampa, ID 83651. 208-467-8556. Biweekly newspaper. Query w/SASE.

COLLEGE/UNIVERSITY

Cryptogram Detective, 8137 SE Ash, Portland, OR, 97215. 503-256-2393. Editor: Joan Barton. Bimonthly periodical/membership. Uses 19 freelance mss per issue. Pays copies on publication. Byline given. Submit ms, SASE.

Dot matrix, photocopied, simultaneous OK. Reports in 6 mos. Accepts fiction. Sample $1.25.
ENTERTAINMENT

Crystal Musicworks, 2235 Willida Lane, Sedro Woolley, WA 98284. Book publisher.
MUSIC

Culinary Arts Ltd, PO Box 2157, Lake Oswego, OR 97035. 503-639-4549. Editor: Cheryl Long. Publishes softcover books. Does not accept unsolicited submissions. Pays royalties. Query w/clips, SASE, phone.
FOOD/COOKING

Cumtux, Clatsop County Historical Society, 1618 Exchange St, Astoria, OR 97103. Quarterly.
NW/REGIONAL HISTORY

The Current, KMUN-FM, PO Box 269, Astoria, OR 97103. Editor/Ads: Doug Sweet. Monthly newsletter of North Coast community radio. Sub $25/yr; circ 2,500. Not a freelance market.
COMMUNITY

Current Concepts in Oral & Maxillofacial Surgery, 101 E 8th St #120, Vancouver, WA 98660-3294. Editor: Dr Jack Stecher. 206-254-8540. Monthly. Also publishes Current Concepts in Orthodontics and Current Concepts in Clinical Pathology — a Physician's Newsletter. Circ 12,000. Not a freelance market.
MEDICAL

Current Lit Publications Inc, 1513 E St, Bellingham, WA 98225. 206-671-6664. Book publisher.
COMMUNITY, MEDIA/COMMUNICATIONS

Current News, Idaho Power Company, PO Box 70, Boise, ID 83707. Editor: Nikki B Stilwell. Published 8 times a yr. Circ 3,200.
BUSINESS, CONSUMER, PUBLIC AFFAIRS

Curry Coastal Pilot, 507 Chetco Ave, Box 700, Brookings, OR 97415. 503-469-3123. Weekly newspaper.
COMMUNITY

Curry County Echoes, Curry County Historical Society, 920 S Ellensburg Ave, Gold Beach, OR 97444. Editor: Virginia Fendrick. 503-247-6113. Monthly on local history. Sub w/membership in historical society, $5. Not a freelance market.
NW/REGIONAL HISTORY

Curry County Reporter, 510 N Ellensburg Ave, Box 766, Gold Beach, OR 97444. 503-247-6643. Weekly newspaper. Query with/SASE.
COMMUNITY

CutBank, c/o English Department, University of Montana, Missoula, MT 59812. 406-243-5231. Editor: David Curran. Semiannual literary journal. Sub $12. Circ 400. Uses freelance material. Pays 1 copy on publication. Byline given. Submit query w/ms & SASE. Photocopied OK. Reports in 6 mos. Publishes in 6–10 mos. Accepts fiction (to 40 ds pages), poetry (3–5), photos, interviews, plays, reviews, and art. "Work must be of high quality to be considered. No stylistic limitations." Guidelines available. Sample $4.50.
FICTION, LITERARY, POETRY

CVAS, Bellingham Public Library, Fairhaven Branch, Bellingham, WA, 98227. Periodical.
REFERENCE/LIBRARY

Cybele Society, W 1603 9th Ave, Spokane, WA 99204-3406. Book publisher. Query with/SASE.
OTHER/UNSPECIFIED

The Daily, 144 Communications, DS-20, University of Washington, Seattle, WA 98195. 206-543-2335. Newspaper. Query with/SASE.
COLLEGE/UNIVERSITY

The Daily Astorian, Box 210, Astoria, OR 97103. 503-325-3211. Newspaper.
COMMUNITY

Daily Barometer, Oregon State University, Memorial Union East 106, Corvallis, OR 97331. 503-754-2231. Newspaper.
COLLEGE/UNIVERSITY

Daily Bulletin, PO Box 770, Colfax, WA 99111. 509-397-4333. Newspaper.
COMMUNITY

The Daily Chronicle, 321 N Pearl, PO Box 580, Centralia, WA 98531. 206-736-3311. Newspaper.
COMMUNITY

Daily Emerald, University of Oregon, Box 3159, Eugene, OR 97403. 503-686-5511. Newspaper.
COLLEGE/UNIVERSITY

Daily Evergreen, Room 113, Edward R Murrow C Cntr, PO Box 2008 C S, Pullman, WA 99165-9986. Editor: Michael Strand. Newspaper.
COLLEGE/UNIVERSITY

Daily Journal American, 1705 - 132nd NE, PO Box 310, Bellevue, WA 98009. 206-455-2222. Newspaper.
COMMUNITY

Daily Journal of Commerce, PO Box 10127, Portland, OR 97210. Editor: Jeff McIvor. 503-226-1311. Ads: Bob Smith. Daily newspaper, general business with emphasis on local news. Circ 4,000. Uses 1 mss per issue. Payment: Negotiable; on publication. Byline given. Query w/ms, SASE. Makes assignments. Phone query, dot matrix, photocopies, simultaneous submissions (if noncompeting) OK. Reports in 1–2 wks. Nonfiction: 600–700 wds. Photos: B&W 5x7 or larger.
BUSINESS, ECONOMICS

The Daily News, Port Angeles, PO Box 1330, Port Angeles, WA 98362. Editor: Tony Wishik. 206-452-2345. Ads: Bob Blumhagen. 800-826-7714. Newspaper serving Clallam/Jefferson counties. Circ 12,500. Sub $6.75. Accepts freelance material. Payment: Money on publication. Byline given. Rights purchased: First. Query w/SASE. Dot matrix, photocopies, electronic OK. Nonfiction: up to 1,000 wds; $20–25. Photos: $5–35 per assignment. "Must be directly related to Clallam/Jefferson counties." Sample available.
COMMUNITY

The Daily Olympian, 1268 East Fourth Ave, PO Box 407, Olympia, WA 98507. 206-754-5400. Newspaper.
COMMUNITY

Daily Shipping News, 2014 NW 24th, Portland, OR, 97210. Periodical.
BUSINESS

The Daily Tidings, 1661 Siskiyou Blvd, Box 7, Ashland, OR 97520. 503-482-3456. Newspaper.
COMMUNITY

Dairyline, United Dairymen of Idaho, 1365 N Orchard, Boise, ID 83760. Bimonthly. Circ 3,000.
AGRICULTURE/FARMING, BUSINESS

Dalmo'ma, Empty Bowl Press, PO Box 646, Port Townsend, WA 98368. Editor: Michael Daley. 206-385-4943. Circ 1,500. Sub $7/issue. Irregularly published anthology of "literature and responsibility, " and regional/rural quality of life, by NW writers. Accepts freelance submissions on themes. Nonfiction, fiction, poetry, photos, plays, cartoons — almost anything serious considered. Recent edition included a record. Rights revert to author. Pays in copies on publication. Reports in 2 mos. Query w/SASE. Dot matrix, photocopies and simultaneous submission OK. Guideline available; sample/$7.
CULTURE, FICTION, POETRY

Dark Horse Comics, 2008 SE Monroe St, Milwaukie, OR 97222. 503-652-8815. Publishers of contemporary comic books. Catalog available.
ARTS, FANTASY/SCI FI, FISHING

Darvill Outdoor Publications, 1819 Hickox Rd, Mt. Vernon, WA 98273. Book publisher.
OUTDOOR

Davenport Times, PO Box 66, Davenport, WA 99122. 509-725-0101. Weekly newspaper.
COMMUNITY

Dayton Chronicle, PO Box 6, Dayton, WA 99328. 509-382-2221. Weekly newspaper.
COMMUNITY

Dayton Tribune, 408 4th, Box 68, Dayton, OR 97114. 503-864-2310. Weekly newspaper.
COMMUNITY

Dead Mountain Echo, PO Box 900, Oakridge, OR 97463. 503-782-4241. Editor: Christy Roberts-Truelove. Ads: Larry Roberts. Weekly newspaper. Sub $25/20; circ 1,500. Uses freelance material. Byline given. Pays copies. Query letter, SASE. Responds in 1–2 wks; publishing time varies. Accepts nonfiction, cartoons, news items, op/ed, photos (B&W screened). Sample $1.
COMMUNITY

Deals & Wheels, 11717 NE 50th Ave #1. Editor: Shelly Wilson. Periodical.
OTHER/UNSPECIFIED

Dee Publishing Company, 774 Cottage NE, Salem, OR 97301. Book publisher.
OTHER/UNSPECIFIED

Delphian Press, 20950 SW Rock Cr Rd, Sheridan, OR 97378. Book publisher.
OTHER/UNSPECIFIED

Democrat, 517 E Broadway #210, Vancouver, BC V5T 1X4. 604-879-4601. Editor: Stephen Brewer. Periodical.
OTHER/UNSPECIFIED

Demographics Northwest, 317 SW Alder, Ste 1285, Portland, OR 97204. 503-222-5412. Contact: John Ettinger. Monthly newsletter. Sub $63/yr. Byline given, pays money, copies on publication, acquires all rights. Submit query letter, outline, synopsis, SASE. Response time varies, publishes in 1 mo. Accepts nonfiction, news items. Topics: trends, trend tracking in the NW, news of research, surveys, studies.
BUSINESS, ECONOMICS, MEDIA/COMMUNICATIONS

Denali, Lane Community College, 4000 E 30th Ave, Eugene, OR 97405. 503-747-4501 x2830. Editor: Karen Loche. College literary magazine. Editors could change yearly. SASE for guidelines.
COLLEGE/UNIVERSITY, FICTION, OREGON

The Denali Press, PO Box 021535, Juneau, AK 99802-1535. 907-586-6014. Fax 907-463-6780. Editor: Alan Schorr. Publishes softcover originals. Accepts unsolicited submissions. Pays royalties. Submit query w/clips, outline, sample chapters, synopsis. Photocopies OK. Reports in 3 wks; publishes in 9–14 mos. Accepts nonfiction and biography. Topics: primarily reference books, but also travel guides and Alaskana, Hispanic, refugees, immigrants, cultural diversity. Catalog available.
ALASKA, MINORITIES/ETHNIC, REFERENCE/LIBRARY

Desert Trails, Desert Trail Association, PO Box 589, Burns, OR, 97720. Editor: Jack Remington. Quarterly periodical.
OTHER/UNSPECIFIED

The Desktop Publishing Journal, 4027-C Rucker Ave, Ste 821, Everett, WA 98201. 206-568-2950. Editor: Linda Hanson. Ads: Jared Hays. Circ 50,000. Sub $10.99. Monthly journal. Uses 2–5 freelance mss per issue. Some technical expertise needed to write for us. Pays money on publication: $200 for feature articles of 4,000–7,000 wds; $100 for articles 1,000–4,000 wds; $25 for cartoons. Likes to trade articles for 1/4 page ads. Graphic req's: 85-line screen. Rights purchased: First. Reprints OK. Byline given. Query w/ clips, SASE. All forms of submis. OK. Reports in 2 mos. Publishes in 2 mos. Accepts nonfiction, photos, cartoons. "We need articles written for all levels, but prefer beginner's level. How-to articles are preferred, but print anything and everything related to D Pub." Guidelines. Sample $1.50.
COMPUTERS, PUBLISHING/PRINTING, TECHNICAL

Devil's Thumb Press, Box 1136, Petersburg, AK 99833. Book publisher.
OTHER/UNSPECIFIED

Dewdney Publishing, PO Box 231, Cranbrook, BC V1C 4H7. Book publisher.
OTHER/UNSPECIFIED

Dialogue - Thoughtprints, Center Press, 14902 33rd Ave NW, Gig Harbor, WA 98335. Editor: E J Featherstone. 206-858-3964. Quarterly of "poetry with inspirational (nonreligious) — humourous — philosophical message." Circ 2,000–3,000. Pays on publication. Byline given. Query w/ms, SASE.

Dot matrix, simultaneous submissions OK. Publishes submissions in 3–12 mos. Nonfiction: on poetry and poetry markets, 250 wds, no pay. Poetry: 24 lines; pays in prizes/subs. Short rhymed humor: pays $1. Tips: "No 'sensational' morbid themes. Good imagery — meter will be edited if poem merits publication. Mankind's needs addressed, looking for upbeat material — no heavy religious or Pollyanna."
PHILOSOPHY, POETRY

Diamond Editions, Box 12001, Portland, OR 97212. 503-287-9015. Contact: Carolan Gladden. Publishes trade paperback fiction and nonfiction. Averages 4 titles/yr; 75% of books from first-time authors. Royalties vary. Reports in 2–3 weeks. Publishes 1 yr after acceptance. Queries only w/SASE. Dedicated to helping new/unpublished writers achieve publication. Nonfiction: how-to, self-help, celebrity bio. No technical or textbooks. Fiction: mainstream, horror/thriller, action, science fiction. No romance, westerns children's, poetry, or short fiction.
FANTASY/SCI FI, FICTION, HOW-TO

The Digger, Oregon Association of Nurserymen, 2780 SE Harrison, Ste 102, Milwaukie, OR 97222. 503-653-8733. Editor: Miles McCoy. Monthly agricultural trade magazine. Circ 3,400. Uses freelance material. Byline given. Pays money on publication. Acquires all rights. Submit query letter, SASE, phone. Responds in 3–4 wks; publishes in 1–6 mos. Accepts nonfiction, news items, interviews, photos. Topics: plant nursery business. Sample available.
AGRICULTURE/FARMING, BUSINESS, GARDENING

Dillon Tribune-Examiner, 22 S Montana, Dillon, MT, 59725. Newspaper.
COMMUNITY

Dime Novels, 1511 SW Park Ave #320, Portland, OR 97201. 503-223-2991. Editor: Linda Sterling-Wanner, Randy Byrd. Publishes miniature softcover books. Accepts unsolicited submissions. Pays advance, royalties. Submit outline, sample chapter. Responds in 6 wks. Accepts fiction; 20,000 words in length, approx. 80 ds typed pages. Guidelines available.
FICTION

Dimi Press, 3820 Oak Hollow Lane SE, Salem, OR 97302. 503-364-7698. Fax 503-364-9727. Publisher of softcover books and cassettes. Accepts unsolicited submissions. Pays royalties on publication. Query w/SASE. Simultaneous submission OK. Reports in 4 wks. Topics: relaxation and other psychological self-help. Tips: know your market, targeted by direct mail. Guidelines and catalog available.
HEALTH, HOW-TO, PSYCHOLOGY

Dioscoridus Press Inc, 9999 SW Wilshire, Portland, OR 97225. 503-292-0745. Editor: Richard Abel. Ads: Michael Fox. Publishes hardcover originals, reprints. Accepts unsolicited submissions. Acquires all rights. Submit query w/clips. Dot matrix, photocopied OK. Reports in 3–4 wks. Topics: botany, plant sciences, and ecology. Catalog available.
GARDENING, SCHOLARLY/ACADEMIC, TECHNICAL

The Direct Express, 928 Broadwater, Billings, MT 59101. Newspaper.
OTHER/UNSPECIFIED

Discovery, 1908 Second St, Tillamook, OR 97141. 503-842-7535. Periodical.
OTHER/UNSPECIFIED

Dispatch, PO Box 248, Eatonville, WA 98328. 206-832-4411. Weekly newspaper.
COMMUNITY

Diver Magazine, Seagraphic Publications Ltd, #295 - 10991 Shellbridge Way, Richmond BC V6X 3C6. 604-273-4333. Editor: Neil McDaniel. Magazine published 9X/yr. Circ 20,000. Uses freelance material. Byline given. Pays money, copies on publication. Query letter, complete ms, SASE. Dot matrix, disk/modem OK. Accepts nonfiction, fiction, news items, reviews, photos. Topics: subjects of interest to divers. Guidelines available. Sample $3.
OUTDOOR, RECREATION, TRAVEL

Diversity: The Lesbian Rag, PO Box 66106, Stn F, Vancouver, BC V5N 5L4. 604-872-3026. Editor: Evie Mandel. Ads: Jo'anne Lambert. Bimonthly magazine. Circ 2,000, subs. $18/yr US. Uses freelance material. Byline given, pays copies. Submit ms, query/SASE (Canadian stamps), phone. Photocopied sub OK. Responds in 1–6 mos. Accepts fiction, nonfiction, poetry, cartoons, articles, art, news items. Tips: material by and for lesbians, include bio for publication with work. Guidelines available, sample $2.

GAY/LESBIAN, SEX, WOMEN

Dog River Review, PO Box 125, Parkdalee, OR 97041-0125. Editor: Laurence F Hawkins, Jr. 503-352-6494. Semiannual of fiction, poetry, art. Circ 200. Sub $6. Accepts freelance material. Payment: Copies on publication. Rights purchased: First. Submit ms, SASE. Dot matrix, photocopies OK. Reports in 1–3 mos. Fiction: to 2,500 wds. Poetry: prefer verse to 30 lines but will consider longer, all forms. Also accepts plays, B&W art. "No pornography; eroticism OK. No sermonizing, self-indulgent material. No religious verse." Guidelines available; sample/$2.

CRAFTS/HOBBIES, FICTION, POETRY

Dolan Press, 1645 Gales Ct, Forest Grove, OR 97116. 503-357-7682. Contact: Eileen Dolan Savage. Self-publisher of books.

OTHER/UNSPECIFIED

Doll Mall, Paddlewheel Press, PO Box 230220, Tigard, OR, 97223. 503-292-8460. Quarterly.

OTHER/UNSPECIFIED

Doorway Publishers, PO Box 707, Poulsbo, WA 98370. 206-297-7952. Editors: Doris Moore, Connie Lord. Publisher of softcover books. Does not accept unsolicited submissions. Submit query/SASE. Responds in 2–3 wks. Accepts nonfiction. Topics: how-to, crafts/hobbies.

CRAFTS/HOBBIES, HOW-TO

Doral Publishing Inc, 32025 Village Crest Lane, Wilsonville, OR 97070. 503-694-5707. Editor: Dr Alvin Grossman. Publishes hard/softcover books. Accepts unsolicited submissions. Submit sample chapters, SASE. Simultaneous, photocopies OK. Responds in 3 wks; publishes in 1 yr. Topics: dog books. Catalog available.

ANIMALS

Douglas Geidt, Box 246, Union Bay, BC V0R 3B0. 604-335-1042.

CANADIAN HISTORY

Douglas & McIntyre Publishers, 1615 Venables St, Vancouver, BC V5L 2H1. Contact: Shaun Oakey. 604-254-7191. Publisher of hard and softcover originals and paperbacks, primarily by Canadian writers. Payment: Advances average $500; royalties 8–15%. Query or mss w/SASE. Nonfiction, fiction. Topics: biography, ethnic, experimental, historical, and women's literary fiction. Catalog available free.

BIOGRAPHY, CANADIAN HISTORY, WOMEN

Doves Publishing Company, PO Box 821, Newport, OR, 97365. Book publisher.

OTHER/UNSPECIFIED

The Downtowner, 621 SW Morrison St, Ste 140, Portland, OR 97205. Editor: Maggi White. 503-243-2600. Weekly focusing on Portland, entertainment, culture. Sub $26/yr; circ 25,000. Uses freelance material. Byline given. Pays money on publication. Query w/SASE. Nonfiction, photos. Tips: local, short pieces, 2–3 pages typed.

CULTURE, ENTERTAINMENT, HUMOR

Dragonfly, 4120 NE 130th Place, Portland, OR 97230. Quarterly haiku journal.

POETRY

The Drain Enterprise, PO Box 26, Drain, OR 97435-0026. Newspaper.

COMMUNITY

Dream Research, PO Box 107, Grapeview, WA 98546. Editor: Adrienne Quinn. Book publisher.

OTHER/UNSPECIFIED

Drelwood Publications, PO Box 10605, Portland, OR 97210. Book publisher.

OTHER/UNSPECIFIED

Drift Creek Press, PO Box 511, Philomath, OR 97370. 503-929-5637/800-338-0136. Editors: Craig J Battrick, Nancy R Astin. Publishes books and irregular newsletter. 3 softcover books 1991. Negotiable payment. Copyrights

for authors. Query w/SASE, outline, sample chapter, or by phone. Photocopied, disk, dot matrix subs OK. Reports in 1 mo; publishes in 1 yr. Subjects: poetry, nonfiction, cookbooks, NW regional.

FOOD/COOKING, POETRY, NORTHWEST

Duane Shinn Publications, 5090 Dobrot, Central Point, OR 97501. Book publisher.

OTHER/UNSPECIFIED

The Duckabush Journal, PO Box 2228, Sequim, WA 98382-2228. 206-683-0647. Editor: Ken Crump. Literary regional periodical published 3 times a yr. Sub $12. "A creative insight to the Olympic Peninsula and adjacent areas." Pays copies on publication. Submit ms, query w/SASE. Accepts poetry, short stories, historical studies, character sketches, other nonfiction, B&W art, photographs. Tips: Prose should have a tone or feeling of Olympic Peninsula. Guidelines available. Sample $4.50.

FICTION, POETRY, VISUAL ARTS

d'Void, Fraser Valley College, RR No 2, Abbotsford, BC V2S 4N2. Magazine of poetry and translations. Submit ms w/SASE.

LITERARY, POETRY

Eagle Signs, 1015 Hutson Rd, Hood River, OR 97031. Book publisher.

OTHER/UNSPECIFIED

Early Warning, Ste 1, EMU, Eugene, OR, 97403. Periodical.

OTHER/UNSPECIFIED

Earshot Jazz, 3429 Fremont Pl #308, Seattle, WA 98103. 206–547-64763. Editor: Sandra Burlingame. Ads: Jeff Ferguson. Monthly magazine. Sub $15/yr; circ 7,000. Uses freelance material. Byline given. Pays money on publication. Acquires 1st rights. Submit query letter w/clips, complete ms, SASE. Photocopy, disk/modem OK. Reports in 1 mo; publishes in 1–3 mos. Accepts nonfiction, news items, interviews, reviews, photos (B&W $10–25). Sample free.

MUSIC

Earth View Inc, 6514 18th Ave NE, Seattle, WA 98115. 206-527-3168. Contact: Bryan Brewer. Self-publisher only of computer, health, and new age books.

COMPUTERS, HEALTH, NEW AGE

Earth-Love Publishing House, 302 Torbett #100, Richland, WA 99352. 509-943-9567. Publisher of new age and metaphysical books.

NEW AGE

The Earthling, Society of Separationists Inc, PO Box 14054, Portland, OR, 97214. Editor: James Almblad. Periodical.

OTHER/UNSPECIFIED

`, 2637 SW Water, Portland, OR 97210. Editor/ads: Heath Lynn Silberfeld. 503-222-1963. Quarterly on environmental issues of concern to Oregonians. Circ 2,000. Sub $25. Accepts freelance material. No pay. Byline given. Phone query, dot matrix, photocopies OK. Uses nonfiction, photos. "Environmental issues reporting/opinion pieces of 1–10 typewritten pages, with emphasis on legislative activity, lobbying, and enforcement of environmental law, statutes, rules." Photos: B&W prints. Sample available.

ENVIRONMENT/RESOURCES, OREGON, POLITICS

East is East, PO Box 95247, Seattle, WA 98145-2247. 206-522-1551. Periodical.

OTHER/UNSPECIFIED

East Oregonian, 211 SE Byers, Box 1089, Pendleton, OR 97801. 503-276-2211. Daily newspaper.

COMMUNITY

East Washingtonian, PO Box 70, Pomeroy, WA 99347. 509-843-1313. Weekly newspaper.

COMMUNITY

Eastbank Focus, Pry Publishing Co, 600 NW 14th Ave, Portland, OR 97209. 503-226-8335. Editors: Tom or Marcia Pry. Ads: Greg Hudson. Monthly tabloid, founded 1988. Circ 10,000. Uses freelance material. Byline given. Pays money on publication. Acquires 1st rights. Submit query letter, clips, SASE. Dot matrix OK. Responds in 1–2 wks. Accepts new items, nonfiction,

photos, articles. Topics: events and people of inner NE and SE Portland, Albina, Lloyd Center, Hawthorne. Guidelines available.
COMMUNITY

The Eastern Beacon, Eastern Oregon State College, Hoke College Center, La Grande, OR 97850. 503-962-3526. Editor: Jennie Beyerl. Ads: Artie Peterson. Bimonthly to college students, professors, staff and community. Circ 1,800. Accepts freelance material. No pay. Byline given. Dot matrix, photocopies, simultaneous subs OK. Uses nonfiction, fiction, poetry, photos, cartoons. Sample available, SASE.
COLLEGE/UNIVERSITY, ENTERTAINMENT, SPORTS

Eastern School Press, 146 Talent Ave, PO Box 684, Talent, OR 97540. Contact: David Reigle. Book publisher.
OTHER/UNSPECIFIED

Eastern Washington State Historical Society, W 2316 1st Ave, Spokane, WA 99204. Book publisher.
NW/REGIONAL HISTORY

Eastland Press, 611 Post Ave Ste #3, Seattle, WA 98104. 206-587-6013. Editor: Dan Bensky. Ads: Patricia O'Connor. Publishes 3 hardcover orig. books a yr. Accepts unsolicited mss. Pays royalties, advance on publication. Rights purchased: All. Submit: ms. Dot matrix, photocopy, computer disk OK. Reports in 1 mo. Publishing time varies. Accepts nonfiction, photos. "We publish only medical books, principally Oriental medicine and manual medicine (bodywork)." Guidelines/catalog available.
HEALTH, MEDICAL

Eastside a la Carte, 4231 135th Place SE, Bellevue, WA 98006. Book publisher.
OTHER/UNSPECIFIED

Eastside Courier-Review, PO Box 716, Redmond, WA 98052. 206-885-4178. Weekly newspaper.
COMMUNITY

Eastside Writers Newsletter, PO Box 8005, Totem Lake Post Office, Kirkland, WA 98034. Editor: Kathy Mendelson. Monthly by and for members of Eastside Writers Association. Circ 250. Sub with membership. Not a freelance market.
WRITING

Echo, PO Box 39, Leavenworth, WA 98826. 509-548-7911. Weekly newspaper.
COMMUNITY

Echo Digest, 10300 SW Greenburg Rd, #280, Portland, OR 97223. Editor: Owen R Brown. Periodical.
OTHER/UNSPECIFIED

Echo Film Productions, 407 W Bannock St, Boise, ID 83702. Freelance market for scripts. Query w/SASE.
DRAMA, VISUAL ARTS

The Eclectic Muse, 340 W 3rd St #107, North Vancouver, BC V7M 1G4. 604-984-7834. Editor: Joe M Ruggier. Ads: Bill Marles. Magazine published 3X/yr. Sub $20/yr; circ 200. Uses freelance material. Byline given. Pays copies on publication. Submit query letter, SASE. Photocopy, dot matrix, simultaneous subs OK. Responds in 4 mos; publishing time varies. Accepts fiction, poetry, articles, interviews, reviews. "Can you write in free form like the Authors of Scripture?" Guidelines available. Sample $7.
FICTION, POETRY

Eclectic Press Inc, PO Box 14462, Portland, OR 97214. 503-286-4018. Contact: Barbara Cogan Neidig. Reprint and copublish books for the gift trade — floral crafts, gardening. Is not a freelance market. No submissions please.
CRAFTS/HOBBIES

Economic Facts/Idaho Agriculture, University of Idaho Extension Service, College of Agriculture, Moscow, ID 83843. Editor: Neil Meyer. Quarterly.
AGRICULTURE/FARMING, BUSINESS, IDAHO

Ecotope Group, 2812 E Madison, Seattle, WA 98112. Book publisher.
OTHER/UNSPECIFIED

Edge Art Press, 154 N 35, #204, Seattle, WA 98103. 206-547-4453. Book publisher.
OTHER/UNSPECIFIED

Edmonds Arts Commission Books, 700 Main St, Edmonds, WA 98020. 206-775-2525. Self-publisher. Assignment only. Pays money, copies on acceptance. Rights purchased: First. Byline given. Dot matrix, photocopy OK. Reports in 1–2 mos. Publishes in 2–3 mos. Accepts nonfiction, fiction, poetry, cartoons, line drawings. Publication projects vary with contest subject. 500 word max. "Contest awards plus free copies." Sample $7.95+ hand.
FAMILY, NW/REGIONAL HISTORY, HUMOR

The Edmonds View, 1827 160th Ave NE, Bellevue, WA 98008-2506. Weekly newspaper.
COMMUNITY

Educare Press, PO Box 31511, Seattle, WA 98103, 206-781-2665. Editor: Shane O'Mahoney. Self-publisher.
EDUCATION

Educational Digest, The Riggs Institute, 4185 SW 102nd Ave, Beaverton, OR 97005. 503-646-9459. Periodical.
EDUCATION

Edwards Publishing Company, PO Box 998, Milton, WA 98354. Book publisher.
OTHER/UNSPECIFIED

Ruth Edwins-Conley Publishing, 495 Aeneas Valley Rd, Tonasket, WA 98855. 206-659-1229. Self-publisher of 1–2 softcover subsidy books a yr; "poems, fiction, diaries of literary merit, translations." Press run: 100. Not a freelance market.
FICTION, POETRY

The Eighth Mountain Press, 642 SE 29th, Portland, OR 97214. 503-233-3936. Editor: Ruth Gundle. Publishes softcover original books on feminist literary works. Accepts unsolicited submissions. Pays royalties. Query w/ clips & SASE. Photocopy OK. Reports in 1–2 mos. Accepts fiction, poetry, and essays. Annual poetry prize (see Contests). Guidelines, catalog available 45¢ postage.
FEMINISM, GAY/LESBIAN, WOMEN

Ekstasis Editions, PO Box 474, Stn E, Victoria, BC V8W 2N8. 604-385-3378. Editor: Richard Olafson. Ads: Carol Ann Sokolaff. Publishers of hard- & softcover books, journal. Accepts unsolicited submissions. Pays 20% of run, royalties on publication. Submit query letter, complete ms, sample chapters, SASE. Photocopy, simultaneous OK. Responds in 8–10 wks; publishes in 1 yr. Accepts fiction, nonfiction, poetry, photos, plays. Catalog available.
BOOK ARTS/BOOKS, BRITISH COLUMBIA, POETRY

El Centinela, Pacific Press Publishing Association, 1350 Kings Rd, Nampa, ID 83605. Editor: Tulio Peverini. Monthly. Circ 113,000.
OTHER/UNSPECIFIED

The Elder Statesman, 301 – 1201 West Pender, Vancouver, BC V6E 2V2. Newspaper.
OTHER/UNSPECIFIED

Elephant Mountain Arts, PO Box 1304, Hood River, OR 97040. 503-233-9841. Contact: Chuck Williams. Self-publisher of hard- & softcover books. Not a freelance market.
ENVIRONMENT/RESOURCES, NW/REGIONAL HISTORY, NATIVE AMERICAN

Elixir! of Oregon Wordworks, PO Box 514, Manzanita, OR 97130. 503-368-7017. Editor: Cathleen Thomsen. Quarterly magazine. Circ 5,000. Uses freelance material. Byline given. Pays copies. Submit query letter, complete ms. Photocopy, simultaneous subs OK. Responds in 2 wks; publishes in 3 mos. Accepts fiction, nonfiction, poetry, cartoons, photos.
FICTION, POETRY, OTHER/UNSPECIFIED

Ellensburg Anthology, Four Winds Bookstore, 202 E 4th, Ellensburg, WA 98926. Editor: Tom Lineham. 206-754-1708. Periodical of poetry and prose for emerging NW writers. Circ 200–300. Sub $3.50 + post. Uses 5 mss per issue. Payment: Copies. Byline given. Rights purchased: First. Submit ms, SASE. Dot matrix, photocopies, simultaneous submission, electronic OK.

Reports in 2–4 mos. Fiction (2,000 wds), poetry (100 lines), plays (sections only), illustrations. "We are looking especially for new talent." Deadline: July 31 each yr. Guidelines available; sample/$3.50/SASE.
DRAMA, FICTION, POETRY

Ellensburg Daily Record, Fourth & Main, PO Box 248, Ellensburg, WA 98926. 509-925-1414. Daily newspaper.
COMMUNITY

Elliott & Fairweather Inc, PO Box 1524, Mercer Island, WA 98040-1524. 206-236-9008. Editor: Priscilla Johnston. Publishes softcover books. Unsolicited submissions accepted. Submit query letter, outline, sample chapters, phone. Responds in 30 days. Topics: city guidebooks.
NORTHWEST, RECREATION, TRAVEL

The Eloquent Umbrella, English Dept, Linn-Benton Community College, 6500 Pacific Blvd SW, Albany, OR 97321-3799. 503-928-2361 ext 208. Contact: Lin Eastburn. Annual literary journal. Accepts freelance material. Query w/SASE.
FICTION, LITERARY, POETRY

Em-Kayan, Morrison-Knudsen Corporation, PO Box 73, Boise, ID 83707. Editor: Vern Nelson. Monthly for employees, stockholders and customers of M-K.
BUSINESS

EMC Retort, Eastern Montana College, Billings, MT 59101. Editor: Angela Enger. Newspaper.
COLLEGE/UNIVERSITY

Emerald City Comix & Stories, PO Box 95402, Seattle, WA 98145-2402. 206-523-1201. Editor: Nils Osmar. Circ 7,000. Sub $3.50. Quarterly newspaper of fiction and comic strips. Uses 50 freelance mss/issue. Pays 2 copies on publication. Rights purchased: First. Byline given. Submit ms. "Must be accompanied by SASE!" Dot matrix, photocopy OK. Reports in 6 wks. Publishes in: 3–6 mos. Accepts nonfiction, fiction, poetry, cartoons. "We publish short fiction up to 4,000 wds. Interested in thoughtful, well-crafted stories & poems, humorous & dramatic cartoons & comic strips." Guidelines available. Sample $1.50 in stamps.
FANTASY/SCI FI, FICTION, SATIRE

Emerald House, PO Box 1769, Sand Point, ID 83864. Book publisher.
OTHER/UNSPECIFIED

Emergency Librarian, PO Box C34069, Dept 284, Seattle, WA 98124-1069, or PO Box 46258, Stn G, Vancouver, BC V6R 4G6. 604-734-0255. Editor: Ken Haycock. Ads: Dana Sheehan. Circ 10,000. Sub $40 prepaid. Publishes magazine 5 times a yr. Uses 3 freelance mss per issue. Request guidelines before writing. Pays money on publication. Rights purchased: All. Byline given. Query w/clips. Dot matrix, photocopy OK. Reports in 6 wks. Publishes within 1 yr. Accepts: Nonfiction, cartoons. Guidelines available.
BOOK ARTS/BOOKS, EDUCATION, REFERENCE/LIBRARY

Emmett Messenger, PO Box 577, Emmett, ID 83617. Weekly newspaper.
COMMUNITY, OTHER/UNSPECIFIED

Empire Press, PO Box 430, Waterville, WA 98858. 509-745-8782. Weekly newspaper.
COMMUNITY

Empty Bowl Press, PO Box 646, Port Townsend, WA 98386. Small press publisher of nonfiction, fiction, poetry and other material. Book publisher.
FICTION, POETRY

The Empty Space Theatre, PO Box 1748, Seattle, WA 98111-1748. 206-587-3737. Contact: Kurt Beattie. Stage theater accepts unsolicited full-length plays, one-acts, translations, adaptations, musicals, from regional playwrights (ID, MT, OR, WA, WY). Pays royalties. Query w/SASE. Reports in 3 wks. to query, 4 mos. to scripts.
DRAMA

The Emshock Letter, Randall Flat Rd, PO Box 411, Troy, ID 83871. 208-835-4902. Editor: Steven E Erickson. Newsletter published irregularly. Sub $25/yr, circ 17. Submissions accepted only from subscribers. Topics: philosophical, metaphysical.
ASTROLOGY/SPIRITUAL, CULTURE, HUMOR

Enchantment Publishing of Oregon, Rt 1 Box 28H, Enterprise, OR, 97828. Editor: Irene Barklow. Book publisher.
OTHER/UNSPECIFIED

Encore Arts in Performance Magazine, Encore Publishing Inc. 1987 SW Montgomery Pl, Portland, OR 97201. 503-226-1468. Editor: Philbrook Heppner. Ads: Tom Brown. Published 60 times a season. Circ 986,000. Not a freelance market. Sample: 73¢.
ARTS, DRAMA, MUSIC

Encounters/Black Matrix Press, PO Box 5737, Grants Pass, OR 97527. 503-476-7039. Editor: Guy Kenyon. Sub $6. Circ 500. Uses 5–8 mss an issue. Pays in 3 copies (additional copies at 1/2 price) on publication. First rights acquired. Byline given. Submit mss with SASE. Accepts dot matrix, photocopies. Uses fiction, cartoons, B&W art work both for cover and interior. Send portfolio of at least 6 images. Maximum length 5,000 wds. "Any material not accompanied by SASE cannot be returned...We accept SF, horror, fantasy and humor. There is no particular slant to the type of fiction we need — just tell us a good story and if we like it we will try to fit it into our printing schedule."
FANTASY/SCI FI, FICTION, HUMOR

Encyclopedia Bananica, Banana Productions, PO Box 3655, Vancouver, BC V6B 3Y8. 604-876-6764. Editor/Ads: Anna Banana. Semiannual newsletter. $12/4 issues. Uses freelance material. Byline given, pays copies, acquires 1st rights. Query, ms, SASE. Topics: Anything about bananas, parody, spoof, news stories, graphics. Guidelines available. Sample $3.
HUMOR

Endeavor, Treasure Valley Community College, 650 College Blvd, Ontario, OR 97914. 503-889-6493. Biweekly newspaper "carrying campus news and nonfiction articles." Circ 1,400. Payment: Copies. Byline given. Query w/ms. Simultaneous submission OK. Nonfiction: 300–500 wds on experiences, problems of Eastern Oregon college students. Tips: "Query before submitting lengthy feature." Sample free.
COLLEGE/UNIVERSITY

Energeia Publishing Inc, PO Box 985, Salem, OR 97308-0985. 503-588-2926. Contact: Norman C Tognazzini. Publisher of softcover books. Accepts unsolicited submissions. Topics: self-help and humor.
CHILDREN (BY/ABOUT), HOW-TO, HUMOR

Enfantaisie, 2603 SE 32nd Ave, Portland, OR 97202. 503-235-5304. Editor: Michael Gould. Published bimonthly for children learning French. Circ 2,000. Not accepting submissions at this time. "We do not guarantee return of any unsolicited material."
CHILDREN (BY/ABOUT), CHILDREN/TEEN, LANGUAGE(S)

Engineering Geology/Soils Engineering Symposium, Idaho Transportation Department, PO Box 7129, Boise, ID 83707. Annual periodical. Circ 500.
IDAHO, SCIENCE

Engineering News-Record, 6040 Fifth NE, Seattle, WA 98115. 206-525-0433. Periodical.
BUSINESS

English Literature Studies Monograph Series, Department of English, University of Victoria, PO Box 1700, Victoria, BC V8W 2Y2. Book publisher.
COLLEGE/UNIVERSITY, EDUCATION, LITERARY

Ensemble Publications Inc, 3972 SW Dolph Ct, Portland, OR 97219-3659. Book publisher.
OTHER/UNSPECIFIED

Enterprise, PO Box 977, Lynnwood, WA 98046. 206-775-7521. Weekly newspaper.
COMMUNITY

Enterprise, c/o BC Central Credit Union, 1441 Creekside Dr, Vancouver, BC V6B 3R9. Editor: David Morton. Bimonthly concerning credit unions in BC, aimed at managers and directors. Circ 2,000. Payment: $200–300 on publication. Query w/SASE. Phone query, dot matrix OK. Publishes submissions in 1–2 mos. Nonfiction: 1,000–2,000 wds about credit unions and coopera-

tives. Photos: contact sheet and negatives w/article. Guidelines/ sample available.
BUSINESS

The Enterprise Courier, Box 471, Oregon City, OR 97045. 503-636-1911. Daily newspaper.
COMMUNITY

Entertainment Publications Inc, 8196 SW Hall Blvd, Beaverton, OR 97005. 503-646-8201. Book publisher.
ENTERTAINMENT

Entheos, PO Box 709, Philomath, OR 97370. No descriptive information.
OTHER/UNSPECIFIED

Entreprenurial Workshops, 4000 Aurora Ave N, Ste 112, Seattle, WA, 98103. Editor: Fred Klein. Publisher of books on building businesses and entrepreneurship.
BUSINESS

Environmental Law, Northwestern School of Law, 10015 SW Terwilliger Blvd, Portland, OR 97219. 503-244-1181. Contact: Managing Editor. Sub $20 (1 vol; 4 issues). Publishes journal on environmental law and natural resources only. Accepts unsolicited mss. No pay. Submit ms w/SASE. Photocopy OK. Reports in 2–3 wks. Accepts nonfiction. Sample $8–$10.
ENVIRONMENT/RESOURCES, LAW

Envoy, Fairbanks Arts Association, PO Box 2786, Fairbanks, AK 99707. An Alaskan newsletter "designed to keep isolated writers in touch with writers here and in the Northwest."
WRITING

The EOTU Group, 1810 W State #115, Boise, ID, 83702. Editor: Larry D Dennis. Publishes softcover books. Accepts unsolicited submissions. Pays advance, copies, royalties. Acquires 1st rights, others negotiated. Submit query letter, outline, sample chapters, complete ms, SASE. Photocopy, dot matrix OK. Responds in 3 mos; publishes in 8 mos. Accepts fiction and poetry; mostly interested in chapbooks: short novels or story collections, about 20–25,000 words. Sample $5.
AVANT-GARDE/EXPERIMENTAL, FANTASY/SCI FI, FICTION

EOTU, 1810 W State #115, Boise, ID, 83702. Editor: Larry D Dennis. Bimonthly magazine. Sub $18/yr; circ 200+. Uses freelance material. Pays $5–25 + copy on acceptance. Byline given. Acquires 1st rights. Submit ms, SASE. Dot matrix, photocopies OK. Reports in 6–8 wks; publishes in 2–6 mos. Accepts fiction, cartoons, artwork ($5 for black ink or pen); experimental fiction, "something that has never been written before.... Genre unimportant." 5,000 wds max. Guidelines, SASE. Sample $4.
AVANT-GARDE/EXPERIMENTAL, FANTASY/SCI FI, FICTION

Epicenter Press, 18821 64th Ave NE, Seattle, WA 98155. (206) 485-6822. Also: Box 60529, Fairbanks, AK 99706. Kent Sturgis, President. Publishes hard- & softcover originals, reprints. Accepts unsolicited submissions w/ SASE. Pays royalties. Acquires all rights. Submit ms, SASE. Reports in 4–6 wks. Accepts nonfiction.
ALASKA, OTHER/UNSPECIFIED

Equinews, PO Box 1778, Vernon, BC V1T 8C3. 604-545-9896. Editor: Dr B J White. Monthly newspaper. Sub $15/Cdn, $20/US. Circ 16,792. Uses freelance material. Pays $30–100/article on publication. Byline given. Submit ms, SASE. Dot matrix, photocopied OK. Reports in 2 mos. Publishes in 1–2 mos. Accepts nonfiction, photos, cartoons. Topics: all equine aspects. Photos, $5. Sample $2.
ANIMALS, RECREATION

ERGO! Bumbershoot's Literary Magazine, PO Box 9750, Seattle, WA 98109-0750. Editor/ads: Louise DiLenge. 206-448-5233. Annual of "works by Bumbershoot literary arts program participants, book reviews, bookfair participant directory, articles of literary interest." Circ 3,000. Accepts freelance material. Payment: Copies. Byline given. Query w/SASE. Phone query, dot matrix, photocopies, simultaneous submission, electronic OK. Uses nonfiction, fiction, poetry, photos, plays, cartoons. Photos: B&W glossy, no smaller than 3x5. Tips: "Reviews should be for small press publi-

cations. Articles should be of particular interest to the literary community. Make contact between the months of Feb./May." Sample: $1.
FICTION, LITERARY, POETRY

ERIC Clearinghouse on Educational Mgmt, 1787 Agate St, Eugene, OR 97403. Contact: Stuart C Smith. 503-686-5043. Publisher of softcover books on educational research. "The Educational Resources Information Center (ERIC) is a decentralized nationwide network, sponsored by the National Institute of Education, and designed to collect educational documents and to make them available to teachers, administrators, researchers, students." Query w/SASE. Photocopies OK. Education research. Guidelines/catalog available.
ABSTRACTS/INDICES, EDUCATION

ESQ, Washington State University Press, Pullman, WA 99164-5910. 509-335-3518. Quarterly. Sub $15.
COLLEGE/UNIVERSITY

Esquimalt Lookout, CFB, Esquimalt FMO, Victoria, BC V0S 1B0. Editor: A C Tassic. 604-385-0313. Periodical.
OTHER/UNSPECIFIED

Essence, Central Oregon Community College, NW College Way, Bend, OR 97701. 503-382-6112 X304. Editor: Bob Shotwol. College literary magazine. Editors could change yearly. SASE for guidelines.
COLLEGE/UNIVERSITY, FICTION, OREGON

Estrada Publications and Photography, 5228 Rambler Rd, Victoria, BC V8Y 2H5. 604-658-8870. Self-publisher. Not a freelance market.
CHILDREN/TEEN, HOW-TO, SPORTS

Estrela Press, 2318 2nd Ave, Box 23, Seattle, WA 98121. Book publisher.
OTHER/UNSPECIFIED

Et Cetera, King County Library System, 300 8th Ave N, Seattle, WA 98109. Contact: Public Information Officer. Periodical.
REFERENCE/LIBRARY

ethos, Campus Box 8841, Idaho State University, Pocatello, ID 83209. Editor: Mary Beitia.
COLLEGE/UNIVERSITY

Eurock, PO Box 13718, Portland, OR 97213. Editor: Archie Patterson. 503-281-0247. Quarterly of new music by experimental musicians from around the world. Circ 700. No pay. Byline given. Phone queries. "Interested in features, interviews, LP reviews. Knowledge necessary in this very specialized area of music.... Familiarity with the publication's concept is necessary.... Pre-arrangement of artists' material suggested." Sample: $1.
MUSIC

Europe Through the Back Door Travel Newsletter, 120 4th Ave N, Edmonds, WA 98020. 206-771-8303. Editor: Eileen Owen. Sub free. Circ 12,000. Uses 2 freelance mss per issue. Pays copies on publication. Rights acquired: None. Byline given. Submit ms, SASE. Dot matrix, photocopies, simultaneous OK. Reports in 1 mo. Publishes within 1 yr. Accepts nonfiction, poetry, photos, cartoons. Budget European travel tips, unusual places, how-to, personal experiences, specific tips, keep it light, 500–700 wds. B&W photos, camera-ready. Guidelines available. Sample free.
TRAVEL

Event, Kwantlen College, Box 9030, Surrey, BC V3T 5H8. Semiannual periodical. Not a freelance market.
COLLEGE/UNIVERSITY

Event, Douglas College, PO Box 2503, New Westminster, BC V3L 1X1. 604-527-5293. Editor: Dale Zieroth. Managing editor: Bonnie Bauder. Literary journal published 3X/yr. Sub $12/yr, $20/2 yrs; circ 1,000. Uses freelance material. Pays money ($25–500), copies on publication. Acquires 1st rights. Byline given. Submit ms, SASE. Photocopied OK. Reports in 3–4 mos; publishes in 10–15 mos. Accepts fiction, poetry, photos, plays, drama; nonfiction for creative nonfiction contest only. Tips: readers are sophisticated, open-minded; invite involvement and present experiences. Usual fiction about 5,000 wds. Payment: $25/poem, $20/page for other. Prefer 5X7 glossy B&W prints. Guidelines available. Sample $4.
FICTION, LITERARY, POETRY

Events Magazine, 7514 SW Barnes Rd #B, Portland, OR 97225-6265. 503-224-6109. Editor: Greg Kroell. Monthly. Sub $12.
ENTERTAINMENT, MUSIC

The Everett Herald, PO Box 930, Everett, WA 98206. Newspaper.
COMMUNITY

Evergreen Pacific Publications, 18002 15th Ave NE #B, Seattle, WA 98155-3838. 206-368-8158. Book publisher. Query w/SASE. Topics: charts, guides and logbooks for boating, fishing and scuba diving.
BOATING, FISHING, RECREATION

Evergreen Publishing, PO Box 3449, Kirkland, WA 98083. 206-624-8400. Editor: Martin Rudow. Book publisher.
OTHER/UNSPECIFIED

Ex Libris, Box 225, Sun Valley, ID 83353. Book publisher.
OTHER/UNSPECIFIED

The Exhibit Review, 3800 SW Cedar Hills Blvd. #241, Beaverton, OR 97005. 503-643-2783. Editor: Mary K Bucknell. Ads: Jim Sleeper. Quarterly directory. Sub $50/yr; circ 40,000. Uses freelance material. Pays copies, acquires all rights. Query letter, SASE. Responds in 6 wks; publishes in 4 mos. Accepts nonfiction, news items, interviews, reviews. Topics: international trade shows & exhibits.
BUSINESS, CALENDAR/EVENTS

Exhibition, Bainbridge Island Arts Council, 261 Madison Ave S, Bainbridge Island, WA 98110. Submission may also be sent to 4791 NE North Tolo Rd, Bainbridge Island, WA 98110. 206-842-6017, 206-842-7901. Editor: John Willson. Tri-annual magazine. Sub $15/yr; circ 1,000. Uses freelance material. Byline given, pays copies on publication. Submit ms w/SASE, short bio. Photocopied sub OK, no simultaneous. Reports in 3 mos. Accepts nonfiction, fiction (1,000 wds), poetry, cartoons, photos, B&W art, some half tones. Sample $3.
FICTION, POETRY

Expanducators Publishing, 135 N Howard Ave, Burnaby, BC V5B 1J6. Contact: Mrs Fraser. Book publisher.
OTHER/UNSPECIFIED

Expansions Publishing Co, PO Box 1360, Ellensburg, WA 98926. 509-968-4714. Editor: Janet Spath. Self-publisher only.
ASTROLOGY/SPIRITUAL, PHILOSOPHY, NEW AGE

Explorations, Department of English, University of Alaska Southeast, 11120 Glacier Hwy, Juneau, AK 99801. Contact: Art Petersen. Annual literary publication. Circ 250. Accepts poetry, fiction, fine arts. "Subject matter less important than quality. Best for submitters to purchase a copy first." Sample: $2.50.
ARTS, FICTION, POETRY

Exponent, Montana State University, 330 Strand Union Bldg, Bozeman, MT 59717-0001. 406-994-2611. Semiweekly newspaper.
COLLEGE/UNIVERSITY

The Extender, Jackson County Extension Service, 1301 Maple Grove Dr, Medford, OR 97501. 503-776-7371. Periodical.
AGRICULTURE/FARMING, GOVERNMENT

(f.) Lip, Box 1058, Stn A, Vancouver, BC V6C 2P1. Journal seeking feminist poetry, prose, reviews, and essays which experiment and are innovative in form, content, and ideas. Rates: $10 per featured writer. Query w/SASE.
FEMINISM, FICTION, POETRY

Facts Newspaper, 2765 East Cherry, Seattle, WA 98122. 206-324-0552. Weekly newspaper.
OTHER/UNSPECIFIED

Fade in Publications, 312 S 6th, Bozeman, MT 59715. Book publisher.
OTHER/UNSPECIFIED

Fairbanks News-Miner, Box 710, Fairbanks, AK 99707. 907-456-6661. Daily newspaper.
COMMUNITY

Fairchild Times, PO Box 218, Spokane, WA 99204. 509-535-7089. Weekly newspaper.
COMMUNITY

Fairhaven Communications, 810 N State St, Bellingham, WA 98225. Book publisher.
OTHER/UNSPECIFIED

Falcon Press Publishing Co Inc, 318 N Last Chance Gulch, PO Box 1718, Helena, MT 59624. 406-442-6597. Editor: Rick Newby. Publishes 20–30 hard- & softcover, subsidy books per yr. Accepts unsolicited submissions. Payment & rights vary. Submit query letter, outline, sample chapters, complete ms, SASE, phone. Photocopied, simultaneous subs OK. Reports in 2–3 mos; publishes in 3–6 mos. Accepts nonfiction, poetry, biography, memoirs, photos. Topics: hiking and nature guides, gift books, Western history. Guidelines, catalog available.
NW/REGIONAL HISTORY, MONTANA, OLD WEST

Family Tree Pony Farm, Publications Division, 1708 Burwell, Bremerton, WA 98310. Book publisher.
OTHER/UNSPECIFIED

Famous Faces Magazine, 139 Water, Vancouver, BC V6B 1A7.
BIOGRAPHY, CONSUMER

Fantasy and Terror, PO Box 20610, Seattle, WA 98102. Editor: Jessica A Salmonson. An "octavo format magazine, payment in copies, uses macabre poems-in prose, themes covering ghosts and graves, morosity and fear, somewhat experimental, highly refined, dark, cruel, evil, jaded, darkly romantic. Not for everyone." Queries w/SASE.
FANTASY/SCI FI, FICTION, POETRY

Fantasy Football, 18411 – 60th Place NE, Seattle, WA 98155. 206-525-6928. Editor: Bruce Taylor. Annual magazine. Newsstand $3.95. Circ 37,000. Will use 3–4 freelance mss per issue. Pays copies. Byline given. Interested in columnist material on pro football, offensive play photographs, cartoons. Tips: football expertise and wit is important.
SPORTS

Fantasy Macabre, Box 20610, Seattle, WA 98102. Editor: Jessica A Salmonson. Periodical. Payment: 1¢ per wd; copies. Queries w/SASE. Fiction: under 3,000 wds, "supernatural literature with a slant towards translations from European authors. Translators always welcome…. Lyric poetry (nothing experimental, no free verse)."
FANTASY/SCI FI, FICTION, POETRY

Farm & Ranch Chronicle, Box 157, Cottonwood, ID 83522. 208-962-3851. Monthly. Query/SASE.
AGRICULTURE/FARMING

Farm Review, PO Box 153, Lynden, WA 98264. 206-354-4444. Monthly.
AGRICULTURE/FARMING

Fathom Publishing Company, PO Box 821, Cordova, AK 99574. Book publisher.
OTHER/UNSPECIFIED

Fax Collector's Editions Inc, PO Box 851, Mercer Island, WA 98040. Book publisher.
OTHER/UNSPECIFIED

Features Northwest, 5132 126th Place NE, Marysville, WA 98270. 206-659-7559. Contact: John & Roberta Wolcott. Self-publishers, not a freelance market.
WRITING, OTHER/UNSPECIFIED

Federal Way News, 1634 South 312th, Federal Way, WA 98003. 206-839-0700. Weekly newspaper.
COMMUNITY

Fedora, PO Box 577, Siletz, OR 97380. Editor: John E Hawkes. Periodical.
OTHER/UNSPECIFIED

Fernglen Press, 473 Sixth St, Lake Oswego, OR 97034. 503-635-4719. Self-publisher softcover book on hiking trails, Hawaii, nature.
NATURAL HISTORY, OUTDOOR, TRAVEL

Ferry Travel Guide, Olympic Publishing Company, 7450 Oak Bay Rd, Port Ludlow, WA 98365. 206-437-9172. Editor: Dan Youra. Published 3X a year. Sub $6/yr; circ 330,000. Byline given. Query letter, SASE. Simultaneous submissions OK. Accepts nonfiction, articles, photos. Sample $2.
NORTHWEST, TRAVEL, WASHINGTON

The Fiction Review, Brick Lung Press, PO Box 12268, Seattle, WA 98102. Editor: S P Stressman. Ads: Stephanie Miskowski. Quarterly magazine. (Also publishes 1 chapbook a yr.) Sub $15. Circ 300. Uses 1–2 freelance mss per issue. Pays in copies on publication. Acquires 1st rights. Byline given. Submit ms, SASE. Reports in 2–8 wks. Publishes in 3–6 mos. Accepts nonfiction, fiction, other. "Essays on fiction. Reviews (500–750 wds) of collections & anthologies from small press or by writers needing more exposure. Stories any subject — prefer an edge to style — 500–4,000 wds." Tips: "Do not follow trends in contemporary, published fiction. Be unique." B&W graphics, 6x6" max. Guidelines available. Sample $4.
FICTION, LITERARY, LITERATURE

N H Fieldstone Publishing, PO Box 22, Medina, WA 98039. Book publisher.
OTHER/UNSPECIFIED

Figment: Tales from the Imagination, Figment Press, PO Box 3566, Moscow, ID 83843-0477. 208-882-8201. Editor: J C & Barb Hendee. Ads: J C Hendee. Quarterly magazine founded in 1989 for comics and art in the genres of SF, Fantasy, and SF/F related Horror. Sub $14.50/yr; circ 500. Accepts freelance material. Pays money, copies on acceptance. Byline given. Acquires 1st rights. Query SASE for guidelines before submitting. Photocopy, dot matrix OK. Reports in 8 wks; publishes in 6 mos. Accepts fiction, poetry, art, vignettes, novelettes. Stories: 3,000–5,000 wds/$17. Vignettes of 1,000 wds/$5. Sample $4.
FANTASY/SCI FI, FICTION, POETRY

Financial Times of Canada Ltd, 1035 Richards, Vancouver, BC B6B 3E4. Business news.
BUSINESS, CANADA, ECONOMICS

Findhorn Publications, PO Box 57, Clinton, WA 98236. Book publisher.
OTHER/UNSPECIFIED

Fine Madness, Box 31138, Seattle, WA 98103. Contact: editors. Semiannual journal of poetry, fiction reviews, essays. Circ 800, subs. $9/yr. Byline given, pays copies on publication, acquires 1st rights. Accepts freelance mss. Submit typewritten w/SASE only. Reports in 2 mos. Publishes in 1 yr. or less. Accepts fiction, poetry. Tips: poetry, 10 poems max; fiction, 20 pages max. Annual awards for best of volume." Guidelines available. Sample $4.
FICTION, LITERARY, POETRY

FINESSE Magazine for the Washington Woman, 14346 Burke Ave N, Seattle, WA 98133. 206-259-4377. Contact: Barb Bond. Bimonthly, offers the Fiction (1000 wd limit)/Poetry (12 line limit) Contest open to all WA women.
FICTION, POETRY, WOMEN

FINNAM Newsletter, Finnish-American Historical Society of West, PO Box 5522, Portland, OR 97208. 503-654-0448. Editor: Gene A Knapp. Quarterly, membership. Circ 400. Uses freelance material. Byline given. Pays copies. Submit query letter, ms, SASE, phone. Dot matrix, photocopied OK. Accepts nonfiction, photos, monographs. Guidelines, sample available.
NW/REGIONAL HISTORY, MINORITIES/ETHNIC

Finnish American Literary Heritage Foundation, PO Box 1838, Portland, OR 97207. Book publisher.
GENEALOGY, LANGUAGE(S), MINORITIES/ETHNIC

Finnish Connection, PO Box 1531, Vancouver WA 98668-1531. Editor/ads: Eugene Messer. 206-254-8936. Sub Assoc. $10/yr. Circ 5,500. Published 6 times per yr. Accepts 2–3 freelance mss per issue pertaining to Scandinavians and Finns in the US and Canada: nonfiction, fiction, poetry and photos (B&W/color glossies) w/articles. Query w/clips, ms, SASE. Phone queries, photocopied & simultaneous submissions OK. Reports "promptly." Gives byline and pays $20–$50 on publication. Guidelines available; sample/$1.
CULTURE, LANGUAGE(S), MINORITIES/ETHNIC

FIR Report, 1301 Maple Grove Dr, Medford, OR 97501. 503-776-7116. Periodical.
OTHER/UNSPECIFIED

Firehouse Theater, 1436 SW Montgomery St, Portland, OR 97201. Contact: Patricia Iron. 503-248-4737. Accepts scripts. Seeks new works by NW playwrights. Query w/SASE.
DRAMA

Fireweed: Poetry of Western Oregon, 1330 E 25th Ave, Eugene, OR 97403. 503-344-1053. Contact: E Muller. Quarterly journal. Sub $10/yr; circ 200. Uses freelance material. Byline given. Pays copy on publication. Acquires 1st rights. Submit complete ms, short bio, SASE. Dot matrix, simultaneous subs OK. Responds in 8 wks; publishes in 2–5 mos. Accepts poetry written by western Oregon poets; no subject, length or style limitations. Sample $2.50.
OREGON, POETRY

First Alternative Thymes, 1007 SE 3rd St, Corvallis, OR 97333. 503-929-4167. Editor: Christine Peterson. Monthly. Sub $6. Circ 1,000. Uses 10 freelance mss per issue. Pays in copies. Submit query w/clips, ms, phone, SASE. Dot matrix, photocopied, simultaneous OK. Reports in 1–2 wks. Accepts nonfiction, photos, cartoons. Sample available.
ADVENTURE, CHILDREN (BY/ABOUT), ENTERTAINMENT

Firsthand Press, 137 Sixth St, Juneau, AK 99801. Book publisher.
OTHER/UNSPECIFIED

Harriet U Fish, PO Box 135, Carlsborg, WA 98324. 206-542-9195. Self-publisher of 1 softcover book, reprint a yr. on local history. Print run: 1,000. Not a freelance market. Catalog available.
NW/REGIONAL HISTORY

The Fisherman's News, C-3 Bldg, Rm. 110, Fisherman's Terminal, Seattle, WA 98119. Bimonthly.
BUSINESS

Fishing and Hunting News, Outdoor Empire Publications Inc, Box C-19000, 511 Eastlake E, Seattle, WA 98109. Weekly.
OUTDOOR, RECREATION, SPORTS

Fishing Tackle Trade News, PO Box 2669, Vancouver, WA 98668-2669. Editor: John Kirk. 206-693-4721. Ads: Robert E Wood. Published 10 times a yr. for retailers of fishing tackle, hunting gear, camping gear, marine equipment. Circ 23,000. Sub $35. Accepts freelance material. Payment: Money on acceptance. Byline given. Queries w/SASE. Phone queries, dot matrix, photocopies OK. Uses nonfiction, photos, cartoons, illustrations. "Stories cover management, merchandising, business topics, species slants (how retailers can use info on two particular species to assist their selling efforts). We also cover news of the resources, and publish success profiles, articles on to use products, and product round-ups." Approx. 1,000–1,500 wds. Photos: B&W, verticals, $25; $50 color transparencies; no Polaroid. Guidelines/sample available free, SASE.
BUSINESS

Fjord Press, PO Box 16501, Seattle, WA 98116. 206-625-9363. Editor: Steve Murray. Adv: Nete Leth. Publishes hard- & softcover books. Accepts unsolicited submissions. Pays royalties, copies on publication. Submit query, SASE. Photocopied, simultaneous subs OK. Reports in 1–12 wks; publishes 18–24 mos. Accepts translations (include sample of original language text); fiction & nonfiction from western US writers, "preferably published ones, but will consider first-timers if high literary quality." Catalog available.
FICTION, NW/REGIONAL HISTORY, LITERARY

Flashes, North Idaho Children, 321 22nd Ave, PO Box 1288, Lewiston, ID 83501. Semiannual periodical.
CHILDREN (BY/ABOUT)

Flight Press, 3630 W Broadway #2, Vancouver, BC V6R 2B7. Nonfiction publisher. Book publisher.
OTHER/UNSPECIFIED

The Florian Group, 5620 SW Riverside Ln. #8, Portland, OR 97201. 503-638-1972. Editor: F Michael Sisavic. Publishes hard- & softcover nonfiction travel books. Press run: 5,000–10,000. Accepts unsolicited submissions. Dot matrix, photocopied OK.
TRAVEL

The Florist & Grower, 686 Honeysuckle N, Salem, OR 97301. 503-390-0766. Editor: Donald H Johnson. Monthly periodical.
AGRICULTURE/FARMING, BUSINESS

The Flyfisher, 1387 Cambridge St, Idaho Falls, ID 83401. Editor: Dennis G Bitton. 208-523-7300. Quarterly journal of the Federation of Fly Fishers. Circ 10,000. Accepts nonfiction/fiction, to 2,000 wds, on flyfishing. Buys photos w/articles. Pays various rates on publication. Query w/SASE. Guidelines available; samples $3 from Federation of Fly Fishers, PO Box 1088, West Yellowstone, MT 59758.
CRAFTS/HOBBIES, FISHING, SPORTS

Flyfishing, Frank Amato Publications, PO Box 02112, Portland, OR 97202. 503-653-8108. Editor: Marty Sherman. Ads: Joyce Sherman. Magazine published 5 times a yr. Uses 15 freelance mss per issue. Pays money on publication. Acquires 1st rights. Byline given. Submit query w/clips, ms, SASE. Reports in 2 wks. Accepts nonfiction articles (approx 1,500 wds) related to all aspects of flyfishing — location, water management, equipment, etc. "…buys ONLY stories which are accompanied by color transparencies, B&W glossies and/or original art work." Guidelines available.
FISHING, OUTDOOR

Flyfishing News, Views & Reviews, 1387 Cambridge Dr, Idaho Falls, ID 83401. 208-523-7300. Editor: Dennis G Bitton. Ads: Mae Farrow. Semimonthly. Sub $15/yr; circ 5,000. Uses freelance material. Byline given. Pays money ($50–150), copies on publication. Acquires 1st rights. Query letter, outline, complete ms, SASE, or phone. Reports in 2 wks; publishes in 6–24 mos. Accepts fiction, nonfiction, cartoons, news items, biography, essays, op/ed, interviews, and reviews. Length: 500–3,500 wds. Photos: B&W and color slides w/article. Topics: must deal with flyfishing. Guidelines available; sample $2.
FISHING, OUTDOOR, RECREATION

Flying Pencil Publications, PO Box 19062, Portland, OR 97219. 503-245-2314. Editors: Madelynne Diness, Dan Casali. Publishes softcover reprints and originals. Accepts unsolicited submissions. Pays royalties. Query letter, ms, SASE, phone. Responds in 2 wks; publishes in 4–12 mos. Accepts fiction, nonfiction and personal narrative, regional guidebooks, short story collection, young adult, children. Topics: ecologically sound outdoors orientation, specializing in fishing. Catalog available.
FISHING, OUTDOOR, RECREATION

Flying-W Publishing Co, PO Box 3118, Courtenay, BC V9N 5N3. Contact: Gordon Wagner. Book publisher.
OTHER/UNSPECIFIED

Focus on Books, PO Box 51103, Seattle, WA 98115. 206-324-2900. Editor: Kristen Nelson. Quarterly newsletter. Sub $12/yr; circ 4,000. Promotes books for a fee. Not a freelance market.
CHILDREN (BY/ABOUT), NORTHWEST, PUBLISHING/PRINTING

FoodTracks, WordScape Publishing, PO Box 69021, Portland, OR 97201. Contact: Rachel O'Neal, Editor. Bimonthly newsletter for consumers of natural and whole foods, seeking freelance material and illustrations. Pays copies. Send query w/clips. Guidelines available.
CONSUMER, ENVIRONMENT/RESOURCES, FOOD/COOKING

Footnotes, Pacific Northwest Booksellers Assoc, Rt 1 Box 219B, Banks, OR 97106. Contact: Debbie Garman. Monthly. Circ 500. Uses freelance material. Dot matrix, photocopied OK.
BOOK ARTS/BOOKS, PUBLISHING/PRINTING

Footprint Publishing Co. Ltd, PO Box 1830, Revelstoke, BC V0E 2S0. Published 3 hardcover original books in last 3 yrs. Does not accept unsolicited submissions.
BRITISH COLUMBIA, CANADIAN HISTORY

Judy Ford & Company, 11530 84th Ave NE, Kirkland, WA 98034. 206-823-4421. Editor: Judy Ford. Book publisher.
SEX

Forest Log, Department of Forestry, 2600 State St, Salem, OR 97310. 503-378-2562. Monthly, free. Does not use freelance material. Sample available.
AGRICULTURE/FARMING, FORESTRY, GOVERNMENT

Forest Voice, Native Forest Council, PO Box 2171, Eugene, OR 97402. 503-688-2600. Editors: Timothy Hermach & Harold Lonsdale. Sub $25/yr, free to contributors and members. Nonprofit educational newsletter devoted to preservation of publicly owned forests. Contributions welcomed with SASE. Sample available.
CONSERVATION, ENVIRONMENT/RESOURCES, FORESTRY

Forest Watch Magazine, 14417 SE Laurie Ave, Oak Grove, OR 97267. 503-652-7049. Monthly magazine. Sub $25/yr. Not a freelance market. Sample $2.
ENVIRONMENT/RESOURCES, FORESTRY, LAND USE/PLANNING

Forest World, World Forestry Center, 4033 SW Canyon Rd, Portland, OR 97221. 503-228-1367. Editor: Anna Browne. Sub $15/yr; circ 5,000. Quarterly magazine. Uses freelance material. Byline given. Pays money, copies on publication. Acquires 1st rights. Submit query letter, outline, complete ms, SASE, phone. Responds in 2 wks; publishes in 12 wks. Accepts nonfiction, fiction, news items, interviews, op/ed, photos. Topics: forest conservation, forest recreation and related resources. Stories require illustrative support. Payment for a story & photo package: $50–$250. Payment for photos or artwork purchased separately: $25–$100. Guidelines available. Sample $2.50.
CONSERVATION, CRAFTS/HOBBIES, FORESTRY

The Foreword, 15455 65th Ave S, Tukwila, WA 98188. Monthly periodical.
OTHER/UNSPECIFIED

Forks Forum & Peninsula Herald, PO Box 300, Forks, WA 98331. 206-374-2281. Weekly newspaper.
COMMUNITY

Forrest-Park Publishers, 5163 Ranchos Rd, Bellingham, WA 98226. 206-398-8915. Editor: Dan and Janet Homel. Publishes 2-3 softcover books per yr. Press run 2000-4000. Subjects: NW regional outdoor recreation - particularly fishing and fly fishing. Query w/SASE; clear, concise, well written submissions with high quality illustrations and/or photographs considered.
FISHING, NORTHWEST, OUTDOOR

Fort Lewis Ranger, PO Box 98801, Tacoma, WA 98499. 206-584-1212. Army base weekly newspaper.
MILITARY/VETS

The Foundation Afield, Rocky Mountain Elk Foundation, Rt 3, Wilderness Plateau, Troy, MT 59935. Periodical.
ANIMALS, CONSERVATION

Foundation House Publications, Box 9, 100 Mile House, BC V0K 2E0. Contact: Norman Smookler. Book publisher.
OTHER/UNSPECIFIED

Fountain Books, 2475 W 37th Ave, Vancouver, BC V6M 1P4. Self-publisher of softcover books for lawyers and legal secretaries. Not a freelance market.
LAW

Fountain Publications, 3728 NW Thurman St, Portland, OR 97210. Book publisher.
OTHER/UNSPECIFIED

The Fox Hunt, 506 W Crockett, Seattle, WA 98119. Book publisher.
OTHER/UNSPECIFIED

Fox Publishing Company, 320 SW Stark St, #519, Portland, OR 97204. 503-223-0051. Editor: Susan Monti. Ads: Lindsey McGrath. Publisher of annual directory. Sub $11/copy; circ 18,500. Uses freelance material. Byline given. Pays money, copies on acceptance. Acquires 1st rights. Submit query letter, SASE, assignment only. Responds in 1–2 wks. Accepts articles, reviews, photos. Sample $7.50.
TRAVEL

Fox Reading Research Company, PO Box 1059, Coeur d'Alene, ID 83814. Book publisher.
OTHER/UNSPECIFIED

Franklin County Graphic, PO Box 160, Connell, WA 99326. 509-234-3181. Weekly newspaper.
COMMUNITY

The Charles Franklin Press, 7821 175th St SW, Edmonds, WA 98020. Contact: Linda Meyer or Denelle Peaker. 206-774-6979. Publisher of 3 nonfiction, hard- & softcover, original books per yr; self-help and booklets for national organizations. "We specialize in children's books which teach safety and common sense, especially sexual assault and abduction prevention skills. Most of our books are 25 to 40 pages. They must be written in a non-threatening style. We rely heavily on an organization's existing network to distribute our books. Print run: 5,000. Accepts freelance material. Payment: Money, 8% without split, 5 or 6% with split, or negotiable. Rights purchased: All. Query w/sample chapters or complete ms and SASE. Photocopies OK. Reports in 1 month. Publishes in 6 mos. Tips: "Author should indicate to publisher the market and extent of the market as well as organizations that might be interested in the book." Catalog available.
CHILDREN/TEEN, FAMILY, WOMEN

The Fraser Institute, 626 Bute St, Vancouver, BC V6E 3M1. 604-688-0221. Contact: Sally Pipes. Publisher of trade books and journal (sub $48–95/yr; circ 4,500; not a freelance market). Topics: religion, social sciences, business, social issues. Catalog available. SASE/IRC for guidelines.
BUSINESS, ECONOMICS, SCHOLARLY/ACADEMIC

Fredrickson/Kloepfel Publishing Company, 7748 17th SW, Seattle, WA 98106. 206-767-4915. Contact: J Fred Blair. Publishes softcover books. Accepts unsolicited submissions. Payment by profit-share. Rights revert to author. Submit query, SASE. Photocopy, simultaneous OK. Responds in 1 wk. Accepts fiction, poetry, nonfiction, cartoons, articles. Topics: anthologies on specific subjects announced through national newsletter grapevine.
CULTURE, PHILOSOPHY, POETRY

Free Press, PO Box 218, Cheney, WA 99004-0218. 509-235-6184. Weekly newspaper.
COMMUNITY

Free! The Newsletter of Free Materials/Services, Department 284, Box C34069, Seattle, WA 98124-1069. Published 5 time a yr. Lists free materials which have been evaluated by professionals and are readily available. Short descriptions. Sub $18. No submissions info. Query w/SASE.
CONSUMER, EDUCATION

Freedom Socialist, New Freeway Hall, 5018 Ranier Ave S, Seattle, WA 98118. 206-722-2453. Political tabloid.
FEMINISM, POLITICS, SOCIALIST/RADICAL

Freighter Travel News, 3524 Harts Lake Rd, Roy, WA 98580. Editor: Leland Pledger. Monthly newsletter with firsthand reports of freighter voyages. Sub $18. Freelance mss accepted. Pays copies. Byline given. Submit ms, SASE. Dot matrix, photocopies OK. Reports in 15 days. Publishes in 6 mos. Nonfiction. Tips: Wants articles on "recent travel experience aboard freighters, barges, or other unique water craft." Sample $1.50
TRAVEL

The Freighthoppers Manual, PO Box 191, Seattle, WA 98111. Editor: Dan Leen. Book publisher.
TRAVEL

Friendly Press, 2744 Friendly St, Eugene, OR 97405. Book publisher.
OTHER/UNSPECIFIED

Friends of Wells Gray Park Society, Box 1386, Kamloops, BC V2C 6L7. Self-publisher only. Not a freelance market.
000

Friendship Publications Inc, PO Box 1472, Spokane, WA 99210. Book publisher.
OTHER/UNSPECIFIED

From The Woodpile, Matanuska-Susitna Community College, PO Box 2899, Palmer, AK 99645. Contact: Barbara Mishler. 907-745-4255. Sub $5/yr. Annual literary journal of poetry, short fiction, essays and photographs. "Designed to offer writers and photographers from remote Alaskan areas a market for their creative efforts. Though we come from University of Alaska's rural education system, we will consider mss from anywhere inside or outside Alaska." Query w/ms, SASE.
FICTION, PHOTOGRAPHY, POETRY

Frontier Printing & Publishing, 322 Queen Anne Ave N, Seattle, WA 98109. Editor: Jerry Russell. Publishes 4 books a yr. Press run: 3,000. Accepts unsolicited submissions. Pays royalties. Submit query. Reports in 1 mo. Publishes in 1 yr. Guidelines available.
NW/REGIONAL HISTORY, HOW-TO, NORTHWEST..

The Frontiersman, 1261 Seward Meridian Rd, Wasilla, AK 99687. 907-376-3288. Editors: Sean Hanlon/Duncan Frazier. Ads: Barb Stephl. Biweekly newspaper. Uses freelance material. Pays money on publication. Acquires 1st rights. Byline given. Submit query w/clips, SASE. Photocopied OK. Reports in 2 wks. Publishes in 2 wks. Accepts nonfiction about rural Alaska.
ALASKA, ENVIRONMENT/RESOURCES, NW/REGIONAL HISTORY

O W Frost Publisher, 2141 Lord Baranof Dr, Anchorage, AK 99503. Book publisher.
OTHER/UNSPECIFIED

Fryingpan, 7378 SW Pacific Coast Hwy, Waldport, OR 97394. Editors: Carol Alice/John Fry. Monthly magazine.
130

Fugue: Literary Digest of the University of Idaho, Brink Hall - Rm 200, University of Idaho, Moscow, ID 83843. 208-882-8201. Editor: J C Hendee. Ads: Leiloni Reed. Tri-annual magazine. Sub $11/yr; circ 200+. Accepts submissions by U of I or Lewis Clark State College students only. Byline given. Pays copies on publication. Submit complete ms, SASE. Photocopied, dot matrix subs OK. Reports in 3–12 wks; publishes in 3–6 mos. Accepts nonfiction, fiction, poetry, plays, B&W photos. Guidelines available.
COLLEGE/UNIVERSITY, LITERARY, STUDENT

Function Industries Press, PO Box 9915, Seattle, WA 98109. Contact: Tom Grothus. Self-publisher.
HUMOR, VISUAL ARTS

Fur Bearers, 2235 Commercial Dr, Vancouver, BC, V5N 4B6. Periodical.
OTHER/UNSPECIFIED

Future Science Research Publishing Company, PO Box 86372, Portland, OR 97286. 503-235-1971. Self-publisher of books on environment, new age science. Not a freelance market. Catalog available.
ENVIRONMENT/RESOURCES, SCIENCE, NEW AGE

GL Images, 203 Casa Nova, 400 E Denny Way, Seattle, WA 98122. 206-328-1746. Contact: J David Austin. Monthly magazine of gay and lesbian life. Circ 5,900. Uses 1–3 freelance mss per issue. Pays money on publication, byline given. Submit ms w/SASE. Dot matrix, photocopies, electronic/modem, computer disk OK. Reports in 1 month; publishes in 1–2 months. Accepts nonfiction, fiction, photos, cartoons. Guidelines and sample issues available.
FICTION, GAY/LESBIAN

Gable & Gray Publishing, 1307 W Main, Medford, OR 97501. 503-779-1353. Editor: Stephen Guettermann. Publishes 10–30 softcover books a yr. Avg press run 10,000. Payment & rights negotiable. Submit outline, sample chapters, SASE. Dot matrix, photocopied, simultaneous OK. Reports in 2–3 mos. Publishes in 6 mos. Topics: health, sports & training, business manuals & how-to, New Age, environmental, others of a marketable nature. Tips: query should identify audience & why the ms is needed. "Controversial & provocative topics are great as long as the writer has the ability to present issues with strength & clarity." Guidelines available.
BUSINESS, HEALTH, SPORTS

Gadfly Press, 8925 SW Homewood St, Portland, OR 97225. Contact: Robert Lynott. 503-292-8890. Publisher of books on meteorology.
SCIENCE

Gahmken Press, PO Box 1467, Newport, OR 97365. 503-265-2965. Contact: Range D Bayer. Publishes softcover books. Accepts unsolicited submissions. Pays 4 copies. Acquires 1st rights. Submit ms, SASE. Dot matrix, photocopies, computer disk OK. Reports in 3 wks; publishes in 6 mos. Accepts nonfiction, monograph-length mss dealing with detailed studies of OR ornithology or ornithologists. Guidelines, samples available.
NATURAL HISTORY, OREGON, SCHOLARLY/ACADEMIC

Gaining Ground, PO Box 9184, Portland, OR 97207. Book publisher.
OTHER/UNSPECIFIED

Gallerie: Women's Art, 2901 Panorama Dr, N Vancouver, BC V7G 2A4. 604-929-7129. Editor: Caffyn Kelley. Quarterly journal. Sub $20/yr. Circ 1,500. Uses freelance material. Submit query w/clips. Reports in 1–2 mos. Accepts photos and mss from women artists and philosophical articles by writers on women's art. All articles include B&W photos. Guidelines available. Sample $6.
ARTS, VISUAL ARTS, WOMEN

Galley Proofs, 131 W 8th St, McMinnville, OR 97128. 503-472-8277. Editor: Jo McIntyre. Oregon Press Women membership newsletter. Circ 200. Uses 2–3 freelance mss per issue. Pays in copies on publication. Byline given. Submit by phone query. Simultaneous OK. Reports in 1–4 wks. Publishes in 1–2 mos. Accepts nonfiction, photos. Topics: member profiles, organization news, First Amendment issues. Photos: B&W, prefer screened. Tips: "We are mainly interested in writing as a profession, newspaper people, public relations, freelance.
MEDIA/COMMUNICATIONS, WOMEN, WRITING

Galloway Publications Inc, 2940 NW Circle Blvd, Corvallis, OR 97330. Book publisher.
OTHER/UNSPECIFIED

Gardyloo Press, 2620 SW De Armond Dr, Corvallis, OR 97333. Poetry books.
POETRY

Garren Publishing, 1008 SW Comus, Portland, OR 97219. 503-636-3506. Contact: John H Garren. Self-publisher of books on whitewater rivers. Not a freelance market.
OUTDOOR

Gasworks Press, 16292 37th NE, Seattle, WA 98155. Book publisher.
OTHER/UNSPECIFIED

The Gated Wye, Office of State Fire Marshal, 3000 Market St NE #534, Salem, OR 97310. 503-378-2884. Editor: Nancy Campbell. Monthly of "timely items and important features for the fire service." Sub $10. Circ 1,150. Uses freelance mss. Pays copies on publication. Byline given. Query w/SASE. Phone queries, dot matrix, photocopies OK. Reports in 2 mos. Publishes in 2 mos. Accepts nonfiction, poetry; fire service related, training and education. Sample free.
GOVERNMENT, LABOR/WORK, PUBLIC AFFAIRS

Gazette, PO Box 770, Colfax, WA 99111. 509-397-4333. Weekly newspaper.
COMMUNITY

Gazette-Tribune, PO Box 250, Oroville, WA 98844. 509-476-3602. Weekly newspaper.
COMMUNITY

Gem Paperbacks, PO Box 1201, Burley, ID 83318. Book publisher.
OTHER/UNSPECIFIED

Gem State Geological Review, Idaho Geological Survey, c/o University of Idaho, Moscow, ID 83843. Editor: Roger C Stewart. Annual periodical.
GEOLOGY/GEOGRAPHY, IDAHO, SCIENCE

Gemaia Press, 209 Wilcox Lane, Sequim, WA 98382. Book publisher.
OTHER/UNSPECIFIED

Genealogical Forum of Portland Bulletin, Rm. 812, 1410 SW Morrison, Portland, OR 97205. Monthly.
GENEALOGY

General Aviation News & Flyer (formerly Western Flyer and Sport Flyer), PO Box 98786, Tacoma, WA 98498-0786. 206-588-1743. Editor: Dave Sclair. Biweekly tabloid devoted to general aviation. Circ 35,000. Rights purchased: One time rights, 1st or 2nd. Query w/SASE on longer pieces; send ms or phone on breaking news. Dot matrix, simultaneous submissions OK. Reports in 2–3 wks. Publishes in 2–3 mos. Nonfiction: 500–2,000 wds on sport and general aviation news, safety, pilot reports, people, airports, destinations, etc. Review back issues for hints on departments, columns, fillers.

Photos: B&W prints $10, color slides or prints $25–50. Guidelines available for #10 SASE; sample/$2.
AVIATION, RECREATION, SPORTS

Geo-Heat Center Bulletin, Oregon Institute of Technology, 3201 Campus Dr, Klamath Falls, OR 97603. 503–885-1750. Editor: Paul S Lienau. Quarterly, free; circ 2,000. Uses freelance material. No pay. Submit query letter, SASE, phone. Photocopied, dot matrix, disk/modem subs OK. Accepts nonfiction. Topic: technical, geothermal heat. Sample free.
COLLEGE/UNIVERSITY, ENVIRONMENT/RESOURCES, TECHNICAL

Geologic Publications, Division of Geology & Earth Resources, MS PY-12, Department of Natural Resources, Olympia, WA 98504. Publishes softcover books & an irregular newsletter. Uses freelance material on assignment. Query letter, SASE.
GEOLOGY/GEOGRAPHY, NATURAL HISTORY, SCIENCE

Geophysical Institute, University of Alaska, 903 Koyukuk Ave, Fairbanks, AK 99701. Book publisher.
ALASKA, NATURAL HISTORY, SCIENCE

The Georgia Straight, 1235 W Pender St, 2nd Fl, Vancouver, BC V6E 2V6. Contact: Charles Campbell. 604-681-2000. Weekly entertainment guide. Sub $25/yr Cdn, $40/yr US. "Unsolicited mss, photographs and graphics must be accompanied by SASE & Canadian stamp. Payment at approved rates will be made 30 days after publication, upon presentation of invoice."
BRITISH COLUMBIA, COUNTER CULTURE, ENTERTAINMENT

The Georgian Press Company, 2620 SW Georgian Place, Portland, OR 97201. Contact: E K MacColl. Publisher of Portland histories. Not a freelance market.
NW/REGIONAL HISTORY, OREGON

Getting Together Publications, 3006 – 21st Ave S, Seattle, WA 98144. 206-329-0172. Book publisher.
OTHER/UNSPECIFIED

Ghost Town Quarterly, Box 714, Philipsburg, MT 59858. 406-859-3736. Editor/Ads: Donna McLean. Quarterly magazine. Sub $8. Circ 5,000–7,000. Uses freelance material. Pays 5¢/word on publication. Acquires first rights. Byline given. Submit ms, SASE. Dot matrix, photocopied OK. Reports in 2–3 mos. Publishes 1–12 mos. Accepts nonfiction, fiction, poetry, photos, cartoons, historical documents (letters, diary pages). Features a "Students' Corner" for K–12 writers. Topics: traditions, history & heritage of ghost towns in North America; events of a historical nature; unique places to visit; unusual museums. Tips: use extreme care with factual information. Guidelines available. Sample $3.50.
CHILDREN (BY/ABOUT), OLD WEST, TRAVEL

Daniel W Giboney, PO Box 5432, Spokane, WA 99205. 509-926-3338. Self-publisher of a book on divorce. Not a freelance market.
LAW

Gilgal Publications, PO Box 3386, Sunriver, OR 97707. 503-593-8639. Editor: Judy Osgood. Periodical.
OTHER/UNSPECIFIED

GIS/CAD Mapping Solutions, Venture Communications Inc, PO Box 02332, Portland, OR 97202. 503-236-5810. Fax 503-245-1110. Editor: Michael J Carey. Sub $99. Publishes monthly newsletter & manuals. No unsolicited mss on manuals. Freelance accepted for newsletter. Needs technical knowledge on subject to write for us. Pay negotiable on publication. Rights purchased: All. No byline in newsletter. Phone query OK. Dot matrix, photocopy OK. Accepts nonfiction. "Technology, mapping, training for public sector and vendors. Key = applications, not product literature." Sample: $8 end-users. Copies for interested writers.
COMPUTERS, PUBLIC AFFAIRS, TECHNICAL

Glacier Natural History Association Inc, Glacier National Park, West Glacier, MT 59936. Publisher, educational organization. Does not accept unsolicited submissions. Catalog available.
NATURAL HISTORY

The Glasgow Courier, 341 3rd Ave So, Glasgow, MT 59230. 406-228-9301. Editor: Doris Vallard. Ads: Stanley D Sonsteng. Weekly newspaper. Sub $18/

yr; circ 4,200. Does not accept unsolicited submissions. Query letter, SASE. Accepts news items, photos.
COMMUNITY

Glass Studio Magazine, Box 23383, Portland, OR 97223. Editor: Jim Wilson. 503-620-3917. Monthly for professional glass artists, studios, museums. Payment: $100–300 on publication. Rights purchased: First. Submit ms, SASE. Dot matrix, simultaneous submissions OK. Reports in 3 wks. Publishes in 2 mos. Nonfiction: 1,500–2,500 wds dealing with glass art, business for artists, hazards in industry. Photos: Slides or B&W glossy with article. Guidelines available; sample/$2.
ARTS, BUSINESS

Glen Abbey Books Inc, 735 N Northlake Way, Seattle, WA 98103. 206-548-9360. Editor: Bill Pittmann. Publishes softcover original books. Accepts unsolicited submissions. Pays royalties. Acquires all rights. Submit query letter, outline, sample chapters, synopsis, or complete ms with SASE. No photocopies. Computer disk OK (IBM). Reports in 2 mos; publishes in 6–12 mos. Accepts nonfiction only. Topics: 12-step recovery groups (from alcohol, drugs, etc). Guidelines and catalog available.
HEALTH, PSYCHOLOGY

Global Fishing Publications, 2442 NW Market St #113, Seattle, WA 98107. 206-789-8405. Contact: Donal Driscoll. Ads: C Mahoney. Self-publisher. Not a freelance market.
FISHING

Globe & Mail, 920-1200 Burrard St, Vancouver, BC V6Z 2C7. Periodical.
BRITISH COLUMBIA, OTHER/UNSPECIFIED

Globe Publishing Co, 3625 Greenwood N, Seattle, WA 98103. Publishes poetry and prose on love. No submissions info. Query w/SASE.
FICTION, POETRY

Glover Publications, PO Box 21745, Seattle, WA 98111. Book publisher.
OTHER/UNSPECIFIED

Gluten Intolerance Group of North America, PO Box 23053, Seattle, WA 98102. Book publisher.
HEALTH

Goal Lines, The Oregon Youth Soccer Association, 1750 Skyline Boulevard #25, Portland, OR 97221. 503-292-5542. Editor: Judy Davidson. Ads: Don Patch. Newspaper published 5 times/yr. Sub $6. Circ 25,000. Uses freelance material. Byline given. Query w/clips, SASE. Dot matrix, computer disk OK. Reports in 2 wks. Publishes in next issue. Accepts nonfiction, photos. Guidelines available. Sample $1.
CALENDAR/EVENTS, SPORTS

Golden Eagle, Audubon Society, Golden Eagle Chapter, PO Box 8261, Boise, ID 83707. Editor: Scott Tuthill. Monthly.
CONSERVATION, NATURAL HISTORY, OUTDOOR

The Golden Eagle, Oregon Autobody Craftsman Association, 4370 NE Halsey, Portland, OR 97213. 503-284-7762. Editor: John Yoswick. Monthly trade magazine. Circ 3,500. Uses freelance material. Byline given. Submit query letter, clips, complete ms, SASE. Photocopied, dot matrix subs OK. Responds in 3 wks; publishes in 1–3 mos. Accepts cartoons, news items, biography, photos, interviews, op/ed, articles. Sample $1.
TRADE/ASSOCIATIONS

Golden Horizons Inc, 5238 Pullman Ave NE, Seattle, WA 98105. 206-525-8160. Self-publisher only.
SENIOR CITIZENS

Golden Messenger, 3025 Lombard, Everett, WA 98201. Monthly.
OTHER/UNSPECIFIED

Goldendale Sentinel, 117 W Main St, Goldendale, WA 98620. 509-773-4212. Local newspaper.
COMMUNITY, OTHER/UNSPECIFIED

Goldermood Rainbow, 331 W Bonneville St, Pasco, WA 99301. Book publisher.
OTHER/UNSPECIFIED

Golf Sports Publishing, PO Box 3687, Lacey, WA 98503. Self-publisher of 1 softcover book a yr. for golfers. Print run: 10,000. Not a freelance market.
SPORTS

Goliards Press, 3515 18th St, Bellingham, WA 98225. Book publisher.
OTHER/UNSPECIFIED

Gonzaga University Press, Gonzaga University, Spokane, WA 99202. Book publisher.
COLLEGE/UNIVERSITY

Good Medicine Books, Box 844, Invermere, BC V0A 1K0. Publisher of books on history and nature.
GENERAL HISTORY, NATURAL HISTORY

Good Times Publishing Co, PO Box 8071-107, Blaine, WA 98230. 604-736-1045. Editor: Dorothy Miller. Nonfiction self-help books, particularly nutrition and psychology. Reports in 2 mos. Pays 2–4%. 2 titles in 1991.
FOOD/COOKING, PSYCHOLOGY

Goodfruit Grower, PO Box 9219, Yakima, WA 98909. 509-457-8188. Editor: Phil Shelton. Ads: Randy Morrison. Sub $18. Circ 13,000. Trade magazine published 21 times a yr. Uses 4–6 freelance mss per issue. Pay: $2 column inch, $5 pictures, more for color or cover material; on publication. Rights acquired: First. Byline given. Submit query w/clips. Phone query, dot matrix OK. Reports in 4 wks. Publishes in 4–12 wks. Accepts nonfiction, photos. "…the official trade publication of the Washington State tree fruit industry, but circulates far beyond the boundaries of the state and is a respected source of information for orchardists everywhere, including overseas. Subject matter includes growing and marketing of commercial tree fruit. Grower profiles, too."
AGRICULTURE/FARMING, BUSINESS

Gooding Country Leader, PO Box 56, Gooding, ID 83330-0056. 208-934-4449. Newspaper.
COMMUNITY

The Gorge Current, 209 Oak St #206, Hood River, OR 97031. 503-386-6223. Editor: Mike Worral. Weekly magazine. Sub $24/summer season; circ 7,000. Uses freelance material. Byline given. May pays money on publication. Submit query letter, outline, SASE, phone. Dot matrix, simultaneous, disk/modem subs OK. Responds in 2–4 wks, publishes in 1–6 wks. Accepts nonfiction, cartoons, news items, biography, interviews, op/ed, reviews, photos (B&W, color print, $10). Topics: Columbia Gorge, Portland to Arlington, Oregon and Washington; recreation, land use, environment; timely info most desirable. Guidelines available. Sample 50¢.
NORTHWEST, RECREATION, SPORTS

Gospel Tract Distributors, 8036 N Interstate Ave, Portland, OR, 97217. 503-283-5985. Contact: President. Book publisher.
RELIGION

Bruce Gould Publications, PO Box 16, Seattle, WA 98111. Book publisher.
OTHER/UNSPECIFIED

Grandparents Journal, Senior Writers Network, E 1419 Marietta Ave, Spokane, WA 99207. 509-487-3383. Editor: Elinor Nuxoll. Quarterly newsletter. Sub $6. Circ 200+. Uses freelance from writers age 50+. Byline given, pays copies, prizes, acquires 1st rights. Submit cips, ms, SASE. Dot matrix, photocopied, simultaneous subs OK. Reports in 2–3 mos. "Wants news clips for 'grandparents in the news.'" Guidelines available, sample $1.50.
CHILDREN/TEEN, FAMILY, SENIOR CITIZENS

The Grange News, PO Box 1186, Olympia, WA 98507-1186. Editor: Dave Howard. 206-284-1753. Monthly for rural WA audience on agricultural news/information about the Grange. Circ 48,000. Payment: Money on acceptance. Byline given. Query w/SASE. Publishes submissions in 1 month. Nonfiction: 600–800 wds on agriculture, personal finances, home economics.
AGRICULTURE/FARMING, WASHINGTON

Grant County Journal, PO Box 998, Ephrata, WA 98823. 509-754-4636. Weekly newspaper.
COMMUNITY

Grants Pass Daily Courier, 409 SE Seventh St, Box 1468, Grants Pass, OR 97526. 503-474-3200. Daily newspaper.
COMMUNITY

Grapevine Publications Inc, PO Box 118, Corvallis, OR 97339. Contact: Gregg A Kleiner. 503-754-0583. Publisher of 2–5 nonfiction, softcover books a yr, mainly technically oriented for calculator & computer owners. Print run: 3,000–10,000. Accepts freelance material. Rights purchased: First. Query with outline, sample chapters and SASE. Dot matrix, photocopies OK. Reports in 4 wks. Publishes in 6–12 mos. Presents "technical material to readers in a non-intimidating, friendly manner. We like to use humor, illustrations, etc. We're interested in what you have if it fits into our upbeat, understandable, uniquely different style. We're into teaching through no-jargon, straightforward, conversational writing."
COMPUTERS, TEXTBOOKS

Graphic Arts Center Publishing Co, 3019 NW Yeon Ave, PO Box 10306, Portland, OR 97210. 503-226-2402. Editor: Jean Andrews. Publishes hard- & softcover books. Does not accept unsolicited submissions. Pays money, copies, royalties, advance. Acquires all rights. Submit query letter, SASE. Responds in 3 mos; publishes in 6 mos. Accepts nonfiction. Guidelines, catalog available.
CHILDREN/TEEN, NORTHWEST, OUTDOOR

Grassroots Oracle, 29581 Fraser Hwy, Aldergrove, BC V0X 1A0. Contact: Arthur Joyce. Publication of writers' group.
FICTION, POETRY, WRITING

Herbi Gray, Handweaver, PO Box 2343, Olympia, WA 98507. 206-491-4138. Self-publisher of softcover originals books on handweaving. Accepts no submissions. Catalog available.
CRAFTS/HOBBIES, HOW-TO

Gray Power, 16901 SE Division St #111, Portland, OR 97236. Semiannual.
SENIOR CITIZENS

Grayfellows Inc, 20567 Newbedford Cr, Bend, OR 97702-9457. Contact: Linda Gray. Book publisher.
OTHER/UNSPECIFIED

Grays Harbor County Vidette, PO Box 671, Montesano, WA 98563. 206-249-3311. Weekly newspaper.
COMMUNITY

Great Expeditions Magazine, Box 8000-411, Sumas, WA 98295-8000 (or Box 8000-411, Abbotsford, BC V2S 6H1). 604-852-6170. Editor: Craig Henderson. Bimonthly magazine. Sub $18. Circ 8,000. Uses 36 freelance mss per issue. Pays $20–35, plus copies, for 1st or 2nd rights on publication. Buys photos with articles. Byline given. Submit query w/clips, SASE. Dot matrix, photocopies, simultaneous subs OK. Reports in 6 wks. Publishes in 1–6 mos. Accepts nonfiction: "Unusual, off-the-beaten path travel, budget travel outside of North America, socially-responsible tourism and working abroad. Articles 800–2,500 wds." Guidelines available. Sample $4.
TRAVEL

Great Falls Montana Catholic Register, PO Box 13997, Great Falls, MT 59403. Newspaper.
RELIGION

Great Falls Tribune, 205 River Dr S, PO Box 5468, Great Falls, MT 59403. Editor: Terry Dwyer. 406-761-6666. Daily newspaper.
COMMUNITY

Great Northwest Publishing & Distributing Company, PO Box 103902, Anchorage, AK 99510. Book publisher.
ALASKA, OTHER/UNSPECIFIED

Green Bough Press, 3156 W Laurelhurst Dr NE, Seattle, WA 98105. 206-523-0022. Self-publisher of 1 softcover book a yr. for children on animals and writing. Not a freelance market. Catalog available.
ANIMALS, CHILDREN/TEEN, WRITING

Green Stone, 5612 56th NE, Seattle, WA 98105. 206-524-4744. Editor: Joe Devine. Publishes hard- & softcover books on English education. Self-publisher only. Does not accept unsolicited submissions.
EDUCATION

Greenwood Publications, 12324 25th NE, Seattle, WA 98125. Book publisher.
OTHER/UNSPECIFIED

Greer Gardens, 1280 Goodpasture Island Rd, Eugene, OR 97401. 503-686-8266. Editor: Harold Greer. Self-publisher.
OTHER/UNSPECIFIED

Gresham Outlook, 1190 NE Division St, PO Box 880, Gresham, OR 97030. 503-665-2181. Semiweekly newspaper.
COMMUNITY

Greycliff Publishing Co, Box 1273, Helena, MT 59624. Publisher of hardcover books on fishing. Query letter, SASE.
FISHING

The Griffin Press, PO Box 85, Netarts, OR 97143. 503-842-2356. Book publisher.
OTHER/UNSPECIFIED

Griggs Printing & Publishing, 426 1st Ave, Box 1351, Havre, MT 59526. Book publisher.
OTHER/UNSPECIFIED

Gros Ventre Treaty Committee, Ft Belknap Agency, Harlem, MT 59526. Book publisher.
NATIVE AMERICAN

Group 1 Journal, 45 W Broadway, Ste 205, Eugene, OR 97401. 503-344-7813.
OTHER/UNSPECIFIED

The Group Theatre Company, 3755 University Way, Seattle, WA 98105. 206-685-4969. Contact: William S Yellow Robe, Jr. Uses full length comedies and dramas. Submit query letter, synopsis, SASE. Responds in 2–4 wks.
DRAMA

Growing Edge Magazine, PO Box 90, Corvallis, OR 97339. 503-757-8477. Editor: Don Parker. Ads: Jane DeHart. Quarterly magazine. Sub $24.95/yr; circ 20,000. Uses freelance material. Byline given. Pays $.075/wd on publication. Acquires first, other rights. Submit query letter, outline, synopsis, SASE, or phone. Photocopy, dot matrix, disk/modem, simultaneous subs OK. Responds in 2–3 wks; publishes in 3 mos. Accepts nonfiction, news items, biography, interviews, op/ed, reviews, photos (B&W-color, $5–50). Topics: high-tech gardening techniques, people using them use. Guidelines available. Sample $6.50.
AGRICULTURE/FARMING, GARDENING, TECHNICAL

Growing Images, 627 Kay St, Fairbanks, AK 99709. Book publishers.
OTHER/UNSPECIFIED

Gryphon West Publishers, PO Box 12096, Seattle, WA 98102. Publisher of 1 hard- & softcover original a yr. Query w/SASE.
OTHER/UNSPECIFIED

Guide Magazine, One in Ten Publishing Co, PO Box 23070, Seattle, WA 98102. 206-323-7343. Editor: Bill Swigart. Ads: Lee Johnson. Monthly magazine, gay-lesbian oriented issues, social info. Sub $12.95. Circ 12,000. Uses 3 freelance mss per issue. Pays money on publication, $5 for photos. Rights acquired: First. Byline given. Submit query w/clips, SASE. Dot matrix, photocopies, simultaneous, computer disk OK. Reports in 4 wks. Publishes in 2 mos. Accepts nonfiction, fiction, photos, cartoons. Sample $1.
GAY/LESBIAN, GOVERNMENT, MINORITIES/ETHNIC

Hack'd, PO Box 17640, Portland, OR 97217. 503-289-5220. Editor: Jim Dodson. Ads: Chris Dodson. Quarterly for those whose interests include motorcycle sidecars as an unequaled form of transportation. Sub rate. $10. Circ 3,000. Accepts freelance mss. Pays copies. Rights acquired: None. Byline given. Query, SASE. Dot matrix, photocopies, simultaneous submission, electronic, computer disk OK. Accepts nonfiction, fiction, poetry, photos, plays, cartoons. Sample available.
HOW-TO, RECREATION, TRAVEL

Haiku Zasshi Zo Publishing Company, PO Box 17056, Seattle, WA 98107. (206) 542-9692. Editor: George Klacsanzky. Semiannual. Sub $6. Accept 1–2 freelance mss an issue. No pay. No byline. Submit 15–20 haiku with SASE.

Dot matrix, photocopies, simultaneous subs ok. Reports in 1–3 mos. Publishes in 1–24 wks. Accepts haiku poetry, reviews of haiku books, essays focusing on haiku composition, or various other artforms and practices that influence the writing of haiku, poetic diaries incorporating haiku. May be anywhere from 3–21 syllables long. Also line drawings in B&W. Guidelines/samples available.
LITERARY, POETRY, WRITING

Haker Books, 2707 1st Ave N, Great Falls, MT 59401. Book publisher.
OTHER/UNSPECIFIED

Hampshire Pacific Press, 3043 SW Hampshire St, Portland, OR 97201. Book publisher.
OTHER/UNSPECIFIED

Hancock House Publishers Ltd, 19313 Zero Ave, Surrey, BC V3S 5J9. 604-538-1114. Editor: Herb Bryce. Book publisher. Accepts unsolicited submissions. Pays advance, royalties. Acquires all rights. Submit query letter, outline, sample chapters, SASE. Accepts nonfiction, biography. Topics: guidebooks, Native American. Academic standards. Catalog available.
BIOGRAPHY, NW/REGIONAL HISTORY, NATIVE AMERICAN

Hand Voltage Publications, 7362 Woodlawn Ave NE, Seattle, WA 98115. 206-525-3923. Editors: Rody Nikitins, Judith Young. Book publisher.
OTHER/UNSPECIFIED

Hands Off, PO Box 68, Tacoma, WA 98401. Book publisher.
OTHER/UNSPECIFIED

Hapi Press, 512 SW Maplecrest Dr, Portland, OR 97219. Contact: Joe E Pierce. 503-246-9632. Self-publisher of textbooks for university classes or reference books. Does not accept unsolicited submissions. Pays royalties. Acquires all rights. Submit query letter, outline, sample chapters, synopsis, SASE. Dot matrix, simultaneous photocopied subs OK. Reports in 2 mos; publishes in 1 yr. Accepts nonfiction. Catalog available.
LITERATURE, TEXTBOOKS

Haralson Enterprises, PO Box 31, Yarrow, BC V0X 2A0. Self-publisher of softcover nonfiction & fiction books. Not a freelance market.
CANADA, CANADIAN HISTORY, NATIVE AMERICAN

Harbor Features, PO Box 1061, Olympia, WA 98507. Book publisher.
OTHER/UNSPECIFIED

Harbor Press, 6712 38th Ave NW, Gig Harbor, WA 98335. 206-851-9598. Publisher of hard- & softcover books. Accepts unsolicited submissions. Pays royalties. Acquires 1st, 2nd rights. Submit sample chapters, SASE. Responds in 3 mos. Accepts nonfiction. Topics: longevity, rejuvenation, natural healing, alternative health.
HEALTH

Harbour Publishing, Box 219, Madeira Park, BC V0N 2H0. Book publisher. Poetry, environment, fiction.
ENVIRONMENT/RESOURCES, FICTION, POETRY

Harbour & Shipping, 355 Burrard St, C310, Vancouver, BC V6C 3G6. Contact: Liz Bennett. Periodical magazine. No submission information. Query w/SASE.
BUSINESS

Hard Row to Hoe, Seven Buffaloes Press, PO Box 249, Big Timber, MT 59011. Editor: Art Cuelho. Published 3 times a yr. "Mostly regional reviews of Rural America that librarians, individuals, and the general public can use as a guide to purchasing books and mags about the common people who still work the land." Sub $3. Query w/SASE. Sample/$1 SASE.
LITERARY, RURAL

Hardball, Northwest Baseball, PO Box 31541, Seattle, WA 98103. Editor: Sean Kimball. Sub $18/yr, circ 150+. Newspaper. Uses freelance material. Byline given. Pays copies on publication. Submit complete ms, SASE. Photocopied OK. Accepts nonfiction, fiction, poetry, photos, cartoons, news items, biography, interviews, reviews. Topics: baseball — historical, personal interest, statistical, opinions, etc; focus is Northwest. Sample available.
COLLECTING, NW/REGIONAL HISTORY, SPORTS

Hardin Herald, Box R, Hardin, MT 59034. 307-665-1008. Newspaper.
COMMUNITY

Hartley & Marks Inc, Box 147, Point Roberts, WA 98281. 206-945-2017. Editor: Susanne Tauber. Publishes hard- & softcover books. Accepts freelance submissions. Pays royalties on publication. Submit query letter, ms, SASE. Photocopied OK. Reports in 3 mos. Accepts nonfiction. Topics: agriculture, farming, architecture, gardening, health, how-to, medical, psychology, senior citizens, technical. Catalog available.
AGRICULTURE/FARMING, HOW-TO, PSYCHOLOGY

Harvest House Publishers, 1075 Arrowsmith, Eugene, OR 97402. 503-343-0123. Editor: LaRae Weikert. Publishes 50 hard- & softcover originals, reprints books a yr. Accepts unsolicited submissions. Pays royalties on publication. Submit query w/clips, ms, SASE. Photocopied, simultaneous OK. Reports in 2–8 wks. Accepts nonfiction, fiction. Topics: "...we have a specialty–books that 'help the hurts of people.' We publish Bible-study-oriented books and fiction with a Christian theme or message consistent with Scripture." Catalog available.
RELIGION

Havin' Fun Inc, PO Box 70468, Eugene, OR 97401. 503-344-6207. Publishes softcover original books for children. Does not accept unsolicited submissions. Catalog available.
CHILDREN/TEEN

Havre Daily News, 119 2nd St, Havre, MT 59501. 406-265-6796. Daily newspaper.
COMMUNITY

HDTV, PO Box 5247, Portland, OR 97208. 503-222-3343. Newsletter with articles relating to video conferencing, production, and interviews.
MEDIA/COMMUNICATIONS

Headlight Herald, Pacific Coast Newspapers Inc, 1908 Second St, Tillamook, OR 97141. Editor: Mark H Dickson. 503-842-7535. Newspaper.
OTHER/UNSPECIFIED

Health Education League of Portland, 9242 SW Terwilliger Blvd, Portland, OR 97219. Periodical.
HEALTH

Health News and Notes, NW Portland Area Indian Health Board, 520 SW Harrison, #440, Portland, OR 97201-5258. Editor: Sheila Weinmann. Quarterly.
HEALTH, NATIVE AMERICAN

Healthview, Corporate Communications Department, Good Samaritan Hospital, 1015 NW 22nd Ave, Portland, OR 97210. Editor: Dick Baltus. 503-229-7711. Quarterly for "patients, medical staff, employees, benefactors and friends" of Good Samaritan Hospital.
HEALTH

HearSay Press, PO Box 3877, Eugene, OR 97403. Contact: Cliff Martin. 503-233-2637. Publisher of 4–6 hard- & softcover, originals, reprints a yr. on: social sciences, especially oral history, sociology, anthropology; music, criticism, reference works, contemporary themes/subjects; literature, esp. local (Pacific NW themes and authors). Print run: 2,000–5,000. Accepts freelance material. Payment: Advance, royalties. Rights purchased: All. Query, outline, table of contents w/SASE. Dot matrix, photocopies, simultaneous submissions OK. Reports in 2 wks. Publishes in 6–12 mos. Accepts nonfiction, fiction.
LITERARY, MUSIC, SOCIOLOGY

Heartland Magazine, Fairbanks News Miner, PO Box 710, Fairbanks, AK 99701. Editor: Dave Stark. Weekly.
ALASKA

Helena Independent, 317 Allen St, Helena, MT 59601. 406-442-7190. Editor: Charles Wood. Newspaper.
COMMUNITY

Helstrom Publications, 3121 SE 167th Ave, Portland, OR 97236. Book publisher.
OTHER/UNSPECIFIED

Hemingway Western Studies Series, c/o Research Center, Boise State University, Boise, ID 83725. Contact: Tom Trusky. 208-385-1572. Publisher of nonfiction, softcover originals on Western American culture. Print run:

2,000. Accepts freelance material. Payment: Copies; royalties after expenses met. Acquires 1st rights. Query with outline, sample chapters, SASE. Dot matrix, photocopies, simultaneous submissions OK. Reports in 6 mos. Publishes in 1 yr. Catalog available.
COLLEGE/UNIVERSITY, CULTURE, NORTHWEST

The National Hemlock Society, PO Box 11830, Eugene, OR 97440. 503-342-5748. Contact: Derek Humphry. Quarterly periodical.
MEDICAL, PHILOSOPHY

Henry Art Gallery, DE-15, University of Washington, Seattle, WA 98195. Book publisher.
ARTS, COLLEGE/UNIVERSITY

Heppner Gazette-Times, 147 W Willow, Box 337, Heppner, OR 97836. 503-676-9228 or 503-676-9492. Weekly newspaper.
COMMUNITY

Herald, 107 Division, Grandview, WA 98930. 509-882-3712. Weekly newspaper.
COMMUNITY

Herald & News, 1301 Esplanade, Box 788, Klamath Falls, OR 97601. 503-883-4000. Daily newspaper.
COMMUNITY

Herald News, PO Box 639, Wolf Point, MT 59201. 406-653-2222. Newspaper.
COMMUNITY

The Herb Market Report, O.A.K Inc, 1305 Vista Dr, Grants Pass, OR 97527. 503-476-5588. Editor: Richard Alan Miller. Ads: Iona Miller. Monthly newsletter. Sub $12/yr; circ 2,000+. Uses freelance material. Pays money. Acquires all rights. Query by phone. Disk/modem subs OK. Reports in 2 wks; publishes in 1 mo. Accepts nonfiction, news items, interviews, photos. Topics: alternative agriculture, herbs & spices, marketing, cottage industry, rural economic development, processing, small farming, foraging, secondary timber products. Tips: 2,000–4,000 wds. Artwork. Sample $1.50.
AGRICULTURE/FARMING, FORESTRY, HOW-TO

Heritage House Publishing Co, Box 1228, Stn A, Surrey, BC V3S 2B3. Contact: Art Downs.
BRITISH COLUMBIA, OTHER/UNSPECIFIED

Heritage Music Review, 4217 Freemont N #5, Seattle, WA 98103. Periodical review of music.
CULTURE, MUSIC

Heritage Quest, PO Box 40, Orting, WA 98360. 206-893-2029. Editor: Leland K Meitzler. Bimonthly with articles on genealogy and local history, all geared toward helping researchers. Sub rate $30. Circ 10, 000. Uses 8 freelance mss per issue from historians or genealogists. Pays from 75¢ to $1.25 per column inch, on publication. Byline given. Rights purchased: All. Submit ms, SASE. Reports in 1 mo. Publishes in 2–6 mos. Guidelines available. Sample $6.
GENEALOGY, AMERICAN HISTORY, GENERAL HISTORY

The Hermiston Herald, 158 E Main, Box 46, Hermiston, OR 97838. 503-567-6457. Weekly newspaper.
COMMUNITY

The Heron Press, 2427 Panorama Dr, North Vancouver, BC V7G 1V4. Contact: Frankie Smith. Book publisher.
OTHER/UNSPECIFIED

Heron's Quill, 10511 SE Crystal Lake Lane, Milwaukie, OR 97222. Book publisher.
OTHER/UNSPECIFIED

Herspectives, Box 2047, Squamish, BC V0N 3G0. 604-892-5723. Quarterly newsletter. Sub $22/yr; circ 50. Uses freelance material. Byline given, pays copies on publication. Submit query, SASE. Simultaneous sub OK. Responds in 2 wks; publishes in 1–3 mos. Accepts nonfiction, poetry, cartoons, biography, interviews, op/ed, reviews, memoirs. Topics: feminist perspective; no racist, sexist, homophobic material accepted. Guidelines available. Sample $5.
FEMINISM, POETRY, WOMEN

Hewitt Research Foundation, PO Box 9, Washougal, WA 98671. Periodical.
OTHER/UNSPECIFIED

Hi Baller Forest Magazine, 117-543 Seymour St, North Vancouver, BC V6B 3H6. Editor: Paul Young. 604-669-7833.
BRITISH COLUMBIA, TRADE/ASSOCIATIONS, FORESTRY

Hi Prep, PO Box 714, Meridian, ID 83642. 208-888-1165. Newspaper.
OTHER/UNSPECIFIED

Hidden Assets, PO Box 15357, Seattle, WA 98115-0357. Book publisher.
OTHER/UNSPECIFIED

Shaun Higgins, Publisher, W 428 27th Ave, Spokane, WA 99203. Book publisher.
OTHER/UNSPECIFIED

High & Leslie Press, 490 Leslie St SE, Salem, OR 97301. 503-363-7220. Publishes softcover original books. Does not accept unsolicited submissions.
OTHER/UNSPECIFIED

Highline Times & Des Moines News, PO Box 518, Burien, WA 98166. 206-242-0100. Weekly newspaper.
COMMUNITY

Highway Information, Idaho Transportation Department, PO Box 7129, Boise, ID 83707. Editor: Pat Youngblood. Bimonthly. Circ 1,200.
IDAHO, PUBLIC AFFAIRS

Highway Milemarker Guide Co (HMG Co), 525 East Bridge St, Blackfoot, ID 83221-2806. 208-785-5125. Contact: John Aulik. Publishes and packages books on travel in Idaho. Query w/SASE and outline. Payment varies. Report time is 60-90 days.
IDAHO, TRAVEL

Hillsboro Argus, 150 SE Third, Hillsboro, OR 97123. 503-684-1131. Semi-weekly newspaper.
COMMUNITY

Janice McClure Hindman, PO Box 208, Durke, OR 97905. Book publisher.
OTHER/UNSPECIFIED

Hispanic News, PO Box 22526, Portland, OR 97222. 503-777-6759. Contact: Juan Prats. Weekly newspaper. Sub $25/yr. Bilingual news and features (local, national, and international) for both Hispanic and non-Hispanic communities. Accepts freelance submissions. For news, query by phone. For features, typed query w/SASE.
BILINGUAL, CHICANO/CHICANA, MINORITIES/ETHNIC

The Hispanic News, 2318 Second Ave, Seattle, WA 98121. Editor: Tony Badillo. 206-768-0421. Sub $30/yr. Circ 10,000. Weekly newspaper "dedicated to serving the more than 127,000 Hispanics in Washington State." Accepts freelance submissions of news items, nonfiction, photos, interviews, and articles. Query w/SASE.
BILINGUAL, CHICANO/CHICANA, MINORITIES/ETHNIC

Historic Preservation League of Oregon Newsletter, PO Box 40053, Portland, OR 97240. Quarterly.
ARCHITECTURE, NW/REGIONAL HISTORY, OREGON

Historical Gazette, PO Box 527, Vashon, WA 98070. 206-463-5656. Editor: Roger Snowden. Ads: Don King. Monthly. Sub $10. Circ 10,000. Uses freelance material. Pays money on publication. Byline given. Submit query w/clips, ms, phone. Dot matrix, photocopied OK. Accepts nonfiction, photos, other. Guidelines available. Sample 50¢.
NW/REGIONAL HISTORY

Historical Perspectives, Oregon State Archives, 1005 Broadway NE, Salem, OR 97310. 503-378-4241. Editor: Elizabeth Uhlig. Free semiannual newsletter. Circ 1,700. No freelance mss accepted. Sample available.
GENEALOGY, GOVERNMENT, NW/REGIONAL HISTORY

Historical Society of Seattle & King County, 2161 E Hamlin St, Seattle, WA 98112. Book publisher.
NW/REGIONAL HISTORY

Holden Pacific Inc, 814 35th Ave, Seattle, WA 98122. 206-325-4324. Self-publisher of 1 wine/travel book a yr. Not a freelance market.
FOOD/COOKING, TRAVEL

Holistic Resources, PO Box 25450, Seattle, WA 98125. 206-523-2101. Editor: Susan James. Periodical.
HEALTH

The Hollywood Star, Pry Publishing Co, 600 NW 14th Ave, Portland, OR 97209. 503-226-8335. Editors: Tom or Marcia Pry. Ads: Greg Hudson. Monthly tabloid, founded 1984. Circ 15,000. Uses freelance material. Byline given. Pays money on publication. Acquires 1st rights. Submit query letter, clips, SASE. Dot matrix OK. Responds in 1–2 wks. Accepts new items, nonfiction, photos, articles. Topics: events and people of central NE Portland including Hollywood, Alameda, Grant Park, Rose City Park, Madison neighborhoods. Guidelines available.
COMMUNITY

Opal Laurel Holmes Publisher, PO Box 2535, Boise, ID 83701. Book publisher.
OTHER/UNSPECIFIED

Holtz-Carter Publications, 4326 Dyes Inlet Rd NW, Bremerton, WA 98312. Contact: Nancy Holtz-Carter. 206-377-2432. Publisher of 1 softcover book a yr. on cottage crafts for consumers and crafters. Print run: 5,000. Accepts freelance material. Unspecified payment schedule. Query w/SASE. Photocopies OK. Nonfiction, poetry, photos. Guidelines available.
CRAFTS/HOBBIES, POETRY

Home Business Advisor, Nextstep Publications, 6340 34th Ave SW, Seattle, WA 98126. 206-928-2290. Contact: Jan Fletcher. Bimonthly newsletter. Sub $24/yr. Cir. 1,000. Uses 2–4 freelance mss per issue. Pays copies, subs, advertisements on publication. Byline given. Submit query w/clips, ms. Dot matrix, photocopied, 3.5" computer disk submissions OK. Reports in 2 wks. Publishes in 2 mos. Accepts nonfiction, poetry, cartoons. Topics: home business how-to's and first hand experiences geared toward parents. Editorials, interviews on alternative work options for parents (telecommuting, job-sharing, etc). Photos: B&W, family business themes, up to $25 for cover. Guidelines available. Sample $3.
BUSINESS, HOW-TO, POETRY

Home Education Magazine, PO Box 1083, Tonasket, WA 98855. Editor/Ads: Helen Hegener. Bimonthly magazine. Sub $24/yr; circ 5,200. Uses freelance material. Pays money, copies (about $10 per 750 wds) on publication. Byline given. Submit query letter, ms, SASE. Dot matrix, photocopied, simultaneous, electronic, computer disk subs OK. Accepts nonfiction, photos, cartoons, artwork. Photos: clear B&W, rates negotiable. Writers must know home schooling or alternative education. Guidelines/catalog available. Sample $4.50.
CHILDREN (BY/ABOUT), EDUCATION, FAMILY

Home Education Press, PO Box 1083, Tonasket, WA 98855. Editor: Helen Hegener. Self-publisher of softcover books relating to home schooling or alternative education. Submit query, SASE. Dot matrix, photocopied, simultaneous, electronic/modem, computer disk OK. Catalog available.
CHILDREN (BY/ABOUT), EDUCATION, FAMILY

Home Office Opportunities, 9330-D Bridgeport Way SW #40, Tacoma, WA 948499. 206-582-1757. Editor: Kay Kennedy. Quarterly newsletter. Sub $12/yr. Uses freelance material. Pays copies on publication. Submit query letter, complete ms, SASE. Photocopied, dot matrix subs OK. Responds in 1 mo; publishes in 3–6 mos. Accepts nonfiction, interviews, reviews, photos (B&W). Topics: how-to, informative, personal experience about owning and operating a home-based business. Tips: 600 words or less, business software reviews. Guidelines available. Sample $3.
BUSINESS, HOW-TO

Home Source, 2285 University Dr, Boise, ID 98702. 208-338-1561. Contact: Mark Russell. Circ 200,000. Biannual magazine of regional and national real estate info for home buyers and sellers. Pays on acceptance for 1st or 2nd serial rights for nonfiction features, how-to pieces, etc from 800 to 1,800 wds. Uses photos. SASE for guidelines. Sample free.
BUSINESS, CONSUMER

Home Sweet Home, PO Box 1254, Milton, WA 98354. 206-922-5941. Editors: Mark & Laurie Sleeper. Quarterly magazine. Sub $20/yr; circ 700. Uses freelance material. Byline given. Pays money, copies on publication. Acquires 1st rights. Submit complete ms, SASE. Disk/modem, dot matrix, simultaneous subs OK. Responds in 4 mos; publishes in 6 mos. Accepts interviews, articles, reviews, poetry. Guidelines available. Sample $6.
BUSINESS, HOME, HOW-TO

Homer News, 3482 Landing St, Homer, AK 99603-7948. 907-235-7767. Weekly newspaper.
COMMUNITY

Homes & Land Magazine, 3606 Main St #205, Vancouver, WA 98663. Editor: Alicia Ord. Periodical.
BRITISH COLUMBIA, HOME

Homestead Book Company, PO Box 31608, Seattle, WA 98103. 206-782-4532. Editor: David Tatelman. Publisher of 2–3 softcover, original books a yr. Accepts unsolicited submissions. Pays royalties. Rights acquired: All. Byline given. Query w/clips, SASE. Dot matrix, photocopies OK. Reports in 3 mos. Publishes in 6 mos. Accepts nonfiction, cartoons. Topics: restaurants, drugs, music, food, counter-culture.
COUNTER CULTURE, FOOD/COOKING, MUSIC

Honeybrook Press, PO Box 883, Rexburg, ID 83440. 208-356-5133. Editor: Donnell Hunter. Publishes 3 books a yr; poetry chapbooks, and some subsidy printing. Accepts unsolicited mss only on a subsidy basis. Reports in 2 wks. Publishes in 2 mos. "Except for subsidy printing, I publish only those authors I am interested in who are already established."
POETRY

Hood River News, 409 Oak St, Box 390, Hood River, OR 97301. 503-386-1234. Weekly newspaper.
COMMUNITY

Hoogan House Publishing, PO Box 14823, Portland, OR 97214. 503-231-4320. Contact: Carolyn Steiger. Publishes texts midwifery. Not accepting submissions. Catalog available.
HEALTH, MEDICAL

Horizons SF, Box 75, Student Union Bldg, UBC, Vancouver, BC V6T 1W5. Biannual science fiction & fact publication which showcases unpublished Canadian writers. Query w/SASE.
COLLEGE/UNIVERSITY, FANTASY/SCI FI, SCIENCE

Horsdal & Schubaat Publishers Ltd, Box 1, Ganges, BC V05 1EO. Contact: Marilyn Horsdal. 604-537-4334. Publisher of 1–2 hard- & softcover originals and reprints. Does not accept unsolicited mss. Query w/SASE first. Reports in 2 wks. Publishes in 6–9 mos. Accepts nonfiction, Canadian histories and biographies. Catalog available.
BIOGRAPHY, CANADA, GENERAL HISTORY

Horse Times, PO Box 351, Star, ID 83669. Editor: Jo O'Connor. Periodical.
ANIMALS, RECREATION

Horsemanship, 105 Old Oak Circle, Grants Pass, OR 97526. 503-476-8902. Self-publisher of 1 hardcover book a year for horse owners. Print run: 6,000. Not a freelance market.
ANIMALS

Hortus Northwest, PO Box 955, Canby, OR 97013. 503-266-7968. Editor: Dale Shank. Annual directory-journal, commercial sources for PNW native plants. Circ 700. Uses freelance material. Byline given. Pays money on publication. Acquires 1st rights. Submit query letter, outline, synopsis, SASE. Photocopy, dot matrix subs OK. Responds in 3 mos; publishes within 1 yr. Accepts nonfiction, articles. Topics: Pacific Northwest native plants. Guidelines available.
ENVIRONMENT/RESOURCES, REFERENCE/LIBRARY

Hot Off The Press, 7212 S Seven Oaks, Canby, OR 97013. Publisher of books on crafts.
CRAFTS/HOBBIES

Hot Springs Gazette, 12 S Benton, Helena, MT 59601-6219. 406-482-5766. Editor: Suzanne Hackett. Periodical. Sub $12. Circ 1,000. Uses 12 freelance mss per issue. Pays copies on publication. Acquires 1st rights. Byline given. Submit ms. Dot matrix, photocopied OK. Reports in 2 mos. Accepts nonfiction, fiction, poetry, cartoons. Guidelines available. Sample $4.
ENTERTAINMENT, HOME, LITERARY

Hound Dog Press, 10705 Woodland Ave, Puyallup, WA 98373. 206-845-8039. Self-publisher of 1 hardcover book on bloodhounds for search & rescue work. Not a freelance market.
ANIMALS

House by the Sea Publishing Company, 8610 Hwy 101, Waldport, OR 97394. Book publisher.
OTHER/UNSPECIFIED

House of Charles, 4833 NE 238th Ave, Vancouver, WA 98662. Book publisher.
OTHER/UNSPECIFIED

House of Humor, PO Box 7302, Salem, OR 97303. 503-585-6030. Editor: Paul Everett. Book publisher.
HUMOR

How To Travel Inexpensively, Nomadic Books, 1911 N 45th St, Seattle, WA 98103. Periodical.
CONSUMER, TRAVEL

The Howe Street Press, 212 E Howe St, Seattle, WA 98102. Book publisher.
OTHER/UNSPECIFIED

Howlet Press, 2741 SW Fairview Blvd, Portland, OR 97201. 503-227-6919. Contact: Doris Avshalomov. Fine letterpress self-publisher of limited editions of poetry and other literary works. Query w/SASE. "I will publish chapbooks (letterpress) or print full-length books for self-publishing (upon acceptance)."
LITERATURE, POETRY

HTH Publishers, PO Box 460, Freeland, WA 98249. Book publisher.
OTHER/UNSPECIFIED

Hubbub, A Poetry Magazine, Trask House Books Inc, 2754 SE 27th, Portland, OR 97202. Editor: Carlos Reyes. 503-235-1898. Nationally circulated biannual magazine of poetry. No editorial strictures. Circ 350. Submit 3–5 poems w/SASE. Pays in copies.
POETRY

Hug-a-Book Publications, 390 West A St, Lebanon, OR 97355. Contact: Cindy Butherus. Publishes books for children.
CHILDREN/TEEN

Hulogos'i Cooperative Publishers, Box 1188, Eugene, OR 97440. 503–343–0606. Publisher of 8 softcover originals a year on NW region, environment, political activism, co-operatives and New Age consciousness. Print run: 5,000. Accepts freelance material. Payment: 8–10 % of retail, every 6 mos. Rights purchased: first; can be individually negotiated. Submit ms, SASE. Dot matrix, photocopies, simultaneous submissions, electronic OK. Reports in 1 month. Publishes in 6–12 mos. Uses nonfiction, poetry, photos, cartoons.
ENVIRONMENT/RESOURCES, NORTHWEST, SOCIALIST/RADICAL

The Humanist Newsletter, PO Box 3936, Portland, OR 97208.
PHILOSOPHY

Hundman Publishing, 5115 Montecello Dr, Edmonds, WA 98037. 206-743-2607. Editor: Cathy Hundman Lee. Book publisher.
OTHER/UNSPECIFIED

Hungry Horse News, 926 Nucleus Ave, PO Box 189, Columbia Falls, MT 59912. 406-862-2151. Newspaper.
COMMUNITY

Hunt Magazine, PO Box 58069, Renton, WA 98058. 206-226-4534. Editor: Bill Boylon. Bimonthly. Sub $19.97/yr; circ 100,000. Uses freelance material. Acquires 1st rights. Submit complete ms, SASE. Responds in 1–2 mos; publishes in 1 yr. Accepts articles, cartoons, photos w/ms. Sample $3.50.
COMMERCE, OUTDOOR

Hunter Publications Inc, Box 4308, Seattle, WA 98104. Book publisher.
OTHER/UNSPECIFIED

The Hyacinth Poetry Review, 6426 198th St East, Spanaway, WA 948387. 206-847-4892. Editor: Sandra VanOrman. Quarterly newsletter. Sub $12/yr. Uses freelance material. Pays copies on publication. Acquires 1st rights. Submit complete ms, SASE. Photocopy, dot matrix OK. Responds in 2–3 wks. Accepts poetry (1–24 lines, no longer than one page), cartoons. Guidelines available.
POETRY

Hydrazine, Northwest Science Fiction Society, PO Box 24207, Seattle, WA 98124. Periodical.
FANTASY/SCI FI

Hyperlink, PO Box 7723, Eugene, OR 97401.
OTHER/UNSPECIFIED

I Can See Clearly Now, 262 W Beach Lane, Coupeville, WA 98239. Book publisher.
OTHER/UNSPECIFIED

Iconoclast, Foundation of Human Understanding, PO Box 5237, Grants Pass, OR, 97527. Monthly.
OTHER/UNSPECIFIED

Idaho, Boise State University, College of Business, Department of Economics, Boise, ID 83725. Editor: Charles L Skoro. Quarterly.
BUSINESS, COLLEGE/UNIVERSITY, IDAHO

Idaho Archaeologist, Idaho Archaeological Society, PO Box 7532, Boise, ID 83707. Editor: Mark G Plew. Semiannual. Circ 100.
ANTHROPOLOGY/ARCHÆOLOGY, IDAHO

Idaho Argonaut, Student Union Bldg, University of Idaho, Moscow, ID 83843. 208-885-7825. Semiweekly newspaper written & published by students. Sub $18/yr. Circ 7,000. Not a freelance market.
COLLEGE/UNIVERSITY, IDAHO, STUDENT

Idaho Business Review, 4218 Emerald St, Ste B, Boise, ID 83706. Editor: Carl A Miller. Weekly periodical. Circ 2,000.
BUSINESS, IDAHO

Idaho Cities, Association of Idaho Cities, 3314 Grace St, Boise, ID 83707. Editor: Ray Holly. Monthly. Circ 2,200.
IDAHO, PUBLIC AFFAIRS

Idaho Citizen, PO Box 9303, Boise, ID 83707. Editor: Kenneth L Robinson. Monthly. Circ 1,200.
IDAHO, PUBLIC AFFAIRS

Idaho Clean Water, Division of Environment/IDHW, 450 West State St, Boise, ID 83720. Editor: Tom Aucutt. 208-334-5867. Quarterly focusing on improving Idaho's water quality. Circ 2,000. Sub free. Query w/SASE. Guidelines/sample available free.
CONSERVATION, ENVIRONMENT/RESOURCES, IDAHO

Idaho Conservation League Newsletter, PO Box 844, Boise, ID 83701. Editor: Renee Guillierie. Monthly. Circ 1,300.
CONSERVATION, IDAHO

Idaho Council on Economic Education Newsletter, 1910 University Dr, Boise, ID 83725. Editor: Dr Gerald Drayer. Semiannual periodical. Circ 7,000.
ECONOMICS, EDUCATION, IDAHO

Idaho County Free Press, PO Box 690, Grangeville, ID 83530. 208-983-1070. Newspaper.
OTHER/UNSPECIFIED

Idaho Currents, Idaho Department of Water Resources, Statehouse, Boise, ID 83720. Editor: K T Meyer. Monthly. Circ 9,000. Query with/SASE.
CONSERVATION, ENVIRONMENT/RESOURCES, IDAHO

Idaho Falls Post-Register, 333 Northgate Mile, Idaho Falls, ID 83401. 208-522-1800. Newspaper.
COMMUNITY, OTHER/UNSPECIFIED

Idaho Farm Bureau News, Idaho Farm Bureau Federation, PO Box 167, Boise, ID 83701-0167. Editor: Mike Tracy. Monthly newspaper. Circ 29,000. Does not accept freelance material.
AGRICULTURE/FARMING, IDAHO

Idaho Farmer-Stockman, PO Box 2160, Spokane, WA 99210. Contact: Thomas D Henry. Biweekly agricultural periodical. Circ 18,000. Uses news and farmer profiles. Guidelines available w/SASE.
AGRICULTURE/FARMING, IDAHO

Idaho Fish & Game News, PO Box 25, Boise, ID 83807. Editor: Jack Trueblood. Bimonthly newspaper.
FISHING, OUTDOOR

Idaho Forester, College of Forestry/Wildlife/Range Science, University of Idaho, Moscow, ID 83843. Annual. Circ 1,200.
AGRICULTURE/FARMING, FORESTRY, IDAHO

Idaho Foxfire Network, c/o Reva Luvaas, PO Box 1207, Wallace, ID 83873. 208-752-6978. Periodical.
EDUCATION, WRITING

Idaho Genealogical Society Quarterly, Idaho Genealogical Society, 325 W State, Boise, ID 83702. 208-384-0542. Editor: Jane Walls Golden. Sub $10/yr; circ 450. Publisher of hard- & softcover books and quarterly magazine. Uses freelance material. Byline given. Pays money on acceptance. Submit query letter, SASE. Responds in 3 wks; publishes in 3 mos.
GENEALOGY

Idaho Grain, 112 W 4th, Moscow, ID 83843. 208-882-0888. Editor: Ivar Nelson. Ads: Opal Gerwig. Bimonthly magazine. Sub $10/yr. Circ 16,000. Uses freelance material. Pays money on publication. Acquires 1st rights. Byline given. Submit query letter, complete ms, SASE, phone. Reports in 3 wks; publishes in 2 mos. Accepts biography, photos (on request), interviews, op/ed, articles, reviews. Topics of interest to Idaho grain producers and related industries. Study sample before querying. Guidelines available; sample $2.
AGRICULTURE/FARMING, BUSINESS, IDAHO

Idaho Grange News, PO Box 367, Meridian, ID 83642. Editor/ads: Glen Deweese. 208-888-4495. Bimonthly of agriculture and fraternal news. Circ 8,000. Sub w/membership. Not a freelance market.
AGRICULTURE/FARMING, IDAHO

Idaho Humanities Council Newsletter, Len B Jordan Bldg, 650 W State St, Rm 300, Boise, ID 83720. 208-345-5346. Editor: Sharron Bittich. Circ 5,200.
IDAHO, LIBERAL ARTS

Idaho Law Review, University of Idaho, College of Law, Moscow, ID 83843. Editor: Nancy M Morris. Published 3 times a year. Circ 1,000. No submission info
IDAHO, LAW

Idaho Librarian, Idaho Library Association, c/o Idaho State University, Pocatello, ID 83209. Quarterly. Circ 600.
BOOK ARTS/BOOKS, IDAHO, REFERENCE/LIBRARY

Idaho Motorist, Idaho Automobile Association, PO Box 15240, Boise, ID 83715. Editor: Grant C Jones. Irregular periodical.
CONSUMER, IDAHO, TRAVEL

Idaho Museum of Natural History, PO Box 8183, Idaho State University, Pocatello, ID 83209. Editor: B Robert Butler. 208-236-3717. Periodical of primitive pottery/ceramics. Circ 250. Uses 2–5 mss per issue. Byline given. Submit ms w/SASE. Phone query, photocopies OK. "Notes on replication of experiments in primitive pottery manufacture, processes, techniques, etc. Observations, discoveries, tips, materials, techniques, especially as they relate to prehistoric or folk pottery, but also as they can be applied to contemporary ceramics." Photos: glossy. Tips: "Good, straight forward writing; first person, present tense."
ANTHROPOLOGY/ARCHÆOLOGY, IDAHO, NATURAL HISTORY

Idaho Outdoor Digest, PO Box 454, Rupert, ID 83350. 208-436-3171. Contact: Ed Mitchell, editor. Ads: vickie Higgins. Monthly magazine. Sub $12/yr. Circ 15–25,000. Uses 15–18 freelance mss per issue. Pays money on publication. Acquires first rights. Byline given. Query by phone or w/SASE. Dot matrix, photocopies, simultaneous, modem, disk subs OK. Accepts nonfiction, photos, cartoons. Topics: adventure, bicycling, boating, environment, fishing, how-to, Idaho, Montana, outdoor recreation. Guidelines and sample available.
HOW-TO, OUTDOOR, RECREATION

Idaho Pharmacist, Idaho State Pharmaceutical Association, 1365 N Orchard, Rm 316, Boise, ID 83706. Editor: JoAn Condie. Monthly. Circ 350.
BUSINESS, HEALTH, IDAHO

Idaho Potato Commission Report, Idaho Potato Commission, PO Box 1068, Boise, ID 83701. Bimonthly.
AGRICULTURE/FARMING, BUSINESS, IDAHO

Idaho Power Bulletin, Idaho Power Company, PO Box 70, Boise, ID 83707. Editor: Jim Taney. Quarterly. Circ 60,000.
BUSINESS

Idaho Press-Tribune, PO Box 9399, Nampa, ID 83652-9399. Editor: Richard Coffman. 208-467-9251. Daily newspaper.
COMMUNITY

Idaho Register, Box 2835, Boise, ID 83701. Editor: Colette Cowman. 208-342-2997. Weekly newspaper. Circ 14,300.
COMMUNITY

Idaho Senior News, PO Box 6662, Boise, ID 83707. Editor: Owen Krahn. Monthly.
SENIOR CITIZENS

Idaho State Historical Society, 450 N 4th St, Boise, ID 83702. 208-334-3428. Editor: Judith Austin. Publishes hard- & softcover books. Accepts unsolicited submissions. Pays royalties, copies. Submit query letter, outline, sample chapters, synopsis, complete ms, SASE, phone. Photocopy OK. Responds in 1 mo; publishing time varies. Accepts nonfiction, biography, memoirs. Topics: Idaho history. Catalog (Univ. of Idaho Press) available.
NW/REGIONAL HISTORY, IDAHO

Idaho State Historical Society, 450 N 4th St, Boise, ID 83702. Book publisher.
NW/REGIONAL HISTORY, IDAHO

Idaho State Journal, 305 S Arthur, Pocatello, ID 83204. 208-232-4161. Newspaper.
IDAHO

Idaho State University Press, c/o University Bookstore, Box 8013, Pocatello, ID 83209.
COLLEGE/UNIVERSITY, PUBLISHING/PRINTING

The Idaho Statesman, Box 40, Boise, ID 83707. 208-377-6200. Daily newspaper.
COMMUNITY

Idaho, The University, Office of University Communications, University of Idaho, Moscow, ID 83843. 208-885-8973. Editor: Stephen Lyons. Ads: Terry Maurer. Quarterly magazine. Free; circ 60,000. Uses freelance material. Byline given, pays money/copies on publication. Submit query letter w/SASE. Dot matrix, simultaneous subs OK. Responds in 1 mo; publishes in 2 mos. Accepts nonfiction, photos, interviews, articles. Photos: B&W, color slides, pays $50–100. "All stories must have a Univ. of Idaho link. Our standards are high. We are not the usual university magazine." Guidelines and samples, free.
COLLEGE/UNIVERSITY, IDAHO, NORTHWEST

Idaho Thoroughbred Quarterly, Idaho Thoroughbred Breeders Association, 5000 Chinden Blvd #B, Boise, ID 83714.
AGRICULTURE/FARMING, ANIMALS, BUSINESS

Idaho Voice, Idaho Fair Share Inc, PO Box 1927, Boise, ID 83701. Editor: Ralph Blount. 208-343-1432. Quarterly to membership of Idaho Fair Share. Circ 10,000. Sub $15. 90% of magazine freelance material. Byline given. Uses nonfiction, poetry, photos, cartoons. Photos: B&W, 3x5 preferred.
CONSUMER, ECONOMICS, POLITICS

Idaho Wheat, Idaho Wheat Growers Association, Ste M, Owyhee Plaza, Boise, ID 83702. EIndexIndexditor: Vicki Higgins. Bimonthly. Circ 13,850.
AGRICULTURE/FARMING, BUSINESS, IDAHO

Idaho Wildlife, Idaho Department of Fish & Game, PO Box 25, Boise, ID 83707. 208-334-3748. Editor: Diane Ronayne. Bimonthly magazine with widespread readership (40% outside ID, 60% inside), interested in outdoor activities, including but not limited to fishing and hunting, with strong ties to Idaho. Sub $10/yr; circ 30,000. Accepts only photographs. "Only photographers with substantial files of subjects photographed in Idaho are placed on the want list mailing list." Submit sample sleeve of 20 slides. Pays $35 per photo for 1 time rights, cover, $60; plus copies and byline. Guidelines available. Sample $1.50.
ENVIRONMENT/RESOURCES, FISHING, IDAHO

Idaho Wool Growers Bulletin, Idaho Wool Growers Association, PO Box 2596, Boise, ID 83701. Editor: Stan Boyd. Monthly. Circ 1,800.
AGRICULTURE/FARMING, BUSINESS, IDAHO

Idaho Yesterdays, Idaho State Historical Society, 450 N 4th St, Boise, ID 83702. Editor: Judith Austin. Quarterly. Sub $15/yr; circ 1,500. Uses freelance material. Pays copies. Submit query letter, complete ms, SASE, phone. Photocopy OK. Responds in 2 wks; publishing time varies. Accepts nonfiction. Topics: Idaho history. Sample $1.50–3.75.
NW/REGIONAL HISTORY, IDAHO

Idahoan, National Railroad Historical Society, PO Box 8795, Boise, ID 83707. Editor: Milt Sorensen. Monthly. Circ 60.
CRAFTS/HOBBIES, AMERICAN HISTORY, NW/REGIONAL HISTORY

Idahobeef, Idaho Cattle Association, 2120 Airport, Boise, ID 83705. Editor: Tom Hovenden. Monthly. Circ 900.
AGRICULTURE/FARMING, BUSINESS, IDAHO

Idahoan/Palouse Empire News, PO Box 8197, Moscow, ID 83843. 208-882-5561. Daily newspaper.
COMMUNITY

Idaho's Economy, College of Business, Boise State University, Boise, ID 83725. 208-385-1158. Editor: C Skoro. Quarterly magazine. Sub free. Circ 4,500. Uses freelance material. Pays in copies. Byline given. Submit ms, SASE. Dot matrix, photocopied, computer disk. Reports in 2 mos; publishes in 6 mos. Accepts nonfiction. Sample available.
BUSINESS, ECONOMICS, IDAHO

IEA Reporter, Idaho Educational Association, PO Box 2638, Boise, ID 83701. Editor: Gayle Moore. Monthly. Circ 9,000.
EDUCATION, IDAHO, LABOR/WORK

IFCC News, PO Box 17569, 5340 N Interstate Ave, Portland, OR 97217. 503-243-7930. Periodical.
ARTS, COMMUNITY

Il Centro, Italian Cultural Centre Society, 3075 Slocan St, Vancouver, BC V5M 3E4. 604-430-3337. Editor: Anna Terrana. Newsletter of the Italian Canadian community published 3–4 times a yr. Sub $12. Circ 4,000. Accepts no freelance mss. Sample free.
CANADA, COMMUNITY, MINORITIES/ETHNIC

Illinois Valley News, 319 Redwood Highway, Box M, Cave Junction, OR 97523. Editor/ads: Robert R Rodriquez. 503-592-2541. Weekly newspaper. Circ 3,300. Sub $9. Uses 2 mss per issue. Payment: Average 20¢ per column inch on publication. $3 per photo. Byline given. Photocopies, simultaneous submissions OK. Reports in 2 wks. Nonfiction, photos (B&W). "News & general interest for Illinois Valley." Sample: 35¢/SASE.
COMMUNITY

Image Imprints, PO Box 370, Eugene, OR 97448. Contact: Marje Blood. Book publisher.
OTHER/UNSPECIFIED

Image West Press, PO Box 5511, Eugene, OR 97405. Book publisher.
OTHER/UNSPECIFIED

Images, Lane County ESD, PO Box 2680, Eugene, OR 97402. 503-689-6500. Editor: Dr Marilyn Olson. Publication of poetry and art by students in Lane County. Guidelines available. Sample $5.
ARTS, CHILDREN/TEEN, POETRY

Imagesmith, PO Box 1524, Bellevue, WA 98009. Book publisher.
OTHER/UNSPECIFIED

Imaginationary Books, 1917 Warren Ave N, Seattle, WA 98109. Book publisher.
OTHER/UNSPECIFIED

Impact, OSPIRG, 1536 SE 11th Ave, Portland, OR 97214. Periodical.
OREGON, PUBLIC AFFAIRS, STUDENT

In Common, Tsunami Publications, Box 104004, Anchorage, AK 99510. Editor/Ads: Jay Brause. 907-337-0872. Gay/lesbian monthly. Accepts freelance material. Byline given. Submit ms, SASE. Dot matrix, photocopies OK. Uses nonfiction, fiction, poetry, photos, cartoons. "Must be gay/lesbian oriented material, preferably with an Alaska or Pacific NW slant." Photos: B&W glossy news/documentation photos, as well as artistic photos suitable for a general public audience.
GAY/LESBIAN

In Context, PO Box 11470, Bainbridge Is, WA 98110. Editor: Alan Atkisson. Quarterly journal. Sub $18/yr; circ 7,000. Uses freelance material. Byline given. Pays money, copies on publication. Submit complete ms, SASE. Accepts nonfiction, poetry, cartoons, photos (B&W), interviews. Guidelines available. Sample $5.
CULTURE, ENVIRONMENT/RESOURCES

In Focus, 5000 Deer Park Dr SE, Salem, OR 97301. 503-581-8600. Newspaper.
OTHER/UNSPECIFIED

In Stride Magazine, 12675 SW 1st, Portland, OR 97005. Periodical.
OTHER/UNSPECIFIED

Incline Press Book Publisher, PO Box 913, Enumclaw, WA 98022. 206-825-1989. Contact: Bernard Winn. Self-publisher, subsidy books. Topics: European railway guides.
CHILDREN/TEEN, RECREATION, TRAVEL

Incredible Idaho, Division of Tourism & Industrial Development, Room 108 Capitol Bldg, Boise, ID 83720. Quarterly.
BUSINESS, IDAHO, TRAVEL

Incunabula Press, 310 NW Brynwood Lane, Portland, OR 97229. Book publisher.
OTHER/UNSPECIFIED

Independent, PO Box 27, Port Orchard, WA 98366. 206-876-4414. Weekly newspaper.
COMMUNITY

Independent, PO Box D, Tenino, WA 98589. 206-264-2500. Weekly newspaper.
COMMUNITY

Independent, PO Box 67, Wapato, WA 98951. 509-879-2262. Weekly newspaper.
COMMUNITY

The Independent Record, PO Box 4249, Helena, MT 59604. 406-442-7190. Daily newspaper.
COMMUNITY

Independent Senior, 1268 W Pender, Vancouver, BC V6E 2S8. Periodical.
SENIOR CITIZENS

Indian Feather Publishing, 7218 SW Oak, Portland, OR 97223. Book publisher.
OTHER/UNSPECIFIED

Info, International Sled Dog Racing Assoc, PO Box 446, Nordman, ID 83848. Editor: Nancy Molburg. Bimonthly. Circ 2,000.
ANIMALS, OUTDOOR, SPORTS

Info Alternatives, 19031 33rd Ave W #301, Lynnwood, WA 98036. Book publisher.
OTHER/UNSPECIFIED

Infoletter, International Plant Protection Center, Oregon State University, Corvallis, OR, 97331. 503-754-3541. Editor: A E Deutsch. Free quarterly. Circ 8,600. Not a freelance market. Sample free.
AGRICULTURE/FARMING, COLLEGE/UNIVERSITY, GARDENING

Information Center, Northwest Regional Educational Lab, 101 SW Main St, Portland, OR 97204. 503-275-9555. Editor: M Margaret Rogers. Book publisher.
EDUCATION

Information Press, PO Box 1422, Eugene, OR 97440. 503–689-0188. Contact: Richard Yates. Publishes hard- & softcover reference books related to government, business. Not a freelance market.
BUSINESS, GOVERNMENT, REFERENCE/LIBRARY

Inky Trails Publications, Box 345, Middletown, ID 83644. Editor: Pearl Kirk. Literary magazine published 3 times a year. Circ 300. "Uses 90% freelance poems. Non-subscribers must buy issue in which their efforts appear. Does not pay." Submit ms, SASE. Reports in 2–8 wks. Publishes in 2–3 yrs. Uses nonfiction, fiction, poetry, illustrations. "Adventure, fantasy, historical, humorous, mystery, religious (not preachy), romance, western and animals. We prefer unpublished material…and do not want to receive: horror, make fun of, porno or gay/lesbian material." Offers periodic cash awards for best subscriber efforts. Guidelines available w/SASE/44¢. Sample for 9x12 SASE/70¢.
FANTASY/SCI FI, FICTION, HUMOR

Inland Country, Inland Power & Light Company, E 320 Second Ave, Spokane, WA 99202. Editor: Chuck Bandel. Monthly.
COMMUNITY, CONSUMER, FAMILY

Inland (formerly Idaho English Journal), English Dept, Boise State University, Boise, ID 83725. 208-385-1246. Editor: Driek Zirinsky. Semiannual magazine for English teachers. Sub $8/yr; circ 600. Uses freelance material. Byline given, pays copies. Acquires 1st rights. Submit query letter, complete ms, SASE, phone. Photocopy, disk/modem subs OK. Responds in 6 wks; publishes in 6 mos. Accepts fiction, nonfiction, cartoons, poetry, photos, interviews, op/ed, reviews, memoirs, art, student work. Sample $4.
EDUCATION, ENGLISH, STUDENT

INCTE Newsletter, Inland NW Council Teachers of English, PO Box 9261, Moscow, ID 83843-1761. Quarterly devoted to the teaching of English.
EDUCATION, ENGLISH

Inland Register, PO Box 48, Spokane, WA 99210-0048. 509-456-7140. Ads: Margaret Nevers. Regional Catholic news magazine published 17X/yr. founded in 1942. Sub $15. Circ 8,500. Accepts freelance material. Byline given. Author qualification: Roman Catholic. Pays money (10¢/wd) on publication. Submit ms, SASE. Photocopies OK. Reports in 1 mo; publishes in 1 mo. Accepts nonfiction, photos, ($10 negotiable). Sample $1.
RELIGION

Inner Growth Books, Box 520, Chiloquin, OR 97624. Self-publisher of 2 softcover original books.
PHILOSOPHY, PSYCHOLOGY, RELIGION

Inner Voice, Assn of Forest Service Employees for Environmental Ethics (AFSEEE), PO Box 11615, Eugene, OR 97440. 503-484-2692. Editor: Tom Ribe. Quarterly newsletter. Sub $20/yr; circ 50,000. Occasionally uses freelance material. Submit query letter, SASE. Responds in 3 wks; publishes in 6 mos. Accepts nonfiction, cartoons, photos (B&W), op/ed. Topics: current forest service policy or procedure issues. Sample $2.
ENVIRONMENT/RESOURCES

Inner Woman, PO Box 51186, Seattle, WA 98115-1186. 206-524-9071. Editor: Krysta Gibson. Quarterly newspaper. Sub $7.50/yr. Circ 16,000. Uses freelance material. Byline given. Pays by subscription on acceptance. Acquires 1st rights. Submit ms w/SASE. Photocopies OK. Reports in 1–2 mos. Accepts nonfiction, poetry, photos, cartoons. Topics: women's issues dealing with empowering women from within; healing, spirituality, psychology, redefining the feminine in our society. Photos 5X7 or larger B&W glossy. Guidelines available SASE. Sample $1.
FEMINISM, WOMEN, NEW AGE

Innkeeping World, PO Box 84108, Seattle, WA 98124. Contact: Charles Nolte. Published 10 times per yr for the hotel industry worldwide. Uses non-fiction on marketing, managing, advertising, hospitality, trends, labor relations. SASE for ample and guidelines. Query w/SASE.
BUSINESS, TRADE/ASSOCIATIONS

Inscriptions, Creative Writing Program Newsletter, Department of English, GN-30, University of Washington, Seattle, WA 98195. Periodical.
COLLEGE/UNIVERSITY, WRITING

Inside Basic, Ariel Publishing Inc, Box 398, Pateros, WA 98846. 509-923-2249. Monthly magazine for Macintosh developers. Columns on programming skills, introductory programming and advanced development. Sub $36.95.
COMPUTERS, TECHNICAL

Insight Northwest, PO Box 25450, Seattle, WA 98125-2330. Bimonthly on human potential. From statement of philosophy: "We create our own reality. We can heal ourselves. Synergy works better." Query w/SASE. Sample/free.
HEALTH, PHILOSOPHY, PSYCHOLOGY

Inspirational Publisher, 2500 S 370th St, Ste 134, Federal Way, WA 98003. Nonfiction self publisher. 1 title 1990. Press run 1M.
RELIGION

Institute for Judaic Studies, PO Box 751, Portland, OR 97207. Soft- and hardcover books on Judaic history.
GENERAL HISTORY, MINORITIES/ETHNIC

Institute for Quality in Human Life, 6335 N Delaware Ave, Portland, OR 97217. Book publisher.
OTHER/UNSPECIFIED

Institute for the Study of Traditional American Indian Arts, PO Box 66124, Portland, OR 97266. Book publisher.
ARTS, NATIVE AMERICAN

Insurance Adjuster, 1001 4th Ave #3029, Seattle, WA 98154-1190. 206-624-6965. Monthly.
BUSINESS

Insurance Week, 1001 4th Ave #3029, Seattle, WA 98154-1190. 206-624-6965.
BUSINESS

The Insurgent Sociologist, University of Oregon Sociology Dept, Eugene, OR 97403. Quarterly journal of radical analysis in sociology.
COLLEGE/UNIVERSITY, SOCIALIST/RADICAL, SOCIOLOGY

Integrity Publications, PO Box 9, 100 Mile House, Yarrow, BC V0K 2E0. Book publisher.
OTHER/UNSPECIFIED

Interact, Special Education Department, PSU, PO Box 751, Portland, OR, 97207-0751. Editor: Susan Wapnick. Periodical.
COLLEGE/UNIVERSITY, EDUCATION

Interface, 1910 Fairview Ave E, Seattle, WA 98102-3699. Periodical.
OTHER/UNSPECIFIED

Interior Voice, Box 117, Kelowna, BC V1Y 7N3. Quarterly devoted to human consciousness, environment and related topics. Uses fiction, nonfiction, poetry, cartoons, etc.
ENVIRONMENT/RESOURCES, FICTION, POETRY

Intermountain Logging News, Statesman-Examiner Inc, Box 271, Colville, WA 99114. 509-684-4567. Monthly.
BUSINESS, LUMBER

International Bicycle Fund, 4887 Columbia Dr S, Seattle, WA 98108-1919. 206-628-9314. Books on bicycle travel, especially trips sensitive to the environments and cultures of the of hosts.
BICYCLING, TRAVEL

International Communication Center, School of Communications DS-40, University of Washington, Seattle, WA 98195. Book publisher.
COLLEGE/UNIVERSITY, MEDIA/COMMUNICATIONS

International Examiner, 318 6th Ave S, Ste 127, Seattle, WA 98104. Editor: Ron Chew. 206-624-3925. Ads: Xandria LaForga. Bimonthly for Asian American communities of Seattle/King County. Circ 17,500. Sub $12. Accepts freelance material. Payment: $10 on publication. Byline given. Query w/SASE. Dot matrix, photocopies OK. "Topics of interest and significance

to Asian Americans, particularly in the NW. Historical articles, feature interviews, investigative journalism, straight news, analysis." Sample/50¢.
ASIA, ASIAN AMERICAN, MINORITIES/ETHNIC

International Self-Counsel Press Ltd, 1481 Charlotte Rd, N Vancouver, BC V7J 1H1. Publisher of softcover original, nonfiction. Book publisher. Query w/SASE. Guidelines/catalog available. Also see Self-Counsel Press Inc.
BUSINESS, HOW-TO

Intertext, 2633 E 17th Ave, Anchorage, AK 99508. Contact: Sharon Ann Jaeger. Publishes hard- & softcover books. Accepts freelance material. Payment: 10% royalty after costs of production, promotion, and distribution. Acquires 1st rights; option on second printing. Submit query letter, sample chapters, SASE. No simultaneous ms submissions. Reports in 3–6 mos; publishes in 1–2 yrs. Accepts fiction, poetry, translations, literary criticism and theory. "Query first, poets send 3–5 poems, fiction writers send sample chapter to show quality of language, w/SASE and by first-class mail. Vivid use of imagery and strong, alchemical use of language are essential; poetry collections should be powerful, sustained groups of 48–80 poems; fiction mss may be either aggregates of short stories or novellas — a novel would have to be extremely remarkable to be considered at this time." Guidelines available w/SASE.
FICTION, LITERARY, POETRY

Interwest Applied Research, 4875 SW Griffith Dr, Beaverton, OR 97005. 503-641-2100. Editor: Mary L Lewis. Publisher of hard- & softcover education materials & videos, 30–60 topics per yr. in 2–4 subject areas. Pay: Money, on acceptance. Rights acquired: All. Byline depends on extent of contribution. Phone query, computer disk OK. Reports in 1 month. Publishes in 3–12 mos. "Actively soliciting writers for development of textbooks, study guides, examination questions and video scripts for production/distribution as college-level course materials. Topics include math, music, geography, law, child development, philosophy, and others. Payment by assignment; assignments vary from 2 days to 6 mos. Call for Writer Information Form describing current needs and soliciting information on writer's qualifications. Writers are interviewed after selection based on this form."
EDUCATION, SCHOLARLY/ACADEMIC, TEXTBOOKS

Intuition Trainings, 7800 185th Place SW, Edmonds, WA 98020. 206-775-8365. Editor: Janet V Burr. Book publisher.
OTHER/UNSPECIFIED

InUnison, PO Box 6957, Portland, OR 97228. 503-221-1298. Editor: Judy Henderson. Ads: Ellen Nichols. Bimonthly magazine examining issues important to Oregon's thinking women. Sub $12/yr; circ 15,000. Uses freelance material. Negotiated payment for feature articles on publication. Byline given. Submit query letter, SASE. Dot matrix, computer disk subs OK. Reports in 4 wks; publishing time varies. Accepts nonfiction. Topics: social & community issues, business, art, education, families, politics and economics; theme is equity for women. Tips: interested in informative, thought-provoking, entertaining articles about women, their jobs and families; buys some humor relating to women's lives; no fashion or food articles. "We want insightful, substantive writing about women who set their goals and accomplish them." Guidelines available. Sample $3.
WOMEN

IPEA News, Idaho Public Employees Association, 1434 W Bannock, Boise, ID 83702. Editor: Jim Vineyard. Quarterly. Circ 4,700.
IDAHO, LABOR/WORK

ISBS Inc, 5602 NE Hassalo St, Portland, OR 97213. Editor: Jeanette Bokma. Book publisher.
OTHER/UNSPECIFIED

Island Books, 3089 Gibbons Rd, Duncan, BC V9L 1E9. Book publisher.
OTHER/UNSPECIFIED

The Island Grower, BC's Magazine of Coastal Gardening and Living, RR 4, Sooke, BC V02 1N0. 604-642-4129. Contact: Phyllis Kusch. Monthly (except Jan) magazine on living and garden on the N Pacific coast. Buys 1st rights for how-tos, profiles, travel. Tips: practical slant with emphasis on natural gardening and thorough research. Pay varies after publication. Byline

given. Reports in 1 mo. Query w/clips & SASE. Sample and guidelines for SASE.
GARDENING, NORTHWEST

Island Publishers, Box 201, Anacortes, WA 98221-0201. 206-293-3285. Publisher of poetry and nonfiction. Book publisher.
OTHER/UNSPECIFIED

Island Spring, PO Box 747, Vashon, WA 98070. Book publisher.
OTHER/UNSPECIFIED

Issaquah Press, PO Box 1328, Issaquah, WA 98027. 206-392-6434. Weekly newspaper.
COMMUNITY

IWA Woodworker, International Woodworkers of America, 25 Cornell Ave, Gladstone, OR 97027-2547. Membership newsletter.
LABOR/WORK

IWUA Alert, Idaho Water Users Association, 410 S Orchard, Ste 144, Boise, ID 83705. Editor: Sherl L Chapman. Quarterly devoted to water resource management issues. Circ 1,250. Not a freelance market.
AGRICULTURE/FARMING, CONSERVATION, IDAHO

Jackson Creek Press, 2150 Jackson Creek Dr, Corvallis, OR 97330. 503-752-4666. Editor/Ads: Cheryl McLean. Publishes 1 softcover original book a yr. on travel, outdoor recreation; focus on NW. Accepts unsolicited mss. Pays copies, royalties. Submit prospectus and sample chapters. Photocopies, simultaneous submissions OK. Reports in 2 mos. "Looking to fill gaps in NW travel/outdoor recreation book publishing field. Want new ideas, thoroughly researched mss in accessible, easy-to-read style. General audience. Call for guidelines.
NORTHWEST, OUTDOOR, TRAVEL

Jackson Mountain Press, Box 2652, Renton, WA 98056. 206-255-6635. Contact: Carole Goodsett. Book publisher. Accepts freelance material. Acquires 1st rights. Submit query letter, outline, SASE. Dot matrix, photocopies OK. Reports in 1 mo; publishes in 6–12 mos. Accepts nonfiction. Topics: geology: state field guides, 48–200 pg; general popular geology subjects up to 100 pg. Food: local interest cookbooks, to 100 pg; guides to best of area, best of type, to 200 pg. Tips: "Our expertise is in marketing local guides to specific areas, ie, a specific city, half a state, or NW." Catalog available.
FOOD/COOKING, GEOLOGY/GEOGRAPHY, NORTHWEST

Jalapeno Press, PO Box 12345, Portland, OR 97212-0345. Book publisher.
OTHER/UNSPECIFIED

Jaleo Press International, 2453 Heights Dr, Ferndale, WA 98248. Contact: John Dolan. Book publisher.
OTHER/UNSPECIFIED

Jennifer James Inc, 9250 45th Ave SW, Seattle, WA 98136-2633. Book publisher.
PSYCHOLOGY

Janes Publishing, 25671 Fleck Rd, Veneta, OR 97487-9510. Contact: Bobbi Corcoran. 503-343-2408. Book publisher.
OTHER/UNSPECIFIED

Janus Press, PO Box 1050, Rogue River, OR 97537. Book publisher.
OTHER/UNSPECIFIED

The Jason, Willamette University - D248, 900 State St, Salem, OR 97301. 503-370-6905. Editor: Margaret Jester. Annual for students writers only. No pay. Byline given. Submit ms. Dot matrix, photocopied OK. Accepts fiction, poetry, photos, plays, cartoons, other. Sample $2.
COLLEGE/UNIVERSITY, FICTION, POETRY

Jawbone Press, Waldron Island, WA 98297. Book publisher.
OTHER/UNSPECIFIED

JC/DC Cartoons Ink, 5536 Fruitland Rd NE, Salem, OR 97301. Book publisher.
HUMOR

Jean's Oregon Collections, 3486 Wood Ave, Eugene, OR 97402. Book publisher.
OREGON, OTHER/UNSPECIFIED

Jefferson Review, 145 S Main St, Box 330, Jefferson, OR 97352. 503-327-2241. Weekly newspaper.
COMMUNITY

Jefferson Star, 134 W Main, Rigby, ID 83442. 208-745-8701. Newspaper.
COMMUNITY

Jeopardy, Western Washington University, 350 Humanities Bldg, Bellingham, WA 98225. 206-676-3118. Editor: Lori L Fox. Annual literary magazine. Sub $3. Circ 4,000. Accepts unsolicited mss. Pays copies, on publication. Rights acquired: First. Byline given. Submit: ms, SASE. Dot matrix, photocopies, simultaneous OK. Accepts fiction, poetry, photos (slides if color or B&W prints), art work. No over-long stories or poems.
FICTION, POETRY, VISUAL ARTS

Jesuit Books, Seattle University, Seattle, WA 98122.
RELIGION

Jewell-Johnson & Company Inc, 502 Benton St, Port Townsend, WA 98368. Book publisher.
OTHER/UNSPECIFIED

Jewish Review, 6800 SW Beaverton-Hillsdale Hwy #C, Portland, OR 97225-1408. Editor: Elaine Cogan. 503-226-3701. Ads: Dru Duniway. Monthly. Circ 5,000. Sub free. Uses 1–3 mss per issue. Writers must have "good writing, knowledge or interest of Oregon Jewish community." Payment: 10¢/wd on publication. Byline given. Rights purchased: First. Query w/SASE. Reports in 1 month. News: 150–250 wds; features: to 1,000 wds. Cartoons. Photos: $25, B&W. Sample/SASE.
CULTURE, OREGON, RELIGION

Jewish Transcript, 2031 – 3rd Ave #200, Seattle, WA 98121-2418. 206-624-0136. Weekly newspaper.
COMMUNITY, RELIGION

Jimmy Come Lately Gazette, PO Box 1750, Sequim, WA 98382. Editor: JoAnne Booth. 206-683-7238. Ads: Dianne Christensen. Weekly community newspaper. Circ 10,500. Sub $15. Infrequently accepts freelance material. Writers must have "very strong local emphasis." Payment: Usually $25. Byline given. Query w/SASE. Dot matrix, photocopies OK. Uses nonfiction, poetry, photos, cartoons. "Emphasis on local people, events and issues. Our 3 person news staff provides about all the material we have space for, although we do work with some freelancers for historical pieces, etc." Sample/$1.
CALENDAR/EVENTS, COMMUNITY, PHOTOGRAPHY

Henry John & Company, PO Box 10235, Dillingham, AK 99576. Book publisher.
OTHER/UNSPECIFIED

Joint Development Trading Company Ltd, RR 3, 1970 Nicholas Place, Victoria, BC V8X 3X1. Book publisher.
OTHER/UNSPECIFIED

Jomac Publishing Inc, 621 SW Morrison, #1450, Portland, OR 97205. 503-224-5811. Editor: Jo Ann Lippert. Book publisher. Does not accept unsolicited submissions. Query w/SASE.
OTHER/UNSPECIFIED

Edward-Lynn Jones & Associates, 5517 17th Ave NE, Seattle, WA 98105. Book publisher.
OTHER/UNSPECIFIED

Stan Jones Publishing Co, 3421 E Mercer St, Seattle, WA 98112. 206-323-3970. Editor: Stan Jones. Self-publisher of 1–2 softcover fishing, outdoor-oriented books a yr. Average print run 15,000. Not a freelance market. Catalog available.
FISHING, FOOD/COOKING, NORTHWEST

Jordan Valley Heritage House, 43592 Hwy 226, Stayton, OR 97383. Book publisher.
NW/REGIONAL HISTORY, OTHER/UNSPECIFIED

The Journal, 278 Main St, Morton, WA 98356. 206-496-5993. Newspaper.
COMMUNITY

Journal for Architecture & Design, 2318 Second Ave, Box 54, Seattle, WA 98121.
ARCHITECTURE, ARTS

Journal of Business, S 104 Division St, Spokane, WA 99202. 509-456-5257. Editor: Norman Thorpe. Ads: Scott Crytser. Biweekly newspaper. Sub $18/yr; circ 15,000. Uses freelance material. Byline given. Pays $20–75 per piece, "depending on quality, work put into it, and amount of work we have to do on it." Pays on publication. Acquires 1st rights. Phone query. Dot matrix OK. Reports in 2–3 wks; publishes in 2–3 mos. Accepts business news about the Spokane-Coeur d'Alene market and surrounding area. Sample $2.
BUSINESS, COMMERCE

Journal of Computer Based Instruction, Miller Hall 409, Western Washington University, Bellingham, WA 98225.
COLLEGE/UNIVERSITY, COMPUTERS, EDUCATION

The Journal of Ethnic Studies, Western Washington University, Bellingham, WA 98225.
COLLEGE/UNIVERSITY, MINORITIES/ETHNIC, SOCIOLOGY

Journal of Everett & Snohomish County History, Everett Public Library, 2702 Hoyt, Everett, WA 98201. Biannual.
NW/REGIONAL HISTORY

Journal of Financial & Quantitative Analysis, University of Washington, School of Business, 127 Mackenzie Hall, DJ-10, Seattle, WA 98105. 206-543-4660. Published 5 times a yr.
BUSINESS, COLLEGE/UNIVERSITY, ECONOMICS

Journal of Health, Physical Education, Recreation, Dance & Athletics, Dept of Health, Physical Ed, University of Idaho, Moscow, ID 83843. Editors: Sharon Stoll/ Frank Pettigrew. Published semiannually.
DANCE, EDUCATION, HEALTH

Journal of Pesticide Reform, Northwest Coalition for Alternatives to Pesticides, PO Box 1393, Eugene, OR 97440. 503-344-5044. Editor: Caroline Cox. Quarterly journal & book publisher. Sub $15/yr; circ 2,500. Occasionally uses freelance material. Pay negotiable, 1 copy or more. Byline given. Submit query letter, outline, sample chapters, synopsis, complete ms, SASE. Phone query OK. Dot matrix, photocopies, computer disk subs OK. Uses illustrations. Topics: scientific or public interest material on pesticides, pesticide reform, sustainable forestry & agriculture, pesticide policies & alternatives. "Call first to get approval, guidelines. Prefer experienced specialists in field. Occasional research papers, interviews with specialists." Guidelines available. Sample $3.
AGRICULTURE/FARMING, ENVIRONMENT/RESOURCES, TECHNICAL

Journal of the BC English Teachers' Association, Port Coquitlam Secondary, 3550 Wellington St, Port Coquitlam, BC V3B 3Y5. Contact: Pat Curtis.
EDUCATION, ENGLISH

Journal of the Idaho Academy of Science, Idaho Academy of Science, Ricks College, Rexburg, ID 83460-1100. 208-356-2022. Editor: Lawrence Pierson. Semiannual journal. Circ 200. Uses freelance scientific research material. Byline given. Acquires 1st rights. Submit query letter, three photocopies of complete ms, SASE. Responds in 1 mo; publishes in 6 mos. Accepts nonfiction (original scientific research); book reviews; regional emphasis. Topics: biology, geology, physics, science education, chemistry, medicine, etc. Guidelines available. Sample $2.50.
SCHOLARLY/ACADEMIC, SCIENCE, TECHNICAL

Journal of the Nez Perce County Historical Society, Nez Perce Historical Society, 3rd & C Sts, Lewiston, ID 83501. Editor: Bea Davis. Semiannual. Circ 130.
NW/REGIONAL HISTORY, NATIVE AMERICAN

The Journal of the Oregon Dental Association, 17898 SW McEwan Rd, Portland, OR 97224. Editor: Howard F Curtis, DMD. 503-620-3230. Quarterly.
BUSINESS, HEALTH

Journal of the San Juans, PO Box 519, Friday Harbor, WA 98250. 206-378-4191. Newspaper.
COMMUNITY

Journal of the Seattle-King County Dental Society, PO Box 10249, Bainbridge Island, WA 98110. 206-682-7813. Monthly.
BUSINESS, HEALTH

Journey Press, 116 N 78th St, Seattle, WA 98103. 206-783-4554. Contact: Mary LeLoo. Monthly newspaper aimed at individuals in recovery from dysfunctional families. Seeking submissions of poetry, articles, photos. SASE for guidelines.
HEALTH, POETRY, PSYCHOLOGY

Juneau Empire, 3100 Channel Dr, Juneau, AK 99801. 907-586-3740. Contact: Carl Sampson. Newspaper.
COMMUNITY

Junior League of Eugene Publishers, 2839 Willamette St, Eugene, OR 97405. Book publisher.
OTHER/UNSPECIFIED

Juniper Ridge Press, Box 338, Ashland, OR 97520. 503-482-9585. Editor: Rosana Hart. Self-publisher of 1–3 softcover original books, and 3–5 videotapes, a yr; for llama owners. Print run 2,000. Accepts no unsolicited mss. Pays copies, royalties. Submit any way — dot matrix, photocopies, simultaneous OK. Accepts: Nonfiction "primarily related to llamas. Will consider submissions from writers knowledgeable about the animals. Most of our products are created in house." Catalog available.
AGRICULTURE/FARMING, ANIMALS, RECREATION

Jupiter Publications, 7527 Lake City Way NE, Seattle, WA 98115. Book publisher.
OTHER/UNSPECIFIED

Just Dogs, PO Box 954, Auburn, WA 98072. 206-852-0294. Editor: Bob Hughes. Bimonthly magazine; circ 8,000. Uses freelance material. Byline given, pays money/copies on publication, acquires 1st rights. Submit query/SASE. Disk/modem, dot matrix, simultaneous subs OK. Responds in 2 mos; publishes within 4 mos. Accepts fiction, poetry, nonfiction, articles, photos, cartoons, interviews, news items. "Material should be targeted to dog owners in the Puget Sound region." Guidelines, back issues available for 9x12 envelope with 45¢ postage.
ANIMALS, RECREATION

Just in Time Publishing, 401 Olson Rd, Longview, WA 98632. Book publisher.
OTHER/UNSPECIFIED

Just Out, PO Box 15117, Portland, OR 97215. 503-236-1252. Editor: Beth A Allen. Ads: Yvonne Mammarelli. Monthly tabloid for the gay/lesbian community. Sub $17.50/yr; circ 15,000. Uses freelance material. Byline given, may pay money on publication. Submit query letter, clips, SASE. Dot matrix, simultaneous subs OK. Responds in 1 mo; publishes in 1 mo. Accepts news items, interviews, photos, articles. Sample $2.
GAY/LESBIAN, MINORITIES/ETHNIC, OREGON

Kabalarian Philosophy, 908 W 7th Ave, Vancouver, BC V5Z 1C3. Book publisher.
PHILOSOPHY

Kalispell Daily Interlake, PO Box 8, Kalispell, MT 59901. 406-755-7000. Contact: Dan Black. Newspaper
COMMUNITY

Kalispell News, PO Box 669, Kalispell, MT 59901. Editor: JoAnn Speelman. 406-755-6767. Weekly newspaper.
COMMUNITY

Kamloops Museum & Archives, 207 Seymour St, Kamloops, BC V2C 2E7. 604-828-3576. Contact: Elisabeth Duckworth. Book publisher — Canadian (esp BC) history and natural history. Does not accept unsolicited submissions. Submit query letter w/SASE, or phone.
BRITISH COLUMBIA, CANADIAN HISTORY, NATURAL HISTORY

Karwyn Enterprises, 17227 17th Ave W, Lynnwood, WA 98036. Book publisher.
OTHER/UNSPECIFIED

KBOO Program Guide, 20 SE 8th, Portland, OR 97214. Editor/ads: Tony Hansen. 503-231-8032. Accepts freelance material. No pay. Byline given. Uses nonfiction, fiction, poetry.
CULTURE, MEDIA/COMMUNICATIONS, MUSIC

Joan Keil Enterprises, PO Box 205, Medina, WA 98039. Book publisher.
OTHER/UNSPECIFIED

Keizertimes, 680 Chemawa Rd NE, Keizer, OR 97303-4437. 503-390-1051. Weekly newspaper.
COMMUNITY

Kellogg Evening News, 401 Main St, Kellogg, ID 83837. 208-783-1107. Newspaper.
COMMUNITY

Kenmore Northlake News, PO Box 587, Woodinville, WA 98072. 206-483-0606. Weekly newspaper.
COMMUNITY

Kent News Journal, 600 S Washington, Kent, WA 98032. Contact: Diane Glamser. Newspaper.
COMMUNITY

Ketch Pen, Washington Cattlemen's Association Inc, PO Box 96, Ellensburg, WA 98926. Editor: Ann E George. Monthly.
AGRICULTURE/FARMING

Ketchikan News, PO Box 7900, Ketchikan, AK 99901. 907-225-3157. Biweekly newspaper.
COMMUNITY

Key to Victoria, 1001 Wharf St, 3rd Floor, Victoria, BC V8W 1T6. Editor: Janice Strong. 604-388-4342. Monthly magazine about Vancouver Island and Victoria. Circ 30,000. Acquires 1st or all rights to nonfiction of 500–2,500 wds with photos. Query w/SASE. Sample free.
BRITISH COLUMBIA, TRAVEL

Keyboard Workshop, PO Box 700, Medford, OR 97501. 503-664-6751. Self-publisher of 50 new cassettes, videos or softcover original books a yr. Accepts no freelance material.
HOW-TO, MUSIC

Ki2 Enterprises, PO Box 13322, Portland, OR 97213. Editor: K Canniff. Publisher of 2 originals per yr; "totally unique nonfiction about OR/WA." Average print run 5,000. Accepts freelance material. Payment negotiated at time of purchase. Rights purchased: All. Submit outline, sample chapter, SASE. "Tell me why readers need this book too." Dot matrix, photocopies, simultaneous OK. Reports in 4–6 wks. Publishes in 1 yr. Accepts nonfiction, 80–160 pg; B&W artwork and photos. Tips: "We don't do 'coffee table' books."
NORTHWEST, TRAVEL

KID Broadcasting Corporation, PO Box 2008, Idaho Falls, ID 83401. Book publisher.
MEDIA/COMMUNICATIONS

Kid Care Magazine, PO Box 1058, Clackamas, OR 97015. 503-239-2334. Editor: Margaret Ramsom. Ads: Clay Sheldon. Quarterly. Sub $5. Circ 10,000+. Uses freelance material. Writers must be knowledgeable about the topic. Pays copies. Acquires first rights. Byline given. Query w/clips, ms, SASE. Dot matrix, photocopied OK. Reports in 2–4 wks. Publishes within 12 mos. Accepts nonfiction, fiction, poetry, photos, cartoons, tips & ideas. Topics: infants through teens; adults taking care of/living with children; day care; how to. Tips: 100–650 wds length, short, easy to read. Photos: B&W, children & adults in everyday action. Guidelines available. Sample $3.
CHILDREN (BY/ABOUT), CHILDREN/TEEN, HEALTH

KILSA News, Shoreline Community College Library, 16101 Greenwood Ave N, Seattle, WA 98133. Periodical.
COLLEGE/UNIVERSITY

The M Kimberly Press, 3331 279th Ave NE, Redmond, WA 98053. 206-880-6235. Contact: Mare Blocker. Artist books/handmade books/limited

editions. Poetry, literature, and illustrations. No submission accepted. Info available.
BOOK ARTS/BOOKS

Kindred Joy Publications, 554 W 4th, Coquille, OR 97423. 503-396-4154. Contact: Marilee Miller. Press inactive in 1991. Self-publisher of softcover original and subsidy books on regional/natural history. Press run approx 1,000. Not a freelance market. Catalog available.
NW/REGIONAL HISTORY, NATURAL HISTORY

Kinesis, 301 – 1720 Grant St, Vancouver, BC V5L 2Y6. Periodical 10 times a yr. Query/SASE.
WOMEN

Kinesis, PO Box 4007, Whitefish, MT 59937-4007. Editors: Austin B Byrd & R Kirk Williams. Northwest arts and literature magazine devoted to the exposure of established and emerging writers and poets. Accepts unsolicited freelance mss. Payment negotiable on acceptance. Byline given. Submit ms w/SASE. Dot matrix, photocopied, simultaneous OK. Replies within 10 wks. Accepts fiction, poetry, photography. Sample $2 ppd.
ARTS, LITERATURE, PHOTOGRAPHY

King Books, 817 S 265th St, Kent, WA 98032. Book publisher.
OTHER/UNSPECIFIED

Kiowa Press, PO Box 555, Woodburn, OR 97071. 503-981-3017. Self-publisher of 1 hardcover book a year. Press run: 1,100. Not a freelance market. Catalog available.
FICTION, MILITARY/VETS, POETRY

Kitsap County Herald, PO Box 278, Poulsbo, WA 98370. 206-779-4464. Weekly newspaper.
COMMUNITY

Klamath Falls Publishing Co, PO Box 788, Klamath Falls, OR 97801. 503-883-4000. Publishes Cascade Cattleman, Cascade Horseman, Polled Hereford Journal. Uses freelance features focusing on people in the trades. Include photos.
AGRICULTURE/FARMING, ANIMALS

Klassen & Foster Publications, PO Box 18, Barriere, BC V0E 1E0. Book publisher.
OTHER/UNSPECIFIED

KMG Publications, 290 E Ashland Lane, PO Box 1055, Ashland, OR 97520. Book publisher.
OTHER/UNSPECIFIED

Kodiak Mirror, 216 W Rezanoff, Kodiak, AK 99615. 907-486-3227. Daily newspaper.
COMMUNITY

Korea Times, 430 Yale Ave N, Seattle, WA 98109-5431. 206-525-9222. Weekly newspaper.
ASIA, ASIAN AMERICAN, COMMUNITY

Krause House Inc, PO Box 880, Oregon City, OR 97045. Book publisher.
OTHER/UNSPECIFIED

KSOR Guide to the Arts, 1250 Siskiyou Blvd, Ashland, OR 97520. Periodical.
ARTS, MEDIA/COMMUNICATIONS

La Posta: A Journal of American Postal History, PO Box 135, Lake Oswego, OR, 97034. 503-657-5685. Editor: Richard W Helbock. Ads: Cathy R Clark. Bimonthly magazine. Sub $10. Circ 1,200. Uses 5–6 freelance mss per issue. Byline given. Submit ms. Dot matrix, electronic subs OK. Accepts nonfiction. Sample $3.
CRAFTS/HOBBIES, NW/REGIONAL HISTORY

Lacon Publishers, Rt 1, PO Box 15, Harrison, ID 83833. Book publisher.
OTHER/UNSPECIFIED

Lacoz Chicana, Idaho Migrant Council, PO Box 490, Caldwell, ID 83606-0490. 208-454-1652. Editor: Lydia Mercado. Ads: Rico Barrera. Monthly newsletter. Sub $6/yr; circ 2,000. Uses freelance material. Submit query letter, SASE. Accepts nonfiction, poetry, cartoons, news items, photos, interviews, op/ed. Sample available.
BILINGUAL, IDAHO, MINORITIES/ETHNIC

Laing Communications, 500 – 108th Ave NE, Ste 1050, Bellevue, WA 98004. Contact: Norman Bolitin or Christine Laing. 206-451-9331. Publisher of studies and monographs on publishing. Book packager. "We acquire books & regularly contract w/writers/authors for projects on behalf of our publishing clients." Subjects: biography, business, economics, computers, history, travel, how-to. Submit query w/credentials and brief synopsis.
MEDIA/COMMUNICATIONS, PUBLISHING/PRINTING, REFERENCE/LIBRARY

Lake County Examiner, 101 N "F" St, Box 271, Lakeview, OR 97630. 503-947-3370. Weekly newspaper.
COMMUNITY

Lake Oswego Review, 111 A St, PO Box 548, Lake Oswego, OR 97034. 503-635-8811. Weekly newspaper.
COMMUNITY

Lambrecht Publications, RR #5, Duncan, BC V9L 4T6. 604-748-8722. Self-publisher. Not a freelance market. Catalog available.
BRITISH COLUMBIA, FOOD/COOKING, HEALTH

The Lamron, Western Oregon State College, WOSC College Center, Monmouth, OR 97361. 503-838-1171. Newspaper.
COLLEGE/UNIVERSITY

Lance Publications, PO Box 61189, Seattle, WA 98121. 206-442-4613. Cookbooks. Book publisher. Query w/SASE before submitting.
FOOD/COOKING

LAND, "Bill Anderson's Trap and Farm Journal, " 4466 Ike Mooney Rd, Silverton, OR 97381. 503-873-8829. Editor: Bill Anderson. Magazine (aka Living Among Nature Daringly) published 5X/yr. Sub $9/yr; circ 500. Accepts freelance material. Byline given, pays money on publication. Acquires 1st rights. Submit complete ms, SASE. Photocopy, dot matrix, disk/modem (Mac) OK. Responds in 3 wks; publishes in 10 wks. Seeks vernacular writing style, how-to's. Sample available.
AGRICULTURE/FARMING, AMERICAN HISTORY, CANADIAN HISTORY

Land Mark Publishing, PO Box 776, Pocatello, ID 83204. 208-233-0075. Publishes softcover books. Topics: education, sex education, and biography.
BIOGRAPHY, EDUCATION, SEX

Landmark, 1000 Friends of Oregon, 300 Willamette Bldg, 534 SW 3rd Ave, Portland, OR 97204. Editor: Marie Reeder. 503-223-4396. Quarterly on land use planning. Circ 15,000. Sub w/membership in 1,000 Friends of OR./$3 single issue. Uses 2 mss per issue. Payment: Copies on publication. Byline given. Rights purchased: First. Submit ms, SASE. Phone queries, dot matrix, photocopies, simultaneous submissions OK. Reports in 2 wks. Nonfiction: 500–2,500 wds on farm/forest land conservation; efficient, environmentally sound development. For educated, professional readership, interested in concrete examples or research/economic facts. Photos: B&W glossy. Sample available.
CONSERVATION, ECONOMICS, LAND USE/PLANNING

Landmark Publishing, PO Box 776, Pocatello, ID 83204. Book publisher.
OTHER/UNSPECIFIED

Landmarks, 835 Securities Bldg, Seattle, WA 98101. Editor: Barbara Krohn. 206-622-3538. Quarterly on NW history, archaeology, historic preservation. Circ 12,000. Sub $10. Accepts freelance material. No pay. Byline given. Rights purchased: First. Query w/ms, SASE. Phone queries, dot matrix, photocopies OK. Reports in 1–3 mos. Uses nonfiction, photos (B&W, no preferred size). Guidelines available, sample/free.
ANTHROPOLOGY/ARCHÆOLOGY, NW/REGIONAL HISTORY, NORTHWEST

Lane Regional Air Pollution, 225 N 5th #501, Springfield, OR 97477. Editor: Marty Douglass. Periodical.
ENVIRONMENT/RESOURCES

Larry Langdon Publications, 17314 SW Loma Vista St, Aloha, OR 97007-5791. Book publisher.
OTHER/UNSPECIFIED

The Lariat, 12675 SW First St, Beaverton, OR 97005. Editor: Barbara Zellner. 503-644-2233. Fax 503-644-2213. Monthly devoted to horses and related subjects.
ANIMALS, RECREATION

J Larsen Publishing, PO Box 586, Deer Lodge, MT 59722. Book publisher.
RECREATION

Larsen Publishing Co, 9243 Shaw Sq, Aumsville, OR 97325. Contact: Lee Larsen. Book publisher.
OTHER/UNSPECIFIED

Latah County Genealogical Society Newsletter, 110 S Adams, Moscow, ID 83843. 208-882-5943. Editor: Dorothy Viets Schell. Quarterly. Circ 80. Sub with membership fee of $8. Not a freelance market. Sample: $2.
GENEALOGY, IDAHO

Latah County Historical Society, 110 S Adams, Moscow, ID 83843. Publisher of books on local and regional history.
NW/REGIONAL HISTORY

Latah Legacy, 110 S Adams, Moscow, ID 83843. Editor: Stan Shepard. 208-882-1004. Quarterly on local historical subjects. Circ 550. Sub w/membership in historical society. Sometimes accepts freelance material if of interest to audience. Payment: Copies. Byline given. Submit ms w/SASE. Phone queries, dot matrix, photocopies OK. Nonfiction and photos (related to article). Sample: $2.
NW/REGIONAL HISTORY, IDAHO

Laughing Dog Press, PO Box 1622, Vashon, WA 98070. 206-463-3153. Publishes handmade books, both cloth and paper bound, of nature poetry. Pays in copies. Acquires 1st rights. Dot matrix, photocopies OK. Reports in 6 mos; publishes in 1–2 yrs. No unsolicited submissions.
CONSERVATION, ENVIRONMENT/RESOURCES, POETRY

The Lavender Network, PO Box 5421, Eugene, OR 97405. 503-485-7285. Publisher/Ads: Ronald B Zahn. Editor: Martha Burdick. Monthly magazine published by an all-volunteer non-profit corporation. Sub $25/yr; circ 10,000. Uses freelance material. Pays copies on publication. Acquires 1st rights. Byline given. Submit ms, SASE. Photocopied, disk/modem OK. Reports in 1 mo. Accepts nonfiction, fiction, poetry, photos, cartoons, photos (B&W prints). Topics: gay and lesbian, feminist related topics, especially expressing wellness themes. Sample for postage.
FEMINISM, GAY/LESBIAN, MEN

LaVoz Newsmagazine, 157 Yesler Way #400, Seattle, WA 98104. 206-461-4891. Editor: Raquel Orbegoso. Ads: Ana Meekins. Bilingual/Spanish tabloid published 10X/yr. Sub $10. Circ 15,000 statewide. Accepts freelance material. Payment on publication negotiable. Acquires 1st rights. Byline given. Submit phone query. Dot matrix, photocopied OK. Accepts nonfiction, cartoons. Topics: subjects of interest to Latinos. Sample available.
BILINGUAL, CHICANO/CHICANA COMMUNITY

Law Forum Press, 2318 Second Ave, Seattle, WA 98121. 206-622-8240. Editor: Don Berry. Publishes softcover how-to guides for small business owners, 50 pps. Accepts unsolicited submissions, phone query. Pays 10% gross revenue royalties. Dot matrix, photocopied, simultaneous, electronic subs OK. Reports in 4 wks. Publishes in 3 mos.
BUSINESS

Lazara Press, Box 2269 MPO, Vancouver, BC V6B 3W2. Contact: Penny Goldsmith. Book publisher.
OTHER/UNSPECIFIED

Lazy Mountain Press, PO Box 2650, Palmer, AK 99645. Contact: Kathy Hunter. Books on Alaska. Self-publisher.
ALASKA

LC Review, Lewis & Clark College, 0615 SW Palatine Hill Rd, Portland, OR 97219. 503-244-6161. Periodical.
COLLEGE/UNIVERSITY

Leader, c/o Port Townsend Publishing, PO Box 552, Port Townsend, WA 98368-552. 206-385-2900. Weekly newspaper.
COMMUNITY

Learning, Etc, 1818 NE 17th #10, Portland, OR 97212. Contact: John M Gingel.
EDUCATION

Lebanon Express, 90 E Grant St, Box 459, Lebanon, OR 97355. 503-258-3151. Semiweekly newspaper.
COMMUNITY

Left Coast Review, 818 W Crockett St #305, Seattle, WA 98119-2875. 206-284-6323 206-789-1884. Monthly magazine.
OTHER/UNSPECIFIED

Legacy House Inc, PO Box 786, 139 Johnson Ave, Orofino, ID 83544. 208-476-5632. Self-publisher of 4 hard- & softcover original books a year for animal lovers, children, history buffs. Print run: 1,000. Not a freelance market.
ANIMALS, CHILDREN/TEEN, AMERICAN HISTORY

Legendary Publishing Co, PO Box 7706, Boise, ID 83707-1706. 208-342-7929. Self-publisher of books. Not a market.
COMMUNITY

L'Epervier Press, 5419 Kensington Pl N, Seattle, WA 98103. 206-547-8306. Book publisher.
OTHER/UNSPECIFIED

Lesbian Contradiction: A Journal of Irreverent Feminism, 1007 N 47, Seattle, WA 98103. Editor: Betty Johanna, Jane Meyerding. Quarterly newspaper format with journal content. Sub $6/yr; circ 2,000. Uses freelance material. Pays copies on publication. Byline given. Submit ms, SASE. Dot matrix, photocopies OK. Reports in 2–8 wks; publishes within 1 yr. Accepts nonfiction, photos (B&W), cartoons, line drawings; emphasis on non-academic material, with analysis or commentary based on personal experience." Uses essays, interviews, commentaries (10 pp. or less); book, movie, music reviews (3 pp. or less), queries, testimonies. Guidelines available. Sample $2.
FEMINISM, GAY/LESBIAN

Letter to Libraries, Oregon State Library, State Library Bldg, Salem, OR 97310. 503-378-4243. Editor: Wesley A Doak. Newsletter to libraries only. Uses freelance material. Byline given. Pays copies. Submit query letter, complete ms, SASE. Responds in 3 mos. Accepts nonfiction, news items, interviews, articles.
BOOK ARTS/BOOKS, REFERENCE/LIBRARY

Lewis County News, PO Box 10, Winlock, WA 98596. 206-785-3151. Weekly newspaper.
COMMUNITY

Lewis River News & Kalama Bulletin, PO Box 39, Woodland, WA 98674. 206-225-8287. Weekly newspaper.
COMMUNITY

Lewiston Morning Tribune, Box 957, Lewiston, ID 83501. 208-743-9411. Arts Editor: John McCarthy. Daily newspaper, art section once a wk. Circ 25,000. Accepts freelance book reviews. Pays in copies. Byline given. Submit ms. Dot matrix, photocopied, simultaneous OK. Publishes within 1 mo. Book reviews on Northwest writers, fiction or nonfiction with subjects centered in the NW & Rocky Mountains (Washington, Oregon, Idaho & Montana).
COMMUNITY, LITERARY, NORTHWEST

Lewistown News-Argus, PO Box 900, Lewistown, MT 59457. Editor: Vonnie Jacobson. Newspaper.
COMMUNITY

LFL Associates, 52 Condolea Court, Lake Oswego, OR 97034-1002. Book publisher.
OTHER/UNSPECIFIED

Life Messengers Inc, PO Box 1967, Seattle, WA 98111-1967. Book publisher.
OTHER/UNSPECIFIED

Life Press, 5705 SW Seymour St, Portland, OR 97221. 503-285-3906. Book publisher.
OTHER/UNSPECIFIED

Life Scribes, Box 848, Livingston, MT 59047. 406-222-6433. Editor. Quarterly newsletter. Sub $15. Accepts freelance material. Pays copies. Rights acquired: First. Byline given. Submit ms; SASE. Dot matrix, photocopies, simultaneous, electronic OK. Reports in 6 mos. Publishes in 2–3 mos. "We

like short articles dealing with the journaling process or journal entries with date and name." Guidelines, sample available.
WRITING

Lifecraft, PO Box 1, Heisson, WA 98622. Book publisher.
OTHER/UNSPECIFIED

Lifeline Magazine, 352 Halladay, Seattle, WA 98109. Editor: Alison Leary. Periodical.
OTHER/UNSPECIFIED

Lifeprints, Blindskills Inc, PO Box 5181, Salem, OR 97304. 503-581-4224. Editor: Carol M McCarl. Ads: Robert McCarl. Quarterly newsletter for blind teens and adults. Sub $15/yr; circ 500. Uses freelance material. Byline given, pays money. Submit query letter, SASE, phone. Accepts nonfiction, poetry, interviews, articles. Sample available.
DISABLED

Lifeworks Letter, Woodland Park Hospital, 10300 NE Hancock, Portland, OR 97220. 503-257-5128. Editor: Sharon Wood. Bimonthly newsletter. Sub free. Circ 14,000. Uses 2 freelance mss per issue. Pays money on acceptance. Acquires first rights. Byline given. Submit by assignment only, SASE. Dot matrix OK. Publishes in 2–6 mos. Accepts poetry, photos. Tips: short poetry; photos: shots/captions about women's issues. "Limited freelance opportunity." Sample 55¢.
HEALTH WOMEN

The Light Spectrum, Box 215–mp, Kootenai, ID 83840. Periodical.
OTHER/UNSPECIFIED

The Light, PO Box 7534, Olympia, WA 98507. 206-456-3078. Contact: W W Koopman. Monthly periodical.
OTHER/UNSPECIFIED

Light-House Publications, 1721 Wallace, Vancouver, BC V6R 4J7. Book publisher.
BRITISH COLUMBIA, OTHER/UNSPECIFIED

Lighthouse, PO Box 1377, Auburn, WA 98071-1377. Editor: Tim Clinton. Bimonthly magazine. Uses freelance material. Sub $7.95/yr. Byline given, pays money, copies on publication. Acquires 1st/other rights. Submit complete ms, SASE. Photocopy OK. Responds in 4–8 wks; publishes in 18 mos. Accepts fiction, poetry; children's stories and poetry. Guidelines available. Sample $2.
CHILDREN/TEEN, FICTION, POETRY

Lightship Press Ltd, 109 – 1418 Newport, Victoria, BC V8S 5E9. Book publisher.
OTHER/UNSPECIFIED

Lillooet Tribal Council Press, PO Box 1420, Lillooet, BC V0K 1V0. Publishes Native-American books.
NATIVE AMERICAN

Limberlost Press, HC 33, Box 1113, Boise, ID 83706. Contact: Richard Ardinger. Query/SASE. Nonfiction, poetry.
CULTURE, LITERARY, POETRY

Limousin West, Box 5027, Salem, OR 97304. 503-362-8987. Editor: Tim Hinshaw. Ads: Tommy Badley. Bimonthly. Sub $6. Circ 4,200. Uses 6 freelance mss per issue. Pays money, copies on publication. Acquires 1st rights. Byline given. Phone. Dot matrix, photocopied OK. Reports in 2 wks. Accepts nonfiction, photos. Guidelines available. Sample $1/SASE.
AGRICULTURE/FARMING, ANIMALS

Lincoln County Historical Society, 545 SW 9th St, Newport, OR 97365. Book publisher.
NW/REGIONAL HISTORY

Judy Lindahl Unlimited, 3211 NE Siskiyou, Portland, OR 97212. Self-publisher only.
OTHER/UNSPECIFIED

Line, c/o English Dept, Simon Fraser University, Burnaby, BC V5A 1S6. 604-291-3124. Editor: R Miki. Ads: I Niechoda. Semiannual journal. Sub $12. Circ 300. Uses 5 freelance mss per issue. Pays money, copies on publication. Acquires all rights. Submit query w/clips. Dot matrix, photocopied OK. Reports in 3–4 mos. Publishes in 5–12 mos. Accepts nonfiction: literary

criticism, reviews; "Contemporary (Canadian & American) writing & its modernist sources; 30 pp. max; payment rate yet to be determined. Sample $8.
LITERARY, LITERATURE, WRITING

Line Rider, Idaho Cattle Association, PO Box 15397, Boise, ID 83705. Editor: Carol Reynolds. Published 10 times a year. Circ 1,600.
AGRICULTURE/FARMING, ANIMALS, IDAHO

The Linews, Linfield College, PO Box 395, McMinnville, OR 97128. 503-472-0585. Weekly campus newspaper. Sub $7.50; circ 1,600.
COLLEGE/UNIVERSITY

Listen: Journal of Better Living, Pacific Press Publishing Association, 1350 Kings Rd, Nampa, ID 83605. Editor: Gary Swanson. Monthly magazine of the Seventh-Day Adventist Church. Circ 185,000.
FAMILY, RELIGION

Listen To Your Beer, Box 546, Portland, OR 97207. Periodical.
CONSUMER, CRAFTS/HOBBIES

Listening Post - KUOW FM, Box 9595, Seattle, WA 98195. Editor: Anna Manildi. 206-543-9595. Monthly of public radio station. Circ 12,000. Sub w/ membership. Uses 1 mss per issue. Byline given. Phone queries OK. Nonfiction, fiction, photos, cartoons. "Short articles of interest to KUOW listener supported radio. Classical music, news and info, arts, theater."
ARTS, MEDIA/COMMUNICATIONS, PUBLIC AFFAIRS

Literary Creations, PO Box 1339, Albany, OR 97321. 503-451-1372. Contact: Margaret L Ingram. Monthly newsletter. Sub $8/yr. Sample $2. Pays in copies. SASE for guidelines.
LITERARY, WRITING

Literary Markets, PO Drawer 1310, Point Roberts, WA 98281-1310. 604-277-4829. Editor: Bill Marles. Bimonthly newsletter. Sub $15/yr. Circ 1,000. Uses freelance material. Pays in copies on publication. Submit ms, SASE. Photocopied OK. Reports in 2 mos; publishes immediately after acceptance. Topics: about writing & the writing life. Accepts fiction, nonfiction. Length limit–250 wds or 30 lines. Guidelines, sample available.
POETRY, WRITING

Lithiagraph Classifieds, 507 Clay St #b-1, Ashland, OR 97520. Periodical.
COMMUNITY

Little Red Hen Inc, PO Box 4260, Pocatello, ID 83201. Book publisher.
OTHER/UNSPECIFIED

Little Wooden Books, 1890 Rd 24 SW, Matawa, WA 99344. Book publisher.
OTHER/UNSPECIFIED

Livestock Express, 4346 SE Division, Portland, OR 97206. Monthly.
AGRICULTURE/FARMING, ANIMALS, BUSINESS

Livingston Enterprise, PO Box 665, Livingston, MT 59047. Editor: John Sullivan. Newspaper.
COMMUNITY

Llama World, PO Box 567, Athena, OR 97813. Quarterly.
ANIMALS

The Lockhart Press, Box 1207, Port Townsend, WA 98368. 206-385-6412. Contact: Russell A Lockhart, PhD. Publishes handmade books of poetry. Accepts unsolicited submissions. Pays money, copies, royalties. Acquires all rights. Submit complete ms, SASE. Photocopy, dot matrix, disk/modem, simultaneous subs OK. Responds in 2–3 mos.
POETRY

Log House Publishing Company Ltd, Box 1205, Prince George, BC V2L 4V3. Publisher of nonfiction books on modern log building construction.
HOW-TO, TEXTBOOKS

The Log, Rogue Community College, 3345 Redwood Highway, Grants Pass, OR 97526. 503-479-5541 x201. Weekly newspaper.
COLLEGE/UNIVERSITY

Loggers World, 4206 Jackson Hwy, Chehalis, WA 98532. Periodical.
BUSINESS, LABOR/WORK, LUMBER

Logging & Sawmill Journal, 1111 Melville St, Ste 700, Vancouver, BC V6E 3V6. 604-683-8254. Editor: Norm Poole. Ads: Robert Stanhope. Monthly

trade magazine. Sub $33/yr; circ 19,000. Uses freelance material. Byline given, payment on publication. Assignment only, query by phone, letter. Responds in 1 mo; publishes in 1–3 mos. Accepts news items, interviews, geared to small–medium independent contractors and mills. Sample available.
FORESTRY, LUMBER, TRADE/ASSOCIATIONS

Logistics & Transportation Review, University of British Columbia, 1924 West Mall, Vancouver, BC V6T 1W5. Editor: W G Waters, II. 604-228-5922. Periodical.
BRITISH COLUMBIA, BUSINESS, COLLEGE/UNIVERSITY

London Northwest, 929 S Bay Rd, Olympia, WA 98506. Book publisher.
OTHER/UNSPECIFIED

Lone Star Press, PO Box 165, LaConner, WA 98257. Book publisher.
OTHER/UNSPECIFIED

Long House Printcrafters & Publishers, 680 Spring St #216, Friday Harbor, WA 98250-8058. Book publisher.
OTHER/UNSPECIFIED

Longanecker Books, PO Box 127, Brewster, WA 98812. Book publisher.
OTHER/UNSPECIFIED

Longview Daily News, 770 11th Ave, PO Box 189, Longview, WA 98632. 206-577-2500. Daily newspaper.
COMMUNITY

Loompanics Unlimited, PO Box 1197, Port Townsend, WA 98368. Contact: Michael Hoy. Publishes soft- & hardcover books. Accepts unsolicited submissions. Pays advance, copies, royalties. Acquires all rights. Submit query letter, outline, sample chapters, SASE. Photocopy, disk/modem OK. Responds in 6 wks; publishes in 6 mos. Accepts nonfiction, must be out-of-the-ordinary. Guidelines available. Catalog $3.
COUNTER CULTURE, HOW-TO

Lord Byron Stamps, PO Box 4586, Portland, OR 97208. 503-254-7093. Editor: Tom Current. Self-publisher of softcover books on British philately. Query w/SASE.
COLLECTING, CRAFTS/HOBBIES

Loud Pedal, Oregon Region, SCCA, 154 Idylwood Dr SE, Salem, OR 97302. Editor: Margie Swanson. Monthly.
OTHER/UNSPECIFIED

Louis Foundation, Main St, PO Box 210, Eastsound, WA 98245. Book publisher.
OTHER/UNSPECIFIED

Love Line Books, 790 Commercial Ave, Coos Bay, OR 97420. Book publisher.
OTHER/UNSPECIFIED

Lumby Historians, c/o Rosemary Deuling, RR 2, Lumby, BC V0E 2G0. Book publisher.
CANADIAN HISTORY

LUNO: Learning Unlimited Network of Oregon, 31960 SE Chin St, Boring, OR 97009. 503-663-5153. Newsletter published 9 times a yr. Sub $10. Circ 100. Accepts unsolicited mss. Pays copies. Byline given. Submit w/ SASE. Photocopies OK. Accepts nonfiction, poetry, cartoons. Topics: "Education, especially family/home schooling, education alternatives, learning styles, related politics."
CHILDREN/TEEN, COUNTER CULTURE, EDUCATION

Lyceum Press, 2442 NW Market St #51, Seattle, WA 98107. 206-547-6651. Editor: David D Horowitz. Publishes one softcover original book of poetry every 1–2 yrs. Not accepting unsolicited submissions.
POETRY

Lynx, PO Box 169, Toutle, WA 948649. 206-274-6661. Editor: Terri Lee Grell. Quarterly journal of renga. Sub $15/yr. US; circ 1,000. Accepts freelance material. Byline given. Pays money, copies on publication. Acquires 1st rights. Submit query letter, complete ms, SASE. Photocopy OK. Responds in 1–2 mos; publishes in 3–6 mos. Accepts poetry: renga. Guidelines available. Sample $2.
ASIA, AVANT-GARDE/EXPERIMENTAL, POETRY

Lynx House Press, 9305 SE Salmon Ct, Portland, OR 97216. 503-253-0669. Editor: Christopher Howell. Publishes 8 hard- & softcover original books a year. Does not accept unsolicited submissions. Pays small advance plus 10% of cloth & paper press run on publication. Submit ms, SASE. Photocopied OK. Reports in 3 mos. Publishes in 6–18 mos. Accepts fiction, poetry, plays. "We are an ambitious and highly selective literary press." Catalog available.
DRAMA, FICTION, POETRY

M/T/M Publishing Company, PO Box 245, Washougal, WA 98671. Book publisher.
OTHER/UNSPECIFIED

MacManiman Inc, 3023 362nd SE, Fall City, WA 98024. Book publisher.
OTHER/UNSPECIFIED

Madison County History Association, PO Box 228, 207 Mill St, Sheridan, MT 59749. Book publisher.
NW/REGIONAL HISTORY, MONTANA

Madison Park Press, 3816 E Madison St, Seattle, WA 98112. Book publisher.
OTHER/UNSPECIFIED

Madisonian, PO Box 367, Virginia City, MT, 59755. Periodical.
OTHER/UNSPECIFIED

The Madras Pioneer, 452 Sixth St, Box W, Madras, OR 97741. 503-475-2275. Weekly newspaper.
COMMUNITY

Madrona Publishers Inc, PO Box 22667, Seattle, WA 98122. Contact: Sara Levant. 206-325-3973. Publisher of 10 hard- & softcover originals & subsidy a year. Print run: 7,500. Accepts freelance material. Payment: Royalties. Rights purchased: First. Query with outline, sample chapter, SASE. Dot matrix, photocopies, simultaneous submissions OK. Reports in 6–8 wks. Publishes in 1 year. Nonfiction: At least 150 typewritten pgs. "Since we do not specialize, we will consider almost any topic of interest to a broad adult market. Particular interests are alcoholism (especially alcoholism as a physical, not mental, disease); feminist issues; and small business, especially the business side of crafts. No novels, poetry, drama, children's books." Guidelines/catalog 39¢.
BUSINESS, CRAFTS/HOBBIES, FEMINISM

Magnifica Books of Oregon, 1450 NE A St, Grants Pass, OR 97526. 503-474-0139. No submissions info.
OTHER/UNSPECIFIED

Magnolia House Publishing, 1820 Dartmouth W, Seattle, WA 98199. Book publisher.
OTHER/UNSPECIFIED

Magnolia News, 225 West Galer, Seattle, WA 98119. 206-282-900. Weekly newspaper.
COMMUNITY

Magpie, 3656 Liberty Rd S #10, Salem, OR 97302. 503-588-3705. Editor: John W Wilkerson. Counter culture periodical.
COUNTER CULTURE

The Mail Tribune, 33 N Fir St, Box 1108, Medford, OR 97501. 503-776-4411. Lifestyles Editor: Cleve Twitchell. Daily newspaper.
COMMUNITY

The Malahat Review, University of Victoria, PO Box 3045, Victoria, BC V8W 3P4. 604-721-8524. Editor: Constance Rooke. Quarterly magazine of fiction/poetry. Sub $15/yr; circ 1,800. Uses freelance material. Pays fiction: $40 per 1,000 wds + 1 yr sub on acceptance; poetry: $20 per pg + 1 yr sub. Reports in 3 mos; publishes in 6 mos. Accepts fiction, poetry, plays. No restrictions on topic, slant or length. Tips: "Send one story at a time, or 6–10 pgs of poetry." Guidelines available; sample $6.
FICTION, LITERARY, POETRY

Malheur Enterprise, 263 A St W, Box 310, Vale, OR 97918. 503-473-3377. Weekly newspaper.
COMMUNITY

Management Information Source Inc, PO Box 5277, Portland, OR 97208. Book publisher.
BUSINESS

Management/Marketing Associates Inc, 707 SW Washington St, Bank of California Tower, Portland, OR 97205. Book publisher.
BUSINESS

Manna Publications Inc, PO Box 1111, Camas, WA 98607. Book publisher.
OTHER/UNSPECIFIED

Manx Publishing Co, 1761 S 10th St, Sheridan, MT 59801. Book publisher.
OTHER/UNSPECIFIED

The Marijuana Report, PO Box 8698, Portland, OR 97207. Editor: John Sajo. 503-239-5134. Bimonthly tabloid on marijuana issues, politics, special initiatives, drug education; published by the Oregon Marijuana Initiative. Circ 50,000. Payment: 10¢ wd on publication. Submit ms, SASE. Phone queries, dot matrix, simultaneous submissions OK. Reports in 1 month. Nonfiction: 500–3,000 wds; any subject. Fiction, poetry: Inquire. Photos: B&W, preferably screened, $25–50. Tips: "Need well researched articles on impact of marijuana laws, ie, who is in prison for marijuana. Also urinalysis." Sample available.
FICTION, POETRY, PUBLIC AFFAIRS

Marine Digest, PO Box 3954, Seattle, WA 98124. 206-682-2484. Periodical.
BUSINESS, MARITIME

Maritime Publications, 3560 Alm Rd, Everson, WA 98247. Self-publisher. Not a freelance market.
BUSINESS, MARITIME

Marketing Index International Pub, PO Box 19031, Portland, OR 97219. Bimonthly.
BUSINESS

Marketing Reports & Trade Leads, USA Dry Pea & Lentil Council, PO Box 8566, Moscow, ID 83843. Editor: Don Walker. Published 18 times a year.
AGRICULTURE/FARMING, BUSINESS

Markins Enterprises, 2039 SE 45, Portland, OR 97215. Contact: Myrna Perkins. 503-235-1036. Self-publisher of 4 softcover children's picture books per year – educational, science oriented, entertaining. Press run: 500.
CHILDREN/TEEN, ENTERTAINMENT, SCIENCE

The Martlet, University of Victoria, Box 1700, Victoria, BC V8W 2Y2. Editors: Mike O'Brian/Kim Balfour. 604-721-8359. Periodical.
COLLEGE/UNIVERSITY

Marysville Globe, 8213 State St, Marysville, WA 98270. 206-659-1300. Editor: Brent Anderson. Ads: Dan Berentson. Weekly newspaper. Sub $16/yr. Uses freelance material. Byline given. Pays on publication. Submit query letter, SASE, phone. Accepts nonfiction, cartoons, interviews, articles, photos.
COMMUNITY

The Mason Clinic, 1100 9th Ave, PO Box 900, Seattle, WA 98111. Book publisher.
OTHER/UNSPECIFIED

Mason County Journal & Belfair Herald, PO Box 430, Shelton, WA 98584. 206-426-4412. Weekly newspaper.
COMMUNITY

Masonic Tribune, 2314 Third Ave, Seattle, WA 98121. 206-285-1505. Editor: Ruth Todahl. Ads: Sid Worbass. Weekly newspaper. Sub $15. Circ 5,500. Material supplied by fraternal members. No pay. Byline given. Uses B&W glossy photos. Guidelines available. Sample 50¢.
DISABLED

The Mast, Pacific Lutheran University, Tacoma, WA 98447. 206-535-7387. Weekly student newspaper.
COLLEGE/UNIVERSITY

Master Gardener Notes, OSU Extension, Multnomah County Office, 211 SE 80th Ave, Portland, OR 97215. Monthly.
GARDENING

Master Press, PO Box 432, Dayton, OR 97114. Book publisher.
OTHER/UNSPECIFIED

Masterstream, PO Box 1523, Longview, WA 98632. Periodical.
OTHER/UNSPECIFIED

Masterworks Inc, Rt 1 Box 1236, Lopez, WA 98261. Book publisher.
OTHER/UNSPECIFIED

Math Counseling Institute Press, 4518 Corliss Ave N, Seattle, WA 98103. Book publisher.
EDUCATION

MatriMedia, PO Box 6957, Portland, OR 97228. 503-221-1298. Editor: Ellen Nichols. Publishes softcover books on women and art. Payment on publication. Acquires all rights. Query w/SASE. Responds in 2–3 mos. Uses nonfiction, photos, interviews.
ARTS, NORTHWEST, WOMEN

Matrix, c/o The Daily, 132 Communications DS/20, University of Washington, Seattle, WA 98195. 206-543-2700. Monthly literary supplement of poetry and short fiction in the UW paper, The Daily. Circ 25,000. No pay. Byline given. Simultaneous submissions OK. Publishes submissions in 1–2 mos. Fiction: 1,500 wds, any subject. Poetry: Varies. Photos: B&W. Tips "We prefer to print the work of UW students, but on occasion have published non-student works. We receive about 100 submissions a month but have space for about 20–25."
COLLEGE/UNIVERSITY, FICTION, POETRY

Maverick Publications, Drawer 5007, Bend, OR 97708. Contact: Ken Asher. 503-382-6978. Publisher of 10 hard- & softcover originals per year for the general trade. Print run: 2,000. Accepts freelance material. Payment: Money. Rights acquired: Book rights plus 50% of subsidiary. Query w/outline, sample chapters, SASE. Dot matrix, photocopies, simultaneous submissions, electronic OK. Reports in 6 wks. Publishes in 6 mos. Nonfiction, fiction. Catalog available.
DRAMA, FICTION, NORTHWEST

Mazama, 909 NW 19th, Portland, OR 97209. Periodical on rock and mountain climbing and related subjects for club w/members. Sub w/membership.
OUTDOOR, RECREATION, SPORTS

Jo McIntyre, 131 W 8th St, McMinnville, OR 97128. Contact: Jo McIntyre. Book publisher.
OTHER/UNSPECIFIED

McKenzie River Reflections, PO Box 12, McKenzie Bridge, OR 97413. 503-822-3358. Editors/ads: Ken & Louise Engelman. Weekly of local tourist, recreation news. Sub $12/yr; circ 1,100. Uses freelance material. Pays copies. Byline given. Query w/SASE. Dot matrix, photocopies OK. Accepts nonfiction, fiction, poetry, photos (B&W), plays, cartoons. Sample free.
COMMUNITY, NORTHWEST, RECREATION

MCS Enterprises, PO Box 30160, Eugene, OR 97403. Book publisher.
OTHER/UNSPECIFIED

MCSA-Medical Committee & Service Association, 10223 NE 58th St, Kirkland, WA 98033. Book publisher.
HEALTH, MEDICAL

Medford Mail Tribune, PO Box 1108, Medford, OR 97501. 503-776-441. Daily newspaper.
COMMUNITY, OTHER/UNSPECIFIED

Media Inc, Media Index Publishing Inc, PO Box 24365, Seattle, WA 98124. 206-382-9220. Editor: Gordon Todd. Ads: Cathy Kaufman. Monthly. Sub $20/yr; circ 15,000. Uses freelance material. Byline given. Pays money on publication. Acquires all rights. Query by phone. Responds in 1 wk; publishes in 1 mo. Accepts news items, articles, reviews, photos (B&W or color glossy, rates negotiable). Topics: hard news-oriented, in-depth articles about advertising and advertising crafts such as photography, film/video, design, printing, etc. Sample $3.
FILM/VIDEO, MEDIA/COMMUNICATIONS, PHOTOGRAPHY

Media Weavers, Rt 3 Box 376, Hillsboro, OR 97124. 503-621-3911. Contact: Dennis Stovall, Linny Stovall. An imprint of Blue Heron Publishing, Media Weavers publishes books on writing and publishing for writers, pub-

lishers, librarians, booksellers, and teachers of writing, English, and journalism. Query w/SASE. Reports in 1 mo. Payment & rights negotiable. Gives byline. Dot matrix, photocopies, simultaneous, electronic, computer disk OK.
NORTHWEST, PUBLISHING/PRINTING, WRITING

Mediaor Company, Box 631, Prineville, OR 97754. Book publisher.
OTHER/UNSPECIFIED

Medic Publishing Company, PO Box 89, Redmond, WA 98073. 206-881-2883. Editor: Murray Swanson. Book publisher. Accepts unsolicited submissions. Pays royalties. Query letter, SASE. Dot matrix, photocopies OK. Reports in 1 mo. Topics: bereavement, medical — patient instruction. All are booklets, typically 24 pgs, 9,000 wds. "We are the country's leading publisher of grief literature, with some titles exceeding 1 million copies." Catalog available.
HEALTH, MEDICAL, PSYCHOLOGY

Medium, PO Box 22047, Seattle, WA 98122. 206-323-3070. Weekly newspaper.
COMMUNITY

Mentor: The Oregon Resource for Men, PO Box 10863, Portland, OR 97210. 503-621-3612. Editor: Dick Gilkeson. Bimonthly newsletter. Circ 2,500. Uses freelance material. Byline given. Query by phone. Mac disk sub preferred. Responds in 1 wk; publishes in 2 mos. Accepts fiction, poetry, nonfiction, cartoons, photos, interviews, reviews, memoirs. Topics: men's issues, redefining masculinity, freedom from racism, classism, sexism. Sample $1.
MEN

Mercury Services Inc, PO Box 1523, Longview, WA 98632-0144. 206-577-8598. Ads: Bruce Grimm. Bi-monthly newsletter. Sub $6/yr. Circ 2,500. Uses 1 freelance ms per issue. Pays on publication in copies. Acquires 1st rights. Byline given. Submit query w/clips, SASE. Dot matrix, photocopies, simultaneous, computer disk subs OK. Reports in 4–6 wks. Publishes 45–50 days. Accepts nonfiction: transportation related; safety issues. B&W photos.
COMMERCE, GOVERNMENT, LAW

Merril Press, PO Box 1682, Bellevue, WA 98009. 206-454-7009. Editor: Ron Arnold. Ads: Julie Versnel. Publishes 4–6 hard- & softcover originals, reprints, subsidy books/yr. Accepts unsolicited mss. Pays money, royalties. Acquires all rights. Prefers phone query. Dot matrix, photocopies, simultaneous, electronic/modem, computer disk OK. Publishes in 3–6 mos. Accepts nonfiction: how-to, politics, special interest, hobby material, economics.
CRAFTS/HOBBIES, ECONOMICS, HOW-TO

Message, Montana Info, Box 229, Condon, MT 59826. Quarterly.
OTHER/UNSPECIFIED

Message Post: Portable Dwelling Info-Letter, PO Box 190-MW, Philomath, OR 97370. Editor: Holly Davis. Newsletter published 3X/yr. Sub $5/6 issues. Circ 1,000. Uses freelance material. Pays subscription or ad on acceptance. Submit ms, SASE. Dot matrix, photocopied, simultaneous, subs OK. Accepts nonfiction. Topics: information related to camping for long periods or living in tipis, vans, trailers, boats, remote cabins, etc. No photos, line drawings & screens only. Want candid reports from those doing what they are writing about. Polish not important. Guidelines available. Sample $1.
HOW-TO, OUTDOOR

The Messenger, PO Box 1995, Vancouver, WA 98668. Editor: Marilyn Forbes. 206-696-8171. Ads: John Castile. Monthly for senior citizens. Circ 14,000. Sub $5. Uses 1–2 mss per issue. Payment: Free sub. Byline given. Rights purchased: First. Query w/SASE. Phone queries, photocopies OK. Nonfiction, photos (B&W glossy, any size, not prescreened), cartoons. "All material must relate directly to senior citizens. Strong preference for upbeat informational or feature articles from NW writers. 250 wds preferred maximum. Deadline, 12th of each month for following month's issue." Tips: "All material for this non–profit publication must be non-promotional. I encourage novice freelancers to submit pieces." Sample: Free.
CONSUMER, NW/REGIONAL HISTORY, SENIOR CITIZENS

METAlink, Rt 4 Box 4155, Hermiston, OR 97838. 503-567-7618. Editor: Chris Cromer. "A newsletter for Earth People of the Columbia Basin Plateau." Query w/SASE.
NEW AGE

Metamorphous Press Inc, PO Box 10616, Portland, OR 97210-0616. 503-228-4972, orders 800-937-7771, fax 503-223-9117. Acquisitions: Gene Radeica. Publishes hard- & softcover books. Accepts unsolicited submissions. Submit query w/clips, outline, sample chapters, SASE. Dot matrix, photocopied, disk/modem, simultaneous subs OK. Reports in 3–6 mos; publishes in 1 yr. Accepts nonfiction. Topics: self-help, psychology, health & fitness, business and sales, education, and children. Guidelines/catalog available.
EDUCATION, HEALTH, PSYCHOLOGY

Methow Valley News, PO Box 97, Twisp, WA 98856. 509-997-7011. Weekly newspaper. Sub $15–30/yr; circ 3,000. Uses freelance material. Byline given. Pays money on publication. Submit query letter, SASE. Responds in 2 wks; publishes in 2 wks. Accepts news items, nonfiction, photos (B&W), interviews, op/ed.
COMMUNITY

Metrocenter YMCA, PO Box 85334, Seattle, WA 98145. Editor: Jack C Thompson. 206-547-4003. Quarterly on pop culture, music, politics. Circ 500. Accepts freelance material. Byline given. Query w/SASE. Phone queries, simultaneous submissions, electronic OK. Nonfiction, cartoons, essays, analysis. Guidelines and sample available.
CULTURE, MUSIC, POLITICS

Metropolis, 2207 SW Iowa, Portland, OR 97201. 503-244-0535. Editor: Mary Catherine Koroloff. Free in Portland area. Monthly magazine of literature and arts. Interested in all types of short fiction (7,000 wds max), poetry, and experimental writing forms (concrete poetry, graphic short stories, etc). Submit ms w/SASE. "It is the avowed policy to treat writers with respect and dignity, for that is something that professional writers see all too infrequently."
ARTS, LITERARY, POETRY

Mica Publishing Company, PO Box 1528, Sisters, OR 97759. Contact: Joanne Stevens Sullivan. Self-publisher of 1 hard- & softcover book of poetry per year. Print run: 2,000. Not a freelance market. Catalog available.
POETRY

Micro Cornucopia, PO Box 223, Bend, OR 97709. Editors: Cary Gattan, Larry Fogg, Dave Thompson. Bimonthly magazine. Sub $18. Circ 30,000. Uses avg 6 freelance mss per issue. Pays $100–150 plus copies on publication. Acquires 1st rights. Byline given. Submit ms/SASE. Dot matrix, photocopied, electronic, computer disk OK. Reports in 1 mo, publishes in 4 mos. Accepts nonfiction, fiction. Topics: "Low level (hacker) hardware and software projects for MS-DOS machines…columns for start-up companies and silly computer stories." Tips: Technical, but also personal & humorous; 10–20,000 character length; "also interested in the nature of thought, creativity, and problem-solving." Guidelines available. Sample $3.95.
COMPUTERS, SATIRE, TECHNICAL

Microaccess, PO Box 5182, Bellingham, WA 98227. 206-671-1155. Contact: Mitch Lesoing/Carol Anderson. Computer newsletter. No unsolicited mss. Query with clips, SASE. Topics: computer education materials.
COMPUTERS, EDUCATION

Microsoft Press, PO Box 97017, Redmond, WA 98073-9717. Contact: Salley Oberlin. Publisher of 50–100 hard- & softcover nonfiction books per yr on software, science, and math, aimed at "people interested in computers, science and people." Query, w/ms, outline, sample chapters, SASE. Dot matrix, photocopies, simultaneous submissions, electronic OK. Publishes submissions in 6–9 mos. Catalog available.
COMPUTERS

Mid-County Memo, Pry Publishing Co, 600 NW 14th Ave, Portland, OR 97209. 503-226-8335. Editors: Rich Riegel. Ads: Greg Hudson. Monthly tabloid, founded 1985. Circ 15,000. Uses freelance material. Byline given. Pays money on publication. Acquires 1st rights. Submit query letter, clips,

SASE. Dot matrix OK. Responds in 1–2 wks. Accepts new items, nonfiction, photos, articles. Topics: events and people of east Portland, including Gateway, Parkrose, and Argay. Guidelines available.
COMMUNITY

Mid-Valley Arts Council, 265 Court St NE, Salem, OR 97301. 503-364-7474. Contact: Mark McCrary. Monthly newsletter. Circ 10,000. Uses freelance material. Byline given. Submit query letter, SASE. Photocopy, dot matrix subs OK. Responds in 1 wk; publishing varies. Accepts poetry, news items, interviews, photos (B&W glossy), articles, reviews. Sample 50¢.
ARTS

MIDCO Enterprises, PO Box 1266, Gresham, OR 97030. Editor: Lynette M Middleton. Book publisher.
OTHER/UNSPECIFIED

Midgard Press, 4214 Midway Ave, Grants Pass, OR 97527. 503-476-3603. Contact: Signe M Carlson. Self-publisher of hard- & softcover books. Not a freelance market. Topics: dairy goat owners, Northern Scandinavia.
AGRICULTURE/FARMING, ANIMALS, LITERATURE

Midwifery Today, PO Box 2672, Eugene, OR 97402. Editor: Jan Tritten. 503-345-1979. Ads: Bobbi Corcoran. 503-343-2408. Quarterly for midwifery practitioners and consumers. Sub $18. Uses 13 mss per issue. Payment: Copies on publication. Byline given. Rights purchased: First. Query w/ms, SASE. Phone queries, dot matrix, photocopies, simultaneous submissions OK. Reports in 6 wks. Nonfiction, fiction, poetry, photos, cartoons. "Articles to help birth practitioners do their work well. We have 20 different columns and take a variety of articles, both scientific and spiritual. We always need good research articles. Biographical sketch of writer included." Guidelines available, sample: $5.
HEALTH, WOMEN

Milco Publishing, 18910 37th S, Seattle, WA 98188. Book publisher.
OTHER/UNSPECIFIED

The Miler, Oregon Institute of Technology, Klamath Falls, OR 97601. 503-822-6321 x189.
COLLEGE/UNIVERSITY

Miles City Star, PO Box 1216, Miles City, MT 59301. Editor: Gerald Anglum. Newspaper.
COMMUNITY

Milestone Publications, PO Box 35548, Sta E, Vancouver, BC V6M 4G8. Book publisher.
ENVIRONMENT/RESOURCES

The Mill City Enterprise, 117 NE Wall, Box 348, Mill City, OR 97360. 503-897-2772. Weekly newspaper.
COMMUNITY

Robert Miller Productions, 1 Jefferson Prkwy, Lake Oswego, OR 97035. Book publisher.
OTHER/UNSPECIFIED

Minds Ink Publishing, PO Box 2701, Eugene, OR 97402. 503-689-4785. Editor: Phillip Hennin. Publishes 10 softcover books/yr. Accepts unsolicited mss. Submit query w/clips, SASE. Dot matrix, photocopied, simultaneous, electronic, computer disk (IBM) OK. Reports in 6 wks. Business, success stories, business resource material. Photos: graphics preferred, price negotiable. Also accepts articles for inclusion in "The Gold Book series ... a series of established business books for Oregon, " by assignment only. Write for guidelines.
BUSINESS, CALENDAR/EVENTS, HOW-TO

Miner & Gem State Miner, PO Box 349, Newport, WA 99156. 509-447-2433. Weekly newspaper.
CRAFTS/HOBBIES, GEOLOGY/GEOGRAPHY, RECREATION

Mineral Land Publications, PO Box 1186, Boise, ID 83701. Book publisher.
OTHER/UNSPECIFIED

Mining Review, 124 W 8th St, North Vancouver, BC V7M 3H2. Editor: Vivian Rudd. 604-985-8711. Periodical.
BUSINESS, SCIENCE

The Minnesota Review, Department of English, Oregon State University, Corvallis, OR 97331. Editor: Fred Pfeil. Literary review.
COLLEGE/UNIVERSITY, LITERARY, POETRY

Minutes Magazine, 50 SW Second Ave, Ste 416, Portland, OR 97204. 503-243-2616. Editor: Len Rothbaum. Periodical.
OTHER/UNSPECIFIED

MIR Publication Society, PO Box 730, Grand Forks, BC V0H 1H0. Book publisher.
OTHER/UNSPECIFIED

The Mirror, Marylhurst College for Lifetime Learning, Marylhurst, OR 97036. Editor: Courtney Rojas. Periodical.
COLLEGE/UNIVERSITY

MIS:Press, 524 N Tillamook, Portland, OR 97227. 503-282-5215. Contact: Robert Williams. Publishes 24 hard- & softcover computer/business books a yr. Pays royalties, advance. Rights acquired: All. Submit query w/clips, ms, SASE. Reports in 2–3 wks. Publishes in 3–6 mos. In-depth books on PC/MAC topics/products or business topics (management-oriented). Catalog available.
BUSINESS, COMPUTERS, TECHNICAL

Miscellania Unlimited Press, 5014-D Roosevelt Way NE, Seattle, WA 98105. 206-525-0632. Contact: Edd Vick. Book publisher.
OTHER/UNSPECIFIED

The Missing Link, Daffodil Press, 6426 – 198th St E, Spanaway, WA 98387. 206-847-4892. Contact: Sandra Van Orman. Sub $12/yr. Bimonthly newsletter. Accepts freelance material. Pays copies. Acquires 1st rights. Byline given. Submit ms/SASE. Dot matrix, photocopied OK. Reports in 2–3 wks. Publishes quickly. Accepts poetry. Guidelines available. Sample $2.50.
POETRY

Mississippi Mud, 1336 SE Marion St, Portland, OR 97202. Editor: Joel Weinstein. Literary/arts magazine published 2–3X/yr. Sub $19/4 issues; circ 1,500. Uses freelance material. Pays money, copies on publication. Byline given. Acquires 1st rights. Submit ms, SASE. Dot matrix, simultaneous subs OK. Reports in 2–4 mos; publishes in 3–12 mos. Accepts fiction (2,500–5,000 wds); poetry (no restrictions). Guidelines available. Sample $6.
FICTION, POETRY

Missoulian, PO Box 8029, Missoula, MT 59807. 406-721-5200. Daily newspaper.
COMMUNITY

Mocha Publishing, 8475 SW Morgan Dr, Beaverton, OR 97005. 503-643-7591. Contact: Berdell Moffett. Publisher of books on self-help, building self-confidence.
HOW-TO, PSYCHOLOGY

Modern & Contemporary Poetry of the West, Boise State University, Department of English, 1910 University Dr, Boise, ID 83725. Editor: Tom Trusky. Periodical 3 times a year. Circ 500.
LITERARY, POETRY

Modern Language Quarterly, 4045 Brooklyn Ave NE, Seattle, WA 98105.
ENGLISH, LANGUAGE(S)

Molalla Pioneer, 217 E Main St, Box 168, Molalla, OR 97038. Weekly newspaper.
COMMUNITY

Mole Publishing Company, Rt 1 Box 618, Bonners Ferry, ID 83805. Book publisher.
OTHER/UNSPECIFIED

Monad, Box 1227, Eugene, OR 97440. 503-344-6742. Editor: Kristine Kathryn Rusch. Ads: Dean W Smith. Science fiction and fantasy quarterly. Uses freelance material. Byline given. Pays money, advance, royalties. Acquires 1st or anthology rights. Submit query letter, complete ms. Simultaneous subs OK. Responds in 2 mos; publishes in 8 mos. Accepts fiction, cartoons, nonfiction, photos. Guidelines available.
FANTASY/SCI FI, FICTION, WRITING

Monday Magazine, 1609 Blanshard St, Victoria, BC V8W 2J5. 604-382-6188. Editor: Sid Tafler. Weekly alternate news magazine. Sub $30/yr Cdn,

$46/outside. Circ 40,000. Uses freelance material. Byline given. Pays 12–15¢/wd on publication. Acquires 1st rights. Submit query letter, ms, SASE. Photocopy, disk/modem subs OK. Reports in 1–4 wks; publishes in 1–4 wks. Accepts nonfiction, news items, biography, photos, interviews, op/ed, reviews. Topics: features of local or regional interest about politics, government, social issues, arts & entertainment. Guidelines available.

CANADA, ENTERTAINMENT, URBAN

Monroe Monitor/Valley News, PO Box 399, Monroe, WA 98272. Editor: Fred Willenbrock. 206-794-7116. Ads: Pat Oliffeer. Weekly newspaper. Circ 3,500. Sub $17 out of county. Not a freelance market.

COMMUNITY

Montana Agricultural Statistics Service, PO Box 4369, Helena, MT 59604. 406-449-5303. Editor: Lyle H Pratt. Semimonthly newsletter. Sub $12/yr; circ 1,800. Not a freelance market.

AGRICULTURE/FARMING, ANIMALS, MONTANA

Montana Arts Council, 35 S Last Chance Gulch, Helena, MT 59620. 406-444-6430. Editor: Julie Cook. Publishes 1 softcover book a yr. Accepts unsolicited submissions. Submit query w/clips, SASE. Dot matrix, photocopied, simultaneous, electronic subs OK. Accepts fiction, poetry, other. Guidelines available.

ARTS, FICTION, POETRY

Montana Author, PO Box 20839, Billings, MT 59104. Editor: Richard Wheeler. Quarterly publication of Montana Authors Coalition. Submit to R Wheeler, PO Box 1449, Big Timber, MT 59011. Articles and news on Montana authors and their work.

MONTANA, WRITING

Montana Business Quarterly, Bureau of Business & Economic Research, University of Montana, Missoula, MT 59812. Quarterly on Montana business.

BUSINESS, ECONOMICS, MONTANA

Montana Department of Labor & Industry, PO Box 1728, Helena, OR 59604. Book publisher.

BUSINESS, LABOR/WORK, MONTANA

Montana English Journal, Montana State University, Department of English, Bozeman, MT 59717. 406-586-2686. Editor: Sharon Beehler. Periodical.

EDUCATION, ENGLISH

Montana Farmer-Stockman, NW Unit Farms Magazines, PO Box 2160, Spokane, WA 99210. 509-459-5361. Semimonthly farm magazine. Also see listing for OR, WA, ID editions.

AGRICULTURE/FARMING, BUSINESS, MONTANA

Montana Historical Society, 225 N Roberts St, Helena, MT 59620. 406-444-4708. Editor: Charles Rankin. Book publisher. Pays money, copies on publication. Submit query letter, complete ms, sample chapters, SASE. Dot matrix, disk/modem subs OK. Responds in 3 mos; publishes in 6–12 mos. Accepts biography, interviews, reviews, articles. Topics: authentic history, footnotes and bibliography required. Guidelines, sample available.

NW/REGIONAL HISTORY, MONTANA, SCHOLARLY/ACADEMIC

Montana Historical Society Press, 225 N Roberts, Helena, MT 59620. 406-444-4708. Editor: W Lang, M Keddington. Publisher of nonfiction hard- & softcover original, reprint books. Does not accept unsolicited submissions.

NW/REGIONAL HISTORY, MONTANA, NATIVE AMERICAN

The Montana Journal, PO Box 4087, Missoula, MT 59806. 406-728-5520. Editor: Mike Haser. Semimonthly magazine. Sub $15/yr; circ 20,000. Uses freelance material. Byline given. Pays money, copies on publication. Acquires 1st rights. Submit ms, SASE. Responds in 1 mo, publishes in 1 mo. Accepts nonfiction, articles, memoirs, photos ($5). Guidelines available. Sample available

MONTANA, OTHER/UNSPECIFIED

Montana Kaimin, University of Montana, Missoula, MT 59812. Student newspaper.

COLLEGE/UNIVERSITY

Montana Library Association Focus, Montana State University Library, Bozeman, MT 59717. 406-994-3162. Editor: Gregg Sapp. Quarterly newsletter. Sub $12/yr; circ 650. Uses freelance material. Byline given, pays copies, acquires 1st rights. Submit query letter, synopsis, outline, complete ms, SASE, phone. Dot matrix, photocopy, simultaneous subs OK. Responds in 1 mo; publishes in 4–6 mos. Accepts news items, interviews, photos, articles. Topics: libraries, education, regional publishing trade. Guidelines available. Sample available.

BOOK ARTS/BOOKS, MONTANA, PUBLISHING/PRINTING

Montana Magazine, PO Box 5630, Helena, MT 59604. 406-443-2842. Editor: Carolyn Cunningham. Bimonthly magazine. Circ 85,000. Open to good freelance features. Pays money on publication. Byline given. Submit query w/ms, SASE. Phone queries, dot matrix, simultaneous subs OK. Reports in 4–6 wks, publishes in 1 yr. Accepts nonfiction, photos (write for guidelines; $75 cover, $50 center section). Topics: Montana — outdoor, history, places to go, geology, hunting, wildlife, personality profiles, etc. Guidelines available.

MONTANA, TRAVEL

Montana Newsletter, Montana State Library, 1515 E 6th Ave, Helena, MT 59620. Periodical.

REFERENCE/LIBRARY, SCHOLARLY/ACADEMIC

The Montana Poet, PO Box 100, Three Forks, MT 59752. 406-284-6655. Editor: Don Akerlow. Bimonthly newspaper. Sub $10/yr; circ 5,000. Uses freelance material. Pays copies on publication, acquires 1st rights, byline given. Submit ms w/SASE. Dot matrix, photocopied, simultaneous subs OK. Reports in 8 wks; publishes in 2–6 mos. Accepts: poetry about Montana or by a Montanan, cartoons, photos (of author). Submissions must be neatly printed or typed. Guidelines available. Sample $2.

POETRY, PUBLISHING/PRINTING, WOMEN

Montana Repertory Threatre, Part 101, University of Montana, Missoula, MT 59812. 406-243-6809. Director: Jim Bartruff. "Accepts unsolicited submissions for original dramatic works. SASE. Especially interested in works dealing with Western issues both modern and historic."

DRAMA

Montana Review, 1620 N 45th St, Seattle, WA 98103. 206-633-5929. Editor: Rich Ives. Ads: Rich Ives. Semiannual literary periodical. Circ 500. Sub $9. Accepts freelance material. Payment: Money, copies on publication. Byline given. Rights purchased: First. Submit ms w/SASE. Dot matrix, photocopies OK. Reports in 2–8 wks. Nonfiction, fiction, poetry, translations, book reviews. "Any length, subject. Literary quality is our only criteria. Pay varies according to current grant status."

FICTION, LITERARY, POETRY

Montana Senior Citizens News, PO Box 3363, Great Falls, MT 59403. 406-761-0305, 800-672-8477 (in Montana). Editor: Jack W Love, Jr. Ads: Jane Basta. Bimonthly tabloid. Sub $6. Circ 14,000. Uses 5 freelance mss per issue. Pays 4¢/word on publication. Acquires 1st rights. Byline given. Submit ms w/SASE, phone query. Dot matrix, photocopied, electronic/modem OK. Reports in 10 days. Accepts nonfiction, fiction, poetry, photos, cartoons. Topics: stories and articles of interest to seniors, particularly colorful, unique biographical sketches. Photos required with personality profiles; submit contact sheet or negatives, pay $5. Tips: length generally 500–1,000 wds; positive, upbeat, focus on the value of life experiences; humor/satire preferred for political topics. Sample $2.

MONTANA, SENIOR CITIZENS

Montana Standard, PO Box 627, Butte, MT 59703-0627. 406-782-8301. Contact: Rick Foote. Daily newspaper.

COMMUNITY

Montana Student Literary/Art Magazine, c/o Shirley M. Olson, 928 4th Ave., Laurel, MT 59044. 406-628-7063. A publication for the work of Montana students grade K-12. Each school in MT will receive a copy. Send SASE for guidelines.

CHILDREN (BY/ABOUT), MONTANA

Montana, the Magazine of Western History, Montana Historical Society, 225 N Roberts St, Helena, MT 59620. 406-444-4708. Editors: Charles Rankin/Tammy Ryan. Quarterly newsletter. Sub $20/yr; circ 9,000. Uses freelance material. Pays money, copies on publication. Submit query letter, complete ms, SASE. Dot matrix, disk/modem subs OK. Responds in 3 mos; publishes in 6–12 mos. Accepts biography, interviews, reviews, articles. Topics: authentic history, footnotes and bibliography required. Guidelines, sample available.
NW/REGIONAL HISTORY, MONTANA, SCHOLARLY/ACADEMIC

Montevista Press, 5041 Meridian Rd, Bellingham, WA 98226. 206-734-4279. Editor: J Burkhart. Publisher of 1 hard- & softcover book a yr. Freelance material not accepted. Catalog available.
ANIMALS, AMERICAN HISTORY, NW/REGIONAL HISTORY

Moonstone Press, 7620 SE Hwy 160, Port Orchard, WA 98366. Editor: Gayle Vogel Thomsen. 206-746-9201. Publisher of "poetry, prose and mythological illustrations about the Goddess and other literary, amusing and mystical subjects." No submissions info. Query w/SASE.
ASTROLOGY/SPIRITUAL, ENTERTAINMENT, FEMINISM

Moore Publications, PO Box 2530, Redmond, WA 98052. Book publisher.
OTHER/UNSPECIFIED

Mooseyard Press, PO Box 6462, Kent, WA 98064. 206-631-9013. Editors: Olga Joanow, Katherine Speed, L Pagliaro. Magazine published once or twice a year. Sub $7. Circ 500+. Accepts unsolicited mss. Pays in copies. Byline given. Submit ms, SASE. Dot Matrix, photocopies, electronic/modem, computer disk (MAC only) OK. Reports in 2 mos. Publishes in 3–4 mos. Accepts nonfiction, fiction, poetry. Guidelines available. Sample $3.
FICTION, PHILOSOPHY, POETRY

Morgan Notes, 3128 Penny Creek Rd, Bothell, WA, 98012, 206-743-6098. Contact: Jeanette Schouer. Periodical.
OTHER/UNSPECIFIED

Morse Press, PO Box 24947, Seattle, WA 98124. Contact: Ronn Talbot Pelley. 206-282-9988. Publisher of 4 softcover books, originals, reprints annually. "Confirmation materials, chancel dramas, Lenten programs, counseling guides." Print run: 5,000. Accepts freelance material. Payment: Money, royalties. Rights purchased: All. Sample chapters w/SASE. Photocopies, simultaneous submissions OK. Reports in 6 wks. Publishes in 1 year. Nonfiction, plays. Catalog available.
EDUCATION, RELIGION

Morton Journal, PO Drawer M, Morton, WA 98356. 206-496-5993. Weekly newspaper.
COMMUNITY

Mosaic Enterprises Ltd, 1420 St Paul St, Kelowna, BC V1Y 2E6. Book publisher.
OTHER/UNSPECIFIED

Mother of Ashes Press, PO Box 135, Harrison, ID 83833-0135. 208-689-3738. Contact: Joe M Singer. Small publisher. Does not accepts unsolicited submissions. Query letter, SASE, assignment only. Catalog available.
FICTION, PICTURE, POETRY

Mount Vernon Press, 1121 112th NE, Bellevue, WA 98004. Book publisher.
OTHER/UNSPECIFIED

The Mountain Guide, Blue Mountain Community College, Box 100, Pendleton, OR 97801. 503-276-1260. Periodical.
COLLEGE/UNIVERSITY

Mountain Home News, PO Box 0, Mountain Home AFB, ID 83648. 208-587-3331. Newspaper.
COMMUNITY, MILITARY/VETS

Mountain Light, Idaho Historical Society, 450 N 4th St, Boise, ID 83702. 208-334-3428. Editor: Judith Austin. Quarterly newsletter. Sub w/membership; circ 2,000. Submit query letter, complete ms, SASE, phone.
NW/REGIONAL HISTORY, IDAHO

Mountain Meadow Press, PO Box 1170, Wrangell, AK 99929. 907-874-2565. Editor: Linwood Laughy. Self-publisher. Does not accept unsolicited submissions. Topics: parent-participatory education and Idaho history/travel. Catalog available.
EDUCATION, NW/REGIONAL HISTORY, IDAHO

Mountain Press Publishing Company, 1600 North Ave W, Missoula, MT 59806. Book publisher. Titles/yr: 12.
MONTANA, OUTDOOR, OTHER/UNSPECIFIED

Mountain Press, 16175 SW Holly Hill Rd, Hillsboro, OR 97123. 503-628-3995. Editor: J K Basco. Book publisher. Does not accept unsolicited submissions. Submit query letter, SASE. Responds in 3 wks. Topics: business, entrepreneurs.
BUSINESS

The Mountaineers Books, 306 2nd Ave W, Seattle, WA 98119. 206-285-2665. Editor: Margaret Foster-Finan. Ads: Michael Bronsdon. Publishes hard- & softcover books. Accepts unsolicited submissions. Pays money, royalties, advance. Acquires 1st rights. Submit query letter w/clips, outline, sample chapters, SASE. Dot matrix, photocopies, simultaneous subs OK. Reports in 2–8 wks; publishes in 1 yr. plus. Accepts nonfiction: how-tos, guides and adventure narratives for non-motorized, non-competitive outdoor sports (skiing, biking, hiking, climbing, mountaineering, kayaking, walking, etc; also, nature, conservation, history. Guidelines, catalog available.
NATURAL HISTORY, OUTDOOR, RECREATION

Mr Cogito, Mr Cogito Press, Pacific University, PO Box 627, Forest Grove, OR 97116. 503-226-4135. Editors: Robert Davies, John Gogol. Irregularly published magazine. Sub $9/3 issues; circ 500. Submit ms, SASE. Dot matrix OK. Reports in 2–8 wks. Infrequently pays. Acquires 1st anthology and publishing rights. Accepts poetry: 1 pg; image and sound and diction important; line drawings & photos (up to 3.5" wide x 10" long). Topics: poems in English and translated into English, various themes, leans toward social and political poetry, Central America. Sample copies $3.
POETRY

Mr Cogito Press, Pacific University, PO Box 627, Forest Grove, OR 97116. Editors: Robert Davies, John Gogol. Publishes softcover books. Does not accept unsolicited submissions. Publishes in 6–12 mos. Poetry: translations and English. Tips: "We are a very small press, highly selective; our magazine submissions are our source for selecting authors." Catalog available.
POETRY

MSU Exponent, Montana State University, Bozeman, MT 59717. Student Newspaper.
COLLEGE/UNIVERSITY

Mt Tabor Bulletin, 12311 NE Glisan #103, Portland, OR 97230. 503-256-2833. Contact: Shelli Smith. Newspaper.
COMMUNITY

Mud Creek, The Loess Press, PO Box 19417, Portland, OR 97219. Contact: Marty Brown. Semiannual magazine of fine art and fine writing. Sub $8/2 yrs. Sees freelance material. Pays 2 copies. Acquires 1st rights. Reports promptly. Submit ms/SASE. Accepts poetry (no verse), short fiction, essays, interviews, B&W photos, artwork. No genre material. Send sample of 2–5 poem. Submit through Aug for Oct issue; through Feb for Apr issue. Sample $5.
FICTION, LITERATURE, POETRY

Mukluks Hemcunga, PO Box 1257, Klamath Falls, OR 97601. Monthly.
OTHER/UNSPECIFIED

Multiples Press, 1821 S 4th W, Missoula, MT 59801-2229. Book publisher.
OTHER/UNSPECIFIED

Multnomah Press, 10209 SE Division, Portland, OR 97266. 503-257-0526. Editors: Al Janssen, Karan Gleason. Ads: Toni Pittman. Book publisher. Accepts freelance material. Pays advance, royalties, copies. Query letter, complete ms, SASE. Dot matrix, photocopies, simultaneous, electronic subs OK. Responds in 1 mo; publishes in 9–12 mos. Accepts fiction, nonfiction, children's literature. Topics: "Christian literature that is contemporary while faithful to the Scriptures." Guidelines, catalog available.
FICTION, RELIGION

Rie Munoz Ltd, 233 S Franklin St, Juneau, AK 99801. 907-586-3037. Self-publisher. Does not accept unsolicited submissions.
ARTS

Murray Publishing Company, 2312 3rd Ave, Seattle, WA 98121. Contact: John Murray. Publisher of textbooks and other nonfiction. Book publisher.
TEXTBOOKS

Museum of History & Industry, 2700 24th Ave E, Seattle, WA 98112. 206-324-1125. Book publisher.
GENERAL HISTORY, NW/REGIONAL HISTORY, INDUSTRY

Musher Monthly, PO Box 305, Bethel, AK 99559. 907-543-2845. Contact: Mike Murray. A publication for and by children of Bethel, AK.
ALASKA, CHILDREN (BY/ABOUT)

Mushing, PO Box 149, Ester, AK 99725. Contact: Todd Hoener. International periodical for recreational and competitive dog sledders. Uses freelance interviews, features (1,500–2,000 wds), profiles, and shorter departmental reports. Pays money on acceptance. Query w/SASE. Guidelines available.
OUTDOOR, RECREATION, SPORTS

Mushroom, The Journal, Box 3156, University Stn, Moscow, ID 83843. 208-882-8720. Editor: Don Coombs. Quarterly. Sub $16. Circ 2,000. Uses 4 freelance mss per issue. Pays money/copies on publication. Acquires 1st rights. Byline given. Submit query w/clips, ms. Dot matrix, photocopied, computer disk (DOS/ASCII) OK. Reports in 1 mo. Publishes in 2–6 mos. Accepts nonfiction, poetry, photos, cartoons. "Material should be relevant in some way to what's going on outdoors with plants, animals and insects." Personal experience okay if it includes valuable learning for the reader. B&W prints or color negatives. Guidelines available. Sample $4 (3 or more $3 ea).
HOW-TO, NATURAL HISTORY, OUTDOOR

Musings, Campbell River Museum, 1235 Island Highway, Campbell River, BC V9W 2C7. 604-287-8043. Newsletter published 3 times a year on local history, Museum activities. Sub $10/yr; circ 375. Not a freelance market. Sample: $1.25, SASE.
NW/REGIONAL HISTORY

Mustard Seed Faith Inc, PO Box 3, St Helens, OR 97051. 503-397-3735. Editor: Diane Barrick. Quarterly Christian newspaper. Sub $7/yr. Uses freelance material. Byline given. Submit query letter, SASE. Responds in 2–3 wks; publishes in 2–3 mos. Accepts fiction, nonfiction, poetry, cartoons, news items, biography, photos ($10). Topics: religious, Christian, testimonies. Sample $1.
RELIGION

My Awe/Zine Orgy, 1501 NE 102 St, Seattle, WA 98125. Periodical.
OTHER/UNSPECIFIED

My Little Salesman, PO Box 70208, Eugene, OR 97401. Monthly.
OTHER/UNSPECIFIED

Myrtle Point Herald, PO Box 128, Myrtle Point, OR 97458-0128. 503-572-2717. Weekly newspaper.
COMMUNITY

Mystery News, POB 1201, Port Townsend, WA 98368. 206-385-6116. Contact: Larry & Harriet Stay. Bimonthly tabloid. Circ 1,200. Sub $13.95/yr. Previews and reviews of current mystery novels. No freelance submissions. Sample free.
MYSTERY

Mystery Time, PO Box 1870, Hayden, ID 83835. 208-772-6184. Editor: Linda Hutton. Annually published collection. Price $5. Uses freelance material. Pays $.0025–.01 per word for 1st rights, 1 copy for reprint rights. Submit short story (to 1,500 wds) w/SASE. Photocopied, simultaneous OK. Tips: short stories, suspense/mystery theme only, avoid present tense; poetry about mysteries or mystery writers. "Six authors are nominated annually for the Pushcart Prize in Fiction."
FICTION, POETRY

Nanaimo Historical Society, PO Box 933, Nanaimo, BC V9R 5N2. 604-758-2828. Contact: Mrs Mar. Self-publisher of historical hard- & softcover original books. Not a freelance market.
BRITISH COLUMBIA, GENEALOGY, CANADIAN HISTORY

National Book Company, PO Box 8795, Portland, OR 97207-8795. 503-228-6345. Publishes hard- & softcover books. Accepts unsolicited submissions. Reports in 1–2 mos; publishes in 6–12 mos. Accepts nonfiction. Submit query letter, outline, sample chapters, complete ms, SASE. Dot matrix, photocopy, disk/modem subs OK. Topics: textbooks, multimedia instructional programs and computer software in Jr. High –Jr. College range; library and business reference books, educational policy studies, ethnic issues, computer software. Catalog available.
MINORITIES/ETHNIC, REFERENCE/LIBRARY, TEXTBOOKS

National Boycott Newsletter, 6506 28th Ave NE, Seattle, WA 98115. Editor: Todd Putnam. 206-523-0421. Quarterly on consumer action in the market place, boycotts and socially responsible investing. Circ 4,000–5,000. Sub $3. Uses 1–2 mss per issue. Payment: Money, copies on publication. Byline given. Query w/ms, SASE. Phone queries, dot matrix, photocopies, electronic OK. Nonfiction, photos, cartoons. "Corporations/multinationals and their environmental, social, economic impacts; boycotts and consumer action; boycotts called by human rights, peace, labor, environmental, and civil, women's and animal rights organizations." Sample available.
CONSUMER, LABOR/WORK, PEACE

National Fisherman Magazine, 4215 21st W, Seattle, WA 98199. 206-283-1150. Periodical.
FISHING

National Percent for Art Newsletter, 1120 S Elm St, Spokane, WA 99204-4244. Editor: Richard Twedt. Quarterly of news on state, regional and local public art commissions and % for art programs. Sub $24.
ARTS

National Radio Guide, 240 – 1075 W Georgia, Vancouver, BC V6E 3C9. 604-688-0382. Editor: C Robertson. Ads: J Knight. Monthly magazine. Sub $23.95/yr. Circ 20,000. Accepts freelance submissions. Pays money on publication for 1st rights. Gives byline. Query first. Responds in 1 mo; publishes in 2 mos. "Canada's only complete guide to CBC radio programming. …publishes articles that refer to on air programming that month."
MEDIA/COMMUNICATIONS

National Seafood Educators, PO Box 60006, Richmond Beach, WA 98160. 206-546-6410. Editors: Evie Hansen, Janis Harsila. Publishes softcover books. Accepts unsolicited submissions. Submit query letter, outline, sample chapters, complete ms, SASE. Topics: cartoons, children's books, marine historical.
CHILDREN (BY/ABOUT), FISHING, MARITIME

Natural Living, 611 Market St, Kirkland, WA 98033. Periodical.
HEALTH

Navillus Press, 1958 Onyx St, Eugene, OR 97403. Editor: William L Sullivan. Self-publisher. Accepts no submissions.
OREGON, OUTDOOR

NBS West, PO Box 1039, Vashon, WA 98070. Book publisher.
OTHER/UNSPECIFIED

Nechako Valley Historical Society, PO Box 1318, Vanderhoof, BC V0J 3A0. Book publisher.
CANADIAN HISTORY

The Neighbor, Pry Publishing Co, 600 NW 14th Ave, Portland, OR 97209. 503-226-8335. Editor: John Henrikson. Ads: Greg Hudson. Semimonthly tabloid, founded 1975. Circ 16,500. Uses freelance material. Byline given. Pays money on publication. Acquires 1st rights. Submit query letter, clips, SASE. Dot matrix OK. Responds in 1–2 wks. Accepts new items, nonfiction, photos, articles. Topics: events and people of NW Portland and surrounding neighborhoods. Guidelines available.
COMMUNITY

Nerve Press, 5875 Elm St, Vancouver, BC V6N 1A6. Publisher of children's fiction & sci-fi. Book publisher.
CHILDREN/TEEN, FANTASY/SCI FI, FICTION

Nesbitt Enterprises, 7421 Tennessee Ln, Vancouver, WA 98664-1442. Book publisher.
OTHER/UNSPECIFIED

Nettle Creek Publishing, 600 1st Ave, Ste 310, Seattle, WA 98104. Book publisher.
OTHER/UNSPECIFIED

Network News, Oregon Coalition Against Domestic & Sexual Violence, 2336 SE Belmont, Portland, OR 97214. Quarterly newsletter. Query w/ SASE. 050, 098, 124.
FEMINISM, POLITICS, WOMEN

NAPRA Trade Journal, New Age Publishers & Retailers Alliance, PO Box 9, Eastsound, WA 98245. 206-376-2702. Editor: Marilyn McGuire. Circ 7,000. Quarterly features new age book reviews, author tours, and boo events.
PUBLISHING/PRINTING, NEW AGE

New Age Retailer, Continuity Publishing Inc, PO Box 224, Greenbank, WA 98253. 206-678-7772. Contact: Duane Sweeney. Ads: Pat Brown. Magazine published 7x/yr. Sub $15/yr. Circ 3,200. Uses 1 freelance ms per issue. Pays copies/ad credit on publication. Byline given. Submit by phone query. Dot matrix, photocopies, computer disk subs OK. Publishes in 1–4 mos. Accepts nonfiction. Topics: info of use or interest to owners of new age bookstores. Tips: 1,500–3,000 words. Sample $2.50.
BUSINESS, NEW AGE

New Breed News, North American Indian League, Box 7309, Boise, ID 83707.
NATIVE AMERICAN

New Capernaum Works, 4615 NE Emerson St, Portland, OR 97218. Book publisher.
OTHER/UNSPECIFIED

The New Era Newspaper, 1200 Long St, Box 38, Sweet Home, OR 97386. 503-367-2135. Weekly newspaper.
COMMUNITY

The New Pacific, 1201 Third Ave, Ste 3912, Seattle, WA 948101-3099. 206-583-8566. Editor: Eileen V Quigley. Quarterly journal. Sub $19.95/US, $23.95/CDN. Uses freelance material. Byline given. Pays money on publication, acquires 1st rights. Submit query letter, outline, clips, complete ms, SASE, phone. Simultaneous, disk/modem subs OK. Responds in 1 mo; publishes in 6 wks. Accepts nonfiction, poetry, cartoons, reviews, photos (B&W only, $150–200). Topics: public policy, economics and culture for Pacific Northwest and British Columbia. Guidelines available. Sample $5.95 + postage.
BRITISH COLUMBIA, NW/REGIONAL HISTORY, NORTHWEST

New Riders Publishing, Division of Que Corporation, 1603 116th Ave NE, Ste 111, Bellevue, WA 98004. 206-453-0710. Contact: Jesse Berst. Publishes 20 softcover original books per yr. Accepts query letters only — include outline, bio, writing sample, statistics about target market. Technical expertise required. Pays advance, royalties. Dot matrix, computer disk subs OK. Topics: computer books on leading edge topics — graphics, desktop publishing, CAD, networking, and others. Catalog available.
COMPUTERS, TECHNICAL

New River Times, 310 1/2 First Ave, Fairbanks, AK 99701. Periodical.
OTHER/UNSPECIFIED

New Star Books, 2504 York Ave, Vancouver, BC V6K 1E3. 604-738-9429. Publisher of 8 nonfiction softcover originals a year for left-wing readers. Query, manuscript, outline, sample chapters w/SASE. Publishes in 1 year. Nonfiction: labor, social history, feminism, gay liberation, ethnic studies. Catalog available.
FEMINISM, LABOR/WORK, SOCIALIST/RADICAL

The New Times, PO Box 51186, Seattle, WA 98115-1186. 206-524-9071. Editor: Krysta Gibson. Monthly newspaper. Sub $9.50/yr; circ 17,000. Uses freelance material. Pays on acceptance in subs. Acquires 1st rights. Byline given. Submit photocopied ms, SASE. Reports in 1–2 mos; publishes in 1–2 mos. Accepts nonfiction, cartoons, interviews. Topics: New Age, spirituality, human potential, holistic health, interviews. Photos B&W, 5x7 or larger, nature or human interest; 1 yr. subs for payment. Tip: looking for positive information which will help our readers grow spiritually, emotionally & physically. Guidelines SASE. Sample $1.
ASTROLOGY/SPIRITUAL, HEALTH, NEW AGE

Newberg Graphic, 109 N School, Box 110, Newberg, OR 97132. 503-538-2181. Weekly newspaper.
COMMUNITY

Newberg Times, PO Box 370, Beaverton, OR 97075-0370. Weekly newspaper.
COMMUNITY

Newport Bay Publishing Ltd, 356 Cyril Owen Place, RR 3, Victoria, BC, V8X 3X1. Native titles.
BRITISH COLUMBIA, CHILDREN (BY/ABOUT), NATIVE AMERICAN

Newport News-Times/Lincoln County Leader, 831 NE Avery, Box 965, Newport, OR 97365. 503-265-8571. Weekly newspaper.
COMMUNITY

News Bulletin, Salem Area Seniors Inc, 1055 Erixon NE, Salem, OR 97303. Monthly.
SENIOR CITIZENS

The News-Examiner, PO Box 278, Montpelier, ID 83254. 208-847-0552. Editor: Rosa Moosman. Weekly newspaper. Uses freelance material by assignment only. Byline given. Accepts news items, photos (B&W). Topics: Bear Lake area.
COMMUNITY

The News Guard, 930 SE Highway 101, Box 848, Lincoln City, OR 97367. 503-994-2178. Weekly newspaper.
COMMUNITY

News Register, 611 E Third, Box 727, McMinnville, OR 97128. 503-472-5114. Daily newspaper.
COMMUNITY

News & Reports, Idaho Department of Education, 650 West State St, Boise, ID 83720. Editor: Helen J Williams. Monthly newsletter. Circ 20,000. Not a freelance market.
EDUCATION, IDAHO

News Tribune, PO Box 499, Snohomish, WA 98290. 206-258-9396. Weekly newspaper.
COMMUNITY

News-Journal, 600 S Washington, Kent, WA 98031. 206-872-6600. Daily newspaper.
COMMUNITY

News-Miner, PO Box 438, Republic, WA 99166. 509-775-3558. Weekly newspaper.
COMMUNITY

The News-Review, 345 NE Winchester, Box 1248, Roseburg, OR 97470. 503-672-3321. Daily newspaper.
COMMUNITY

Coulee City News-Standard, PO Box 488, Coulee City, WA 99115. Editor/ads: Sue Poe. 509-632-5402. Weekly newspaper focusing on local agriculture and schools. Circ 700. Sub $12–15. Not a freelance market.
AGRICULTURE/FARMING, COMMUNITY, EDUCATION

News-Times, PO 408, Forest Grove, OR 97116. 503-357-3181. Weekly newspaper.
COMMUNITY

Newscast, PO Box 998, Ephrata, WA 98823. 509-754-4636. Weekly newspaper.
COMMUNITY

Newsletter, Portland Friends/Cast Iron Architecture, 213 SW Ash, Rm 210, Portland, OR 97204. Editor: William J Hawkins. Semiannual.
ARCHITECTURE

The Newspoke, Anchorage School District, 1800 Hillcrest, Anchorage, AK 99503. Periodical.
EDUCATION

Nexus Press, 13032 NE 73rd, Kirkland, WA 98033. Book publisher.
OTHER/UNSPECIFIED

Nike Times, Nike Inc, 3900 SW Murray Rd, Beaverton, OR 97005. Editor: Chris Van Dyke. Company publication.
BUSINESS

Nisqually Valley News, PO Box 597, Yelm, WA 98597. 206-458-2681. Weekly newspaper.
COMMUNITY

Nobility Press, PO Box 17603, Portland, OR 97217. 503-289-5216. Editor: Kelly Osmont. Book publisher.
FAMILY, PSYCHOLOGY

Noetic Press, PO Box 10851, Eugene, OR 97440. 503-937-3437 (503-937-3214 FAX). Contact: Jan Sellon. Publishes hard- and softcover books — "highly original with a firm intellectual base on the subjects of creativity, ethics, and evolution. We strive to be thoroughly scientific in our mysticism and thoroughly mystical in our science." Accepts poetry and nonfiction. No unsolicited submissions. Gives byline and acquires all rights. "Pays all costs of publication; gives no advances, shares profits with author. Material must relate to backlog and backlist." Responds in 3 wks; publishes in 2 yrs. Query first. Guidelines and catalog available.
EDUCATION, PHILOSOPHY, SCIENCE

Nomadic Newsletter, Nomadic Books, 1911 N 45th St, Seattle, WA, 98103. Periodical.
OTHER/UNSPECIFIED

Nordic West, PO Box 7077, Bend, OR 97708. Editor: Richard Coons. Monthly magazine devoted to cross-country skiing in the western USA. Query w/SASE.
OUTDOOR, RECREATION, SPORTS

Norjak Project, 11678 SE Capps Rd, Clackamas, OR, 97015. Editor: Tom Worcester. Book publisher.
NW/REGIONAL HISTORY

North American Post, 662 1/2 S Jackson St, Seattle, WA 98104. 206-623-0100. Editor: Akiko Kusunose. Japanese language newspaper, published 3 times a week, with an English section once a week. Sub $60/yr; circ 2,000. Accepts freelance material very infrequently. No pay. Byline given. Submit ms, SASE. Accepts nonfiction, poetry, photos. Sample available.
ASIAN AMERICAN, LANGUAGE(S), MINORITIES/ETHNIC

North Beach Beacon, PO Box 1207, Ocean Shores, WA 98569. 206-289-3359. Weekly newspaper.
COMMUNITY

The North Coast Times Eagle, 955 24th St, Astoria, OR 97103. Editor: Michael Paul McCusker. Monthly broadsheet founded in 1971. Query w/ SASE. Topics: international, national, regional, and local politics, economics, development, environment, militarism, censorship, and regional arts.
ARTS, ENVIRONMENT/RESOURCES, POLITICS

North Country Publishing, 112 W 4th, Moscow, ID 83843. 208-882-0888. Editor: Ivar Nelson. Ads: Opal Gerwig. Publisher of hard- and softcover books. Uses freelance material. Pays money on publication. Acquires all rights. Byline given. Submit query letter, complete ms, SASE, phone. Reports in 3 wks; publishes in 2 mos. Accepts biography, photos (on request), interviews, op/ed, articles, reviews. Topics: local history, natural history, politics, environment issues, sports, food, science, business, regional travel, recreation, arts, people, "— must be of interest to interior Northwest readers." Guidelines and catalog available w/SASE.
NORTHWEST, RECREATION, TRAVEL

North Country Review, PO Box 1688, Billings, MT 59103. 406-252-3026. Editor: Jim Rains. A Montana journal of Western life and literature looking for short stories, articles, poems, and short subjects. Guidelines available.
FICTION, LITERARY, POETRY

North Pacific Publishers, PO Box 13255, Portland, OR 97213. Book publisher.
OTHER/UNSPECIFIED

North Publishing, 4217 W Bertona St, Seattle, WA 98119-1840. Book publisher.
OTHER/UNSPECIFIED

North Seattle Press/Lake Union Review, 4128 Fremont N, Seattle, WA 98103. 206-547-9660. Editor: Clayton Park, James Bush. Ads: Karina Erickson, Terry Denton. Biweekly newspapers. Sub $12/both; circ 20,000. Uses freelance material. Byline given. Pays money on publication. Submit query letter, clips, SASE, phone. Responds in 1 wk; publishes in 1–2 wks. Accepts news items, photos!, articles. Assignments readily given! Sample available.
COMMUNITY

North Side News, PO Box 468, Jerome, ID 83338. 208-324-3391. Newspaper.
COMMUNITY, OTHER/UNSPECIFIED

Northern Kittitas County Tribune, PO Box 308, Cle Elum, WA 98922. 509-674-2511. Weekly newspaper.
COMMUNITY

Northern Lights, Northern Lights Institute, PO Box 8084, Missoula, MT 59807-8084. Editor/Ads: Debra Clow. 406-721-7415. Quarterly about ID, WY, MT and the NW, public policy issues. Circ 4,000. Sub minimum donation $15. Uses 5–10 freelance mss per issue. Payment 10¢/wd and copies on publication. Byline given. Rights purchased: First. Query w/clips, ms, SASE. Dot matrix, photocopies OK. Reports in 6–8 wks. Publishes in 3–6 mos. Accepts nonfiction, photos, cartoons. Encourage writers & artists to send SASE for guidelines. "We want articles that capture not only the facts, but also the mood, landscape, humor and personalities of the subject in question…we are interested in problems in the West that need solutions, but we are also interested in writing about the things in the West that make it such a wonderful place to live." Sample $5.
ENVIRONMENT/RESOURCES, HUMOR, NORTHWEST

Northland Publications, PO Box 12157, Seattle, WA 98102. Book publisher.
OTHER/UNSPECIFIED

Northshore Citizen, PO Box 647, Bothell, WA 98041. 206-486-1231. Weekly newspaper.
COMMUNITY

Northwest Airlifter, PO Box 98801, Tacoma, WA 98499. 206-584-1212. Weekly newspaper.
AVIATION

Northwest Anthropological Research Notes, University of Idaho, Laboratory of Anthropology, Moscow, ID 83843. Editor: Roderick Sprague. Semiannual. Circ 300. Query w/SASE. Guidelines available.
ANTHROPOLOGY/ARCHÆOLOGY, SCHOLARLY/ACADEMIC

Northwest Arctic NUNA, Maniilaq Assoc, PO Box 256, Kotzebue, AK 99752. 907-442-3311. Free monthly. Circ 3,000. Uses 2 freelance mss per issue. Pays copies. Byline given. Submit by phone, SASE. Dot matrix, photocopied OK. Report and publishing time varies. Accepts nonfiction, fiction, poetry, photos. Sample free.
ALASKA, NATIVE AMERICAN

Northwest Attitudes, PO Box 1739, Ferndale, WA 948248. 206-384-9588. Editor: E M Gareth. Bimonthly magazine founded in 1990. Free. Uses freelance material. Byline given. Pays money on publication. Acquires 1st rights. Submit query letter, complete ms, SASE. Photocopy, dot matrix OK. Responds in 2 mos; publishes in 4–6 mos. Accepts news items, interviews, articles. Topics: material interesting to family members in the Pacific NW.
CHILDREN (BY/ABOUT), CHILDREN/TEEN, FAMILY

Northwest Beachcomber, 200 W Highland Dr, #101, Seattle, WA 98119. Contact: Eloise Holman. Book publisher.
CRAFTS/HOBBIES, RECREATION

Northwest Bed & Breakfast Travel Unlimited, 610 SW Broadway, Ste 609, Portland, OR 97205. 503-243-7616. Self-publisher, bed & breakfast directory. Not a freelance market.
CALENDAR/EVENTS, NORTHWEST, TRAVEL

Northwest Boat Travel, PO Box 220, Anacortes, WA 98221. Editor: Gwen Cole. Quarterly magazine on boat travel from Olympia, WA to Skagway, AK: sites, resorts, cruises, anchorages. Uses 6 mss for the May and June issues only. Payment: $75–100 on publication. Byline given. Submit ms, SASE. Photocopies OK. Nonfiction: 2–4 pgs; "cruises, history of boating sites, anchorages, towns, sea life." Photos: B&W 3 1/2x5 or larger; parks, landmarks, city scenes; $5–10; color slides for cover/$100.
MARITIME, TRAVEL

Northwest Chess, PO Box 84746, Seattle, WA 98124-6046. 206-935-8440. Monthly magazine. Sub $12.50/yr; circ 600. Query w/SASE. Accepts news items, poetry, cartoons, photos, interviews. Topics: chess.
ENTERTAINMENT, RECREATION

Northwest Comic News, PO Box 11825, Eugene, OR 97440. 503-344-1922. Editor: Taft Chatham. Biweekly newspaper founded in 1989. Sub $15/yr; circ 25,000. Uses freelance material. Pays money, copies on publication. Submit complete ms, query letter, SASE. Responds in 2 wks; publishes in 2 mos. Accepts cartoons, political satire (1,000 wds). Sample available.
IDAHO

Northwest Computer News, Access Publishing, 7904 SW 14th Ave, Portland, OR 97219. 503-245-3381. Contact: Ed Reid. Monthly newspaper. No submissions info.
BUSINESS, COMPUTERS

Northwest Construction News, 3000 Northrup Way #200, Bellevue, WA 98004. 206-827-9900. Trade periodical.
BUSINESS, ECONOMICS

Northwest Cyclist Magazine, PO Box 9272, Seattle, WA 98109. 206-286-8566. Publisher/Ads: Carolyn Price. Magazine founded in1988, published 9X/yr. Sub $12. Circ 20,000. Freelance material accepted. Pays money, copies on publication. Byline given. Submit query, SASE. Disk/modem OK. Reports in 1 mo. Publication time varies. Accepts cartoons, news, photos, interviews, op/ed, articles. Color transparencies for cover; B/W inside. Guidelines with SASE. Sample $2.
BICYCLING, RECREATION, TRAVEL

Northwest Discovery, Journal of NW History & Natural History, 1439 E Prospect St, Seattle, WA 98112. Editor: Harry Majors. Not accepting mss.
NW/REGIONAL HISTORY, NATURAL HISTORY

The Northwest Dispatch, 913 S 11th St, Box 5637, Tacoma, WA 98405. 206-272-7587. Periodical.
COMMUNITY

Northwest Energy News, 851 SW 6th, Portland, OR 97204. Editor: Carlotta Collette. 503-222-5161. Bimonthly magazine reporting on power planning, fish, wildlife restoration activities in OR, WA, ID, MT. Published by NW Power Planning Council. Circ 15,000 to electric energy professionals, fisheries managers, NW Indian tribes. Generally does not accept freelance, but will entertain story ideas. Photos: B&W, "salmon (live, not on hooks) and other NW wildlife"; pay varies. Tips: "Not responsible for unsolicited photos or mss. We have in-house writers, but an occasional story idea, w/clips, may make it." SASE.
CONSERVATION, NORTHWEST, OUTDOOR

The Northwest Environmental Journal, FM-12, University of Washington, Seattle, WA 98195. 206-543-1812. Semiannual of NW environmental research and policy. Sub $16. Uses 1–2 freelance mss per issue. Payment: Reprints; no pay. Byline given. Submit ms, SASE. Phone queries OK. "Scholarly articles written for a broad audience, sans jargon.... All NW environmental topics may be relevant (NW= AK, BC, WA, OR, ID, Western MT). Usual length 20–25 pgs (top length of 50). Ours is a refereed journal; 3 scholarly reviewers read each ms." Photos: as needed to make a point. Guidelines available, sample/$9.
ENVIRONMENT/RESOURCES, NORTHWEST, PUBLIC AFFAIRS

Northwest Ethnic News, 144 NE 54th St #6, Seattle, WA 98105. 206-522-2188. Editor: Kent Chadwick. Monthly newspaper. Sub $12/yr; circ 12,000. Uses freelance material. Byline given. Pays copies. Acquires 1st rights. Submit query letter, complete ms, SASE, phone. Simultaneous subs OK. Responds in 1 mo; publishes in 1 mo. Accepts nonfiction, news items, photos (B&W, $5), poetry, interviews, op/ed, reviews. Topics: an ethnic angle. Guidelines available. Sample $2.50.
CULTURE, MINORITIES/ETHNIC

The Northwest Film Video & Audio Index, Media Index Publishing Inc, 1201 First Ave S #328, Seattle, WA 98124. 206-382-9220. Editor: Richard K Woltjer. Annual directory. Sub $25; circ 6,000. Not a freelance market.
DRAMA

Northwest Gallery Art Magazine, 7276 SW Beaverton-Hillsdale Hwy #126, Portland, OR 97225. 503-293-3067. Jane Talisman, Editor.
ARTS, NORTHWEST

Northwest Gay and Lesbian Reader, 1501 Belmont Ave, Seattle, WA 98122. 206-322-4609. Editor: Ron Whiteaker. Bimonthly magazine founded in 1989. Sub $2/yr; circ 4,000. Uses freelance material. Byline given. No pay, acquires no rights. Submit complete ms, SASE. Dot matrix, photocopy, disk/modem subs OK. Responds in 2 wks; publishes in 6 wks. Accepts fiction, poetry, essays, cartoons, interviews, op/ed, articles, book reviews, photos (half-tone, credit but no payment). Topics: reflecting the lesbian/gay experience. Guidelines available.
FEMINISM, GAY/LESBIAN, SEX

Northwest Golf Magazine, 5206 Ballard NW, Seattle, WA 98107. 206-781-1554. Editor: Dick Stevens. Ads: Stein Svenson. Monthly magazine. Sub $18/yr; circ 10,000. Uses freelance material. Byline given. Pays money on publication. Submit query letter, SASE. Sample available.
SPORTS.

Northwest Golfer, 920 108th NE, Bellevue, WA 98004. 206-455-5545. Periodical.
NORTHWEST, RECREATION

Northwest Historical Consultant, 2780 26th St, Clarkston, WA 99403. Publisher of histories. Book publisher.
NW/REGIONAL HISTORY, NORTHWEST

Northwest Indian Fisheries Commission, 6730 Martin Way E, Olympia, WA 98506. 206-438-1180. Contact: Steve Robinson. Quarterly newsletter. Free. Circ 10,000. Uses some freelance material. Pay varies. Submit complete ms, SASE. Dot matrix, photocopy, simultaneous, disk/modem subs OK. Responds only on request. Publishes in 1–3 mos. Accepts nonfiction, cartoons, news items, photos.
FISHING, MINORITIES/ETHNIC

Northwest Inland Writing Project Newsletter, c/o Elinor Michel, College of Education, University of Idaho, Moscow, ID 83843. 208-885-6586. Submissions editor: Duane Pitts, Box 385, Odessa, WA 99159. 509-982-0171. Quarterly. Sub $5/$10/$25. Circ 300. Uses freelance material. Pays copies on publication. Byline given. Submit query w/clips, ms, SASE. Dot matrix, photocopied, simultaneous OK. Reports in 3 wks. Publishes in next issue usually. Accepts nonfiction, fiction, poetry, cartoons, other (student/teacher work). Topics: elementary, jr/sr high, college writing; reading-writing connections; teaching ideas/techniques about writing; classroom research in reading/writing. Tips: length may vary: 50–300+ wds, depends on subject. Tips: practical ideas for use in classroom stressed; limited amounts of student work produced in writing workshops accepted. Sample $1.
EDUCATION, ENGLISH, WRITING

Northwest Interpretive Association, 83 S King St, Ste 212, Seattle, WA 98104. Book publisher.
CONSERVATION, NORTHWEST, OUTDOOR

Northwest Lookout, PO Box 3366, Salem, OR 97302. Editor: Dennis L Tomkins. 503-364-2942. Trade publication of Northwest Christmas Tree Association published 3 times a year. Circ 2,000 to Christmas tree growers, wholesalers, retailers, related product mfgs and sellers. Byline given. Query

w/SASE to editor at 324 Sumner Ave, Sumner, WA 98390. Guidelines available.
AGRICULTURE/FARMING, BUSINESS, NORTHWEST

Northwest Magazine, The Oregonian Publishing Co, 1320 SW Broadway, Portland, OR 97210. 503-221-8228. Editor: Ellen Emry Heltzel. Ads: Debi Walery. 503-221-8351. Weekly included with Sunday Oregonian. Circ 400,000+. Uses freelance material. Pays on acceptance. Byline given. Acquires 1st rights. Query w/SASE. Dot matrix, photocopies, electronic subs OK. Accepts nonfiction, photos. Pays $500+ for major cover stories; $150–350 for inside stories (1,500–4,000 wds); $75–125 for shorter personal essays and similar material. Photos: submit color slides (preferably Kodachrome) or B&W contact prints with negatives. Guidelines available. Sample free.
FICTION, RECREATION, TRAVEL

Northwest Motor: Journal for Automotive Industry, 811 1st Ave #600, Seattle, WA 98104. 206–624-3470. Editor: J B Smith. Ads: Peter du Pre. Monthly for the automotive parts and service industry. Circ 6,000. Sub $10. Accepts freelance material. Writers must have industry documentation. Pays copies on publication. Byline given. Acquires all rights. Query w/SASE. Accepts news items, interviews, articles, reviews. Sample: $2.
BUSINESS, TRADE/ASSOCIATIONS

The Northwest Network, PO Box 2505, Kirkland, WA 98083-2502. 206-820-9833. Editor: Andrew Bosworth. Biweekly.
OTHER/UNSPECIFIED

Northwest Nikkei, PO Box 3173, Seattle, WA 98114. 206-624-4169, 206-623-0100. Editor: L Matsuda. Ads: Steve Uyeno. Monthly English language newspaper serving the Japanese-American community. Sub $15/yr; circ 10,000. Uses freelance material. Byline given. Pays money, copies on publication. Submit query letter, SASE, phone. Accepts nonfiction, photos, interviews, articles, reviews.
ASIAN AMERICAN, MINORITIES/ETHNIC

Northwest Notes, St Peter Hospital Library, 415 Lilly Rd, Olympia, WA 98506. Periodical.
HEALTH, REFERENCE/LIBRARY

Northwest Nurserystock Report, 10041 NE 132nd St, Kirkland, WA 98034. 206-821-2535. Editor: John Bjork. Periodical.
AGRICULTURE/FARMING, BUSINESS

Northwest Oil Report, 4204 SW Condor Ave, Portland, OR 97201. Editor: C J Newhouse. Periodical.
BUSINESS

Northwest Outpost, Northwest Chapter, Paralyzed Veterans of America, 901 SW 152nd St, Seattle, WA 98166. 206-241-1843. Periodical.
MILITARY/VETS, NORTHWEST, DISABLED

Northwest Pace, RR 6 Box 247, Astoria, OR 97103. 503-826-7700. Editor: Mark Flint. Periodical.
OTHER/UNSPECIFIED

The Northwest Palate, PO Box 10860, Portland, OR 97132. 503-538-0317. Editor: Judy Peterson-Nedry. Ads: Cameron Nagel. 503-228-4897. Bimonthly magazine; circ 12,000; sub $15/yr. Byline given, pays money, copies on publication, acquires 1st/2nd rights. Submit query, ms, SASE, or phone. Accepts nonfiction, interviews, articles, photos. Topics: food & wine, breweries, distilleries, travel, restaurants, lodging, lifestyles by NW writers. Tips: study magazine, must have NW perspective. Sample $3.50.
FOOD/COOKING, NORTHWEST, TRAVEL

Northwest Passage, Western Oregon State College, English Dept, 345 N Monmouth Ave, Monmouth, OR 97361. 503-838-8599. Editor: Leslie Murray. College literary magazine. Editors change frequently. SASE for guidelines.
COLLEGE/UNIVERSITY, FICTION, OREGON

Northwest Passages Historical Newsletter, PO Box 160, Brownsville, OR 97327. 503-466-5208 or 503-369-2835. Editors: Pat Hainline, Margaret Carey. Bimonthly newsletter. Sub $12. Uses freelance material. Byline given. Pays copies on publication. Acquires 1st rights. Submit query letter, ms,

SASE, or phone. Reports in 1 mo; publishes in 6 mos. Accepts nonfiction, photos. Topics: historical articles about the Northwest, 250–750 wds, well-researched and historically accurate, reminiscences within word limit; also accepts obscure but interesting material from old newspapers and out-of-print books. Guidelines available. Sample $2.
NW/REGIONAL HISTORY, NORTHWEST

Northwest PhotoNetwork, HCA Publishing, 1309 N 77th, Seattle, WA 98103. 206-526-0621. Editor: Harry Cartales. Ads: Gary Halpern. Sub free. Circ 12,000+. Uses 2–3 freelance mss per issue. Pays money/copies on publication. Acquires 1st rights. Byline given. Submit query/SASE, phone. Photocopied, computer disk OK. Reports in 2 wks. Publishing time variable. Accepts nonfiction, photos, cartoons. Prefers writers knowledgeable in Northwest photography. "We are in need of writers whose ties to the photo community will help generate stories beyond those that we assign.". Guidelines available.
PHOTOGRAPHY

Northwest Poets & Artists Calendar, 261 Madison S, Bainbridge Island, WA 98110. 206-842-7901. Contact: Nancy Rekow. Annual calendar of art and poetry selected from competition open to residents of AK, ID, MT, OR, WA and BC, deadline late January each year. Accepts poetry, original artwork. See also listing under Contests. Write for purchase or competition guidelines. Sample $5.
ARTS, POETRY

Northwest Prime Times, 10829 NE 68th St, Kirkland, WA 98033-7100. 206–827-9737. Editor: Neil Strother. Monthly for seniors. Sub $5/yr; irr. 30,000. Uses freelance material. Pays money on publication. Byline given. Submit query letter, SASE. Accepts nonfiction, articles, photos.
LITERARY, SENIOR CITIZENS

The Northwest Print Index, Media Index Publishing Inc, 1201 First Ave S #328, Seattle, WA 98124. 206-382-9220. Editor: Richard K Woltjer. Annual directory. Sub $35; circ 5,000. Not a freelance market.
MEDIA/COMMUNICATIONS, PHOTOGRAPHY, VISUAL ARTS

Northwest Public Power Bulletin, PO Box 4576, Vancouver, WA 98662. Editor: Rick Kellogg. 206-254-0109. Ads: Tina Nelson. Monthly periodical on public power issues in the NW. Circ 4,000. Sub $18. Accepts freelance material. Payment: Generally $100–300 for major articles with photos, on publication. Byline given. Rights purchased: First. Query w/SASE. Phone queries OK. Reports in 1 month. Nonfiction: "People, issues, activities relating to public power entities, regional electrical issues. Area covered: OR, WA, ID, Western MT, Northern CA, BC and AK." Photos: B&W glossies. Rates negotiable. Tips: "Not interested in investor owned utilities, counter-culture energy schemes, anti-nuke propaganda." Sample available.
NORTHWEST, PUBLIC AFFAIRS

Northwest Report, NW Regional Educational Laboratory, 101 SW Main, Ste 500, Portland, OR 97204. Monthly newsletter founded in 1966. Editor: Lee Sherman Candell. Circ 9,000. Not a freelance market.
EDUCATION

Northwest Review, 369 PLC, University of Oregon, Eugene, OR 97403. 503-346-3957. Editor: John Witte, poetry; Cecelia Hagen, fiction. Ads: Rachel Barton-Russell. Literary triannual published 3X/yr (Jan, May, Sep.). Sub $14; circ 1,100. Accepts unsolicited submissions. Pays in copies on publication. Acquires 1st rights. Byline given. Submit complete mss, SASE. Dot matrix, photocopies OK. No simultaneous submissions are considered. Reports in 5–10 wks; publishes in 1–4 mos. Accepts nonfiction, fiction, poetry, plays, interviews, essays, artwork. Receives approx 4,000 submissions annually, publishes 90. Guidelines available. Sample $3.
FICTION, LITERARY, LITERATURE

The Northwest Review of Books, 535 NE 95th St, Seattle, WA 98115-2127. Editor: Jane Friedman. Quarterly magazine focusing on NW authors and publishers. Circ 5,000. Uses 16–20 mss a year. Payment: Money on publication. Byline given. Submit ms, SASE. Phone queries, dot matrix, simultaneous submissions OK. Reports in 1 month. Publishes in 1–3 mos. Nonfiction: 600–900 wds; history, biography, photography, science; $15. Columns:

100 wds; brief review section, $5. Photos: 85 line screen. Tips: "Lively writing for our wide audience."
BOOK ARTS/BOOKS, LITERARY, PUBLISHING/PRINTING

Northwest Roadapple, The Newspaper for Horsemen, 4346 SE Division, Portland, OR 97206. Editor: John. 503-238-7071. Monthly tabloid for horse people. Circ 24,000. Submit ms, SASE. Phone queries, dot matrix, simultaneous submissions OK. Publishes in 2 mos. Nonfiction, poetry, photos (80 lines, 3x5).
ANIMALS, RECREATION

Northwest Runner, 1231 NE 94th, Seattle, WA 98115. 206-526-9000. Editor/ads: Jim Whiting. Monthly. Sub $15.97/yr; circ 7,000. Uses freelance material. Byline given. Pays money on publication. Acquires 1st rights. Query by phone. Reports in 2–4 wks. Accepts: short articles (300–1,000 wds, $25–50); features (1,000 wds up, $35–75); photos (B&W glossy, $15). Tips: Readers range from beginners to veterans, most have been running for at least a couple of yrs. We like training articles, how-to, personal experiences, and especially humor. Sample: $3.
SPORTS

Northwest Sailboard, PO Box 918, Hood River, OR 97031. 503-386-7440. Periodical.
RECREATION, SPORTS

Northwest Science, Washington State University Press, Pullman, WA 99164-5910. 509-335-3518. Quarterly. Sub $25.
COLLEGE/UNIVERSITY, NORTHWEST, SCIENCE

Northwest Seasonal Worker, Northwest Seasonal Workers Association, 145 N Oakdale St, Medford, OR 97501. Editor: Jana Clark. Monthly. Sub $12.50.
AGRICULTURE/FARMING, CHICANO/CHICANA, MINORITIES/ETHNIC

Northwest Silver Press, 88 Cascade Key, Bellevue, WA 98006. Book publisher.
OTHER/UNSPECIFIED

Northwest Skier & Northwest Sports, PO Box 95229, Seattle, WA 948145. 206-547-6229. Editor: Jenny Petersen. Ads: Trish Drew. Monthly magazine. Sub $7.95/yr; circ 30,000. Uses freelance material. Byline given. Pays money, copies, other on publication. Acquires all rights. Submit query letter, SASE, phone. Responds 1–60 days, publishes in 3–6 mos. Accepts fiction, poetry, cartoons, interviews, articles, op/ed. Topics: NW skiing, all kinds, areas, etc. Sample 2.
OUTDOOR, SPORTS

Northwest Stylist and Salon, PO Box 1117, Portland, OR 97207. Editor: David Porter. 503-226-2461. Monthly trade magazine. Sub $10/free to salons. Circ 26,000. Accepts freelance material. Pays money, when assigned. Byline given. Query w/SASE, phone. Accepts news items, interviews, articles (500–750 wds with photo), photos (B&W; $5 or $15–20 for cover). "Query first. I prefer to give a writer the slant I want, and I would like to talk to people to give them hints on things I'd like covered in their area." Topics: hair and beauty for the industry, professional beauty salons, schools and supply houses. Sample $2.
BUSINESS, FASHION

The Northwest Talent Index, Media Index Publishing Inc, 1201 First Ave S #328, Seattle, WA 98124. 206-382-9220. Editor: Richard K Woltjer. Annual directory. Sub $25; circ 2,000. Not a freelance market.
DRAMA

`, PO Box 18000, Florence, OR 97439. 800-727-8401. Editors: Rob & Alicia Spooner, Dave Peden, Judy Fleagle. Ads: Glenda Ryall. Bimonthly magazine; circ 25,000; sub $12.95. Uses freelance material, byline given, pays money, copies on publication, acquires 1st rights. Responds in 1–3 mos; publishes in 3–12 mos. Submit query letter, clips, SASE. Topics: travel in Oregon, Washington, Idaho, and British Columbia. Tips: well-researched historical pieces welcome, ms with photos preferred. List resources used.
NORTHWEST, RECREATION, TRAVEL

Northwest Wine Almanac, First Noel Publishing Co, PO Box 95188, Seattle, WA 98145. Periodical.
FOOD/COOKING

Northwest Yachting, 5206 Ballard NW, Seattle, WA 98107. 206-789-8116. Editor: Daniel Schworer. Monthly tabloid. Pays money. Submit phone query. Accepts nonfiction, photos. Topics: news, activities and information related to boating in the Northwest and southwest Canada.
BOATING, SPORTS

Northwest Living, 130 Second Ave S, Edmonds, WA 98020. 206–672-6716. Fax 206-672-2824. Editor: Terry W Sheely. Ads: Bonnie Kostic. Monthly of NW people doing NW things. Sub $19.95/yr; circ 20,000. Uses freelance material. Pays money on publication. Acquires 1st rights. Byline given. Query letter, SASE. Photocopies OK. Reports in 6 wks; publishes in 6–12 mos. Accepts nonfiction, photos, interviews, articles. Topics: suburban and rural subjects; natural science, natural history, homes, foods, gardening, outdoor recreation, regional travel, cottage industries, crops and related subjects. Guidelines available. Sample $3.95.
NATURAL HISTORY, OUTDOOR, TRAVEL

Nor'westing, PO Box 1027, Edmonds, WA 98020. Editor: Thomas F Kincaid. 206-776-3138. Ads: Wendelborg Hansen. Monthly for NW boaters. Circ 11,000. Sub $15. Uses freelance material. Pays $100 on publication. Byline given. Acquires 1st rights. Query w/SASE. Phone queries, dot matrix, photocopies, simultaneous submissions, electronic subs OK. Reports in 1 mo. Accepts nonfiction, 1,500–3,000 wds; photos (covers $75). Guidelines available.
BOATING, OUTDOOR, RECREATION

Nosado Press, PO Box 634, Olympia, WA 98507-0634. 206-754-0152. Editor: L B Arender. Publishes softcover books. Accepts unsolicited submissions. Submit query letter, outline, sample chapters, SASE. Photocopy, dot matrix, simultaneous subs OK. Responds in 10 days. Accepts nonfiction.
NORTHWEST, OUTDOOR

Noted, 919 NW 63rd St, Seattle, WA 98107. Periodical.
OTHER/UNSPECIFIED

NRG Magazine, 6735 SE 78th, Portland, OR 97206. Editor: Dan Raphael. Biannual magazine of nonfiction, fiction, poetry, photos and graphics. Sub $4/yr; circ 600. "Any form or genre, but it should be work with energy — work that doesn't add up — open ended." Byline given. Pays copies. Acquires no rights. Reports in 1 month. Submit ms, SASE. Dot matrix, photocopied and simultaneous subs OK. Sample: $1.50.
AVANT-GARDE/EXPERIMENTAL, FICTION, POETRY

Nuclear News Bureau, CALS, 454 Willamette, Eugene, OR 97401. Periodical.
INDUSTRY

Nugget, Box 610, Nome, AK 99762. 907-443-5235. Weekly newspaper.
COMMUNITY

Nugget Enterprises, PO Box 184, Enumclaw, WA 98022. Contact: Roy F Mayo. 206-825-3855. Self-publisher of 1–2 softcover originals on gold and gold mining. Print run: 1,000. Not a freelance market. Catalog available.
GEOLOGY/GEOGRAPHY, NW/REGIONAL HISTORY, RECREATION

The Nurse Practitioner: The American Journal of Primary Health Care, 3000 Northrup Way #200, Bellevue, WA 98004. 206-827-9900. Editor: Linda J Pearson. Ads: Barton Vernon. Monthly for nurses in advanced primary care practice. Circ 11,600. Sub. $27. Accepts freelance material. Writers must be nurse practitioners. No pay. Byline given. Query w/SASE. Phone queries, dot matrix, photocopies OK. Clinical articles; reports of appropriate research; role, legal and political issues. Guidelines available; sample/$3.
HEALTH, MEDICAL

Nursery Trades BC, 101A-15290-103A Ave, Surrey, BC V3R 7A2. Editor: J C Crocco. 604-585-2225. Periodical.
AGRICULTURE/FARMING, BUSINESS

Nutrition Notebook, Idaho Dairy Council, 1365 N Orchard, Boise, ID 83706. Editor: Mary Pittam. Semiannual. Circ 3,000.
AGRICULTURE/FARMING, ANIMALS, HEALTH

NW Examiner, 2066 NW Irving, Portland, OR 97209. 503-241-2353. Contact: Allan Classen. Monthly tabloid. Circ 15,000. Accepts submissions w/

SASE. Payment negotiable. Byline given. Topics: issues of interest to NW Portland community.
COMMUNITY

Nyssa Gate City Journal, 112 Main St, Box 1785, Nyssa, OR 97913. 503-372-2233. Weekly newspaper.
COMMUNITY

O.K. Press, PO Box 521, Butte, MT 59703. 406-782-7958. Publisher of one book per year.
OTHER/UNSPECIFIED

O&B Books Inc, 1215 NW Kline Place, Corvallis, OR 97330. Book publisher.
OTHER/UNSPECIFIED

Oak Lodge Publishing, 3320 SE Pinehurst, Milwaukie, OR 97267. 503-653-9046. Contact: Janet Higginson. Book publisher.
OTHER/UNSPECIFIED

Observer, Oregon State Council on Alcoholism, 2560 Center St NE, Salem, OR 97310. Monthly.
HEALTH

The Observer, 1710 6th St, Box 3170, La Grande, OR 97850. 503-963-3161. Daily newspaper.
COMMUNITY

OCLC PAC-NEWS, PO Box 03376, Portland, OR 97203. Editor: Bruce Preslan. 503-283-4794. Periodical.
OTHER/UNSPECIFIED

Ocotillo Press, 215 N 51st St, Seattle, WA 98103. Book publisher.
OTHER/UNSPECIFIED

ODOT News, Oregon Department of Transportation, 140 Transportation Bldg, Salem, OR 97310. 503-378-6546. Editor: Andy Booz. Periodical.
GOVERNMENT, PUBLIC AFFAIRS

Offshoot Publications, 1280 Goodpasture Island Rd, Eugene, OR 97401-1794. Self-publisher of 1 hard- & softcover book a yr.
GARDENING

Oh! Idaho!, Peak Media Inc, PO Box 925, Hailey, ID 83333. 208-788-4500. Editor: Laurie Sammis. Quarterly magazine. Uses freelance material. Pays money on publication. Query w/SASE. Dot matrix, photocopy, disk subs OK (WordPerfect or ASCII). Accepts articles. Topics: all facets of Idaho and her people. Feature article (about 2,000 wds) to include spectacular photography. Guidelines and sample, $3 + 8.5x11 SASE.
IDAHO

Old Bottle Magazine/Popular Archaeology, Drawer 5007, Bend, OR 97708. Editor: Shirley Asher. 503-382-6978. Monthly. Circ 3,000. Sub $12. Uses 10 mss per issue. Payment: $10 published pg. on publication. Byline given. Rights purchased: All. Query w/ms, SASE. Dot matrix, photocopies, simultaneous submissions, electric OK. Reports in 6 wks. Nonfiction: "Dedicated to the discovery, research and preservation of relics of the industrial age in general and the establishment of specialized, representative collection by individuals." Photos: $50 color cover. Sample/$1.
ANTIQUES, ARCHITECTURE, COLLECTING

Old Farm Kennels, NE 5451 Eastside Hwy, Florence, MT 59833. Book publisher.
ANIMALS

Old Harbor Press, PO Box 97, Sitka, AK 99835. 907-747-3584. Publisher of 1 hard- & softcover original, reprint a year. Press run: 3,000. Does not accept unsolicited submissions.
ALASKA, FOOD/COOKING, NW/REGIONAL HISTORY

Old News, Clatsop County Historical Society, 1618 Exchange St, Astoria, OR 97103. Irregular periodical of local and regional history.
NW/REGIONAL HISTORY, NORTHWEST, OREGON

Old Oregon, 101 Chapman Hall, University of Oregon, Eugene, OR 97403. Editor: Tom Hager. 503-686-5047. Quarterly for graduates. Circ 90,000. No unsolicited submissions. Uses 6 freelance mss per issue. Pays 10¢/wd on acceptance + 2 copies. Byline given. Query w/clips, SASE. Photocopies, electronic, computer disk OK. Reports in 3 wks. Publishes in 3–6 mos. Nonfic-

tion: features 2,500–3,000 wds; columns 1,500 wds. Photos: 8x10 B&W glossy. All topics relate to UO issues, people, ideas. Sample available.
COLLEGE/UNIVERSITY

Old Stuff, The Paddlewheel Press, PO Box 230220, Tigard, OR 97223. Editor: Marge Davenport. 503-639-5637. Periodical.
GENERAL HISTORY

Old Time Bottle Publishing, 611 Lancaster Dr NE, Salem, OR 97301. Book publisher.
COLLECTING, CRAFTS/HOBBIES

Old Violin-Art Publishing, Box 500, 225 S Cooke, Helena, MT 59624. Book publisher.
PUBLISHING/PRINTING

Older Kid News, PO Box 1602, Pendleton, OR 97801. 503-276-9035. Editor: John Brenne. Periodical.
COMMUNITY, ENTERTAINMENT, SENIOR CITIZENS

Olive Press, 333 SE 3rd, Portland, OR 97214. Book publisher.
OTHER/UNSPECIFIED

Olympia News, PO Box 366, Olympia, WA 98507. 206-943-2950. Weekly newspaper.
COMMUNITY

Olympic Publishing Company, PO Box 353, Port Ludlow, WA 98365. Publisher of 2 nonfiction books a year: local history/travel, boating, other. Query, outline, sample chapters w/SASE. Reports in 2 mos. Catalog available.
BOATING, NW/REGIONAL HISTORY, TRAVEL

Omak-Okanogan County Chronicle, PO Box 553, Omak, WA 98841. 509-826-1110. Weekly newspaper.
COMMUNITY

Omega Publications, PO Box 4130, Medford, OR 97501. Book publisher.
OTHER/UNSPECIFIED

OMGA Northwest Newsletter, Oregon Master Gardener Association, PO Box 756, Albany, OR 97321. Periodical devoted to home gardening for graduates of the Master Gardener program of the OSU Agricultural Extension Program. Includes news of the programs and the local MG chapters. No payment. Query w/SASE.
AGRICULTURE/FARMING, EDUCATION, GARDENING

One Cook to Another, Sumner House Press, 2527 W Kennewick Ave, Ste 190, Kennewick, WA 99336. 509-783-7800. Contact: Barbara Hill. Quarterly newsletter on cooking.
FOOD/COOKING

Onion World, Columbia Publishing, PO Box 1467, Yakima, WA 98907-1467. Editor: D Brent Clement. Circ 5,500. Monthly magazine of onion production and marketing for the industry. Uses nonfiction with photos. Query w/SASE.
AGRICULTURE/FARMING, BUSINESS, COMMERCE

Online Press Inc, 14320 NE 21st, Ste 18, Bellevue, WA 98007. 206-641-3434. Contact: Sally B Oberlin. Publisher of 6 softcover books per year on computers, technology, and software — streamlined instruction for professional and business users (Quick Course Series). Query w/SASE.
BUSINESS, COMPUTERS, TECHNICAL

Onset Publications, 692 Elkader St, Ashland, OR 97520. Book publisher.
OTHER/UNSPECIFIED

Ontario, PO Box 130, Ontario, OR 97914. Editor: Fran McLean. Quarterly.
OTHER/UNSPECIFIED

Oolichan Books, PO Box 10, Lantzville, BC V0R 2H0. 604-390-4839. Editor: Ron Smith, Rhonda Bailey. Ads: R Smith. Circ 1,000. Publishes hard- & softcover original books. Accepts unsolicited submissions. Pays 10% royalties, copies on publication. Query w/SASE. Reports in 2 mos. Publishes within 1 yr. Accepts nonfiction, fiction, poetry. Topics: literary press, primarily interested in high quality fiction and poetry; also BC history and a few general titles of specific interest to western Canadians. Length can vary from 48 pp. for poetry title to 448 pp. for regional history. Catalog available SASE.
FICTION, CANADIAN HISTORY, POETRY

Open Hand Publishing Inc, PO Box 22048, Seattle, WA 98122. 206-323-3868. Editor: P Anna Johnson. Publishes hard- & softcover originals. Does not accept unsolicited mss. Pays royalties, advance. All rights acquired. Submit query, outline, SASE. Dot matrix, photocopied OK. Accepts nonfiction. Topics: Afro-American issues, bilingual children's books. Catalog available.
BLACK, CHILDREN (BY/ABOUT), AMERICAN HISTORY

Open Path Publishing, Box 3064, Boise, ID 83703-0064. Book publisher.
OTHER/UNSPECIFIED

Open Rd Publishers, PO Box 46598, Stn G, Vancouver, BC V6R 4G8. 604-736-0070. Contact: Russell Jennings. Self-publisher, softcover. Not a freelance market.
TRAVEL

Opening Up, 3819 SE Belmont, Portland, OR 97214. Periodical.
OTHER/UNSPECIFIED

Opinion Rag, PO Box 20307, Seattle, WA 98102. Contact: Debbie Lester. Periodical.
OTHER/UNSPECIFIED

Optical Engineering, PO Box 10, Bellingham, WA 98225. 206-676-3290. Bimonthly.
INDUSTRY, TECHNICAL

The Optimist, Idaho State School for the Deaf & Blind, 202 14th Ave E, Gooding, ID 83330. Editor: Edward Born. Monthly.
DISABLED

ORC Enterprises Ltd, 7031 Westminster Highway, Ste 305, Richmond, BC V6X 1A3. Book publisher.
OTHER/UNSPECIFIED

Orca Book Publishers Ltd, Box 5626, Stn B, Victoria, BC V8R 6S4. 604-380-1229. Editor: R J Tyrrell. Publishes soft- & hardcover originals. Pays advance, royalties. Query letter, outline, sample chapters, SASE. Reports in 3–6 wks; publishes in 6–12 mos. Accepts nonfiction, fiction, biography. Topics: regional history, geology, guidebooks, children's. Catalog available, SASE.
CHILDREN/TEEN, CANADIAN HISTORY, PUBLISHING/PRINTING

Orcas Publishing Company, Rt 1 Box 104, Eastsound, WA 98245. Publisher of books on history and language. Does not accept unsolicited submissions.
NW/REGIONAL HISTORY, LANGUAGE(S)

Oregon Administrator, ASPA, Oregon Chapter, PO Box 73, Portland, OR 97207. Monthly.
TRADE/ASSOCIATIONS

Oregon Adventures, 446 Charnelton, Eugene, OR 97401. 503-689-1943. Editor: Carl Traegde.
ADVENTURE, OREGON

Oregon Arts News, Oregon Arts Commission, 835 Summer NE, Salem, OR 97301. 503-378-3625. Quarterly newsletter founded in 1967. Circ 6,500. Uses freelance material. Byline given. Pays copies. Assignment only. Accepts news items, interviews, op/ed, articles, reviews, photos (B&W). Sample available.
ARTS, CULTURE, OREGON

Oregon Association of Christian Writers Newsletter, 2495 Maple Ave NE, Salem, OR 97303. 503-364-9570. Published 3 times a year. Sub $5. Not a freelance market.
RELIGION, WRITING

Oregon Association of Nurserymen, 2780 SE Harrison, Milwaukie, OR 97222. Book publisher.
AGRICULTURE/FARMING, BUSINESS

Oregon Authors, The Information Place, State Library Bldg, Salem, OR 97310. Annual publication listing those authors who had books published during the preceding year which were written while they lived in Oregon. Works by corporate authors and editors are excluded unless of local interest; textbooks and technical works, unless of timely or regional significance, are excluded. Inclusion depends upon notification of the library of publication, either by the author or by some other means. Authors wishing to ensure their inclusion should provide documentation to the library. The Oregon State Library is interested in maintaining its collection of works by regional writers, and encourages them to make sure the library knows of their books.
LITERATURE, OREGON, REFERENCE/LIBRARY

Oregon Birds, S Willamette Ornithological Society, PO Box 3082, Eugene, OR 97403. Quarterly devoted to the study and enjoyment of Oregon's birds.
ANIMALS, OREGON, RECREATION

Oregon Book Artists Guild Newsletter, PO Box 994, Beaverton, OR 97075-0994. 503-324-8081. Contact: Patricia Grass. On papermaking, marbling, bookbinding, fine printing. Newsletter, $15; circ 200.
ARTS, BOOK ARTS/BOOKS, PUBLISHING/PRINTING

Oregon Business Magazine, 921 SW Morrison St #407, Portland, OR 97205. 503-223-0304. Editor: Robert Hill. Monthly on the business and economy in Oregon. Circ 23,000 business owners, executives. Uses freelance material. Pays 10¢/wd on publication, byline given, acquires 1st rights. Query w/ms, SASE. Simultaneous submissions OK. Reports in 1–2 mos. Publishes in 1–8 mos. Accepts nonfiction: 1,000–2,000 wds on business topics; departments, 500–1,000 wds. Guidelines available; sample/SASE with $1.05 postage.
BUSINESS, OREGON

Oregon Business Review, 264 Gilbert Hall, University of Oregon, Eugene, OR 97403. Periodical on Oregon business issues.
BUSINESS, COLLEGE/UNIVERSITY

Oregon Catholic Press, PO Box 18030, Portland, OR 97218. Book publisher.
RELIGION

Oregon Central News, Oregon Central Credit Union, 336 NE 20th, Portland, OR 97232. Editor: Arleen Payne. Periodical.
BUSINESS

Oregon Chinese News, The Chinese Cons. Benevolent Association, 1941 SE 31st Ave, Portland, OR 97214. Periodical.
ASIAN AMERICAN, MINORITIES/ETHNIC, OREGON

Oregon Coast Getaway Guide, PO Box 18000, 1870 Highway 126, Florence, OR 97439. 800-727-8401. Editor: Dave Peden. Ads: Glenda Ryall. Monthly magazine. Circ 6,000. Uses freelance material, byline given, pays money/copies on publication, acquires 1st rights. Query w/clips, SASE. Responds in 1–3 mos; publishes in 3–6 mos. Accepts news, nonfiction, photos, articles. Tips: must pertain to Oregon Coast. Manuscript with photos preferred. Restaurant reviews good place for new authors. List resources on all submissions. Guidelines available, sample $2.
OREGON, RECREATION

Oregon Coast Magazine, PO Box 18000, Florence, OR 97439. 800-727-8401. Editors: Rob Spooner, Alicia Spooner. Bimonthly covering the entire Oregon coast. Founded 1982. Sub $12.95/yr; circ 65,000. Accepts freelance material. Byline given. Pays money on publication. Acquires 1st rights. Query letter, clips, SASE. Dot matrix OK. Reports in 1 mo; publishes in 6–12 mos. Accepts nonfiction on Oregon coast topics. Photos: Transparencies 35mm or larger, B&W prints or color slides with article. Tips: "Study an issue and understand our style before submitting an article." Guidelines available. Sample $3.
OREGON, TRAVEL

Oregon Commentator, Box 30128, Eugene, OR 97403. Editor: Thomas W Mann. 503-686-3721. Periodical.
OUTDOOR

Oregon Conifer, Sierra Club, 2637 SW Water Ave, Portland, OR 97201. Editor: Teresa A Kennedy. 503-224-1538. Bimonthly journal for the OR chapter of the Sierra Club; covers local wildernesses, current legislation on the environment, chapter club outings. Circ 6,000. Sub w/membership. Accepts freelance material. Payment: Copies. Byline given. Rights purchased: First. Query w/ms, SASE. Phone query, photocopies OK. Nonfiction, fiction, poetry, cartoons. "Pro-environmental reports, essays, book reviews, map re-

views. Articles of outdoor activity interests." Photos: B&W and color prints; no slides; 4x5 prints preferred; screened photos must be 85 lines.
ENVIRONMENT/RESOURCES, OREGON, OUTDOOR

Oregon Contractor, Oregon State Association of PHC Inc, 8755 SW Citizens Dr #202, Wilsonville, OR 97070. 503-399-7344. Bimonthly trade journal for member contractors.
BUSINESS, TRADE/ASSOCIATIONS

OCTE Chalkboard Newsletter, Sutherlin High School, PO Box 1068, Sutherlin, OR 97479. Editor: Bill Mull. Educational newsletter of the Oregon Council of Teachers of English. No submission info (also see Oregon English Journal)
EDUCATION, ENGLISH

Oregon Council on Alcoholism and Drug Abuse Newsletter, 4506 SE Belmont St, Ste 220, Portland, OR 97215. Editor: Doreen Thomas. 503-232-8083. Bimonthly providing info on alcoholism and drug abuse, issues pertaining to families. Query w/ms, SASE. Phone query OK. No pay. Nonfiction. Tips: "Interested in current topics on alcoholism and drug treatment, legislative issues, and family therapy." Sample available.
FAMILY, HEALTH, PUBLIC AFFAIRS

Oregon Cycling, 3460 Chambers, Eugene, OR 97405. 503-345-4335. Editor: Anae Boulton. Published 8 times a year. Circ 8,000. Sub $4.50. Accepts freelance material. Byline given. Dot matrix, photocopies, simultaneous submissions, electronic OK. Nonfiction, poetry, photos, cartoons. Tips: "O.C. appeals mainly to well-heeled middle class. Health, fitness, personal experiences, personal opinions, anything related to cycling." Sample/free.
BICYCLING, RECREATION, SPORTS

Oregon Cycling News, 12200 N Jantzen Ave, Ste 300, Portland, OR 97217. 503-283-1999. Editor: Jim Canton.
OREGON, RECREATION, SPORTS

Oregon East Magazine, Eastern Oregon State College, Hoke Hall, La Grande, OR 97850. Editor/ads: Kathy Gilmore. 503-963-1787. Annual of creative literature and visual art. Circ 800–1,000. Sub $5. 50% of each issue freelance material. Payment: Copies on publication. Byline given. "We reserve the right to print piece in specified issue and maybe again in future anthology, nothing more." Query w/ms, SASE. Dot matrix, photocopies, simultaneous submissions, electronic OK. Deadline: March. Reports by June. Publication: Sept. Fiction: short stories, max of 4,700 wds. Poetry: no line max; accepts haiku. Photos, plays, essays, criticism, interviews, any art medium. Guidelines available; sample/$4.
DRAMA, POETRY, VISUAL ARTS

Oregon Economic Development Department, International Trade Division, 595 Cottage St NE, Salem, OR 97310. Book publisher.
BUSINESS, ECONOMICS, OREGON

Oregon Education, Oregon Education Association, 1 Plaza Southwest, 6900 SW Hanes Rd, Tigard, OR 97223. Monthly.
EDUCATION

Oregon English Journal, Portland State University, PO Box 751, Portland, OR 97207. Contact: Ulrich H Hardt. Semiannual journal of the Oregon Council of Teachers of English. Sub $15/yr; circ 1,200. Accepts freelance submissions of fiction, poetry, cartoons, biographies, nonfiction, photos (B&W glossy 5x7), interviews, articles, plays, and reviews. Pays 2 copies on publication. Responds in 2 mos; publishes within 6 mos. Query with complete ms and SASE. Guidelines available. Sample $5.
EDUCATION, FICTION, POETRY

Oregon Episcopal Churchman, PO Box 467, Lake Oswego, OR 97034. 503-636-5613. Editor: Annette Ross. Monthly. Sub $2.
RELIGION

Oregon Farm Bureau News, 1730 Commercial SE, Salem, OR 97308. Monthly.
AGRICULTURE/FARMING

Oregon Farmer-Stockman, PO Box 2160, Spokane, WA 99210-2160. Editor: Dick Yost. Ads: Eric Bosler. Semimonthly periodical of farming, ranching. Circ 20,000. Sub $9. Uses 1 ms per issue. Writer must have intimate knowledge of agriculture. Payment: Up to $50 on acceptance. Byline given. Rights purchased: First. Query w/ms, SASE. Dot matrix OK. Reports in 1 month. Nonfiction; photos: color prints with negatives. Tips: "Will consider all submissions, but majority of copy is staff produced." Sample available.
AGRICULTURE/FARMING

Oregon Focus, City of Roses Publishing Co. for Oregon Public Broadcasting, 7140 SW Macadam Ave, Portland, OR 97219. 503-293-1904. Editor: Marjorie Columbus. Ads: Ann Romano. Monthly magazine for membership. Sub $35/yr. circ 65,000. Rarely accepts freelance material, very specific to TV & radio programs. Pays money on publication. Byline given. Submissions by assignment only. Dot matrix, photocopied, simultaneous, computer disk OK. Reports in 30 days. Publishes in 30–60 days. Accepts nonfiction on assignment, background material on a new public TV or radio series, occasionally on a personality connected to public TV and radio.
BIOGRAPHY, FILM/VIDEO, MEDIA/COMMUNICATIONS

Oregon Freemason, 709 SW 15th Ave, Portland, OR 97205. 503-228-3446. Editor: Sally Spohn. Monthly.
TRADE/ASSOCIATIONS

Oregon Future Farmer, Agricultural Education, OBE, 700 Pringle Parkway SE, Salem, OR 97310. Quarterly.
AGRICULTURE/FARMING

Oregon Gay News, PO Box 2206, Portland, OR 97208. 503-222-0017. Editor: Christopher L Smith. Weekly.
GAY/LESBIAN

Oregon Geology, Oregon Dept of Geology/Mineral Industries, 910 State Office Bldg, Portland, OR 97201. 503-229-5580. Editor: Beverly F Vogt. Monthly for audience ranging from professional geologists to amateur geologists to planners and politicians. Sub $6. Circ 2,000–3,000. Accepts freelance material from writers qualified to write about geology. No pay. Rights acquired: All. Byline given. Submit ms, SASE. Dot matrix, photocopies, computer disk OK. Reports in 1 month. Accepts nonfiction: geology, mining, mining history, field trip guides, anything related to geology in OR; 40 ds typed pages max length. Also: cartoons; photos: B&W glossy. Guidelines available; sample.
GEOLOGY/GEOGRAPHY, OREGON

Oregon Golfer, PO Box 7215, Bend, OR 97708. 503-389-6890. FAX 389-7022. Editor: Jeff Chase. Monthly tabloid, 10x yr. Accepts freelance material. Response varies. Pays on publication. Query w/SASE.
OREGON, RECREATION, SPORTS

Oregon Grange Bulletin, Oregon State Grange, 1313 SE 12th, Portland, OR 97214. Semimonthly publication of Oregon State Grange, concerning news and issues of importance to agriculture.
AGRICULTURE/FARMING

Oregon Health Sciences University, Center Foundation, 3181 SW Sam Jackson Park, Portland, OR 97201. Book publisher.
COLLEGE/UNIVERSITY, HEALTH, SCIENCE

Oregon Historical Quarterly, 1230 SW Park Ave, Portland, OR 97205. 503-222-1741. Editor: Rick Harmon. Quarterly. Sub $25/yr. Circ 8,600. Uses 3–4 freelance mss per issue. Pays copies. Acquires all rights. Byline given. Phone queries OK. Reports in 8 wks. Publishes in 2 1/2 yrs. Accepts nonfiction — history and culture of Pacific Northwest. Photos used. Sample $2.50.
GENERAL HISTORY, NORTHWEST, OREGON

Oregon Historical Society News, 1230 SW Park Ave, Portland, OR 97205. 503-222-1741. Editor: Elizabeth Buehler. OHS newsletter.
NW/REGIONAL HISTORY, NORTHWEST, OREGON

Oregon Historical Society Press, 1230 SW Park, Portland, OR 97205. Contact: Bruce Taylor Hamilton. 503-222-1741. Publishes hard- & softcover originals. Accepts unsolicited mss. Acquires all rights; negotiable on all contracts. Submit query w/outline, sample chapters, SASE. Photocopies OK. Reports in 2–6 wks; publishes in 2–3 yrs. Accepts nonfiction, fiction, photos. Topics: Pacific NW history and allied subjects. Firm scholarship or experience. Will review article-length (for Oregon Historical Quarterly) to book length mss. Material must be new or new interpretation. Guidelines/catalog available.

NW/REGIONAL HISTORY, NATURAL HISTORY, NORTHWEST

The Oregon Horse, PO Box 17248, Portland, OR 97217. Editor: Jim Burnett. 503-285-0658. Ads: Rich Weinstein. Bimonthly trade magazine on thoroughbred racing and breeding industry. Circ 3,000. Sub $12. Uses 1–3 mss per issue. Payment: $75–150 (for feature) on publication. Byline given. Rights purchased: First. Query w/ms, SASE. Phone query, photocopies OK. Reports in 2 wks. "Particularly need profiles of Oregon breeders, owners, trainers." Sample available.

ANIMALS, OREGON, SPORTS

Oregon Humanities: A Journal of Ideas, History/Culture, Oregon Council for the Humanities, 812 SW Washington St #225, Portland, OR 97205. 503-241-0543. Editor: Richard Lewis. Semiannual magazine. Circ 10,500. Accepts freelance material. Pays money on publication. Byline given. Acquires 1st rights. Query letter, complete ms, SASE. Dot matrix, photocopies, disk subs OK. Reports in 2 wks; publishes in 3 mos. Accepts nonfiction & essays on topics relevant to the humanities, 1,000–3,000 wds. Oregon writers and scholars preferred. Guidelines/sample available.

CULTURE, ENGLISH, GENERAL HISTORY

Oregon Independent Grocer, Oregon Independent Retail Grocers Assoc, 310 SW 4th, Portland, OR 97204. Bimonthly trade.

BUSINESS, FOOD/COOKING, OREGON

Oregon Ink, Oregon Institute of Literary Arts, 888 SW Fifth Ave #1600, Portland, OR 97204-2099. Contact: Kay Reid. 503-221-1440. Free annual tabloid on Oregon books, distributed to libraries and bookstores throughout the state.

BOOK ARTS/BOOKS, LITERATURE, OREGON

Oregon Insider, Oregon Environmental Foundation, 2637 SW Water, Portland, OR 97201. 503-222-2252. Contact: Peter Ravalla. Twice-monthly environmental newsletter for lawyers, businesses, political groups, and public agencies. Sub $175/yr.

CONSERVATION, ENVIRONMENT/RESOURCES, OREGON

Oregon Jersey Review, 993 Rafael St N, Salem, OR 97303. Quarterly.

AGRICULTURE/FARMING, ANIMALS, OREGON

Oregon Law Journal, PO Box 5518, Salem, OR 97304. 503-371-6469. Editors Michael A Campbell/Greg Wasson. Sub $132. Circ 5,000. Weekly journal for lawyers. Uses freelance material. Pays by arrangement on publication. Byline given. Acquires 1st rights. Submit query w/clips, ms, phone, SASE. Dot matrix, photocopied, simultaneous, electronic/modem, computer disk OK. Accepts nonfiction, cartoons. Topics: current issues and news of interest to practicing attorneys in Oregon. Photos and graphics welcome, but not necessary. Sample for 9x12 SASE.

LAW, POLITICS, PUBLIC AFFAIRS

Oregon Law Review, School of Law, University of Oregon, Eugene, OR 97403. Quarterly.

LAW, OREGON

Oregon Legionnaire, 7420 SW Hunziker Rd #A, Tigard, OR 97223-8242. Bimonthly.

MILITARY/VETS

Oregon Libertarian, PO Box 1250, McMinnville, OR 97128. 503-472-8277. Editor/Ads: Jo McIntyre. Monthly newsletter. Sub $12. Circ 200/250. Accepts unsolicited freelance material. Uses 1–5 mss per issue. Pays money ($5–10 per 250–500 wds) or copies on publication. Acquires first rights. Byline given. Submit query w/SASE, phone query. Dot matrix, photocopies OK. Reports in 1–6 wks. Publishes in 1–2 mos. Accepts nonfiction, photos, cartoons. Topics: victims of government, beating city hall, grassroots freedom fighting, benefits of freedom, how personal liberty stimulates creativity, "Would like articles from Greens, bioregionalists, decentralists, anarchists, feminists, tax protesters and others interested in networking with fellow freedom lovers." B/W prints only, pays $10 if screened, $5 if not. Free sample.

GOVERNMENT, OREGON, POLITICS

Oregon Library Foundation Newsletter, Oregon Library Foundation, State Library Bldg, Salem, OR 97310-0642. Editor: Wesley A Doak. Quarterly.

REFERENCE/LIBRARY

Oregon Library News, Oregon Library Association, Hood River County Library, 502 State St, Hood River, OR 97031. Editor: June Knudson. Periodical.

EDUCATION, REFERENCE/LIBRARY

Oregon Masonic News, PO Box 96, Forest Grove, OR 97116. Periodical.

TRADE/ASSOCIATIONS

Oregon Motorist, 600 SW Market, Portland, OR 97201. Editor: Doug Peeples. Monthly for members of Oregon AAA. Circ 225,000. Accepts freelance material "on limited basis." Query w/ms, SASE. Dot matrix, simultaneous submissions OK. Pay and rights purchased are negotiable. Nonfiction: 2 ds pages. Fillers: no pay. Guidelines/sample available.

OREGON, TRAVEL

Oregon Music Educator, 337 W Riverside Dr, Roseburg, OR 97470. Quarterly.

EDUCATION, MUSIC

Oregon Newsletter, CH2M Hill Inc, PO Box 428, Corvallis, OR 97339. Contact: Mary O'Brien. Newsletter published 5 times a yr by engineering firm.

BUSINESS, TECHNICAL

Oregon Optometry, College of Optometry, Pacific University, Forest Grove, OR 97116. Quarterly.

COLLEGE/UNIVERSITY, HEALTH

Oregon Outlook, Oregon School for the Deaf, 999 Locust NE, Salem, OR 97310. 503-378-3825. Editors: Shermalee Roake, Fred Farrior. Newsletter published 8 times a year. Sub $1.50/yr. No submission info, query w/SASE.

EDUCATION, DISABLED

Oregon PeaceWorker, 333 State St, Salem, OR 97301. 503-585-2767. Editor: Peter Bergel. Ads: 503-371-8002. Monthly newspaper.

ENVIRONMENT/RESOURCES, PEACE, POLITICS

Oregon Public Employee, 1127 25th SE, PO Box 12159, Salem, OR 97309. Monthly.

LABOR/WORK, OREGON, PUBLIC AFFAIRS

Oregon Publisher, Oregon Newspaper Publishers Association, 7150 SW Hampton St, Ste 111, Portland, OR 97223. 503-624-6397. Editor: Shelly Sanderlin. Quarterly trade newspaper. Circ 2,000. Submit query letter, SASE. Photocopy, disk/modem subs OK. Responds immediately. Accepts news items, articles. Sample available.

COMPUTERS, MEDIA/COMMUNICATIONS, TRADE/ASSOCIATIONS

Oregon Realtor, Oregon Association of Realtors, PO Box 351, Salem, OR 97308. Editor: Max Chapman. Monthly.

BUSINESS, OREGON, TRADE/ASSOCIATIONS

Oregon Restaurateur, PO Box 2427, Portland, OR 97208. Editor: Cheryl Long. 503-282-4284. Bimonthly trade magazine for "Oregon restaurateurs, food service industry operations, and Restaurants of Oregon Association members…. All editorial content is commissioned on a 'work-for-hire' basis; writing and photography guidelines are given with each assignment…. The editor is not responsible for unsolicited contributions which must include a SASE if return is requested."

BUSINESS, TRADE/ASSOCIATIONS

Oregon Scholastic Press, 201 Allen Hall, University of Oregon, Eugene, OR 97403. Book publisher.

EDUCATION, TEXTBOOKS

Oregon School of Design Newsletter, 734 NW 14th Ave, Portland, OR 97209. 503-222-3727. Periodical related to school of architecture and allied arts.

ARCHITECTURE, ARTS, EDUCATION

Oregon School Study Council Bulletin, 1787 Agate St, University of Oregon, Eugene, OR 97403. 503-686-5045. Monthly publication offers an in depth description of effective programs in the state's schools. Each issue fo-

cuses on topics of significance to administrators and lay board members. Sub with membership.
EDUCATION, OREGON

Oregon Science Teacher, Rt 1 Box 148, Hillsboro, OR 97123. Quarterly.
EDUCATION, OREGON, SCIENCE

The Oregon Scientist, PO Box 230220, Tigard, OR 97223. 503-292-8460. Editor: Marge Davenport. Ads: L B Cady. Quarterly founded in 1988. Sub $8/yr; circ 32,000. Uses freelance material. Requires research/science or technology expertise. Pays money on publication. Acquires 1st rights. Byline given. Submit phone query. Accepts news items, photos, interviews, op/ed, articles. Sample $2.
SCIENCE, TECHNICAL

Oregon Snowmobile News, PO Box 6328, Bend, OR 97708. Editor: Larry Lancaster. Monthly of the Oregon State Snowmobiling Assoc.
OREGON, OUTDOOR, RECREATION

Oregon Sport & Recreation Magazine, Sportland Publishing, PO Box 82747, Portland, OR 97282. 503-287-5408. Editor: Mike Fazzolari. Ads: Gary Dunsworth. Annual magazine. Circ 30,000. Uses freelance material. Byline given, pays money on publication. Submit query, ms, SASE. Photocopy, disk/modem, dot matrix subs OK. Responds in 1–2 wks. Uses fiction, cartoons, nonfiction, photos, interviews, articles. Photos: color slides or B&W glossy. "Editorial directed at winter recreation preferred." Sample free for 9x12" SASE.
OREGON, RECREATION, SPORTS

Oregon Sports & Recreation Magazine, PO Box 82747, Portland, OR 97282. 503-287-5408. Contact: Mike Fazzolari, editor. Ads: Gary Dunsworth. Biannual. Sub $4/yr. Circ 25,000. Uses 5 freelance mss per issue. Pays money ($40/article) on publication. Byline given. Submit query w/ clips, or phone. Computer disk OK. Accepts nonfiction, fiction, photos, cartoons. Topics: outdoor recreation and all sports. Tips: 500–2,000 wds. Photos: B&W 5x7 or 8x10 glossy, color-chrome, $10 B&W, $15 color. Sample $1.
NORTHWEST, RECREATION, SPORTS

Oregon Sportsman & Conservationist, 1177 Pearl St, PO Box 1376, Eugene, OR 97440. Bimonthly on outdoor non-competitive sports, conservation and related issues in OR.
CONSERVATION, OREGON, RECREATION

Oregon State Parks Quarterly, 525 Trade St NE, Salem, OR 97310. 503-378-2796.
OREGON, OUTDOOR, RECREATION

Oregon State Poetry Association Newsletter, 1601 E Reserve St, Apt 1, Vancouver, WA 98661-4047. Editor: Lindsay Thompson. Quarterly. Circ 300. Sub w/membership. Uses 4 mss per issue from OSPA members. Payment: Copies on request. Byline given on longer pieces. Query w/ms, SASE. Phone query, dot matrix, photocopies, simultaneous submissions (if writer indicates where) OK. Reports in 2 wks. Nonfiction; poetry, 3–8 lines, related to writing poetry or poets; cartoons, poetry related. Photos: assignment only. "Opinion pieces on trends in poetry. Market updates. Book reviews. Short articles on poetry groups state-wide, individual poets who enjoy remarkable success, poetry and its role in political and social issues, projects in poetry by OSPA members (special exhibits, children's contests, readings, etc) — Oregon poetry news almost exclusively, unless of national or international importance. Items must be very short, 100–500 wds."
LITERARY, POETRY, WRITING

Oregon State Trooper, PO Box 717, Tualatin, OR 97062. 503-639-9651. Editor: Ralph Springer. Magazine published 3 times a yr. Sub $8/4 issues. Circ 2,000. Accepts freelance material. Pays money or copies. Byline given. Submit query w/clips. Dot matrix OK. Reports in 4 wks. Publishing time varies. Accepts nonfiction, photos. "Seeking photos, mss covering OSP officers at work, off-duty, etc; accident scenes w/OSP slant, etc; features on OSP troopers, hobbies, etc." B&W photo's preferred, usually pays $7.50 per photo.
LABOR/WORK, OREGON, TRADE/ASSOCIATIONS

Oregon State University Press, 101 Waldo Hall, Corvallis, OR 97331. 503-737-3166. Editor: Jo Alexander. Publishes nonfiction, hard- & softcover original & reprint books. Accepts unsolicited submissions. Pays royalties. Rights purchased: negotiable. Submit query, ms, SASE. Dot matrix, photocopies OK. Reports in 1 mo. Publishes in approx 1 yr. Accepts scholarly book-length manuscripts. Topics: a limited range of disciplines, with a special emphasis on the Pacific Northwest. Tips: "Query with sample chapter & table of contents. Acceptance process is lengthy & involves outside reviews & editorial board." Catalog available.
ENVIRONMENT/RESOURCES, NORTHWEST, SCHOLARLY/ACADEMIC

Oregon Stater, OSU Alumni Assoc, 104 Memorial Union Bldg, Corvallis, OR 97331. 503-754-4611. Published 7 times a year. Circ 96,000. Uses 4 freelance mss per issue. Pays money on publication. Rights acquired: first. Byline given. Submit query w/clips. Dot matrix, photocopies, computer disk OK.
COLLEGE/UNIVERSITY, EDUCATION, OREGON

Oregon Teamster, 1020 NE 3rd, Portland, OR 97232. Semimonthly union publication.
LABOR/WORK, OREGON

Oregon Vintage Motorcyclist Newsletter, PO Box 14645, Portland, OR 97124. Editor: Wally Skyman.
LABOR/WORK, TRADE/ASSOCIATIONS

Oregon Wheat, 305 SW 10th, PO Box 400, Pendleton, OR 97801. Editors: Scott Duff. 503-276-7330. Bimonthly magazine dedicated to the "improvement of wheat farming in OR." Circ 9,000. Interested in general trade mss by industry professionals only. Byline given. Query w/SASE. Dot matrix, simultaneous submissions OK. Reports in 1 mo. Publishes in 2 mos. Nonfiction: 3 typewritten, ds pgs on issues pertaining to wheat farming. "Rarely print anything outside of technical wheat farming subjects." Guidelines available; sample/free.
AGRICULTURE/FARMING, BUSINESS, OREGON

Oregon Wine Press, 644 SE 20th Ave, Portland, OR 97214. 503-232-7607. Editor: Richard Hopkins. Ads: Elaine Cohen. Monthly tabloid newspaper founded in 1984. Sub $8/yr; circ 20,000. Uses freelance material. Byline given. Pays money on publication. Acquires all rights. Submit query letter, SASE, phone. Photocopy, simultaneous subs OK. Responds in 2–3 wks; publishes in 1 mo. Accepts news items, interviews, articles, photos (B&W). Topics: Oregon wine, the wine industry, Oregon hospitality industry, wine education. Sample $2.
CALENDAR/EVENTS, FOOD/COOKING, TRAVEL

Oregon's Agricultural Progress, AdS 416, Oregon State University, Corvallis, OR 97331. 503-737-3379. Editor: Andy Duncan. Quarterly magazine. Uses freelance material. Byline given. Submit query letter, clips, SASE. Responds in 2–4 wks; publishes in 3–8 mos. Accepts nonfiction.
AGRICULTURE/FARMING, CONSUMER, GARDENING

Oregon/Washington Labor Press, 4313 NE Tillamook, Portland, OR 97213. Editor: Mary Lyons. 503-231-4990. Monthly newspaper of the Oregon & Washington AFL-CIO organizations. Sub $10/yr.
LABOR/WORK, OREGON

The Oregonian, 1320 SW Broadway, Portland, OR 97201. 503-221-8327. Daily newspaper.
URBAN

Oregon's Agricultural Progress, Agricultural Experiment Stn, Oregon State University, Corvallis, OR 97331. Editor: Robert E Witters. Periodical.
AGRICULTURE/FARMING, COLLEGE/UNIVERSITY, OREGON

Oriel Press, 2020 SW Kanan St, Portland, OR 97201-2039. Book publisher.
OTHER/UNSPECIFIED

Orion Nature Quarterly, 10 SW Ash St, Portland, OR 97204.
ENVIRONMENT/RESOURCES, NATURAL HISTORY

Ornamentals Northwest, Department of Horticulture, Oregon State University, Corvallis, OR 97331. Editor: James L Green. Quarterly.
AGRICULTURE/FARMING, COLLEGE/UNIVERSITY, GARDENING

Orpheus, 1406 Cheny, La Grande, OR 97850. Editor: Christopher Hatten. Science fiction and fantasy tabloid seeking undiscovered talent. Accepts stories, poems, art, cartoon. Max 1,500 wds, B&W artwork. Pays copies. Query w/SASE.
FANTASY/SCI FI, POETRY

Merle Osgood Productions, PO Box 4516, Kent, WA 98032-9516. Book publisher.
OTHER/UNSPECIFIED

Osprey Press, PO Box 32, Sedro Woolley, WA 98284. 206-755-0941. Book publisher.
OTHER/UNSPECIFIED

Othello Outlook, PO Box "O", Othello, WA 99344. 509-488-3342. Weekly newspaper.
COMMUNITY

Other Press, Douglas College, PO Box 2503, New Westminster, BC V3L 5B2. 604-525-3830. Periodical.
COLLEGE/UNIVERSITY

Our Little Friend, PO Box 7000, Boise, ID 83707. Editor: Louis Schutter. Weekly magazine for children published by Seventh-Day Adventist Church. Circ 65,785.
CHILDREN/TEEN, RELIGION

Out North Theatre Company, Box 100140, Anchorage, AK 99510-0140. 907-279-8099. Contact: Gene Dugan. Pays money on production. Submit query letter/SASE. Accepts new scripts as well as previously produced. Tips: small cast and simple technical requirements.
DRAMA, ENTERTAINMENT

Outdoor Empire Publishing Inc, PO Box C-19000, Seattle, WA 98109. Editor: William Farden. Book publisher.
OTHER/UNSPECIFIED

Outdoor Pictures, PO Box 277, Anacortes, WA 98221. Book publisher.
OUTDOOR, PHOTOGRAPHY

Outdoors West, Federation of Western Outdoor Clubs, 512 Boylston Ave E, #106, Seattle, WA 98102. Editor: Hazel A. Wolf. Semiannual tabloid concerning use and protection of wilderness and recreation resources.
CONSERVATION, ENVIRONMENT/RESOURCES, OUTDOOR

Outlaw Newsletter, PO Box 4466, Bozeman, MT 59772. 406-586-7248. Editor: Jeri Walton. Quarterly newsletter of Western happenings, cowboy poetry & book reviews. Sub $7. Does not accept unsolicited submissions. Submit query w/clips.
FICTION, NORTHWEST, POETRY

Outlook, PO Box 455, Sedro Woolley, WA 98284. 206-855-1306. Weekly newspaper.
COMMUNITY

Outlook, Canadian Jewish Outlook Society, #3 – 6184 Ash St, Vancouver, BC V5Z 3G9. 604-324-5101. Editor: Henry Rosenthal. Monthly magazine founded in 1962. Sub $25, US $31. Freelance material accepted. Pays in copies. Byline given. Submit ms. Photocopy, dot matrix OK. Reports in 3 wks; publishes in 3 mos. Accepts poetry, cartoons, interviews, op/ed, articles, reviews, memoirs.
MINORITIES/ETHNIC, PEACE, PUBLIC AFFAIRS

Overland West Press, PO Box 17507, Portland, OR 97217. Book publisher.
PUBLISHING/PRINTING

Overlook, Sierra Club, 2637 SW Water Ave, Portland, OR 97201. Periodical.
CONSERVATION, ENVIRONMENT/RESOURCES

The Overseas Times, PO Box 442, Surrey, BC V3T 5B6. Editor: Ben P Sharma. 604-588-8666. Periodical.
OTHER/UNSPECIFIED

The Ovulation Method Newsletter, Ovulation Method Teachers Association, PO Box 10-1780, Anchorage, AK 99501. Quarterly. Sub $10. Circ 500. Uses freelance material. Pays in copies. Byline given. Submit ms, SASE. Dot matrix, photocopied OK. Accepts nonfiction, cartoons. Sample available.
FAMILY, HEALTH, WOMEN

Owl Creek Press, 1620 N 45th St, Seattle, WA 98103. Contact: Rich Ives. 206-633-5929. Publisher of 6–10 hard- & softcover and mass market, originals and reprints a year. Print run: 1,000. Accepts freelance material. Payment: 10% in copies to 20% in cash. Rights purchased: All. Sample chapters w/SASE. Dot matrix, photocopies OK. Reports in 2–12 wks. Nonfiction, fiction, poetry. "Any length, subject. Literary quality is our only criteria." Two annual contests (see Resources). Poetry Chapbook contest: under 40 pgs, $5 entry fee, July 1 deadline. Poetry Book Contest: over 50 pgs, $8 entry fee, Dec. 31 deadline. Prize: publication with 10% payment in copies of the first printing and additional pay in cash or copies for additional printing. Catalog available.
FICTION, LITERARY, POETRY

Owyhee Outpost, PO Box 67, Murphy, ID 83650. Editor: Dale M. Gray. 208-495-2319. Annual. Circ 500. Sub $5. Uses 2–4 mss per issue. Payment: Copies on publication. Byline given. Rights purchased: First. Query w/ms, SASE. Dot matrix, photocopies OK. Reports in January. Nonfiction: only articles on Owyhee County history, 3–10 typed, ds pgs. Photos: 5x7 or 8x10 B&W. Tip: "Articles must include bibliography or source of information." Sample/$5.
AMERICAN HISTORY, NW/REGIONAL HISTORY, IDAHO

Oyate Wo'wapi, Tahana Whitecrow Foundation, PO Box 18181, Salem, OR 97305. 503-585-0564. Editor: Melanie Smith. Self-publisher & quarterly newsletter founded in 1987. Sub $5/yr. Editor: Melanie Smith. Uses freelance material. Byline given. Pays copies, acquires 1st rights. Submit query letter, SASE. Simultaneous sub OK. Responds in 2–4 wks, publishing time varies. Accepts news items, poetry. See Resources for annual poetry contest. Guidelines available.
NATIVE AMERICAN, POETRY

The Oz Press, PO Box 33088, Seattle, WA 98133. Book publisher.
OTHER/UNSPECIFIED

P.R.O. Newsletter of Oregon, PO Box 86781, Portland, OR 97286. 503-775-2974. Editor: S Alexander. Ads: Michelle Tennesen. Bimonthly. Sub $15/yr; circ 500. Uses freelance material. Pays copies. Acquires 1st rights. Byline given. Submit query w/clips, ms, phone, SASE. Dot matrix, photocopied, simultaneous OK. Reports in 1 mo. Accepts nonfiction. Topics: children, family. Sample, SASE.
CHILDREN (BY/ABOUT), FAMILY

Pacific, The Seattle Times, PO Box 70, Seattle, WA 98111. 206-464-2283. Weekly Sunday supplement to the Seattle Times. Accepts very little freelance material. Query w/SASE.
CULTURE, NORTHWEST, WASHINGTON

Pacific Affairs, University of British Columbia, 2029 West Mall, Vancouver, BC V6T 1W5. 604-228-6508. Quarterly scholarly journal of UBC. Sub $30/ indiv. $50/inst; circ 4,000. Uses freelance material. Byline given. Submit query letter. Responds in 3 wks; publishes in 6 mos. Accepts solicited book reviews. Guidelines available.
ASIA, POLITICS, SCHOLARLY/ACADEMIC

Pacific Builder & Engineer, 3000 Northrup Way #200, Bellevue, WA 98004–1407. 206-827-9900. Contact: Christine Laing. Trade journal. Accepts freelance material. Pays money on publication. Acquires first rights. Byline given. Submit query w/clips, SASE. Dot matrix, photocopied, computer disk OK. Reports in 1 mo. Accepts nonfiction stories on non-residential construction, about 1,500–2,000 wds, must include art. Photos: color transparencies or B&W negatives & contact sheet.
BUSINESS, NORTHWEST, TRADE/ASSOCIATIONS

Pacific Coast Centre of Sexology, Stn C, Box 24400, Vancouver, BC, V5T 4M5. Sexual education books.
EDUCATION, SEX

Pacific Coast Nurseryman Magazine, 303 NW Murray Rd, Ste 6A, Portland, OR 97229. Editor: John Humes. 503-643-9380. Monthly trade magazine of the nursery, horticulture industry. Circ 10,000. Byline given. "Seldom purchase because we have more info than can usually use…. Minimal fee of $25." Query w/ms, SASE. Phone query, dot matrix, simultaneous submis-

sions OK. Publishes in 2–12 mos. Nonfiction: 300–1,200 wds. Photos: B&W glossies; reimburse cost. Tips: "All submissions subject to editing. Small business retailing, new horticulture research, new agricultural breakthroughs. Not interested in articles aimed at home gardener." Sample/$2.
AGRICULTURE/FARMING, BUSINESS, TRADE/ASSOCIATIONS

Pacific Educational Press, Faculty of Education, UBC, 2173 West Mall, Vancouver, BC V6T 1Z5. 604-228-5385. Editor: Sharon Radcliffe. Publishes 12 quarterly journals and 5 hard- & softcover original books a year. Accepts unsolicited book submissions. Pays royalties/advance on publication. Rights acquired vary. Submit query w/clips, SASE. Photocopies OK. Reports in 1 mo. Accepts educational & academic nonfiction. Pays royalties on publication. Catalog/sample available.
COLLEGE/UNIVERSITY, CONSERVATION, EDUCATION

Pacific Fast Mail, PO Box 57, Edmonds, WA 98020. Contact: Donald Drew. Book publisher.
OTHER/UNSPECIFIED

Pacific Fisheries Enhancement, PO Box 5829, Charleston, OR, 97420. Periodical.
BUSINESS, FISHING

Pacific Fishing, 1515 NW 51st, Seattle, WA 98107. 206-789-5333. Contact: Steve Shapiro. Monthly magazine for the commercial fishing industry on the West Coast. Acquires 1st rights to nonfiction on all aspects of the business and the people, especially features with quality photos. Query w/SASE. Query w/SASE.
BUSINESS, COMMERCE, FISHING

Pacific Gallery Publishers, 7273 SW Nevada Terr., Portland, OR 97219-2061. Book publisher.
ARTS, OTHER/UNSPECIFIED

Pacific House Enterprises, 65 W 26th Ave, Eugene, OR 97405. 503-344-0395. Book publisher.
OTHER/UNSPECIFIED

Pacific Index, Pacific University, UC Box 695, Forest Grove, OR 97116. 503-357-6151. Newspaper.
COLLEGE/UNIVERSITY

Pacific International Publishing Company, PO Box 1596, Friday Harbor, WA 98250-1596. Book publisher.
OTHER/UNSPECIFIED

Pacific Marketer, Northwest Furniture Retailer, 121 Borea N, Seattle, WA 98109. Monthly.
BUSINESS

Pacific Meridian Publishing, 13540 Lake City Way NE, Seattle, WA 98125. Book publisher.
OTHER/UNSPECIFIED

Pacific Network News, PO Box 1224, Portland, OR 97207. 503-778-6920. Contact: Brent Vaughters, Editor. Sub $12/yr or free at drop-off points. Circ 20,000. Topics: Portland-Vancouver business, financial, real estate networking. Welcomes freelance submissions. SASE for guidelines.
BUSINESS, ECONOMICS

Pacific Northwest Executive, Graduate School of Bus Administration, 336 Lewis Hall, DJ-10, University of Washington, Seattle, WA 98195. Editor: Jerry Sullivan. 206-543-1819. Quarterly of business management/economics. Circ 25,000. Sub free. Uses 1–2 mss per issue. Payment: $250–500 on acceptance. Byline given. Rights purchased: First. Query w/SASE. Dot matrix, photocopies, simultaneous submissions, electronic OK. Nonfiction: 1,500–3,000 wds. "Our typical issue will be read at the workplace by people who are keeping themselves informed as part of their jobs. Thus, we serve an educational, not an entertainment function. In recent issues we have featured a debate on comparable worth, a series on Japanese business, a story on the implications for managers of an employee with a life-threatening illness, and an overview on wheat in a changing marketplace." Guidelines/sample available.
BUSINESS, ECONOMICS, NORTHWEST

Pacific Northwest Forum, Eastern Washington University, MS-27, Cheney, WA 99004. J. William, T. Young. Quarterly journal. Sub $5/yr. Circ 500. Uses 3 freelance mss per issue. Pays $20 & 10 copies on publication. Byline given. Submit query w/clips, ms, SASE, phone. Dot matrix, photocopied, Mac disk OK. Reports in 3 mos. Publishes in 6–12 mos. Accepts nonfiction, fiction. Topics: history, literature, environmental issues in the NW; for scholars and the general reader.
COLLEGE/UNIVERSITY, NW/REGIONAL HISTORY, LITERATURE

Pacific Northwest Labor History Association, PO Box 75048, Seattle, WA 98125. 206-524-0346. Contact: Ross Reider. Book publisher.
BUSINESS, NW/REGIONAL HISTORY, LABOR/WORK

Pacific Northwest Magazine, 222 Dexter Ave N, Seattle, WA 98109. 206-284-1750. Editor: Ann Nauman. Ads: Peggy Bilous. Monthly. Sub $24.95/yr; circ 80,000. Uses freelance material. Pays money, copies on publication. Acquires 1st rights. Submit query letter, clips, SASE. Responds in 3 wks; publishes in 4 mos. Accepts articles, photos. Guidelines available. Sample $4.
NORTHWEST, RECREATION, TRAVEL

Pacific Northwest Quarterly, University of Washington, 4045 Brooklyn NE, JA-15, Seattle, WA 98105. 206-543-2992.
COLLEGE/UNIVERSITY

Pacific Press Publishing Association, Seventh-Day Adventist Church, PO Box 7000, Boise, ID 83707. 208-467-7400. Publisher of 50 books a year. Query w/SASE.
RELIGION

Pacific Publishers, 515 W Pender, Vancouver, BC V6B 1V5. Book publisher.
RELIGION

The Pacific Review, Pacific University, UC Box 607, Forest Grove, OR 97116. 503-357-6151 X2406. Editor: Michael Steele. College literary magazine. Editors could change yearly. SASE for guidelines.
COLLEGE/UNIVERSITY, FICTION, OREGON

Pacific Rim Press, 353 G Ave, Lake Oswego, OR 97034. 503-244-8462. Self-publisher only. Not a freelance market.
FOOD/COOKING, TRAVEL

Pacific Soccer School, 1721 22nd Ave, Forest Grove, OR 97116. Book publisher.
RECREATION, SPORTS

Pacific Yachting, 1132 Hamilton St, #202, Vancouver, BC V6B 2S2. Monthly magazine founded in 1968. Editor: John Shinnick. Sub $28/yr; circ 25,000. Uses freelance material. Pays money. Acquires 1st, 2nd rights. Submit query letter, complete ms, SASE (Cdn postage or international coupons). Dot matrix, photocopy, disk/modem subs OK. Accepts news items, interviews, op/ed, reviews, photos (prints or slides, color, $25–300). Topics: industry news and features on boating — people, places and events. High level of expertise required. Guidelines available.
BOATING, BUSINESS, RECREATION

Pacifica International, PO Box 783, North Bend, OR 97459-0061. 503-496-0431. Editor: Steve Serrao. Book publisher. Uses some freelance material. Submit query, outline, sample chap; ms, SASE. Accepts nonfiction. Guidelines available.
OTHER/UNSPECIFIED

Packrat Press, 4366 N Diana Lane, Oak Harbor, WA 98277. 206-675-6016. Self-publisher of 2 hard- & softcover, originals, reprints a year. Print run: 500. Not a freelance market. Catalog available.
POLITICS, SOCIOLOGY, TRAVEL

Packrat Press Books, PO Box 74, Cambridge, ID 83610. Book publisher.
OTHER/UNSPECIFIED

Paddlewheel Press, 15100 SW 109th, Tigard, OR 97224. 503-639-5637. Contact: Marge Davenport. Book publisher.
OTHER/UNSPECIFIED

Page One Press, 9330-D Bridgeport Way SW #40, Tacoma, WA 98499. 206-582-1757. Contact: Kay Kennedy. Subsidy book publisher with some purchased. Accepts unsolicited submissions. Submit query letter, outline, SASE.

Responds in 1 mo; publishes in 6 mos. Accepts nonfiction, biography, memoirs.
BUSINESS, PUBLISHING/PRINTING

Painted Smiles, 1105 W Idaho St, Boise, ID 83702. Book publisher.
OTHER/UNSPECIFIED

Pair-o'-Dice Press, 525 SE 16th Ave, Portland, OR 97214. Book publisher.
OTHER/UNSPECIFIED

Paisley Publishing, PO Box 201853, Anchorage, AK 99520. 907-346-2789. Editors: Betsy Arehart, Anne Marie Holen. Self-publisher. Not a freelance market.
OTHER/UNSPECIFIED

Paladin Publishing Corp, 20947 NW Millicomo Ct, Hillsboro, OR 97229. 503-648-3303. Editor: Suzann Laudenslager. Book publisher.
OTHER/UNSPECIFIED

Pallas Communications, 4226 NE 23rd Ave, Portland, OR 97211. 503-284-2848. Editor: Douglas Bloch. Publisher of 2–3 New Age, softcover, original books per year. Accepts unsolicited submissions. Pays royalties. Submit query, sample chapter, outline w/SASE. Dot matrix, photocopied, simultaneous, computer disk OK. Reports in 4–6 wks. Publishes within 1 yr. Accepts nonfiction. Topics: self-help, psychology, astrology, metaphysics, holistic health, women's spirituality, and inspirational writing; "any path that leads to personal or planetary transformation." Catalog available.
ASTROLOGY/SPIRITUAL, HEALTH, PSYCHOLOGY

Palmer-Pletsch Associates, PO Box 12046, Portland, OR 97212. Book publisher.
OTHER/UNSPECIFIED

Palouse Empire Daily News, S 130 Grand, Pullman, WA 99163. 509-334-6397. Newspaper.
COMMUNITY, OTHER/UNSPECIFIED

Palouse Journal, 112 W 4th, Moscow, ID 83843. 208-882-0888. Editors: Ed Hughes/Phil Druker. Ads: Andrea Kruse/Suzy Franko. Tabloid journal published 5/yr. Sub $12/yr. Circ 13,000. Uses freelance material (5∂–8 mss per issue). Pays money on publication. Acquires 1st rights. Byline given. Query w/clips & SASE or phone. Dot matrix, photocopied, or disk submissions OK. Reports in 1 mo; publishing time varies. Accepts biography, photos (on request), interviews, op/ed, articles, cartoons, photos, reviews, short fiction (1,000 wds). Topics: local history, natural history, politics, environment issues, sports, food, science, business, regional travel, arts, people, "— must be of interest to interior Northwest readers." Study sample before querying. Guidelines available; sample $2.
COMMUNITY, IDAHO, TRAVEL

Palouse Summer, 112 W 4th, Moscow, ID 83843. 208-882-0888. Editor: Ivar Nelson. Ads: Opal Gerwig. Annual magazine. Free. Circ 20,000. Uses freelance material. Pays money on publication. Acquires 1st rights. Byline given. Submit query letter, complete ms, SASE, phone. Reports in 3 wks; publishes in 2 mos. Accepts biography, photos (on request), interviews, op/ed, articles, reviews. Topics: local history, natural history, politics, environment issues, sports, food, science, business, regional travel, recreation, arts, people, "— must be of interest to interior Northwest readers." Study sample before querying. Guidelines available; sample $2.
NORTHWEST, RECREATION, TRAVEL

Panda Press Publications, Richards Rd, Roberts Creek, BC V0N 2W0. Contact: L R Davidson. 604-885-3985. Publisher of 1 softcover original a year. Print run: 300. Accepts freelance material. Payment: Copies. Rights purchased: First. Query, sample chapters w/SASE. Photocopies, simultaneous submissions OK. Reports in 3–4 wks. Publishes in 1–3 yrs. Fiction: "Stories of any kind with excellent, three-dimensional characters interacting with each other and the plot in a logical and interesting way."
AVANT-GARDE/EXPERIMENTAL, FANTASY/SCI FI, SATIRE

Pandora's Treasures, 1609 Eastover Terrace, Boise, ID 83706. Dr. R. Dwayne Moulton. Book publisher.
CHILDREN/TEEN

Panegyria, Aquarian Tabernacle Church, PO Box 85507, Seattle, WA 98145. 206-793-1945. Contact: Pete Pathfinder. Newsletter published 8x/yr. Founded 1983. Circ 500–1,000, subs. $12/yr. Uses freelance material. Byline given, pays copies on publication, acquires some rights. Submit query, complete ms; SASE, phone. Disk/modem subs OK. Responds in 2–4 wks; publishes in 4 mos. Accepts fiction, cartoons, news, nonfiction, interviews, reviews. Topics: related to ancient cultures of Europe, magic, self-mastery, goddess-oriented religion (not Satanist). Sample $3.
FEMINISM, RELIGION, NEW AGE

Panoply Press Inc, PO Box 1885, Lake Oswego, OR 97035. 503-620-7239. Publisher of 2–5 softcover original books a year. Accepts unsolicited queries. Pays royalties. Submit query w/clips, SASE. Dot matrix, photocopied OK. Nonfiction. Topic: real estate.
BUSINESS

Panorama Publication Ltd, #210 – 1807 Maritime Mews, Granville Island, Vancouver, BC V6H 3W7. Book publisher.
OTHER/UNSPECIFIED

Paper Radio, PO Box 85302, Seattle, WA 98145. 206-634-2065. Editors: N S Kvern, Dagmar Howard. Three issues annually. Sub $9/yr; circ 400. Fully freelance written. Pays in copies on publication. No rights acquired. Byline given. Submit ms, SASE. Dot matrix, photocopied, simultaneous OK. Reports in 2–3 wks; publishes in 1–6 mos. Accepts nonfiction, fiction, poetry, photos, plays, cartoons, B&W art. Topics: short stories (under 3,000 wds), poetry (under 20 lines), visual art (8x11" or smaller). Prefers things which are radical, experimental, political (that which is oblique rather than direct). "We have published humor, erotica & essays." See an issue before sending anything. Sample $3.
AVANT-GARDE/EXPERIMENTAL, LITERATURE, VISUAL ARTS

Paradise Publications, 8110 SW Wareham, Portland, OR 97223. 503-246-1555. Publisher of softcover books & quarterly newsletter on travel; sub $6/yr; circ 2,000. Founded 1983. Accepts unsolicited book submissions. Pays royalties. Submit query letter, outline, SASE. Photocopy, simultaneous subs OK. Responds in 1 mo; publishes in 6–12 mos. Catalog available. Newsletter sample $1.50.
TRAVEL

Parallel DisCourse, A Magazine of Graphic & Written Arts, PO Box 2473, Seattle, WA 98111. 206-323-6779. Contact: Phoebe Bosche/James Maloney. Tabloid published "whenever the time is ripe." Query w/SASE. Sample $2.
ARTS, LITERARY

Parallel Publishers Ltd, PO Box 3677, Main Post Office, 349 W Georgia St, Vancouver, BC V6B 3Y8. Book publisher.
OTHER/UNSPECIFIED

Paralog, Oregon Paralyzed Veterans of America, 5611 SE Powell Blvd, Portland, OR 97206. Contact: Editor. 503-775-0938. Periodical. Circ 600. Sub free to members. Payment: Copies on publication if requested. Byline given. Query w/ms, SASE. Phone query, dot matrix, photocopies, simultaneous submissions OK. Reports in 2 mos. Nonfiction: subjects of interest to paralyzed veterans. Sample available.
MILITARY/VETS, DISABLED

Parenting Press Inc, 11065 5th Ave NE #F, Seattle, WA 98125. 206–364-2900. Editor: Elizabeth Crary. Publishes hard- & softcover books. Accepts unsolicited submissions. Pays royalties. Submit query letter, SASE. Dot matrix, photocopied, simultaneous subs OK. Reports in 2–3 mos; publishes in 9–24 mos. Accepts nonfiction. Topics: child guidance/parenting, social skills building books for children. Write for submission guidelines before submitting material. Catalog available.
CHILDREN (BY/ABOUT), EDUCATION, FAMILY

Parkside Press, 2026 Parkside Court, West Linn, OR 97068. Book publisher.
OTHER/UNSPECIFIED

Parlie Publications, 15525 SW 114th Ct. Ste 31, Tigard, OR 97224-3310. 503-639-2694. Contact: Alice Pohl. Publisher of books on parliamentary procedure.
REFERENCE/LIBRARY

Parsley, Sage & Time, Pike Market Senior Center, 1931 1st Ave, Seattle, WA 98101. Periodical.
SENIOR CITIZENS

Passage, Seattle Arts Commission, 305 Harrison, Seattle, WA 98109. Editor: Diane Shamash. 206-625-4223. Periodical.
ARTS, CULTURE, VISUAL ARTS

Patchwork, 1615 NW Hillcrest Dr, Corvallis, OR 97330. Quarterly welcomes submissions from writers 55 or older. No pay. 500 word maximum. "Images of today and memories of yesterday, stored in the fabric of our minds, now pieced together for your reading enjoyment."
BIOGRAPHY, GENERAL HISTORY, SENIOR CITIZENS

Pathways, Inky Trails Publications, PO Box 345, Middleton, ID 83644. Editor: Pearl Kirk. Published 3 times a year. Circ 300. Query w/ms, SASE. Reports in 2–8 wks. Publishes in 2–3 yrs. Nonfiction, fiction, poetry. "Fantasy, animals, essays, humor, travels, historical and children's own ideas. 500–1,200 wds. Encourage new writers, especially children. Do not want horror or porn." Guidelines: SASE/44¢ post. Sample: $7 w/9x12 SASE.
CHILDREN (BY/ABOUT), FANTASY/SCI FI, HUMOR

The Patriot, Runaway Publications, PO Box 1172, Ashland, OR 97520–0040. 503-482-2578. Editor: James Berkman. Self-publisher only. Annual issue + special editions. Sub $10; circ 100. Not a freelance market. Catalog available.
AMERICANA, POETRY

Paws IV Publishing Co, PO Box 2364, Homer, AK 99603. 907-235-7697. Contact: Shelley Gill. Publisher of 2 hard- & softcover originals a year. Accepts unsolicited submissions. Submit ms, SASE. Photocopied, simultaneous OK. Reports in 1 mo. Accepts nonfiction, fiction. Topics: Alaska, children's.
ADVENTURE, ALASKA, CHILDREN/TEEN

PAWS, Progressive Animal Welfare Society, PO Box 1037, Lynnwood, WA 98046. Periodical.
ANTHROPOLOGY/ARCHÆOLOGY

PDXS, 2305 NW Kearny, Box 335, Portland, OR 97210. 503-224-7316. Editor/Ads: Jim Redden. Biweekly tabloid of news and arts coverage for Portland metro area. Seeks freelance submissions of political commentary, arts reviews, profiles, coverage of anything local and outrageous. Uses photos with news stories. Query by phone on news or ms w/SASE. Payment varies. Report in 1 wk; publishing time varies.
AVANT-GARDE/EXPERIMENTAL, COUNTER CULTURE, POLITICS

Pea & Lentil News, PO Box 8566, Moscow, ID 83843. Editor: Tracy Bier. 208-882-3023. Quarterly trade publication. Circ 4,500. Not a freelance market.
AGRICULTURE/FARMING, BUSINESS

The Peak, Peak Trailers, Simon Fraser University, Burnaby, BC V5A 1S6. 604-291-3598. Student newspaper published 39 times a year. Circ 8,000. Sub $28. Accepts freelance material typed ds. Byline given. No pay. Nonfiction, student issues.
COLLEGE/UNIVERSITY, CULTURE, EDUCATION

Peak Media, Box 925, Hailey, ID 83333-0925. 208-726-9494. Publishes magazines, focus on the region.
FOOD/COOKING, OUTDOOR, RECREATION

Peanut Butter Publishing, 200 2nd Ave W, Seattle, WA 98104-4204. 206-628-6200. Publisher of 40 hard- & softcover, original, reprints, subsidy books a year. Print run: 5–10,000. Accepts freelance material. Rights purchased: First, all. Outline, sample chapters, ms w/SASE. Dot matrix, photocopies OK. Nonfiction: Food cooking, dining. Catalog available.
ENTERTAINMENT, FOOD/COOKING, RECREATION

Peavine Publications, PO Box 1264, McMinnville, OR 97128–1264. 503-472-1933. Editor: W P Lowry. Publishes softcover books. Accepts unsolicited mss. Pays royalties. Submit query letter, outline, sample chapters, SASE.

Photocopy, dot matrix subs OK. Reports in 1 mo; publishes in 6–12 mos. Accepts nonfiction. Topics: ecological, balanced analyses with mild advocacy preferred.
ENVIRONMENT/RESOURCES, SCIENCE, TEXTBOOKS

The Pedersens, PO Box 128, Sterling, AK 99672. Self-publisher. Not a freelance market.
ALASKA, CHILDREN/TEEN, AMERICAN HISTORY

Peel Productions, Rt 4, Box 396, Sherwood, OR 97140. 503–829-6849. Editor: Susan Joyce. Publishes hard- & softcover original books. Does not accepts unsolicited mss. Pays in copies, royalties on publication. Acquires first rights. Submit query letter. Photocopies OK. Reports in 5–6 wks. Publishes in 1 yr. Accepts nonfiction, fiction. Topics: illustrated children's books and how-to-draw books. Catalog available.
ANIMALS, CHILDREN/TEEN, PICTURE

Pemberton Pioneer Women, RR 1, Pemberton, BC V0N 2L0. Book publisher.
BRITISH COLUMBIA, CANADIAN HISTORY, WOMEN

Pen Print Inc, 230 E. 1st St. #A, Port Angeles, WA 98362-2905. Book publisher.
OTHER/UNSPECIFIED

Pendleton Record, 809 SE Court, Box 69, Pendleton, OR 97801. 503-276-2853. Weekly newspaper.
COMMUNITY

Peninsula Gateway, PO Box 407, Gig Harbor, WA 98335. 206-858-9921. Weekly newspaper.
COMMUNITY

Peninsula Magazine, PO Box 2259, Sequim, WA 98382. 206-683-5421. Editor: Rachel Bard. Quarterly magazine devoted to the Olympic Peninsula. Uses freelance material. Pays 10¢/wd. on publication. Acquires 1st rights. Submit query, SASE. Dot matrix, photocopied, simultaneous, electronic/modem OK. Reports in 1 mo. Publishes next issue. Accepts nonfiction, photos. Topics: Olympic Peninsula — outdoor activities, history, sports events, archaeology, culinary adventures, festivals/celebrations, unique business enterprises, craftspeople. Tips: avg length 400–1,700 wds; feature articles related to Olympic National Park, 2,500 wds. Guidelines available.
OUTDOOR, TRAVEL, WASHINGTON.

Pennypress Inc, 1100 23rd Ave E, Seattle, WA 98112. Contact: Penny Simkin. 206-324-1419. Publisher of 1 nonfiction, softcover original a year. Print run: 3,000. Rarely accepts freelance material. Query w/SASE. Dot matrix, photocopies, simultaneous submissions, electronic OK. Reports in 1–5 mos. Publishes in up to 2 yrs. "Our publications deal with controversial issues in childbearing and topics of interest to young families. They are accurate, up-to-date and encourage decision making by informed consumers in matters relating to maternity care and parenting…I am very selective and usually invite authors to write for Pennypress." Write w/query and ask for guidelines; they vary according to audience targeted. Catalog available.
FAMILY, HEALTH, WOMEN

People's Food Store Newsletter, 3029 SE 21st, Portland, OR 97202. 503-244-9133. Contact: Dave Kehoe. Bimonthly. Circ 500. Seeking freelance material. No pay. Topics: Natural foods and "wellness." Length: 425 wds is ideal. Wants food-oriented graphics, MacPaint or similar. Sample for SASE.
CONSUMER, ENVIRONMENT/RESOURCES, FOOD/COOKING

People's Law Books, Juvenile Rights Prj., 2325 E. Burnside, Portland, OR 97214. Book publisher.
EDUCATION, LAW

Perceptions, Language & Literature Division, Mt. Hood Community College, 26000 SE Stark, Gresham, OR 97030. 503-667-7657. Annual magazine. Circ 500. Uses freelance material. Byline given, pays copies, acquires 1st rights. Submit complete ms./SASE. Responds in 3 mos; publishes in early December. Accepts fiction, poetry, nonfiction, photos, fine art drawings. Send SASE for submission form and special announcements. Sample $3.
COLLEGE/UNIVERSITY, LITERARY

Perceptions, 1945 S 4th W, Missoula, MT 59801. 406-543-5875. Editor: Temi Rose. Chapbook journal of mostly women's poetry published 3 times a year. Uses 30 freelance mss per issue. Sub $3/yr. Pays copies on publication. Byline given. Submit query letter, SASE. Responds in 1 mo; publishing time varies. Accepts nonfiction, fiction, poetry, photos (B&W), cartoons. Guidelines available. Sample $3.
FICTION, POETRY, WOMEN

Performance Press, PO Box 7307, Everett, WA 98201-0307. 206-252-7660. Self-publisher of 3 softcover books a year on Catholic charismatics. Print run: 10,000. Not a freelance market. Catalog available.
FAMILY, HUMOR, RELIGION

Peridot Press, 1463 Marion St NE, Salem, OR 97301. Book publisher.
OTHER/UNSPECIFIED

Permaculture with Native Plants, Box 38, Lorane, OR 97451. Editor: Curtin Mitchell. Periodical.
AGRICULTURE/FARMING, ENVIRONMENT/RESOURCES, GARDENING

Permafrost, University of Alaska-Fairbanks, Department of English, Fairbanks, AK 99775-0640. 907-474-5237. Periodical. Sub $7. Circ 500. Uses freelance material. Pays copies. Submit ms, SASE. Dot matrix, photocopied OK. Reports in 1–3 mos. Accepts nonfiction, fiction, poetry, photos, other. Guidelines available. Sample $4.
COLLEGE/UNIVERSITY, FICTION, POETRY

Perseverance Theatre, 914 Third St, Douglas, AK 99824. Interested in scripts.
DRAMA

Pet Owners' Association, PO Box 2807, Portland, OR 97228. 503-297-7530. Editor: Joan Dahlberg. Publishes softcover books, videotapes, bimonthly magazine. Very limited acceptance of freelance material, assignment only. Byline given. Pays money on acceptance.
ANIMALS, BUSINESS, TRADE/ASSOCIATIONS

Pet Owners' Tribune, Pet Owners' Association, PO Box 2807, Portland, OR 97228. 503-297-7530. Editor: Joan Dahlberg. Bimonthly magazine. Circ 3500; subs $6/yr. Very limited acceptance of freelance material, assignment only. Byline given. Pays money on acceptance. Accepts cartoons, articles. Tips: retail management articles wanted. Catalog available. Sample $2.
ANIMALS, BUSINESS, TRADE/ASSOCIATIONS

Petarade Press, Box 65746 Stn F, Vancouver, BC V5N 5N7. 604-873-2703. Contact: Gordon Murray. Publishes 3 softcover, original performance texts per yr: novels, short stories, poetry. Query w/SASE, but not encouraged unless specifically performance oriented. Pay varies.
DRAMA, LITERARY, POETRY

Pharmaceutical Technology, 859 Willamette St, PO Box 10460, Springfield, OR 97440. 503-343-1200. Book publisher.
BUSINESS, SCIENCE

Phelps Enterprises, 3838 Kendra, Eugene, OR 97404. Book publisher.
OTHER/UNSPECIFIED

Philam Books Inc, 2101-2077 Nelson St, Vancouver, BC V6G 2Y2. Book publisher.
OTHER/UNSPECIFIED

Henry Philips Publishing, 19316 3rd Ave NW, Seattle, WA 98177. Book publisher.
OTHER/UNSPECIFIED

Phinney Ridge Review, Phinney Neighborhood Association, 6532 Phinney Ave N, Seattle, WA 98103. Editor: Ed Medeiros. Quarterly.
COMMUNITY, FAMILY, HEALTH

Phoenix Publishing Company, PO Box 10, Custer, WA 98240. Book publisher.
OTHER/UNSPECIFIED

Photography at Open-Space, 510 Fort St, Victoria, BC V8W 1E6. Book publisher.
PHOTOGRAPHY

Pictorial Histories Publishing Company, 713 S 3rd, Missoula, MT 59801. 406-549-8488. Contact: Stan Cohen. Publishes 12 hard- & softcover books/ yr. Accepts unsolicited submissions. No submission info given. Query w/ SASE.
GENERAL HISTORY, MILITARY/VETS, PHOTOGRAPHY

Pierce County Business Examiner, 5007 Pacific Hwy E, Ste 22, Tacoma, WA 98424. 206-922-1522. Editor: Jeff Rhodes. Ads: Jeff Rounce. Biweekly newspaper of business news for Tacoma-Pierce County. Circ 17,000. Sub $15. Uses 4 freelance mss per issue. Payment: $2/column inch and copies on publication. Byline given. Purchases 1st rights. Query w/SASE. Phone query, dot matrix, photocopies OK. Nonfiction: 2.5 pages ds. "Articles on business topics primarily for Pierce Co, but applicable to all of WA considered. Photos: B&W 5x7 or larger. $2/inch. Sample, SASE.
BUSINESS, WASHINGTON

Pika Press, PO Box 457, Enterprise, OR 97828. 503-426-3623. Editor: Rich Wandschneider. Publishes 3–5 hard- & softcover originals, reprints a year. Press run: 1,500–3,000. Pays royalties. Submit query w/clips, phone. Accepts: books of special interest to the inland Northwest. "Chances for an outside manuscript now are very slim. A year from now we should be better able to evaluate manuscripts."
NW/REGIONAL HISTORY, NORTHWEST, OUTDOOR

Pike Place Market Craft Catalog, 1916 Pike Place, Box 12-234, Seattle, WA 98101-1013. 206-587-5767. Editor: Paul Dunn. Quarterly.
CRAFTS/HOBBIES

Pike Place Market News, 85 Pike St #407, Seattle, WA 98101. 206-587-0351. Contact: Clayton Park. Monthly newspaper. Sub $12/yr. Circ 20,000. Uses freelance material pays copies, occasionally up to $25. Byline given. By assignment only, phone query. Dot matrix, photocopied mss OK. Accepts nonfiction, fiction, photos. Topics: articles about Pike Place Market or other public markets in the US, personal memoirs, or direct experience. Sample available with SASE.
COMMERCE, FICTION

Pill Enterprises, N22790, Hwy 101, Shelton, WA 98584. 206-877-5825. Self-publisher only. Not a freelance market.
FOOD/COOKING

Pinstripe Publishing, PO Box 711, Sedro-Woolley, WA 98284. 206-855-1416. Editor: Helen Gregory. Publishes 1–2 softcover original books/yr. Query only w/outline & SASE. How-to, small business & crafts. Booklist available.
BUSINESS, CRAFTS/HOBBIES, HOW-TO

Pioneer Log, Lewis and Clark College, LC Box 21, Portland, OR 97219. 503-244-6161. Student newspaper.
COLLEGE/UNIVERSITY, EDUCATION, ENTERTAINMENT

Pioneer News, Bank of British Columbia, 1165 - 555 Burrard St, Vancouver, BC V7X 1K1. Periodical.
BUSINESS

Pioneer Press Books, 37 S Palouse, Walla Walla, WA 99362. 509-522-2075. Editor: Robert A Bennett. Publisher of 3–5 hard- & softcover, books/yr. Pays royalties. Query, SASE. Report time varies. Nonfiction: Western history.
NW/REGIONAL HISTORY, NORTHWEST, OLD WEST

Pioneer Publishing Company, Box 190, Big Timber, MT 59011. Book publisher.
OTHER/UNSPECIFIED

Pioneer Square Gazette, Pioneer Square Association, PO Box 4006, Seattle, WA 98104. Editor: Lori Kinnear. Periodical, 3 times per yr.
OTHER/UNSPECIFIED

Pioneer Trails, Umatilla County Historical Society, PO Box 253, Pendleton, OR 97801. 503-276-0012. Contact: Julie Reese. Newsletter published 3X/yr. Sub $10/yr; circ 800. Uses freelance material. byline given. Submit query letter, complete ms, SASE. Photocopy, dot matrix OK. Responds in 2 mos; publishes in 6–12 mos. Accepts biography, photos, articles, memoirs. Topics: history of Umatilla County. Sample $2.
NW/REGIONAL HISTORY, OREGON

Planned Parenthood Association of Idaho, 4301 Franklin Rd, Boise, ID 83705. Book publisher.
EDUCATION, FAMILY

Playboard Magazine, 7560 Lawrence Dr, Burnaby, BC V5A 1T6. Editor: Mick Maloney. 604-738-5287. Mass circulation monthly magazine of entertainment and arts.
ARTS, ENTERTAINMENT

Playful Wisdom Press, PO Box 834, Kirkland, WA 98083-0834. 206-823-4421. Editor: William Ashoka Ross. Publishes softcover, original books. Accepts unsolicited submissions. Charges a reading free of $250. Submit query letter, sample chapters, SASE before the whole ms. Topics: "Playfully instructive insights about the human condition. Our books are for and by grownups who delight in childlike enthusiasm and celebrate being alive. We love love."
HUMOR, RELIGION, SEX

Pleneurethic International, Earth Light Bookstore, 113 E Main, Walla Walla, WA 99362. Book publisher. New Age books.
NEW AGE

Plugging In, Columbia Education Center, 11325 SE Lexington, Portland, OR 97266. 503-760-2346. Editor: Dr Ralph Nelsen. Periodical.
EDUCATION

Plus, Ste 410, 550 Burrard St, Vancouver, BC V6C 2J6. Editor: Don Stanley. Periodical.
OTHER/UNSPECIFIED

PMUG Mouse Tracks, PO Box 8895, Portland, OR 97207. 503-254-2111. Editor: Michael Pearce. Ads: Jim Lyle, 503-641-1587 or 255–5718. Monthly. Sub $24. Circ 900. Uses 7–10 freelance mss per issue. Written by Mac users. No pay. Acquires 1st rights. Byline given. Submit ms, SASE, phone. Electronic sub OK. Accepts nonfiction, cartoons. Guidelines available. Sample $4.
COMPUTERS

PNLA Quarterly, 1631 E 24th Ave, Eugene, OR 97403. 503-344-2027. Editor: Katherine G Eaton. Quarterly. Sub $15. Circ 1,100. Uses freelance material. Byline given. Phone query. Photocopied OK. Accepts nonfiction, cartoons. Sample. $6.50.
BOOK ARTS/BOOKS, LANGUAGE(S), PUBLISHING/PRINTING

Poe Studies, Washington State University Press, Pullman, WA 99164-5910. 509-335-3518. Semiannual. Sub $8. Nonfiction.
COLLEGE/UNIVERSITY, FICTION, LITERARY

Poetic Space, PO Box 11157, Eugene, OR 97440. Editor: Don Hildenbrand. Magazine published 3–4X/yr. Sub $15/yr; circ 800+. Uses freelance material. Pays copies on publication. Byline given. Acquires 1st rights. Submit ms, SASE. Dot matrix, photocopied subs OK. Reports in 2–4 mos. publishes in 2–3 mos. Accepts nonfiction, short (1,200–1,500 wds) fiction, contemporary poetry, literary essays (1,200–1,500 wds), line drawings, simple graphics, book reviews (600–1,000 wds). No traditional (rhymed) unless high quality; no sentimental, romantic. Guidelines available. Sample $4.
AVANT-GARDE/EXPERIMENTAL, FICTION, POETRY

Poeticus Obscuritant Publications, PO Box 85817, Seattle, WA 98145. Contact: Patrick McCabe. Book publisher.
POETRY

Poetry Exchange, c/o Horizon Books, PO Box 85477, Seattle, WA 98145-1477. Editor: Staff. Monthly community newsletter. Circ 1,400. Sub $10/yr. Assignment only. The Poetry Exchange includes a calendar of literary readings, announcements about small press books, workshops, and a mss wanted column. Also contains reviews and articles (query 1st — unsolicited material is not accepted.)
FICTION, POETRY, PUBLISHING/PRINTING

Poetry Northwest, 4045 Brooklyn Ave NE, University of Washington, Ja-15, Seattle, WA 98105. Periodical.
COLLEGE/UNIVERSITY, NORTHWEST, POETRY

Poetry Today, 5136 NE Glisan St, Portland, OR 97220. Periodical.
LITERARY, POETRY

Poets. Painters. Composers, 10254 35th Ave SW, Seattle, WA 98146. 206-937-8155. Contact: Joseph Keppler. Publisher of Poets. Painters. Composers, an arts journal; Colin's Magazine, a review of contemporary culture & technology; and various poetry books and broadsides. Accepts freelance material. Pays copies (negotiable). Query w/ms, SASE. Photocopies OK. Reports immediately. Publishes in 3 mos. Poetry, art, music, essays; experimental, short works, original in concept and design, provocative, ingenious, knowledgeable, beautiful.
ARTS, MUSIC, POETRY

Point of View, Aperture Northwest Inc, PO Box 24365, Seattle, WA 98124-0365. 206-382-9220. Editor: Richard K Woltjer. Monthly.
MEDIA/COMMUNICATIONS, NATURAL HISTORY, VISUAL ARTS

The Pointed Circle, Portland Community College–Cascade Campus, Terrell Hall, 4th Fl, 705 N Killingsworth, Portland, OR 97217. 503-244-6111 x5405. Editor/contact: M McNeill, M Dembrow, D Averill. Annual literary magazine. Pays copies, acquires 1st rights. Submit ms/SASE. Dot matrix, photocopied OK. Simultaneous sub OK with notice. Accepts previously unpublished nonfiction, fiction, poetry, photos, plays, cartoons. Guidelines, back issues available. Sample $2.50.
COLLEGE/UNIVERSITY, FICTION, POETRY

Points Northwest, Washington State University, Owen Science & Engineering Library, Pullman, WA 99164-3200. Periodical.
COLLEGE/UNIVERSITY

Points & Picas Magazine, 422 N Grant St, Moscow, ID 83843. 208-882-3373. Editor: Gary Lundgren. Periodical, 3 times a yr.
OTHER/UNSPECIFIED

Polestar Press, RR 1, Winlaw, BC V0G 2J0. Contact: Julian Ross. Book publisher.
POETRY, SPORTS

Polk County Itemizer-Observer, 147 SE Court St, Box 108, Dallas, OR 97338. 503-623-6364. Weekly newspaper.
COMMUNITY

Polson Flathead Courier, PO Box 1091, Polson, MT 59860. 406-883-4343. Newspaper.
COMMUNITY, OTHER/UNSPECIFIED

Poltergeist Press, 706 S Morain St, Kennewick, WA 99336. Book publisher.
OTHER/UNSPECIFIED

POME News, Home Orchard Society, PO Box 776, Clackamas, OR 97015. 503-630-3392. Editors: Winnifred and Ken Fisher. Quarterly newsletter. Sub $10. Circ 1,200. Uses freelance material. Byline given. Phone query. Photocopied, computer disk OK. Reports in 8 wks. Publishes in 1 yr. Accepts nonfiction articles on home-growing of fruits and nuts and recipes. Sample available.
AGRICULTURE/FARMING, FOOD/COOKING, GARDENING

Pond, Roger & Associates, 314 Pine Forest Rd, Goldendale, WA 98620. 509-773-4718. Contact: Roger Pond. Publishers of books on rural life.
FAMILY, RURAL

Ponderosa Publishers, 2037 Airport Rd, Saint Ignatius, MT 59865-9602. Book publisher.
OTHER/UNSPECIFIED

Pooka Press, 150 Mt. Olympus Dr NW, Issaquah, WA 98027. 206-392-6674. Self-publisher of hand-made books. Not a freelance market.
AVANT-GARDE/EXPERIMENTAL, OTHER/UNSPECIFIED

Pope International Publications, PO Box 203, Abbotsford, BC V2S 4N8. Book publisher.
OTHER/UNSPECIFIED

Poptart, 3505 Commercial Dr, Vancouver, BC V5N 4E8. Periodical. Accepts fiction, poetry, drawings.
FICTION, POETRY

Port Orford News, 519 W 10th, Box 5, Port Orford, OR 97465. 503-332-2361. Weekly newspaper.
COMMUNITY

Port Side: The Port of Portland Magazine, PO Box 3529, Portland, OR 97208. Quarterly with news and economic facts relating to shipping and cargo handling.
BUSINESS, MARITIME

Port/Manhattan Publishers, 6406 N Maryland Ave, Portland, OR 97217. Book publisher.
OTHER/UNSPECIFIED

The Portable Wall, Basement Press, c/o Dan Struckman, 215 Burlington, Billings, MT 59101. 406-256-3588. Editor: Gray Harris. Journal published 1 or 2 times a yr. Sub $5. Circ 200–500. Accepts freelance material. Pays copies on acceptance. Byline given. Submit ms, SASE. Dot matrix, photocopied OK. Publishes in 6–12 mos. Accepts nonfiction, fiction, poetry, cartoons. "This magazine is highest quality hand-set type on fine paper — articles and stories must be short, terse…can reproduce almost any line drawing…." Sample $5.
HUMOR, MONTANA, PICTURE

Portfolio, College of Business, Boise State University, Boise, ID 83725. Semiannual. Circ 2,500.
BUSINESS, COLLEGE/UNIVERSITY

The Portland Alliance, 2807 SE Stark, Portland, OR 97214. 503-239-4991. Contact; Joel Dippold. Monthly magazine. Circ 8,000, subs. $15/yr. Uses freelance material. Byline given, pays copies, acquires all rights. Submit query letter, SASE. Simultaneous, disk/modem subs OK. Responds in 1 wk; publishes in 1 mo. Accepts nonfiction, photos, news items, photos, cartoons, op/ed, reviews. Topics: news and views by and for progressive activists in Portland and the Northwest. Sample 50¢.
ENVIRONMENT/RESOURCES, POLITICS, SOCIALIST/RADICAL

Portland and Area Events, Three World Trade Center, 26 SW Salmon St, Portland, OR 97204-3299. 503–275-9787. Jacquie R. Smith. Monthly newspaper. Query letter, SASE, phone. Accepts news items.
CALENDAR/EVENTS, ENTERTAINMENT

Portland Atari Club Computer News, PO Box 1692, Beaverton, OR 97005. 503-667-3306. Editor: Teri Williams. Monthly.
COMPUTERS

Portland Family Calendar, Pry Publishing Co, 600 NW 14th Ave, Portland, OR 97209. 503-226-8335. Editor: Peggy J Coquet. Ads: Bill Cowley. Monthly tabloid, founded 1980. Sub $10/yr; circ 13,500. Uses freelance material. Byline given. Pays money, copies on publication. Submit query letter, clips, SASE, phone. Responds in 1 mo; publishes in 2 mos. Accepts news items, photos (B&W $5/ea.), interviews, op/ed, articles, reviews. Topics: prefer factual articles related to local parenting issues, resources, products. Guidelines, sample available.
CALENDAR/EVENTS, CHILDREN (BY/ABOUT), FAMILY

Portland Gray Panther Pulse, 1819 NW Everett, Portland, OR 97209. 503-224-5190. Monthly on issues of importance to older citizens.
SENIOR CITIZENS

The Portland Guide, 4475 SW Scholls Ferry Rd, Ste 256, Portland, OR 97225. Monthly visitor's guide for Portland. Focuses on events and directories.
CALENDAR/EVENTS, ENTERTAINMENT, TRAVEL

Portland Life & Business Magazine, Pacific Gateways Publications, Inc., 816 SW First, Portland, OR 97204. 503-997-8401. Editor: Rob Spooner. Ads: Carolyn Clemens. Bimonthly magazine founded in 1989. Sub $14.97/yr; circ 30,000. Uses freelance material. Byline given. Pays money on acceptance. Acquires 1st rights. Submit query letter, clips, phone; assignment only to correspond with editorial calendar. Responds in 1 wk; publishes in 2 mos. Accepts cartoons, biography, photos, interviews, articles, reviews. Guidelines, sample available.
BUSINESS, CALENDAR/EVENTS, CONSUMER

Portland Live Music Guide, PO Box 12072, Portland, OR 97212. 503-288-5846. Editor: Boyd Martin. Monthly magazine, directory. Sub $20/yr; circ 8,000. Uses freelance material. Byline given. Pays copies on publication. Acquires 1st, 2nd rights. Assignment only, submit query. Photocopy, dot matrix, simultaneous subs OK. Responds in 2 wks; publishes in 1 mo. Accepts interviews, cartoons, Photos (8x10 glossy). Tips: most acceptable are interviews with Portland musical artists. Sample $1.
CALENDAR/EVENTS, ENTERTAINMENT, MUSIC

Portland Media Review, University of Portland, 5000 N Willamette Blvd, Portland, OR 97203. Editor: Frank King. Periodical.
COLLEGE/UNIVERSITY, MEDIA/COMMUNICATIONS

Portland News of the Portland Chamber of Commerce, 221 NW 2nd, Portland, OR 97209. Periodical.
TRADE/ASSOCIATIONS, URBAN

Portland Observer, 2201 N Killingsworth, Box 3137, Portland, OR 97208. Weekly.
COMMUNITY

Portland Review, PO Box 751, Portland, OR 97207. 503-725-4531. Contact: Editor. Triannual magazine. Sub $12. Cir. 1,000. Uses freelance material. Pays copies on publication. Submit ms, SASE. Dot matrix, photocopied, simultaneous OK. Accepts nonfiction, fiction (under 6,000 wds), poetry, photos, plays, cartoons. Photos: B&W only. "We're a city publication with an urban look and perspective … encourage cultural variety and political overtones…. We'd like to hear from more Black, American Indian, Hispanic, and Asian writers, or works dealing with other subcultural groups…. Don't be afraid to be radical." Guidelines available. Sample $3.
AVANT-GARDE/EXPERIMENTAL, LITERATURE, PHOTOGRAPHY

Portland Scribe, Multnomah County Medical Society, 4540 SW Kelly Ave, Portland, OR 97201. 503-222-9977. Editor: Rob Delf. Biweekly trade publication, founded in 1983. Sub $30/yr; circ 3,000. Uses freelance material. Byline given. Pays money on publication. Acquires 1st rights. Submit query letter, complete ms, phone. Photocopy subs OK. Responds in 1 day, publishes in 2 wks. Accepts news items, photos, interviews, articles. Topics: health and the politics, economics and business of health care. Sample available.
GOVERNMENT, HEALTH, PUBLIC AFFAIRS

Positively Entertainment & Dining, PO Box 16009, Portland, OR 97233. 503-253-0513. Editor: Bonnie Carter. Monthly. Sub $14. Circ 10,000. Uses freelance material. Byline given. Submit query w/clips, phone. Photocopied OK. Accepts nonfiction, photos, plays, cartoons. Sample available.
ENTERTAINMENT, FOOD/COOKING, SPORTS

Post Point Press, PO Box 4393, Bellingham, WA 98227. 206-676-9531. Editor: Jack W Bazhaw. Book publisher.
ANTHROPOLOGY/ARCHÆOLOGY

Post Register, 333 Northgate Mile, Idaho Falls, ID 83401. Newspaper.
COMMUNITY

Postcard/Paper Club Newsletter, Box 814, E Helena, MT 59635. Editor: Tom Mulvaney. Quarterly.
CRAFTS/HOBBIES

Potato Country, Box 1467, Yakima, WA 98907. Editor: D Brent Clement. 509-248-2452. Published 9 times a year featuring potato industry of OR, WA, ID. Circ 6,000. Payment: $100 on publication. Byline given. Rights purchased: All. Query w/ms, SASE. Dot matrix OK. Reports immediately. Nonfiction: 5–6 ds pages on features and news. Photos: W/mss, B&W. Guidelines available.
AGRICULTURE/FARMING, BUSINESS

Potato Grower of Idaho, Harris Publishing Inc, PO Box 981, Idaho Falls, ID 83402. Editor: Steve Janes. 208-522-5187. Monthly.
AGRICULTURE/FARMING, BUSINESS, IDAHO

Potboiler Magazine, Richards Rd, Roberts Creek, BC VON 2W0. Editor/ads: L R Davidson. 604-885-3985. Semiannual. Circ 250–300. Sub $5. Uses 7–12 mss per issue. Payment: Copies on publication. Byline given. Rights purchased: First. Query w/ms, SASE. Photocopies OK. Reports in 6–8 wks. Fiction, cartoons, comics. "Science fiction, fantasy, horror, weird, unusual, mainstream, graphic stories, fumetti, comics, collage pieces." Guidelines and sample available.
AVANT-GARDE/EXPERIMENTAL, FANTASY/SCI FI, SATIRE

Potlatch Times, Potlatch Corporation, Western Division, PO Box 1016, Lewiston, ID 83501. Editor: Bea Davis. Monthly for employees and business community. Circ 6,500.
BUSINESS

Poverty Bay Publishing Company, 529 SW 294th St, Federal Way, WA 98003. Book publisher.
OTHER/UNSPECIFIED

Poverty Hill Press, PO Box 519, Leavenworth, WA 98826. Book publisher.
OTHER/UNSPECIFIED

Powell River Heritage Research Assn, 7155 Hazelton St, Powell River, BC V8A 1P9. 604-485-2222. Editors: Karen Southern, Peggy Bird. Publishes hard- & softcover books on NW regional history. Does not accept unsolicited submissions. Submit query letter, outline, SASE.
NW/REGIONAL HISTORY

Powell's Books, 1005 W Burnside St, Portland, OR 97209. Editor: Terry Naito. 503-228-4651. Periodical. "This publication will be about books and more books…to provide a 'behind the scenes' look at Powell's Books itself…how and why we choose the used books that we do, and offer tips on selling us your own used books."
BOOK ARTS/BOOKS, LITERARY, PUBLISHING/PRINTING

Prasad Press, PO Box 11804, Eugene, OR 97440. 503-741-3992. Contact: Richard Reed. Book publisher.
OTHER/UNSPECIFIED

Prensa Samizdat, Publishers Research Service, PO Box 21094, Seattle, WA 98111. Contact: Maria Abdin. Publishes saddle-stitched booklets, corner-stapled mss. Submit abstract and/or outline, SASE. Reports "ASAP." Accepts nonfiction. Topics: monographs furthering individual, family and public strength and well-being; public health/sanitation, appropriate technology, alternative health and education, preventive health care, medical subjects for laymen. Tips: particularly interested in environmental health. Guidelines available.
HEALTH, MEDICAL, NATIVE AMERICAN

The Preschool Times, 12311 NE Glisan #103, Portland, OR 97230. 503-256-2833. Contact: Shelli Smith. Quarterly newsletter concerned with activities for families with children aged 2–12. No submission info available.
CHILDREN (BY/ABOUT), FAMILY

Prescott Street Press, PO Box 40312, Portland, OR 97240-0312. 503-254-2922. Publisher of hard- & softcover originals. Accepts freelance submissions. Payment negotiated. Rights purchased: first, all. Reports in 1 mo. Submit query letter, SASE. Publishing time varies. Topics: poetry, art. PSP arranges artwork and pays artist. Catalog available.
ARTS, POETRY

Press Gang Publishers Ltd, 603 Powell St, Vancouver, BC V6A 1H2. 604-253-2537. Editor: Della McCreary. Publishes softcover originals. Accepts unsolicited submissions. Pays royalties. Acquires all rights. Submit query w/ clips, SASE. Dot matrix, photocopied, computer disk OK. Reports in 2–4 mos; publishes in 12 mos. Accepts nonfiction, fiction, priority to Canadian women's writing. Seeking submissions by Native women. "We are a feminist collective interested in publishing fiction and nonfiction that challenges traditional assumptions about women and provides a feminist framework for understanding our experience. We look for work that is not homophobic, racist, classist or sexist." Catalog available.
FEMINISM, GAY/LESBIAN, NATIVE AMERICAN

Press Porcepic Ltd, 4252 Commerce Circle, Victoria, BC V8W 4M2. Contact: Guy Chadsey. 604-727-6522. Publishes softcover trade books. Accepts freelance material. Pays royalties, advance negotiable. Acquires all rights. Submit query letter, outline, sample chapters, SASE. Simultaneous OK. Reports in 3–4 mos; publishes in 12 mos. Accepts science fiction, poetry. "We publish Canadian authors only." Guidelines/catalog available.
BRITISH COLUMBIA, FANTASY/SCI FI, POETRY

Pressing America, PO Box 201672, Anchorage, AK 99520. Contact: Michael Meyers. 907-272-4257. Book publisher. Query w/SASE.
FICTION, LITERARY, POLITICS

Preston & Betts, c/o Camosun College, Victoria, BC V8P 5J2. Book publisher.
COLLEGE/UNIVERSITY

Price Guide Publishers, PO Box 525, Kenmore, WA 98028. Book publisher.
BUSINESS, CONSUMER

Price Productions, 373 Altadena, Astoria, OR 97103. 503-325-3733. Contact: Juanita B Price. Publishes a bibliography of authors and illustrators of children's books in Oregon. SASE for catalog.
CHILDREN (BY/ABOUT), REFERENCE/LIBRARY, WRITING

Primary Treasure, PO Box 7000, Boise, ID 83707. Editor: Louis Schutter. Periodical.
CHILDREN (BY/ABOUT), RELIGION

Primavera Productions, PO Box 669, Union, OR 97883. Book publisher.
OTHER/UNSPECIFIED

Prime Time, North Bend Publishing Co, PO Box 507, North Bend, OR 97459. 503-443-1322. Editor: Gail Snyder. Ads: Bruce Root. Monthly newspaper. Free to seniors. Circ 9,000. Uses freelance material. Pays $25 on publication. Byline given. Submit query for assignment only, SASE. Simultaneous OK. Reports in 2–3 mos; publishes in 1–2 mos. Accepts nonfiction, photos (B&W negatives), senior issues and features with a local slant (Coos County), 500–600 wds. Guidelines available. Sample 75¢.
RURAL, SENIOR CITIZENS

Princess Publishing, PO Box 386, Beaverton, OR 97005. 503-646-1234. Editor: Cheryl Matschek. Publishes hard- & softcover originals. Accepts unsolicited submissions. Submit query letter, outline, sample chapters, complete ms, SASE. Reports in 2 wks; publishes in 3 mos. Accepts nonfiction. Topics: self-help, new age, sales, management, business. Guidelines available, SASE.
ASTROLOGY/SPIRITUAL, BUSINESS, PSYCHOLOGY

The Print, Clackamas Community College, 19600 S Molalla Ave, Oregon City, OR 97045. 503-657-8400. Newspaper.
COLLEGE/UNIVERSITY

The Printer's Devil, PO Box 66, Harrison, ID 83833-0066. 208-689-3738. Tri-annual newsletter founded in 1986. Sub $4.50/yr; circ 600. Uses freelance material. Pays copies on publication. Submit query letter, clips, complete ms, synopsis, outline, SASE. Photocopies, dot matrix, simultaneous subs OK. Reports in 1 mo; publishes in 6 mos. Accepts news items, interviews, op/ed, reviews, memoirs, photos (B&W glossy, query on color), cartoons. Topics: graphic arts for the small press, best formalized and illustrated. Guidelines available. Sample for postage.
HOW-TO, PUBLISHING/PRINTING, VISUAL ARTS

The Printer's Northwest Trader, 736 SE Ankeny St, Portland, OR 97214. 503-234-5792. Editor: Sandy Hubbard. Ads: David Mann. Monthly for graphic arts industry. Sub $10; circ 4,800. Uses freelance material. Pays copies. Byline given. Query by phone. Dot matrix, photocopied subs OK. Responds in 1 wk; publishes in 1–2 mos. Accepts nonfiction, news items, photos (B&W glossy), interviews, reviews. Topics: new products, printing news, trade activity highlights. Guidelines available. Sample $2.50.
ARTS, PUBLISHING/PRINTING, TRADE/ASSOCIATIONS

Printery Farm, 153 Benson Rd, Port Angeles, WA 98362. 206-457-0248. Self-publisher of 2–3 softcover originals a year. Press run: 200. Not a freelance market.
BIOGRAPHY, FAMILY

Prism, University Student Media Committee, Oregon State University, Corvallis, OR 97331. Editor: David Fowler. Quarterly magazine.
COLLEGE/UNIVERSITY

PRISM International, Department of Creative Writing, University of British Columbia, Vancouver, BC V6T 1W5. 604-255-9332. Editor: Blair Rosser. Quarterly magazine. Sub $12/yr. Circ 1,200. Uses freelance material. Pays $30/page on publication. Acquires 1st rights. Byline given. Submit ms, SASE. Dot matrix, photocopied OK. Reports & publishes up to 3 mos. Accepts fiction, poetry, plays, cover art, imaginative nonfiction (as opposed to

reviews, articles). "We like to see imaginative, fresh & new work." US contributors use SASE w/IRCs. Tips: "…read one or two back issues before submitting…always looking for new and exciting writers." Guidelines available. Sample $4.
DRAMA, FICTION, POETRY

Professional Business Communications, 11830 SW Kerr Pkwy, Ste 350, Lake Oswego, OR 97035. 503-293-1163. Contact: Marian Woodall. Publisher softcover books on public speaking and communications skills. Not a market.
HOW-TO

Programmer's Journal, PO Box 30160, Eugene, OR 97403. Periodical.
COMPUTERS

Progress, Clark College, 1800 E McLoughlin, Vancouver, WA 98663. 206-699-0159. Weekly newspaper.
COLLEGE/UNIVERSITY

The Progress, 910 Marion, Seattle, WA 98104. Editor: Bill Dodds. Monthly.
OTHER/UNSPECIFIED

Progressive Woman, 1208 SW 13th, Ste 212, Portland, OR 97205. 503-223-9344. Editor: Dona-Rose Pappas. Ads: Nancie Hammond. Monthly newspaper. Sub $12. Circ 20,000+. Uses freelance material. Pays on publication. Acquires 1st rights. Byline given. Unsolicited submissions accepted. Submit query w/clips, SASE; phone query, dot matrix, photocopied, simultaneous OK. Reports in 10 days. Publishes in several weeks. Accepts fiction, nonfiction, poetry, cartoons, photos, news items, biographies, interviews, op/ed, reviews, memoirs. Topics: articles of interest to Oregon businesswomen. Back issues $3 each.
BUSINESS, FEMINISM, WOMEN

Property Tax Charges, Associated Taxpayers of Idaho, PO Box 1665, Boise, ID 83701. Editor: Sue Fowler. Annual.
CONSUMER, IDAHO, PUBLIC AFFAIRS

Prosser Record-Bulletin, PO Box 750, Prosser, WA 99350. 509-786-1711 Weekly newspaper.
COMMUNITY

The Province, 2250 Granville St, Vancouver, BC V6H 3G2. No info. Query w/SASE.
OTHER/UNSPECIFIED

Provincial Archives of British Columbia, Sound and Moving Image Division, Victoria, BC V8V 1X4. Book publisher.
BRITISH COLUMBIA, CANADIAN HISTORY, VISUAL ARTS

ProWOMAN, MatriMedia, PO Box 6957, Portland, OR 97228. 503-221-1298. Editor: Judy Henderson. Ads: Colleen Hill. A bimonthly magazine. Circ 15,000. Sub $12/yr. Accepts freelance material. Gives byline. Pays copies or other remuneration on publication. Acquires 1st rights. Query w/ SASE and clips. Disk/modem submission OK. Responds in 3-4 wks; publishes in 2-4 mos. Uses news items, nonfiction, interviews, articles, photos. Guidelines available; back issue $2.50.
BUSINESS, WOMEN

PSI Research/The Oasis Press, 300 N Valley Dr, Grants Pass, OR 97526. 503-479-9464. Contact: Virginia Groso. Publisher of hard- & softcover originals and reprints. Pays money, royalties in advance, upon publication. Acquires all rights. Byline given — author's name on book cover. Submit ms w/SASE or query by phone. Dot matrix, photocopies OK. Reports in 2 wks. Publishing time varies, but 1 yr at most. Accepts fiction. Topics: wide variety of business subjects; especially sales, management, decision-making, customer service, interviewing, leadership. Guidelines available.
BUSINESS, FICTION

PSU Magazine, Portland State University Alumni News, PO Box 751, Portland, OR 97207. 503-725-3711. Contact: Kathryn Kirkland. Quarterly magazine founded in 1987. Circ 43,000. Uses assigned freelance material. Byline given. Pays 15¢/wd on publication. Submit query letter. Responds in 2 wks; publishes in 1 mo. Accepts nonfiction. Sample available.
COLLEGE/UNIVERSITY, EDUCATION, ENTERTAINMENT

Ptarmigan Press, 2727 NE Blakeley, Seattle, WA 98105. Book publisher.
OTHER/UNSPECIFIED

Ptarmigan Press, 1372 Island Hwy, Campbell River, BC V9W 2E1. Contact: Ann Kask. Book publisher.
OTHER/UNSPECIFIED

Publication Development Inc, Box 23383, Portland, OR 97223. Editor: Jim Wilson. Book publisher.
OTHER/UNSPECIFIED

Publications in History, University of Montana, Missoula, MT 59812. Book publisher.
AMERICAN HISTORY, NW/REGIONAL HISTORY, MONTANA

Publishers' Press, 1935 SE 59th Ave, Portland, OR 97215. Book publisher.
OTHER/UNSPECIFIED

Publishing Enterprises Inc, PO Box 4122, Kent, WA 98032. Book publisher.
OTHER/UNSPECIFIED

Puffin Press, 151 Wallace Way NE, Bainbridge Island, WA 98110. Book publisher.
OTHER/UNSPECIFIED

Puget Sound Business Journal, 101 Yesler Way, #200, Seattle, WA 98104. Editor: Al Hooper. 206-583-0701. Ads: Steven Maris. Weekly of local and regional business news and business features. Circ 20,000. Sub $26. Uses 1 ms per issue. Payment: $75-150 on acceptance. Byline given. Rights purchased: First. Phone query, dot matrix OK. Reports in 1 wk. Nonfiction: up to four ds pages. Cartoons. Photos: on assignment only. Sample/free SASE.
BUSINESS, ECONOMICS, WASHINGTON

Puget Sound Women's Digest, PO Box 1712, Tacoma, WA 98401. 206-627-8367. Contact: Sue MacStravic, editor. Monthly magazine. Sub $15/yr. Welcomes freelance material. Topics: local women's concerns, issues. No submissions info.
WOMEN

Pulphouse: A Weekly Magazine, Box 1227, Eugene, OR 97440. 503-344-6742. Editor: Kristine Kathryn Rusch. Ads: Dean W Smith. Science fiction and fantasy weekly. Uses freelance material. Byline given. Pays money, advance, royalties. Acquires 1st or anthology rights. Submit query letter, complete ms. Simultaneous subs OK. Responds in 2 mos; publishes in 8 mos. Accepts fiction, cartoons, nonfiction, photos. Guidelines available.
FANTASY/SCI FI, FICTION, WRITING

Pulphouse Publishing, Box 1227, Eugene, OR 97440. 503-344-6742. Editor: Kristine Kathryn Rusch. Publisher of hard- & softcover books (including Axolotl Press Series and Writer's Notebook Press) and five periodicals (Pulphouse, Author's Choice Monthly, and Mondad). Uses freelance material. Byline given. Pays money, advance, royalties. Acquires 1st or anthology rights. Submit query letter, complete ms. Simultaneous subs OK. Responds in 2 mos; publishes in 8 mos. Accepts fiction, cartoons, nonfiction, photos. Topics: science fiction, fantasy. Guidelines, catalog available.
FANTASY/SCI FI, FICTION, WRITING

Puppet Concepts Publishing, PO Box 15203, Portland, OR 97215. 503-236-4034. Contact: Susan Barthel or Bruce Chessé. Books on puppetry and puppet construction. Not accepting manuscripts.
DRAMA, EDUCATION, ENTERTAINMENT

Quality Paperbacks, PO Box 7, Boring, OR 97009. 503-663-3428. Contact: Mabel Johnson. Book publisher.
OTHER/UNSPECIFIED

Quality Publications, 12180 SW 127th, Tigard, OR 97223. Self-publisher.
OTHER/UNSPECIFIED

The Quarterdeck Review, Columbia River Maritime Museum, 1792 Marine Dr, Astoria, OR 97103. 503-325-2323. Editor: Hobe Kytr. Quarterly for museum members on museum news and maritime history. Circ 2,000. Not a freelance market. Sample $1.
NW/REGIONAL HISTORY, MARITIME

Quarterly Review, Center for the Study of Women in Society, University of Oregon, Eugene, OR, 97403. Quarterly.
COLLEGE/UNIVERSITY, WOMEN

The Quartz Press, PO Box 465, Ashland, OR 97520. 503-482-8119. Publisher of 2 softcover books a year. Print run: 100. Accepts freelance material. Payment: Royalties negotiated. Dot matrix, photocopies OK. Reports in 6 mos. Publishes in 1–2 yrs. Nonfiction, fiction, poetry, plays. "We seek revolutionary material with no known market, and hence not publishable commercially."
CULTURE, FICTION, POETRY

The Quartz Theatre, Box 465, Ashland, OR 97520. Interested in scripts.
DRAMA

Queen Anne News, 225 West Galer, Seattle, WA 98119. 206-282-0900. Weekly newspaper.
COMMUNITY

Queen Anne's Lace Quarterly, Doorway Publishers, PO Box 707, Poulsbo, WA 98370. 206-297-7952. Editors: Doris Moore, Connie Lord. Quarterly magazine; circ 500; subs $20/yr. Uses freelance material. Byline given, pays copies on publication. Submit query/SASE. Responds in 2 wks; publishes in 3 mos. Accepts poetry, nonfiction, articles, memoirs. Topics: environment/resources, philosophy, natural history. Guidelines available. Sample $5.
ENVIRONMENT/RESOURCES, NATURAL HISTORY, PHILOSOPHY

Quest, Reed College, 3203 SW Woodstock Blvd, Portland, OR 97202. 503-771-1112. Weekly newspaper.
COLLEGE/UNIVERSITY

Quest for Excellence, St Luke's Regional Medical Center, 190 E Bannock, Boise, ID 83712. Editor: Rita Ryan. Quarterly magazine for patients, staff and friends of the hospital. Circ 17,000.
HEALTH

Quest Northwest, PO Box 200, Salkum, WA 98582. Contact: Dean Marshall. 206-985-2999. Book publisher.
OTHER/UNSPECIFIED

Questar Publishers Inc, PO Box 1720, Sisters, OR 97759. 503-549-1144. Editor: Thomas Hale Womack. Ads: Brenda Jacobson. Publishes hard- & softcover books. Accepts unsolicited submissions. Pays royalties. Acquires all rights. Submit query letter, outline, sample chapters, SASE. Photocopied, dot matrix subs OK. Responds in 1 mo; publishes in 6–18 mos. Accepts fiction, nonfiction, biography.
BIOGRAPHY, CHILDREN/TEEN, FICTION

Quicksilver Productions, Box 340, Ashland, OR 97520. 503-482-5343. Publisher of 4 books a year.
OTHER/UNSPECIFIED

Quimper Press, c/o Port Townsend Publishing, PO Box 552, Port Townsend, WA 98368-0552. Book publisher.
OTHER/UNSPECIFIED

Quincy Valley Post-Register, PO Box 217, Quincy, WA 98848. 509-787-4511. Weekly newspaper.
COMMUNITY

R C Publications, 1828 NE Stanton, Portland, OR 97212. 503-287-1009. Self-publisher. Not a freelance market. Catalog available.
CRAFTS/HOBBIES, HOW-TO

R&M Press, Perkins Building, 1103 A St, Tacoma, WA 948402. 206-272-1609. Editors: Ann Roush, Jon Martin. Publishes hard- & softcover books. Accepts unsolicited submissions. Pays royalties. Submit query letter, outline, sample chapters, SASE. Responds in 4 wks; publishes in 9 mos. Accepts nonfiction. Topics: textbooks, how-to. Guidelines, catalog available.
FOOD/COOKING, TEXTBOOKS

R N Idaho, Idaho State Nurses Association, 200 N 4th St #20, Boise, ID 83702-6001. Periodical 6 times a year. Circ 750.
BUSINESS, HEALTH, LABOR/WORK

Racing Wheels, 7502 NE 133rd Ave, Vancouver, WA 98662. 206-892-5590. Periodical.
CRAFTS/HOBBIES

the raddle moon, 9060 Ardmore Dr, Sidney, BC V8L 3S1. 604-656-4045. Editor: Susan Clark. Semiannual literary journal. Sub $8. Circ 700. Uses freelance material. Submit ms w/SASE. Photocopied OK. Reports in 2 mos. Accepts nonfiction, fiction, poetry, photos, plays, other. "...publishing language-centered and 'new lyric' poetry, essays, fiction, photographs and graphics."
FICTION, LITERARY, POETRY

Radiance Herbs & Massage Newsletter, 113 E Fifth, Olympia, WA 98501. 206-357-9470. Editor: Barbara Park. Ads: Carolyn McIntyre. Bimonthly periodical. Sub free/$5. Circ 10,000. Uses 1–2 freelance mss per issue. Byline given. Phone assignment, SASE. Accepts nonfiction, poetry, photos, cartoons. Sample 50¢.
GARDENING, HEALTH, POETRY

Rae Publications, PO Box 731, Brush Prairie, WA 98606-0731. 206-687-3767. Contact: Pat Redjou. Self-publisher only. Not a freelance market.
FOOD/COOKING

Railway Milepost Books, 4398 Valencia Ave, North Vancouver, BC V7N 4B1. Book publisher.
OTHER/UNSPECIFIED

Rain, Clatsop Community College, Astoria, OR 97103. College literary magazine. SASE for guidelines.
COLLEGE/UNIVERSITY, FICTION, LITERARY

Rain Belt Publications Inc, 18806 40th Ave W, Lynnwood, WA 98036. Book publisher.
OTHER/UNSPECIFIED

Rainbow News, Oregon Rainbow Coalition, PO Box 6797, Portland, OR 97228-6797. Periodical of political news.
LAW, MINORITIES/ETHNIC, POLITICS

Raincoast Books, 112 E 3rd Ave, Vancouver, BC V5T 1C8. Book publisher.
BRITISH COLUMBIA, OUTDOOR

Rainforest Publishing, PO Box 101251, Anchorage, AK 99510. 907-274-8687. Editor: Duncan Frazier. Publishes 1–3 softcover books a year. Press run 3,000. Payment negotiated. Acquires 1st rights. Submit query. Photocopied, simultaneous OK. Reports in 1 mo. Publishes in 6 mos. Accepts nonfiction on any Alaska-related topic. Catalog available.
ALASKA

Rainy Day Press, PO Box 3035, Eugene, OR 97403. 503-484-4626. Contact: Mike Helm. Publishes books of NW folklore, history, poetry. Has not published for others yet, but would "listen to a good idea."
NW/REGIONAL HISTORY, NORTHWEST, POETRY

Rainy Day Publishing, 13222 SE 57th St, Bellevue, WA 98006. Contact: Renae R Knapp. 206-746-0802. Book publisher.
OTHER/UNSPECIFIED

Ralmar Press, 3623 SW Nevada St, Portland, OR 97219. Book publisher.
OTHER/UNSPECIFIED

Ramalo Publications, 2107 N Spokane St, Post Falls, ID 83854. 208-773-9416. Editor: Marie Fish. Book publisher. Accepts unsolicited submissions. Submit complete ms, SASE. Photocopy OK. Responds in 6 wks; publishes in 1 yr. Accepts fiction, poetry, cartoons, articles. Topics: family-oriented
FAMILY, FICTION, POETRY

Rancher-Stockman-Farmer, PO Box 714, Meridian, ID 83642. 208-888-1165. Contact: Frank Thomason. Quarterly newspaper.
AGRICULTURE/FARMING

Rand & Sarah Publisher Ltd, Box 94368, Richmond, BC V6Y 2A8. 604-278-0624. Contact: Sidney Cole. Books on history of BC and regional nonfiction. No submissions accepted.
BRITISH COLUMBIA, CANADIAN HISTORY

Random Lengths, PO Box 867, Eugene, OR 97440-0867. 503-686-9925. Weekly periodical with reports on N American forest products marketing. Print run: 12,300. Sub rate: $145. Not a freelance market. Sample/$2.50.
BUSINESS, LUMBER

Random Lengths Publications Inc, PO Box 867, Eugene, OR 97440-0867. 503-686-9925. Self-publisher weekly, biweekly newsletters, 3 hard- & softcover books/yr. Not a freelance market.
BUSINESS

Ravali Republic, 232 Main St, Hamilton, MT 59840. 406-363-3300. Newspaper.
COMMUNITY, OTHER/UNSPECIFIED

Raven Press, PO Box 135, Lake Oswego, OR 97034. Editor: Richard W Helbock. Book publisher.
OTHER/UNSPECIFIED

Raxas Books, 207 W Hastings St #1103, Vancouver, BC V6B 1H7. Publisher of cookbooks and guides.
CRAFTS/HOBBIES, FOOD/COOKING, HOW-TO

RB Publishing Co, Box 5203, Vancouver, WA 98668. Publishes books on women and work.
LABOR/WORK, WOMEN

The Reader, 1751 W Second Ave, Vancouver, BC V6J 1H7. 604-681-0041. Editor: Kevin Dale McKeown. Bimonthly magazine of book reviews. Sub free.
BOOK ARTS/BOOKS, LITERARY

The Real Comet Press, 3131 Western Ave #410, Seattle, WA 98121-1028. 206-283-7827. Editor: Ann Ross or Catherine Hillenbrand. Ads: Suzanne Albright. Publishes 6–8 hard- & softcover, originals, reprints/yr. Accepts unsolicited submissions. Pays royalties, advance. Submit query w/clips, SASE. Accepts nonfiction, comics. Topics: contemporary culture, especially where art, humor and social commentary intertwine. Catalog available.
ARTS, CULTURE, HUMOR

Realms, PO Box 5737, Grants Pass, OR 97527. Contact: Guy Kenyon, editor. Bimonthly journal. Sub $8/yr. Pays 3 copies for first rights. Submit ms. Dot matrix, photocopied OK. No simultaneous subs. Topics: traditional fantasy fiction — sorcery, elves, dragons, castles, etc. Max 12–15,000 words, possible serialization. Also seeking cover and interior artwork. Sample $1.50.
FANTASY/SCI FI, FICTION,

Record, PO Box 458, Odessa, WA 99159. 509-982-2632. Weekly newspaper.
COMMUNITY

The Record, ASUO Publications, Ste 4 EMU, University of Oregon, Eugene, OR 97403. Periodical.
COLLEGE/UNIVERSITY

The Record-Courier, 1718 Main, Box 70, Baker, OR 97814. 503-523-5353. Weekly newspaper.
COMMUNITY

Recovery Life, PO Box 31329, Seattle, WA 98103. 206-527-8999 or 800-252-6624. Editor: Neil Scott. Bi-monthly inserted into Alcoholism & Addiction Magazine. Uses freelance material. Pays in copies. Byline given. Submit ms, SASE. Dot matrix, photocopied OK. Accepts nonfiction, fiction, poetry. Topics: principles of addiction recovery, first-person stories, physical fitness, nutrition, humor, tips, recipes. Tips: upbeat poetry, tips on planning a sober vacation, holiday season, etc. Guidelines available. Sample $5.
HEALTH, PSYCHOLOGY

Recreation Consultants, 610 Hillside Dr. E, Seattle, WA 98111-5056. 206-329-7894. Self-publisher. Not a freelance market.
RECREATION

Red Cedar Press, 606 First St, Nanaimo, BC V9R1Y9. 604-753-8417. Editor: W & A Baker, L McLeod. Ads: A Baker. Publishes 2 softcover books/yr. Press run 500–1,000. Does not accept unsolicited submissions at the present time.
CANADA, NW/REGIONAL HISTORY, LITERARY

Red Letter Press, 409 Maynard Ave S, Ste 201, Seattle, WA 98104. 206-682-0990. Editor: Helen Gilbert. Publisher of fiction and nonfiction softcover books on socialism, feminism, people of color, lesbians/gays, world events, history, commentary, poetry. Does not accept unsolicited submissions. Query w/SASE.
FEMINISM, MINORITIES/ETHNIC, SOCIALIST/RADICAL

Red Lyon Publications, 2123 Marlow, Eugene, OR 97401-6431. Book publisher.
OTHER/UNSPECIFIED

Red Octopus Theatre Company, PO Box 1403, Newport, OR 97365. "Invites original, one-act scripts for its annual Original Scripts workshop. Performances by professional actors are provided of selected plays. Scripts are solicited during June for fall performance. The playwrights have workshop time with actors and a director to develop the scripts. Professional critique and honorariums are provided." Query w/SASE.
DRAMA

Redmond Spokesman, 226 NW Sixth, Box 788, Redmond, OR 97756. 503-548-2184. Weekly newspaper.
COMMUNITY

The Redneck Review of Literature, PO Box 730, Twin Falls, ID 83303. 208-734-6653. Penelope Reedy. Semiannual journal founded 1975. Sub $14/yr; circ 500. Uses freelance material. Byline given. Pays copies. Acquires 1st rights. Submit query letter, complete ms, SASE. Photocopy OK. Responds in 2–8 wks; publishes in 6 mos. Accepts fiction, poetry, cartoons, essays, articles, plays, reviews. Topics: contemporary western American literature and related topics. Guidelines available. Sample $7.
FICTION, LITERATURE, POETRY

Reed, The Quarterly Magazine of Reed College, Reed College, 3203 SE Woodstock, Portland, OR 97202. Editor: S Eugene Thompson. Periodical.
COLLEGE/UNIVERSITY, EDUCATION

Reference & Research Book News, 5600 NE Hassalo, Portland, OR 97213-3640. 503-281-9230. Editor/ads: Jane Erskine. Quarterly, reviews reference books. Sub $48; circ 2,100. Assigned only. "Consider assigning book reviews to specially qualified librarians." Pays money on acceptance. Possible byline. "This publication lists and reviews 500–600 newly published reference books each issue for the benefit of librarians who buy books. Reviews are 80–150 wds. Payment varies according to qualifications of the reviewer." Sample $5.
ABSTRACTS/INDICES, REFERENCE/LIBRARY

Reference-West, 2450 Central Ave, Victoria, BC, V8S 2S8. Limited edition chapbooks. Book publisher.
LITERARY

Reflections Directory, PO Box 13070, Portland, OR 97213. Editor: Beth Howell. 503-281-4486. Ads: John Ivy. Quarterly on holistic health. Circ 35,000. Sub $8. Accepts freelance material. Byline given. Rights purchased: First. Phone query, dot matrix, photocopies, electronic OK. Nonfiction (max 700 wds), poetry, photos (B&W glossy), cartoons. Topics: holistic health, thinking; people doing business in a holistic manner. Sample available.
HEALTH, PEACE, PSYCHOLOGY

Reflections Publishing, Box 178, Gabriola, BC V0R 1X0. 604-247-8685. Contact: Neil Aitken. Publisher of books on ecology, human rights, and Native American issues. Press runs of 2,000–2,500. Acquires 1st rights. Pays royalties. Responds in 3 wks; publishes within a year. Query w/SASE (CDN) or IRC (US), including outline, sample chapter, and author's qualifications/previous credits. Photocopied OK. Catalog available.
BRITISH COLUMBIA, ENVIRONMENT/RESOURCES, PUBLIC AFFAIRS

Reflector, PO Box 2020, Battle Ground, WA 98604. 206-687-5151. Weekly newspaper.
COMMUNITY

Register, 610 Ash, Othello, WA 99344. Weekly newspaper.
COMMUNITY

The Register-Guard, 975 High St, Box 10188, Eugene, OR 97401. Editor: Bob Keefer. 503-485-1234. Daily newspaper.
COMMUNITY

Reliance Press, 4127 Phinney N, Seattle, WA 98103. Book publisher.
OTHER/UNSPECIFIED

Reliant Marketing & Publishing, PO Box 17456, Portland, OR 97127. Contact: Florence K Riddle. Publisher softcover original books. Accepts freelance material. Query letter, outline, SASE. Dot matrix, photocopies OK. Reports in 3 wks. Accepts nonfiction. Topics: how-to, self-help, money making. Guidelines available.
CRAFTS/HOBBIES, HEALTH, HOW-TO

Rendezvous, Idaho State University, Department of English, PO Box 8113, Pocatello, ID 83209. Annual. Accepts article, prose, poetry and photo essay submissions.
COLLEGE/UNIVERSITY, EDUCATION, ENGLISH

Renewal, A Journal & Resource Guide for Natural Lifeways, PO Box 1314, Ashland, OR 97520. 503-488-1645. Contact: Richard & Maraji Gwynallen. Bimonthly. Mail sub $10/yr. Free regional retail distribution. Circ 20,000. Uses freelance material. Pays in copies. Submit query or ms w/SASE. Mac disk OK. Accepts fiction, nonfiction, poetry. Topics: health, environment, metaphysical, occult, innovative psychology, book & music reviews, anything related to natural/holistic lifeways. Guidelines available. Sample $2.
ENVIRONMENT/RESOURCES, ENVIRONMENT/RESOURCES, NEW AGE

Renton Record-Chronicle, 339 S Burnett, Renton, WA 98055. Newspaper.
COMMUNITY

Reporter, PO Box 38, Mercer Island, WA 98040. 206-232-1215. Weekly newspaper.
COMMUNITY

Repository Press, RR 7, RMD 35, Buckhorn Rd, Prince George, BC V2N 2J5. Contact: John Harris. Publishes softcover books. Not a freelance market. Catalog available.
FICTION, PICTURE, POETRY

Researcher Publications Inc, 18806 40th Ave W, Lynnwood, WA 98036. Book publisher.
OTHER/UNSPECIFIED

Resolution Business Press, 11101 NE 8th St, Ste 208, Bellevue, WA 98004. 206-455-4611. Editor: John Spilker. Book publisher. Accepts unsolicited submissions. Acquires all rights. Submit query letter, clips, SASE. Responds in 3–5 wks; publishes in 6–12 mos. Accepts nonfiction, interviews, articles. Topics: computer and business-related. Guidelines available.
COMPUTERS, REFERENCE/LIBRARY, TECHNICAL

Resource Development, Box 91760, West Vancouver, BC V7V 4S1. Periodical.
OTHER/UNSPECIFIED

Resource Recycling, PO Box 10540, Portland, OR 97210. 503-227-1319. Editor: Jerry Powell. Ads: Rick Downing. Monthly trade journal. Sub $42/yr; circ 6,500. Uses freelance material. Pays money, copies on publication. Acquires first rights. Byline given. Submit query w/clips. Photocopied, electronic, computer disk OK. Reports in 6–8 wks; publishes 6+ mos. Accepts nonfiction articles on multi-material recycling topics. B&W glossy photo's preferred, rates variable. Guidelines & sample available.
CONSERVATION, ENVIRONMENT/RESOURCES

Retirement Life News, 10211 SW Barbur Blvd, Ste 109 A, Portland, OR 97219. 503-245-6442. Editor: Carl Olson. Monthly. Sub $7.50.
COMMUNITY, SENIOR CITIZENS

The Retort, Idaho Academy of Science, c/o Department of Chemistry, Boise State University, Boise, ID 83725. Editors: Edward Matjeka & Richard Banks. Published 3 times a year.
COLLEGE/UNIVERSITY, EDUCATION, SCIENCE

Review, Seattle Community College, 1718 Broadway Ave, Seattle, WA 98122. Periodical.
COLLEGE/UNIVERSITY

Review, PO Box 511, Toppenish, WA 98948. 509-865-4055. Weekly newspaper.
COMMUNITY

Review of Social & Economic Conditions, Institute of Social & Economic Research, University of Alaska, 3211 Providence Dr, Anchorage, AK 99508. 907-786-7710. Editor: Linda Leask. Irregularly published magazine. Sub free except Canada & foreign. Circ 1,800–2,500. Not a freelance market. Catalog & sample available.
ALASKA, COMMERCE, ECONOMICS

Revolution Books/Banner Press, 5519-A University Way NE, Seattle, WA 98105. 206-527-8558. Radical and socialist books.
COMPUTERS, LAW, SOCIALIST/RADICAL

Reynard House, 5706 30th NE, Seattle, WA 98105. Book publisher.
OTHER/UNSPECIFIED

Rhapsody!, Clackamas Community College, 19600 S Molalla, Oregon City, OR 97045. 503-657-8400. Semiannual literary magazine. Circ 500. Query w/ ms, SASE. Phone query, dot matrix OK. Fiction: 3–5 ds typed pages on any subject. Fillers: 3–4 ds typed pages on "people in the arts (writing, photo, art, music, etc). Poetry: 4–25 lines. Photos: "good, creative photographs." Tips: "We accept submissions from Clackamas County residents or students of Clackamas CC only."
FICTION, LITERARY, PHOTOGRAPHY

Rhino Press, PO Box 5207, Stn B, Victoria, BC V8R 6N4. Book publisher.
OTHER/UNSPECIFIED

Rhyme Time Poetry Newsletter, PO Box 1870, Hayden, ID 83835. 208-772-6184. Editor: Linda Hutton. Bimonthly. Pays 1 copy on publication. Submit ms, SASE. Photocopied, simultaneous OK. Accepts "quality poetry, preferably rhymed, and fewer than 16 lines. We aim to encourage beginning poets, as well as…published professionals." Six poets nominated annually for Pushcart Prize in Poetry. Also publishes an annual anthology of contest winners & best poetry. Guidelines/sample, SASE + 2 first-class stamps.
POETRY

Richmond Review, 5811 A Cedarbridge Way, Richmond, BC V6K 1W6. Periodical.
OTHER/UNSPECIFIED

Ricwalt Publishing Company, Fisherman's Terminal, C-3 Bldg, Seattle, WA 98119. Book publisher.
OTHER/UNSPECIFIED

Randy Stapilus Ridenbaugh Press, 1429 Shenandoah Dr, Boise, ID 83712-6658. Book publisher.
OTHER/UNSPECIFIED

Riffs, Washington Jazz Society, PO Box 2813, Seattle, WA 98111. 206-324-2794. Contact: Ed Foulks.
MUSIC

Right White Line, 531 N Inlet, Lincoln City, OR 97367. Book publisher.
OTHER/UNSPECIFIED

Ritz Publishing, 202 W Fifth Ave, Ritzville, WA 99169-1722. 509-659-4336. Publisher: Star Andersen. Contact: David Andersen. "Alternative" press for Vietnam War literature — trade paperback books and semiannual book/journal (Adventures in Hell). Seeking Vietnam War related material — poetry, fiction, or 1st person historical narratives. Length open. Reports in 1 mo; publishing time varies. Query W/SASE. No dot matrix. Typed ms, or laser (suitable for scanning). "I believe wholeheartedly that this writing helps in the healing process of a war wound of the nation, as well as helping new authors get established."
FICTION, AMERICAN HISTORY, MILITARY/VETS

The Ritzville Adams County Journal, PO Box 288, Ritzville, WA 99169. 509-659-1020. Weekly newspaper.
COMMUNITY

River West Books, 663 S 11th St, Coos Bay, OR 97420. 503-269-1363. Contact: Nathan Douthit. Book publisher.
OTHER/UNSPECIFIED

RNABC News, Registered Nurses' Association, 2855 Arbutus St, Vancouver, BC V6J 3Y8. Editor: Bruce Wells. 604-736-7331. Periodical.
BRITISH COLUMBIA, HEALTH, LABOR/WORK

Robinson Publishing Company Inc, 207 SW 150th, Seattle, WA 98166. Book publisher.
OTHER/UNSPECIFIED

Rock Rag, 13879 SE Foster Rd, Dayton, OR 97114. Editors Toby & Troy. Ads: Bryce Van Patten. Periodical.
COUNTER CULTURE, MUSIC

The Rocket/Murder Inc, 2028 5th St, Seattle, WA 98121. 206-728-7625. Editor: Charles R Cross. Ads: Courtney Miller. Monthly magazine. Sub $12. Circ 65,000. Accepts freelance material, usage varies. Freelance qualifications require knowledge of popular music. Pays money on publication. By-line given. Submit query w/clips, ms w/SASE. Dot matrix, photocopies OK. Reports in 1 mo. Accepts nonfiction, photos, cartoons. Tips: record review — 1–2 paragraphs; features — 500–1,000 wds. B&W photos preferred. Guidelines available. Sample cost varies.
MUSIC

Rockhound Rumblings, 6775 River Rd N, Salem, OR 97303. Editor: Les Puffer. Monthly.
COLLECTING, CRAFTS/HOBBIES, RECREATION

Rocking Chair Studio, SS2 S12 C36, Fort St. John, BC V1J 4M7. 604-827-3515. Contact: Ann Simmons.
BRITISH COLUMBIA, FISHING, CANADIAN HISTORY

Rockland Publishing, PO Box 1597, Kalispell, MT 59901. 406-756-9079. Contact: Judy Overbeek. Publishes original softcover advanced computer books. Pays royalties. Query w/clips. Dot matrix, electronic/modem, computer disk submissions OK. Reports in 3–4 weeks. Publishes within 1 yr.
COMPUTERS, HOW-TO, TECHNICAL

Rocky Butte Publishers, 5635 NE Alameda, Portland, OR 97213. Book publisher.
OTHER/UNSPECIFIED

Rocky Mountain Poetry, PO Box 269, Gallitan-Gateway, MT 59730. Accepts poetry, essays, and short stories. Focus is on cowboy poetry, poetry from the Rocky Mountain region, and other walks of life. Pays in copies. Byline given. Query w/SASE.
FICTION, POETRY

Romar Books, 18002 15th Ave NE, Ste B, Seattle, WA 98155-3838. 206-368-8157. Editors: Karen Duncan Larry Reynolds. Publishes soft- & hardcover books. Accepts unsolicited submissions. Submit query w/SASE. Dot matrix, photocopied, simultaneous OK. Reports in 8 wks. Publishes in 1 yr.
CHILDREN/TEEN, FOOD/COOKING, MYSTERY

Ronan Pioneer, 123 Main St SW, Ronan, MT 59864. 406-676-3800. Newspaper.
COMMUNITY, OTHER/UNSPECIFIED

Room of One's Own, PO Box 46160, Stn G, Vancouver, BC V6R 4G5. Feminist literary quarterly. Sub $10. Circ 2,000. Uses freelance material. Pays money on publication. Acquires 1st rights. Byline given. Submit ms. Photocopied OK. Reports in 3–4 mos. Publishes in 3–6 mos. Accepts nonfiction, fiction, poetry, photos. Sample $3.
DRAMA, POETRY, WOMEN

The Rose, Publication of the Portland Jaycees, University Stn, PO Box 622, Portland, OR 97207. 503-231-2800. Editor: Keeya Prowell. Periodical.
BUSINESS, TRADE/ASSOCIATIONS, URBAN

The Rose Arts Magazine, 336 SE 32nd Ave, Portland, OR 97214. 503-231-0644. Editor/Ads: Terry Hammond. Bimonthly dedicated to the promotion of art and artists. Sub $6. Circ 10,000 in metro Portland. Uses 5 freelance mss per issue. Pays 2 1/2 cents a word on publication. Acquires 1st rights. Byline given. Submit ms, SASE. Dot matrix, photocopied, electronic, PC computer disk OK. Reports in 6 wks. Publishes in 1–5 mos. Accepts nonfiction, fiction, photos, cartoons, rarely poetry. Topics: the arts, humanities, history, "any scholarly focus rendered in a bright style might be acceptable." No reviews. Tips: articles up to 3,000 wds; fiction, 3,500. Guidelines available. Sample $1.
ARTS, CULTURE, FICTION

Rose Press, 6531 SE Ivon St, Portland, OR 97206. Book publisher.
OTHER/UNSPECIFIED

Roseburg News-Review, 345 NE Winchester, Roseburg, OR 97470. 503-672-3321. Daily newspaper.
COMMUNITY, OTHER/UNSPECIFIED

Roseburg Woodsman, c/o Chevalier Advertising, 1 Centerpointe Dr #300, Lake Oswego, OR 97035-8613. Editor. Monthly on wood & wood products to customers and friends of Roseburg Forest Products Co. Circ 7,500. Sub free. Uses 2–3 mss per issue. Payment: $50–100 on publication. Rights acquired: One time. Query with ms, SASE. Photocopies OK. Reports in 2 wks. Nonfiction: with photos; must be wood-related; 500–1,000 wds. Photos: Color transparencies only (35mm OK) accompanying ms only. No single photos. $25 per printed photo, $125 cover. Tips: Only buy mss & photos together. Assignments occasionally available at higher rate. Guidelines available; sample/free.
ANIMALS, ARCHITECTURE, LUMBER

Rosewood Press, PO Box 10304, Olympia, WA 98502. Contact: Mark Schwebke. Publisher: poetry, underground posters, network artwork/poetry broadsides, some experimental prose. Pays copies. Byline given. Query w/clips, SASE. Dot matrix OK.
AVANT-GARDE/EXPERIMENTAL, POETRY, VISUAL ARTS

Royal Banner, PO Box 516, Royal City, WA 99357. 509-346-9456. Weekly newspaper.
OTHER/UNSPECIFIED

Ruah, Sacred Art Society, 0245 SW Bancroft, Portland, OR 97201. 503-236-2145. Editor: LaVaun Maier. Quarterly. Sub $12.
OTHER/UNSPECIFIED

The Rude Girl Press, Box 331, Reed College, 3203 SE Woodstock Boulevard, Portland, OR 97202. Periodical.
COLLEGE/UNIVERSITY, FEMINISM

Rumors & Raggs, 19924 Aurora Ave #57, Seattle, WA 98133. 206–742–4FUN. Editor: Seaun Richards. Monthly.
OTHER/UNSPECIFIED

Rural Oregon Biker, 5224 Cherry Heights Rd W, The Dalles, OR 97058. 503-298-1317. Editor: Brian Stovall. Sub $7.50; circ 250. Bimonthly magazine accepts freelance articles. Submit mss with SASE. Pays in copies. Accepts fiction, nonfiction, cartoons, news, photos, interviews, reviews. Topics: motorcycle oriented — political, recreational, historical.
RECREATION

Rural Property Bulletin, PO Box 2042, Sandpoint, ID 83864. 208-263-1177. Contact: Sandy Weaver. Monthly.
RURAL

Ruralite, Box 558, Forest Grove, OR 97116. Feature editor: Walt Wentz. 503-357-2105. Ads: Reva Bassler. Monthly. Sub $5; circ 260,000. Accepts freelance material. Payment: $30–200 on acceptance. Byline given. Purchases first rights. Query with ms, SASE. Dot matrix, photocopies, simultaneous submissions OK. Reports in 1 week. Accepts nonfiction: Northwest focus; general family interest stories slanted to Pacific NW; oddities in history, admirable or unusual characters, humor, community improvement, self-help, rural electrification, unusual events or interesting places, etc (max length 1,000 wds). Photos add greatly to chances of acceptance: B&W, preferably with 35 or 120mm negatives, pay usually included with story. Guidelines available; sample/$1.
FAMILY, HUMOR, RURAL

RV Life Magazine, PO Box 55998, Seattle, WA 98155. 206-745-5665. Editor: Gayle Harrison. Monthly magazine. Sub $12/yr. Circ 25,000. Uses freelance material. Byline given. Submit query letter, SASE, phone. Responds in 1 mo, publishes in 1–4 mos. Accepts articles, photos (prefers B&W prints). Topics: anything related to the RV life-style — buying RVs, campgrounds, historic sites, pets, travel with kids, recipes, outdoor cooking, etc. Guidelines available. Sample 50¢.
OUTDOOR, SCHOLARLY/ACADEMIC, TRAVEL

Ryder Press, 424 NW 14th, Portland, OR 97209. Book publisher.
OTHER/UNSPECIFIED

Sabella Press, 20809 59th Pl W, Lynnwood, WA 98036. Book publisher.
OTHER/UNSPECIFIED

Sachett Publications, 100 Waverly Dr, Grants Pass, OR 97526. 503-476-6404. Self-publisher of 1 softcover original book a year. Print run: 1,000–2,500. Not a freelance market. Catalog available.
COLLECTING, EDUCATION, TRAVEL

Sagebrush Heritage, 368 NE 19th Ave, Hillsboro, OR 97124. 503-648-4587. Contact: Robert J White. Self-publisher of books on Oregon history and the Seabees of WWII.
NW/REGIONAL HISTORY, MILITARY/VETS

Sagittarius Press, 930 Taylor, Port Townsend, WA 98368. 206-385-0277. Book publisher.
CRAFTS/HOBBIES, NW/REGIONAL HISTORY

St Alphonsus Today, St Alphonsus Regional Medical Center, 1055 N Curtis Rd, Boise, ID 83706. Editor: Bob Hieronymus. Quarterly. Circ 12,500. Not a freelance market.
HEALTH, MEDICAL

St Helens Chronicle, 195 S 15th St, St Helens, OR 97051. 503-397-0116. Newspaper.
COMMUNITY, OTHER/UNSPECIFIED

Sakura Press, 36787 Sakura Lane, Pleasant Hill, OR 97455-9727. 503-747-5817. Self-publisher of 1–3 softcover originals a year and tapes & cards. Print run: 500. Not a freelance market. Assignment only. Guidelines available, SASE.
ASIA, LANGUAGE(S)

Salmon Recorder-Herald, PO Box 310, Salmon, ID 83467. 208-756-2221. Newspaper.
COMMUNITY, OTHER/UNSPECIFIED

Salmon Trout Steelheader, Frank Amato Publications, PO Box 82112, Portland, OR 97282. 503-653-8108. Asst. editor: Nick Amato. Ads: Joyce Sherman. Bimonthly magazine. Sub $12.95. Circ 37,000. Uses freelance material. Pays money on publication. Acquires 1st rights. Byline given. Submit query letter, complete ms, SASE. Dot matrix, disk subs OK. Reports in 2 wks. Accepts nonfiction related to fishing and conservation. Topics: how to — salmon, steelhead, trout fishing. Articles should be accompanied by B&W or color (35 mm or 5x7 prints). Guidelines available. Sample $2.50.
FISHING

Salmonberry Publishing Company, PO Box 479, Skagway, AK 99840. 907-983-2674. Editor: Cindy Roland. Publishes softcover books. Accepts unsolicited submissions. Submit query/SASE. Responds in 1 mo; publishes in 1 yr. Accepts fiction, nonfiction, biography, photos, interviews, memoirs—must relate to Alaska.
ALASKA

Salud de la Familia News, PO Box 66, Woodburn, OR 97071. Quarterly.
MINORITIES/ETHNIC

Sammamish Valley News, PO Box 716, Redmond, WA 98052. 206-885-4178. Weekly newspaper, founded in 1945. Editor: Rick Beasley. Ads: Phyllis Neimeyer. Sub $15; circ 18,400. Uses freelance material. Byline given. Pays money on publication. Submit query letter, complete ms, SASE, phone. Responds in 1 wk; publishes in 1 wk. Accepts news items, cartoons, photos (B&W film or print), interviews, op/ed, articles. Topics: local to reader area.
COMMUNITY

Sandpiper Press, PO Box 286, Brookings, OR 97415. 503-469-5588. Contact: Marilyn Riddle. Publisher of softcover books for vision-impaired (18 pt. large print books). Accepts freelance material. Submit query, SASE. Photocopies, dot matrix, simultaneous subs OK. Reports in 2 mos. Accepts nonfiction, fiction, poetry, cartoons. Topics: save the planet, peace, brotherhood, one God seen from many angles individually, The Holy Spirit or Great Spirit our constant companion, verified Native American legends, healing plants, first-person experiences of rising above physical handicaps to find what we CAN do instead of settling for what we can't (no bragging or preaching). Rod

Serling type short stories; no horror; want irony and moral and surprise ending. Guidelines/catalog available.
FANTASY/SCI FI, PEACE, DISABLED

Sandpoint Daily Bee (News Bulletin), 310 Church, Sandpoint, ID 83864. 208-263-9534. Daily newspaper.
COMMUNITY, OTHER/UNSPECIFIED

The Sandy Post, 17270 Bluff Rd, Box 68, Sandy, OR 97055. 503-668-5548. Editor: Scott Newton. Weekly newspaper.
COMMUNITY

Santiam Books, 744 Mader Ave SE, Salem, OR 97302. Book publisher.
OTHER/UNSPECIFIED

Sasquatch Publishing Company, 1931 2nd Ave, Seattle, WA 98101. Contact: David Brewster. Publisher of 6–8 hard- & softcover nonfiction originals per yr, "mostly guidebooks and reprints of Weekly material." Pays royalties. Query with outline, sample chapters, SASE. Nonfiction: "Travel in the NW" and other nonfiction for and about the NW. Tips: "Most of our books are produced totally by in-house staff of writers and researchers, though we have purchased material from other writers on occasion." Catalog available.
NORTHWEST, TRAVEL

Satellite Guide, CommTek, 9440 Fairview Ave, Boise, ID 83704. Editor: Fran Fuller. Monthly satellite reception guide. Circ 10,000.
ABSTRACTS/INDICES, REFERENCE/LIBRARY

Satellite World, CommTek, 9440 Fairview Ave, Boise, ID 83704. Editor: Bruce Kinnaird. Monthly. Circ 15,000.
ABSTRACTS/INDICES, REFERENCE/LIBRARY

Saturday's Child, PO Box 148, Cloverdale, OR 97112. Book publisher.
CHILDREN/TEEN, FAMILY

Sauvie Island Press, 14745 NW Gillihand Rd, Portland, OR 97231. Book publisher.
OTHER/UNSPECIFIED

Saving Energy, 5411 117 Ave SE Bellevue, WA 98006. Periodical.
CONSUMER

Saxifrage, Pacific Lutheran University, Tacoma, WA 98447. 206-535-7387. Annual student creative arts magazine.
COLLEGE/UNIVERSITY

Scappoose Spotlight, 52644 NE First, Box C, Chinook Plaza, Scappoose, OR 97056. 503-543-6387. Weekly newspaper.
COMMUNITY

School Media Services, Dept of Education, Public Office Bldg, Salem, OR, 97310. Periodical for school media specialists.
EDUCATION

The School Paper, Eugene Public Schools, 200 N Monroe, Eugene, OR 97402. Periodical.
EDUCATION

Science Fiction Review, PO Box 11408, Portland, OR 97211. Editor: Richard E Geis. Quarterly.
FANTASY/SCI FI

Scitech Book News, 5600 NE Hassalo, Portland, OR 97213-3640. Editor: Jane Erskine. 503-281-9230. Monthly list, reviews 500–600 newly published scientific, medical, technical books for librarians primarily. Sub $60; circ 2,200. Not a freelance market. Assignment only. "We will consider assigning book reviews to specially qualified scientific and technical people." Pays money on acceptance. Sample $3.
REFERENCE/LIBRARY, SCIENCE

Screef, MPO Box 3352, Vancouver, BC V6B 3V3. 604-681-5295. Contact: Jerome Cranston, editor. Sub $12/yr. Quarterly publication of the Pacific Reforestation Workers Association. Uses freelance material. Query w/SASE.
FORESTRY, LABOR/WORK

Screenings, Oregon Archaeological Society, PO Box 13293, Portland, OR 97213. Monthly.
ANTHROPOLOGY/ARCHÆOLOGY, NATURAL HISTORY, SCIENCE

Sea Grant Program, University of Alaska, 303 Tanaka Dr, Bunnell Bldg. Rm. 3, Fairbanks, AK 99701. Book publisher.
COLLEGE/UNIVERSITY, NATURAL HISTORY, SCIENCE

Sea Kayaker, 6327 Seaview Ave NW, Seattle, WA 98107. 206-789-1326. Ads: 206-789-6413. Editor: Christopher Cunningham. Quarterly magazine, founded 1984. Sub $13/US. Circ 10,000. Uses freelance material. Requires sea kayaking expertise. Pays 5¢–10¢/wd on publication. Acquires 1st rights. Byline given. Submit query letter, clips, outline, SASE. Dot matrix OK. Reports in 2–3 mos; publishes in 6–9 mos. Accepts nonfiction, fiction, photos (B&W, $15–35), cartoons. Topics: sea kayaking. "Best guidelines contained in our back issues." Guidelines available. Sample $3.50.
ADVENTURE, BOATING, TRAVEL

Sea Pen Press & Paper Mill, 2228 NE 46th St, Seattle, WA 98105. Book publisher.
OTHER/UNSPECIFIED

Seablom Design Books, 2106 2nd Ave N, Seattle, WA 98109. Book publisher.
OTHER/UNSPECIFIED

Seafood Leader, 1115 NW 45th St, Seattle, WA 98107. 206-548-9846. Contact: Peter Redmayne. Bimonthly trade journal of the seafood industry. Uses nonfiction on the business and the people, including historical pieces, profiles of individuals and companies, op/ed, news, etc. Uses color photos. Issues have themes. No sport or recreational. Query w/clips, or ms. Pay varies.
BUSINESS, COMMERCE, FISHING

Seagull Publishing, 2628 W Crockett, Seattle, WA 98199. Book publisher.
OTHER/UNSPECIFIED

The Seal Press, 3131 Western Ave #410, Seattle, WA 98121. 206-283-7844. Editor: Faith Conlon. Publishes 10 softcover originals, reprints, a year. Press run 4,000–5,000. Query w/clips, SASE. Dot matrix, photocopied OK. Reports in 4–8 wks. Accepts nonfiction, fiction. "We are a feminist publisher specializing in works by women writers." Catalog available.
FEMINISM, GAY/LESBIAN, WOMEN

Searchers Publications, 4314 Island Crest Way, Mercer Island, WA 98040. Book publisher.
OTHER/UNSPECIFIED

Seaside Signal, 113 N Holladay, Box 848, Seaside, OR 97138. 503-738-5561. Weekly newspaper.
COMMUNITY

Seattle, PO Box 22578, Seattle, WA 98122. Monthly.
COMMUNITY

Seattle Airplane Press, 6727 Glen Echo Lane, Tacoma, WA 98499. Book publisher.
OTHER/UNSPECIFIED

Seattle Art Museum Program Guide, Volunteer Park, 14th E & E Park, Seattle, WA 98112. 206-625-8900. Periodical.
ARTS, CULTURE

Seattle Arts, Seattle Arts Commission, 305 Harrison, Seattle, WA 98109. 206-625-4223. Contact: Steve Munzenmaier. Monthly relating to SAC concerns. Circ 5,000. Accepts freelance material relevant to arts in Seattle by competent author. Guest editor program. Pay depends on budget. Byline given. Phone queries OK. Assignments only. "We have a literary supplement to the newsletter 2 times per year. Authors are accepted only if they respond to the call for submissions (published in the newsletter). Those accepted are selected by jury process." Sample available.
ARTS

Seattle Audubon Society, 8028 35th Ave NE, Seattle, WA 98115-4815. Book publisher.
ANIMALS, CONSERVATION, OUTDOOR

Seattle Chinese Post, 409 Maynard S, Rm 16, Seattle, WA 98104. 206-223-0623. Weekly newspaper.
ASIAN AMERICAN, COMMUNITY, CULTURE

Seattle Gay News, 704 E Pike St, Seattle, WA 98122. Editor: George Bakan. 206-324-4297. Weekly for gay/lesbian audience. Circ 20,000. Sub $35/yr. Accepts freelance material. Payment: Money, copies, on publication. Dot matrix OK. Nonfiction, fiction, photos ($5), cartoons. Sample available.
COUNTER CULTURE, GAY/LESBIAN

The Seattle Medium, 2600 S Jackson, Seattle, WA 98144. Editor: Connie Bennett Cameron. 206-632-3307. "Pacific Northwest's largest Black-owned newspaper."
BLACK

Seattle Post-Intelligencer, 101 Elliott Ave W, Seattle, WA 98119. 206-448-8000. Editor: John Reistrup. Daily newspaper.
URBAN, OTHER/UNSPECIFIED

The Seattle Review, Padelford Hall GN-30, University of Washington, Seattle, WA 98195. 206-543-9865. Editor: Nelson Bentley, Poetry/Charles Johnson, Fiction. Ads: Janie Smith. Semiannual literary magazine. Sub $8/yr; circ 800. Uses freelance material. Pays money, copies, 1 year sub on publication. Byline given. Acquires 1st rights, revert to author. Submit ms, SASE. Dot matrix, photocopies OK. Reports in 3–6 mos. Accepts nonfiction, fiction, poetry, essays on the craft of writing. Will consider most topics and length varies, limited only by issue requirements. No photos. Guidelines available. Sample 1/2 price.
COLLEGE/UNIVERSITY, FICTION, POETRY

Seattle Star, PO Box 30044, Seattle, WA 98103. 206-633-4701. Editor: Michael Dowers. Bi-monthly cartoon tabloid. Accepts freelance material. Pays copies/advertising trade. Submit w/SASE. Photocopied OK. "Looking for humorous cartoons." Sample $1.
HUMOR

Seattle Times, Fairview Ave N & John St, PO Box 70, Seattle, WA 98111. 206-464-2111. Daily newspaper.
URBAN

Seattle Weekly, 1931 Second Ave, Seattle, WA 98101. Editor: David Brewster. Weekly tabloid. Circ 30,000. Payment: Money on publication. Byline given. Query, outline w/SASE. Nonfiction. Guidelines available; sample 75¢.
CULTURE, LITERARY

Seattle's Child/Eastside Project, PO Box 22578, Seattle, WA 98122. 206-322-2594. Editor: Ann Bergman. Ads: Alzyne Sulkin. Monthly magazine. Sub $15. Circ 20,000. Uses 3 freelance mss per issue. Pays 10¢/word on publication. Acquires 1st rights. Byline given. Submit query w/clips, ms, SASE. Dot matrix, photocopied, simultaneous OK. Reports in 3 mos. Publishes in 6–24 mos. Accepts nonfiction. Topics: directed to parents and professionals working with kids. Audience well-read, sophisticated. Tips: 400–2,500 wds. Guidelines available.
CHILDREN/TEEN, COMMUNITY, FAMILY

Seattle's Child Publishing, PO Box 22578, Seattle, WA 98122. 206-322-2594. Contact: Ann Bergman. Publisher of 1–2 softcover, nonfiction originals on same subjects and for same audience as above. Payment: Money, royalties. Query, manuscript, outline, sample chapters w/SASE. Dot matrix, photocopies, electronic OK. Reports in 3 mos. Publishes in 2 yrs. Tips: "Issues relevant to parent, educators, professionals working with children 12 or under."
CHILDREN/TEEN

Second Amendment Foundation, James Madison Bldg, 12500 NE 10th Place, Bellevue, WA 98005. Book publisher.
OTHER/UNSPECIFIED

Second Language Publications, PO Box 1700, Blaine, WA 98230. Also, PO Box 82370, Burnaby, BC V5C 5P8. Book publisher.
LANGUAGE(S)

Select Homes, 207–10215 – 150th, Surray, BC. Editor: Pam Withers. 604-293-1275. Ads: Allen Barnett. Published 8 times a yr. Circ 175,000. Sub $14.97. Uses 4–6 mss per issue. Payment: Money, copies, on acceptance. Byline given. Rights purchased: First Canadian. Query w/SASE. No phone queries. Assignment only. Photocopies, simultaneous submissions (if ex-

plained) OK. Reports in 3 wks. Nonfiction, cartoons, humor essays. "House maintenance, house renovation, house finance, house decorating, news of interest to home owners, architecture, energy issues as related to homeowning, humor essay." Photos: $50–100 per stock photo, on publication; negotiable day-rates for shoots ($450 per day average). Tips: Use mostly Canadian material. See guidelines before querying. Send clips. Guidelines available; sample $2.
ARCHITECTURE, HOME, HOW-TO

Self-Counsel Press Inc, Subsidiary of International Self-Counsel Press Ltd, 1704 N State St, Bellingham, WA 98225. 206–676-4530. Publisher of softcover original books, legal and business self-help. Query w/SASE. Guidelines/catalog available.
BUSINESS, HOW-TO

Sellwood Bee, Pry Publishing Co, 600 NW 14th Ave, Portland, OR 97209. 503-226-8335. Editors: Marcia Pry. Ads: Greg Hudson. Weekly tabloid, founded 1904. Circ 2,500. Uses freelance material. Byline given. Pays money on publication. Acquires 1st rights. Submit query letter, clips, SASE. Dot matrix OK. Responds in 1–2 wks. Accepts new items, nonfiction, photos, articles. Topics: events and people of Sellwood-Moreland neighborhoods in SE Portland. Guidelines available.
COMMUNITY

Charles Seluzicki, Fine Press Series, Fine and Rare Books, 3733 NE 24th Ave, Portland, OR 97212. Contact: Charles Seluzicki. 503-284-4749. Publisher of 2–4 hard- & softcover originals, reprints a year. Print run: 50–300. Accepts freelance material with strict qualifications. Payment: Copies, small cash payment at times. Rights purchased: First. Submit ms, SASE. Photocopies OK. Reports in 1 month. Publishes in 6–24 mos. Book arts, fiction, poetry, plays. "We are interested in the best possible writing for fine press formats. Such publishing requires materials that suggest the strong graphic and tactile expression. Primarily mss are solicited. Our authors have included Ted Hughes, William Stafford, Tess Gallagher, Seannes Heaney and Charles Simic (among others)." Catalog available.
BOOK ARTS/BOOKS, FICTION, POETRY

Senior News, PAMI Publications, PO Box 229, Salem, OR 97308. Editor: Frank Crow. 503-299-8478. Monthly.
SENIOR CITIZENS

Senior News of Island County, 2845 E Hwy 525, Langley, WA 98260. 206-321-1600. Editor: Claudia Fuller. Monthly, free. Circ 3,600. Uses freelance material. No pay. Submit ms, SASE. Dot matrix, photocopied OK. Accepts nonfiction, poetry, photos, cartoons.
PHOTOGRAPHY, POETRY, SENIOR CITIZENS

Senior Scene, 223 N Yakima, Tacoma, WA 98403. 206–622-5427. Monthly tabloid. Sub $7.50/yr; circ 13,200. Uses freelance material. Byline given. Pays money, copies on publication. Submit query letter, ms, SASE. Photocopy, simultaneous subs OK. Responds in 2 wks; publishes in 3 mos. Accepts cartoons, news items, biography, photos, interviews, op/ed, articles, reviews. Sample $2.
SENIOR CITIZENS

Senior Times, 7802 E Mission, Spokane, WA, 99212. Periodical.
SENIOR CITIZENS

Senior Tribune, 6420 SW Macadam Ave #210, Portland, OR 97201-3518. 503-777-5436. Editor: Jill Warren. Monthly tabloid serving residents 55 and older in Multnomah, Clackamas and Washington counties. "Distributed free to banks and savings and loan institutions, senior and community centers, retirement complexes, medical clinics, Social Security offices." Tips: "Individuals and organizations are encouraged to submit articles of interest to older persons. The deadline for all copy is the 15th of each month."
SENIOR CITIZENS

The Senior Voice, 325 E 3rd Ave, Anchorage, AK 99501. Editor: Liz Lauzen. 907-277-0787. Ads: Pat Bressett. Monthly, senior advocate for legislative, health, consumer affairs. Sub $10 for Alaskans over 55/others $20. Seldom accepts freelance material. "Source should be well versed in Alaskan concerns." Byline given.
AMERICANA, SENIOR CITIZENS

Sentinel, Box 799, Sitka, AK 99835. 907-747-3219. Daily newspaper.
COMMUNITY

Sequim Sun, PO Box 2049, Sequim, WA, 98382. Contact: Del Price. Newspaper.
COMMUNITY

Serconia Press, PO Box 1786, Seattle, WA 98111. 206-782-9272. Editors: Jerry Kaufman, Donald Keller. Publishes 1–2 hard- & softcover books per yr. Accepts unsolicited submissions. Pays royalties, copies, on publication. Acquires 1st or reprint rights. Submit query w/SASE. Dot matrix, photocopied OK. Reports 2–4 wks. Publishes in 1 yr. Accepts nonfiction. Topics: criticism, reviews, memoirs, biography, history about or related to science fiction and fantasy. Collections or book-length. "Most of our material has been by authors recognized in this field."
FANTASY/SCI FI, LITERARY, WRITING

Sesame, Windyridge Press, PO Box 327, Medford, OR, 97501. Editor: Gene Olson. 503-772-5399. Monthly newsletter for writers. Sub $26.
LITERARY, WRITING

Seven Buffaloes Press, PO Box 249, Big Timber, MT 59011. Contact: Art Cuelho. Publisher of a newsletter series, poetry, fiction, essays; devoted to the rural heritage, farmers, workers, the land, and to regionalism. The role of the small press is "at best…the seedbed of this country's best potential writers and poets…. You can pick up 50 to over 100 magazines in this country and find the same poets in all of them. You don't see that in magazines or presses where strong focus is on regionalism." Query w/SASE. Catalog/free.
AGRICULTURE/FARMING, FICTION, POETRY

Shalom, Oregon, PO Box 8094, Portland, OR 97207. Quarterly of the Oregon chapter of the National Council of Christians and Jews.
RELIGION

Shane Press, 4719 SE Woodstock, Portland, OR 97206. Book publisher.
OTHER/UNSPECIFIED

Sherman County For The Record, Sherman County Historical Society, Moro, OR 97039. Editor: Sherry Kaseberg & Patty Moore. Semiannual magazine of local history. Prints 1,000 copies, mainly for residents of Sherman County. No pay. Submit ms, SASE. Phone queries OK. Nonfiction: "Our authors are mostly local people. No one is paid. Profit is for the historical society." Sample available.
NW/REGIONAL HISTORY

Sherman County Journal, 107 W 1st, Box 284, Moro, OR 97039. 503-565-3515. Weekly newspaper.
COMMUNITY

Shiloh Publishing House, 1490 Greenview Ct, Woodburn, OR 97071. 503-981-4328. Editor: Jerry Robeson. Self-publisher. Not a freelance market. Catalog available.
RELIGION

Shining Knight Press, PO Box 22733, Eugene, OR 97402. 503-563-5327. Editors: Diana Gregory, Claudia O'Keefe. Publishes 2–5 hard- & softcover originals and reprints a year about writers, desk reference books, how-to-live-cheaper-better books. Submit query, sample chapters, mss, with SASE. Material not returned without SASE. Dot matrix (if good), photocopies, simultaneous subs OK. Reports in 2–4 wks. Publishes in 1 yr. Acquires 1st rights. Pay varies. "No schlock books. We're not 'saddle stitch mail-order' people." Wants professionally presented proposal. Catalog available.
HOW-TO, REFERENCE/LIBRARY, WRITING

Duane Shinn Publications, 5090 Dobrot, Central, OR 97502. Book publisher.
OTHER/UNSPECIFIED

Shires Books, RR 3, Site 1, Nanaimo, BC V9R 5K3. Book publisher.
OTHER/UNSPECIFIED

Shoban News, Box 427, Fort Hall, ID 83203. Weekly periodical. Circ 1,500.
COMMUNITY

Shorey Publications, 110 Union St, PO Box 21626, Seattle, WA 98111. Book publisher.
OTHER/UNSPECIFIED

Sidney Herald, PO Box 1033, Sidney, MT 59270. 406-482-2706. Newspaper.
COMMUNITY, OTHER/UNSPECIFIED

Sign of the Times, A Chronicle of Decadence, PO Box 70672, Seattle, WA 98107-0672. 206-323-6779. Editor: Mark Souder. Biannual. Sub $15/2 yrs. Circ 750. Uses 11 freelance mss per issue. Acquires first rights. Pays copies on publication. Byline given. Submit ms w/SASE. Dot matrix, photocopied, electronic OK. Reports in 6 wks. Accepts fiction, photographs, drama, cartoons. Guidelines available.
FICTION, HUMOR, PHOTOGRAPHY

Signal Elm Press, 1300 E Denny #205, Seattle, WA 98122. Publisher: psychology, religion, metaphysics, New Age. Query w/outline.
RECREATION, PSYCHOLOGY, RELIGION

The Signal, Network International, PO Box 67, Emmett, ID 83617. 208-365-5812. Editor: Joan Silva. Semiannual magazine founded in 1987. Sub $10/yr; circ 500. Uses freelance material. Byline given. Pays copies. Submit query letter, complete ms, SASE, phone. Photocopy, dot matrix, simultaneous subs OK. Responds in 2–6 wks; publishes in 1 yr. Accepts fiction, poetry, cartoons, nonfiction, photos, interviews, op/ed, articles, reviews. Topics: worldwide issues, human and planetary issues; no religious material. Guidelines available. Sample $5.
ARTS, LITERATURE, POETRY

Signmaker Press, PO Box 967, Ashland, OR 97520. Book publisher.
OTHER/UNSPECIFIED

Signpost Books, 8912 192nd SW, Edmonds, WA 98026. 206-776-0370. Contact: Cliff Cameron. Publishes softcover originals on NW outdoor recreation, with emphasis on hiking, bicycling, canoeing/kayaking, and cross country skiing. Accepts freelance material. Pay negotiated. Submit query, sample chapters, SASE. Dot matrix, photocopies, simultaneous submissions, electronic (call first) OK. Reports in 3–4 wks. Accepts nonfiction. Topics: self-propelled outdoor recreation activities in the Pacific NW. Length 100–250 published pgs, including text, photos, maps. Tips: "In addition to showing knowledge of a subject, it is impressive when the author shows that he/she has considered the whole book, including artwork, appendices, promotional material for covers, potential markets, and other details of the finished book."
BICYCLING, OUTDOOR, RECREATION

Signpost for Northwest Trails, 1305 Fourth Ave #512, Seattle, WA 948101. Editor: Ann Marshall. 206-625-1367. Ads: Barbara Allen. Monthly magazine founded in 1966. Sub $25/yr; circ 3,000. Uses freelance material. Pays money, copies on publication. Byline given. Acquires 1st rights. Submit complete ms, SASE. Dot matrix, photocopies, simultaneous submissions OK. Reports in 2–8 wks; publishing time varies. Accepts nonfiction, photos (B&W glossy, 5x7 minimum, $25, must show a scene from WA or OR, and include a person or people), illustrations. Topics: non-motorized backcountry recreation, primarily backpacking, hiking X-C skiing; including climbing, paddling. Guidelines available. Sample $2.50.
OUTDOOR, RECREATION

Signpost Press Inc, 1007 Queen St, Bellingham, WA 98226. 206-734-9781. Publishes softcover books and semi-annual magazine (see Bellingham Review). Book editor: Knute Skinner. Mag editor: Susan Hilton. Sub $5/yr; circ 600. Uses freelance material. byline given. Submit query letter for books, complete ms for magazine, w/SASE. Accepts fiction, poetry, plays. Guidelines available for magazine. Sample $2.
DRAMA, FICTION, POETRY

Signs of the Times, PO Box 7000, Boise, ID 83707. Editor: Kenneth J Holland. 208-465-2577. Monthly magazine, "shows how Bible principles are relevant in today's world." Circ 325,000. Payment: Money on acceptance. Byline given. Rights purchased: First. Submit ms, SASE. Phone queries, simultaneous submissions OK. Reports in 2–3 wks. Publishes in 3–6 mos.

Nonfiction: 500–3,000 wds on "home, marriage, health, inspirational human interest articles that highlight a Biblical principle, and personal experiences solving problems with God's help." Photos: B&W contact sheets, 5x7 & 8x10 prints, 35mm color transparencies. Buys photos with or without articles. Guidelines, sample available.
RELIGION

The Silver Apple Branch, 1036 Hampshire Rd, Victoria, BC V8S 4S9. Editor: Janet P Reedman. Periodical of Irish myths and legends. Accepts freelance material. Payment: Copies. Byline given. Query w/SASE. Reports in 3–6 wks. Fiction, poetry. Max story length 1,500. Original fiction featuring Irish heroes.
CULTURE, FICTION, POETRY

Silver Bay Herb Farm, 9151 Tracyton Blvd, Bremerton, WA 98310. Contact: Mary Preus. 206-692-1340. Book publisher.
GARDENING

Silver Creek Press, PO Box 508, Sun Valley, ID 83353. 208-726-4880. Contact: Jan Roddy or Joan Nelson. Accepts queries w/SASE for sportsmen's calendar datebooks and wall calendars. Pays on publication. Responds in 1 wk; publishes within 3 mos.
FISHING, OUTDOOR, RECREATION

Silver Fox Connections, Emilie Johnson, 1244 SW 301st St, Federal Way, WA 98003. Book publisher.
OTHER/UNSPECIFIED

Silver Owl Publications Inc, PO Box 51186, Seattle, WA 98115. 206-524-9071. Book publisher. New Age books. Query w/SASE.
PEACE, PHILOSOPHY, NEW AGE

Silver Pennies Press, 1365 E 30th Ave, Eugene, OR 97405. Book publisher.
OTHER/UNSPECIFIED

Silver Seal Books, PO Box 106, Fox Island, WA 98333. Book publisher.
OTHER/UNSPECIFIED

Silverdale Reporter, Kitsap Newspaper Group, 2817 Wheaton Way #104, Bremerton, WA 98310-0334. 206-373-7969. Editor: Julie Seibert. Ads: David Bird. Sub $16/yr; circ 17,000. Weekly newspaper. Uses freelance material. Pays $5–$10 per story, depending; $5–10 per B&W glossy, any size, on acceptance. Byline given. Submit clips, ms, SASE, phone. Reports ASAP, publishes in 1–2 wks. Accepts nonfiction, photos, news items, interviews.
COMMUNITY

Silverfish Review, PO Box 3541, Eugene, OR 97403. 503-344-5060. Editor: Roger Moody. Literary review published irregularly. Sub $9/3 issues, indiv, $12 inst. Circ 750. Uses freelance material. Sponsors a poetry chapbook competition. Query w/SASE. Reports in 6 wks; time to publication varies. Accepts fiction, poetry, photos, interviews, reviews. Guidelines available.
FICTION, POETRY

Silverleaf Press, PO Box 70189, Seattle, WA 98107. Editor: Ann E Larson. Publishes softcover original books. Accepts unsolicited submissions. Pays royalties on publication. Submit ms, SASE. Dot matrix, photocopied OK. Reports in 1–3 mos; publishes in 6–12 mos. Accepts fiction, cartoons. Topics: feminist writing, "…does not have to be political, but should contain strong women (including Lesbian) characters." Currently accepting novels and short story collections. Catalog available.
FICTION, GAY/LESBIAN, WOMEN

The Silverton Appeal-Tribune, Mt. Angel News, 399 S Water, Box 35, Silverton, OR 97381. 503-873-8385. Weekly newspaper.
COMMUNITY

Single Scene, PO Box 5027, Salem, OR 97304. Monthly.
ENTERTAINMENT, OTHER/UNSPECIFIED

Single Vision Publications, PO Box 804, Lebanon, OR 97335. 503-258-5888. Self-publisher 1 softcover book/yr. inspirational prose/poetry. Press run: 1,000. Not a freelance market.
POETRY, RELIGION

Siskiyou, Southern Oregon State College, Stevenson Union, Ashland, OR 97520. 503-482-6306. Newspaper.
COLLEGE/UNIVERSITY, CULTURE, EDUCATION

Siskiyou Journal, The Siskiyou Regional Education Project, PO Box 1055, Ashland, OR 97520. 503-482-5969. Editors: Marc Prevost & Jim Kelly. Ads: Susan Brock. Bimonthly. Sub $16/$25. Circ 5,000. Uses 4–6 freelance mss per issue. Pays money, copies on publication. Submit query w/clips, ms, SASE, phone. Dot matrix, photocopied, simultaneous, electronic subs OK. Reports in 2–4 mos. Accepts nonfiction, fiction, poetry, photos, cartoons, other. Sample $2.
ECONOMICS, HEALTH, POLITICS

The Siuslaw News, PO Box 10, 148 Maple St, Florence, OR 97439. 503-997-3441. Fax 503-997-7979. Editor: Robert Serra. Ads: Pamela Girard. Weekly newspaper founded in 1890. Circ 6,000. Sub Lane County $15/other $22. Accepts freelance material. Byline given. Query with ms, SASE. Phone queries, dot matrix, photocopies OK. Accepts news, articles, op/ed, reviews photos.
COMMUNITY

Skagit Argus, PO Box 739, Mount Vernon, WA 98273. 206-336-6555. Weekly newspaper.
COMMUNITY

Skagit County Historical Society, PO Box 424, Mount Vernon, WA 98273. Book publisher.
NW/REGIONAL HISTORY, WASHINGTON

Skagit Farmer and Tribune, PO Box 153, Lynden, WA 98264. 206-354-4444. Weekly newspaper.
COMMUNITY

Skagit Valley Herald, PO Box 578, Mount Vernon, WA 98273-0739. 206-336-5751. Daily newspaper.
COMMUNITY

Skamania County Pioneer, PO Box 250, Stevenson, WA 98648. 509-427-8444. Weekly newspaper.
COMMUNITY

The Skanner, 2337 N Williams, PO Box 5455, Portland, OR 97228. Weekly tabloid of the Portland Black community.
BLACK, COMMUNITY

Skein Publications, PO Box 5326, Eugene, OR 97405. Book publisher.
OTHER/UNSPECIFIED

Ski Canada Magazine, 202 – 1132 Hamilton, Vancouver, BC V6V 2S8. Magazine devoted to Canadian skiing.
CANADA, RECREATION, SPORTS

Skies America, 7730 SW Mohawk, Tualatin, OR 97062. Editor: Robert Patterson. 503-691-1955. Inflight magazine. Accepts freelance material. Payment: $100–300 for feature articles, on publication. Query w/SASE. Nonfiction: features 1,200–1,500 wds; departments 500–700 wds, $50–100. Prefer photos with article, B&W prints and color transparencies. "Timely, original material in the fields of business, investing, travel, humor, health/ medicine, sports, city features, geographical features." Guidelines available; sample/$3.
BUSINESS, TRAVEL

Skipping Stones, c/o Aprovecho Institute, 80574 Hazelton Rd, Cottage Grove, OR 97424. 503-942-9434. Editors: Arun N Toke, Amy Klauke. Quarterly magazine by and for children (multicultural children's forum). Circ 2,500, subs. $15/yr. indiv; $20 inst. Uses freelance mss; pays in copies. Submit query, ms./SASE. Responds in 2 mos; published in 2–3 mos. Accepts nonfiction, fiction, poetry, photos, cartoons. Topics: "Environmental awareness, cultural diversity, multi-ethnic literature." Pen-pal letters, children's activities, project reports welcome. Tips: Shorter items preferred (1–2 ds pages). If writing is other than English, submit translation if possible. Guidelines available. Sample $4.
CHILDREN/TEEN, CULTURE, MINORITIES/ETHNIC

Skookum Publications, Site 176 Comp 4, 1275 Riddle Rd, Penticton, BC V2A 6J6. 604-492-3228. Editor: Doug Cox. Publisher of 2–3 softcover books a year. Does not accept freelance submissions.
CANADIAN HISTORY, NW/REGIONAL HISTORY

Skribent Press, 9700 SW Lakeside Dr, Tigard, OR 97223. Book publisher.
OTHER/UNSPECIFIED

Sky House Publishers, an imprint of Falcon Press Publishing Co Inc.
NW/REGIONAL HISTORY, MONTANA, OLD WEST

Skyviews, PO Box 2473, Seattle, WA, 98111. 206-323-6779. Editor: Jim Maloney. Periodical.
OTHER/UNSPECIFIED

Skyword, 1334 Seymour St, Vancouver, BC V6B 3P3. Airline magazine.
TRAVEL

SL Publishers, Box F110-223, Blaine, WA 98230. Book publisher.
OTHER/UNSPECIFIED

Slightly West, The Evergreen State College, CRC 306, Olympia, WA 98505. 206-866-6000 X6879. Editor: Robert M Keefe. Biannual. $2; circ 2,000. Uses freelance material. Pays in copies. Byline given. Submit ms, SASE. Dot matrix, photocopied OK. Reports in 1 mo. Accepts nonfiction, fiction, poetry, literary essays, photos, cartoons, plays, reviews, memoirs. Aims for diverse cultures and ideas. Photo submissions should reproduce well in black & white. Guidelines, sample available.
COLLEGE/UNIVERSITY, FICTION, POETRY

Slo-Pitch News, Varsity Publications, PO Box 27590, Seattle, WA 98125-2590. Monthly.
SPORTS

Slug Press, 128 E 23rd Ave, Vancouver, BC V5V 1X2. Book publisher.
OTHER/UNSPECIFIED

Small Farmer's Journal, PO Box 68, Reedsport, OR 97467. Farmer's literary quarterly, including poetry.
AGRICULTURE/FARMING

Small Pleasures Press, 88 Virginia St #29, Seattle, WA 98101. Book publisher.
OTHER/UNSPECIFIED

Small World Publications, PO Box 305, Corvallis, OR 97339. 503–929-5108. Editor: Rick Cooper. Self-publisher. Not a freelance market.
HOW-TO, HUMOR

The Smallholder Publishing Collective, Argenta, BC V0G 1B0. 604-366-4283. Editor: Betty Tillotson. Magazine published approx. 4 times a year. Sub $14/6 issues; circ 730. Uses freelance material. No pay. Acquires all rights. Byline given. Submit query, SASE. Photocopies OK. "We're a group of volunteers putting together a magazine for country people regarding rural living (all aspects) & our copy is largely made up of letters and articles from readers…non-profit."
COMMUNITY, GARDENING, RURAL

Smith, Smith & Smith Publishing Company, 17515 SW Blue Heron Rd, Lake Oswego, OR 97034. Book publisher.
OTHER/UNSPECIFIED

Smith-Western Inc, 1133 NW Glisan St, Portland, OR 97209. Book publisher.
OTHER/UNSPECIFIED

Smoke Signals, Pacific Press Publishing Association, 1350 Kings Rd, Nampa, ID 83605. Editor: Francis A Soper. Monthly of the Seventh-Day Adventist Church.
RELIGION

SmokeRoot, University of Montana, Department of English, Missoula, MT 59812. University literary publication.
COLLEGE/UNIVERSITY, LITERARY

Smuggler's Cove Publishing, 107 W John St, Seattle, WA 98119. Book publisher.
OTHER/UNSPECIFIED

Smurfs In Hell, 2210 N 9th, Boise, ID 83702. Periodical.
OTHER/UNSPECIFIED

Snake River Alliance Newsletter, PO Box 1731, Boise, ID 83701. Monthly. Circ 1,200. The group works for peace and sane nuclear policies.
OTHER/UNSPECIFIED

Snake River Echoes, PO Box 244, Rexburg, ID 83440. Editors: Louis Clements/Ralph Thompson. 208-356-9101. Quarterly on Snake River history. Circ 700. Sub $10. Uses 6 mss per issue. Byline given. Submit ms, SASE. Photocopies OK. Nonfiction, photos (B&W). "We print history of Snake River area of Eastern Idaho, Eastern Wyoming." Sample/$1.
NW/REGIONAL HISTORY, IDAHO, NORTHWEST

Writing Pursuits, 1863 Bitterroot Dr, Twin Falls, ID 83301. 208-734-0746. Newsletter, 10X/yr. Sub $5.50. Uses freelance material. Pays copies. Byline given. Query, SASE. Dot matrix, photocopied OK. Reports in 2 wks; publishes in 1–2 mos. Accepts nonfiction, short-short stories, poetry, cartoons. Guidelines available. Sample 25¢ & #10 SASE.
FICTION, POETRY, WRITING

The Sneak Preview, PO Box 639, Grants Pass, OR 97526. 503-474-3044. Editor: Curtis Hayden. Biweekly. Sub $34/yr; circ 11,000. Uses freelance material. Pays money on publication. Byline given. Submit ms. Photocopied OK. Accepts nonfiction, fiction, poetry. Topics: humor and satire appreciated. Guidelines available. Sample 65¢.
COMMUNITY, CULTURE, ENTERTAINMENT

Snohomish County Tribune, PO Box 71, Snohomish, WA 98290. 206-776-7546. Weekly newspaper.
COMMUNITY

Snohomish Publishing Company, PO Box 499, Snohomish, WA 98290. Contact: David Mach. 206-568-4121. Publisher of 50 softcover, reprint books a year. Accepts freelance material. Rights purchased: First. Query with outline, SASE. Photocopies, electronic OK. Nonfiction, fiction, poetry, photos, plays, cartoons. Guidelines available.
LITERATURE, MEDIA/COMMUNICATIONS, PUBLISHING/PRINTING

Snowmobile West, Harris Publishing Company, 520 Park Ave, Idaho Falls, ID 83402. Editor: Darryl Harris. Bimonthly. Circ 95,000.
CRAFTS/HOBBIES, OUTDOOR, RECREATION

Socialist Party of Canada, PO Box 4280, Stn A, Victoria, BC V8X 3X8. Book publisher.
POLITICS, SOCIALIST/RADICAL

Society for Industrial Archeology, Dept of History/Social Sciences, Northern Montana College, Havre, MT 59501. Quarterly.
ANTHROPOLOGY/ARCHÆOLOGY, COLLEGE/UNIVERSITY

Society of Photo-Optical Instrumentation Engineers, PO Box 10, 1022 19th St, Bellingham, WA 98227. Book publisher.
BUSINESS, SCIENCE, TECHNICAL

Society of Professors of Education, Portland State University, School of Education, PO Box 751, Portland, OR 97207. Book publisher.
COLLEGE/UNIVERSITY, EDUCATION

Solo Magazine, Box 1231, Sisters, OR 97759. Quarterly.
OTHER/UNSPECIFIED

Solstice Press, Box 111272, Anchorage, AK 99511. Contact: Director. Book publisher.
ALASKA, OTHER/UNSPECIFIED

Solstice Press, Box 9223, Moscow, ID 83843. 208-882-0888. Contact: Ivar Nelson. Publisher and packager of hard- and softcover nonfiction books of national and/or regional interest. Accepts unsolicited submissions. Query w/ SASE/outline/sample chapters. Photocopied and simultaneous subs OK. Pays royalties. Responds in 2 weeks; publishes in 2 months.
NW/REGIONAL HISTORY, NORTHWEST, TRAVEL

SONCAP News, Southern Oregon Northwest Coalition for Alternatives to Pesticides, PO Box 402, Grants Pass, OR 97526. 503-474-6034. Editor: Louise Nicholson. Quarterly newsletter. Sub $10. Circ 700. Accepts freelance material. Submit ms. Dot matrix, photocopied, simultaneous, electronic/ modem OK. Accepts nonfiction, poetry, cartoons. Topics: forestry & environmental ecology, pesticides & herbicides alternatives; air, soil, water, visual quality; worker right-to-know; roadside vegetation management, organic gardening, clearcutting, etc. Sample available.
ENVIRONMENT/RESOURCES, FORESTRY, GARDENING

Sono Nis Press, 1745 Blanshard St, Victoria, BC V8W 2J8. 604-382-1024. Editor: Patricia M Sloan. Publishes 10 hard- & softcover originals per yr. Accepts unsolicited submissions. Pays royalties. Submit query w/clips, SASE. Dot matrix, photocopied, simultaneous OK. Reports in 3 wks. Accepts nonfiction, poetry, humor.
BRITISH COLUMBIA, NW/REGIONAL HISTORY, POETRY

SOS Publishing, Box 68290, Oak Grove, OR 97268. Book publisher.
OTHER/UNSPECIFIED

Soul Town Review, 510 SW 3rd St, Ste 100, Portland, OR 97204. Editor: Connie Cameron. Periodical on the local music scene.
COUNTER CULTURE, CULTURE, MUSIC

Gordon Soules Book Publishers Ltd, 1352-B Marine Dr, West Vancouver, BC V7T 1B5. 604-922-6588. Editor: Gordon Soules. Publishes softcover nonfiction books. Accepts unsolicited high-quality submissions. Topics: biography, guide books, medicine, sports. Query w/clips, SASE, phone. Submit outline, sample chapters, complete ms. Photocopy, dot matrix, simultaneous subs OK. Responds in 1 mo; publishes in 6 mos. Catalog available.
BRITISH COLUMBIA, MEDICAL, RECREATION

Sound Business (formerly Seattle Business), Vernon Publications, 3000 Northrup Way #200, Bellevue, WA 98004. 206-827-9900. Editor: Michele Andrus Dill. Ads: Ruth Schubert. Monthly magazine. Circ 13,000. Uses freelance material. Pays money per length, copies. Acquires 1st, all rights. Byline given. Submit ms, SASE. Dot matrix OK, computer disk if agreed on. Reports only if accepted. Publishing time varies. Accepts nonfiction, photos. Topics: business issues germane to Greater Seattle area. 1,200–2,000 wds. Editorial calendar available.
AVIATION, ECONOMICS, GOVERNMENT

The Source, 5285 NE Elam Young Pkwy. A800, Hillsboro, OR 97124. 503-693-1390. Editor: Suzann Laudenslager. Periodical.
DISABLED

Source Publishing, 6105 SW Bonita Rd #K305, Lake Oswego, OR 97034-3227. Contact: Jan Kennedy. 503-224-5529. Book publisher.
OTHER/UNSPECIFIED

Sourdough Enterprises, 16401 3rd Ave SW, Seattle, WA 98166. Contact: Howard Clifford. 206-244-8115. Publisher of 2–3 softcover originals, reprints a year for an audience of travel, history, rail fans. Press run: 500–20,000. Accepts freelance material. Rights purchased: First. Query w/SASE. Photocopies, simultaneous submissions OK. Reports in 2–3 wks. Nonfiction.
ALASKA, GENERAL HISTORY, TRAVEL

The Sourdough, Fairbanks Law Library, 604 Barnette St, Fairbanks, AK 99701. Periodical.
LAW, REFERENCE/LIBRARY

South County Citizen, c/o Northshore Citizen, PO Box 647, Bothell, Wa 98041. 206-486-1231. Weekly newspaper.
COMMUNITY

South District Journal, 2314 Third Ave, Seattle, WA 98121. 206-461-1331. Weekly newspaper.
COMMUNITY

South Pierce County Dispatch, PO Box 248, Eatonville, WA 98328. 206-832-4411. Newspaper.
COMMUNITY

South Whidbey Record, Box 10, Oak Harbor, WA 98277. 206-321-5300. Weekly newspaper.
COMMUNITY

Southeastern Log, Box 7900, Ketchikan, AK 99901. Editor: Nikki Murray Jones. 907-225-3157. Periodical.
OTHER/UNSPECIFIED

Southern Oregon Arts, The Arts Council of Southern Oregon Newsletter, 33 N Central Ave #308, Medford, OR 97501. 503-779-2820. Editor: Jill Whalley. Quarterly. Mbrship $15/yr; circ 1,600. Uses freelance material.

Byline given, pays copies. Submit ms, query/SASE. Photocopied, disk, dot matrix subs OK. Responds in 1 wk; publishes in 1 mo. Accepts poetry, news items, biographies, nonfiction, photos, interviews, reviews. Photos: B&W any size, no payment, photos returned. Sample $1.
ARTS, COMMUNITY, CULTURE

Southern Oregon Currents, PO Box 1468, Grants Pass, OR 97526. 800-525-2624. Editor: Cathy Noah. Ads: Michele Thomas. Weekly magazine founded in 1989. Sub $24/yr; circ 19,300. Uses freelance material. Byline given. Pays money, copies on publication. Submit query letter, clips, complete ms, SASE, or phone. Responds in 1–2 mos; publishes in 1–2 mos. Accepts nonfiction, poetry, articles, photos (B&W prints, $15; color slides, $25). Topics: entertainment, primarily things to do and places to go; the arts, local personalities and current trends. Guidelines available. Sample 75¢.
ARTS, ENTERTAINMENT, RECREATION

Southern Oregon Historical Society, 106 N Central Ave, Medford, OR 97501-5926. Bimonthly magazine founded in 1946. Editor: Natalie Brown. Ads: Ted Lawson. Mbrship/circ 3,000. Uses freelance material. Byline given. Pays money, copies on acceptance. Acquires 1st rights. Submit query letter, complete ms, SASE, phone. Photocopy, simultaneous subs OK. Responds in 1 mo; publishing time varies. Accepts biography, interviews, memoirs, oral history, photos (B&W, $10–50). Topics: regional history, thoroughly documented, accurate. Guidelines available. Sample $2.50.
AMERICAN HISTORY, NW/REGIONAL HISTORY, OREGON

Southern Willamette Alliance, 454 Willamette, Eugene, OR 97401. 503-343-0565. Editor: Peter Holden. Ads: Dave Zupan. Monthly newspaper. Sub $10–25/yr; circ 7,000. Uses freelance material. Pay varies. Byline given. Submit query letter, complete ms, SASE, phone. Simultaneous, disk/modem subs OK. Accepts nonfiction, photos, cartoons, poetry, news items, interviews, op/ed, reviews; art work for cover. Topics: particularly interested in investigative pieces focusing on current environmental and human rights issues. Guidelines available. Sample $1.
COUNTER CULTURE, ENVIRONMENT/RESOURCES, POLITICS

The Southwestern, Southwestern Oregon Community College, Coos Bay, OR 97420. 503-888-2525. Biweekly newspaper.
COLLEGE/UNIVERSITY, CULTURE, EDUCATION

Southwestern Oregon Publishing Co, 350 Commercial, Coos Bay, OR 97420. 503-269-1222. Book publisher.
OTHER/UNSPECIFIED

Sovereign Press, 326 Harris Rd, Rochester, WA 98579. Publisher of 5 books a year.
OTHER/UNSPECIFIED

Speaking of Taxes, Associated Taxpayers of Idaho, PO Box 1665, Boise, ID 83701. Editor: Russell Westerberg. Irregular periodical. Circ 1,500.
ECONOMICS, IDAHO, PUBLIC AFFAIRS

Special Child Publications, J B Preston, Editor & Publisher, PO Box 33548, Seattle, WA 98133. 206-771-5711. Publisher of 5–10 softcover originals, subsidy (rarely) books a year. Print run: 500–2,000. Rarely accepts freelance material. Payment: 10% of cash received, payable 6 mos after close of royalty period. Rights purchased: All. Query with outline, SASE. Photocopies OK. Reports in 1 month. Publishes in 1–3 yrs. Professional books, college texts, curriculum guides, assessment instruments. Tips: "Mss must be neatly typed, following Chicago Manual. Authorial style should approximate Psychology Today or Omni. Guidelines, catalog available.
EDUCATION, PSYCHOLOGY, TEXTBOOKS

Special Interest Publications, 202-1132 Hamilton St, Vancouver, BC V6B 2S2. Book publisher.
OTHER/UNSPECIFIED

The Spectator, Seattle University, Seattle, WA 98122. Periodical.
COLLEGE/UNIVERSITY, EDUCATION

Spencer Butte Press, 84889 Harry Taylor Rd, Eugene, OR 97405. 503-345-3962. Self-publisher of softcover books. Not a freelance market.
AMERICAN HISTORY, NATIVE AMERICAN, POETRY

Spice West Publishing Company, PO Box 2044, Pocatello, ID 83201. Book publisher.
OTHER/UNSPECIFIED

Spilyay Tymoo, PO Box 870, Warm Springs, OR 97761. 503-553-1644. Editor: Sid Miller. Sub $9. Biweekly newspaper for tribal membership. Uses local news, Native American issues. Sample $1.
COMMUNITY, MINORITIES/ETHNIC, NATIVE AMERICAN

Spindrift, Shoreline Community College, 16101 Greenwood Ave N, Seattle, WA 98133. 206-546-4785. Annual magazine. Sub $6–7. Circ 500. Accepts freelance material. Pays copy on publication. Byline given. Submit ms, SASE. Dot matrix, photocopied OK. Reports in 3 mos. Accepts nonfiction, fiction, poetry, photos, plays, cartoons, B&W drawings. Tips: 4,500 wds on prose, 6 poems, 15 pages dialogue. Photos & art: B&W, 24x24 max. Audience includes essay, fiction & poetry lovers, art enthusiasts. "Genuine work that avoids greeting card sentiment." Sample $6.
COLLEGE/UNIVERSITY, FICTION, POETRY

Spindrift, Tacoma Writers Club, PO Box 459, Puyallup, WA 98371. Editor: John Cuno. Sub $6. Literary quarterly of club. Accepts articles, poetry, fiction from non–members.
LITERATURE, POETRY, WRITING

Spirit Mountain Press, PO Box 1214, Fairbanks, AK 99707. Contact: Larry Laraby. 907-452-7585. Self-publisher of 3–6 softcover books about AK. Print run: 1,500. Accepts freelance material. Rights purchased: First. Submit ms, SASE. Dot matrix, photocopies OK. Reports in 1–6 mos. Publishes in 6–12 mos. Nonfiction, fiction, poetry. "We are looking for material from or about Alaska primarily." Catalog available.
ALASKA, BIOGRAPHY, POETRY

Spokane Area Economic Development Council, PO Box 203, Spokane, WA 99210. Private nonprofit book publisher & newsletter. Sub $14/yr; circ 2,000. Not a freelance market. Sample $3.50.
ECONOMICS, WASHINGTON

Spokane Chronicle, PO Box 2160, Spokane, WA 99210. 509-455-7010. Daily newspaper.
COMMUNITY

Spokane House Enterprises, 2904 W Garland Ave, Spokane, WA 99205-2336. Book publisher.
OTHER/UNSPECIFIED

Spokane Interplayers Ensemble, PO Box 1691, Spokane, WA 99210. Interested in scripts.
DRAMA

Spokane Woman, South 104 Division St, Spokane, WA 99202. 509-456-0203. Editor: Jean Kavanagh. Monthly magazine founded in 1989. Sub $12/yr. Circ 50,000. Uses freelance material. Byline given. Pays money, copies on publication. Acquires 1st rights. Submit query letter, clips, complete ms, SASE, phone. Responds in 2–4 wks; publishes in 2–6 mos. Accepts fiction, nonfiction, photos, articles. Topics: Spokane women — lifestyles, trends, issues. Guidelines available. Sample $1.50.
WOMEN

Spokes, Rotary Club of Portland, 1119 SW Park Ave, Portland, OR 97205. Weekly periodical.
TRADE/ASSOCIATIONS

Spokes, Canadian Poetry Assoc, PO Box 46658, Stn G, Vancouver, BC V6R 4K8. 604-266-0396. Editor: Katie Eliot. Quarterly newsletter; circ 150; sub $10/yr. Uses freelance material. Byline given, pays copies, no rights. Submit query/SASE, phone, photocopy OK. Responds in 1 mo; publishes within 4 mos. Accepts poetry, cartoons, interviews, reviews, news of past or future poetry events. "We publish modern poetry that reflects the involvement and intricacies of contemporary living…." Sample $2.
BRITISH COLUMBIA, POETRY, WRITING

The Spokesman-Review, PO Box 2160, Spokane, WA 99210. 509-455-7010. Daily newspaper. No submission information. Query w/SASE.
COMMUNITY

Sports Digest, The Enterprise Courier, PO Box 471, Oregon City, OR 97045. 503-656-1911. Editor: Dick Mezejewski. Monthly.
RECREATION, SPORTS

Sports Northwest Magazine, 4556 University Way, Seattle, WA 98105. Editor: John Erben. 206-547-9709. Monthly tabloid on "participant sports: running, bicycling, hiking, skiing, triathletics, and lesser known sports such as ultimate frisbee, lacrosse, etc." Circ 25,000. Payment: $1.50 column inch, on publication. Byline given. Query w/SASE. Phone queries, simultaneous submissions OK, modem preferred. Nonfiction: up to 2,000 wds. Fiction: up to 2,000 wds (humor, a personal account or satire." Photos: color slide for cover pays $85, interior B&W action shots, pay varies. Guidelines available. Sample/SASE.
PHOTOGRAPHY, RECREATION, SPORTS

Spotlight, PO Box 51103, Seattle, WA 98115. 206-527-2693. Editor: Ellen Hokanson. Newsletter published 3–4 times a year. Sub free. Circ 5,000. Promotes books for a fee. Not a freelance market. Catalog & sample free.
NORTHWEST, PUBLISHING/PRINTING

The Sprague Advocate, PO Box 327, Sprague, WA 99032. 509-257-2311. Editor/Ads: Kim Nolt. Weekly newspaper founded in 1888. Sub $20/yr; circ 600. Accepts freelance material. Byline given. Submit query letter, clips, SASE, phone. Dot matrix, photocopied OK. Accepts news items, biography, op/ed, memoirs, photos (B&W). Topics: must be relevant to area, used on space-available basis. No payment for unsolicited copy. Guidelines available. Sample $1.50.
AGRICULTURE/FARMING, COMMUNITY, WASHINGTON

Springfield Historical Commission, Planning Department, Springfield City Hall, Springfield, OR 97477. Book publisher.
NW/REGIONAL HISTORY, OREGON

The Springfield News, 1887 Laura St, Box 139, Springfield, OR 97477. 503-746-1671. Daily newspaper.
COMMUNITY

The Sproutletter, Sprouting Publications, Box 62, Ashland, OR 97520. 503-488-2326. Editor: Michael Linden. Bimonthly newsletter. Sub $14/yr; circ 3,000. Uses freelance material. Pays on publication for 1st & 2nd serial rights. Byline given. Submit query letter, SASE. Photocopy, dot matrix, disk/modem, simultaneous subs OK. Responds in 4–8 wks; publishes in 3–4 mos. Accepts nonfiction, cartoons, news items, photos, interviews, reviews. Topics: holistic health through live and raw foods, sprouting and indoor gardens. Sample $3.
FOOD/COOKING, GARDENING, HEALTH

ST 2 Publishing, 203 Si Town Rd, Castle Rock, WA 98611. Book publisher.
OTHER/UNSPECIFIED

St Johns Review, Pry Publishing Co, 600 NW 14th Ave, Portland, OR 97209. 503-226-8335. Editors: Tom or Marcia Pry. Weekly tabloid. Uses freelance material. Byline given. Pays money on publication. Acquires 1st rights. Submit query letter, clips, SASE. Dot matrix OK. Responds in 1–2 wks. Accepts new items, nonfiction, photos, articles. Topics: events and people of the St Johns neighborhood of Portland. Guidelines available.
COMMUNITY

St Maries Gazette Record, 127 S 7th, St Maries, ID 83861. 108-245-4538. Newspaper.
COLLECTING

St Nectarios Press, 10300 Ashworth Ave N, Seattle, WA 98133-9410. 206-522-4471. Self-publisher of 3–4 softcover originals, reprints a year for Eastern Orthodox Christian audience. Print run: 2,000. Not a freelance market. Catalog available.
RELIGION

St Paul's Press, PO Box 100, Sandy, OR 97055. Book publisher.
OTHER/UNSPECIFIED

Stamp Collector, PO Box 10, Albany, OR 97321-0006. 503-928-3569. Editor: Kyle Jansson. Ads: Joan Hanten. Weekly newspaper. Sub $19.95. Circ 22,000. Uses 8 freelance mss per issue. Pays $20+ on publication. Acquires 1st rights. Byline given. Submit query w/SASE, phone query. Dot matrix OK.

Reports in 14 days. Publishing time variable. Accepts nonfiction geared toward stamp collectors, including beginner and advanced collectors and their interests. B&W photos preferred. Guidelines available. Sample $1.
COLLECTING, CRAFTS/HOBBIES

The Stamp Wholesaler, PO Box 706, Albany, OR 97321. 503-928-4484. Editor: Dane Claussen. Newspaper published 28 times a yr. Sub $16.95. Circ 6,000. Uses 4 freelance mss per issue. Pays money on publication. Acquires 1st rights. Byline given. Submit phone query, SASE. Dot matrix OK. Accepts nonfiction. Topics: "Dedicated to promoting the growth and prosperity of the philatelic industry through the exchange of information and ideas." Includes feature articles about stamp dealers and other news of the stamp industry. Sample available.
BUSINESS, COLLECTING, CRAFTS/HOBBIES

Standard-Register, PO Box 988, Tekoa, WA 99033. 509-284-5782. Editor: Bev Berger. Ads: Barbara Schweiter. Weekly newspaper. Sub $17/yr. in-county. Circ 1,800. Uses freelance material. Pays 50¢/col. inch on publication. Byline given. Submit query w/clips, SASE, phone. Dot matrix, photocopied subs OK. Reports in 2 wks; publishes in 1–2 mos. Accepts nonfiction of local human interest, local recreation, agriculture. B&W photos or negatives, color photos, $3 on publication. Sample 35¢.
AGRICULTURE/FARMING, COMMUNITY, RECREATION

Stanwood/Camano News, PO Box 999, Stanwood, WA 98292. 206-629-2155. Weekly newspaper.
COMMUNITY

The Star, PO Box 150, Grand Coulee, WA 99133. 509-633-1350. Weekly newspaper.
COMMUNITY

Star News, PO Box 985, McCall, ID 83638. Editor: Tom Grote. Newspaper.
COMMUNITY, OTHER/UNSPECIFIED

Star Press, Box 835, Friday Harbor, WA 98250. Book publisher.
OTHER/UNSPECIFIED

Star System Press, PO Box 15202, Wedgewood Stn, Seattle, WA 98115. Book publisher.
OTHER/UNSPECIFIED

Star Valley Publications, PO Box 421, Noti, OR 97461. Book publisher.
OTHER/UNSPECIFIED

Starbright Books, 1611 E Dow Rd, Freeland, WA 98249. Book publisher.
OTHER/UNSPECIFIED

StarLance Publications, 50 Basin Dr, Mesa, WA 99343. 509-269-4497. Publishes 4–6 titles per year; collections of fantasy & sf illustrations, cartoons, graphic novels, and illustrated fantasy & sf short fiction. Reports in 2–4 wks. Payment: negotiable. No further submission info; query w/SASE.
FANTASY/SCI FI, FICTION

Starmont House, PO Box 851, Mercer Island, WA 98040. Book publisher.
OTHER/UNSPECIFIED

Starwind Press, 507 3rd Ave #547, Seattle, WA 98104. 206-523-1201. Book publisher. Query w/SASE. Query w/SASE.
OTHER/UNSPECIFIED

Stat, Oregon Medical Association, 5210 SW Corbett, Portland, OR 97201. Monthly.
HEALTH, MEDICAL, TRADE/ASSOCIATIONS

Statesman-Examiner, PO Box 271, Colville, WA 99114. 509-684-4567. Weekly newspaper.
COMMUNITY

Statesman-Journal, 280 Church St NE, Box 13009, Salem, OR 97309. 503-399-6611. Daily newspaper.
COMMUNITY

Stay Away Joe Publishers, Box 2054, Great Falls, MT 59401. Book publisher.
OTHER/UNSPECIFIED

Stay Smart Shoppers, 2729 S Marylhurst Dr, West Lynn, OR 97068. Book publisher.
CONSUMER

Stayton Mail, PO Box 400, Stayton, OR 97383. 503-769-6338. Weekly newspaper.
COMMUNITY

Step Magazine, 200 – 1084 Homer, Vancouver, BC V6B 2W9.
OTHER/UNSPECIFIED

Stephens Press, Drawer 1441, Spokane, WA 99210. Book publisher.
OTHER/UNSPECIFIED

Stepping Out Magazine, 510 SW 3rd Ave, Ste 1, Portland, OR 97204. Editor: James Bash. 503-241-ARTS. Ads: Rex Ruckert. Semiannual magazine of creative endeavors in the fine arts. Sub $14/2 yrs; circ 180,000. Accepts freelance material. Pays money, varies upon article requirements, on publication. Byline given. Acquires all rights. Submit query letter, SASE, phone for assignment. Photocopies, dot matrix, disk/modem subs OK. Accepts nonfiction. Topics: the arts and artists; creative undertakings. Guidelines available; sample $2.50.
ARTS, BUSINESS, TRAVEL

Steppingstone Magazine, Canby High School, 721 SW 4th St, Canby, OR 97013. 503-266-5811. Editor: Paul Dage. Annual. $1. Circ 300. Not a freelance market.
BUSINESS, CALENDAR/EVENTS

90 Steppingstone Press, 3113 Falling Brook Ln, Boise, ID 83706. 208-384-1577. Editors: Martha Miller, Dorris Murdock. Book publisher.
STUDENT

Sternwheeler Press, 200 Burnham Rd #306, Lake Oswego, OR 97034. 503-636-7580. Contact: S A Carrigan. Book publisher. Does not accept unsolicited submissions. Submit query letter, SASE. Responds in 3 mos; publishes in 1 yr. Accepts nonfiction. Topics: all aspects of personal computers written specifically for non-technical computer users, cookbooks and menu books for singles and small families.
COMPUTERS, FOOD/COOKING

The Steward, Erb Memorial Union, University of Oregon, Eugene, OR 97403. Periodical.
COLLEGE/UNIVERSITY

The Stoma Press, 13231 42nd Ave NE, Seattle, WA 98125. Book publisher.
OTHER/UNSPECIFIED

Stonechild Press, PO Box 1612, Havre, MT 59501. Editor: Paul Fussette. Publisher of greeting cards, and subsidy books. Pays money, copies, royalties, advance. Acquires 1st, 2nd rights. Submit query letter, complete ms, synopsis, sample chapters, SASE. Photocopy OK. Responds in 2 wks; publishes in 3 mos. Accepts greeting card poetry, fiction, nonfiction, cartoons, biography.
POETRY

Stonehouse Publications, Timber Butte Rd, Box 390, Sweet, ID 83670. Self-publisher only. No submissions.
ARCHITECTURE, HOW-TO

Stoneydale Press Publishing Company, 274 Cap De Villa, Lolo, MT 59847. Book publisher.
OTHER/UNSPECIFIED

Stories & Letters Digest, 5401 S 12th St #504 Tacoma, WA 98465. 206-752-9434. Editor: James R Humphreys. Quarterly magazine. Sub $9. Circ 300. Uses 4–8 freelance mss per issue. Pays 1/4–1/2 cent/word on acceptance. Acquires 1st rights. Byline given. Submit ms, SASE. Dot matrix, photocopied OK. Reports in 2–4 wks. Publishes in 3–6 mos. Accepts fiction, other. "Literate, entertaining and wholesome short stories. No restrictions on subject matter as long as it is not pornographic...also publishes letters." Guidelines available. Sample $2.50.
ENTERTAINMENT, FICTION

Story Line Press, 3 Oaks Farm, Brownsville, OR 97327-9718. 503-466-5352. Contact: Lysa McDowell. Publisher of literary books, texts and poetry.
LITERARY, POETRY, TEXTBOOKS

Storypole Press, 11015 Bingham Ave E, Tacoma, WA 98446. Publishes out-of-print books on NW Indians and legends. Acquires all rights. Query w/ SASE. Responds in 3 mos; publishes in 1 yr.
NATIVE AMERICAN

Storyteller Guidebook Series, 10 S Keeneway Dr, Medford, OR 97504. Contact: Barbara Budge Griffin. Book publisher.
EDUCATION, HOW-TO, TEXTBOOKS

Straub Printing & Publishing Company, PO Box 1230, Everett, WA 98206. Book publisher.
OTHER/UNSPECIFIED

Strawberry Fields, PO Box 33786, Seattle, WA 98133-0786. Contact: Ken Boisse. Bimonthly.
OTHER/UNSPECIFIED

Street Times, 1236 SW Salmon, Portland, OR 97205. 503-223-4121. Editor: Louis Folkman. Bimonthly. Circ 1,500. Uses freelance material. Query w/SASE. Accepts nonfiction, fiction, poetry, photos, cartoons. Sample available.
CHILDREN/TEEN

Studio 403, PO Box 70672, Seattle, WA 98107-0672. Publisher (fiction, photos, cartoons, other). Book publisher.
FICTION, HUMOR, PHOTOGRAPHY

Studio Solstone, PO Box 4304, Pioneer Sq. Stn, Seattle, WA 98110. Contact: Michael Yaeger. 206-624-9102. Self-publisher of 2 softcover books a year. Print run: 5,000.
OTHER/UNSPECIFIED

Stylus, PO Box 1716, Portland, OR 97207. Contact: Michael Olson, editor; Michael Palmer, book review editor. Bimonthly newsletter. "An eclectic review of music & books." Not a freelance market.
BOOK ARTS/BOOKS, CULTURE, MUSIC

sub-Terrain, Anvil Press, PO Box 1575, Stn A, Vancouver, BC V6C 2P7. 604-876-8700. Editor: B Kaufman. Irregularly published magazine founded in 1988. Sub 4 issues $8 Cdn, $12 US. Circ 500. Uses freelance material. Pays copies. Acquires 1st rights. Byline given. Submit ms/SASE. Dot matrix, photocopied OK. Reports in 1–2 mos; publishes in 3 mos. Accepts fiction, nonfiction, poetry. Topics: opinions, questions and alternatives for the underprivileged, the disenfranchised, the silent many below the surface of Canadian/North American society. Guidelines available. Sample $3.
FICTION, LITERARY, SOCIALIST/RADICAL

Subterranean Company, PO Box 168, Monroe, OR 97456. Book publisher.
OTHER/UNSPECIFIED

Subway Press, 1706 Bison Dr, Kalispell, MT 59901. 406-756-9079. Contact: Judie Overbeek. Publisher of books for learning adult readers. Pays royalties. Submit detailed outline, sample page, word count. Reports in 2–3 wks. Topics: mysteries, history, poetry, contemporary fiction, how-to handbooks, regional cultures. Author's guide available.
EDUCATION, FICTION, OTHER/UNSPECIFIED

Sugar Producer, Harris & Smith Company, 520 Park Ave, Idaho Falls, ID 83402. Editor: Darryl Harris. Semiannual periodical. Circ 20,000.
AGRICULTURE/FARMING, BUSINESS

Sumner House Press, 2527 W Kennewick Ave, Ste 190, Kennewick, WA 99336. 509-783-7800. Editor: R F Hill. Book publisher.
OTHER/UNSPECIFIED

Sun, PO Box 689, Sunnyside, WA 98944. 509-837-3701. Weekly newspaper.
COMMUNITY

The Sun, 248 S Bridge, Box 68, Sheridan, OR 97378. 503-843-2312. Weekly newspaper.
COMMUNITY

The Sun—Editorial, 2250 Granville St, Vancouver, BC V6H 3G2. Newspaper.
OTHER/UNSPECIFIED

Sun-Enterprise, 1697 Monmouth St, Box 26, Independence, OR 97351. 503-838-3467. Weekly newspaper.
COMMUNITY

Sun King Publishing Company, PO Box 68503, Seattle, WA 98168-0503. Book publisher.
OTHER/UNSPECIFIED

Sun Magic, 911 NE 45th, Seattle, WA 98105. Book publisher.
OTHER/UNSPECIFIED

Sun Moon Press, PO Box 1516, Eugene, OR 97440. Book publisher.
OTHER/UNSPECIFIED

The Sun Tribune, 104 E Central, Box 430, Sutherlin, OR 97479. 503-459-2261. Weekly newspaper.
COMMUNITY

Sun Valley Books, Box 1688, Sun Valley, ID 83358. Self-publisher.
OTHER/UNSPECIFIED

Sun Valley Magazine, PO Box 2950, Ketchum, ID 83340. Editor: Mike Riedel. Published 3 times a year. Circ 2,600.
ENTERTAINMENT, IDAHO, RECREATION

Sunburst, 1322 Coral Dr W, Tacoma, WA 98466-5832. Book publisher.
OTHER/UNSPECIFIED

Sunburst Press, PO Box 14205, Portland, OR 97214. Editor: Johnny Baranski. Ads: Grace Jewett. Self-publisher of 1 softcover original book a year. Press run: 300–1,000. Not a freelance market. Catalog available.
PEACE, POETRY, RELIGION

Sundance Publishing Company, 1270 Colgan Court SE, Salem, OR 97302. Book publisher.
OTHER/UNSPECIFIED

Sunfire Publications, PO Box 3399, Langley, BC V3A 4R7. 604-576-6561. Contact: Garnet Basque. Publisher of hard- & softcover originals, reprints on "historical subjects from British Columbia, Alberta and the Yukon." Catalog available.
BRITISH COLUMBIA, CANADIAN HISTORY, OLD WEST

Sunnyside Daily News, PO Box 878, Sunnyside, WA 98944. 509-837-4500. Daily newspaper.
COMMUNITY

Sunrise Publishing, PO Box 62, Sisters, OR 97759. Book publisher.
OTHER/UNSPECIFIED

Sunrise Tortoise Books, Box 61, Sandpoint, ID 83864. Book publisher.
OTHER/UNSPECIFIED

Survival Education Association, 9035 Golden Givens Rd, Tacoma, WA 98445. Book publisher.
OTHER/UNSPECIFIED

Swale Publications, 4003 Airport Way S, Seattle, WA 98108. Editor: Roberto Valenze/Phoebe Bosche. Periodical.
OTHER/UNSPECIFIED

SwanMark Books, PO Box 2056, Valdez, AK 99686. 907-835-4385. Contact: Harry Swan. Publisher of books about Alaska by Alaskans. Childrens' stories, animal stories, short stories for young adults, stories about Alaskan Native life, works in the humanities for all ages.
ALASKA, CHILDREN/TEEN, FICTION

Swedish Press, 1294 W 7th Ave, Vancouver, BC V6M 1B6. 604-731-6381. Editor/ads: Anders Neumueller. Monthly of Swedish interest, founded 1929. Sub $14. Uses 2 mss per issue. Pays copies. Byline given. Acquires 1st rights. Submit ms, SASE. Photocopies OK. Accepts nonfiction. Topics: Swedes, Swedish descendants, Swedish slants on general stories. Photos: B&W and color landscapes for cover, B&W on inside. Sample $1.
MINORITIES/ETHNIC, PHOTOGRAPHY

Sweet Forever Publishing, PO Box 1000, Eastsound, WA 98245. Book publisher.
OTHER/UNSPECIFIED

Sweet Home New Era, 1200 Long St, Sweet Home, OR 97386. 503-367-2135. Newspaper.
COMMUNITY, OTHER/UNSPECIFIED

Synesis Press, PO Box 1843-N, Bend, OR 97709. 503-382-6517. Contact: Juliana Panchura. Publishes 6 softcover originals per year. Accepts unsolicited submissions w/SASE. Pays royalties on publication. Query by phone OK. Dot matrix photopied, computer disk subs OK. Reports in 3 wks. Topics: nonfiction, health/fitness, diet/nutrition, food/cooking, exercise/training, self-help/how-to.
FOOD/COOKING, HEALTH, SPORTS

Syringa Publishing, 1340 Eldorado #D, Boise, ID 83704. Editor: Susan A Lewis. Book publisher.
OTHER/UNSPECIFIED

T.I.P.S. Employment Guide, PO Box 2548, Redmond, WA 98073-2548. Editor: Jim Massey.
BUSINESS, CONSUMER, LABOR/WORK

TABA Publishing, 24103 SE 384th St, Enumclaw, WA 98022. 206-825-9709. Contact: Eugene E Bauer. Publisher of books on the history of the aircraft industry.
AVIATION, COMMERCE, GENERAL HISTORY

Table Rock Sentinel, 106 N Central Ave, Medford, OR 97501. 503-899-1847. Editor: Natalie Brown. Ads: Ted Lawson. Self-publisher of membership magazine & newsletter. Circ 2,000. Uses one freelance ms per issue. Requires historical accuracy & expertise. Pays money ($10–100) on acceptance (30–60 days). Byline given. Submit query w/clips, SASE. Dot matrix, photocopied OK. Reports in 30 days. Publishing time varies. Accepts nonfiction feature articles, poetry, book reviews. Topics: relating to the history of the southern Oregon region. Photos 8X10 glossy, professional ($5–10). Guidelines available. Sample $2.50.
NW/REGIONAL HISTORY, OREGON

Tabula Rasa Press, 617 Western Ave, Seattle, WA 948104. 206-682-5185. Editor: John P Lathourakis. Publishes hard- & softcover books. Accepts unsolicited submissions. Pays royalties, copies on publication. Submit query letter, complete ms, phone. Photocopy, disk/modem subs OK. Responds in 1 mo; publishes in 1–8 mos. Accepts fiction, poetry, biography, nonfiction, articles, short stories (1,000–5,000 wds). Catalog available.
BIOGRAPHY, FICTION

Tacoma Daily Index, PO Box 1303, Tacoma, WA 98401. 206-627-4853. Daily newspaper.
COMMUNITY

Tacoma Magazine, Western Pacific Publishing, 2501 E 'D' St #203, Tacoma, WA 98421-1326. 206-627-4228. Contact Patricia Collinge. Ads: Jim Vanderwarner. Monthly magazine. Circ 50,000. Uses 50 freelance mss per issue. Pays negotiated rates on publication. Byline given. Submit query w/clips, ms, or by phone. Dot matrix, photocopies, computer disk, simultaneous bus OK. Reports in 2 wks. Publishes in 2–4 mos. Accepts nonfiction, fiction, photos. Topics: feature material of interest to Pacific NW residents. Tips: 1500–2000 wds. Photos: color slides, B&W prints, rates negotiated. Sample free.
CULTURE, FICTION, NORTHWEST

Tacoma News Tribune, PO Box 11000, Tacoma, WA 98411-0008. Editor: Al Gibbs. 206-597-8551. Daily newspaper. "The only freelance writing currently being accepted by our newspaper is for the travel section." Query w/SASE.
COMMUNITY, TRAVEL

Tadalex Books, PO Box 78582, Seattle, WA 98178. 206-772-6110. Editor: Larry G Carlson. Adv: LaDonna Brown. Book publisher. Accepts unsolicited submissions. Pays royalties/copies, acquires all rights. Submit ms, query/SASE. Responds in 8 wks; publishes in 6 mos. Accepts science fiction for science education only. No excessive violence, language, sex. Guidelines available.
EDUCATION, ENTERTAINMENT, FANTASY/SCI FI

Tag Books, PO Box 111, Independence, OR 97351. Book publisher.
OTHER/UNSPECIFIED

Tahlkie Books, Tahlkie Books, Camas, WA 98607. Contact: Jim Attwell. Books on regional and Columbia Gorge history and peoples.
NW/REGIONAL HISTORY

Tai Chi School, PO Box 2424, Bellingham, WA 98227. Book publisher.
SPORTS

Take Five, PO Box 5027, Salem, OR 97304. Contact: Tim Hinshaw. Periodical.
ENTERTAINMENT

Talking Leaves, 1430 Willamette #367, Eugene, OR 97401. 503-342-2974. Editor: Carolyn Moran. Sub $15/yr; circ 8,000. Monthly journal. Uses freelance material. Byline given. Pays copies. Acquires 1st rights. Submit query letter, SASE. Photocopied, dot matrix subs OK, disk/modem preferred. Publishes in 2 mos. Accepts fiction, poetry, cartoons, news items, biography, photos, interviews, op/ed, articles, plays, reviews, memoirs. Topics: bioregional; deep ecology and spiritual activism. Sample $1.50.
CONSERVATION, ENVIRONMENT/RESOURCES, FEMINISM

Talonbooks, 201 – 1019 E Cordova St, Vancouver, BC V6A 1M8. Publisher of books on drama, fiction, poetry, photography.
DRAMA, FICTION, POETRY

Tantalus Research, PO Box 34248, 2405 Pine St, Vancouver, BC V6J 4N8. Book publisher.
OTHER/UNSPECIFIED

Tao of Wing Chun Do, 11023 NE 131st, Kirkland, WA 98033. Book publisher.
OTHER/UNSPECIFIED

TAPjoe, PO Box 104, Grangeville, ID 83530. 208-983-2780. Contact: Editorial Board. Biannual with occasional special issues. Sub $10/4 issues. Poetry only. Prefers 10–50 lines, but will look at longer. Prefers material dealing with nature and social issues, but considers all submissions. Pay in copies. No simultaneous submissions or previously published poems. Query w/ SASE.
POETRY

Target Seattle, 909 4th Ave, Seattle, WA 98104. Book publisher.
OTHER/UNSPECIFIED

Tari Book Publishers, 146 E 34th Ave, Eugene, OR 97405. Book publisher.
OTHER/UNSPECIFIED

TASH (The Association for Persons with Severe Handicaps), 7010 Roosevelt Way NE, Seattle, WA 98115. Book publisher.
DISABLED

Tax Fax Publishing Co, PO Box 84275, Vancouver, WA 98684. Book publisher.
BUSINESS, ECONOMICS

Tax Tutors, 506 7th Ave, Oregon City, OR 97045. 503-657-9521. Contact: Janis E Salisbury. Publishers of books on taxes.
CONSUMER, ECONOMICS, HOW-TO

Teaching Home, PO Box 20219, Portland, OR 97220-0219. Editor: Sue Welch. Sub $15/yr. Bimonthly magazine for Christian home educators. No submission infor.
CHILDREN (BY/ABOUT), EDUCATION, RELIGION

Teaching Research Infant and Child Center, Monmouth, OR 97361. Periodical.
CHILDREN (BY/ABOUT), CHILDREN/TEEN, EDUCATION

Teaching Today, University of Idaho Off-campus Programs, College of Education, Moscow, ID 83843. Contact: Sid Eder. Newspaper published in Nov & Apr each year provides a communication link between the U of I and the education community of Idaho and the Inland Northwest. Guest editorials solicited; pay $25.
EDUCATION, IDAHO, NORTHWEST

Tech Talk, Oregon Institute of Technology, Klamath Falls, OR 97601. 503-882-6321. Weekly student newspaper.
COLLEGE/UNIVERSITY

Technical Analysis of Stocks & Commodities, 3517 SW Alaska St, Seattle, WA 98126. 206-938-0570. Editor: Thom Hartle. Ads: Lou Knoll Kemper. Monthly magazine. Sub $64.95/yr; circ 25,000. Uses freelance material. Writers should be knowledgeable about trading. Pays $3/col inch, $50 min on publication; cartoons, small items, flat $15. Acquires 1st rights. Byline given. Submit ms, SASE. Dot matrix, photocopied, electronic, disk-modem OK. Reports in 1 day; publishes in 3–6 mos. Accepts nonfiction, fiction, how-to articles on trading. Topics-theme blocks: psychology of trading, technical vs fundamental, using statistics, chart work & technical analysis, new technical methods (charting, computer use), trading techniques, basics, reviews (books, articles, software, hardware), humor (incidents, cartoons, photos). Guidelines available. Sample $5.
COMMERCE, COMPUTERS, HOW-TO

Technocracy Digest and The Northwest Technocrat, 3642 Kingsway, Vancouver, BC V5R 5M2. 604-434-1134. Editor: Elizabeth L Hievert. Quarterly magazine, founded 1934. Sub $6/yr. Digest only, $12/yr includes The Northwest Technocrat. Uses freelance material. Byline given. Submit query w/SASE, or phone. Responds in 1 mo; publishes in 3 mos. Accepts nonfiction, news items, articles. Guidelines available. Sample 75¢.
EDUCATION, PHILOSOPHY

Temporal Acuity Press, 1535 121st Ave SE, Bellevue, WA 98005. Book publisher.
OTHER/UNSPECIFIED

Terragraphics, PO Box 1025, Eugene, OR 97440. 503-343-7115. Editor: Peter Powers. Ads: Renee Travis. Self-publisher. Not a freelance market.
BICYCLING, RECREATION, TRAVEL

Testmarketed Downpour, Linfield College, Box 414, McMinnville, OR 97128. 503-472-4121. Editor: Barbara Drake. College literary magazine. Editor could change yearly. SASE for guidelines.
COLLEGE/UNIVERSITY, FICTION, OREGON

TGNW Press, 2429 E Aloha, Seattle, WA 98112. 206-328-9656. Editor: Roger Herz. Self-publisher. Does not accept unsolicited submissions. Submit query letter, SASE. Dot matrix, simultaneous subs OK. Topics: juvenile.
CHILDREN/TEEN, HUMOR, SPORTS

That Patchwork Place Inc, 18800 142nd Ave NE, Ste 2A, Woodinville, WA 98072. Contact: Nancy Martin. 206-483-3313. Publisher of 6 softcover books a year on quilting, creative sewing. Print run: 10,000. Accepts freelance material. Rights purchased: All. Pay: varies. Query w/outline, SASE. Dot matrix, photocopies OK. Reports in 1 month. "Quilting techniques or quilt history; new techniques or speed techniques for patchwork; creative sewing especially that related to folk art, quilting, Christmas and other holidays." Guidelines/catalog available.
CRAFTS/HOBBIES, VISUAL ARTS

The Dalles Chronicle, 414 Federal St, The Dalles, OR 97508. 503-296-2141. Daily newspaper.
COMMUNITY, OTHER/UNSPECIFIED

The Dalles Weekly Reminder, PO Box 984, The Dalles, OR 97508. Editor: Gerald Ericksen. 503-298-4725. Ads: Saundra Bernards. Weekly newspaper. Circ 4,000. Sub $18. Almost never accepts freelance material, but "I'll look at anything of local interest." Byline given. No pay: "If something were exclusive and really good, we could possibly negotiate a small payment." Submit ms, SASE. Phone queries, dot matrix, photocopies, simultaneous submission OK. Reports immediately. "Local means Wasco or Sherman counties only." Photos: B&W photos or negatives preferred.
AGRICULTURE/FARMING, NW/REGIONAL HISTORY, PUBLIC AFFAIRS

The Montana Catholic, PO Box 1729, Helena, MT 59624. 406-442-5820. Editor: Gerald M Korson. Journal published 16X/yr. Sub $10; circ 8,500. Uses freelance material. Submit query letter, complete ms, SASE. Dot matrix, simultaneous subs OK. Responds in 3 wks; publishes in 1–6 mos. Accepts news items, photos, interviews, articles. Catholic angle necessary. Sample $3 for 3 issues.
RELIGION

These Homeless Times, Burnside Community Council, 313 E Burnside St, Portland, OR 97214. 503-231-7158. Editor: Susan Elwood. Quarterly. Sub $10. Uses freelance material.
URBAN

Theytus Books, Box 218, Penticton, BC V2A 6K3. Book publisher: poetry, fiction, photos, nonfiction.
FICTION, NATIVE AMERICAN, POETRY

Thin Power, 2519 First Ave #709, Seattle, WA 98121. Book publisher.
HEALTH, OTHER/UNSPECIFIED

The Third Age Newspaper, 3402 112th St SW, Everett, WA 98204. Monthly newspaper.
OTHER/UNSPECIFIED

This is Alaska, 1041 E 76th, Ste C, Anchorage, AK 99502. Editor: Frank Martone. 907-349-7506. Periodical.
ALASKA

"This Is Just to Say", Assembly on American Literature, National Council of Teachers of English, PO Box 1305, Lake Oswego, OR 97035. 503-245-4526. Editor: Sandi Brinkman. Quarterly newsletter on American authors. Circ 300. Accepts freelance material. Byline given. Query w/ms, SASE. Dot matrix, simultaneous submissions OK. Reports in 1–3 mos. Nonfiction: 1,000 words on authors, literature. Photos. Sample available.
EDUCATION, AMERICAN HISTORY, LITERATURE

This Week Magazine, 9600 SW Boeckman Rd, Portland, OR 97208. Asst. editor: Don Campbell. Ads: 503-682-1223. Weekly newspaper. Free circ 500,000 mailed to homes. Uses freelance material. Pays money on publication. Byline given. Query w/SASE. Phone queries OK. Accepts nonfiction: 600–1,800 wds. Tips: "Most is local by assignment. If writer's clips show a lot of style, might give assignments."
COMMUNITY, CONSUMER, FOOD/COOKING

Thorn Creek Press, 220 N Van Buren, Moscow, ID 83843. Book publisher.
OTHER/UNSPECIFIED

Thumb Press, Box 1136, Petersburg, AK 99833. Book publisher.
OTHER/UNSPECIFIED

Thunderchief Corporation, 18460 SE Stephens St, Portland, OR 97233-5537. Book publisher.
OTHER/UNSPECIFIED

ThunderEgg Publishing, 3929 Overland Rd, Ste 773, Boise, ID 83705. 208-887-4964. Contact: Jana Pewitt. Books on computers and business. No unsolicited mss. Query w/SASE and experience/clips. Responds in 1 mo; publishing time varies. Payment varies.
BUSINESS, COMPUTERS

The Thurston-Mason Senior News, 529 W 4th Ave, Olympia, WA 98501. 206-786-5595. Editor: Rick Crawford. Ads: Don Hellum. Monthly tabloid free to senior citizens. Circ 15,000. Uses freelance material. May pay copies on publication. Byline given. Submit ms, SASE. Dot matrix, photocopied OK. Accepts nonfiction, cartoons. Topics: local news, health, nutrition, leisure, travel, finance, legislation for retirees. Sample for postage.
COMMUNITY, SENIOR CITIZENS

Tickled by Thunder, #4 – 6280 King George Hwy, Surrey, BC V3W 4Y9. Contact: Larry Lindner. Quarterly newsletter. Circ 100. 100% freelance written. Copies sent upon publication (cash as circ increases). Acquires 1st rights, byline given. Submit w/SASE. Dot matrix, photocopies, simultaneous, electronic/modem submission OK. Reports in 1 month, publishes on acceptance. Accepts nonfiction, fiction, poetry, and cartoons. Articles: 2,000 words max on writing, personal experience, etc. Fiction: 2,000 words max, anything goes. Poems, 60 lines max. Guidelines and sample issues available with $2 and SASE.
FICTION, LITERARY, POETRY

Tidepools, Peninsula College, Port Angeles, WA 98362. 206-452-9277. Editor: Alice Derry. Periodical.
COLLEGE/UNIVERSITY

Tidewater, 2052 SE Hawthorne Blvd #101, Portland, OR 97214-3857. Contact: Scott Hartwich, editor. Irregular journal of fiction and poetry). No

preachy or sexist material. Try not to offend. Cover letter w/SASE. Be professional. Payment in copies, usually. All subjects welcome.
FICTION, LITERARY, POETRY

Tillamook Headlight-Herald, 1908 2nd St, Tillamook, OR 97141. 503-842-7535. Newspaper.
COMMUNITY, OTHER/UNSPECIFIED

Tillamook Publishing, PO Box 64, Nehalem, OR 97131. 503-322-3542. Contact: George Atcheson. Book publisher.
OTHER/UNSPECIFIED

Timber!, Willamette Timbermen Association Inc, 589 S 72nd St, Springfield, OR 97478. 503-726-7918. Editor: Ted Ferrioli. Monthly.
FORESTRY, LUMBER

Timber Press, 9999 SW Wilshire, Portland, OR 97225. 503-292-0745. Editor: Richard Abel. Ads: Michael Fox. Publishes 50 hardcover originals, reprints per year. Accepts unsolicited submissions. Acquires all rights. Submit query letter, SASE. Dot matrix, photocopied subs OK. Reports in 3–4 wks. Accepts nonfiction: horticulture, landscape design, garden history, botany & other plant sciences, agriculture, farming, forestry, ecology. Catalog available.
AGRICULTURE/FARMING, FORESTRY, GARDENING

Timber/West Magazine, PO Box 610, Edmonds, WA 98020. 206-778-3388. Editor: Dennis Stuhaug, Ads: Don Pravitz. Specialized logging industry publication. Monthly; circ 10,000+. Uses 2–3 freelance mss. per issue, by assignment only. Byline given. Pays money on publication. Acquires all rights. Submit query letter, SASE. Disk/modem, dot matrix OK. Responds immediately, publication in 1–3 months. Topics: logging, heaving on techniques, equipment. Guidelines available. Topics: 032, 070, 078.
COMMERCE, INDUSTRY, LUMBER

Timberbeast, PO Box 3695, Eugene, OR 97403. 503-686-8416. Editor/Ads: Bill Roy. Journal. Sub $12 yr. Circ 1,200+. Uses freelance material. Pays copies. Byline given. Submit query w/clips, ms, SASE, phone. Dot matrix, photocopied, computer disk OK. Reports in 3 wks; publishes in 6 mos. Accepts nonfiction, photos, cartoons. Topics: Pacific NW historical logging — individuals, companies, equipment, methods; "Reviews of relevant materials, 'great loggers I have known.'" Sample $3.
FORESTRY, NW/REGIONAL HISTORY, LUMBER

Timberline Press, PO Box 70071, Eugene, OR 97401. Self-publisher. Not a freelance market.
OTHER/UNSPECIFIED

Timberman Times, Umpqua Community College, PO Box 967, Roseburg, OR 97470. 503-440-4600. Newspaper.
COLLEGE/UNIVERSITY

Time Designs, 29722 Hult Rd, Colton, OR 97017. Editor: T Woods. Periodical.
OTHER/UNSPECIFIED

Time to Pause, Inky Trails Publications, PO Box 345, Middleton, ID 83644. Editor: Pearl Kirk. Semiannual literary magazine featuring poetry, fiction, nonfiction, and art. Circ 200. Submit ms, SASE. Reports in 2–8 wks. Nonfiction: 3,500–5,500 wds on book reviews, essays, historical or nostalgic humor, inspirational, personal experience and travel. Fiction: 3,500–5,500 wds on fantasy, historical, humorous, mystery, romance, suspense, and western. Poetry: 4–70 lines of verse, free verse, light verse, or traditional. Tips: "Do not want horror, porno, etc." Sample: SASE.
FANTASY/SCI FI, HUMOR, TRAVEL

Times, PO Box 97, Waitsburg, WA 99361. 509-337-6631. Weekly newspaper.
COMMUNITY

Times Eagle Books, PO Box 11735, Portland, OR 97211. Editor: John Hall. Publishes softcover books. Pays 10% royalties. Submit query letter, SASE. Responds in 6 wks. Topics: experimental fiction by avant-garde Oregon novelists.
AVANT-GARDE/EXPERIMENTAL, FICTION

The Times-Journal, 319 S Main, Box 746, Condon, OR 97823. 503-384-2421. Weekly newspaper.
COMMUNITY

The Times Journal Publishing Co, 7476 US Hwy #12, Morton, WA 98356. 206-4948-5243. Book publisher. Does not accept unsolicited submissions. Submit query letter, SASE. Responds in 1 mo. Accepts nonfiction, fiction, biography, photos.
OTHER/UNSPECIFIED

The Times News, 132 3rd St W, Twin Falls, ID 83301. Newspaper.
COMMUNITY

The Times, 109 Spalding Ave, Box 278, Brownville, OR 97327. 503-466-5311. Weekly newspaper.
COMMUNITY

Tin Man Press, Box 219, Stanwood, WA 98292. Book publisher.
OTHER/UNSPECIFIED

Tiptoe Literary Service, PO Box 206-H, Naselle, WA 98638-0206. 206-484-7722. Self-publisher. Rarely uses freelance material. Query letter, SASE, phone. Topic: writers guide pamphlets. Catalog available.
EDUCATION, HOW-TO, WRITING

Titania Publications, PO Box 30160, Eugene, OR 97403. Book publisher.
CHILDREN/TEEN, COMPUTERS

Tolemac Inc, PO Box 418, Ashland, OR 97520. Book publisher.
OTHER/UNSPECIFIED

Topping International Institute, 1419 N State, Bellingham, WA 98226. 206-647-2703. Editor: Bernie Topping. Book publisher.
OTHER/UNSPECIFIED

Tops Learning Systems, 10978 S Mulino Rd, Canby, OR 97013. Book publisher.
EDUCATION

The Torch, Lane Community College, 205 Center Bldg, 4000 E 30th Ave, Eugene, OR 97405. 503-747-4501. Weekly newspaper.
COLLEGE/UNIVERSITY

Totline, 17909 Bothell Way SE, Ste 101, Bothell, WA 98012. 206-485-3335. Editor: Jean Warren. Ads: Sharon Schumacher. Bimonthly newsletter. Sub $15. Circ 6,500. Uses freelance material from writers with early childhood educational experience. Pays money on acceptance. Acquires all rights. Byline given. Submit ms, SASE. Dot matrix, photocopied OK. Reports in 10–12 wks. Accepts nonfiction poetry. Topics: activity ideas, ie, craft, art, educational, games, cultural awareness; articles with activities around a central theme, inspirational poetry for adults. Tips: sketches encouraged for clarification. Guidelines available. Sample $2.
CHILDREN/TEEN, EDUCATION

Touch the Heart Press, PO Box 373, Eastsound, WA 98245. Book publisher.
OTHER/UNSPECIFIED

The Touchstone Press, PO Box 81, Beaverton, OR 97075. Contact: Oral Bullard. 503-646-8081. Publisher of 2–3 softcover originals a year for outdoor people. Print run: 3,000. Accepts freelance material. Payment: Royalties. Rights purchased: All. Query, sample chapters w/SASE. Photocopies OK. Reports in 15–45 days. Publishes in 1 year. Trail guides, wildflower books, wilderness guides, local history (OR, WA, CA, ID, MT, NV). Catalog available.
NW/REGIONAL HISTORY, NATURAL HISTORY, OUTDOOR

Towers Club, USA Newsletter, Box 2038, Vancouver, WA 98668. Editor: Jerry Buchanan. 206-574-3084. Monthly "covers the field of selling info in printed or taped format directly to the consumer. Advertising tips, sources, news of the industry." Sub $60/yr. Not a freelance market.
BUSINESS, PUBLISHING/PRINTING

Town Forum Inc, Cerro Gordo Ranch, PO Box 569, Cottage Grove, OR 97424. Book publisher.
OTHER/UNSPECIFIED

Toy Investments Inc, 6705 S 216th, Kent, WA 98032. Book publisher.
BUSINESS, CRAFTS/HOBBIES, OTHER/UNSPECIFIED

Trabarni Productions, 1531 – 550 Cottonwood Ave, Coquitlam, BC V3J 2S1. Publisher of 3–4 softcover original books and journals. Acquires 1st rights. Pays on publication. Query w/SASE and publication credits. Book subjects: poetry, graphics, visual text, women's writing (though not necessarily of feminist slant). Journals: mythology, nonfiction, west coast.
ASTROLOGY/SPIRITUAL, POETRY, WOMEN

Trace Editions, Fine and Rare Books, 3733 NE 24th Ave, Portland, OR 97212. Contact: Charles Seluzicki. 503-284-4749. Publisher of 2 hard- & softcover books a year. Print run: 500. Accepts freelance material. Payment: Copies; small cash payment at times. Rights purchased: First. Submit ms, SASE. Photocopies OK. Reports in 1 month. Publishes in 6–12 mos. Nonfiction, fiction, poetry, plays. "Quality writing in well designed offset formats produced to high standards. Primarily, mss are solicited. Our authors include Sandra McPherson, Vasko Popa, Charles Wright, Charles Simic and Z Herbert." Catalog available.
BOOK ARTS/BOOKS, FICTION, POETRY

Trail Breakers, Clark County Genealogical Society. PO Box 2728, Vancouver, WA 98668. 206-256-0977. Editor: Rose Marie Harshman. Quarterly newsletter. Sub $12. Circ 500. Accepts freelance material. Byline given. Submit query, ms, SASE. Nonfiction, photos: how-to articles, research articles, Clark County genealogy. Sample $3.
GENEALOGY, NW/REGIONAL HISTORY

Trail City Archives, 1394 Pine Ave, Trail, BC V1R 4E6. 604-364-1262. Publishes softcover books. Does not accept unsolicited submissions. Query letter, SASE, phone. Responds in 1 wk. Accepts nonfiction, photos, articles. Topics: history.
BRITISH COLUMBIA, CANADIAN HISTORY

Training Associates Ltd, 1701 W 3rd, Vancouver, BC V6J 1K7. Contact: Peter Renner. 604-263-7091. Publisher of 2 softcover, how-to books a year. Print run: 2,500. Accepts freelance material. Pays biannually; 10–18%; advance to be negotiated. Negotiates rights purchased. Outline, sample chapters w/SASE. Dot matrix, photocopies OK. Reports in 4 wks. Publishes in 6 mos. Nonfiction: how-to, business and training. Catalog available.
BUSINESS, EDUCATION, HOW-TO

Training & Culture Newsletter, GilDeane Group, 13751 Lake City Way NE #105, Seattle, WA 98125-8612. Sub $59/yr org, $39/yr individual. Bimonthly newsletter with monthly bulletins. No submission info available.
OTHER/UNSPECIFIED

The Trainmaster, PNC-National Railway Historical Society, 800 NW 6th Ave, Portland, OR 97209. 503-226-6747. Monthly. Sub $3. Circ 500. Not a freelance market.
GENERAL HISTORY, TRAVEL

Trainsheet, c/o Tacoma Chapter NRHS Inc, PO Box 340, Tacoma, WA 98401-0340. Editor: Art Hamilton. 206-537-2169. Published 10 times a year. Circ 300. Sub $17. Uses 1 ms per issue. No pay. Submit ms, SASE. Phone queries, dot matrix, photocopies OK. Nonfiction: railroad history; max 2 pgs (1,000 + wds) typed 3 1/2" wide max. Photos: 5x7, B&W; no pay.
GENERAL HISTORY, TRAVEL

Transformation Times, PO Box 425, Beavercreek, OR 97004. 503-632-7141. Editor: Connie L Faubel. Ads: E James Faubel. Published 10X/yr. Sub $8; circ 8,000. Uses freelance material. Pays money, other on publication. Acquires 1st rights. Byline given. Submit ms, SASE. Dot matrix, photocopied, disk/modem OK. Reports in 1 mo; publishes in 1–2 mos. Accepts nonfiction, fiction, cartoons, interviews, photos, articles. Topics: metaphysical, holistic, human potential, occult sciences, environmental quality, socially responsible issues, book and video reviews. No longer than 1,500 wds. Guidelines available. Sample $1.
ASTROLOGY/SPIRITUAL, CALENDAR/EVENTS, NEW AGE

Transonic Hacker, 1402 SW Upland Dr, Portland, OR 97221-2649. Editor: Eric Geislinger. Periodical.
COMPUTERS, OTHER/UNSPECIFIED

Transport Electronic News, 3 – 1610 Kebet Way, Port Coquitlam, BC V3C 5W9. 604-942-4312. Contact: Rob Robertson. Canadian trucking industry quarterly on electronics advances and uses. Query w/clips.
BUSINESS, CANADA, COMMERCE

Trask House Press, 2754 SE 27th, Portland, OR 97202. Contact: Carlos Reyes. 503-235-1898. Irregular publisher of poetry books. Print run: 500. Accepts freelance material. Query w/SASE. Reports in 30–60 days. Poetry.
POETRY

Travel Oregon Magazine, 446 Charnelton, Eugene, OR 97401. 503-688-7134. Periodical.
OREGON, TRAVEL

Travelin' Magazine, PO Box 23005, Eugene, OR 97402. 503-687-1242. Editor: Russ Heggen. Sub $20/yr. Circ 10,000. Bimonthly mag using 10–20 freelance mss per issue. Pays money on publication. Byline given. Query w/ clips. Topics: traveling in the eleven western states for adults (45–65 yrs) who travel mostly by car or RV, emphasis on backroads, unusual places. B&W photos and maps as part of articles. Guidelines available.
NORTHWEST, RECREATION, TRAVEL

Traveller's Bed & Breakfast, PO Box 492, Mercer Island, WA 98040. Book publisher.
TRAVEL

Travelling, Wild Boar Publications Ltd, 23260–88 Ave, Fort Langley, BC V0X 1J0. Editor: Chris Potter. Uses articles (with color photos) on travel around the world. Guidelines available.
TRAVEL

Tremaine Publishing, 2727 Front St, Klamath Falls, OR 97601. Book publisher.
OTHER/UNSPECIFIED

Trestle Creek Review, North Idaho College, 1000 W Garden Ave, Coeur d'Alene, ID 83814. 208-769-3384. Editor: Chad Klinger. Annual journal. Subs. $4; circ 500. Uses freelance material. Pays copies. Submit ms, SASE. Submissions read only between January 1st and March 15th. Sample $4.
FICTION, POETRY

Tri-County News, 231 W Sixth, Box 394, Junction City, OR 97448. 503-998-3877. Weekly newspaper.
COMMUNITY

Tri County Special Services, 48 E 1st North, St Anthony, ID 83445. Book publisher.
OTHER/UNSPECIFIED

Tri-City Herald, PO Box 2608, Pasco, WA 99302-2608. 509-582-1500. Editor: Matt Taylor. Daily newspaper, founded 1947. $Sub $8.50/mo; circ 40,000. Not a freelance market.
COMMUNITY

Triad Ensemble, PO Box 61006, Seattle, WA 98121. 206-322-1398. Contact: Victor Janusz. "A relatively young Seattle theater company with a strong interest in new regional works."
DRAMA

Tribune, PO Box 400, Deer Park, WA 99006. 509-276-5043. Weekly newspaper.
COMMUNITY

Trilogy Books, 4316 Riverside Rd S, Salem, OR 97306. 503-362-3300. Contact: Kay L McDonald. Book publisher.
OTHER/UNSPECIFIED

The Trolley Park News, 1836 N Emerson, Portland, OR 97321. Editor/ads: Richard Thompson. 503-285-7936. Semimonthly on historic electric railway preservation. Circ 200. Sub w/membership $10–25. Uses 1 ms per issue. Payment: negotiable; on publication. Byline given. Rights purchased: First. Phone queries, dot matrix, photocopies, simultaneous submission, electronic OK. Reports in 1–2 mos. Nonfiction: "Historic articles on NW, particularly OR, street and interurban railways (including where vehicles are now, tracing abandoned rights-of-way; how-to restore streetcars; and memories of lines

ridden)." Photos: 8x10, 5x7, 3x5; B&W glossy preferred. Maps & car body plans also useful. Sample/SASE.
COLLECTING, NW/REGIONAL HISTORY, TRAVEL

Trout, PO Box 6255, Bend, OR 97708. Editor: Thomas R Pero. 503-382-2327. 503-382-9177. Periodical.
AGRICULTURE/FARMING, CONSERVATION, OUTDOOR

Trout Creek Press, 5976 Billings Rd, Parkdale, OR 97041. 503-352-6494. Contact: Laurence F Hawkins, Jr. Publishes softcover poetry books. Accepts freelance material. Pays copies. Acquires 1st rights. Query letter, SASE. Dot matrix, photocopies OK. Reports in 1 mo; publishes in 1 yr. Accepts fiction, poetry, cartoons, interviews, articles, plays, reviews. Topics: "Open to any poetic project with artistic merit. Probably favor experimental work, provided it is not too esoteric." Guidelines, catalog available. Sample $2.
AVANT-GARDE/EXPERIMENTAL, POETRY

Truck Logger, 124 W 8th St, North Vancouver, BC V7M 3H2. Editor: Vivian Rudd. 604-985-7811. Periodical.
BUSINESS, LABOR/WORK, LUMBER

Truck World, 3 – 1610 Kebet Way, Portl Coquitlam, BC V3C 5W9. 604-942-4312. Contact: Rob Robertson. Monthly Canadian trucking industry trade journal. Pays on publication and gives byline for 1st right on nonfiction of 200–2,000 words. Subjects: product news, photo features, truck financing and maintenance, new technologies, profiles, industry news. Uses photos. Query w/clips. Reports in 2 wks. Pay varies.
BUSINESS, CANADA, COMMERCE

Trucks' Almanac, 3 – 1610 Kebet Way, Port Coquitlam, BC V3C 5W9. 604-942-4312. Contact: Rob Robertson. Canadian trucking industry annual. Query w/clips. Pay varies.
BUSINESS, CANADA, COMMERCE

Truth on Fire (Hallelujah), PO Box 223, Postal Stn A, Vancouver, BC V6C 2M3. 604-498-3895. Editor: Wesley H Wakefield. Bimonthly evangelical magazine. Sub $5. Circ 1,000–10,000. Uses freelance material. Pays $15 & up on acceptance. Byline given. Submit query w/clips. Dot matrix, photo-copied, simultaneous OK. Reports in 6 wks. Publishing time varies. Accepts nonfiction, photos. "Biblically oriented to evangelical & Wesleyan viewpoint." Topics: peace, anti-nuclear, racial equality & justice, religious liberty, etc. Tips: "prefer action or solution-oriented articles; must understand evangelical viewpoint & life style." Guidelines/sample available.
RELIGION

Truth on Fire (Hallelujah) Publishing, Same as preceding. Also publishes 2–3 softcover assigned originals, reprints a year. Will consider queries. Rates vary on assignment.
RELIGION

Tumwater Action Committee Newsletter, 500 Tyee Dr, Tumwater, WA 98502.
PUBLIC AFFAIRS, WASHINGTON

Tundra Drums, PO Box 868, Bethel, AK 99559. Weekly newspaper.
COMMUNITY

Tundra Times, 411 W 4th Ave, Anchorage, AK 99510. 907-274-2512. Periodical of Eskimo, Indian and Aleut news.
ALASKA, NATIVE AMERICAN

Turman Publishing Company, 1319 Dexter Ave N, Seattle, WA 98109. Softcover book publisher. Accepts unsolicited submissions. Pays money on acceptance. Acquires all rights. Submit query letter, outline, sample chapters, synopsis, SASE. Disk (Word4) OK. Responds in 6 wks; publishes in 4 mos. Accepts nonfiction, fiction, biography. Topics: for young adult low readers. Guidelines, catalog available.
BIOGRAPHY, FICTION

Turock Fitness Publishers, 6206 114th Ave NE, Kirkland, WA 98033-7203. Book publisher.
HEALTH

TV Week, 320 – 9940 Lougheed Hwy, Burnaby, BC V3J 1N3. Weekly periodical.
ENTERTAINMENT, LITERATURE

Twin Falls Times-News, 132 3rd St W, Twin Falls, ID 83301. 208-733-0931. Newspaper.
COMMUNITY, OTHER/UNSPECIFIED

Twin Peaks Press, PO Box 129, Vancouver, WA 98666. 206-694-2462. Contact: Helen Hecker. Publishes hard- & softcover reprints. Accepts unsolicited submissions. Submit query, SASE. Pays on publication. Dot matrix, photocopied, simultaneous OK. Accepts nonfiction.
HEALTH, MEDICAL, TRAVEL

Two Louies Magazine, 2745 NE 34th Ave, Portland, OR 97212. Editor: Buck Munger. Periodical.
OTHER/UNSPECIFIED

Two Magpie Press, PO Box 177, Kendrick, ID 83537. 208-276-4130. Not a freelance market. Query w/SASE.
OTHER/UNSPECIFIED

Two Rivers Press, 28070 S Meridian Rd, Aurora, OR 97002. Book publisher.
OTHER/UNSPECIFIED

US Department of Agriculture, Forest Service, Pacific Northwest & Range Experiment, Stn, PO Box 3890, Portland, OR 97208. Book publisher.
AGRICULTURE/FARMING, CONSERVATION, NATURAL HISTORY

Umatilla County Historical Society News, PO Box 253, Pendleton, OR 97801. Quarterly.
NW/REGIONAL HISTORY, OREGON

Umbrella Books, Div. of Harbor View Publications Group, PO Box 1460–A, Friday Harbor, WA 98250-1460. 206-378-5128. Editor: Jerome K Miller. Publishes 4 softcover original books a year. Accepts unsolicited submissions. Pays 10% royalty plus payment for photos. Submit query w/clips, SASE. Dot matrix, computer disk OK. Reports in 6 wks. Publishes very promptly. Accepts nonfiction. Topics: tour guides to the Pacific Northwest. Guidelines available.
NORTHWEST, TRAVEL

Umpqua Free Press, 425 NW Second Ave, Box 729, Myrtle Creek, OR 97457. 503-863-5233. Weekly newspaper.
COMMUNITY

Umpqua Trapper, Douglas County Historical Society, 759 SE Kane, Roseburg, OR 97470. 503–673-4572. Quarterly historical journal for county. Circ 300. Accepts freelance material. No pay. Byline given. Nonfiction: historical relating to Douglas County or family stories.
NW/REGIONAL HISTORY

Underground Express, National Speleological Society, 853 Fairview Ave SE, Salem, OR 97302. Editor: Clay Patrick. Quarterly.
RECREATION, SPORTS

Unicornucopia, 2536 NW Overton, Portland, OR 97210-2441. Book publisher.
OTHER/UNSPECIFIED

Union-Bulletin, PO Box 1358, Walla Walla, WA 99362. 509-525-3300. Daily newspaper.
COMMUNITY

Unique Press, 1103 A St, Tacoma, WA 948402. 206-272-1609. Editors: Ann Roush, Jon Martin. Subsidy publishing imprint of R & M Press. Accepts nonfiction, memoirs, poetry, biography, and photos.
CHILDREN (BY/ABOUT), POETRY, OTHER/UNSPECIFIED

United Press International, 1320 SW Broadway, Portland, OR 97201. 503-226-2644. News Bureau.
OTHER/UNSPECIFIED

Universal Entity, PO Box 728, Milton, WA 98354. 206-941-0833. Editor: Ginny Huseland. Monthly newsletter.
ASTROLOGY/SPIRITUAL

Universe, Washington State University, Pullman, WA 99163-9986. Contact: Tim Steury. Glossy magazine of research and scholarship conducted at WSU. Audience is well-educated, but magazine is not solemn. Written queries are welcome, but mostly written in-house and on assignment. Payment negotiable.
SCHOLARLY/ACADEMIC, WASHINGTON

U of A, Institute of Marine Science, University of Alaska, Fairbanks, AK 99701. Book publisher.
COLLEGE/UNIVERSITY, NATURAL HISTORY, SCIENCE

University of Alaska Library, Elmer E Rasmuson Library, Fairbanks, AK 99701. Book publisher.
COLLEGE/UNIVERSITY, REFERENCE/LIBRARY

University of Alaska Museum, 907 Yukon Dr, Fairbanks, AK 99701. 907-474-6939. Director: Wallen Steffan. Publisher of softcover books & annual newsletter. Free; circ 50,000. Query w/SASE. Catalog, sample available.
ALASKA, ANTHROPOLOGY/ARCHÆOLOGY, NATURAL HISTORY

University of Alaska Press, Gruening Bldg, 1st Fl, U of A, Fairbanks, AK 99776-1580. 907-474-6389. Editor: Carla Helfferich. Ads: Debbie Van Stone. Publishes hard- & softcover original, reprint books. Accepts unsolicited submissions. Submit ms, SASE. Nonfiction: emphasis on scholarly and nonfiction works related to Alaska, the circumpolar north, and the North Pacific rim. Catalog available.
ALASKA, COLLEGE/UNIVERSITY, SCHOLARLY/ACADEMIC

University Herald, 1225 N 43rd, Seattle, WA 98103. 206-522-9505. Weekly newspaper.
COMMUNITY

U of I, Center for Business Development & Research, College of Business & Economics, University of Idaho, Moscow, ID 83843. Book publisher.
BUSINESS, ECONOMICS, IDAHO

University of Idaho Press, U of I, Moscow, ID 83843. 208-885-7564. Editor: James J Heaney. Ads: Mitzi Boyd, 208-885-6245. Publishes hard- & softcover, original, reprint, subsidy books. Accepts unsolicited submissions. Pays 8–12% net royalties, advance on publication. Acquires all, 2nd rights. Submit query letter, outline sample chapters, SASE. Photocopied, dot matrix disk/modem subs OK. Reports in 3 mo; publishes in 12 mos. Accepts nonfiction, fiction: scholarly and regional, including Native American studies, resource and policy studies, Pacific Northwest history and natural history, literature and criticism. Ms between 25,000–100,000 wds. Catalog available.
NW/REGIONAL HISTORY, NATIVE AMERICAN, SCHOLARLY/ACADEMIC

The University News, Boise State University, 1910 University Dr, Boise, ID 83725. 208-385-1464. Weekly newspaper. Circ 15,000.
COLLEGE/UNIVERSITY

University of British Columbia Press, 6344 Memorial Rd, Vancouver, BC V6T IW5. 604-228-3259, 228–4161, 228–4545. Editors: Jane Fredeman (humanities), Karen Morgan (social sciences). Ads: Marie Stephen. Publishes hard- & softcover originals, reprints, subsidy books. Accepts unsolicited submissions. Pays royalties. Acquires all rights. Submit query w/clips. Photocopied OK. Accepts nonfiction. Topics: humanities and social sciences: monographs and upper level textbooks. Catalog available.
CANADIAN HISTORY, LITERARY, TEXTBOOKS

University of Oregon Books, University of Oregon Humanities Center, Eugene, OR 97403-5211. 503-686-3934.
OTHER/UNSPECIFIED

U of O, Bureau of Governmental Research/Service, PO Box 3177, Eugene, OR 97403. Book publisher.
PUBLIC AFFAIRS

U of O, Center for Educational Policy & Management, College of Education, University of Oregon, Eugene, OR 97403. Book publisher.
EDUCATION

U of O, Center of Leisure Studies, Dept of Recreation/Parks, Rm. 138, University of Oregon, Eugene, OR 97403. Book publisher.
RECREATION

U of O, Forest Industries Management Center, College of Business Administration, University of Oregon, Eugene, OR 97405. Book publisher.
BUSINESS, FORESTRY, NATURAL HISTORY

University of Portland Review, 5000 N Portland Blvd, Portland, OR 97203. Contact: Dr Thompson Faller. 503-283-7144. Semiannual tabloid magazine for college educated laymen. Circ 1,000. Accepts 200 mss per year. Payment: 5 copies. Byline given. Phone queries OK. Reports in 6 mos. Publishes in 1 year. Nonfiction: to 2,000 wds on any subject. Fiction: to 2,000 wds on any subject. Poetry: any length and style. Tips: "Its purpose is to comment on the human condition and to present information on expanding knowledge in different fields. With regard to fiction, only that which makes a significant statement about the contemporary scene will be employed." Sample/50¢.
CULTURE, EDUCATION, FICTION

University of Portland Writers, English Department, U of Portland, 5000 N Willamette Blvd, Portland, OR 97203-5798. Periodical.
COLLEGE/UNIVERSITY, WRITING

University Press of the Pacific, Box 66129, Seattle, WA 98166. Not a freelance market.
OTHER/UNSPECIFIED

U of W, Office of Publications, G-16 Communications Bldg, University of Washington, Seattle, WA 98195. Book publisher.
COLLEGE/UNIVERSITY, EDUCATION, PUBLISHING/PRINTING

University of Washington Press, Box 50096, Seattle, WA 98105. Contact: Alice Schroeter. General publisher of trade and academic books, biographies, arts, travel, Native American, history,
ARTS, NW/REGIONAL HISTORY, NATIVE AMERICAN

Update, BC Teachers' Federation, 2235 Burrard St, Vancouver, BC V6T 3H9. Book publisher.
BRITISH COLUMBIA, EDUCATION, LABOR/WORK

Upper Snake River Valley Historical Society, Box 244, Rexburg, ID 83440. Editor: Louis Clements. 208-356-9101. Periodical.
NW/REGIONAL HISTORY, IDAHO

Upword Press, PO Box 1106, Yelm, WA 98597. 206-458-3619. Editor: Lyn Evans. Ads: Warren Evans. Publishes hard- & softcover originals. Accepts unsolicited submissions. Submit query w/clips, ms, SASE. Dot matrix, photocopied OK. Reports in 6 wks. Nonfiction, fiction: New Age, metaphysical.
ASTROLOGY/SPIRITUAL, AVANT-GARDE/EXPERIMENTAL, NEW AGE

Urban Design Centre Society, 1630 E Georgia St, Vancouver, BC V5L 2B2. Book publisher. Query w/SASE.
ARCHITECTURE, CULTURE, SOCIETY

The Urban Naturalist, Audubon Soc. of Portland, 5151 NW Cornell Rd, Portland, OR 97210. 503-292-6855. Editor/Ads: Mike Houck. Quarterly journal. Sub $20/yr. Circ 1,500. Uses 4–6 freelance mss per issue. No pay. Byline given. Submit by assignment only. Publishes in 2 mos. Topics: "Volunteer only, articles & illustrations on Portland area natural history topics." Volunteer authors and artists, decisions by entire group. Guidelines available. Sample $5.
CONSERVATION, ENVIRONMENT/RESOURCES, NATURAL HISTORY

Urquhart Associates Inc, 3811 Seattle First Bank Bldg, PO Box 75092, Northgate Stn, Seattle, WA 98154. Contact: Edward F Urquhart. 206-523-3200. Publisher of 2 softcover books a year. Print run: 2,000. Accepts freelance material. Pay negotiable. Rights purchased: First. Query w/outline, sample chapters, SASE. Reports in 1 month. Publishes in 3 mos. Nonfiction, photos.
BUSINESS, CONSUMER, TRAVEL

User-Friendly Press, 6552 Lakeway Dr, Anchorage, AK 99502. 907-263-9172. Contact: Ann Chandonnet. Self-publisher of 1 or less softcover book a year on Alaskan history and poetry. Does not accept unsolicited submissions. Back list available $7.95.
ALASKA, AMERICAN HISTORY, NATIVE AMERICAN

VA Practitioner, Aster Publishing Corp, PO Box 10460, Eugene, OR 97470-2460. Editor: James McCloskey. Monthly.
OTHER/UNSPECIFIED

Vagabond Press, 605 E 5th Ave, Ellensburg, WA 98926-3201. 509-962-8471. Editor: John Bennett. Publishes 3 softcover books/yr. Press run 1,000. Accepts unsolicited submissions. Pays on publication. Acquires 1st rights. Submit query, SASE. Photocopies OK. Reports in 1 mo. Accepts nonfiction, fiction. Catalog available.
FICTION

Vail Publishing, 8285 SW Brookridge, Portland, OR 97225. 503-292-9964. Self-publisher of 1 softcover book a year. Print run: 2,000. Not a freelance market. Catalog available.
EDUCATION, TEXTBOOKS

Valley American, 724 6th St, Clarkston, WA 99403. 509-758-9797. Weekly newspaper.
COMMUNITY

Valley Herald, 205 N Main, Box 230, Milton-Freewater, OR 97862. 503-938-3361. Weekly newspaper.
COMMUNITY

Valley Herald, PO Box 141268, Spokane, WA 99214. 509-924-2440. Weekly newspaper.
COMMUNITY

The Valley Magazine, Peak Media Inc, PO Box 925, Hailey, ID 83333. 208-788-4500. Quarterly magazine. Uses freelance material. Pay starts at 10¢/wd on publication. Written queries preferred, mss possibly considered. SASE a must. Computer printouts must be legible. Computer disk okay (WordPerfect or ASCII only). "Articles should be timeless, upscale and positive. The subject matter should focus to the Wood River Valley and surrounding areas." Feature article (about 2,000 wds) "must lend itself to spectacular photography." Guidelines and sample ($3 + 8.5x11 SAE) available.
IDAHO

Valley News, PO Box 365, Meridian, ID 83642. 208-888-1941. Editor: Marty Waters. Ads: Jayne Dachlet. Weekly newspaper, founded 1900. Sub $12/yr; circ 2,500. Uses freelance material. Pays copies on publication. Submit query letter, SASE, phone. Responds in 1 wk; publishes in 2 wks. Accepts nonfiction, cartoons, news items, photos (B&W $10), interviews, articles. Topics: Western Ada County; former Meridian/Eagle residents. Sample available.
COMMUNITY

Valley Optimist, PO Box 98, Selah, WA 98942. 509-697-8505. Weekly newspaper.
COMMUNITY

Valley Record & North Bend Record, PO Box 300, Snoqualmie, WA 98065. 206-888-2311. Weekly newspaper.
COMMUNITY

Valley Times, 9730 SW Cascade Blvd, Box 370, Beaverton, OR 97075. Weekly newspaper.
COMMUNITY

Valley View Blueberry Press, 21717 NE 68th St, Vancouver, WA 98662. Book publisher.
OTHER/UNSPECIFIED

Van Dahl Publications, PO Box 10, Albany, OR 97321. 503-928-3569. Editor: Kyle Jansson. Publisher of 1–2 books per year for stamp collectors. Does not accept unsolicited submissions.
COLLECTING, CRAFTS/HOBBIES

Van Patten Publishing, 4204 SE Ogdon St, Portland, OR 97206. 503–775-3815. Editor: George Van Patten. Self-publisher. Accepts unsolicited submissions. Pays copies. Acquires 1st rights. Submit query letter, outline, SASE. Photocopies, simultaneous subs OK. Reports in 30 days, publishing time varies. Topic: organic gardening.
GARDENING

The Vancouver Child, 757 Union St, Vancouver, BC V6A 2C3. 604-251-1760. Editor: Wendy Wilkins. Ads: Stephen Linley. Monthly magazine founded in 1988. Sub $5/yr; circ 30,000. Uses freelance material. Byline given. Pays money on publication. Acquires 1st rights. Submit query letter, complete ms, SASE. Photocopy, dot matrix, disk/modem, simultaneous subs OK. Responds in 2 wks; publishes in 2 mos. Accepts fiction, cartoons, news items, nonfiction, photos (B&W, custom print, $25–35), interviews, reviews. Topics: performing arts, literature, music, etc available to families; also

educational alternatives and innovations; upbeat, purpose is empower parents. Guidelines available.
CHILDREN (BY/ABOUT), EDUCATION, FAMILY

Vancouver Columbian, 701 West Eighth, PO Box 180, Vancouver, WA 98668. 206-694-3391. Daily newspaper.
COMMUNITY

Vancouver Courier, 2094 West 43rd Ave, Vancouver, BC V6M 2C9.
OTHER/UNSPECIFIED

Vancouver History, Vancouver Historical Society, PO Box 3071, Vancouver, BC V6B 3X6. Quarterly.
BRITISH COLUMBIA, CANADIAN HISTORY, NW/REGIONAL HISTORY

Vancouver Magazine, Ste 300 Southeast Tower, 555 W 12th, Vancouver, BC V5Z 4L4. Editor: Malcolm F Parry. 604-877-7732. Mass market monthly of local entertainment & culture.
CULTURE, ENTERTAINMENT

Vancouver Scene, 1250 Homer St, Vancouver, BC V6B 2Y5. Editor: Cliff Faber. Quarterly. Uses short topical tourist-oriented articles, 500–800 words. Byline. Query w/SASE.
BRITISH COLUMBIA, TRAVEL

Vancouver Symphony, 400 E Broadway, Vancouver, BC V5T 1X2. Editor: Marilyn Johnson. 604-875-1661. Periodical.
CULTURE, MUSIC

Vandina Press, PO Box 1551, Mercer Island, WA 98040. 206-232-3239. Editor: Francine Porad. Publishes 1–2 softcover poetry chapbooks a year. Also publishes a poetry journal, Brussels Sprout, 3 times a year. Book publisher.
POETRY

Vanessapress, PO Box 81335, Fairbanks, AK 99708. Alaska's only feminist press.
NW/REGIONAL HISTORY, WOMEN

Vanguard, Portland State University, PO Box 751, Portland, OR 97207. 503-229-4539. Semiweekly newspaper.
COLLEGE/UNIVERSITY

Vardaman Press, 2720 E 176th St, Tacoma, WA 98445. Book publisher.
OTHER/UNSPECIFIED

Vashon Point Productions, Rt 1 Box 432, Vashon, WA 98070. 206-567-4829. Editor: Joyce Delbridge. Publisher of 1 softcover book per 2 yrs. Accepts unsolicited submissions "when needed." Pays in copies on publication. Byline given. Submit ms, SASE, phone. Dot matrix, photocopied, simultaneous OK. Accepts nonfiction, fiction, poetry, photos, cartoons, line drawings relating to incidents on Northwest ferries. Tips: slant toward humor/realistic stories/cartoons, some fantasy. Sample $8.95.
AMERICANA, LITERATURE, NORTHWEST

Vashon-Maury Island Beachcomber, PO Box 447, Vashon, WA 98070. 206-463-9195. Editor: Jay Becker. Ads: Randy Pendergrass. Weekly newspaper. Circ 4,200. Sub $14–22.50. Uses some freelance material. Pays money on publication. Byline given. Acquires 1st rights. Assignment only, query letter, SASE, phone. Disk/modem subs OK. Responds in 1 mo; publishes in 1–2 mos. Accepts nonfiction. Topics: relating to the Island and Islanders; nothing else. $50 for package of 450 wds about interesting Islander with picture (send 35mm negs and we'll develop). Does not need to live on Island now. Guidelines available. Sample 50¢.
COMMUNITY

VCC, Vancouver Community College, 100 W 49th Ave, Vancouver, BC V5Y 2Z6. 604-324-5415. Periodical.
COLLEGE/UNIVERSITY

Vector Associates, PO Box 6215, Bellevue, WA 98008. 206-635-0383. Book publisher. Contact: Douglas Vogt. Does not accept unsolicited submissions.
SCIENCE

Vector Publishing, PO Box 1271, Mount Vernon, WA 98273. Book publisher.
OTHER/UNSPECIFIED

Veda News, PO Box 802, Bandon, OR 97411. Editor: Mildred Robinson. Bimonthly.
OTHER/UNSPECIFIED

Velosport Press, 1100 E Pike, Seattle, WA 98122. Contact: Denise de la Rosa. 206-329-2453. Publisher of 1 softcover book a year on cycling. Print run: 6,000. Accepts freelance material. Pay negotiable. Sample chapters w/ SASE. Photocopies OK. Reports in 1 month. Publishes in varies.
BICYCLING

Venture Communications Inc, PO Box 02332, Portland, OR 97202. 503-236-5810. Editor: Michael J Carey. Publishes original books related to technology (GIS/CAD, RFP), mapping, training for public sector and vendors. Accepts freelance material. Payment negotiable. Acquires all rights. Submit phone query. Dot matrix, photocopied OK. Reports in 1 wk. Publishes in 1–2 mos. Tips: applications, not product literature.
COMPUTERS, PUBLIC AFFAIRS, TECHNICAL

Vernier Software, 2920 SW 89th St, Portland, OR 97225. 503-297-5317. Editor: Chris Vernier. Book publisher.
COMPUTERS

Vernon Printing & Publishing, 1701 Hwy 83 N, Seely Lake, MT 59868. 406-754-2369. Contact: Suzanne Vernon. Publisher of softcover books. Averages 1–2 titles/yr; print runs less than 3,000. Topics: outdoor and hiking.
OUTDOOR, RECREATION

Vernon Publications Inc, 3000 Northrup Way #200, Bellevue, WA 98004. 206-827-9900. Various business and trade periodicals.
BUSINESS, COMMERCE, ECONOMICS

Vet's Newsletter, 700 Summer St NE, Salem, OR 97310-1201. 503-373-2000. Editor: Barb Nobles. Bimonthly.
MILITARY/VETS

Victoria House Publishing, PO Box 1385, Victoria, BC V8W 2W3. Contact: Eugenie Somier. Publishes BC Books.
BRITISH COLUMBIA, PUBLISHING/PRINTING

Victory Music Review, PO Box 7515, Bonney Lake, WA 98390. 206-863-6617. Editor/Ads: Chris Lunn. Monthly. Sub $15/yr; circ 6,000. Uses freelance material. Pays copies. Phone query. Dot matrix OK. Publishes in 15–90 days. Topics: folk, jazz record reviews — 125 wds; local concert reviews — 200 wds. Sample $1.25.
CALENDAR/EVENTS, ENTERTAINMENT, MUSIC

Video Librarian, PO Box 2725, Bremerton, WA 98310. 206-377-2231. Editor/Ads: Randy Pitman. Monthly. Sub $35. Circ 350. Uses 1 freelance ms per issue. Pays copies on publication. Byline given. Dot matrix, photocopied OK. Reports in 2 wks. Accepts nonfiction. Free sample.
FILM/VIDEO, MEDIA/COMMUNICATIONS

Videosat News, CommTek, 9440 Fairview Ave, Boise, ID 83704. Editor: Tom Woolf. Monthly. Circ 24,500.
CONSUMER, ENTERTAINMENT, FILM/VIDEO

Vidiot Enterprises, 501 North M St, Tacoma, WA 98403. Book publisher.
OTHER/UNSPECIFIED

Views, Sexual Minorities Center, Western Washington University, Viking Union 217, Bellingham, WA 98225. Periodical.
GAY/LESBIAN, WOMEN

The Village Idiot, Mother of Ashes Press, PO Box 66, Harrison, ID 83833-0066. Editor: Joe M Singer. Magazine 3X/yr. founded 1970. Sub $7.50; circ 100. Uses freelance material. Pays in copies on publication. Acquires 1st rights. Byline given. Submit ms, SASE. Reports in 1–4 mos. Publishes in 4 mos. Accepts fiction, poetry, cartoons, news items, biography, nonfiction, interviews, op/ed plays, reviews, memoirs, photos (query on color), art. "This magazine is as personal an expression as any poem you will ever hope to write."
FICTION, PICTURE, POETRY

The Villager, PO Box 516, Wilsonville, OR 97070-0516. Editor: K C Swan. Monthly.
OTHER/UNSPECIFIED

Vincentury, St Vincent Hospital & Medical Center, 9205 SW Barnes Rd, Portland, OR 97225. Periodical for patients, relatives, employees and community.
HEALTH

Vintage Northwest, (King's Press), PO Box 193, Bothell, WA 98041. 206-487-1201. Editor: Margie Brons. Ads: Gene Bruns. Semiannual magazine founded in 1980. No sub. Circ 550 at local senior centers. Accepts freelance only from age 50+. Pays in copies on publication. Submit ms, SASE, no more than 1,000 wds. Photocopies OK. Reports in1 wk; publishes 6–12 mos. Accepts nonfiction, fiction, poetry, illustrations, photos (returned after use). Topics: variety, senior's experiences, humorous stories or poems; no sexist language, sermonic, or political. Guidelines available. Sample $2.50.
FICTION, POETRY, SENIOR CITIZENS

Virtue, PO Box 850, Sisters, OR 97759. 503-549-8261. Editor: Marlee Alex. Ads: Debbie Mitchell. Bimonthly non-denominational Christian women's magazine. Circ 175,000. Uses freelance material. Byline given. Acquires 1st rights. Submit query letter, SASE. Responds in 6–8 wks. Accepts fiction, poetry, cartoons, nonfiction, interviews, articles. Guidelines available. Sample $3.
RELIGION, WOMEN

Vision Books, 790 Commercial Ave, Coos Bay, OR 97420. Publisher of books on philosophy, peace, and nuclear disarmament.
PEACE, PHILOSOPHY, PSYCHOLOGY

Visions, 19600 NW Von Neumann Dr, Beaverton, OR 97006. 503-690-1121. FAX 503-690-1029. Editor: Steve Dodge. Ads: Norman Elder. Quarterly magazine. Free. Circ 15,000. Uses 2 freelance mss per issue. Pays money on acceptance. Acquires at least 1st rights. Byline given. Submit query w/clips, 9x12 SASE. Dot matrix, photocopied, simultaneous, computer disk OK. Reports in 2–4 wks. Publishes 1–4 mos. Accepts nonfiction, photos, cartoons. Topics: science and technology, from computer advances and high technology to biology and environment. Length: 1,000–3,000 wds. Science briefs (250 wds) with emphasis on the unusual. Personality profiles of scientists (1,000 wds). Photos: photomicrographs, B&W and color, needed; photos that reveal the unusual or relatively unseen, $50–350. Tips: "Science with an emphasis on people and non-technical explanations of technology especially welcome. Would like to see clips from experienced NW writers willing to work on assignment." Guidelines & free sample for 9x12 SASE.
COMPUTERS, ENVIRONMENT/RESOURCES, SCIENCE

Vitamin Supplement, Odyssey Publishing Inc, 2135 W 45th Ave, Vancouver, BC V6M 2J2. 604-266-0343. Editor: Jean Macleod. Bimonthly journal. Sub $9/yr; circ 125,000. Uses freelance material by assignment only. Byline given. Reports in 6 wks; time to publication varies. Guidelines available.
HEALTH

Leo F Vogel, 2526 Dilling Rd, Connell, WA 99326. 509-234-5112. Self-publisher of hard- & softcover original books. Print run: 2,000. Not a freelance market.
NW/REGIONAL HISTORY, HUMOR

The Voice, Multnomah School of the Bible, 8435 NE Glisan, Portland, OR 97220. 503-251-5325. Editor: Shelley Sonnenberg. Ads: Shelley Lockwood. Monthly newspaper; circ 1,000; sub $10/yr. Accepts freelance from MSB staff, students, alumni only. Byline given, pays copies on publication. Submit query/SASE. Disk (IBM) OK. Responds in 4 wks; publishing time varies. Accepts fiction, poetry, cartoons, news, biography, nonfiction, photos, interviews, op/ed, articles, reviews, memoirs. Guidelines available, sample $2.
COLLEGE/UNIVERSITY, RELIGION

The Voice, Oregon Advocates for the Arts, 707 – 13th St SE #118, Salem, OR 97301-4027. Periodical.
BUSINESS

The Voice, Ore-Ida Foods, PO Box 10, Boise, ID 83707. Editor: Susan C Gerhart. Company journal published 3 x per year for employees, management and business contacts. Circ 6,000.
ARTS, CULTURE, OREGON

Void Press, Box 45125, Seattle, WA 98145. 206-522-8055. Editor: John Stehman. Publisher, small press runs, personal invitation. Poetry, other. Catalog $1.
POETRY

W.H. 1, 21349 NW St Helens Rd, Portland, OR 97231. Book publisher.
OTHER/UNSPECIFIED

Wahkiakum County Eagle, PO Box 368, Cathlamet, WA 98612. 206-795-3391. Weekly newspaper.
COMMUNITY

Donald E Waite Photographer & Publisher Company, 35-22374 Lougheed Hwy, Maple Ridge, BC V2X 2T5. Book publisher.
PHOTOGRAPHY

Walking Bird Publishing, 340 N Grand St, Eugene, OR 97402. Book publisher.
OTHER/UNSPECIFIED

Wallowa County Chieftain, 106 NW First St, Box 338, Enterprise, OR 97828. 503-426-4567. Weekly newspaper.
COMMUNITY

Warner Pacific College Art & Literature Magazine, Warner Pacific College, 2219 SE 68th Ave, Portland, OR 97215. College literary magazine. SASE for guidelines.
COLLEGE/UNIVERSITY, FICTION, OREGON

Warner World, Warner Pacific College, 2219 SE 68th, Portland, OR 97215. 503-775-4366. Newspaper.
COLLEGE/UNIVERSITY

Warren Publishing House, Totline Books, PO Box 2250, Everett, WA 98203. 206-355-7007. Editor: Gayle Bittinger. Ads: Susan Sexton. Bimonthly newsletter, founded 1980. Sub $24/yr; circ 8,500. Uses freelance material. Byline given. Pays money on acceptance. Acquires all rights. Submit query letter, SASE. Responds in 6 wks; publishes in 1 yr. Accepts nonfiction, poetry, articles, activity ideas. Topics: pre-school children — songs, activity ideas; sketches for clarification encouraged. Guidelines, catalog available.
CHILDREN (BY/ABOUT), EDUCATION, MUSIC

The Washboard, Washington State Folklife Council, 11507 NE 104th St, Kirkland, WA 98033-5010. 206-586-8252. Periodical.
CRAFTS/HOBBIES, CULTURE, AMERICAN HISTORY

Washington Arts, 110 9th & Columbia, Mail Stop GH-11, Olympia, WA 98504-4111. 206-753-3860. Editor: Mark Clemens. Bimonthly newsletter & bulletin. Free. Circ 3,500. Uses freelance material infrequently. Byline given. Submit query letter, SASE, for articles ideas. Accepts news items, info about competitions; photos (B&W, 5X7).
ARTS, CALENDAR/EVENTS, WASHINGTON

Washington Cattleman, Box 2027, Wenatchee, WA 98801. 509-662-5167. Monthly.
AGRICULTURE/FARMING, ANIMALS, BUSINESS

Washington Clubwoman, 11404 NE 97th St, Vancouver, WA 98662. Monthly.
WOMEN

Washington Cookbook, PO Box 923, Spokane, WA 99210. Cookbook publisher. Book publisher.
CRAFTS/HOBBIES, WASHINGTON

Washington Crop & Livestock Reporting Service, 417 W Fourth Ave, Olympia, WA 98501. Book publisher.
AGRICULTURE/FARMING, ANIMALS, WASHINGTON

Washington Farmer Stockman, 211 Review Bldg, Spokane, WA 99210. 509-455-7057. Semimonthly ag business publication.
AGRICULTURE/FARMING, BUSINESS, WASHINGTON

Washington Fishing Holes, PO Box 32, Sedro Woolley, WA 98284. Editor/Ads: Brad Stracener. Monthly. Sub $15/yr. Circ 10,000. Uses 4–5 freelance mss per issue. Pays money on publication. Acquires 1st rights. Byline given.

Submit query w/clips, SASE. Photocopied, electronic subs OK. Accepts nonfiction, photos. Guidelines/sample available.
OUTDOOR, RECREATION, SPORTS

Washington Food Dealer, 480 E 19th St, Tacoma, WA 98421. 206-522-4474. Editor/Ads: Arden D Gremmert. Grocery trade magazine published 11 times per year. Sub $20/yr. Circ 4,000. Accepts freelance material. Pays in copies. Acquires 1st rights. Byline given. Query w/clips, SASE, phone query on ideas. Dot matrix, photocopies, simultaneous, computer disk OK. Reports in 1 mo. Publishing time varies. Accepts nonfiction, grocery related only, particularly focusing on Northwest. Length variable. Photos B&W or color, originals, (no-pre-screened), no payment. Sample free.
BUSINESS, FOOD/COOKING, TRADE/ASSOCIATIONS

The Washington Grange News, 3104 Western Ave, Seattle, WA 98121. 206-284-1753. Official publication of the Washington State Grange. Semimonthly newspaper.
AGRICULTURE/FARMING, PUBLIC AFFAIRS, WASHINGTON

The Washington Horse, PO Box 88258, Seattle, WA 98188. 206-226-2620. Editor: Joe LaDuca/Bruce Batson. Ads: Joe LaDuca at 206-772-2381. Monthly periodical on thoroughbred horse racing & breeding. Circ 3,400. Sub $30/yr. Uses 2 mss per issue. Pays money on publication. Byline given. Assignment only. Photocopies OK. Nonfiction, B&W photos. Sample/free.
ANIMALS, BUSINESS, SPORTS

Washington Insurance Commissioner, Insurance Bldg, Olympia, WA 98504. Book publisher.
BUSINESS, CONSUMER, WASHINGTON

Washington Library News, Washington State Library AJ-11, Olympia, WA 98504. Periodical.
REFERENCE/LIBRARY

Washington Newspaper, 3838 Stone Way North, Seattle, WA 98103. 206-643-3838. Monthly periodical.
BUSINESS, PUBLISHING/PRINTING

Washington Professional Publications, PO Box 1147, Bellevue, WA 98009. 206-643-3147. Self-publisher of real estate books. Not a freelance market.
BUSINESS, CONSUMER, WASHINGTON

Washington Sea Grant Program, University of Washington, 3716 Brooklyn Ave NE, Seattle, WA 98105. Contact: Louie Echols. 206-543-6600. Book publisher.
NATURAL HISTORY, SCIENCE

Washington State Bar News, 500 Westin Bldg, 2001 Sixth Ave, Seattle, WA 98121-2599. 206-448-0441. Contact: Managing Editor. Ads: Dennis Eagan. Monthly magazine, founded 1947. Sub $24/yr; circ 16,500. Uses freelance material from lawyers only. Byline given. Acquires all rights. Submit complete ms, phone. Disk subs OK.
LAW

Washington State Historical Society, 315 N Stadium Way, Tacoma, WA 98403. Book publisher.
NW/REGIONAL HISTORY, WASHINGTON

Washington State Library, Washington 1 Northwest Room, WS Library AJ-11, Olympia, WA 98504. 206-753-4024. Editor: Gayle Palmer. Publishes 1 softcover list of Washington-author books per year. Not a freelance market. Catalog available.
REFERENCE/LIBRARY, WASHINGTON, WRITING

Washington State Migrant Ed News, c/o Heritage College, Rt 3 Box 3540, Toppenish, WA 98948. Editor: Larry Ashby. Monthly.
CHICANO/CHICANA, EDUCATION, WASHINGTON

Washington State University Press, Washington State University, Cooper Publications Bldg, Pullman, WA 99164-5910. 509-335-3518. Director: Thomas H Sanders. Publishes hard- & softcover originals, reprints. Accepts unsolicited submissions. Pays copies, royalties. Rights acquired vary. Submit query letter, sample chapters, synopsis, SASE. Dot matrix subs OK. Reports in 2-4 wks; publishes in 1-2 yrs. Accepts nonfiction. Topics: regional studies (history, political science, literature, science); Western Americana; Asian

American, Black, Women's Studies; Pacific NW art, natural sciences. Publishes 7 scholarly journals: Poe Studies; ESQ: A Journal of the American Renaissance; Western Journal of Speech Communication; Communication Reports; Northwest Science; Western Journal of Black Studies; Journal of International Education Administrator. Catalog available.
AMERICANA, AMERICAN HISTORY, MINORITIES/ETHNIC

Washington Stylist and Salon, PO Box 1117, Portland, OR 97207. 503-226-2461. Editor: David Porter. Monthly trade magazine. Circ 36,000. Free to licensed salons, others $10. Accepts freelance material. Pays only when assigned, on publication. Byline given. Submit query letter, SASE. Accepts nonfiction, 500-750 wds w/photos. Topics: anything to do with hair and beauty for the industry, professional beauty salons, schools and supply houses. Photos: B&W, $5, or $15-20 for cover. Tips: needs stringers in OR/WA. "Query first. I prefer to give a writer the slant I want, and I would like to talk to people to give them hints on things I'd like covered in their area."
BUSINESS, FASHION

Washington Teamster Newspaper, 552 Denny Way, Seattle, WA 98109. 206-622-0483. Weekly union newspaper.
LABOR/WORK, WASHINGTON

Washington Thoroughbred, WA Thoroughbred Breeders Assn, PO Box 88258, Seattle, WA 98138. 206-226-2620. Editor: Sue Van Dyke. Ads: Joe LaDuca. Monthly. Sub $40/yr. Uses one freelance article per issue. Assignment only. Pays money on publication. Byline given. Photocopy OK. Reports in 1 wk. Publishes in 2-4 mos. Accepts nonfiction, fiction: thoroughbred horse racing and breeding, local angle preferred. Photos: B&W, color acceptable with good lighting.
ANIMALS, SPORTS

Washington Trails Association, 1305 - 4th Ave #518, Seattle, WA 98101. Contact: Jim Eychaner. 206-743-3947. Publisher of 1-3 softcover original books a year. Print run: 1,000. Not a freelance market at this time.
OUTDOOR, RECREATION

The Washington Trooper, PO Box 1523, Longview, WA 98632-0144. 206-577-8598. Editor: Bruce Grimm. Quarterly. Accepts freelance material. Payment: $5-75 on publication. Query w/SASE. Nonfiction: Wants mss on "legislation, traffic and highway safety for members of WA State Patrol Troopers Assoc as well as for state legislators, educators, court officials and like-minded folks in the state of WA." 500-3,500 wds. Tips: Contributors must be "familiar with goals and objectives of the WA State Patrol and with law enforcement in general in the Pacific NW."
PUBLIC AFFAIRS, WASHINGTON

Washington Water News, Washington State University, Pullman, WA 99164. Periodical.
AGRICULTURE/FARMING, ENVIRONMENT/RESOURCES, PUBLIC AFFAIRS

Washington Wildfire, PO Box 45187, Seattle, WA 98145-0187. Editor: Nancy Boulton. 206-633-1992. Periodical.
OTHER/UNSPECIFIED

WashPIRG Reports, 340 15th Ave E, Ste 350, Seattle, WA 98112. 206-322-9064. Editor: Kathryn Gilbert. Published tri-quarterly on environmental and consumer issues. Circ 25,000. Sub $15/mbr. Uses freelance material. Query letter, SASE, phone. Dot matrix, photocopies, simultaneous subs OK. Accepts nonfiction. Topics: hazardous waste, environment, consumer issues, accountable government. Sample free.
CONSUMER, ENVIRONMENT/RESOURCES, PUBLIC AFFAIRS

Waterfront Press Company, 1115 NW 45th, Seattle, WA 98107. Book publisher.
OTHER/UNSPECIFIED

Waterlines Magazine, 4111 Stone Way N, Seattle, WA 98103-8013.
OTHER/UNSPECIFIED

Watermark, Oregon State Library, State Library Bldg, Salem, OR 97310. Monthly.
BOOK ARTS/BOOKS, REFERENCE/LIBRARY

Watermark Press, 6909 58th NE, Seattle, WA 98115. Book publisher.
OTHER/UNSPECIFIED

R J Watts & Assoc, 4010 Bayridge Crescent, W Vancouver, BC V7V 3K4. Contact: Reg Watts. Book publisher.
OTHER/UNSPECIFIED

Wavefront, PO Box 22070, Postal Stn B, Vancouver, BC, V6A 3Y2. 604-254-3521. Editors/Ads: Carolyn McLuskie/Al Razutis. Periodical published 3 times a yr. Sub $18/$20 US. Circ 200. Uses 6 freelance mss per issue. Pays copies. Byline given. Submit ms, SASE. Photocopied OK. Reports immediately. Accepts nonfiction, fiction, poetry, photos. Sample $6.
FICTION, POETRY, SCIENCE

Waves, c/o Eridani Prod, PO Box 47111, Seattle, WA 98146-7111. 206-325-8037. Periodical.
OTHER/UNSPECIFIED

WCW Unlimited, 155 Loop Rd, Myrtle Creek, OR 97457. Contact: Christopher Wright. Self-publisher of softcover originals. Does not accept unsolicited submissions. Topics: mental health, social services from the perspective of front-line providers and recipients. Catalog available.
HEALTH, PSYCHOLOGY

We Alaskans, The Anchorage Daily News, 1001 Northway Dr, Anchorage, AK 99514-9001. Editor: George Bryson. Ads: Bill Megivern. Weekly newspaper magazine, founded 1980. Circ 75,000. Uses freelance material. Byline given. Pays money on publication. Acquires 1st rights. Submit complete ms, phone. Responds in 1 mo; publishes in 1 mo. Accepts fiction, biography, interviews, op/ed, articles, memoirs. Photos: $100 cover, $50 color slides, $25 B&W. Topics: Alaska and Alaskans. Guidelines available.
ALASKA

We Proceeded On, Lewis/Clark Trail Heritage Foundation, 5054 SW 26th Place, Portland, OR 97201. Editor: Robert E Lange. Quarterly.
AMERICAN HISTORY

Weather Workbook Company, 827 NW 31st St, Corvallis, OR 97330. Book publisher.
OTHER/UNSPECIFIED

Webb Research Group, PO Box 314, Medford, OR 97501. 503-664-5205. Editor: Mr B Webber. Publishes hard- & softcover subsidy books. Does not accept unsolicited submissions. Nonfiction only: subjects on Pacific Northwest (OR, WA, ID) and Oregon Trail. Must be library reference quality, but readable by 8th graders for use in schools. Require bibliography, index, ISBN mandatory, CIP almost mandatory. Must have photos. Query w/SASE.
NATIVE AMERICAN, NORTHWEST, OLD WEST

Wednesday Magazine, PO Box 874, Poulsbo, WA 98370. 206-697-2225. Editor: Paul Goheen. Community newspaper.
COMMUNITY

Weekly, PO Box 587, Woodinville, WA 98072. 206-483-0606. Weekly newspaper.
COMMUNITY

Welcome Press, 2701 Queen Anne N, Seattle, WA 98109. 206-282-5336. Self-publisher of 1–2 softcover originals, reprint books of Scandinavian interest. Print run: 2,500. Not a freelance market.
CULTURE, MINORITIES/ETHNIC

Welcome to Planet Earth, Great Bear Publishers, PO Box 5164, Eugene, OR 97405. Editor: Mark Lerner. Monthly.
ENVIRONMENT/RESOURCES, OTHER/UNSPECIFIED

Wells & West Publishers, 1166 Winsor St, North Bend, OR 97459. Book publisher.
OTHER/UNSPECIFIED

Wenatchee Daily World, PO Box 1511, Wenatchee, WA 98801. 509-663-5161. Daily newspaper.
COMMUNITY

West Coast Baby Magazine, 601 Main St #400, Vancouver, WA 98660. 206-696-1150. Editor: Mike Weber. Ads: Francis Fisher. Monthly magazine for new parents. Circ 25,000. Uses 2–3 mss per issue. Payment: Money on publication. Byline given. Rights purchased: First. Query w/SASE. Dot matrix, photocopies, simultaneous submissions (with notification) OK. Nonfiction: "Serious 'how-to' or medical articles, humor/fiction regarding new parenthood. Fiction (very seldom). Photos: need 4-color cover and feature photography. Rates negotiable. Guidelines available.
CHILDREN/TEEN, FAMILY, WOMEN

West Coast Review, Department of English, Simon Fraser University, Burnaby, BC V5A 1S6. Editor: Tom Martin. 604-291-4287. Quarterly. Circ 700. Sub $12. Uses 20 mss per issue. Payment: $10–15/pg for unsolicited mss, on acceptance. Byline given. Rights purchased: First. Submit ms, SASE. Dot matrix OK. Reports in 2 mos. Nonfiction. Fiction and poetry, no restriction on theme, style. Tips: "Read at least 1 issue before submitting (sample copy of current issue available for $3.50). American contributors enclose sufficient Canadian postage or IRC." Guidelines available; sample/ $2.50.
COLLEGE/UNIVERSITY, FICTION, POETRY

West Hills Bulletin/Mt. Tabor Bulletin, 12311 NE Glisan #103, Portland, OR 97230. 503-256-2833. Editor: Shelli Smith. Ads: Quentin Smith. Monthly newspaper. Sub $5/yr. Circ 31,000. Uses 8–15 freelance mss per issue. Pay "other" on publication. Byline given. Submit ms, SASE, phone query. Dot matrix, photocopied, simultaneous, electronic, computer disk OK. Reports in 3–4 wks. Accepts nonfiction, local human interest, cartoons. Sample for postage.
CALENDAR/EVENTS, COMMUNITY, PUBLIC AFFAIRS

West Lane News, 25027 Dunham, Box 188, Veneta, OR 97487. 503-935-1882. Weekly newspaper.
COMMUNITY

West Magazine, 910–1200 Burrard St, Vancouver, BC V6Z 2C7. 604-685-0308. Contact: Ric Dolphin, Managing Editor. Ads: Linda Davies. Monthly general interest magazine. Circ 310,000 controlled distribution. Uses 15 freelance mss per issue. Pays $0.50–1.00/wd on acceptance. Acquires 1st rights, byline given. Submit query w/clips and SASE, assignment only. Dot matrix photocopied OK. Reports in 1 mon, published in 2–4 months. Accepts nonfiction, fiction, photos, illustrations. Wide range of slants, lengths, and rates. Guidelines and sample available.
CANADA, FICTION, NORTHWEST

Mark West Publishers, PO Box 1914, Sandpoint, ID 83864. Book publisher.
OTHER/UNSPECIFIED

West Side, Box 5027, Salem, OR 97304. 503-362-8987. Editor/Ads: Tim Hinshaw. Monthly. Sub $6. Circ 7,500. Uses 3 freelance mss per issue. Requires journalism/photo experience. Pays money, copies on publication. Acquires 1st rights. Byline given. Phone query. Dot matrix, photocopied OK. Reports in 1 wk. Accepts nonfiction, photos. Free sample.
PHOTOGRAPHY

West Wind Review, English Department, Southern Oregon State College, Ashland, OR 97520. 503-482-6181. Editor: Geri Couchman. Annual journal/ contest. Uses freelance material. Pays copies. Submit ms, SASE. Photocopy, dot matrix subs OK. Responds in 2 wk, publishes in 6 mos. Accepts fiction, poetry, photos, plays. Guidelines available.
COLLEGE/UNIVERSITY, FICTION, POETRY

Western Banker Magazine, Western Banker Publications, 1100 N Cole Rd, Boise, ID 83704-8644. Monthly. Circ 5,500.
BUSINESS

Western Business, PO Box 31678, Billings, MT 59107. Editor: James Strauss. 406-252-4788. Monthly.
BUSINESS, COMMERCE

Western Cascade Tree Fruit Association Quarterly, 9210 131st NE Lake Stevens, WA 98258.
AGRICULTURE/FARMING, BUSINESS

Western Doll Collector, PO Box 2061, Portland, OR 97208-2061. 503-284-4062. Editor/Ads: Richard Schiessl. Monthly. Sub $20. Uses freelance. Byline given. Accepts nonfiction, fiction, poetry, photos. Sample available.
CRAFTS/HOBBIES

Western Engines, PO Box 192, Woodburn, OR 97071. Monthly.
OTHER/UNSPECIFIED

Western Farmer-Stockman Magazines, PO Box 2160, Spokane, WA 99210-1615. 509-459-5377. Monthly magazines. Sub $9/yr; circ 79,200. Infrequently uses freelance material. Byline given. Submit query letter, SASE. Responds in 1 mo. Topics: agriculture-related.
AGRICULTURE/FARMING

Western Fisheries, Ste 202-1132 Hamilton St, Vancouver, BC V6B 2S2. Editor: Henry L Frew. 604-687-1581. Periodical.
BUSINESS, CONSERVATION, FISHING

Western Genesis, 1400 1st Ave N, Great Falls, MT 59401. 406-452-3462. Quarterly newsletter; circ 700, subs. $15/yr. Occasionally uses freelance material. Byline given. No pay. Acquires all rights. Submit query, SASE. Response and publication time vary. Accepts poetry, cartoons, news items, biography, nonfiction, photos, interviews, articles, reviews, memoirs. Sample $1.50.
NW/REGIONAL HISTORY

Western Geographical Series, Department of Geography, University of Victoria, PO Box 1700, Victoria, BC V8W 2Y2. Book publisher.
COLLEGE/UNIVERSITY, GEOLOGY/GEOGRAPHY

Western Horizons Books, PO Box 4068, Helena, MT 59604. 406-442-7795. Publishes softcover original books. Does not accept unsolicited submissions. Query w/SASE. Photocopied OK. Accepts nonfiction, fiction. Topics: sports — boxing, historical — Montana, Upper Rocky Mountain Region, Southwest.
NW/REGIONAL HISTORY, MONTANA, SPORTS

Western Horizons Press, 15890 SE Wallace Rd, Milwaukie, OR 97222. 503-654-1626. Editor: Leonard Delano. Book publisher.
OTHER/UNSPECIFIED

Western Investor, Willamette Publishing Inc, 400 SW 6th, Portland, OR 97204. Contact: Shannon P Pratt. Quarterly.
BUSINESS

Western Journal of Black Studies, Washington State University Press, Pullman, WA 99164-5910. 509-335-3518. Quarterly. Sub $15.
BLACK, NW/REGIONAL HISTORY, SOCIOLOGY

Western Livestock Reporter, PO Box 30758, Billings, MT 59107. 406-259-4589. Editor: Marcia Krings. Ads: Bonnie Zieske. Weekly newspaper, founded 1940. Annual "Breeders Book." Sub $18/yr; circ 12,000. Occasionally uses freelance material. Byline given. Pays money on publication. Acquires all rights. Submit query letter, SASE, phone. Assignment only. Disk/modem subs OK. Responds in 2 wks; publishing time varies. Accepts news items, interviews, photos (B&W). Topics: agricultural features, cattle, people who raise them. Sample available.
AGRICULTURE/FARMING, ANIMALS

Western Living, 504 Davie St, Vancouver, BC V6B 2G4. 604-669-7525. Editor: Andrew Scott. Monthly of western Canadian living, with emphasis on home design. Sub free. Accepts freelance material. Pay averages 30¢/wd, on acceptance. Acquires 1st rights. Query first with outline, SASE. Accepts nonfiction, fiction, poetry. Topics: cuisine, fashion, recreation, the arts, foreign and local travel, architecture and interior design; prefers a regional Western angle. Photos with story: $25–200, B&W 8x10 glossies preferred; prefer 2 1/4 or 4x5 slides. Guidelines available. 023, 103.
ARCHITECTURE, BRITISH COLUMBIA, RECREATION

Western Mills Today, Timber West Publications, PO Box 610, Edmonds, WA 98020. 206-778-3388. Contact: John Nederlee. Highly specialized trade publication. Monthly; circ 10,000. Uses freelance material by assignment only. Byline given. Pays money on publication. Acquires all rights. Submit query letter, SASE. Disk/modem, dot matrix OK. Responds almost immediately, publishes in 1–3 months. Topics: mill operations profiles, heavy technical emphasis. Guidelines available.
COMMERCE, INDUSTRY, LUMBER

Western News, PO Box M, Libby, MT 59923. Editor: June McMahon. 406-293-4124. Weekly newspaper.
COMMUNITY

Western Newsletter, The Book Shop, 908 Main St, Boise, ID 83702. Editor: Jean Wilson & Lori Benton. Published 3 times a year. Circ 350.
LITERARY, LITERATURE

Western Publishing, PO Box 61031, Seattle, WA 98121. Contact: Robert D Ewbank. Periodical. Accepts freelance material. Query w/SASE. Topics: Music, performing arts, poetry, painting.
ARTS, MUSIC, POETRY

Western Remodeler Magazine, 510 SW Third Ave, Portland, OR 97204. 503-283-6202. A monthly targeted to the remodeling construction industry and related professions and trades. Controled circ of 7,500 in Oregon & SW Washington.
BUSINESS, TRADE/ASSOCIATIONS

Western RV News, 1350 SW Upland Dr, Ste B, Portland, OR 97221. 503-222-1255. Editor: Jim Hathaway. Ads: Elsie Hathaway. Newspaper published 14X/yr. Sub $8; circ 16,000. Uses freelance material. Byline given. Pays money on publication, acquires 1st, 2nd rights. Submit query letter, complete ms, SASE, phone. Simultaneous subs OK. Responds in 3 wks; publishes in 6–12 wks. Accepts news items, cartoons, articles, op/ed, photos (B&W, 3X5 glossy preferred). Topics: must have RV slant. Guidelines available. Sample free.
NORTHWEST, RECREATION, TECHNICAL

Western Trucking, 4250 Dawson St, Burnaby, BC V5C 4B1. Periodical.
BUSINESS, CONSUMER

Western Viking, PO Box 70408, Seattle, WA 98108. 206-784-4617. Weekly newspaper.
COMMUNITY

Western Wood Products Association, 1500 Yeon Bldg, Portland, OR 97204. Book publisher.
BUSINESS

Westgate Press, 15050 SW Koll Pkwy. Ste G2, Beaverton, OR 97006. 503-646-0820. Editor: Dr Pam Munter. Quarterly newsletter. Sub $10/yr; circ 250. Not a freelance market. Sample $2.50.
PSYCHOLOGY

Westridge Press, 1090 Southridge Pl S, Salem, OR 97302. Book publisher.
OTHER/UNSPECIFIED

Westside Record Journal, PO Box 38, Ferndale, WA 98248. 206-384-1411. Weekly newspaper.
COMMUNITY

Westwind, Northwest Science Fiction Society, PO Box 24207, Seattle, WA 98124. Editor: Bob Suryan. Periodical.
FANTASY/SCI FI

Westwind Publishing, Box 3586, Boise, ID 83703. Book publisher.
OTHER/UNSPECIFIED

Westworld Magazine/Canada Wide Magazines, 401-4180 Lougheed Highway, Burnaby, BC V5C 6A7. 604-299-7311. Editor: Robin Roberts. Ads: Pat Meyers. Periodicals published 4–6 times a year. Circ 96,000–420,000. Not a freelance market.
CANADA

Whalesong Journal, PO Box 39, Cannon Beach, OR 97110. Periodical.
OTHER/UNSPECIFIED

What's Happening, 1251 Lincoln, Eugene, OR 97401. Editor: Sonja Snyder. 503-484-0519. Weekly tabloid, founded 1982. Sub $25/yr; circ 25,000. Uses freelance material. Byline given. Pays 3¢–7¢ wd, on publication. Acquires 1st rights. Submit query letter, clips, complete ms, phone. Dot matrix, photocopy, simultaneous, disk/modem subs OK. Accepts fiction, poetry, cartoons, news items, interviews, op/ed, articles, reviews, photos (B&W prints). Topics: arts, politics, environment, social, cultural — with alternative/progressive focus. Guidelines available. Sample $1.
ARTS, ENVIRONMENT/RESOURCES, PUBLIC AFFAIRS

Wheat Life, 109 E First, Ritzville, WA 99169. 509-659-0610. Editor/Ads: Sherrye Wyatt Phillips. Publishes 11 issues per year. Sub $12/yr. Circ 14,000. Uses 2 freelance mss per year. Pays in copies. Acquires 1st rights. Byline given. Submit ms, SASE. Nonfiction only: agriculture — wheat & barley, but

with warmth. Recipes/cooking profiles, or features using barley or wheat in a unique way. B&W prints. Sample 50¢.
AGRICULTURE/FARMING, FOOD/COOKING

Wheatherstone Press, 20 Wheatherstone, Lake Oswego, OR 97034. Book publisher.
OTHER/UNSPECIFIED

Wheel Press, 9203 SE Mitchell St, Portland, OR 97266. Contact: Arthur Honeyman. 503-777-6659. Self-publisher of 2 softcover, original, reprint, subsidy books a year. Audience: "Students, educators, sensitive readers of all ages interested in social issues with emphasis on (but not limited to) handicapped people." Print run: 500. Sometimes accepts freelance material. Submit ms, SASE. Reports in 1 month. Nonfiction, fiction, poetry, plays, cartoons. No photographs or multi-colored pictures. Topics: "Almost any subject." Catalog available.
CHILDREN/TEEN, FICTION, DISABLED

Whidbey News Times & Whidbey Today, PO Box 10, Oak Harbor, WA 98277. 206-675-6611. Weekly newspaper.
COMMUNITY

Whistler Publishing, Box 3641, Courtenay, BC V9N 6Z8. Contact: K Ben Buss. 604-334-2852. Publisher of 10 nonfiction, softcover originals per year to outdoor recreation enthusiasts, environmentally aware. Accepts freelance material. Payment: Money, royalties. Ms outline, sample chapters w/SASE. Nonfiction: "Any material applicable to the outdoors from handicrafts to hiking and from cottage industries to flora & fauna…should be of a practical nature easily illustrated or photographed."
ENVIRONMENT/RESOURCES, OUTDOOR, RECREATION

G M White, PO Box 365, Ronan, MT 59864. 406-676-3766. Self-publisher of softcover Indian and Eskimo culture and history books. Not a freelance market.
CRAFTS/HOBBIES, NATIVE AMERICAN, NORTHWEST

White Mammoth, 2183 Nottingham Dr, Fairbanks, AK 99709. 907-479-6034. Contact: M L Guthrie. Publishes softcover books. Not a freelance market.
ALASKA, NATURAL HISTORY

White Ribbon Review, Oregon Women Temperance Union, 36400 Brand S Rd, Springfield, OR 97478. Bimonthly.
RELIGION, SOCIETY, WOMEN

White Salmon Enterprise, PO Box 218, White Salmon, WA 98672. 206-493-2112. Weekly newspaper.
COMMUNITY

Whitecap Books, 1086 W 3rd St, N Vancouver, BC V7P 3J6. 604-980-9852. Editor: Colleen MacMillan. Ads: Robert McCullough. Publishes hard- & softcover books. Accepts unsolicited submissions. Pays advance, royalties. Acquires all rights. Submit query letter, outline, sample chapters, SASE. Photocopy OK. Responds in 1–3 mos; publishes in 12–18 mos. Accepts nonfiction, photos. Topics: gardening, natural history, history, colour scenic, regional guides.
GARDENING, GENERAL HISTORY, NATURAL HISTORY

Whitefish Pilot, 312 2nd St, Whitefish, MT 59937. 406-862-3505. Newspaper.
COMMUNITY

Whitehall Ledger, 15 W Legion, Whitehall, MT 59759. Periodical.
OTHER/UNSPECIFIED

Whitman College Press, Office of Publications, Whitman College, Walla Walla, WA 99362. Book publisher.
COLLEGE/UNIVERSITY, EDUCATION

Whole Air, PO Box 98786, Tacoma, WA 98499-0786. Editor: Bruce Williams. 206-588-1743. Periodical on hang gliding. Uses 2–3 freelance mss per issue. Payment: $3 an inch, 1 month after publication. Byline given. Rights purchased: First. Submit ms, SASE. Phone queries, dot matrix, simultaneous submission OK. Reports in 2–3 wks. Publishes in 1–3 mos. Nonfiction:

1,500–3,500 wds. Query on fiction, poetry, columns. Photos: B&W prints, color slides, prints. Guidelines available; sample/$2.
AVIATION, RECREATION, SPORTS

Whole Self, The Mirdad Center, 429 SE 6th St, Grants Pass, OR 97526. 503-474-7700. Contact: Michael Mirdad, editor. Bimonthly magazine of holistic living. No submission info available.
HEALTH, NEW AGE

Wicazo Sea Review, Eastern Washington University, English & Indian Studies, Cheney, WA 99004. 509-359-2871. Editor: Elizabeth Cook-Lynn. Semiannual. Sub $8/15. Circ 600. Uses freelance material. Byline given, pays copies, acquires 1st rights. Submit complete ms, query w/clips, SASE. Photocopied sub OK. Reports in 3 mos; publishes in 6 mos. Accepts nonfiction, fiction, poetry, news items, interviews, photos (B&W glossy), cartoons, reviews. Sample $8.
ANTHROPOLOGY/ARCHÆOLOGY, AMERICAN HISTORY, NATIVE AMERICAN

Wiggansnatch, PO Box 20061, Seattle, WA 98102. Editor/ads: James Moore. Quarterly journal on neo-paganism. Circ 500. Sub $6. Uses 10 mss per issue. Payment: Copies on publication. Byline given. Rights purchased: First, non-exclusive reprint. Submit ms, SASE. Dot matrix, photocopies, simultaneous submission OK. Reports in 1 month. Nonfiction, fiction, cartoons. "We emphasize personal experiences in magick, ritual, ecology, etc. Anything of interest to a neo-pagan audience. Departments include: real magic, myth, dreams, spirit, politics, shamanism, wicca, tarot." Guidelines available; sample/$2.
ASTROLOGY/SPIRITUAL, COUNTER CULTURE, GAY/LESBIAN

Wilander Publishing Co, 17934 NW Chestnut Lane, Portland, OR 97231. 503-621-3964. Contact: Jodi L Fisher. Self-publisher of children's book. Not accepting freelance submissions.
CHILDREN/TEEN

Wilbur Register, PO Box 186, Wilbur, WA 99185. 509-647-5551. Weekly newspaper.
COMMUNITY

Wild Oregon, Oregon Natural Resources Council, 522 SW Fifth #1050, Portland, OR 97214. 503-223-9001. Editor: Scott Greacen. Quarterly journal, founded 1975. Sub $15/yr; circ 6,500. Seldom uses freelance material. Byline given. Pays copies, acquires all rights. Submit query letter, SASE. Accepts nonfiction, photos (B&W, no payment).
CONSERVATION, ENVIRONMENT/RESOURCES, OREGON

Wilderness House, 11129 Caves Hwy, Cave Junction, OR 97523. Book publisher.
OTHER/UNSPECIFIED

Wildfire, Bear Tribe Medicine Society, PO Box 9167, Spokane, WA 99209-9167. Editor: Matthew Ryan. Ads: Joseph LaZenka. Quarterly magazine. Sub $10. Circ 10,000. Uses freelance material. Pays money. Acquires 1st rights. Submit ms/SASE. Photocopied Apple/Mac computer disk OK. Accepts nonfiction, fiction, poetry, photos, cartoons. Topics: New Age, permaculture, Native American, philosophy, UFOs. Tip: "No sensationalism." Guidelines available. Sample $2.95.
ASTROLOGY/SPIRITUAL, ENVIRONMENT/RESOURCES, NATIVE AMERICAN

Wildfire, PO Box 148-mp, Tum Tum, WA 99034. Magazine.
OTHER/UNSPECIFIED

Wildlife Safari Game Search Newsletter, PO Box 1600, Winston, OR 97496. 503-679-6761. Editor: Sally Lawson. Periodical.
ANIMALS

Wildlife-Wildlands Institute, 5200 Upper Miller Creek Rd, Missoula, MT 59803. Book publisher.
ANIMALS, CONSERVATION, NATURAL HISTORY

Wildwood Press, 209 SW Wildwood Ave, Grants Pass, OR 97526. 503-479-3434. Self-publisher of 1 softcover original book. Does not accept unsolicited submissions.
ADVENTURE, OUTDOOR

Willamette Collegian, 900 State St, Salem, OR 97301. 503-370-6053. Bimonthly student newspaper of Willamette University.
COLLEGE/UNIVERSITY

The Willamette Journal of the Liberal Arts, Willamette University D-180, Salem, OR 97301. 503-370-6272. Editor: Lane McGaughy. Ads: Elsa Struble. Sub $5/issue. Circ 700. Journal published 1–2 times a year. Uses freelance material. Pays in copies. Acquires all rights. Byline given. Submit ms, SASE. Photocopied, computer disk OK. Accepts nonfiction, fiction, poetry, photos. Topics: any scholarly essays in the liberal arts. Guidelines available. Sample $3.75.
COLLEGE/UNIVERSITY, LIBERAL ARTS, SCHOLARLY/ACADEMIC

Willamette Kayak & Canoe Club, PO Box 1062, Corvallis, OR 97339. Book publisher. Query w/SASE.
RECREATION, SPORTS

Willamette Law Review, College of Law, Willamette University, Salem, OR 97301. Quarterly journal. 503-370-6300. Sub $22/yr; circ 850.
LAW

Willamette Week, 2 – 2nd Ave, Portland, OR 97209. Editor: Mark Zusman. 503-243-2122. Weekly alternative news, art and regional living magazine. Circ 50,000. Uses 60% freelance mss per copy. Payment: 2–4¢/wd. Query w/ms, SASE. Dot matrix, simultaneous submission (if informed) OK. Publishes in 1 month. Nonfiction: to 5,000 wds; art, entertainment, politics, Portland based subjects. Guidelines and sample available w/SASE.
ARTS, ENTERTAINMENT, POLITICS

The Willamette Writer, 9045 SW Barbur Blvd, #5A, Portland, OR 97219. 503-452-1592. Monthly newsletter for the membership of Willamette Writers. Circ 900. Sub w/membership. Not a freelance market.
BOOK ARTS/BOOKS, PUBLISHING/PRINTING, WRITING

The Willapa Harbor Herald, PO Box 627, Raymond, WA 98577. 206-942-3466. Weekly newspaper.
COMMUNITY

William & Allen, PO Box 6147, Olympia, WA 98502. Book publisher.
OTHER/UNSPECIFIED

Willoughby Wessington Publishing Company, PO Box 911, Mercer Island, WA 98040. Book publisher.
OTHER/UNSPECIFIED

Willow Springs, Eastern Washington University, PO Box 1063, MS-1, Cheney, WA 99004. 509-458-6429. Editor: Nance Van Winckel. Ads: Deb Moore. Semiannual magazine. Sub $7; circ 8,000. Uses freelance material. Pays money, copies on publication. Acquires all rights. Byline given. Submit ms, SASE. Photocopied OK. Reports in 1–2 mos. Publishes in 1–6 mos. Accepts nonfiction, fiction, fine poetry, photos (B&W or slides), interviews, reviews. Guidelines available. Samples $4.
FICTION, LITERARY, POETRY

Wilson Publications, PO Box 712, Yakima, WA 98907. 509-457-8275. Self-publisher. Not a freelance market.
AMERICAN HISTORY, TRAVEL

Wind Row, Washington State University, English Dept, Pullman, WA 99164. 509-335-4832. Annual magazine. Sub $3.50; circ 500. Uses freelance material only from current students or alumni. Byline given. Pays copies. Submit complete ms. Dot matrix, photocopy subs OK. Responds in 4 mos; publishes in 6–12 mos. Accepts fiction, poetry, cartoons, articles, photos, reviews, memoirs. ID number must accompany submission. Sample $3.50.
COLLEGE/UNIVERSITY

Wind Vein Press, PO Box 462, Ketchum, ID 83340. Contact: Scott Preston. 208-788-3704. Self-publisher of high quality limited editions. "All of the books published by Wind Vein will be privately arranged." Not a freelance market.
BOOK ARTS/BOOKS, IDAHO, POETRY

Windows Watcher Newsletter, CompuTh!nk Inc. 3731 130th Ave NE, Bellevue, WA 98005-1353. Editor: Jesse Berst. Publishes softcover books, monthly newsletter. Sub $195. Accepts unsolicited submissions. No submission info given, query w/SASE.
COMPUTERS, HOW-TO, TECHNICAL

Windsor Publications Inc, 1000 S Bertlesen Rd #14, Eugene, OR 97402. Contact: Ed Lusch. Publishes wildlife artwork & prints, specifically game, fish & birds. Query SASE.
ANIMALS, FISHING, VISUAL ARTS

Windyridge Press, PO Box 327, Medford, OR 97501. Book publisher.
OTHER/UNSPECIFIED

Winn Book Publishers, PO Box 80096, Seattle, WA 98108. Contact: Larry Winn. 206-763-9544. Book publisher. Not a freelance mkt at this time.
OTHER/UNSPECIFIED

Winterholm Press, PO Box 101251, Anchorage, AK 99510. Book publisher.
OTHER/UNSPECIFIED

The Wire Harp, Communications Bldg. 5-121 - 3050 SFCC, W 3410 Ft George Wright Dr, Spokane, WA 99204. 509-459-3594 or 3600. Contact: Almut McAuley. Annual magazine; circ 1500. Pays copies. Submit query/SASE, phone. Photocopied, complete ms. subs OK. Responds in 4 wks. Accepts fiction, poetry, cartoons, nonfiction, photos, interviews, articles, B&W art. Guidelines, sample available for postage.
ARTS, LITERARY, PHOTOGRAPHY

Wise Buys, 511 NW 74th St, Vancouver, WA 98665-8414. Editor: Pat Stenback. Periodical.
CONSUMER

Wistaria Press, 4373 NE Wistaria Dr, Portland, OR 97213. Book publisher.
OTHER/UNSPECIFIED

Wizard Works, PO Box 1125, Homer, AK 99603. Contact: Jan O'Meara. Book publisher.
ALASKA, OTHER/UNSPECIFIED

WLA Highlights, Washington Library Assoc, 1232 143rd Ave SE Bellevue, WA 98007. Periodical.
REFERENCE/LIBRARY

Wolfdog Publications, PO Box 142406, Dept R, Anchorage, AK 99514-2506. Book publisher.
OTHER/UNSPECIFIED

Woman to Woman Magazine, 535 W 10th, 2nd Fl, Vancouver, BC V52 1K9. 604-736-0218. Editor: S Massingham-Pearce. Ads: Megan Abbott. Monthly tabloid. Sub $11.88/yr. Circ 60,000. Uses 8–10 freelance mss per issue. Pays 15–25¢/wd; half on acceptance, half on publication. Acquires 1st rights. Byline depends on size. Submit query w/clips, SASE. Dot matrix, photocopied OK. Reports in 4–6 wks. Publishes in 2–4 mos. Accepts fiction, nonfiction, photos. Topics: health, beauty, human interest, business profiles, crafts. Tips: 200–1,200 wds, entertaining, BC oriented, tabloid style writing — fast, informal, plenty of quotes, personal accounts & anecdotes; aim to stimulate interest & entertain. Pictures must be accompanied by negatives, no slides, original only. Guidelines available. Sample 99¢.
FASHION, FOOD/COOKING, WOMEN

Womanshare Books, PO Box 681, Grants Pass, OR 97526. Book publisher.
WOMEN

Women's Yellow Pages, 1208 SW 13th Ave, Ste 212, Portland, OR 97205. 503-223-9344. Annual business and professional women's directory with edition for Seattle & Portland. Circ 50,000. Sub free. Uses 10 mss per issue. Payment: Copies on publication. Byline given. Query w/SASE. Phone queries, dot matrix, photocopies, simultaneous sub; electronic OK. Reports in 2–6 wks. Nonfiction, 1–6 pgs, typed ds. Women in bus. or professions, and related women's issues. Sample free.
BUSINESS, WOMEN

Women's Chronicle, 206 – 120 Hamilton St, Vancouver, BC V6B 2S2. 604-682-2242. Contact: Linda Richards-Gorowski. Circ 25,000. Bimonthly magazine for businesswomen. Buys 1st and 2nd serial rights. Accepts non-

fiction (general, historical, personal experience, travel, how-to), fillers, photos. Pay varies. Query w/clips or ms.
BUSINESS, WOMEN

Womyn's Press, PO Box 562, Eugene, OR 97440. 503-485-3207. Editors: Betsy Brown, Kaseja O, Jessica Jenkins. Ads: Gail Elber. Bimonthly newspaper. Sub $5–15/yr. Circ 1,000. Uses freelance material from women only. Pays in copies. Byline given. Query, SASE. Dot matrix, photocopied OK. Reports ASAP. Publishes within 2 mos. Accepts nonfiction, fiction, poetry, photos, cartoons. Tips: poetry, not more than a page; articles 2,000 wds. Sample $1.
FEMINISM, GAY/LESBIAN, WOMEN

Wood Lake Books Inc, Box 700, Winfield, BC V0H 2C0. Ralph Milton, editor. Book publisher.
OTHER/UNSPECIFIED

Word River Journal, 112 S Main, Hailey, ID 8333. 208-788-3444. Newspaper.
COMMUNITY, OTHER/UNSPECIFIED

Woodburn Drag Script, 7730 State Hwy 214 NE, Woodburn, OR 97071. Periodical.
RECREATION, SPORTS

Woodburn Independent, 650 N 1st St, Box 96, Woodburn, OR 97071. 503-981-3441. Weekly newspaper.
COMMUNITY

Woodford Memorial Editions Inc, PO Box 55085, Seattle, WA 98155. 206-364-4167. Contact: Jess E Stewart. Book publisher "presently accepting only information or mss on Jack Woodford from those who knew him personally. Otherwise concerned mainly with the person and career of Mr Woodford (Josiah Pitts Woolfolk)…and his ability to inspire people to write…books in one's own style…" Catalog available.
BIOGRAPHY

Woodstock Independent News, PO Box 2354 Ave, Portland, OR 97202. Editor: Jerry Schmidt. 503-233-1797. Ads: same. Monthly newspaper. Circ 20,000. Sub free.
COMMUNITY

Word Power Inc, PO Box 17034, Seattle, WA 98107. Book publisher.
LANGUAGE(S), OTHER/UNSPECIFIED

Word Works, PO Box 2206 MPO, Vancouver, BC, V6B 3W2. 604-683-2057. Quarterly writers group newsletter. Circ 900, subs. $35/yr. Uses freelance material. Byline given, pays copies. Submit query, synopsis, outline, SASE. Photocopy, dot matrix, simultaneous subs OK. Responds in 3 mos; publishes in 3–6 mos. Accepts cartoons, nonfiction, photos, interviews, articles. Tips: articles on computers, writers' organizations, political issues affecting writers. "We prefer to publish member-written material, but will consider other submissions." Samples available, no cost.
WRITING

Words & Pictures Unlimited, 1257 NW Van Buren Ave, Corvallis, OR 97330. Book publisher.
OTHER/UNSPECIFIED

Words Press, 8787 SW Becker Dr, Portland, OR 97223. Book publisher.
OTHER/UNSPECIFIED

Wordware, PO Box 14300, Seattle, WA 98114. Contact: Marguerite Russell. 206-328-9393. Book publisher.
OTHER/UNSPECIFIED

The World, Box 1840, Coos Bay, OR 97420. 503-269-0238. Daily newspaper.
COMMUNITY

World Wide Publishing Corporation, PO Box 105, Ashland, OR 97520. Not a freelance market.
ADVENTURE, HOME, TRAVEL

World Without War Council, 2929 NE Blakeley St, Seattle, WA 98105. Self-publisher of books.
PEACE, PUBLIC AFFAIRS, REFERENCE/LIBRARY

Write-on Press, PO Box 86606, N Vancouver, BC V7L 4L2. 604-858-7739. Editor: Dennis Maracle. Publishes softcover books. Accepts unsolicited submissions. Pays copies, royalties. Acquires all rights. Submit query letter, complete ms, SASE. Photocopy OK. Responds in 2–6 wks. Accepts fiction, poetry, biography, nonfiction, photos, plays. Catalog available.
NATIVE AMERICAN, WOMEN

Writers Information Network, PO Box 11337, Bainbridge Island, WA 98110. 206-842-9103. Contact: Elaine Wright Colvin. Bimonthly newsletter of The Professional Assn for Christian Writers, est 1983. Sub $15/yr; circ 600+. Uses freelance material. Byline given. Submit query letter, complete ms, SASE. Accepts news items, articles, reviews. Topics: writing helps, tips, connections, how-to advice, announcements, info on religious publishers. Sample free, SASE.
BOOK ARTS/BOOKS, RELIGION, WRITING

Writers' Open Forum, PO Box 516, Tracyton, WA 98393. Contact: Sandra E Haven. Bimonthly publication designed as an idea and critique exchange for writers. Sub $9/yr. Pays $5 plus 3 copies on publication for 1st rights for short stories and articles. Byline given. No poetry. Readers requested to send in critiques on those ms published. Critiques are collected (some published) and redirected to authors. Also pays in copies for tips on writing (up to 150 wds). Submit ms w/SASE (1,500 wrds max), photocopies OK, on any subject or genre (except no slice of life, violence, graphic sex, or experimental formats). No simultaneous subs. Guidelines available for SASE. Sample issue $2.
FICTION, WRITING

Writer's Info, PO Box 1870, Hayden, ID 83835. 208-772-6184. Editor: Linda Hutton. Monthly with advice for beginning freelancers. Sub $12. Uses freelance material. Payment "starts at $1" on acceptance. Byline given. Acquires 1st rights. Submit ms, SASE. Photocopies, simultaneous submission OK. Reports in 1 mo. Nonfiction, poetry. To 300 word on any aspect of freelancing, short poems and riddles related to writing. Guidelines available/sample, SASE, 2 first-class stamps.
FEMINISM, POETRY, WRITING

Writer's NW, Media Weavers, Rt 3 Box 376, Hillsboro, OR 97124. 503-621-3911. Editors: Linny Stovall, Dennis Stovall. Quarterly tabloid from Media Weavers (imprint of Blue Heron Publishing Inc.) for writers, teachers, publishers, librarians, students. Uses freelance material. Query w/SASE first. Pays in copies. Tips: 500–1,000 wd articles on all aspects of writing and publishing; regular columns include book reviews, profiles of publishers, and technical reviews (software, how-to). Welcomes news from writers, teachers, publishers and librarians for items in "Calendar" and "News & Notes" sections. Sub $10/yr US, $12/yr CDN. Single copy $2.50.
NORTHWEST, PUBLISHING/PRINTING, WRITING

Writer's Publishing Service Company, 1512 Western Ave, Seattle, WA 98101. 206-284-9954. Contact: John Lathourakis. Publishes hard- & softcover originals, reprints, subsidy books. Accepts unsolicited submissions. Pays money, copies on publication. Acquires all rights. Submit query w/clips, ms, phone, SASE. Photocopied sub OK. Reports in 1–2 mos; publishes in 6–12 mos. Accepts nonfiction, fiction, poetry, cartoons, other. "We are specialists in self-publishing. However, we do purchase or co-publish 3–5 projects a year."
FICTION, GENEALOGY, POETRY

Writing Magazine, Box 69609, Stn K, Vancouver, BC V5K 4W7. 604-738-2032. Editor: Colin Browne. Published 3 times a yr. Circ 650. Accepts freelance submissions. Pays money and subscription. Submit several poems, a long poem, 1–2 stories, a chapter, SASE. Photocopied OK. Reports in 2 mos. Accepts fiction, poetry. Sample $3.
FICTION, POETRY, WRITING

The Written Arts, 1115 Smith Tower, 506 Second Ave, Seattle, WA 98104. Editor: Deborah Moulton. 206-344-7580. Biannual literary magazine of the King County Arts Commission. Open to King County residents. Uses 30 mss per issue. Byline given. Pays modest honorarium. Rights revert to author on publication. Query w/SASE. Nonfiction, fiction, poetry. Submit up to 5 po-

ems and/or 3,000 wds, unbound, without covers. Do not include name or acknowledgements on samples; cover letter to include titles and first lines of submission and short author's bio. Write for current deadlines. Guidelines and sample available.
FICTION, LITERARY, POETRY

WSEO Dispatch, Washington State Energy Office, 400 E Union, 1st Floor, ER-11, Olympia, WA 98504. Editor: Linda Waring. Bimonthly.
GOVERNMENT, WASHINGTON

Wynkyn Press, RR 3, Wildwood Crescent, Ganges, BC V0S 1E0. Book publisher.
OTHER/UNSPECIFIED

Michael Yaeger, PO Box 4304, Pioneer Square, Seattle, WA 98104. 206-624-9102. Self-publisher. Not a freelance market.
AVANT-GARDE/EXPERIMENTAL, HUMOR, NORTHWEST

Yakima Herald-Republic, 114 North Fourth St, PO Box 9668, Yakima, WA 98909. 509-248-1251. Daily newspaper.
COMMUNITY

Yakima Nation Review, PO Box 386, Toppenish, WA 98948. 509-865-5121. Newspaper.
NATIVE AMERICAN, NORTHWEST

Yakima Valley Genealogical Society Bulletin, PO Box 445, Yakima, WA 98907. 509-248-1328. Editor: Ellen Brzoska. Quarterly journal. Sub $11/yr. Uses freelance material. No pay. Submit ms, SASE. Photocopied, computer disk OK. Accepts articles related to family history. Sample available.
GENEALOGY, WASHINGTON

Ye Galleon Press, PO Box 287, Fairfield, WA 99012. 509-283-2422. Publisher of hard- & softcover originals, reprints. Accepts freelance material. Acquires 1st rights. Submit query, SASE. Reports in 1 mo. Accepts nonfiction, poetry, biography, memoirs, Northwest Coast voyage books; "I publish (at my expense) Pacific NW and rare western US history. Modern books with living authors are nearly all paid for by authors, but editions are sometimes split." Catalog available.
AMERICANA, AMERICAN HISTORY, POETRY

Yellow Hat Press, PO Box 34337, Stn D, Vancouver, BC V6J 4P3. Editor: Beverly D Chiu. Book publisher.
OTHER/UNSPECIFIED

Yellow Jacket Press, Rt 4 Box 7464, Twin Falls, ID 83301. Editor: Bill Studebaker. Book publisher.
LITERATURE

YIPE, Washington Poets Association, Box 71213, Rainier, OR 97048. Editor: Carolyn Norred. Periodical.
POETRY

Yokoi, PO Box 726, Bozeman, MT 59715. 406-587-8947. Editor: Marjorie Smith. Quarterly magazine, founded 1990. Sub $16/yr; circ 600+. Uses freelance material. Byline given. Pays copies on publication. Acquires 1st or 2nd rights. Submit complete ms, SASE. Photocopy, dot matrix, simultaneous subs OK. Accepts fiction, poetry, cartoons, op/ed, reviews, essays on the Montana arts scene. Guidelines available. Sample $5.
ARTS, LITERARY, MONTANA

Young American, America's Newspaper for Kids, PO Box 12409, Portland, OR 97212. 503-230-1895. Editor: Kristina Linden. Biweekly, founded 1983. Sub $15/yr. Circ 1.2 million. Uses freelance material. Pays money, negotiable, on publication. Byline given sometimes. Acquires 1st/NA rights. Submit ms, SASE. Dot matrix, photocopies OK. Reports in 4 mos. Publishes within year. Accepts: nonfiction to 500 wds; fiction to 1,000 wds; poetry, photos (B&W $5), plays, cartoons. Guidelines available. Sample $1.50.
CHILDREN/TEEN, HUMOR, SCIENCE

Young Pine Press, c/o International Examiner, 318 6th Ave S #123, Seattle, WA 98104. Book publisher.
OTHER/UNSPECIFIED

Young Voices, PO Box 2321, Olympia, WA 98507. 206-357-4683. Editor: Steve Charak. Bimonthly magazine, founded 1988. Sub $15/yr; circ 1,000.

Uses freelance material from elementary and middle school age children. Byline given. Acquires 1st rights. Submit complete ms, SASE. Responds in 3 mos; publishes in 3 mos. Accepts fiction, poetry, cartoons, nonfiction, interviews, articles, plays, reviews. Guidelines available. Sample $3.
CHILDREN (BY/ABOUT), FICTION, POETRY

Your Public Schools, Superintendent of Public Instruction, Old Capitol Bldg FG-11, Olympia, WA 98504. Periodical news of/for Washington public schools.
EDUCATION

Zap News, Box 1994, Eugene, OR 97440. Periodical.
OTHER/UNSPECIFIED

Zen 'n' Ink, PO Box 11714, Winslow, WA 98110. 206-842-9360. Contact: John T Wood. Founded in 1990, publishes philosophy and psychology softcover books. Not a freelance market.
PHILOSOPHY, PSYCHOLOGY

The Zig Zag Papers, PO Box 247, Zig Zag, OR 97049. 503-622-3425. Contact: Joe Stein. Publisher of 1 book per year on science, technology, or NW. Print run: 3,000. Not a freelance market.
SCIENCE

Resources

The following lists include over 500 Northwest resources for writers, publishers, teachers, librarians, artists, and researchers. We have excluded the names of all the schools that have writing classes, although many of their special programs for writers are listed. Almost every community college, college, university, and extension program offers classes in creative writing, journalism, and photography. There are too many to include them all. Also, we have not listed the many "for profit" private classes and workshops available throughout the region. Information about these can be found by contacting local schools and writers' groups.

If you send us information about events, organizations, classes, contests, or other resources which we overlooked (or corrections), we'll include it in the updates section of our quarterly tabloid, *Writer's NW*.

Arts Organizations

100 Mile & District Arts Council, Box 2262, 100 Mile House, BC V0K 2E0. 604-395-4077. Contact: James Scott.

Abbotsford - Matsqui Arts Council, Box 336, Abbotsford, BC V2S 4N9. 604-852-9358. Contact: Freddy Latham.

Alaska Arts Southeast, Box 2133, Sitka, AK 99835. Contact: Director.

Alaska Arts-in-Prisons, 540 W 10th St, Juneau, AK 99801.

Alaska State Council on the Arts, 411 West 4th Ave, Suite 1E, Anchorage, AK 99501. Contact: Chris D'Arcy. 907-279-1558. For resident writers, they offer an annual fellowship program. Write for grant guidelines and application deadlines.

Alberni Valley Community Arts Council, c/o Rollin Art Centre, 3061 8th Ave, Port Alberni, BC V9Y 2K5. 604-724-3412. Contact: Rob Dom.

Allied Arts Assn, 89 Lee Blvd., Richland, WA 99352. Contact: Rosemary Merckx. 509-943-9815.

Allied Arts Council North Central Washington, PO Box 573, Wenatchee, WA 98807. Contact: Kathleen Gilstrap. 509-662-1213.

Allied Arts Council of The Mid-Columbia Region, PO Box 730, Richland, WA 99352. Contact: Jackie Geiler, Director. 509-943-0524.

Allied Arts Council Yakima Valley, 5000 W Lincoln Ave, Yakima, WA 98908. 509-966-0930. Contact: Ann Byerrum. Annual spring writers workshop.

Allied Arts of Renton, 400 S 3rd St, Renton, WA 98055. Contact: Annette McCully, President. 206-255-2590.

Allied Arts of Seattle, 107 S Main St, Seattle, WA 98104. Contact: Francis Van Ausdal. 206-624-0432.

Allied Arts of Tacoma/Pierce County, 901 Broadway Plaza, Pantages Centre 5th Fl, Tacoma, WA 98402. Contact: Jane Matsch. 206-272-3141.

Arrow Lakes Arts Council, Box 895, Nakusp, BC V0G 1R0. 604-265-3086. Contact: Terry Taylor.

Arts at Menucha, PO Box 4958, Portland, OR 97208. Annual artists summer camp/workshops in fine and applied arts and literature sponsored by Creative Arts Community.

Arts Council Clark County, PO Box 1995, Vancouver, WA 98668-1995. 206-694-1835. Contact: Carolyn Neubauer.

Arts Council Mid-Columbia Region, PO Box 3069, Richland, WA 99302-3069. Contact: Chris Dow. 509-943-0524.

Arts Council of Pendleton, PO Box 573, Pendleton, OR 97801. 503-276-8826. Contact: Carolyn Wallace.

Arts Council of Snohomish, PO Box 5038, Everett, WA 98206. Contact: Laura McNally. 206-252-7469.

Arts Council of Southern Oregon, 33 N Central Ave #308, Medford, OR 97501. 503-482-5594. Contact: Donovan Gray.

Arts Council the Grand Coulee, PO Box 405, Grand Coulee, WA, 99133. Contact: Jerry Rumberg.

Arts & Crafts Guild of Oregon, PO Box 601, Oakridge, OR 97463. 503-782-4431. Contact: Clara Bailey.

Associated Arts of Ocean Shores, PO Box 241, Ocean Shores, WA 98569. Contact: Margie McBride.

Auburn Arts Commission, 25 W Main, Auburn, WA 98001. 206-931-3043. Contact: Josie Emmons Vine. Writers' Conference last weekend in October.

Bainbridge Island Arts Council, Executive Director, 261 Madison South, Bainbridge Island, WA 98110. 206-842-7901. Contact: Janis Shaw. In addition to other activities, including writing workshops, they publish a Poets & Artists Calendar from their annual Poets & Artists Competition.

Ballard Arts Council, c/o Ballard Chamber of Commerce, 2208 NW Market St #204, Seattle, WA 98107. 206-523-8280. Contact: Larry L Jones.

Bay Area Arts Council/South Coast Tourism Assn, 886 S 4th St, Coos Bay, OR 97420. Contact: Lionel Youst. 503-267-6500.

Beaverton Arts Commission, Beaverton City Hall, PO Box 4755, Beaverton, OR 97076. 503-526-2222. Contact: Jayne Bruno Scott.

Bella Coola Valley Arts Council, Box 591, Bella Coola, BC V0T 1C0. 604-982-2453. Contact: Barbara Gilbert.

Bellevue Allied Arts Council, 9509 NE 30th, Bellevue, WA 98004-1741. Contact: Gigi Mauritzen. 206-455-2589.

Bellevue Arts Commission, PO Box 90012, Bellevue, WA 98009. 206-453-8259. Contact: Carol Cullivan.

Bellingham Arts Commission, City Hall, 121 Prospect St, Bellingham, WA 98225. 206-676-6981. Contact: John Keppelman.

Bulkley Valley Community Arts Council, Box 3971, Smithers, BC V0J 2N0. 604-847-2986. Contact: Todd Glover.

Burnaby Arts Council, 6528 Deer Lake Ave, Burnaby, BC V5G 2J3. 604-298-7322. Contact: Clare Warner.

Burns Lake & District Arts Council, Box 202, Francois Lake, BC V0J 1R0. 604-695-6389. Contact: Julia Fortin.

Campbell River Community Arts Council, Box 927, Campbell River, BC V9W 2X9. 604-285-3101. Contact: Gordon James.

Cannon Beach Arts Assn, PO Box 684, Cannon Beach, OR 97110. Contact: Rainmar Bartle. 503-436-1204.

Castlegar Arts Council, Box 3352, Castlegar, BC V1N 3H6. 604-365-3553. Contact: Donna Moyer.

Central Curry Council for the Arts & Humanities, PO Box 374, Gold Beach, OR 97444. 503-247-6854. Contact: Robert E Simons.

Centrum Foundation, PO Box 1158, Port Townsend, WA 98368. 206-385-3102. Contact: Carol Jane Bangs. Activities include: "A residency program for 3-4 writers each year; a press-in-residence, Copper Canyon Press, with press tours, and in some years letterpress workshops with Tree Swenson, Copper Canyon co-publisher and designer of books for several presses; special workshops featuring writers and experts in other fields, convened to address major societal issues; writing workshops for high school students from Washington State."

Chetwynd Community Arts Council, Box 1795, Chetwynd, BC V0C 1J0. 604-788-2267. Contact: Yvonne Elden.

Chilliwack Community Arts Council, 45899 Henderson Ave, Chilliwack, BC V2P 2X6. 604-792-2069. Contact: Bradley Whittaker.

Citizen's Council for the Arts, 307 S 19th St, Coeur d'Alene, ID 83814.

Clackamas County Arts Council, Clackamas Community College, 19600 S Molalla Ave, Oregon City, OR 97045. 503-656-9543. Contact: Harriet Jorgenson.

Coeur d'Alene City Arts Commission, City Hall, 710 E Mullan Ave, Coeur d'Alene, ID 83814.

Columbia Basin Allied Arts, 28th & Chanute, Moses Lake, WA 98837. 509-762-5351. Contact: Brenda Teals.

Columbia Gorge Arts Council of Washington & Oregon, PO Box 211, Corbett, OR 97019. 503-248-0232. Contact: Ed Bonham.

Columbia Gorge Showcase, PO Box 825, Hood River, OR 97031. 503-386-5113. Contact: Kate Mills.

Columbia Valley Arts Council, Box 233, Windermere, BC V0B 1K0. 604-342-6300. Contact: Ann Jardine.

Comox Valley Community Arts Council, Box 3053, Courtenay, BC V9N 5N3. 604-334-2983. Contact: Kathleen Kerr.

Coop Arts Council Clark County, 4900 Wintler Dr, Vancouver, WA 98661. Contact: Barbara Bray Hart. 206-693-5557.

Coquille Valley Art Assn, HC 83, Box 625, Coquille, OR 97423. 503-396-2866. Contact: Yvonne Marineau.

Coquitlam Area Fine Arts Council, PO Box 217, Port Coquitlam, BC V3C 3V7. 604-931-8255. Contact: Guy Risebrough.

Corvallis Arts Center, 700 SW Madison, Corvallis, OR 97330. 503-754-1551. Contact: Susan Johnson.

Cowichan Valley Arts Council, Box 703, Duncan, BC V9L 3V1. 604-746-1611. Contact: Allison Callihoo.

Cranbrook & District Arts Council, Box 861, Cranbrook, BC V1C 4J6. 604-426-8324. Contact: Deanne Perreault.

Creston Community Arts Council, Box 2236, Creston, BC V0B 1G0. 604-428-5186. Contact: Glenna Fay Taylor.

Crossroads Arts Center, PO Box 235, Baker, OR 97814. 503-523-3704. Contact: Peter Decius.

Cultural Services Branch, Ministry of Municipal Affairs, Recreation And Culture, Parliament Buildings, 800 Johnson St, Victoria, BC V8V 1X4. Contact: Dawn Wallace, Coordinator of Literary & Publishing Programs. 604-356-1727. Funding programs for BC books publishers and writers.

Dallas Arts Assn, PO Box 192, Dallas, OR 97338. 503-623-5594. Contact: LaVonne Wilson or Janet Burton, 623-5700/623-5567.

Delta Community Arts Council, Box 287, Delta, BC V4K 3N7. 604-946-0525. Contact: Jo Booker.

Des Moines Arts Commission, 22513 Marine View Dr, Des Moines, WA 98188. Contact: Jack Kniskern.

Desert Arts Council, Blue Mountain CC, 405 N 1st, Suite 107, Hermiston, OR 97838. 503-567-1800. Contact: Karen Bounds.

District 69 Community Arts Council, Box 1662, Parksville, BC V0R 2S0. 604-248-8185. Contact: Denyse Widdifield.

Eagle Valley Arts Council, Box 686, Sicamous, BC V0E 2V0. 604-836-2570. Contact: Betty Tehonchuk.

Eastern Oregon Regional Arts Council, EOSC - Loso Hall, #220, 1410 "L" Ave, La Grande, OR 97850. 503-962-3624. Contact: Anne Bell.

Edmonds Arts Commission, Anderson Cultural Center, 700 Main St, Edmonds, WA 98020. 206-775-2525. Contact: Linda McCrystal. Sponsors Write-on-the Sound writers conference each fall.

El-Wyhee Arts Council, 1520 E 8th N, Mt Home, ID 83647.

Elgin Arts Council, Rt 1 Box 1A, Elgin, OR 97827. 503-437-7772. Contact: Pamela Davis or Christine McLaughlin.

Ellensburg Arts Commission, 420 North Pearl, Ellensburg, WA 98926. Contact: Phyllis Stamm. 509-986-3065.

Enumclaw Arts Commission, 1339 Griffin, Enumclaw, WA 98022. 206-825-1038. Contact: Evelyn Lercher.

Everett Cultural Commission, 3002 Wetmore, Everett, WA 98201. Contact: Lynda Vanderberg. 206-259-8701.

Fernie & District Arts Council, Box 1453, Fernie, BC V0B 1M0. 604-423-6133. Contact: Beth Gregg.

Florence Arts & Crafts Assn, PO Box 305, Florence, OR 97349.

Fort Nelson Arts Council, Box 1829, Fort Nelson, BC V0C 1R0. 604-774-2357. Contact: John Barry.

Fort St John Community Arts Council, 10003 - 100th St, Fort St John, BC V7J 3Y5. 604-785-1990. Contact: Kevin Truscott.

Golden District Arts Council, Box 228, Golden, BC V0A 1H0. 604-344-6365. Contact: Catherine Green.

Grand Forks Area Art Council, Box 2636, Grand Forks, BC V0H 1H0. 604-442-8233. Contact: John Nilsen.

Grants Pass Arts Council, 201 Barbara Dr, Grants Pass, OR 97526. 503-479-5541. Contact: Doug Norby.

Greater Condon Arts Assn, PO Box 165, Condon, OR 97823. 503-384-5114. Contact: Darla Ceale.

Greater Victoria Community Arts Council, #511 - 610 View St, Victoria, BC V8W 1J6. 604-381-2787. Contact: Bruce Stanley.

Harney County Arts & Crafts, PO Box 602, Burns, OR 97720. 503-573-7693. Contact: Royaline Oltman.

Hillsboro Community Arts, PO Box 1026, Hillsboro, OR 97123. 503-648-4019. Contact: Marilyn Helzerman.

Hope & District Arts Council, Box 2, Hope, BC V0X 1L0. 604-869-9971. Contact: William H Scott.

Idaho City Arts Council, PO Box 219, Idaho City, ID 83631.

Idaho Commission on the Arts, 304 W State St, Boise, ID 83720. 208-334-2119. Contact: Betty Brown. Grants, fellowships, apprenticeships, artists-in-education program residencies.

Institute of Alaska Native Arts, Box 80583, Fairbanks, AK 99708. Contact: Director.

Interurban Center for the Arts, 12401 SE 320th St, Auburn, WA 98002. 206-833-9111. Contact: Helen S Smith.

Island County Arts Council, PO Box 173, Langley, WA 98260. Contact: Frank Rose. 206-321-6439. $25/per family, newsletter.

Juneau Arts & Humanities Council, PO Box 020562, Juneau, AK 99802-0562. 907-586-ARTS. Exec. Director: Natalee Rothaus. Projects Coordinator: Marie Popovich. Official arts agency of Juneau. Publishes newsletter, circ. 300.

Kamloops Community Arts Council, Box 467, Kamloops, BC V2C 5L2. 604-374-2704. Contact: Dita Aronowski.

Kaslo Arts Council, Box 1000, Kaslo, BC V0G 1M0. 604-353-2372. Contact: Barbara Bavington.

Keizer Art Assn, PO Box 8900, Keizer, OR 97303. Contact: Lois Graham. 503-390-3010.

Kelowna & District Arts Council, Box 112 Stn A, Kelowna, BC 604-861-4123. Contact: Diane Dejardine.

Kent Arts Commission, 220 S 4th Ave, Kent, WA 98031. 206-872-3350. Contact: Patrice Thorell.

Kent–Harrison Arts Council, Box 502, Agassiz, BC V0M 1A0. 604-796-9851. Contact: Carye Osmack.

Ketchikan Area Arts & Humanities Council, 338 Main St, Ketchikan, AK 99901.

Kimberley Arts Council, Box 102, Kimberley, BC V1A 2V5. 604-427-3209. Contact: Veronica Paauw.

King County Arts Commission, 1115 Smith Tower Bldg., 506 2nd Ave., Seattle, WA 98104. 206-296-7580. The Commission has a Literary Arts Committee; publishes The Written Arts, a literary magazine and The Arts, a newsletter; it funds and sponsors writing related events and projects. Workshops on how to do publicity. Contact them to get on their mailing list for publications.

Kitimat Community Arts Council, Box 342, Kitimat, BC V8C 2G8. 604-632-6225. Contact: Steffan Wegner.

Klamath Arts Council, PO Box 1706, Klamath Falls, OR 97601. Contact: Anita Ward.

Klamath Falls Arts Assn, 2310 Marina Dr, Klamath Falls, OR 97601.

Kootenay Cultural Network–Rockies, Box 1043, Sparwood, BC V0B 2G0. 604-425-7117. Contact: Geri Rothel.

La Grande Arts Commission, 1605 Walnut, La Grande, OR 97850. 503-963-6963. Contact: Michael Frasier.

Lake Arts Council, 307 S 'E', Lakeview, OR 97630. 503-947-2931. Contact: Stanley Wonderly.

Lake Chelan Arts Council, PO Box 627, Chelan, WA 98816. 509-687-3171. Contact: Karen Koch.

Lane Arts Council, 411 High St, Eugene, OR 97401. 503-485-2278. Contact: Douglas Beauchamp. Provides education, information, and services to the professional arts community. Newsletter, Artists Notes, a monthly publication listing professional opportunities for writers & artists; consulting for projects.

Langley Arts Council, Box 3101, Langley, BC V3A 4R3. 604-534-0781. Contact: Iris Preston.

Lebanon Arts Council, 54 W Sherman, Lebanon, OR 97355. 503-451-3934.

Logan Lake Arts Council, Box 299, Logan Lake, BC V0K 1V0. 604-523-9532. Contact: Janet Kohar.

Lost River Community Arts Council, Box B, Arco, ID 83213.

Lynnwood Arts Commission, City Hall, PO Box 5008, Lynnwood, WA 98046. 206-775-1971. Contact: Alice Taylor.

Mackenzie Arts Council, Box 301, Mackenzie, BC V0J 2C0. 604-997-5818. Contact: June Golding.

Magic Valley Arts Council, PO Box 1158, Twin Falls, ID 83301.

Maple Ridge Arts Council, Box 331, Maple Ridge, BC V2X 7G2. 604-467-3825. Contact: Candace Gordon.

Marysville Advisory Committee, City of Marysville, 514 Delta Ave, Marysville, WA 98270. Contact: Steve Dinwiddie.

Medford Arts Commission, 2950 Barnett Rd, Medford, OR 97504. 503-664-5681. Contact: Peter Schmitz.

Mercer Island Arts Council, Community Center at Mercer View, 8236 SE 24th St, Mercer Island, WA 98040. 206-233-3545. Contact: Judith Clibborn.

Metropolitan Arts Commission, 1120 SW 5th, Portland, OR 97204. 503-796-5111. "Grants to artists and arts organizations (including small presses) for public, non-profit projects (no fellowship program). Bimonthly newsletter listing MAC programs, other deadlines, competitions."

Mid-Valley Arts Council, 265 Court NE, Salem, OR 97301. 503-364-7474. Contact: Catherine Leedy.

Mission District Arts Council, Box 3352, Mission, BC V2V 4J5. 604-826-6717. Contact: Peggy Staber.

Monmouth/Independence Community Arts Assn, PO Box 114, Monmouth, OR 97361. 503-838-4141. Contact: Deb Curtis.

Montana Arts Council, 48 N Last Chance Gulch, New York Block, Helena, MT 59620. 406-763-4437. Contact: Bill Pratt. State arts organization, publishes Artistsearch, a monthly newsletter. Also publishes 1 book annually as part of their First Book Award for MT residents. Send for guidelines for grant/fellowship applications, and to get on mailing list for newsletter.

Montana Institute of the Arts, PO Box 1456, Billings, MT 59103. 406-245-3688. Contact: Ron Paulick. "The Montana Institute of the Arts was founded in 1948 by members of the academic and professional community across Montana. It has been effective in helping to establish art centers and museums in the state and continues to stimulate enthusiasm and acceptance of the arts." There are branches in many cities, with various interest groups, writing being one of them. The organization offers workshops, visiting artists, contests, festivals. The monthly newsletter has a special section for writers. For more information, contact Aline Moore, 11333 Gooch Hill Rd, Gallatin Gateway, MT 59730.

Moscow City Arts Commission, 122 E 4th St, Moscow, ID 83843.

Mountlake Terrace Arts Commission, Parks & Recreation Department, 228th St SW, Mountlake Terrace, WA 98043. 206-776-9173. Contact: David Fair.

Nanaimo District Arts Council, Box 557, Nanaimo, BC V9R 5L5. 604-758-5412. Contact: Faye Luchyk.

Nechako Community Arts Council, Box 2288, Vanderhoof, BC V0J 3A0. 604-567-2653. Contact: Joyce Reid.

Nelson & District Arts Council, Box 422, Nelson, BC V1L 5R2. 604-352-2402. Contact: Dennis Zomerschoe.

New Westminster Arts Council, Box 722, New Westminster, BC V3L 4Z3. 604-524-0514. Contact: Alex Webber.

Nicola Valley Community Arts Council, Box 1711, Merritt, BC V0K 2B0. 604-378-5686. Contact: Brian Dodd.

Normal Art Society, 3505 Commercial St, Vancouver, BC V5N 4E8. 604-873-3129. Nonprofit society established in 1988 to encourage art and the creative process. Publishes pop-tart Magazine (see Listings), organizes the Small Press Festival, performances, exhibitions.

North Olympic Arts Council, 114 W Front St, Odyssey Book Shop, Port Angeles, WA 98362. Contact: Craig Whalley. 206-457-1045.

North Santiam Arts League Inc, PO Box 424, Stayton, OR 97383. 503-769-7268 or 769-7321. Contact: Anita Riter.

North Vancouver Community Arts Council, 333 Chesterfield Ave, N Vancouver, BC V7M 3G9. 604-988-6844. Contact: Donna Oseen.

Nyssa Fine Arts Council Inc, PO Box 2356, Nyssa, OR 97913. 503-372-2981. Contact: Marie Wilson.

Oakley Valley Arts Council, PO Box 176, Oakley, ID 83346.

Oceola Arts Council, Box 535, Winfield, BC V0H 2C0. 604-766-4205. Contact: Doug Middleton.

Okanagan Mainline RAC, Box 134, Kelowna, BC V0H 1G0. 604-766-2644. Contact: Gordon Harris.

Oliver Community Arts Council, Box 1711, Oliver, BC V0H 1T0. 604-498-6319. Contact: Mona Meredith.

Olympia Arts Commission, Olympia Parks & Recreation Dept., 222 N Columbia, Olympia, WA 98507-1967. 206-753-8380. Contact: Linda Oestreich, Program Manager.

Oregon Arts Commission, 835 Summer St NE, Salem, OR 97301. 503-378-3625. Individual, non-repeating, fellowships granted annually. A writer can suggest any project to a non-profit organization, and apply to OAC for a project grant four times a year. Write for guidelines or check with local arts councils in Oregon.

Oregon Book Artists Guild, PO Box 994, Beaverton, OR 97075-0994. 503-324-8081. Contact: Patricia Grass. A group of diverse people whose interests include papermaking, marbling, bookbinding, fine printing. Newsletter $15/yr; circ 200.

Oregon Business Committee for The Arts, 221 NW 2nd Ave, Portland, OR 97209-3958. Contact: Director. 503-228-9411.

Oregon Coast Council for the Arts, PO Box 1315, Newport, OR 97365. 503-265-9231. Contact: Sharon Morgan. "We are a regional arts council with a strong history of literary programs and support for emerging writers."

Oregon Institute of Literary Arts, 1600 Pioneer Tower, 888 SW Fifth Ave, Portland, OR 97204-2099. Contact: Kay Reid, Executive Director. 503-223-3604. Annual Oregon book awards ceremony; awards for young readers literature, creative nonfiction, poetry, fiction, playwrights; fellowships for writers and publishers; book exhibits; and publication of tabloid on Oregon books, Oregon Ink.

Osoyoos Community Arts Council, Box 256, Osoyoos, BC V0H 1V0. 604-495-6939. Contact: Ruth Schiller.

Pacific Rim Arts Society, Box 468, Ucluelet, BC V0R 3A0. 604-726-7448. Contact: Donna Fitzpatrick.

Pend Oreille Arts Council, c/o Eve's Leaves, 326 N 1st Ave, Sandpoint, ID 83864.

Peninsula Cultural Arts Center, 533 N Sequim Ave, Sequim, WA 98382. 206-683-8364. Contact: Patricia Gallup.

Penticton & District Community Arts Council, 220 Manor Park Ave, Penticton, BC V2A 2R2. 604-492-7997. Contact: Laura McCartney.

Pierce County Arts Commission, 3711 Center St, Tacoma, WA 98400.

Port Hardy Arts Council, Box 1146, Port Hardy, BC V0N 2P0. 604-949-9433. Contact: Ron Willson.

Port Orford Arts Council, PO Box 771, Port Orford, OR 97465.

Port Townsend Arts Commission, City Hall, 607 Water St, Port Townsend, WA 98368.

Portland Society for Calligraphy, PO Box 4621, Portland, OR 97208. Contacts: Patricia Grass, Ann Mueller. Newsletter, circ. 400.

Powell River Community Arts Council, Box 406, Powell River, BC V8A 5C2. 604-487-9287. Contact: Don Reid.

Prince George & District Arts Council, 2880 - 15th Ave, Prince George, BC V2M 1T1. 604-563-1702. Contact: Mary Pfeiffer.

Prince Rupert Community Arts Council, Box 341, Prince Rupert, BC V8J 3P9. 604-627-1274. Contact: Ralph Troschke.

Progressive Fine Arts Assn, 2637 SE Tibbetts, Portland, OR 97202. 503-232-0330. Contact: Kathryn Bogle.

Queen Charlotte Islands Arts Council, Box 35, Queen Charlotte City, BC V0T 1S0. 604-559-4716. Contact: Elizabeth Cardell.

Quesnel & District Community Arts Council, Box 4069, Quesnel, BC V2J 3J2. 604-992-8885. Contact: Don Hendry.

Reedsport Arts Council, PO Box 7, Reedsport, OR 97467. Contact: Donna Fulhart.

Renton Municipal Arts Commission, 200 Mill Ave S, Renton, WA 98055. Contact: Harriette Hilder. 206-235-2580.

Revelstoke & District Community Arts Council, Box 1931, Revelstoke, BC V0E 2S0. 604-837-2557. Contact: Vern Enyedy.

Richmond Community Arts Center, 7671 Minoru Gate, Richmond, BC V6Y 1R8. 604-276-4012. Contact: Ron Jeffels.

Robson Valley Community Arts Council, Box 638, McBride, BC V0J 2E0. 604-569-2265. Contact: Dave Marchant.

Salmon Arts Council, PO Box 2500, 200 Main St, Salmon, ID 83467. 208-756-2987. Contact: Pat Hauff.

Sea-Tac Arts Council, 1809 S 140th, Seattle, WA 98168. 206-241-5960. Contact: Dorothy Harper.

Seaside Guild of Artists, Inc, PO Box 1122, Seaside, OR 97138.

Seattle Arts Commission, Seattle Center House, 305 Harrison St, Seattle, WA 98109. 206-625-4223. Contact: Barbara Thomas. Send for their guidelines for grants, and get on their newsletter mailing list for information on area events.

Shuswap District Arts Council, Box 1181, Salmon Arm, BC V1E 4R3. 604-832-2663. Contact: Mary Landers.

Silver Sage Art Council, Rt 5, Box 314, Blackfoot, ID 83321.

Slocan Lake Gallery Society, Box 123, Silverton, BC V0G 2B0. 604-358-7788. Contact: Donna Jean Wright.

Slocan Valley Community Arts Council, Box 18, Winlaw, BC V0G 2J0. 604-226-7708. Contact: Bridley Morrison Morgan.

Snohomish Arts Commission, 116 Union Ave, Snohomish, WA 98290-2943. 206-568-3115. Contact: Volkert Volkersz.

South Cariboo Community Arts Council, Box 1441, Lillooet, BC V0K 1V0. 604-256-4346. Contact: Merle P Elesko.

South Coast Community Arts Council, Box 46, Snooke, BC V0S 1N0. 604-642-5211. Contact: Kathy Kirk.

South Coast Council for the Arts and Humanities, c/o Coos-Curry Council of Governments, 510 S Ellensburg, Gold Beach, OR 97444. 503-267-6500. Contact: Lionel Youst.

South Peace Community Arts Council, Box 2314, Dawson Creek, BC V1G 4P2. 604-782-1838. Contact: Anne Matheson Exner.

Southcoast Tourism Assn/Bay Area Arts Council, PO Box 1641, Coos Bay, OR 97420. 503-756-2900. Contact: Judith Kobrin.

Sparwood Arts Council, Box 1043, Sparwood, BC V0B 2G0. 604-425-7117. Contact: Sherry Benko.

Spokane Arts Commission, City Hall - 4th Fl, W 808 Spokane Falls Blvd., Spokane, WA 99201-3333. 509-456-3857. Contact: Sue Ellen Heflin. Free newsletter, circ. 2,500.

Springfield Arts Commission, City of Springfield, Office of Community & Economic Development, 225 N 5th St, Springfield, OR 97477. 503-726-3783. Contact: Bruce Newhouse.

Squamish Arts Council, Box 193, Garibaldi Highlands, BC V0N 1T0. 604-892-5482. Contact: Maureen Brown.

Summerland Community Arts Council, Box 1217, Summerland, BC V0H 1Z0. 604-494-4494. Contact: Sherrill Foster.

Sunshine Coast Arts Council, Box 1565, Sechelt, BC V0N 3A0. 604-885-2986. Contact: Therese Egan.

Surrey & District Arts Council, 13750 88th Ave, Surrey, BC V3W 3L1. 604-596-7461. Contact: Rey Ortmann.

Tacoma Arts Commission, Tacoma Municipal Bldg., 747 Market St, Rm 134, Tacoma, WA 98402-3768. 206-591-5191.

Terrace & District Arts Council, Box 35, Terrace, BC V8G 4A3. 604-635-9960. Contact: Barbara Kenney.

Thompson Valley North Arts Council, Box 75, McNab Rd, Little Fort, BC V0E 2C0. 604-677-4379. Contact: Darlene Jennings.

Tiimutla Arts Council, Rt 3, Box 71, Pendleton, OR 97801. 503-276-1881. Contact: Leah Conner.

Tillamook Arts Assn, PO Box 634, Tillamook, OR 97141-0634. Contact: Ed Sharples.

Trail & District Community Arts Council, Box 326, Trail, BC V1R 4L6. 604-368-6922. Contact: Muriel Griffith.

Tumbler Ridge Community Arts Council, Box 240, Tumbler Ridge, BC V0L 2W0. 604-242-4754. Contact: Colleen Doylend.

Umpqua Valley Arts Assn, PO Box 1105, Roseburg, OR 97470. 503-672-2532. Contact: Heidi Land.

Upper Valley Arts, 321 9th St, Leavenworth, WA 98826. 509-548-5202. Contact: R J Ritz.

Valley Art Assn, PO Box 333, Forest Grove, OR 97116. 503-357-3703. Contact: Merrie French. Free newsletter, circ. 3,000.

Valley Community Arts Council, PO Box 744, Hamilton, MT 59840. Contact: Carlotta Grandstaff, Editor.

Vancouver Community Arts Council, 837 Davie St, Vancouver, BC V6Z 1B7. 604-683-4358. Contact: Anthony Norfolk.

Vashon Allied Arts Inc., PO Box 576, Vashon, WA 98070. 206-463-5131. Contact: Jeffery Basom.

Vernon Community Arts Council, 3300 - 37th Ave, Vernon, BC V2T 2Y5. 604-542-6243. Contact: Marianne Morrison.

Wallowa Valley Arts Council, PO Box 306, Enterprise, OR 97828. 503-426-4775. Contact: Michael Kurtz or Terri Barnett.

Washington State Arts Commission, Mail Stop GH-11, 110–9th & Columbia Bldg., Olympia, WA 98504-4111. 206-753-3860. Send for guidelines for grants and get on mailing list for their newsletter of information on the arts.

Wenatchee Arts Commission, PO Box 519, Wenatchee, WA 98801. Contact: Peggy Mead.

West Vancouver Community Arts Council, 200 Keith Rd, West Vancouver, BC V7T 1L3. 604-922-1110. Contact: Lynne Flipse.

Western Communities Arts Council, Box 468, Ucluelet, BC V9B 4Z3. 604-479-6085. Contact: Lois Klages.

Whistler Community Arts Council, Box 383, Whistler, BC V0N 1B0. 604-932-5378. Contact: Joan Richoz.

White Rock Community Arts Council, Stn Art Centre, 14970 Marine Dr, White Rock, BC V4B 1C4. 604-536-2432. Contact: Corlin Bordeaux.

Willamette Arts Council, 456 SW Monroe, Ste 102, Corvallis, OR 97333. 503-757-6800. Contact: Barbara Ross.

Williams Lake Community Arts Council, Box 4537, Williams Lake, BC V2G 2V5. 604-398-6323. Contact: Sidney Gooch.

Yakima Arts Council, 5000 W Lincoln, Yakima, WA 98908. 509-966-0930. Contact: Anne Byerrun.

Yellowstone Art Center's Regional Writers Project, 401 N 27th St, Billings, MT 59101. 406-656-1238. Contact: Adrea Sukin, Pat Palagi. Promotes Western literature through a retail outlet and mail order catalog and lecture series featuring authors and small press publishers.

Classes

Adventist Writers' Assn of Western Washington, 18115 116th Ave SE, Renton, WA 98058. 206-235-1435. Contact Marian Forschler. How-to newsletter on writing and marketing to Seventh-day Adventist publications. Meetings held 6 times a yr. to critique and/or hear speakers. Annual week-long writing class in June. Anyone may join.

Allied Arts Council Yakima Valley, 5000 W Lincoln Ave, Yakima, WA 98908. 509-966-0930. Contact: Ann Byerrum. Annual spring writers workshop.

Billings Arts Assn Writers, 3706 Duck Creek Rd, Billings, MT 59101. 406-656-2524. Contact: Alice Madsen. Branch interest group of Montana Institute of the Arts. Offers criticism, support, workshops and state-level writing contest for poetry and prose. Meets monthly.

Centrum Foundation, PO Box 1158, Port Townsend, WA 98368. 206-385-3102. Contact: Carol Jane Bangs. Activities include: "A residency program for 3-4 writers each year; a press-in-residence, Copper Canyon Press, with press tours, and in some years letterpress workshops with Tree Swenson, Copper Canyon co-publisher and designer of books for several presses; special workshops featuring writers and experts in other fields, convened to address major societal issues; writing workshops for high school students from Washington State."

Clarion West, 340 15th Ave E, Ste 350, Seattle, WA 98112. 206-322-9083. Contact: Richard Terra. Intensive program in fantasy and science fiction.

Clark College Open Contest and Workshop, 4312 NE 40th St, Vancouver, WA 98661. 206-695-2777. Contact: Arlene Paul. Spring poetry contest (reading fee required), poetry workshop and writing craft lectures.

Confluence Press Inc, 8th Ave & 6th St, LCSC, Lewiston, ID 83501. 208-799-2336. Contact: James R Hepworth. Courses in the publishing arts at Lewis Clark State College are available through Confluence Press. Offers on-the-job training to student interns at the Press; and occasional half-day workshops in publishing for junior high, high school and college editors. Sponsor of Writers-in-the-Schools Projects. Also sponsors The Visiting Writers Series, offering 5 residencies to writers a year. They regularly meet with classes.

Dillon Authors Assn, PO Box 212, Dillon, MT 59725. Contact: Sally Garrett Dingley. 406-683-4539. "Monthly writers meetings on 2nd Tuesday from Sept. through May of each year. Six meetings have guests with special expertise, three meetings are critiquing sessions. A diverse membership of local and regional writers, published and aspiring.... Newsletter published approximately ten times a year. 55+ members, 12 newsletter exchanges."

Eagle River Fine Arts Academy, Box 773989, Eagle River, AK 99577.

Eastside Writers Assn, PO Box 8005, Totem Lake Post Office, Kirkland, WA 98034. Contact: Pat Ahern, Pres. 206-747-5368. Writers group meets the 2nd Tuesday of each month, Sept. through May, from 7:30 to 9:00 pm at First Congregational Church in Bellevue. Off I-405 at NE 8th and 108th. Dues $10 to pay for church, newsletter and speakers for each meeting. Meetings are open to non-members, donation of $2. Eastside Writers is for "anyone who writes, or wants to write. We have members who have been writing for years, and we have outright beginners. Some of our members have sold everything they've written, and some don't even want to sell."

The Federation of British Columbia Writers, Box 2206, Main PO, Vancouver, BC V6B 3W2. 604-683-2057. Contact: Lynne Melcombe. "A non-profit society of professional and aspiring writers, the Federation acts as an umbrella organization for writers of all genres.... Similar organizations in other provinces and in many European countries exist because writers need to unite to achieve their common goals. Unlike writers groups representing specific genres, such as ACTRA, the Writers' Union or PWAC, the Federation's broadly-based membership allows it to direct its voice to larger concerns vital to every BC writer." To this end, the Federation publishes a quarterly newsletter, works with other writers' organizations to promote: photocopying & copyright legislation, establishment of a provincial Writers' Centre and Archives, payment for public use of written material, public readings, and wider funding and support for writers.

Fine Arts Institute Camp, PO Box 2133, Sitka, AK 99835. 907-747-3372. Contact: Anne Morrison. Two week summer camp includes writing workshops for young writers led by nationally-known authors.

Fishtrap Gathering, PO Box 457, Enterprise, OR 97828. Contact: Rich Wandschneider. Annual summer conference with presentations from Northwest and the East Coast authors, editors, and publishers; followed by writing workshops.

Idaho Writers' League, c/o Deana Jensen, President, 306 E. 129th S, Idaho Falls, ID 83404. 208-357-3914. Has 30 local chapters throughout Idaho; regular meetings, workshops, a conference, and occasionally book publishing.

King County Arts Commission, 1115 Smith Tower Bldg., 506 2nd Ave., Seattle, WA 98104. 206-296-7580. The Commission has a Literary Arts Committee; publishes The Written Arts, a literary magazine and The Arts, a newsletter; it funds and sponsors writing related events and projects. Workshops on how to do publicity. Contact them to get on their mailing list for publications.

Kootenay School of Writing, #306-152 W Hastings St, Vancouver, BC V6B 3A0.

Lane Literary Guild, c/o Lane Arts Council, 411 High St, Eugene, OR 97401. 503-485-2278. Contact: Erik Muller, Alice Evans. Membership $10/indiv. Newsletter, circ 20,000. Nonprofit organization representing the professional interests of poets, fiction writers and dramatists living in Lane County.

The Literary Center, PO Box 85116, Seattle, WA 98145-1116. Contact: Sarah Sarai. 206-524-5514. The Literary Center, 1716 N 45th St, is a writer's resource organization — to help writers help themselves. It includes: a small press gallery (containing small press books, magazines, broadsides, tapes, etc.); a resource library (containing foundation directories, information about local readings and workshops, national markets, etc. is located at the Seattle Public Schools Teacher Resource Center at Marshall School, 520 NE Ravenna Blvd, Seattle); Literary Hotline (524-5514), a 24-hour pre-recorded listing of local literary events. Newsletter, $15/yr; circ 2,000.

Montana Writing Project, English Department, University of Montana, Missoula, MT 59812. 406-243-5231. Contact: Dr Beverly Ann Chin.

Moscow Moffia Writers' Workshop, 621 East 'F' St, Moscow, ID 83343. Contact: Jon Gustafson. Weekly writers' discussion groups. Sponsors workshops throughout the Northwest.

National Writers Club, Seattle Chapter, PO Box 33322, Seattle, WA 98155. 206-783-3401. Contact: Leon Billig. "Monthly programs, special workshops and symposia, social events, critique groups, networking, special interest activities, professional visibility."

Northwest Playwrights' Guild — Washington, PO Box 95252, Seattle, WA 98145. 206-762-5525. Contact: Cheryl Read. The organization's goal is to satisfy needs of NW playwrights and organizations interested in supporting the new works of Northwest playwrights. Initial membership fee of $25, plus $15 per year dues. Services include quarterly and monthly newsletters, seminars and classes with visiting playwrights.

Northwest Writing Institute, Campus Box 100, Lewis & Clark College, Portland, OR 97219. 503-768-7745. Contact: Kim Stafford, Director. The Northwest Writing Institute at Lewis & Clark College supports campus writing courses and seeks to assist writers and the literary community in the region through workshops and other programs. Coordinates Oregon Writing Project; Writer to Writer (a seminar for high school students); the Imaginative Writing Seminars; and a wide variety of workshops for teachers and writers.

O-Ya-Ka Story League, Multnomah County Central Library, 801 SW 10th Ave, Portland, OR 97205. 503-244-9415. Meets monthly. Affiliated with National Story League, Western District. Story workshop sponsored by Western District held at Marylhurst alternate summers.

Oregon Assn of Christian Writers, 2495 Maple NE, Salem, OR 97303. 503-364-9570. Contact: Marion Duckworth. Organized for "the purpose of promoting higher standards of craftsmanship in the field of Christian journalism and encouraging a greater sense of spiritual responsibility in the Christian writer." The group hold writer's seminars 3 times a year, in Salem, in Eugene and in Portland.

Oregon Writers Workshop, Pacific Northwest College of Art, 1219 SW Park, Portland, OR 97205. 503-226-4396. Contact: Kathy Budas. Graduate level workshops in poetry writing, fiction, nonfiction and drama.

Oregon Writing Project, Department of English, University of Oregon, Eugene, OR 97403. 503-346-3911. Nathaniel Teich, Project Director. Affiliated with the National Writing Project network. Includes more than 140 projects in 44 states and abroad which have adopted the successful model of the University of California, Berkeley/Bay Area Writing Project. This model has achieved national recognition for improving students' writing by increasing teachers' knowledge and instructional skills in composition. Experienced teachers are eligible for the 4-week summer institute.

Pacific Northwest Writers Conference, 17345 SW Sylvester Rd SW, Seattle, WA 98166. 206-242-9757. Contact: Carol McQuinn. Membership organization sponsoring conferences and contests for adult and young writers.

Playwrights-In-Progress, 14030 NE 12th #410D, Seattle, WA 98125. 206-363-5905. Contact: Nikki Louis. Weekly meetings for readings of members' plays. PIP also sponsors workshops.

Rattlesnake Mountain Writers' Workshop, 5124 Grosscup, Richland, WA 99352. Contact: Nancy Girvin. 509-967-9324.

Sitka Summer Writers Symposium, Box 2420, Sitka, AK 99835. 907-747-3794. Contact: Carolyn Servid.

Spruce St School, 411 Yale Ave N, Seattle, WA 98109. 206-621-9211. Contact: Harvey Sadis. Book arts program for K-4.

Summer Writing Workshop, c/o James McAuley, Creative Writing Program, Eastern Washington University, Cheney, WA 99004. 509-359-2829. Program is held in Ireland.

Tacoma Writer's Club, 14710–30th St Ct E, Sumner, WA 98390. 206-473-9632. Weekly/monthly workshops including poetry, articles, and fiction. "Members study marketing their work, and discuss ideas about illustrating, query letters, etc." The group publishes a monthly newsletter. Meets at the South Hill branch of the Tacoma Public Library.

Washington Poets Assn, 6002 S Fife St, Tacoma, WA 98409. Contact: Amelia Haller. Organization to raise awareness and appreciation of poetry; publishes a newsletter 4 times a year, holds an annual meeting/banquet in May, and workshops/events across the state. Refer to Poetry in Vancouver USA, A Poetry Event at Longview, and Rattlesnake Mountain.

Willamette Writers, 9045 SW Barbur Blvd #5A, Portland, OR 97219. 503-452-1592. Monthly programs, newsletter, annual conference and contest, small critique groups, and ongoing workshops. Newsletter circ 900.

Writers of the Pacific Northwest Workshop, Tillamook Bay Community College, 2510 First St, Tillamook, OR 97141. 503-842-2503. Annual summer workshops with working writers and media professionals as teachers. Usually held in June.

Writing and Publishing Program, Simon Fraser University, Harbour Centre, 515 W Hastings, Vancouver BC V6B 5K3. 604-291-5100. Contact: Christine Hearn. Offers writing and publishing programs to adult learners, courses in fall and spring. Also Canadian Centre for studies in publishing.

Contests

AAUW Essay Contest, c/o Margaret Murphy, 1301 Rimrock Rd, Billings, MT 59102.

The American Assn of University Women, Montana Division, 20200 W Dickerson #58, Bozeman, MT 59715. Contact: Student Contest Coordinator. Sponsors an annual essay contest with prizes, open to Montana students, grades 10-12.

American Pen Women, Rt 1 Box 53, Reardon, WA 99029. 509-796-5872. Contact: Charlotte Chester. State newsletter, Branch Pen Points, sponsors contest, meets monthly.

Bainbridge Island Arts Council, Executive Director, 261 Madison South, Bainbridge Island, WA 98110. 206-842-7901. Contact: Janis Shaw. In addition to other activities, including writing workshops, they publish a Poets & Artists Calendar from their annual Poets & Artists Competition.

Benton County Fair Poetry Contest for Youngsters, 471 NW Hemlock, Corvallis, OR 97330. 503-753-3335. Contact: Linda Smith. Poetry contest for children; also exhibits adult poems at the fair.

Benton County Fair Poetry Contest for Youngsters, 471 NW Hemlock, Corvallis, OR 97330. 503-753-3335. Contact: Linda Smith. Poetry contest for children; also exhibits adult poems at the fair.

Billings Arts Assn Writers, 3706 Duck Creek Rd, Billings, MT 59101. 406-656-2524. Contact: Alice Madsen. Branch interest group of Montana Institute of the Arts. Offers criticism, support, workshops and state-level writing contest for poetry and prose. Meets monthly.

Breviloquence, Writer's NW, Rt 3 Box 376, Hillsboro, OR 97124. 503-621-3911. Contact: Linny Stovall. Two annual contests: one for 18-yr olds and younger; one open to all ages. Specific entry requirements for the given year are announced in Writer's NW, but all entries must be stories of 99 wds or less. Prizes of books are awarded to the first 3 places in each contest.

BC Historical Federation Writing Competition, PO Box 933, Nanaimo, BC V9R 5N2. Contact: Pamela Mar. Annual competition of books or articles for Writers of British Columbia History. Book deadline early January each year. Articles are selected from submissions published in the BC Historical News magazine. Guidelines available.

BC Historical Writing Competition, Box 105, Wasa, BC V0B 2K0. Contact: Mrs. Naomi Miller.

Bumbershoot, PO Box 9750, Seattle, WA 98109-0750. 206-622-5123. Contact: Judith Roche. Major book and literary fair as part of Seattle's Labor Day arts festival. Includes small press displays and sales, book arts exhibits, readings, roundtables, lectures, Writers-in-Performance program, publishing and book arts contests, The Bumbershoot Literary Magazine, and the Bumbershoot/Weyerhaeuser Publication Award.

Bumbershoot/Weyerhaeuser Publication Award, PO Box 9750, Seattle, WA 98109-0750. 206-622-5123. Contact: Judith Roche. Open competition award for a collection of previously unpublished fiction or poetry (alternate years; poetry in 1992) to be published by a press from Washington, Oregon, Alaska, Montana, Idaho, or British Columbia. The publisher will be awarded $5,000 toward production; the author will receive an honorarium of $2,000 and will be asked to read in the Bumbershoot program. Bumbershoot will also promote the winning book, press, and author. Write for award criteria.

Clark College Open Contest and Workshop, 4312 NE 40th St, Vancouver, WA 98661. 206-695-2777. Contact: Arlene Paul. Spring poetry contest (reading fee required), poetry workshop and writing craft lectures.

Composers, Authors and Artists of America Inc, Rt 1 Box 53, Reardan, WA 99029. Contact: David Chester. Sponsors a state poetry contest. Write for info.

CutBank Competition, c/o English Department, University of Montana, Missoula, MT 59812. 406-243-5231. A B Guthrie, Jr. Short Fiction Award & Richard Hugo Memorial Poetry Award. CutBank holds an annual competition for the best short story and best poem published each year in CutBank.

Eighth Mountain Poetry Prize, 624 SE 29th Ave, Portland, OR 97214. 503-233-3936. Contact: Ruth Gundle. Annual prize for a book-length poetry manuscript by a feminist woman writer. Must be postmarked between January 1 and March 1. Winner's ms will be published by Eighth Mountain Press. Guidelines available.

Evelyn Sibley Lampman Award, Oregon Library Assn. - Salem Library, PO Box 14810, Salem, OR 97309.

Event, Douglas College, PO Box 2503, New Westminster, BC V3L 1X1. 604-527-5293. Contact: Dale Zieroth. Creative nonfiction contest. Query for details.

F G Bressani Literary Contest, Italian Cultural Centre Society, 3075 Slocan St, Vancouver, BC V5N 3E4.

Great Expeditions, PO Box 46499, Stn G, Vancouver, BC V6R 4G7. Contact: Marilyn Marshall.

Hutton Publications Contest, PO Box 1870, Hayden, ID 83835. 208-772-6184. Contact: Linda Hutton. Holds several fiction and poetry contests in conjunction with publications. Query for details.

The Louisa Kern Fund, Creative Writing Office, UW, Department of English, GN-30, Seattle, WA 98195. 206-543-9865. Contact: Janie Smith. Annual grant.

Montana Arts Council, 48 N Last Chance Gulch, New York Block, Helena, MT 59620. 406-763-4437. Contact: Bill Pratt. State arts organization, publishes Artistsearch, a monthly newsletter. Also publishes 1 book annually as part of their First Book Award for MT residents. Send for guidelines for grant/fellowship applications, and to get on mailing list for newsletter.

Montana Institute of the Arts, PO Box 1456, Billings, MT 59103. 406-245-3688. Contact: Ron Paulick. "The Montana Institute of the Arts was founded in 1948 by members of the academic and professional community across Montana. It has been effective in helping to establish art centers and museums in the state and continues to stimulate enthusiasm and acceptance of the arts." There are branches in many cities, with various interest groups, writing being one of them. The organization offers workshops, visiting artists, contests, festivals. The monthly newsletter has a special section for writers. For more information, contact Aline Moore, 11333 Gooch Hill Rd, Gallatin Gateway, MT 59730.

Multicultural Playwrights Festival, c/o Jim Bond, 3940 Brooklyn NE, Seattle, WA 98105. Contact: 206-545-4969. Plays by Native American, Hispanic, Black, and Asian playwrights. Pays honorarium, board, travel, and production. Oct 15th deadline.

Northwest Poets & Artists Calendar, Bainbridge Island Arts Council, 261 Madison S, Bainbridge Island, WA 98110. Material for the annual Calendar is jury selected from entries in Annual Poets & Artists Competition, which is open to residents of AK, ID, MT, OR, WA or BC (deadline late January each year). The calendar is a full-color, 12 month wall calendar, 12 x 12, with large squares to write in. Each month features a full color reproduction of an original artwork with a poem. For info on calendar or competition, write to the above address.

Oregon Council of Teachers of English (OCTE), PO Box 2515, Portland, OR 97208. 503-238-1208. Contact: Joe Fitzgibbon. For teachers of English, language arts, literature and creative writing at all levels. Publishes Oregon English and Chalkboard. Sponsors "Teachers-as-Writers," regular conferences, and sponsors the Oregon Writing Festival for young writers.

Oregon Institute of Literary Arts, 1600 Pioneer Tower, 888 SW Fifth Ave, Portland, OR 97204-2099. Contact: Kay Reid, Executive Director. 503-223-3604. Annual Oregon book awards ceremony; awards for young readers literature, creative nonfiction, poetry, fiction, playwrights; fellowships for writers and publishers; book exhibits; and publication of tabloid on Oregon books, Oregon Ink.

Oregon Press Women, PO Box 25354, Portland, OR 97225. 503-292-4945. Contact: Glennis McNeal. Professional group for broadcasters, journalists, public relations practitioners, freelancers, photographers, journalism educators. Meets twice yearly. Sponsors contests for members, high school students.

Oregon State Poetry Assn, 1645 SE Spokane St, Portland, OR 97206. 503-283-3682. Contact: Wilma Erwin. Contact for information on local groups and meetings. "OSPA contests are held spring and fall and offer cash prizes in several categories ($300 total, April 1986). The number and theme of categories vary from year to year. Guidelines are published in the spring and fall issues of the OSPA Newsletter. Non-members may request them in March and August by sending SASE to above address." No entry fee to members.

Oregon Student Magazine Contest, Eastern Oregon State College, English Dept., La Grande, OR 97850. Contact: David Axelrod. Contest cosponsored by the Oregon Council of Teachers of English. Open to students and teachers publishing student writing in a magazine format. Awards six prizes of $100 each.

Oregon Students Writing & Art Foundation, PO Box 2100, Portland, OR 97208-2100. Contact: Chris Weber. 503-232-7737. An organization of students and teachers involved in publishing an anthology of student writing compiled from the winners of the Starfire Contest. Students are involved in all aspects of the book, editing, design, publicity, etc.

Oregon Writers Colony, PO Box 15200, Portland, OR 97215. 503-771-0428. Membership organization for writers in all genres. Publishes newsletter, Colonygram. Operates writers' retreat (Colony House) on Oregon coast. Holds workshops at coast and in Portland. Sponsors readings at the Heathman Hotel (LiteraTea).

Owl Creek Press, 1620 N 45th St, Seattle, WA 98103. 206-633-5929. Contact: Rich Ives. Poetry Chapbook contest: under 40 pgs, $5 entry fee, July 1 deadline. Poetry Book Contest: over 50 pgs, $8 entry fee, Dec. 31 deadline. Prize: publication with 10% payment in copies of the first printing and additional pay in cash or copies for additional printing.

Pacific Northwest Booksellers Assn, Rt 1 Box 219B, Banks, OR 97106. 503-324-8180. Contact: Debby Garman. Sponsors semiannual trade shows and annual book awards.

Pacific Northwest Writers Conference, 17345 SW Sylvester Rd SW, Seattle, WA 98166. 206-242-9757. Contact: Carol McQuinn. Membership organization sponsoring conferences and contests for adult and young writers.

Pacific Northwest Young Reader's Choice Award, Pacific Northwest Library Assn, University of Washington, 133 Suzzallo Library, FM-30, Seattle, WA 98195. 206-543-1794. Contact: Carol Doll. Children vote for their favorite title from a list of 15 selected from works nominated by teachers, librarians, children, or other interested persons. Titles published three years prior to contest year. Guidelines available for SASE.

Physicians for Social Responsibility, 921 SW Morrison, Ste 500, Portland, OR 97205. Sponsors an annual writing contest for Oregon students grades 7-12. Prizes. Send for guidelines.

PRISM International Short Fiction Contest, Department of Creative Writing, University of British Columbia, Vancouver, BC V6T 1W5. 604-228-2514. Contact: Heidi Neufeld Raine. Annual short fiction contest. Deadline each year on Dec. 1. Prizes: $2,000 first, five $200 honorary mention prizes. Send an SASE for entry form and rules.

Puget Sound Literary Arts Competition, PO Box 215, Langley, WA 98260.

Pulp Press International 3-Day Novel Competition, 100–1062 Homer St, Vancouver, BC V6B 2W9. Contact: Brian Lam. 604-687-4233. "A Contest for Normal People." Annual 3-day novel writing contest is just that. "Completed manuscripts must be accompanied by an affidavit signed by at least one living witness." Send SASE. Prize is a publishing offer from Pulp Press Book Publishers. Guidelines for SASE.

Signpost Press–49th Parallel Poetry Contest, 1007 Queen St, Bellingham, WA 98225. 206-734-9781. Contact: Susan Hilton. Cash awards poetry contest, entry fee, submissions must be postmarked between October 1, 1988 and January 3, 1989. Write for guidelines.

Silverfish Review Poetry Chapbook Competition, PO Box 3541, Eugene, OR 97403. 503-344-5060. Editor: Roger Moody. Literary review sponsors a poetry chapbook competition. Query w/SASE. Guidelines available.

Society of Professional Journalists, Willamette Valley Chapter, PO Box 1717, Portland, OR 97201. 503-244-6111 x4181. Contact: Oren Campbell. "Assn representing all areas of journalism and all levels of experience." Meets monthly September through May, annual contest, monthly newsletter.

Tacoma Writer's Club, 14710–30th St Ct E, Sumner, WA 98390. 206-473-9632. Weekly/monthly workshops including poetry, articles, and fiction. "Members study marketing their work, and discuss ideas about illustrating,

query letters, etc." The group publishes a monthly newsletter. Meets at the South Hill branch of the Tacoma Public Library.

Tahana Whitecrow Foundation, PO Box 18181, Salem, OR 97305. 503-585-0564. Contact: Melanie Smith. Annual spring/summer poetry contest. Closing date May 31. Native theme only, limit 30 lines. Winners published in anthology. Publishes Oyate Wo'wapi, quarterly newsletter (see Listings). Guidelines available for SASE.

Teachers as Writers Competition, Chemeketa Community College, PO Box 14007, Salem, OR 97309. Contact: Paul Suter. Sponsored by the Oregon Council of Teachers of English. Prose and poetry contest open to Oregon teachers of kindergarten through college and to any OCTE member. (See OCTE, Organizations.)

Valentine's Poetry Contest, Washington Park Zoo, 4001 SW Canyon Rd, Portland, OR 97221. 503-226-1561. Contact: Anne Brown. Annual contest for preschool through high school age students. Entries are about favorite animals at the Washington Park Zoo. Each winner receives a copy of the anthology of winning poems.

Vernon Writer's Group, Box 1583, Vernon, BC V1T 8C2. Contact: Francis Hill. Local organization. Also holds contests.

Washington Poets Assn, 6002 S Fife St, Tacoma, WA 98409. Contact: Amelia Haller. Organization to raise awareness and appreciation of poetry; publishes a newsletter 4 times a year, holds an annual meeting/banquet in May, and workshops/events across the state. Refer to Poetry in Vancouver USA, A Poetry Event at Longview, and Rattlesnake Mountain.

Western States Book Awards, Western States Art Federation, 236 Montezuma Ave, Santa Fe, NM 87501. 505-988-1166. Awards presented biennially in even-numbered years to publishers & authors in three categories: fiction, nonfiction, poetry. Cash award to publisher and author and promotional aid.

Willamette Writers, 9045 SW Barbur Blvd #5A, Portland, OR 97219. 503-452-1592. Monthly programs, newsletter, annual conference and contest, small critique groups, and ongoing workshops. Newsletter circ. 900.

Distributors

ABZ Books, PO Box 1404, Stn A, Vancouver, BC V6C 2P7. 604-263-0014. Contact: Jackson House.

Billings News, Inc, 711 Fourth Ave N, Billings, MT 59101. Contact: Jim Maddox. Distributes to central and eastern Montana. Does a Montana shelf in selected locales. Authors and publishers with appropriate titles should contact him with citations.

Blackwell North America Inc, 6024 SW Jean Rd, Bldg. G, Lake Oswego, OR 97034. 503-684-1140.

Creative Communications, 322 Queen Anne Ave N, Seattle, WA 98109-4512.

Drift Creek Press, PO Box 511, Philomath, OR 97370. 503-929-5637/800-338-0136. Contact: Craig J Battrick. Distributing cookbooks, regional NW, poetry.

Eclectic Press Inc, PO Box 14462, Portland, OR 97214. 503-286-4018. Contact: Barbara Cogan Neidig. Wholesale distributor of imported floral craft books and gift books.

Far West Book Service, 3515 NE Hassalo, Portland, OR 97232. 503-234-7664. Contact: Katherine McCanna/Larry Burns. Distributor of general NW Americana.

Robert Hale & Co. Wholesaler Inc, 1803 132nd Ave NE #4, Bellevue, WA 948005-2236. 206-881-5212. Distributor of nautical books.

Highway Milemarker Guide Co (HMG Co), 525 East Bridge St, Blackfoot, ID 83221-2806. 208-785-5125. Contact: John Aulik. Wholesaler of nonfiction about Idaho and the northern Rocky Mountains with some titles reflecting things to do in Idaho, ie, hiking, skiing, hunting, prospecting, fishing, archaeology. Sells in all of Idaho: bookstores, but mostly small gift, gas, and sports shops.

Himber's Books, 1380 W Second Ave, Eugene, OR 97402.

International Specialized Book Services Inc, 5602 NE Hassalo St, Suite F5, Portland, OR 97213.

MacRae's Indian Book Distributors, PO Box 652, 1605 Cole St, Enumclaw, WA 98002.

Milestone Publications Ltd, PO Box 35548, Stn E, Vancouver, BC V6M 4G8. 604-251-7675. Contact: Anne Werry. Adv: Helen Werry. Distributor/wholesaler.

Moving Books, PO Box 20037, Seattle, WA 98102. 206-325-9077. Contact: Frank Kroger. Book distributor specializing in health, alcoholism/addition, new age, self-help, and metaphysical.

Nobby Clark's British Book Service, PO Box 505, White Rock, BC, V4B 5G3.

Northwest News, 101 S California, Missoula, MT 59802. Contact: Ken Grinsteiner. Pocketbook distributor. Promotes Montana authors' sections in bookstores.

Pacific Northwest Books, PO Box 314, Medford, OR 97501. 503-664-5205, order desk. 503-644-4442 24-hour answering machine. Contact: Bert Webber. Distributes only books about the Pacific Northwest and the Oregon Trail. Books must have ISBN, CIP desired.

Pacific Periodical Services Inc, 4630 95th SW, Lakewood Industrial Park, Bldg. 6, Tacoma, WA 98499. 206-581-1940. Distributes children's books.

Paragon Publications, 7311 69th Ave NE, Marysville, WA 98270. 206-659-8350. Contact: Bob Graef. Distributor of specialty collections for schools and libraries.

Raincoast Books, 112 E 3rd Ave, Vancouver, BC V5T 1C8.

Rainforest Publishing, PO Box 101251, Anchorage, AK 99510. 907-274-8687.

Rainier News, 1122 80th St SW, Everett, WA 98203.

Sandhill Book Marketing, PO Box 197, Stn A, Kelowna, BC V1Y 7N5. 604-763-1406. Contact: Nancy Wise.

Servatius News Agency, 601 Second St, Clarkston, WA 99403. 509-758-7592.

Silver Bow News Distributing Company Inc, 219 E Park St, Butte, MT 59701.

Silverbow News, 219 E Park, Butte, MT 59701. Contact: Joe Floreen. Paperback distributor, interested in Montana authors.

Small Changes, 3443 12th Ave W, Seattle, WA 98119. 206-282-3665. Contact: Shari Basom. Distributor of magazines and calendars. Catalog available.

Spilled Ink, Studio 403, PO Box 70672, Seattle, WA 98107-0672. 206-323-6779.

Spring Arbor Distributors, 5600 NE Hassalo, Portland, OR 97213. 800-521-3690.

TMS Book Service, PO Box 1504, Beaverton, OR 97075. 503-646-8081.

Townson Publishing Co Ltd, Box 8023, Blaine, WA 98230. 604-263-0014. Contact: Jackson House.

Yellowstone Art Center's Regional Writers Project, 401 N 27th St, Billings, MT 59101. 406-656-1238. Contact: Adrea Sukin, Pat Palagi. Promotes Western literature through a retail outlet and mail order catalog and lecture series featuring authors and small press publishers.

Events

45th St Books, 1716 N 45th, Seattle, WA 98103. 206-633-0811.

Alternatives to Loud Boats, c/o Phoebe Bosche, PO Box 2473, 3rd & Union Stn, Seattle, WA 98101. 206-323-6779.

ARS Poetica, Eastern Oregon State College, La Grande, OR 97850. Contact: Tom Madden. Poetry and fiction readings series.

Arts at Menucha, PO Box 4958, Portland, OR 97208. Annual artists summer camp/workshops in fine and applied arts and literature sponsored by Creative Arts Community.

Auburn Arts Commission, 25 W Main, Auburn, WA 98001. 206-931-3043. Contact: Josie Emmons Vine. Writers' Conference last weekend in October.

Authors' & Artisans' Fair, Allegory Bookshop, PO Box 249, Gleneden Beach, OR 97388. 503-764-2020. Contact: Veronica Johnson.

Bainbridge Island Arts Council, Executive Director, 261 Madison South, Bainbridge Island, WA 98110. 206-842-7901. Contact: Janis Shaw. In addition to other activities, including writing workshops, they publish a Poets & Artists Calendar from their annual Poets & Artists Competition.

Bainbridge Writer's Guild, c/o Nancy Rekow, 8489 Fletcher Bay Rd NE, Bainbridge, WA 98110. 206-842-4855. Formed in 1986 to serve writers of all levels in Bainbridge Island area. Sponsors poetry readings. Publishes local work.

Bend-in-the-River Writers Guild, c/o Doris M Hall, 62340 Powell Butte Rd, Bend, OR 97701. 503-389-5845. "A writers support group, largely poets, but some other kinds of writing are represented. We meet for mutual enrichment, support, and critiques; and to share information about markets, workshops, readings."

Bozeman Readings, c/o Bob Garner, PO Box 98, Bozeman, MT 59715.

Bumbershoot, PO Box 9750, Seattle, WA 98109-0750. 206-622-5123. Contact: Judith Roche. Major book and literary fair as part of Seattle's Labor Day arts festival. Includes small press displays and sales, book arts exhibits, readings, roundtables, lectures, Writers-in-Performance program, publishing and book arts contests, The Bumbershoot Literary Magazine, and the Bumbershoot/Weyerhaeuser Publication Award.

Canadian Authors Assn, Okanogan Branch, PO Box 1436 Stn A, Kelowna, BC V1X 7V8. Contact: Myles Machan. National association for writers and those who seek to become writers. Sponsors annual conference, quarterly journal, awards.

Castalia Series, 239 Savery, University of Washington, Seattle, WA 98105.

Centrum Foundation, PO Box 1158, Port Townsend, WA 98368. 206-385-3102. Contact: Carol Jane Bangs. Activities include: "A residency program for 3-4 writers each year; a press-in-residence, Copper Canyon Press, with press tours, and in some years letterpress workshops with Tree Swenson, Copper Canyon co-publisher and designer of books for several presses; special workshops featuring writers and experts in other fields, convened to address major societal issues; writing workshops for high school students from Washington State."

Christian Writers Conference, c/o Humanities Dept, Seattle Pacific University, Seattle, WA 98119. 206-281-2109. Contact: Linda Wagner. Offers information, inspiration, and instruction for writers for both inspirational markets and secular with major focus on the inspirational markets. Conference is held Monday–Wednesday of the last week of June each year. Includes opportunity for appointments with editors.

Christian Writers Conference, Warner Pacific College, 2219 SE 68th, Portland, OR 97215. 503-775-4366. Contact: George Ivan Smith.

Edmonds Arts Commission, Anderson Cultural Center, 700 Main St, Edmonds, WA 98020. 206-775-2525. Contact: Linda McCrystal. Sponsors Write-on-the Sound writers conference each fall.

The Federation of British Columbia Writers, Box 2206, Main PO, Vancouver, BC V6B 3W2. 604-683-2057. Contact: Lynne Melcombe. "A non-profit society of professional and aspiring writers, the Federation acts as an umbrella organization for writers of all genres…. Similar organizations in other provinces and in many European countries exist because writers need to unite to achieve their common goals. Unlike writers groups representing specific genres, such as ACTRA, the Writers' Union or PWAC, the Federation's broadly-based membership allows it to direct its voice to larger concerns vital to every BC writer." To this end, the Federation publishes a quarterly newsletter, works with other writers' organizations to promote: photocopying &

copyright legislation, establishment of a provincial Writers' Centre and Archives, payment for public use of written material, public readings, and wider funding and support for writers.

The Festival of the Written Arts, Box 2299, Sechelt, BC V0N 3A0. 604-885-9631. Contact: Betty Keller. Annual 3-day program of readings and discussions by Canadian writers. Writers-in-Residence programs, small workshop groups with professional instruction. Write for information.

Fishtrap Gathering, PO Box 457, Enterprise, OR 97828. Contact: Rich Wandschneider. Annual summer conference with presentations from Northwest and the East Coast authors, editors, and publishers; followed by writing workshops.

Foothills Poetry Series, Peninsula College, Port Angeles, WA 98362. Contact: Alice Derry or Jack Estes. 206-452-9277.

Idaho Council of Teachers of English, c/o Judy Decime, Caldwell High School, Caldwell, ID 83605. Organization with newsletter, sponsors annual conference.

Idaho Writers' League, c/o Deana Jensen, President, 306 E. 129th S, Idaho Falls, ID 83404. 208-357-3914. Has 30 local chapters throughout Idaho; regular meetings, workshops, a conference, and occasionally book publishing.

Keizer Artfair, 4748 Lowell Ave NE, Keizer, OR 97303. 503-393-2457 or 393-6144. Third weekend in September each year. Writers can contact Keizer Art Assn for an application.

Kootenay School of Writing, #306-152 W Hastings St, Vancouver, BC V6B 3A0.

Lane Literary Guild, c/o Lane Arts Council, 411 High St, Eugene, OR 97401. 503-485-2278. Contact: Erik Muller, Alice Evans. Membership $10/indiv. Newsletter, circ 20,000. Nonprofit organization representing the professional interests of poets, fiction writers and dramatists living in Lane County.

The Literary Center, PO Box 85116, Seattle, WA 98145-1116. Contact: Sarah Sarai. 206-524-5514. The Literary Center, 1716 N 45th St, is a writer's resource organization — to help writers help themselves. It includes: a small press gallery (containing small press books, magazines, broadsides, tapes, etc.); a resource library (containing foundation directories, information about local readings and workshops, national markets, etc. is located at the Seattle Public Schools Teacher Resource Center at Marshall School, 520 NE Ravenna Blvd, Seattle); Literary Hotline (524-5514), a 24-hour pre-recorded listing of local literary events. Newsletter, $15/yr; circ 2,000.

LitEruption, Sponsored by Northwest Writers Inc, PO Box 3437, Portland, OR 97208. A 2 day book fair and celebration in March in Portland with readings by well known Northwest authors; exhibits from book stores, publishers, writers and artists groups; children's literary room; films; and book art exhibits.

Meet the Author Program Series, Rainier Beach Library, 9125 Rainier Ave S, Seattle, WA 98118. 206-386-1906. Fall & winter scheduling.

Montana Author's Coalition, PO Box 20839, Billings, MT 59104-0839. MAC publishes a newsletter and sponsors events. Dues $20/yr.

Montana Cowboy Poetry Gathering, Box 1255, Big Timber, MT 59011. Contact: Gwen Petersen. 406-632-4227.

Montana Institute of the Arts, PO Box 1456, Billings, MT 59103. 406-245-3688. Contact: Ron Paulick. "The Montana Institute of the Arts was founded in 1948 by members of the academic and professional community across Montana. It has been effective in helping to establish art centers and museums in the state and continues to stimulate enthusiasm and acceptance of the arts." There are branches in many cities, with various interest groups, writing being one of them. The organization offers workshops, visiting artists, contests, festivals. The monthly newsletter has a special section for writers. For more information, contact Aline Moore, 11333 Gooch Hill Rd, Gallatin Gateway, MT 59730.

Mountain Writers Series, Mt Hood Community College, 26000 SE Stark, Gresham, OR 97030. 503-232-7337. Contact: Sandra Williams. "The Mountain Writers Series presents regular literary readings, each preceded by a brief musical performance, featuring artists of local, regional and national reputa-

tion, at noon on scheduled Fridays during the academic year (Oct.-June) on the MHCC campus. The public is welcome at all performances, and those wishing to receive announcements of events should write to be included on the mailing list. Artists wishing to perform in the Series should apply by August 15 with a sample of their work, phone number, and brief statement of biographical/publication/performance history."

Multicultural Playwrights Festival, c/o Jim Bond, 3940 Brooklyn NE, Seattle, WA 98105. Contact: 206-545-4969. Plays by Native American, Hispanic, Black, and Asian playwrights. Pays honorarium, board, travel, and production. Oct 15th deadline.

Normal Art Society, 3505 Commercial St, Vancouver, BC V5N 4E8. 604-873-3129. Nonprofit society established in 1988 to encourage art and the creative process. Publishes pop-tart Magazine (see Listings), organizes the Small Press Festival, performances, exhibitions.

Northwest Writers, Inc, PO Box 3437, Portland, OR 97208. Organization of professional writers intended to offer support, pool resources and share information and job opportunities. Meets the 3rd Thursday of each month, Northwest Service Center, NW 18th & Everett, Portland, 7:30 pm. Sponsors Portland's spring book and author fair, LitEruption.

Oregon Authors' Table, Mission Mill Museum Assn, 1313 SE Mill St Salem, OR 97301. Contact: Betty Reilly, Chairman.

Oregon Book Awards, Oregon Institute of Literary Arts, 888 SW fifth Ave #1600, Portland, OR 97204-2099. 503-221-1440. Contact: Kay Reid. Recognizes and promotes Oregon writers and publishers. Write for information.

Oregon Coast Council for the Arts, PO Box 1315, Newport, OR 97365. 503-265-9231. Contact: Sharon Morgan. "We are a regional arts council with a strong history of literary programs and support for emerging writers."

Oregon Council of Teachers of English (OCTE), PO Box 2515, Portland, OR 97208. 503-238-1208. Contact: Joe Fitzgibbon. For teachers of English, language arts, literature and creative writing at all levels. Publishes Oregon English and Chalkboard. Sponsors "Teachers-as-Writers," regular conferences, and sponsors the Oregon Writing Festival for young writers.

Oregon Institute of Literary Arts, 1600 Pioneer Tower, 888 SW Fifth Ave, Portland, OR 97204-2099. Contact: Kay Reid, Executive Director. 503-223-3604. Annual Oregon book awards ceremony; awards for young readers literature, creative nonfiction, poetry, fiction, playwrights; fellowships for writers and publishers; book exhibits; and publication of tabloid on Oregon books, Oregon Ink.

Oregon State Poetry Assn, 1645 SE Spokane St, Portland, OR 97206. 503-283-3682. Contact: Wilma Erwin. Contact for information on local groups and meetings. "OSPA contests are held spring and fall and offer cash prizes in several categories ($300 total, April 1986). The number and theme of categories vary from year to year. Guidelines are published in the spring and fall issues of the OSPA Newsletter. Non-members may request them in March and August by sending SASE to above address." No entry fee to members.

Oregon Writers Colony, PO Box 15200, Portland, OR 97215. 503-771-0428. Membership organization for writers in all genres. Publishes newsletter, Colonygram. Operates writers' retreat (Colony House) on Oregon coast. Holds workshops at coast and in Portland. Sponsors readings at the Heathman Hotel (LiteraTea).

Pacific Northwest Booksellers Assn, Rt 1 Box 219B, Banks, OR 97106. 503-324-8180. Contact: Debby Garman. Sponsors semiannual trade shows and annual book awards.

Pacific Northwest Writers Conference, Pacific Northwest Writers, 17345 SW Sylvester Rd SW, Seattle, WA 98166. 206-242-9757. Contact: Carol McQuinn. Late summer conference and awards.

Poet Tree, PO Box 2585, Portland, OR 97208-2585. Contact: Director. 503-284-1454.

Portland Poetry Festival, Northwest Service Center, 1819 NW Everett, Portland, OR 97209. 503-285-4451.

Puget Sound Writing Program for Young Writers, English Department, GN-30, University of Washington, Seattle, WA 98195. 206-543-0141. Contact: Linda Clifton. Week-long workshop held in summer for students entering grades 5-11.

Rattlesnake Mountain Writers' Workshop, 5124 Grosscup, Richland, WA 99352. Contact: Nancy Girvin. 509-967-9324.

Red Sky Poetry Theatre, Five-O Tavern, 507 15th Ave E, Seattle, WA 98112. 206-322-9693.

Salem Art Fair, Mission Mill Museum Assn, 1313 Mill St SE, Salem, OR 97301. 503-585-7012. Contact: Patti Wilbrecht. Oregon Authors' Table at annual July art fair.

Sitka Summer Writers Symposium, Box 2420, Sitka, AK 99835. 907-747-3794. Contact: Carolyn Servid.

Vancouver International Writers Festival, 1243 Cartwright St, Vancouver, BC V6H 4B7. 604-681-6330. Contact: Alma Lee, Producer. Festival brings writers from around the world each year for an exchange of culture and ideas with readers.

Warm Beach Christian Writers & Speakers Conference, Warm Beach Camp & Conference Center, 20800 Marine Dr NW, Stanwood, WA 98292.

Washington Poets Assn, 6002 S Fife St, Tacoma, WA 98409. Contact: Amelia Haller. Organization to raise awareness and appreciation of poetry; publishes a newsletter 4 times a year, holds an annual meeting/banquet in May, and workshops/events across the state. Refer to Poetry in Vancouver USA, A Poetry Event at Longview, and Rattlesnake Mountain.

Western Montana Writers Conference, Office of Continuing Education, Western Montana College, Dillon, MT 59725. 406-683-7537. Contact: Sally Garrett-Dingley or Susan K Jones. Annual conference featuring a writer-in-residence with expertise in a specific writing genre.

Willamette Writers, 9045 SW Barbur Blvd #5A, Portland, OR 97219. 503-452-1592. Monthly programs, newsletter, annual conference and contest, small critique groups, and ongoing workshops. Newsletter circ. 900.

Yellow Bay Writers Conference, Ctr for Continuing Ed & Summer Programs, University of Montana, Missoula, MT 59812. 406-243-2900. Contact: Judy L Jones, Program Mgr. Annual, usually in August, for one week with nationally known writers. Classes included 2 fiction, 1 poetry, 1 creative nonfiction or personal essay.

Yellowstone Art Center's Regional Writers Project, 401 N 27th St, Billings, MT 59101. 406-656-1238. Contact: Adrea Sukin, Pat Palagi. Promotes Western literature through a retail outlet and mail order catalog and lecture series featuring authors and small press publishers.

Young Audiences of Oregon Inc, 418 SW Washington, Rm 202, Portland, OR 97204. 503-224-1412. Nonprofit educational organization sponsors professional literary artists (e.g., storytelling, poetry) and performing artists in schools in Oregon and Washington. Artists work in both assembly and classroom settings, with performances, workshops, and residencies.

Young Authors Conference, School of Education, Seattle Pacific University, Seattle, WA 98119. Contact: Nancy Johnson. For young writers grades 1-8 in Western Washington and Oregon. Workshops, critiques.

Young Writers Competition, Oregon Arts Commission, 835 Summer St NE, Salem, OR 97301. A program of the Oregon Arts Commission, this writing workshop takes various forms. Offered to middle schools only in 1991, teams of students and teachers work together in a week-end residency.

Young Writers' Conference, English Dept., Ms-25, Eastern Washington University, Cheney, WA 99004. 509-359-6032. Contact: Mary Ann Nelson.

Writers Organizations

The Assn of Canadian Cinema, TV, Radio, Television And Radio Artists, 911-525 Seymour St, Vancouver, BC V6B 3H7. Contact: 604-681-1101.

Adventist Composers, Arrangers and Poets Inc, PO Box 11, Days Creek, OR 97429. Contact: Eleanor B Davis.

Adventist Writers' Assn of Western Washington, 18115 116th Ave SE, Renton, WA 98058. 206-235-1435. Contact Marian Forschler. How-to newsletter on writing and marketing to Seventh-day Adventist publications. Meetings held 6 times a yr. to critique and/or hear speakers. Annual week-long writing class in June. Anyone may join.

Adventist Writers' Assn of Washington, 21024 9th Ave SE, Bothell, WA 98021-7603. Contact: Maylan Schurch.

Alaska Council of Teachers of English, PO Box 3184, Kodiak, AK, 99615. Editor: Kate O'Dell.

Alaska Historical Society, Box 10355, Anchorage, AK 99511.

Alaska Press Women, PO Box 104056, Anchorage, AK 99510. 907-753-2622. Contact: Carolyn Rinehart. Purposes are: "to promote the highest ideals of journalism; to provide exchange of journalistic ideas and experiences of men and women in communications; and to coordinate efforts on matters of national interest to women." There are active chapters in Juneau, Anchorage, Mat-Su and Fairbanks. There is an annual competition for work performed the previous year.

The Alaska State Writing Consortium, Department of Education, PO Box F, Juneau, AK 99811. This is the version of the Writing Project in other states and publishes a newsletter.

The American Assn of University Women, Montana Division, 20200 W Dickerson #58, Bozeman, MT 59715. Contact: Student Contest Coordinator. Sponsors an annual essay contest with prizes, open to Montana students, grades 10-12.

American Pen Women, Rt 1 Box 53, Reardon, WA 99029. 509-796-5872. Contact: Charlotte Chester. State newsletter, Branch Pen Points, sponsors contest, meets monthly.

American Penwomen, Seattle, 7584 Meadowmeer Lane NE, Bainbridge Island, WA 98110. 206-842-4269. Contact: Kay Stewart. Monthly newsletter, 8 meetings a year.

Amniote Egg Writers Group, 1123 F St, Anchorage, AK 99501.

Argenta Writers' Group, Nowick Gray, Argenta, BC V0G 1B0.

Bainbridge Writer's Guild, c/o Nancy Rekow, 8489 Fletcher Bay Rd NE, Bainbridge, WA 98110. 206-842-4855. Formed in 1986 to serve writers of all levels in Bainbridge Island area. Sponsors poetry readings. Publishes local work.

BC Writers Guild, Box 1717, Hope, BC V0X 1L0. Contact: Estelle McLachlan. 604-869-9848.

Beaverhead Writers' Workshop, Library, Western Montana College, Dillon, MT 59725. 406-683-6794. Contact: Ron Rischer. A critique group for fiction and poetry writers; meets in the Western Montana College Library, 3rd Fridays, 7 pm. Contact: Ron Fischer 406-683-6794.

Before Columbus Foundation, American Ethnic Studies, GN-80, University of Washington, Seattle, WA 98195. 206-543-4264. Contact: Shawn Wong. Promotes the efforts of minority and multicultural writers and topics.

Bend-in-the-River Writers Guild, c/o Doris M Hall, 62340 Powell Butte Rd, Bend, OR 97701. 503-389-5845. "A writers support group, largely poets, but some other kinds of writing are represented. We meet for mutual enrichment, support, and critiques; and to share information about markets, workshops, readings."

Billings Arts Assn Writers, 3706 Duck Creek Rd, Billings, MT 59101. 406-656-2524. Contact: Alice Madsen. Branch interest group of Montana Institute of the Arts. Offers criticism, support, workshops and state-level writing contest for poetry and prose. Meets monthly.

Boise Poets, c/o Jack Hoffman, 7061 Valley Heights Dr, Boise, ID 83709-6658.

BC Book Promotion Council, Box 2206 MPO, Vancouver, BC V6B 3W2. 604-683-2057. Contact: Robert Webster. Acts as a clearing house for information of importance to all sectors of the book industry.

Burnaby Writers, 6450 Gilpin St, Burnaby, BC V5G 2J3.

Butte Writers, Legget Apt S, 50 W Broadway, Butte, MT 59701. 406-782-5373. Contact: Connie. Guest invited to some meetings. Members read and critique each other's work.

Canadian Authors Assn, Okanogan Branch, PO Box 1436 Stn A, Kelowna, BC V1X 7V8. Contact: Myles Machan. National association for writers and those who seek to become writers. Sponsors annual conference, quarterly journal, awards.

Canadian Authors Assn (BC Branch/Vancouver), 726 Parkside Rd, W Vancouver, BC V7S 1P3. Contact: Frank Wade.

Canadian Authors Assn, Vancouver Lower Mainland Branch, 24750 58th Ave, Rm #3, Aldergrove, BC VOX 1AO. Contact: Editor.

Canadian Authors Assn, Vancouver Branch, 726 Parkside Rd, W Vancouver, BC V7S 1P3. 604-922-6983. Contact: Frank Wade.

Canadian Authors Assn, Victoria Branch, 1740 Kenmore Rd, Victoria BC V8N 2E7. Contact: Sherry Biggar.

Canadian Poetry Assn, Eastwing, 1850 Charles St, Vancouver, BC V5L 2T7. Contact: David Bouvier.

Canadian Poetry Assn, Grassroot Oracles, 45801 Reece Ave, Chilliwack, BC V2P 2Z4. Contact: Chad Norman.

Canadian Poetry Assn–Vancouver, PO Box 46658 Stn G, Vancouver, BC V6G 4K8. 604-266-0396. Contact: Katie Eliot. Network of local poets, meets last Friday of alternate months. Publisher of SPOKES Newsletter.

Capital Writers Circle, PO Box 549, Juneau, AK 99802. 907-586-1266. Contact: Mike Macy. "Organization devoted to the enjoyment of literature and the development of writers of all genres." Meets every other week.

Caribou Writers Group, c/o Williams Lake Library, 110 Oliver St, Williams Lake, BC V2G 1G0.

Cascade Poets, 6123 N Commercial, Portland, OR 97217. Contact: Wilma Erwin. 503 283 3682. "We meet on the last Monday of the month at Cascade Center, 705 N Killingsworth, Portland, OR 97217. We welcome all poets. Poets should bring 12 copies of a poem they'd like to have critiqued. Free. We're looking forward to seeing you."

Castlegar Writer's Guild, 3012-4th Ave, Castlegar, BC V1N 2S2.

Central Oregon Coast Writers, Mary Esther Miller, Rt 1 Box 59X, Otis, OR 97368. 503-994-5476.

Children's Book Writers of the Eastside, c/o Carol Krefting Youngberg, 6133 111th Ave NE, Kirkland, WA 98033. 206-822-1170.

Christian Scribes, 9340 SE Morrison, Portland, OR 97216. Contact: Shirley Cody.

Christian Writers, c/o Mrs. Carl T Jones, 207 NE "A" St, College Place, WA 99324. 509-525-4350.

Clearwater Writers Guild, Rt 2 Box 159, Grangeville, ID 83530.

Coastal Fellowship of Christian Writers, PO Box 186, Toledo, OR 97391. 503-336-3410. Contact: Beth Dickinson. "Coastal Fellowship of Christian Writers meet at the Toledo Public Library. Group focus — encouragement and critique."

Columbia Gorge Writers Group, 2470 Lichens Dr, Hood River, OR 97031. 503-386-3112. Contact: Lana Fox. Organized to share and promote the development of good writing habits and to encourage the submission of materials for publication. Regular meetings, 3rd Monday at 7 pm; critiquing, 1st Thursday at 7 pm.

Comox Valley Writers' Club, RR 1, Site 90, Black Creek, BC V0R 1C0. Contact: Audrey M Clark.

Comox Writers Group, 319 Church St, Comox, BC V9N 5G6.

Composers, Authors and Artists of America Inc, Rt 1 Box 53, Reardan, WA 99029. Contact: David Chester. Sponsors a state poetry contest. Write for info.

Coos Head Writers, 950 Spaulding Rd, Coos Bay, OR 97420. 503-267-7236. Contact: Mary Scheirman. Support group.

Creative Arts Guild, 520 SW 5th, Albany, OR 97321. 503-926-2211 or 928-7924. Contact: Connie Petty.

Creative People Support Group, Supportletter, 2905 Mayfair Ave N, Seattle, WA 98109. 206-283-0505. Contact: Beth Bauer. "Informal pot luck dinner; encouragement, emotional support, positive critique of works in progress — to promote creativity; writers, artists, musicians, song writers, poets, needle workers, cooks, photographers, craftpersons — we encourage and enjoy creativity and creative people. Supportletter mailed to those showing continuing interest in group (by attendance, or by verbal contact with editor)."

Creston Writers League, Box 2807, Creston, BC V0B 1G0.

Dillon Authors Assn, PO Box 212, Dillon, MT 59725. Contact: Sally Garrett Dingley. 406-683-4539. "Monthly writers meetings on 2nd Tuesday from Sept. through May of each year. Six meetings have guests with special expertise, three meetings are critiquing sessions. A diverse membership of local and regional writers, published and aspiring…. Newsletter published approximately ten times a year. 55+ members, 12 newsletter exchanges."

Downtown Eastside Poets, Carnegie Centre, 401 Main St, Vancouver, BC V6A 2T7. Contact: Sheila Baxter.

Eastside Writers Assn, PO Box 8005, Totem Lake Post Office, Kirkland, WA 98034. Contact: Pat Ahern, Pres. 206-747-5368. Writers group meets the 2nd Tuesday of each month, Sept. through May, from 7:30 to 9:00 pm at First Congregational Church in Bellevue. Off I-405 at NE 8th and 108th. Dues $10 to pay for church, newsletter and speakers for each meeting. Meetings are open to non-members, donation of $2. Eastside Writers is for "anyone who writes, or wants to write. We have members who have been writing for years, and we have outright beginners. Some of our members have sold everything they've written, and some don't even want to sell."

Entheos, PO Box 709, Philomoth, OR 97370. Contact: Karen C Hayden. 206-830-4758. Writers' and photographers' organization.

Esquimalt Writers Group, 527 Fraser St, Victoria, BC V9A 6H6.

The Federation of British Columbia Writers, Box 2206, Main PO, Vancouver, BC V6B 3W2. 604-683-2057. Contact: Lynne Melcombe. "A non-profit society of professional and aspiring writers, the Federation acts as an umbrella organization for writers of all genres…. Similar organizations in other provinces and in many European countries exist because writers need to unite to achieve their common goals. Unlike writers groups representing specific genres, such as ACTRA, the Writers' Union or PWAC, the Federation's broadly-based membership allows it to direct its voice to larger concerns vital to every BC writer." To this end, the Federation publishes a quarterly newsletter, works with other writers' organizations to promote: photocopying & copyright legislation, establishment of a provincial Writers' Centre and Archives, payment for public use of written material, public readings, and wider funding and support for writers.

Ferndale Writers Group, c/o Ferndale Library, PO Box 1209, Ferndale, WA 98248.

Fictioneers, 13211 39th Ave NE, Seattle, WA 98125. 206-282-2729. Contact: Beth Casey. Monthly meetings for writers, held at Seattle Downtown Public Library, 3rd Saturday of the month at 10:30 am. Group has been in existence for over 40 years, and is not sponsored by the Library. Meetings include manuscript reading, critiques, discussions.

Fort St John Writers, #310 9215-94A St, Fort St John, BC V1J 6E4.

Friends of the Library, c/o Dianne Sichel, 3057 SW Fairview, Portland, OR 97201. 503-228-0841. Organizes readings by nationally known writers.

Gem State Writer's Guild, Rt 1 Box 1283, Homedale, ID 83628. 208-337-3613. Contact: Janet Leep.

Grants Pass Writers Workshop, Dorothy Francis, 114 Espey Rd, Grants Pass, OR 97526. 503-476-2038.

Great Falls Writers Group, c/o Eileen Brandt, PO Box 429, Power, MT 59468. 406-727-3906.

Hellgate Writers, PO Box 7131, Missoula, MT 59807. 406-543-6333. Contact: Lee Evans. Writers group with newsletter, workshops; brings in writers from out of state, puts on events in the community.

Idaho Council of Teachers of English, c/o Judy Decime, Caldwell High School, Caldwell, ID 83605. Organization with newsletter, sponsors annual conference.

Idaho Falls Fiction Workshop, c/o Sharon Bowman, 692 Lomax, Idaho Falls, ID 83401. 208-529-9803.

Idaho Falls Advanced Fiction Workshop, 692 Lomax, Idaho Falls, ID 83401. 208-529-9803. Contact: Sharon Bowman. Writers group.

Idaho Falls Poetry Workshop, PO Box 953, Idaho Falls, ID 83405. 208-524-2569. Contact: Joan Juskie-Nellis. Monthly meetings to read and critique poetry, share marketing information, and exchange information.

Idaho Press Women, PO Box 554, Coeur d'Alene, ID 83814. 208-667-0470. Contact: Louise Shadduck.

Idaho Writers' League, c/o Deana Jensen, 306 E. 129th S, Idaho Falls, ID 83404. 208-357-3914. The League has 13 local chapters throughout Idaho; regular meetings, workshops, a conference, and occasionally book publishing.

Kitsap Writers Club, c/o Phil Kirschner, 916 Hull Ave, Port Orchard, WA 98366. 206-876-3622.

Lane Literary Guild, c/o Lane Arts Council, 411 High St, Eugene, OR 97401. 503-485-2278. Contact: Erik Muller, Alice Evans. Membership $10/indiv. Newsletter, circ 20,000. Nonprofit organization representing the professional interests of poets, fiction writers and dramatists living in Lane County.

Langley Literary Guild, 9582 - 132A St, Surrey, BC V3V 5R2.

The League of Canadian Poets/Vancouver Area, 2588-124B St, Surrey, BC V4A 3N7. 604-538-8214. Contact: Tom Konyves.

The League of Canadian Poets/victoria, 228 Douglas St, Victoria, BC V8V 2P2. 604-386-8066. Contact: Linda Rogers.

The Literary Center, PO Box 85116, Seattle, WA 98145-1116. Contact: Sarah Sarai. 206-524-5514. The Literary Center, 1716 N 45th St, is a writer's resource organization — to help writers help themselves. It includes: a small press gallery (containing small press books, magazines, broadsides, tapes, etc.); a resource library (containing foundation directories, information about local readings and workshops, national markets, etc. is located at the Seattle Public Schools Teacher Resource Center at Marshall School, 520 NE Ravenna Blvd, Seattle); Literary Hotline (524-5514), a 24-hour pre-recorded listing of local literary events. Newsletter, $15/yr; circ 2,000.

Literary Lights, 6918 Spada Rd, Snohomish, WA 98290-6123.

McCall Arts Council, McCall Area Chamber of Commerce, Box D, McCall, ID 83638. 208-634-7631. Contact: Jennifa G Lorenzi.

Montana Assn of Teachers of English, c/o Rebecca Stiff, Helena High School, Helena, MT 59601.

Montana Author's Coalition, PO Box 20839, Billings, MT 59104-0839. MAC publishes a newsletter and sponsors events. Dues $20/yr.

Montana Writing Project, English Department, University of Montana, Missoula, MT 59812. 406-243-5231. Contact: Dr Beverly Ann Chin.

Moscow Moffia Writers' Workshop, 621 East 'F' St, Moscow, ID 83343. Contact: Jon Gustafson. Weekly writers' discussion groups. Sponsors workshops throughout the Northwest.

Mystery Writers of America–Northwest, c/o Frank Denton, 14654 8th Ave SW, Seattle, WA 98166.

N By NW Writers, 655 Main St #305, Edmonds, WA 98020. 206-776-4365. Contact: R Kermit Fisher. Monthly meetings on 3rd Wednesday at The Anderson Center, 7th & Main, Edmonds; publishes monthly newsletter to benefit members. Dues $12/yr.

Nanaimo Writers, 3413 Littleford St, Nanaimo, BC V9T 4C4.

National League of American Pen Women, Spokane, c/o Thalia Kleinoeder, E 1020 Bedivere Dr, Spokane, WA 99218.

National League of American Pen Women, Tacoma, c/o Jane Keffler, 7606 37th W, Unit 3d, Tacoma, WA 98466. 206-564-5542.

National Writers Club, Seattle Chapter, PO Box 55522, Seattle, WA 98155. 206-783-3401. Contact: Leon Billig. "Monthly programs, special workshops and symposia, social events, critique groups, networking, special interest activities, professional visibility."

Nightwriters, Rt 1, Box 432, Vashon, WA 98070. 206-567-4829. Contact: Joyce Delbridge. Regular meetings at Vashon Library, open invitation, small fee, critique group.

No Frills, 1118 Hoyt Ave, Everett, WA 98201. 206-259-0804. Contact: Ron Fleshman. "Active working writers meet Tuesdays for critiques. Share brags, moans, and dues for space rental." Meets weekly.

Northwest Christian Writers Assn, 17462 NE 11th St, Bellevue, WA 98008. 206-644-5012. Contacts: Agnes Lawless, Pauline Sheehan.

Northwest Native American Writers, PO Box 6403, Portland, OR 97228-6403. 503-232-3513. Contact: Elizabeth Woody.

Northwest Outdoor Writers' Assn, 3421 E Mercer St, Seattle, WA 98112. 206-323-3970. Contact: Stan Jones. Assn of professional outdoor writers, editors, artists and photographers in Western US and Canada.

Northwest Playwrights Guild — Oregon, 8959 SW 40th Ave, Portland, OR 97219. Contact: Michael Whelan. Annual dues $15. Support group for regional playwrights, provides both regional and state newsletters, occasionally co-sponsors workshops, readings, and productions.

Northwest Playwrights' Guild — Washington, PO Box 95252, Seattle, WA 98145. 206-762-5525. Contact: Cheryl Read. The organization's goal is to satisfy needs of NW playwrights and organizations interested in supporting the new works of Northwest playwrights. Initial membership fee of $25, plus $15 per year dues. Services include quarterly and monthly newsletters, seminars and classes with visiting playwrights.

Northwest Renaissance, 214 N St NE, Auburn, WA 98002. 206-833-4798. Contact: Marjorie Rommel. Poetry workshop with approximately 50 members, Bellingham to Olympia. Meets monthly in members' homes. Membership by application and election, dues $20/yr, includes newsletter. Occasional publication of member anthology, etc. Literature available.

Northwest Writers, Inc, PO Box 3437, Portland, OR 97208. Organization of professional writers intended to offer support, pool resources and share information and job opportunities. Meets the 3rd Thursday of each month, Northwest Service Center, NW 18th & Everett, Portland, 7:30 pm. Sponsors Portland's spring book and author fair, LitEruption.

O-Ya-Ka Story League, Multnomah County Central Library, 801 SW 10th Ave, Portland, OR 97205. 503-244-9415. Meets monthly. Affiliated with National Story League, Western District. Story workshop sponsored by Western District held at Marylhurst alternate summers.

Ocean Shores Writers, c/o Marlene Thomason, PO Box 1262, Ocean Shores, WA 98569. 206-289-2165.

Okanagan Writers' League, Rm 10, Leir House, 220 Manor Park Ave, Penticton, BC V2A 2R2. 604-493-6035. Contact: Ken Nevin.

Oregon Assn of Christian Writers, 2495 Maple NE, Salem, OR 97303. 503-364-9570. Contact: Marion Duckworth. Organized for "the purpose of promoting higher standards of craftsmanship in the field of Christian journalism and encouraging a greater sense of spiritual responsibility in the Christian writer." The group hold writer's seminars 3 times a year, in Salem, in Eugene and in Portland.

Oregon Council of Teachers of English (OCTE), PO Box 2515, Portland, OR 97208. 503-238-1208. Contact: Joe Fitzgibbon. For teachers of English, language arts, literature and creative writing at all levels. Publishes Oregon English and Chalkboard. Sponsors "Teachers-as-Writers," regular conferences, and sponsors the Oregon Writing Festival for young writers.

Oregon Journalists Coalition, Oregonian, 1320 SW Broadway, Portland, OR 97201. Contact: Stan Chen/Copy Desk. 503-221-8079.

Oregon Press Women, PO Box 25354, Portland, OR 97225. 503-292-4945. Contact: Glennis McNeal. Professional group for broadcasters, journalists, public relations practitioners, freelancers, photographers, journalism educators. Meets twice yearly. Sponsors contests for members, high school students.

Oregon State Poetry Assn, 1645 SE Spokane St, Portland, OR 97206. 503-283-3682. Contact: Wilma Erwin. Contact for information on local groups and meetings. "OSPA contests are held spring and fall and offer cash prizes in several categories ($300 total, April 1986). The number and theme of categories vary from year to year. Guidelines are published in the spring and fall issues of the OSPA Newsletter. Non-members may request them in March and August by sending SASE to above address." No entry fee to members.

Oregon Students Writing & Art Foundation, PO Box 2100, Portland, OR 97208-2100. Contact: Chris Weber. 503-232-7737. An organization of students and teachers involved in publishing an anthology of student writing compiled from the winners of the Starfire Contest. Students are involved in all aspects of the book, editing, design, publicity, etc.

Oregon Writers Alliance, 4950 SW Hall Blvd., Beaverton, OR 97005. Writers' support group meets twice a month.

Oregon Writers Colony, PO Box 15200, Portland, OR 97215. 503-771-0428. Membership organization for writers in all genres. Publishes newsletter, Colonygram. Operates writers' retreat (Colony House) on Oregon coast. Holds workshops at coast and in Portland. Sponsors readings at the Heathman Hotel (LiteraTea).

Pacific Northwest Booksellers Assn, Rt 1 Box 219B, Banks, OR 97106. 503-324-8180. Contact: Debby Garman. Sponsors semiannual trade shows and annual book awards.

Pacific Northwest Writers Conference, 17345 SW Sylvester Rd SW, Seattle, WA 98166. 206-242-9757. Contact: Carol McQuinn. Membership organization sponsoring conferences and contests for adult and young writers.

Pacific Poets, Rt 1 Box 4099, Coquille, OR 97423. Contact: Miriam Roady.

Pilot Knobs Writers Group, Rt 1 Box 591, Victor, ID 83455. 208-354-8522. Contact: Christina Adams. One year old non-membership group in rural SE corner of Idaho. It sponsors a visiting writers series, and plans to have a mentorship program for students enabling them to work with writers through the mail.

Playwrights Union of Canada, 746 E Pender St, Vancouver, BC V5A 1V7. 604-251-3496. Contact: Peter Anderson.

Playwrights-In-Progress, 14030 NE 12th #410D, Seattle, WA 98125. 206-363-5905. Contact: Nikki Louis. Weekly meetings for readings of members' plays. PIP also sponsors workshops.

Pocatello Poetry Workshop, c/o Pocatello Public Library, 812 E Clark St, Pocatello, ID 83201. 208-232-8496. Contact: Jenny Lewis.

Poetry Scribes, 3328 E 36th, Spokane, WA 99223. 509-448-8292. Contact: Betty Egbert. Poetry critique group, meets monthly. Publishes Turquoise Lanterns, an annual anthology.

Poets & Writers Inc, 4045 Brooklyn Ave NE, Seattle, WA 98105. 206-543-4050.

Port Alberni Writers, #38 4467 Wallace St, Port Alberni, BC V9Y 3Y4.

Portland Science Fiction Society, PO Box 4602, Portland, OR 97208. 503-655-6189.

Prince Rupert Writers' Group, Box 1080, Prince Rupert, BC V8J 4H6.

Quadra Island Writers' Group, Support Group, Box 267, Quathiaski Cove, Quadra Island, BC V0P 1N0. 604-285-3570.

Red-Wood Writers Workshop, 2044 Yale Ave E, Seattle, WA 98102. 206-481-3240. Contact: Linda Foss. Support group for area writers. Meetings include readings, creative exercises, sharing ideas and information.

Regional Arts Council of Central Oregon, PO Box 1212, Bend, OR 97709-1212. 503-382-5055.

Renton Writers Workshop, c/o Beth Cole, 18618 SE 128th St, Renton, WA 98056. Contact: Beth Cole/Marilyn Kamcheff. 206-255-5711. Meets in the Administrative Center of the Renton School District, 435 Main Ave South, Renton. "We try to improve our craft by pursuing regular writing habits, giving constructive criticism, and sharing publishing information." Meets twice a month from 9:30 am. to 12:30 pm.

River Bend Writers, 4309 E 17th St #2, Vancouver, WA 98661. 206-693-4071. Contact: Norma Mizer.

Romance Writer's Assn, Greater Vancouver Chapter, c/o 12548 - 216th St, Maple Ridge, BC V2X 5K7.

Romance Writers of America, Box 24843, Stn C, Vancouver, BC V5T 4E9.

Romance Writers of America, c/o Selwyn Young, 620 N 202, Seattle, WA 98133.

Romance Writers of America, c/o Darlene Layman, 7270 Thasof Ave NE, Bremerton, WA 98310.

Romance Writers of America, c/o Sally Fozoft, 1065 Cherry, Anchorage, AK 99504.

Romance Writers of America, c/o Sally Garett Dingley, PO Box 212, Dillon, MT 59725.

Romance Writers of America, c/o Margo MacIntosh, 1206 E Pike St #1004, Seattle, WA 98122-3918.

Romance Writers of America, Cascade, c/o Elly Ibarra, 4825 NE 17th, Portland, OR 97211. 503-284-4200.

Romance Writers of America, Portland/Vancouver Chapter, c/o Clackamas Book Exchange, 7000 SE Thiessen Rd, Milwaukie, OR 97267. 503-659-2559. Contact: Iona Lockwood. "To give encouragement and support to writers, published and unpublished, who are interested in the romance genre via monthly meetings, newsletters, workshops, etc. Meets monthly.

Romance Writers of America, Tacoma Chapter, c/o Lutheran Church of Christ the King, 1710 85th St E, Tacoma, WA 98445. 206-847-7351. Contact: Arlene Dubacker.

Roseburg Writers Group, c/o Pat Banta, Rt 1 Box 4010, Coquille, OR 97423-9756. 503-673-6486.

Salem Writers and Publishers, 3820 Oak Hollow Ln SE, Salem, OR 97302. 503-364-7698. Contact: Dick Lutz. Monthly meeting and newsletter focusing on marketing. Dues $10/yr.

Sandpoint Writer's Project, 5706 E Dufort Rd, Sagle, ID 83860. 208-263-8223. Contact: Tom Birdseye. "Informal discussions and critique sessions."

Scribe's Forum, 1206 E Pike St #1004, Seattle, WA 98122-3918. Contact: Margo McIntosh. Group to improve skills, share market info.

Seahurst Writers, 13404 Military Rd S, Seattle, WA 98168. Contact: Barbara Benepe. Writers group meets twice a month at Burien Library. All writers welcome.

Seattle Freelances, c/o Patricia Mauser, 20021 Hollyhills Dr NE, Bothell, WA 98011-7602. 206-863-2656.

Seely Lake Writer's Club, c/o Vernon Printing & Publishing, 1701 Hwy 83 N, Seely Lake, MT 59868. Informal group of writers and history buffs. No bylaws, rules or dues.

Skagit Valley Writers League, PO Box 762, Sedro Woolley, WA 98284. Contact: Diane Freethy.

Society of Children's Book Writers, 2513 SE Taylor St, Portland, OR 97214-2840. 503-228-1746. Contact: Liz Vaughan.

The Society of Children's Book Writers, NW Chapter, c/o Robert Rubinstein, 90 E 49th St, Eugene, OR 97405.

Society of Children's Book Writers, 1215 NE 168th, Seattle, WA 98155. 206-362-6442. Contact: Shellen Reid.

Society of Children's Book Writers, Eastside, 6133 111th Pl NE, Kirkland, WA 98033. 206-822-1170. Contact: Carol A Youngberg.

Society of Professional Journalists, Willamette Valley Chapter, PO Box 1717, Portland, OR 97201. 503-244-6111 x4181. Contact: Oren Campbell. "Assn representing all areas of journalism and all levels of experience." Meets monthly September through May, annual contest, monthly newsletter.

Southwest Washington Writers, 4309 E 17th St #2, Vancouver, WA 98661. Contact: Norma Mizer.

Spindrift Writers, Box 160, Qualicum Beach, BC, V0R 2T0. 604-752-9723.

Spokane Christian Writers, Beautiful Savior Lutheran Church, S 4320 Conklin St, Spokane, WA 99203. 509-448-6622. Contact: Niki Anderson. Christian writers critique group. Meets monthly.

Tacoma Writer's Club, 14710–30th St Ct E, Sumner, WA 98390. 206-473-9632. Weekly/monthly workshops including poetry, articles, and fiction. "Members study marketing their work, and discuss ideas about illustrating, query letters, etc." The group publishes a monthly newsletter. Meets at the South Hill branch of the Tacoma Public Library.

Them Dam Writers Club, c/o Jean Nicholson, PO Box 307, Electric City, WA 99123.

Valley Poets of Medford, 725 Royal Ave #74, Medford, OR 97504. 503-773-8329.

Vancouver Industrial Writers' Union, #203–1160 Burrard St, Vancouver, BC V6Z 2E8. Contact: Dr Kirsten Emmott. Group meets regularly for support and criticism; interest in work writing — committed to promoting the new fiction, poetry, and drama written by people about their daily work. Membership is by invitation.

Vancouver Island Literary Society, 2610 Lynburn Crescent, Nanaimo, BC V9S 3T6.

Vernon Writer's Group, Box 1583, Vernon, BC V1T 8C2. Contact: Francis Hill. Local organization. Also holds contests.

Washington Christian Writers Fellowship, PO Box 11337, Bainbridge Island, WA 98110. 206-842-9103. Contact: Elaine Wright Colvin. Writers group sharing networking, inspiration, marketing how-to. Sponsors annual conference.

Washington Library Media Assn., 33 S Second Ave, Yakima, WA 98902. Contact: Joan Newman.

Washington Poets Assn, 6002 S Fife St, Tacoma, WA 98409. Contact: Amelia Haller. Organization to raise awareness and appreciation of poetry; publishes a newsletter 4 times a year, holds an annual meeting/banquet in May, and workshops/events across the state. Refer to Poetry in Vancouver USA, A Poetry Event at Longview, and Rattlesnake Mountain.

Washington State Council of Teachers of English, c/o Port Angeles High School, 304 E Park Ave, Port Angeles, WA 98362.

Wenatchee Christian Writers Fellowship, 24216 104th Pl. W, Edmonds, WA 98020-5723. 509-884-3279. Contact: Millie Hynes.

The West Coast Book Prize Society, 1622 W 7th Ave, Vancouver, BC V6J 1S5. 604-734-1611. Annual $1,500 book award.

West Coast Women and Words, Box 65563, Stn F, Vancouver, BC V5N 5K5. 604-872-8014. An organization of women dedicated to furthering the work of women writers. A major annual project is a summer school/writing retreat for women, WEST WORD. Brochure/application upon request in February.

West End Writers' Group, c/o West End Community Centre, 870 Denman St, Vancouver, BC V6G 2L8.

Western Screenplay Development Society, 1804–13 W 4th Ave, Vancouver, BC V6J 1M3.

Whatcom Writers, c/o Margot Rowe, 1237 W Racine St, Bellingham, WA 98226. 206-734-9818. "A group of published and unpublished writers of adult age. Members' manuscripts are read aloud followed by constructive criticism aimed at helping the author to produce a saleable piece of work. Market news, contests, workshops, etc. are brought to the attention of members. We share success and failure with equal interest. Meetings held the 3rd Tuesday of each month."

White Rock & Surrey Writers Club, 13245 Marine Dr, Surrey, BC V4A 1E6. 604-531-8879. Contact: Lynda James. "We are a group of professional and non-professional writers. Meeting every third Wednesday of each month at Centennial Arena, White Rock, BC. Criticizing and exchanging ideas and markets available for manuscripts in process…. Also publication of book 150 pages — Gems of Poetry & Prose."

Willamette Literary Guild, 835 SW 11th St, Corvallis, OR 97333. Provides community support for writers interested in literary arts in the mid-Willamette area. Publishes a newsletter 3 or 4 times each year, holds 3 Literary Cabarets per year, and supports other literary events. Dues $10/yr.

Willamette Writers, 9045 SW Barbur Blvd #5A, Portland, OR 97219. 503-452-1592. Monthly programs, newsletter, annual conference and contest, small critique groups, and ongoing workshops. Newsletter circ. 900.

Women In Communications Inc, PO Box 3924, Portland, OR 97208. 503-292-1324.

Wordsmiths of Battle Ground, 13210 NE 199th St, Battle Ground, WA 98604. 206-687-3767. Contact: Pat Redjou. Writer support group.

Writer's Support Group, 411 Winger Rd, Williams Lake, BC V2G 3S6. Contact: Ann Walsh.

The Writers' Union of Canada, 3102 Main St, 3rd Fl, Vancouver, BC V5T 3G7. 604-874-1611.

Young Audiences of Oregon Inc, 418 SW Washington, Rm 202, Portland, OR 97204. 503-224-1412. Nonprofit educational organization sponsors professional literary artists (e.g., storytelling, poetry) and performing artists in schools in Oregon and Washington. Artists work in both assembly and classroom settings, with performances, workshops, and residencies.

Miscellaneous

Alaska Media Directory, 6200 Bubbling Brook Circle, Anchorage, AK 99516. 907-346-1001. Contact: Alissa Crandall. Annual directory with listings of media related companies in Alaska; includes publications, radio, television, ad and marketing agencies, artists, photographers, writers, printers, typesetters, etc. Cost: $68 for current edition; $34 for past edition.

Alaska Theatre of Youth, Box 104036, Anchorage, AK 99510. Contact: Director.

American Society of Magazine Photographers/Oregon, 431 NW Flanders, Portland, OR 97209. Contact: Bruce Forester.

American Society of Magazine Photographers, Washington Chapter, Aperture PhotoBank Inc, 1530 Westlake Ave N, Seattle, WA 98109. Contact: Marty Lokins. 206-282-8166.

Arts Hotline, 1693 West 7th Ave, Vancouver, BC V6J 1S4. Contact: Editor.

Artists-In-Education (AIE), Oregon, Oregon Arts Commission, 835 Summer St NE, Salem OR 97301. 503-378-3625. Artists working in all disciplines may apply for short and long term residencies in schools in different regions of the state. Applications available from OAC to be submitted to desired region coordinator—addresses follow: AIE: Benton & Linn Counties, Corvallis Art Center, 700 SW Madison, Corvallis, OR 97333. 503-754-1551. Coordinator: Saralyn Hilde; AIE: Columbia Gorge, Columbia Gorge Arts Council, PO Box

1063, Hood River, OR 97031. 503-386-5113. Coordinator: Dede Killeen; AIE: Deschutes, Crook & Jefferson Counties, Central Oregon Arts Compact, Evergreen Center, 437 S 9th St, Redmond, OR 97756. 503-923-5437 x260. Coordinator: Denissia Withers; AIE: Douglas County, Umpqua Valley Arts Assn, PO Box 1542, Roseburg, OR 97470. 503-672-2532. Coordinator: Heidi Land; AIE: Coos & Curry Counties, S Coast Co for Arts/Humanities, 170 S Second St, Ste 204, Coos Bay, OR 97420. 503-267-6500. Coordinator: Lionel Youst; AIE: Eastern Oregon, Eastern Oregon Regional Arts Council, RSI House, Eastern Oregon State College, La Grande, OR 97850. 503-963-1624. Coordinator: Anne Bell; AIE: Jackson & Josephine Counties, Arts Council of Southern Oregon, 236 E Main, Ashland, OR 97520. 503-482-5594. Coordinator: Brooke Friendly; AIE: Lane County, Lane Regional Arts Council, 411 High St, Eugene, OR 97401. 503-452-2278. Coordinator: Carol Ten Eyck; AIE: Lincoln & Tillamook Counties, Oregon Coast Council for the Arts, PO Box 1315, Newport, OR 97365. 503-265-9231. Coordinator: Babette Cabral; AIE: Marion & Polk Counties, Salem Art Assn, 600 Mission St SE, Salem, OR 97301. 503-581-2228. Coordinator: Sara Spiegel; AIE: Portland Metro & Clatsop County, Contemporary Crafts Assn, 3934 SW Corbett Ave, Portland, OR 97201. 503-228-2308. Coordinator: Vicki Poppen; AIE: Statewide: Film/Video Only, NW Film & Video Center, 1219 SW Park, Portland, OR 97205. 503-221-1156. Coordinator: Ellen Thomas.

Assn for the Multi-Image/Idaho Chapter, c/o Paul Franklin, Custom Recording & Sound, 3907 Custer Dr, Boise, ID 83705. Photographers organization.

Assn for the Multi-Image/Montana Chapter, c/o Doug Brekke, PO Box 1295, Big Timber, MT 59011. Photographers organization.

Assn for the Multi-Image/Washington Chapter, Pacific Northwest Bell, 1600 7th Ave #2604, Seattle, WA 98101. Contact: Tony Beck. Photographers organization.

Beall Park Art Center, 409 N Bozeman, Bozeman, MT 59715. Contact: Jo Anne Salisbury Troxel, President. 406-586-3972. Workshops and exhibits.

Canadian Centre for Studies In Publishing, English Department, Simon Fraser University, Burnaby, BC V5A 1S6. Contact: Rolly Lorimer, Director. Among other work, published a survey on BC publishers which resulted in increased government arts support.

Center for Pacific Northwest Studies, Western Washington University, Bellingham, WA 98225. 206-647-4776 or 676-3125, James W Scott, Director. Collections include manuscript materials, business records, maps, photographs, etc. on the PNW, especially NW Washington. Phone ahead of visit.

Clark County Genealogical Society & Library, PO Box 2728, Vancouver, WA 98668. Contact: Rose Marie Harshman.

Earth Images, PO Box 10352, Bainbridge Island, WA 98110. Contact: Terry Domico. 206-842-7793. Stock photo agency.

Eastwing, 3389 William St, Vancouver, BC V5K 2Z4. Contact: Gail D Whitter.

Guild of Natural Science Illustrators, Box 95721, Seattle, WA 98145.

Hedgebrook, Women Writers' Retreat, 2197 East Millman Rd, Langley, WA 98260.

Idaho State Library, 325 W State St, Boise, ID 83720.

Idaho Writers' Archive, Hemingway Western Studies Center, Boise State University, 1910 University Dr, Boise, ID 83725. Contact: Chuck Guilford. Recently developed project to archive Idaho's literary output; includes a newsletter "intended to help make Idaho writers more aware of the many contests, grants, workshops, and publishing opportunities available to them."

KSER 90.7 FM, 14920 Highway 99 #150, Lynnwood, WA 98037-2300. 206-742-4541. Joan & David Blacker produce a combination book review and author-interview segment. One segment is telephone interviews with NW authors or books with a NW emphasis.

National Endowment for the Arts, Literature Program, 1100 Pennsylvania Ave NW, Washington, DC 20506. 202-682-5451. Grants to individual writers and small presses.

Oregon Book Artists Guild, PO Box 994, Beaverton, OR 97075-0994. 503-324-8081. Contact: Patricia Grass. A group of diverse people whose interests include papermaking, marbling, bookbinding, fine printing. Newsletter $15/yr; circ 200.

Oregon Center for the Book in the Oregon State Library, Oregon State Library, Salem, OR 97310. 503-378-4367. Contact: Wes Doak. A statewide program including exhibits, special collections and speakers all designed to increase awareness and appreciation of books and reading. The Center is supported with contributions by the public. It is affiliated with The Center for the Book in the Library of Congress. Writer's Northwest Handbook is an official resource of the Oregon Center for the Book.

Oregon Committee for the Humanities, 812 SW Washington St #225, Portland, OR 97205-3210. 503-241-0543. Contact: Robert W Keeler. Grantmaking philanthropic organization. "Grants available for public programs involving humanities scholars; consultation grants for organizations needing humanities expertise, research grants to humanities scholars."

Oregon State Archives, 1005 Broadway NE, Salem, OR 97310. 503-378-4241. Contact: John Lazud. Publishes high school curriculum packet, historical resources, informational guides — source records on genealogy, Oregon history, law.

Storytelling Workshop, Graduate School of Library Science, University of Washington FM-30, Seattle, WA 98195. Contact: Spencer G Shaw.

Walden Residency for Oregon Writers, Northwest Writing Institute of Lewis & Clark College, Campus Box 100, Lewis & Clark College, Portland, OR 97219. 503-768-7745. Contact: Kim Stafford. Three residencies awarded annually on the basis of a project proposal and a writing sample. Six and twelve week residencies take place at a mountain farm in Southern Oregon, partial board, utilities, no phone.

Washington Coalition Against Censorship, 5503 17th NW #640, Seattle, WA 98107. 206-624-2184. Contact: Barbara Dority. Coalition of organizations joined to fight the attack on First Amendment rights. Acts as an information clearinghouse for Washington state, and puts out newsletter; sells books, videos, T-shirts.

Washington State Library, Northwest Rm, WSL AJ-11, Olympia, WA 98504. Contact: Jeanne Engermann, Librarian.

Washington Volunteer Lawyers for the Arts, 1331 3rd Ave #512, Seattle, WA 98101-2117. 206-223-0502. Contact: Clare M Grause.

Young & Associates, Artists in Schools, 619 Warehouse Ave #238, Anchorage, AK 99501.

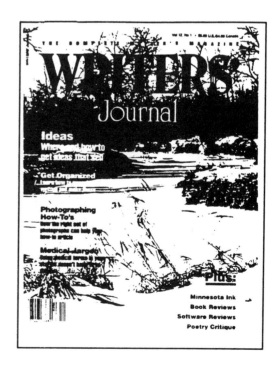

Northwest Writing Institute
of Lewis & Clark College

Please join us for the following programs:
- ☐ Courses in Imaginative Writing
- ☐ Magazine Article Writing
- ☐ Oregon Writing Project
- ☐ Bard Workshops in Writing and Thinking
- ☐ Workshops for Young Writers
- ☐ Oregon Folk Arts and Folklife

— *Kim R. Stafford, Director*

For information contact:
Northwest Writing Institute
Campus Box 100
Lewis & Clark College
Portland, Oregon 97219
503-768-7745

We can free the writer in you

I'm often asked when it was that I first knew I wanted to be a writer. I laugh and tell people it was the day I sold my first short story and I went out and bought a chandelier. But the truth is, as far back as I can remember, I believed there was a writer in me.

Of course, I didn't become a writer overnight. For the longest time, I didn't write at all. I did other things. I told myself I didn't have time to write. I had a family to raise, and besides, what could an everyday person like me have to write about that anyone would want to read?

I guess you could say that's when fate stepped in. I met an experienced writer, a pro, who listened to me and believed me when I said I wanted to write. She got me writing. She read what I wrote, encouraged me when it was good, gave me pointers when it wasn't so good. She freed the writer in me.

Today, I'm living my dream. I'm a professional writer and Director of NRI's School of Writing. I owe so much to my old friend. That's why I feel privileged now to be able to offer you the same kind of help she gave me.

One-on-one, professional guidance

Together with my colleagues at NRI, I've developed a new and complete at-home writing course to give you professional guidance from our team of successful writers.

As my friend was to me, these writers will be your instructors…even more,

---

Carol Bennett brings a remarkable range of writing and teaching skills to NRI. She has lectured on writing at two colleges and has published her short stories, poems, and feature articles in newspapers and business, trade, travel, and general interest magazines.

---

your mentors. They'll guide you, advise you, and help you believe in yourself as a writer.

In personal letters to you and in the margins of the work you send in, they'll give you specific, thoughtful recommendations on improving your technique. Word for word, line for line, they'll help you master the basics of good writing, then dare you to take risks and encourage you to excel. Soon, you'll be doing the kind of clean, clear, strong writing today's publishers pay well for — and readers love to read.

But that's not all. Your mentors will teach you something I learned only long after I'd been writing professionally: how to use a computer not only to write efficiently, but to write freely and with abandon, and to perfect and polish your work for publication.

IBM-compatible computer and software included

I love my computer — and so does every writer I know who uses one. That's why I'm happy to tell you that NRI, unlike any other writing school, includes an IBM-compatible computer and software in your at-home writing course.

Your computer won't do the writing for you, but take it from me, it will take the drudgery out of writing, allowing you to edit and reorganize your work at the touch of a button. Even better, it will free you to experiment; to play with words, sentences, phrases; to write off the top of your head; to be as creative as you truly can be.

I admit, I was a little bit nervous about using a computer in the beginning, but I soon discovered how easy it was. Now, I wouldn't be without one. I truly believe my computer has helped me be a faster, more creative, better writer. I know yours will do the same for you.

Free NRI School of Writing catalog

I'd like to tell you everything about NRI's new at-home writing course, but there's just not enough room here. So I invite you to send for your free NRI catalog. In it you'll find all the details about NRI's at-home writing course, including complete descriptions of your computer, lessons, and writing projects.

One final thought: as a professional writer, I know the thrill of seeing my name in print and being paid for what I love to do. I can tell you, there's no more rewarding life than the writing life. So if something deep down inside of you says "I want to be a writer," I urge you to send for your free NRI catalog today.

Just fill out and mail the coupon or write to us at NRI School of Writing, McGraw-Hill Continuing Education Center, 4401 Connecticut Avenue, NW, Washington, DC 20008.

Sincerely,

Carol Bennett

Carol Bennett
Director, NRI School of Writing

Style Precision Value Performance
Style Precision Value Performance
Style Precision Value Performance
Style Precision Value Performance
Style Precision Value Performance

Acquisition editors, car buyers, book buyers, and grocery shoppers all dance to the same tune. They pass up the dented ones and take the best one home. If you want to see your work picked-up by an agent, published by the big boys, or purchased from the book rack, you better deliver the goods—well-crafted, sharp and shiney. Manuscripts International Ltd. has a full menu of review and editing services to meet every need and budget. Find out where you stand—receive a comprehensive review for a fair price. Send us your manuscript today for a 5 to 10 page in-depth review of your short story, novel, or non-fiction work. Please include a SASE and appropriate payment (we will accept your credit card): under 10,000 words—$25; 10,000 to 20,000—$35; 20,000 to 100,000—$50; over 100,000—$60. You will hear from us within six weeks.

Manuscripts International Ltd., 408 East Main Street, Dayton, WA 99362-1385 (509) 382-2436

2 Good Reasons

WORLD CLASS QUALITY
OFF-SHORE PRICE

Let Seven Seas Exports
Produce Your Next Book

1-800-232-8796

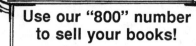

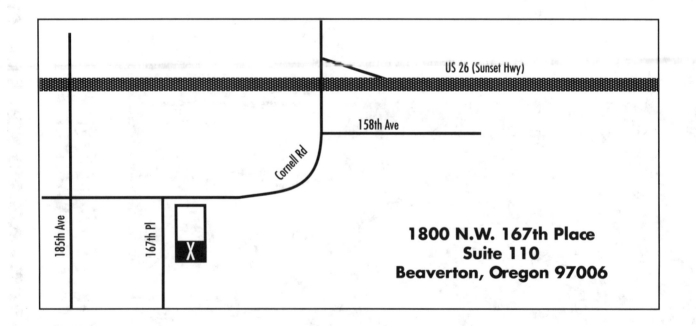

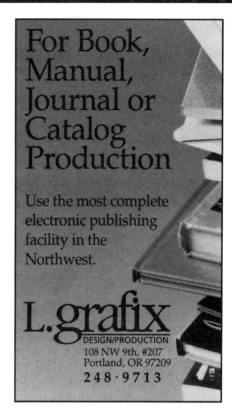

GIVE US BOOKS
GIVE US WINGS

Join America's most successful and soon-to-be-successful writers who read PUBLISHERS WEEKLY for profit and pleasure

Today, a serious author has to get up from the typewriter and get down to business. *The business of books.*

PUBLISHERS WEEKLY has been keeping authors informed about the business of books for over 100 years. Each issue gives you a broad and colorful overview of all that's new and newsworthy in the field...

Who's writing what. What kinds of books are selling now-and what kinds will sell best a year from now. Rights and permissions-for paperbacks, movies, TV. Author tours and publicity. Industry trends and prospects-and how they affect writers, agents, publishers and booksellers...

Book design and manufacturing. News of people in the field. Bookselling and marketing. The international scene. Media tie-ins. Calendars of upcoming events. Convention reports...

Of particular interest to you are the regular, in-depth interviews with writers who are making news today or will be making news tomorrow. They're men and women writing in all fields-from fiction to finance, poetry to politics and they all have valuable thoughts, experiences, ideas and working tips to share with you.

Each issue also brings you advance reviews-by PW's own expert critics-of approximately 100 hardcover and paperback books. These reviews appear *five or ten weeks before publication dates.* So you'll always know which books will be worth looking for-long before they're on bookstore library shelves.

Then there are the advertisements in PUBLISHERS WEEKLY-some 2800 pages a year. Surveys indicate that these book ads are particularly valuable to writers.

If you're serious about writing, the best thing to write today is your name and address on the PW subscription coupon below.

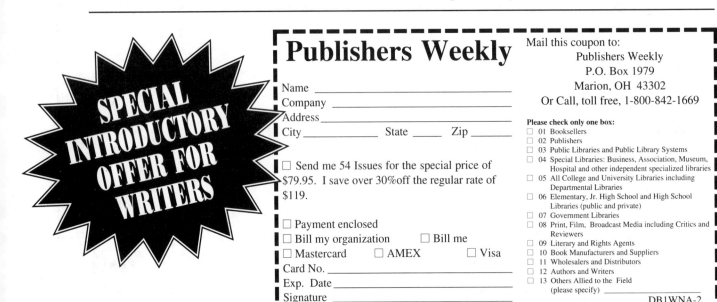

SPECIAL INTRODUCTORY OFFER FOR WRITERS

Publishers Weekly

Name _____
Company _____
Address_____
City _____ State _____ Zip _____

☐ Send me 54 Issues for the special price of $79.95. I save over 30%off the regular rate of $119.

☐ Payment enclosed
☐ Bill my organization   ☐ Bill me
☐ Mastercard   ☐ AMEX   ☐ Visa
Card No. _____
Exp. Date_____
Signature _____

Mail this coupon to:
Publishers Weekly
P.O. Box 1979
Marion, OH 43302
Or Call, toll free, 1-800-842-1669

Please check only one box:
☐ 01 Booksellers
☐ 02 Publishers
☐ 03 Public Libraries and Public Library Systems
☐ 04 Special Libraries: Business, Association, Museum, Hospital and other independent specialized libraries
☐ 05 All College and University Libraries including Departmental Libraries
☐ 06 Elementary, Jr. High School and High School Libraries (public and private)
☐ 07 Government Libraries
☐ 08 Print, Film, Broadcast Media including Critics and Reviewers
☐ 09 Literary and Rights Agents
☐ 10 Book Manufacturers and Suppliers
☐ 11 Wholesalers and Distributors
☐ 12 Authors and Writers
☐ 13 Others Allied to the Field (please specify) _____

DB1WNA-2